THE PURITANS

The Puritans

A TRANSATLANTIC HISTORY

David D. Hall

PRINCETON UNIVERSITY PRESS

PRINCETON & OXFORD

Copyright © 2019 by Princeton University Press

Published by Princeton University Press
41 William Street, Princeton, New Jersey 08540
6 Oxford Street, Woodstock, Oxfordshire OX20 1TR

press.princeton.edu

LCCN: 2019930947
ISBN: 978-0-691-15139-7

British Library Cataloging-in-Publication Data is available

Editorial: Eric Crahan and Pamela Weidman
Production Editorial: Ellen Foos
Jacket Design: Layla Mac Rory
Production: Merli Guerra
Publicity: Tayler Lord and Kate Farquar-Thomson
Copyeditor: Molan Goldstein

Jacket illustration: Edward Winslow, featured in E. Benjamin Andrews, *History of the United States, from the Earliest Discovery of America to the Present Time*, 1913.

This book has been composed in Miller

Printed on acid-free paper. ∞

Printed in the United States of America

10 9 8 7 6 5 4 3 2

CONTENTS

Introduction

WHEN CHRISTENDOM IN THE WEST was swept by currents of renewal and reform in the sixteenth century, the outcome was schism. A single catholic church gave way to a world divided between Catholics and Protestants and, among Protestants themselves, to several versions of true religion. This book is about one of those versions as it unfolded in early modern Scotland and England and, many years later, was transplanted to New England—the Protestantism that, in its British context, acquired the nickname of "puritanism."

Nicknames usually contain an ounce of truth alongside much that is distorted or downright untrue. William Bradford, who became one of the founders of new-world Plymouth, disliked this particular nickname because it implied that such people were reenacting the mistakes of an early Christian sect, the Novatians, who referred to themselves as the Cathari, the "pure," hence "puritans."[1] Not this genealogy but another he would have acknowledged lies at the heart of the Puritanism I am describing, the British version of international Calvinism or, as I prefer to say, the Reformed tradition or Reformed international. On the Continent, the Reformed competed in the mid-sixteenth century with Lutherans and the Anabaptists for the allegiance of the people who abandoned Catholicism and became Protestants. The advocates of Reformed-style Protestantism in England were also competing with a fourth possibility that eventually became known as Anglicanism. For much of the late sixteenth and early seventeenth-centuries, the line between this version of Protestantism and what Puritans preferred was uncertain, for they agreed on some aspects of theology and practice. In Scotland, the party aligned with Reformed principles came much closer to succeeding, able to dominate when it came to doctrine and worship until the early decades of the seventeenth century, when its policies were disrupted by an unfriendly monarch. My answer to the question "What was Puritanism?" is to emphasize everything the movement inherited from the Reformed and how this inheritance was reshaped in Britain and again in early New England—as it were, the Reformed tradition with a Scottish, English, or colonial accent.

To its parent, the Puritan movement owed the ambition to become the state-endorsed version of Christianity in England and Scotland. Theological principle lay at the heart of this ambition. On both sides of the Protestant-Catholic divide, theologians and civic leaders agreed that true religion could be readily defined. All others were false—entirely false or perhaps only in part. Either way, defending true religion against its enemies was crucial. Were error to overtake truth, vast numbers of people would never receive or understand the gospel promise of unmerited grace.[2] Almost as crucial was a second principle, that God empowered godly kings or, as was also said, the "Christian prince," to use the powers of the civil state in behalf of true religion. In early modern Britain and subsequently in early New England, Puritans took both of these assumptions for granted. A third principle concerned the nature of the church. Its role on earth was as a means of grace for all of humankind, a role complicated by the doctrine that only the faithful few would eventually be included within the gospel promise of salvation. Whether (and how) the faithful few should be set apart from hypocrites or the "unworthy" was a question that eventually differentiated some versions of Puritan practice from others.

Because the Puritan movement took a strong stand on the Bible as "law" and insisted that the state churches in England and Scotland eliminate all aspects of Catholicism, it became intensely controversial. Although opposed by many, it enjoyed surprising success in mid-sixteenth-century Scotland. In the 1550s, the government in that country was led by a Catholic queen serving in the place of her daughter, Mary Stuart, who returned from France in 1561 and began to rule in her own right. For reform to succeed, she would have to be circumvented or, as finally happened, defeated in civil war. Thereafter, the reformers were able to enact most of their agenda. Elizabeth I, who became monarch of England in 1558, was a Protestant. But she disliked the reformers who clamored for a "thorough reformation" and thwarted them at every turn. Nonetheless, these people learned how to work around her, aided in doing so by high-placed officials in the government, some of the bishops in the state church and, depending on the issue, members of Parliament. Thanks to these circumstances, the Puritan movement began to thrive—paradoxically, as much within the state church as on its margins.

In the early chapters, I describe the substance of a "thorough" or, to quote John Knox, a "perfect reformation" and the politics that arose in the wake of this concept. Worship had a singular importance in this politics, the source of crisis after crisis in early modern Britain. Important, too, was the nature of the visible church as a community headed, in principle, by Christ as king. The implications of this argument were resisted by monarchs who insisted on what became known as the royal supremacy. By the middle of the seventeenth century as well as earlier, British and colonial Puritans were also disputing how best to describe the relationship between unmerited grace and the "duties" or activity of the redeemed, a quarrel often focused on how to achieve assurance of salvation. As this brief summary suggests, I do my best throughout this book to associate the Puritan movement with theological principles and biblical precepts. Always, however, I situate these commitments in an ongoing politics shaped by social, cultural, and economic circumstances, and especially by the interests of the civil state.

Chronology and comparison drive the structure of *The Puritans*, with two exceptions. The story begins (chap. 1) with an overview of the Reformed (or "Calvinist") tradition and how it was conveyed to British Protestants through books such as John Foxe's *Acts and Monuments (1563 in English)* and firsthand encounters with Reformed practice that happened in the 1550s during the reign of Mary Tudor (1553–58), when English and Scottish ministers—the "Marian exiles"—fled to the Continent. As Foxe and the martyrs whose faith he was documenting repeatedly declared, Catholicism was wrong because it was based on "human inventions" whereas their version of Christianity was restoring the "primitive" (in the sense of first or earliest) perfection of the apostolic church. In the opening chapter, I also outline how the Reformation in Scotland differed from the Reformation in England, differences cited some eighty-five years later by Charles I when he was being pressured to endorse Scottish-style Presbyterianism (see chap. 8).

How the politics of religion unfolded after 1560 is traced in the chapters that follow (2 and 3), which carry the story of reformation in England and Scotland from circa 1555 to the beginning of the seventeenth century. Then come two chapters that are topical, not chronological, the first (chap. 4) on the "practical divinity," or how Puritan ministers and laypeople understood the workings of redemption and developed a dense system of "means," followed by another (chap. 5) situating the Puritan version of a "reformation of manners" or moral reform within a larger anxiety about "decline." Chronology returns in chapter 6, which covers the early decades of the seventeenth century, when James VI of Scotland became James I of England and controversy about worship and the structure of the state church erupted anew in Scotland. As well, chapter 6 covers "Dutch Puritanism," a convenient shorthand for the more radical or safety-seeking laypeople and ministers who went to the Netherlands as early as the 1580s. The final three chapters deal with the run-up to the civil war that broke out in 1642 and its political and theological dimensions (chaps. 7, 8, and 9). In chapter 7, the colonists who founded Massachusetts and other New England colonies finally appear and return in chapter 9, which covers their story after 1640. An epilogue traces the workings of "memory" on both sides of the Atlantic: Puritans not in their own voice but as represented by nineteenth- and twentieth-century novelists, denominational historians, cultural critics, and the like.

To narrate the history of Puritan-style reformation in England and Scotland is not unusual, but treating them side by side as companions who share the same project is less common. From the beginning, the two were entangled, Scottish and English exiles mingling in Geneva, Frankfurt, and elsewhere during the period when England was ruled by Mary Tudor or in pre-1553 England, where John Knox lived at a moment when Protestants in his Scottish homeland could not worship publicly. The partisans of a perfect reformation in England admired what Knox and his heirs accomplished, for the Scottish reformers avoided most of the compromises that dogged the "Elizabethan Settlement" (see chapter 2). It was a different matter when James VI of Scotland became James I of England in 1603, for he brought with him a deep-seated hostility to Scottish "puritans" and set about remodeling the Scottish kirk, a project that blew up in the face of his son and successor, Charles I. With tensions building in the 1620s and 1630s, the narrative in chapter 7 concludes with an extraordinary moment in Scottish religious and political history, the insurgency of 1637–38 that led to the "National Covenant" of 1638 and the return of presbyterian governance for the state church. The implications for England were immense, for the Scottish "revolution" provoked two brief episodes of civil war with the government of Charles I. When his army was defeated, the king had to summon a new Parliament, which began to chip away at royal authority and revamp or curtail aspects of worship, doctrine, and structure within the Church of England. Because Charles I regarded royal authority and an episcopal church structure as two sides of the same coin, space for compromise was scant. The outcome was civil war in England between Royalists and Parliamentarians—a British war once the Scottish government decided to support the English Parliament against the king.

Treating the two reformations side by side sharpens our understanding of the politics that united the advocates of reform in England with their counterparts in Scotland or, as also happened, pulled them apart. Each side endorsed a Reformed-inflected theology of the church, or ecclesiology, but when the moment came (1643–46) to define an alternative to episcopacy, Scottish theologians were virtually unique in upholding a *jure divino* (mandated by divine law) system of church government alongside "magisterial" (state-sustained) Protestantism. As the Scottish historian Gordon Donaldson has pointed out, the reformers in his country never entertained the possibility of separating from an unlawful church, a possibility favored by small groups of Puritans in England early in the reign of Elizabeth I and acted on anew in the late sixteenth and early seventeenth centuries.[3] Already, however, one wing of the Puritan movement in England was moving toward a more decentered, "local" siting of the church. By the early seventeenth century, a handful of ministers were beginning to imagine what such a church would look like. Their ideas played a part in the decision of the colonists who founded Massachusetts in the 1630s to adopt what became known as the "Congregational Way." Soon, others in England were following suit, a step that undermined any possibility of agreement on what should replace the bishop-centered structure of the Church of England. Of the several factors that led to the breakdown of the alliance formed in 1643 between Scotland and the English Parliament, this seems the least understood despite its significance to most British Protestants.

Different though they were in certain respects, each quest for true religion shared a commitment to "discipline" and a social agenda known as a reformation of manners (chap. 5). At a moment when Reformed theology was under attack from various directions, the leaders on each side endorsed a statement of doctrine known as the Westminster Confession (1647). This moment dominates chapter 9, in which I also revisit the "Antinomian controversy" in mid-1630s Massachusetts and describe alternatives to the orthodoxy spelled out in the Confession.[4]

My journey through early modern British and early American history has included the company of historians as interested as I am in doctrine, the practical divinity, the Reformed tradition, and the politics that culminated in civil war and the reign of Oliver Cromwell. Argument among these historians is endemic,[5] argument that encompasses the meaning and significance of events, people, circumstances, and—topics of special pertinence to this book—the descriptive categories on which we depend.

Calvinism is one of these categories. Does it refer to John Calvin and his many publications or to a wider movement in which he was influential but not the final authority in every debate? If the term denotes a wider movement that extended into the seventeenth century and beyond, could it designate an alternative to Calvin—for example, a way of doing theology introduced by a second or third generation of Reformed theologians? That Calvinism in and of itself seems inadequate is suggested by adjectives such as "moderate," "hyper," "experimental," "Dordtian," and "English" that some historians have attached to it. The "practical divinity" I describe in chapter 4 (the term is not mine but dates from c. 1600), is a case in point, "Calvinist" from one vantage but something else from another.[6] In much older scholarship, Calvinism is regarded as inferior to or somehow compromising the theology of John Calvin, a thesis summed up in the phrase, "Calvin versus Calvinism." In this book, however, I temper this distinction after learning of its limitations from Richard A. Muller's numerous articles and books. Muller has put his finger on another problem, the assertion by mid-nineteenth-century German historians that predestination was the "central idea" in Calvin's theology. A misreading of both Calvin and Puritan theologizing, this argument has generated consequences that seem impossible to unwind, one of them the assertion that the doctrine was singular to Puritans and avoided by "Anglicans." As I have learned from informal events where I am asked to describe Puritan theology, someone *always* asks about predestination, and in far too many monographs it turns up as the centerpiece of Puritanism.[7]

As the abundance of scholarship on the "Calvin versus Calvinism" question indicates, the limitations of the term are real. Nonetheless, it designates a stream of theological reflection embodied in creeds and confessions that, although differing in details or emphasis, were acknowledged by Reformed communities in early modern Europe, Britain, and New England as authoritative. I use it cautiously (see chap. 4) and the special circumstances of the 1640s, when orthodoxy was threatened by new enemies in the guise of Socinianism, Arminianism, and a Spirit-centered understanding of conversion that became known as Antinomianism, make it less relevant to that time of struggle. What I foreground in chapter 9, especially, is the sense of crisis that arose among the makers of the practical divinity and how one minister's response could vary from another's. For historians of international Calvinism, the practical divinity has a special importance, for the books in which it was embodied were rapidly reprinted in translation and, by the mid-seventeenth century, were influencing Continental Reformed practice. An emphasis on an "experimental" piety made it unusual, and unusual it remained once it made its way into Pietism and, eventually, evangelical Protestantism.

Among the ministers and academic theologians who turn up in this book, theological practice involved defending the truth against enemies such as Roman Catholicism and making it available in creeds and catechisms. In these genres, as in schoolbooks such as William Ames's *The Marrow of Divinity (1629, in Latin)*, truth or doctrine was compressed into its essentials. Simultaneously, theological practice was carried on in sermons or sermon series tied to Scripture and often employing biblical examples to make a point. As a genre, sermons were very different from creeds and catechisms, for they added layer upon layer of reflection to the principles spelled out in a creed. A good example is the theological and biblical category of covenant, which acquired a fresh importance at the outset of the seventeenth century when a "covenant" or "federal" theology came into being.[8] Another reason why simple rules became entangled with overlays of meaning was the ambition of Puritan ministers to reach a broad audience. In everyday life, people needed guidance on how to become a "sincere" Christian and what it meant to behave righteously. Hence the emphasis within the practical divinity on what in our own era is often described as "spirituality." In this mode, biblical and theological language owed more to the psalms of David than to a sixteenth-century creed.

Making sense of the layers of interpretation that sermons added to key terms is challenging, for historians of Puritan theology have realized that these can encompass inconsistencies or, to quote the historian of theology E. Brooks Holifield, "ambivalence." Ambivalence did not suddenly appear in early modern Britain, for Calvin wavered in some of his thinking. What he and his heirs said about assurance of salvation is a good example, as is what they said about the sacraments of baptism and Holy Communion or the visible church as a means of grace. We may not be able to understand why someone could simultaneously extol the benefits of infant baptism and deny it any efficacy, or why the English minister Arthur Dent added list after list of inconsistent "signs" of assurance to a manual of devotion (see chap. 4), but both were aspects of British and early American "Calvinism."[9] Another approach to ambivalence or ambiguity is to recognize the layers of meaning embedded in words such as "liberty" and "purity." At first glance, these are words we think we understand. But our versions vary from how such words were understood in early modern Britain. Time and again, we take for granted their meaning, a mistake that historians of ideas do their best to correct.[10]

Close kin to Calvinism and almost as problematic, orthodoxy is a word I use to denote an agreed-upon framework of doctrine. Nineteenth-century Protestant liberals disliked this word, as do their more recent heirs, to whom it denotes an overly abstract or "rigid" version of theology because it established firm boundaries between truth and error. Liberals also disliked the category because it exposed them to accusations of apostasy: if the truth was so clearly evident, then all other interpretations of the Trinity, justification, and Scripture were wrong, and possibly very wrong. The alternative, which liberals in Europe and America shared, was to understand religious truth and religion itself as always and everywhere historically incomplete or caught up in "development." In this book, however, the word *orthodoxy* denotes principles or doctrines formally endorsed by synods and state churches or closely related assumptions in the realm of ethics. Yet as I do my best to indicate in chapters 4 and 9, the contours of orthodoxy were constantly being discussed or contested, or to use a more fashionable word, "negotiated" by ministers who according to their own self-estimation remained orthodox.[11] In mid-seventeenth-century England, Richard Baxter (see chap. 9) fits this description, as does another English minister, John Preston.

Some students of the religious politics I describe regard the terms *Puritan* and *Puritanism* as too uncertain to be useful. This point of view has the great merit of recognizing that, as soon as the word surfaced in Elizabethan religious politics, its meaning owed more to anti-puritanism than to the makers of the movement themselves. Anti-puritanism of the kind to which William Bradford was responding (see above) was politically motivated. The goal of its makers was to prevent certain theological ideas and practices from winning the support of kings and parliaments at a moment when advocates of a "thorough reformation" were becoming a vocal presence. Anti-puritanism is alive and well in our own times and, on the both sides of the Atlantic, is responsible for most popular misconceptions of the movement. Freeing the word from the abuse directed at it over the centuries, a task I pursue implicitly in this book, can seem impossible. Too many people in the United States have come under the sway of Arthur Miller's *The Crucible* and Nathaniel Hawthorne's *The Scarlet Letter*. The same seems true of English culture, thanks to nineteenth and early twentieth-century Anglicans who rained contempt upon the movement.

From their perspective, it was unhealthy—too disciplining, too sectarian, and too subversive, as witnessed by the civil wars that erupted in the 1640s and the execution of Charles I in 1649. For people with this point of view, there was nothing to learn from a movement they regarded as being outside of or hostile to the "real" Church of England.

We owe to the late Patrick Collinson (d. 2011), who concluded his distinguished career at Cambridge University, a sharp retort to such assumptions. In essays and books that included *The Elizabethan Puritan Movement* (1967) and *The Religion of Protestants* (1982), he argued exactly the opposite.[12] The movement arose within the Church of England and aspired to reform it *from within*. As he quietly pointed out, important leaders of the state church acknowledged that the institution was imperfect and sided with the reformers on certain issues. The bishops who felt this way had allies in the queen's Privy Council, an alliance tied to the centrality of the movement or, to say this differently, the common ground shared by various wings of the state church. Only when a small group of "radical" intellectuals, most of them associated with Cambridge University, began to question the royal supremacy, the legitimacy of the *Book of Common Prayer*, and the scriptural basis of episcopacy did an aggressive, sharp-edged version of Puritanism come into being. Even so, the organizers of *this* Puritanism rejected the more extreme alternative of "Separatism." Like the Scottish reformers, they wanted an inclusive state church and a "Christian prince" (monarch) who would *preserve* uniformity in practice and belief. For everyone who absorbed the lessons of Collinson's scholarship, the movement ceased to be "revolutionary" or inherently "radical."[13]

To this forceful argument, Collinson added another. Acknowledging the push and pull of conscience versus conformity or of "lawful" versus "things indifferent" (see chap. 2), he excelled at describing the tensions that accumulated within the movement. One version of these arose around the difference between "voluntary religion" and magisterial Protestantism, a tension allied with another: the difference between a church consisting only of the faithful and one that was broadly inclusive. Properly understood, therefore, the English version struggled with its own internal differences even as it contended against its critics in the state church or government. To capture some of these nuances, Collinson used adjectives and nouns such as "pragmatic," "dogmatic," "moderate," "revolutionary," and "sectarian," a vocabulary I use myself, although sparingly, to suggest a dynamics that spun out of control in the 1640s and 1650s. My version also includes the people who are usually classified as "Separatists" because they denied the lawfulness (legitimacy) of the Church of England and formed their own worshipping communities. Collinson excluded these groups because they fell outside his magisterial version of the Puritan movement. My reasons for doing the opposite are implied in the final pages of chapter 2.[14]

Movements are not the same as institutions. No person or self-designated elite headed the movement I am describing and, when disagreements erupted, it had no internal means of restoring consensus. A Puritanism at once tightly bounded and restless complicates the task of deciding who really qualifies as a Puritan—and when. Early modern British history is littered with examples of people, policies, and practices that seem impeccably Puritan from one perspective but not from another. Was John Milton a Puritan? Not if orthodoxy is required. Could a bishop in the Church of England be one? Yes, if the hallmark of identity is doctrine, not ecclesiology. Could Puritans support the monarchy? The answer is yes, despite assertions to the contrary by kings and their allies, to which I add the observation that in mid-seventeenth-century England, "republicans" such as James Harrington (d. 1675) were not involved in the movement. When the scene shifts to the landowning class known as the gentry, some were outspoken in behalf of reform, but in contexts such as Parliament, where consensus and social rank were highly valued, hard-edged identities often became blurred. According to Jacqueline Eales, the high-status Harley family mingled in their home county with others of the same rank who were Catholics, and when Robert Harley attended sessions of the House of Commons, he worked alongside men of quite different convictions.[15] In Scotland as in England, the nuances were many—too many, in fact, for all of them to be adequately acknowledged in this book.

Where does the presence of Puritanism in early modern Britain seem most obvious? Most of us are likely to say it is as an advocate of disciplinary religion, by which we mean a forceful ethics of obedience to divine law, coupled with a machinery of overseeing that obedience. In point of fact, a reformation of manners (another name for this agenda) was widely endorsed, an observation I expand on in chapter 5 in the wake of work by social historians who discount the singularity or importance of a Puritan-derived "civic godliness."[16] In the same chapter, however, I identify a cluster of assumptions that differentiate the Puritan version of a reformation of manners from its near neighbor. The line between the two was not always clearly drawn, a case in point being the preference of ministers of all persuasions to protect the Sunday Sabbath. Nor was one version more enduring than another, although in the epilogue, I instance some of the legacies of the Puritan version.

When it comes to the practical divinity, its identity as "Puritan" is genuinely in doubt. Ministers in good standing in the Church of England—Arthur Dent, for one; William Perkins, for another—contributed to the making of this version of the Protestant message about salvation. Yet to deny it any connections with the movement is a mistake. We have only to ask why it was impossible for the Church of England to endorse the Westminster Confession of 1647—a text keyed to the practical divinity as well as to disputes about the Trinity and divine sovereignty—to expose how "Anglicanism" of the kind associated with

John Donne, Lancelot Andrewes, Richard Hooker, William Laud, and William Chillingworth was different.[17]

From my perspective, the controversies about who was a Puritan or "presbyterian" or possibly something else hold two lessons. One of these is that historians (literary, social, political, religious, etc.) should pause before they acclaim or denounce this or that practice as singularly "Puritan." This happens constantly in American scholarship—as in the assertion that a "Puritan" mode of child-rearing existed, an argument usually based on a handful of examples or (at an extreme) a single sentence from a sermon, when in fact people of middling social status in England treated children in the same manner. Ways of dying were also widely shared among Protestants, as were ways of understanding sickness, healing, and gender. Everyone wanted to protect the Sunday Sabbath, although not always for the same reasons. We do better as historians if we qualify all such claims for singularity.

Historians of early New England wrestle with other versions of this problem. Usually unaware of how British scholars have complicated the meaning of the term, they use Puritan or Puritanism without any hesitation, as if Puritanism arrived on this side of the Atlantic in a tidy box or perhaps as a single text (usually, John Winthrop's essay or discourse, "A Modell of Christian Charity"), a Puritanism shorn of the complexities arising out of the English and Scottish reformations and a hard-fought politics of religion in early modern Britain. This practice abets the quest for "origins," for we marvel as the colonists unpack the luggage labeled Puritanism and magically turn into "founders" of the America-to-be—founders of a literary tradition or of something resembling democracy, and especially founders of a ready-made "identity," as though (for example) the colonists equipped their venture with a singular understanding of the "millennium."[18]

This was how things stood when I began my doctoral work in 1959. Ignorant of the British side of the story, I took for granted an essentially denominational perspective. The "pilgrims" had been "Separatists" and the founders of Massachusetts "Congregationalists," so any backward glance across the Atlantic could start and end with these two groups or their theorizers. By the close of the 1960s, I was beginning to recognize the limitations of this approach and, in a brief preface to a new edition of Perry Miller's *Orthodoxy in Massachusetts* (1933, 1970), questioned his reliance on denominational categories. In a monograph on the ministry in seventeenth-century New England, I also questioned a vigorously "Americanist" interpretation of its development in response to arguments along those lines.

But the real awakening to a more fully Atlantic or Reformed framework—my own awakening, if not always shared by others—happened in the wake of scholarship that reclaimed the richness of theological speculation on the other side of the Atlantic and, in doing so, altered our understanding of theological controversy in New England. Pride of place in this enterprise belong to Michael McGiffert, E. Brooks Holifield, Baird Tipson, W.G.B. Stoever, Theodore Dwight Bozeman, and Charles Hambrick-Stowe.[19] Later, and continuing to this day, they were joined by Norman Fiering, Charles Lloyd Cohen, Francis J. Bremer, Richard Cogley, and Stephen Foster. The point of view that informs Foster's *The Long Argument: English Puritanism and the Shaping of New England Culture, 1570–1700* (1990), is indicative of how an origins narrative tied to a thick history of the Puritan movement in England looks very different from one that begins at water's edge or depends on denominational categories.[20]

My own confidence in a theological perspective rests on work by another group of historians who share a deep interest in the Reformed tradition as embodied in a Puritanism that remains a resource to this day. Richard A. Muller stands apart from this group in various ways, but his work in historical theology set a standard for evangelical scholars such as Mark E. Dever, Joel Beeke, Lyle Bierma, Randall Gleason, Tom Schwanda, and especially Paul C. H. Lim. My citations to them in chapters 4 and 9 are a small token of their presence in these pages.

I have already alluded to the anti-puritanism of nineteenth-century British Anglicans. This rhetoric was flourishing in the late sixteenth century and became a significant weapon in the religious politics associated with Charles I, who knew that his father had characterized the movement as anti-monarchical.[21] Renewed after the restoration of Charles II to the throne in 1660 and periodically reenergized during the nineteenth and twentieth centuries, it remains with us to this day. The American version, which I describe more fully in the epilogue, mainly dates from a schism in the early nineteenth century that divided Unitarians (today, Unitarian Universalists) from Congregationalists. As post-Calvinist Protestants, Unitarians justified their newfound independence by denouncing the intolerance of the seventeenth-century colonists and the cruelties of Calvinist theology. To them we owe the popular assumptions that the colonists persecuted large numbers of innocent people and burned witches at the stake. Neither happens to be true.[22] On the British side as on the American, anti-puritanism included the assumption that Puritans were joyless except when it came to punishing others, an assumption translated by some social and cultural historians, or anyone constructing a scenario of repression versus liberation, into the thesis that the goal of the movement was to impose social discipline on those beneath them in rank or status. This too is an argument with major weaknesses.[23]

In the nineteenth century and continuing into ours, anti-puritanism was likely to reemerge whenever the emphasis fell on the benefits of progress, or of being more enlightened. Puritanism became akin to the Dark Ages once liberals on both sides of the Atlantic embraced the story of progress from superstition to rationality or from dogma to free inquiry, a story endorsed even more widely in our own times despite the horrors of the twentieth century. We may recognize that the price we pay for "modernity" includes severe damage to the environment and ongoing inequality, but it seems impossible to jettison the assumption that things are better now than they were in the past.

A simple response to anti-puritanism in any of its forms is to reemphasize that this book is about the Protestant Reformation as it unfolded in early modern Britain. No serious student of the past doubts the importance of this Reformation and its Catholic counterpart. Nor should any serious student of early America, for the conflicts associated with these two reformations played an oversized role in determining who moved from Britain or elsewhere in Europe to the colonies—people who identified themselves (e.g.,) as Catholics, Quakers, Puritans, Scots-Irish Presbyterians, German Pietists, and Moravians—and an outsized role as well in the making of Native American and African-American forms of Christianity.[24]

By way of conclusion, I note a few questions of interest to historians of early modern Britain and early America I do not address. That Protestantism and, especially perhaps, anti-Catholicism, played a major role in fashioning English or Scottish popular nationalism seems obvious, but as Arthur Williamson has shown for early modern Scotland, much else was involved.[25] Only in chapter 3, which concludes with the making of a "myth" of the kirk uniquely aligned with divine law, do I deal with the intersecting of national identity with the rhetoric of the reformers. How the people of early modern Scotland and England became Protestants—how, in other words, centuries of Catholic practice were replaced and Protestantism as culture and doctrine implanted—is a fascinating question that animates Peter Marshall's remarkable *Beliefs and the Dead in Reformation England* (2002), Margo Todd's *The Culture of Protestantism in Early Modern Scotland* (2002), and much of the scholarship of Christopher Haigh and Arnold Hunt.[26] Here, however, I pass it by, as I also do a question of more immediate interest to me, how Protestantism was "lived" or, alternatively, what counted as "popular' religion in this period.[27] Addressing either of these became impossible once I decided to foreground theology, the institutional church, and the politics of religion as it was carried on (or by) monarchs, general assemblies, parliaments, and the like.

Given the ambiguities that inhere in so many key words I use, the practical question becomes when to capitalize. Collinson tilted toward a lowercase *p* for puritanism, but other historians vary in their practice, as I did while this book was being written. Because a copyeditor has insisted on consistency, I have capitalized *Puritanism* and *Puritan* but not terms such as *Presbyterian* until I reach the 1640s, which was when the Scottish theologians who participated in the Westminster Assembly advocated *jure divino* Presbyterianism. At this point, therefore, it seems appropriate to acknowledge their point of view with a capital letter. Their many English allies in the Westminster Assembly were a mixed lot, some persuaded by the Scots and others more middling in their sentiments. No good way of naming them exists. Mindful of Collinson's observation that historians should not repeat the error of pushing the history of nineteenth-century denominations back into the sixteenth and seventeenth centuries, I have wavered in how I treat the colonists who brought into being a "Congregational Way," not wanting to baptize them prematurely as Congregationalists but needing a label of some kind. On the other hand, Baptists and Quakers (although this term postdates 1660) seem sufficiently distinctive to merit capitals, even though each was tugged this way and that in deciding matters of doctrine and practice.

In the pages that follow, biblical quotations conform to the King James Version of the Bible. Contrary to the practice of some historians of early modern Scotland, I spell Mary Stuart's name in this manner and translate most examples of Scots English into ordinary English. When quoting from a sixteenth- or seventeenth-century text, I drop the long-tailed *i* and change *u*'s into *v*'s, but I do my best to preserve capitalization and punctuation. Place of publication for early modern texts cited in my narrative is London unless otherwise noted. Readers wanting to know more about arguments within the field of Puritan studies should consult Peter Lake, "The historiography of Puritanism," chapter 20 of *The Cambridge Companion to Puritanism*, ed. John Coffey and Paul C. H. Lim (Cambridge: Cambridge University Press, 2008); and the essays cited in the bibliographical note in *Puritans in the New World: A Critical Anthology*, edited by David D. Hall (Princeton, NJ: Princeton University Press, 2004).

CHAPTER ONE

From Protestant to Reformed

LONG BEFORE ANYONE was being called a Puritan in sixteenth-century England and Scotland, there were people who, when pressed to name themselves, would have used the newly coined word "Protestant." By the 1530s, men and women of this temperament were eagerly reading the Bible in English, using copies printed overseas and smuggled into their countries, where Catholicism remained the official religion. Encountering Scripture in the vernacular was transformative, as it also was to hear preachers who promised the "Pure Gospel." At a church trial in 1530s England, a fifteen-year-old boy who was caught owning a primer and a New Testament recalled how "divers poor men in the town of Chelmsford . . . bought the new testament of Jesus Christ and on Sundays did sit reading [aloud] in lower end of church, and many would flock about them to hear their reading then I came among the said readers to hear them . . . then thought I will learn to read English, and then I will have the new testament and read thereon myself." Scenes of this kind were becoming more frequent as the years passed, the less audacious gathering in the privacy of household-based communities to converse about the Christ whose death on the cross freed them from unrelenting penance and the "tyranny" of a sacerdotal priesthood.[1] Thus, step by step, did the Reformation emerge in England and Scotland alongside the Reformation in Europe initiated by Martin Luther and Ulrich Zwingli.

Everywhere, these Protestants celebrated the Word, with its revelation of "the great and ineffable omnipotent power, promise, justice, mercy and goodness of Almighty God." Everywhere as well, the same people likened it to a "light" that eliminated the "darkness" of Catholicism and its "dumme and dead idoles." So declared the English ministers who, living in exile in the safety of Protestant Geneva, prepared a fresh translation of the Bible into English (1560), telling its prospective readers that they would experience the "unspeakable mercy" of being recalled to the truth by the "marvelous light of his Gospel." Catholics mocked these evocations of Scripture as mere "Bible-babble," and

Protestants mocked Catholics in return for introducing practices and rites without warrant in the Word.[2] In his *Apology of the Church of England* (1562), the English minister John Jewell challenged Roman Catholics to refer all disputes "to the trial of God's word." Protestants were also insisting that the Bible become available in "such a tonge as we can and do understand," a practice resisted by the Catholic hierarchy. William Tyndale, who made the earliest translation to reach British Protestants, argued that "it was not possible to stablish the laypeople in any truth, except the Scripture were so plainly laide before their eyes in their mother tongue."[3] "Christ never spoke in English," a Catholic official interrogating a Protestant pointed out, only to be told that "neither spoke he any Latin; but always in such a tongue as the people might be edified thereby." With Catholic assumptions about the authority of priests and tradition thrust aside, Scripture became the doorway to knowing God and the most important source of rules for Protestants to follow as they organized churches, ministry, and worship.[4]

This lesson learned, Protestants in England and Scotland turned it against the "human inventions" they saw everywhere. A much-repeated phrase, human inventions captured an understanding of Christian history as it had unfolded from the times of the apostles to the beginning of the sixteenth century—in essence, a history of "idolatry" and "superstitions" overtaking the "primitive" perfection of the apostolic period. Now, with the Word to guide them, Protestants were restoring that perfection. Theirs was a movement of reform as a return to or reappropriation of the past, a regaining of the "primitive" as original or first: "We have searched out of the Holy Bible, which we are sure cannot deceive, one sure form of religion, and have returned again unto the primitive church of the ancient fathers and apostles." In the long run, this confidence in the principle of *ad fontes*, or returning to what came first, could not forestall various interpretations of Scripture. What exactly did the church fathers and apostles teach about worship and the nature of the church? As the leaders of the Reformation in Scotland and England learned to their dismay, it was possible to answer such questions in different ways.[5]

Everywhere as well, Protestants celebrated the message of *sola gratia*: by (free) grace we are redeemed from our sinfulness, not, as Catholicism maintained, by some combination of grace and our own efforts. Emphasizing the gulf between "law" or "works" and "Gospel," Martin Luther called on Christians to recognize the new freedom that became theirs in the aftermath of Christ's death on the cross. The law that bound the Jews was no longer binding now that the Gospel was available to everyone. Eager to remove any uncertainty about the saving effects of grace, Luther emphasized Christ's love for the redeemed, who had only to respond in faith. To this argument he added an understanding of the church as a community of the faithful existing apart from the unredeemed world, a theme he owed in part to St. Paul's evocation of Christ as the "corner stone" of a "holy temple" of people who, in the aftermath of being transformed by the Holy Spirit (Eph. 2:20; 1 Cor. 6:19–20; 2 Cor. 3:3), practiced "love" (charity), "peace," and "edification," or a mutual commitment to enhance the holiness of those who came together in fellowship. Luther and other Protestants drew on early Christianity for another motif, the church as a community that, here on earth, suffered at the hands of its enemies. To suffer as outcasts was a fundamental aspect of the Christian condition until the arc of Christian history was completed with the return of Christ and the final restoration of his kingdom.[6]

The authority of the word, or regulative principle, the gift of grace from a merciful God, the imperative of eliminating idolatry, and the special liberty Christians would enjoy within the fellowship of a purified church—these themes were shared by everyone who turned away from Catholicism and became Protestants. As the rest of this book will indicate, these same motifs defined the movement that became known as Puritanism. To them the British reformers added others fashioned by the intellectual and cultural movement known as Christian humanism, which contributed an "activism and . . . reformist ethic" to the intellectual climate of sixteenth- and seventeenth-century Europe. Humanists drew on classical, pre-Christian writers as well as on the Christian tradition for an understanding of the common good and the virtues that would promote it. Imagining an active citizenry prompted by ethical ideals to attempt a new kind of society, humanism overlapped with aspects of the social ethics that Luther and other early leaders of the Reformation were articulating.[7]

The Reformed International

While sharing so much, Protestants on the Continent and in Britain were at odds on other issues. Bitter words were exchanged and violence erupted when a coalition of Lutherans and Catholics in Germany went to war with local Anabaptists in the 1520s and early 1530s. Nonetheless, Protestants had good reasons for uniting. The more divided they were, the more vulnerable they became to the Catholic assertion that any questioning of Rome's authority opened the floodgates to heresy. The implications of division and disagreement prompted Protestants in Switzerland to fashion a compromise theology of the Eucharist and baptism. Lutherans spurned the *Consensus Tigurinus* (1549), as this agreement was named, although its carefully balanced view of the sacrament reappeared in major creedal statements of the Reformed tradition. By the 1560s, hopes for a more unifying faith had given way to lasting division into three major families or traditions: the Lutheran, the Reformed, and the Radical or "Free." During the same decade, Reformed churches on the Continent fashioned statements of doctrine and reemphasized the principle of "discipline" (see below). Simultaneously, some leaders of the Reformed began to insist on a "presbyterian" system of governance.

The Reformed tradition (or, alternatively, "Calvinism") played a singular role in the making of the Reformation in England, Ireland, and Scotland and the development of New England.[8] As early as the 1530s, Luther's theology, although available in translation, was giving way to connections direct and indirect with the Reformed international, connections nurtured by Thomas Cranmer, who became Archbishop of Canterbury (the highest clerical office in the Church of England) in 1533. When Protestantism resumed its advance in England after the death of Henry VIII in 1547, Cranmer invited Reformed theologians such as Peter Martyr Vermigli and Martin Bucer to take up posts at Oxford and Cambridge. Simultaneously, he allowed refugees from continental Europe to organize congregations of their own in London. Thereafter, anyone interested in Reformed modes of worship and governance could ponder the example of these "stranger" churches.[9]

The influence of the Reformed arose as well out of the experience of Protestants who, for safety's sake, left England and Scotland for the Continent. In the early 1540s, when Henry VIII was retreating from his Protestantism and James V, the Catholic ruler of Scotland, was suppressing dissent, exiles from both countries settled in cities sympathetic to the Reformed—for example, John Hooper in Zurich and John Knox in Geneva. A more consequential exodus from England occurred after Mary Tudor came to the throne in 1553 and restored Catholicism as her country's official religion. The clergy who fled to Europe settled in cities under the sway of the Reformed tradition, places such as Strasbourg, Frankfurt, Zurich, Emden, Basel, and especially Geneva, where as many as a fourth of the exiles ended up. When these men returned after Elizabeth I became queen in 1558 and the Church of England reverted to Protestantism, they had an important voice in debates about worship and ministry, with several becoming bishops. A smaller number of Scottish exiles or Scots who went abroad in search of academic training settled or taught in Geneva or other Reformed centers and, after returning to their homeland, became influential advocates of Reformed practices. Another wave of repression in 1570s England propelled a handful of reformers across the Channel to Geneva and Heidelberg and subsequently to the Netherlands, where some of them found positions within churches set up for and by soldiers and merchants. "Separatists" sought refuge in the same country in the 1580s and beyond. Although differing among themselves, the great majority of these exiles admired the Reformed understanding of the church.[10]

Books were another means of communicating the themes of the Reformed tradition. After 1560, the London book trade issued translation after translation of texts by Continental theologians and church leaders and imported other copies, some of them in Latin, to sell to the English reading public. A careful count of both kinds of evidence demonstrates that, where printed books are concerned, John Calvin was "the dominant theological influence in Elizabethan England," published and republished more times than any native theologian. His one serious rival was William Perkins of Cambridge, but the writings of Theodore Beza, who assumed the leadership of the Geneva church after Calvin's death in 1564, rank third in a tabulation of editions, with Heinrich Bullinger of Zurich in sixth place, just after Luther.[11] Scottish Protestants read the same books in Latin, English, or, by 1567, in Scots Gaelic[12] and formed close ties with the French Reformed community, which recruited students and faculty from Scotland for its seminaries. The seven provinces (soon to be known as the Low Countries or Netherlands) that broke off from the Spanish empire after 1581 became another major source of theological and biblical scholarship. There, English and Scottish refugees found printers willing to publish tracts and manifestos that could not be issued in their home countries. Meanwhile, well-placed patrons of learning such as Robert Dudley, the Earl of Leicester, were encouraging translators to make Continental polemics available in English and backing local writers who supported the Reformed tradition.[13]

The grandest publishing project of the Marian exiles was the English-language Geneva Bible. William Whittingham, who initiated this project, relied on that city's printers to issue the New Testament in 1558 and, two years later, the entire Bible. Under Henry VIII, the Church of England had already authorized the Great Bible (1539);[14] a revised version known as the Bishops Bible was published in 1568. Both were designed for display in parish churches. Once the Geneva Bible began to be printed in England, the number of editions far surpassed those of the Bishops Bible: at least seventy-seven between 1560 and 1611, as contrasted with twenty of the Bishops Bible, with another twenty or so issued after the appearance of the "authorized" or King James version of 1611. Eventually published in sizes compact enough to suit households and solitary readers, the Geneva Bible included an apparatus of summaries and commentary designed to make the text more intelligible. In the course of time, other documents were appended and the marginal comments revised. After 1579, some printings included a catechism headed "Certain Questions and Answers Touching the Doctrine of Predestination." The commentary on Romans 8:29 and 9:15 and Psalm 147:20 also called attention to this doctrine. As well, after 1599 some printings included "completely new, and very full, notes on Revelation" prepared by Franciscus Junius (François du Jon), a French Protestant. According to his commentary, Revelation told the story of God's people as they passed from tribulation to a culminating "freedom and immunity from all evil."[15]

The community of exiles in Geneva reshaped another book that, like the Geneva version of the Bible, acquired a remarkable importance within British Protestantism, *The Whole Booke of Psalmes* (1562), a much expanded version of Thomas Sternhold's *Certayne Psalmes chose[n] out of the Psalter of David* (London, 1547). With the energetic London printer and fervent Protestant John Day in charge and John Hopkins and Thomas Norton serving as translators, *The Whole Booke of Psalmes* rapidly became the psalter of choice in English congregational worship and household devotions, as evidenced by the 186 printings (at a minimum) by 1609 and another 294 by 1640, with other copies printed in Scotland, where some of the same translations were incorporated into the Scottish psalter. Especially after 1600, many of these editions were in smaller formats that suited individual purchasers.[16] Wherever it came into use, *The Whole Booke of Psalmes* nurtured the communal singing that Calvin had introduced in Geneva. Like the Geneva Bible, moreover, the psalter in some of its editions included prose instruction in theology, one of them "The confession of Christian faith" borrowed from another product of the exile community: the Anglo-Genevan Form of Prayers, a devotional text that become the official order of worship in Scotland. Much favored by groups that regarded themselves as "godly," the Sternhold-Hopkins psalter remained nonpartisan, as demonstrated by the fact that copies were frequently incorporated into printings of the official liturgy of the Church of England, the *Book of Common Prayer*.[17]

To these influential books we must add one more, a collection of martyr stories assembled by the Marian exile John Foxe. Initially published in Basel (1559), the first English-language printing of *Actes and Monuments of these latter and perilous days, touching matters of the Church*, or, to use its colloquial title, the *Book of Martyrs* (London, 1563; revised in three subsequent printings) recounted the history of Christianity as an ongoing struggle between true Christians and their enemies within the church. Foxe began with the earliest Christian martyrs, although the women and men of special interest to him were those who died for their Protestantism under Henry VIII and Mary Tudor. Some, like John Bradford, became household names because of the power of the stories he told about them. As he explained on the title page as well as in a preface he added to the 1570 edition, the "true church" was not the corrupt and tyrannical "church of Rome" but the church of the "poor oppressed and persecuted." It was their story he wanted to update, a story of "horrible troubles that have been wrought and practiced by the Romish prelates." With the coming of the Reformation, these people were awaiting their moment of triumph even as they continued to suffer. Foxe reiterated a commonplace of English thinking, the fable that true Christianity had persisted longer in his native country and recovered earlier from corruption than elsewhere in Europe. (Scottish Protestants made the same assumptions about their national church.) But by dedicating the edition of 1563 to Elizabeth I and hailing her as another Constantine, the emperor who installed Christianity as the official religion of the Roman Empire, Foxe tweaked the meaning of his book. Now, the church of the suffering few became the church of an entire nation. For the moment, Foxe allowed these two versions of past, present, and future to exist side by side in his pages.[18]

Via this traffic in books and people, Protestants in England and Scotland became familiar with the distinctive features of Reformed theology and practice. And distinctive the Reformed tradition was, although faithful to the core Protestant principles of free grace and the primacy of Scripture. What made it singular were six arguments or assumptions, all of which shaped the reformations underway in England and Scotland.[19]

> 1. *A critique of "idolatry" that encompassed the whole of Catholic worship.* John Calvin regarded man-made images of God and the worship of them as idolatry. He based this reasoning on the second commandment, which, in the version of the Decalogue he and the Reformed preferred, emphasized the prohibiting of "graven images" once this was detached from the injunction to "have none other gods before me" (Deut. 5:7). In his hands and those of British reformers, the category of idols encompassed freestanding statues, representations of God or Christ in stained glass, and images of any kind; as was argued by the English reformer William Fulke, "there is no difference between idol and image." This outcry against idolatry became a distinctive feature of the Reformed tradition and, in Britain, of the more radical advocates of Protestantism. John Hooper was unflinching in his *Declaration of the ten holy commandments* (1549/1550): "every man in England knoweth praying to saints and kneeling before images is idolatry, and instruments of the devil to lead men from the commandments of God." For Hooper as for Calvin, the outward practice of idolatry was paralleled by "mental images" that substituted mere "imagination" for the reality of God as known from Scripture.[20] Armed with this broad understanding of idolatry, Reformed communities throughout Europe engaged in spasms of iconoclasm. Similar outbursts occurred in mid-sixteenth-century Scotland and England, and again during the mid-seventeenth-century English Revolution.[21]

Calvin extended his critique of idolatry to the Catholic understanding of the Eucharist. According to Catholic doctrine, the sacrament involved the miraculous transformation of wafer and wine into the body and blood of Christ. This, the "real presence," dictated how those who participated in the mass should behave—kneeling to adore the presence of Christ and receive the consecrated wafer, with the wine reserved for the priest whose sacred (or "sacerdotal") powers enabled transubstantiation to occur. Calvin exalted Christ's spiritual presence and its consequences for believers, but he insisted that Jesus was speaking symbolically when he offered his body and blood to the disciples and asked them to remember him—"do this in remembrance of me"—and, as Calvin and his colleagues insisted, remember him by receiving the bread and the wine in their seats, not by coming forward to kneel at an altar. No miracle of transubstantiation happened, if only because the resurrected Christ was beside the Father in heaven and nowhere else: present in the sacrament, but present "spiritually."[22]

The reformers in mid-sixteenth-century Scotland and England shared Calvin's interpretation of the Catholic mass as idolatrous. Whenever they opened their Bibles, they came upon story after story in the Old Testament of righteous kings and prophets who, in the spirit of God's command in Deuteronomy 12:3, punished idolaters by "overthrow[ing] their altars, and . . . hew[ing] down the graven images of their gods." It was axiomatic that Catholics were idolaters and also axiomatic that all Christians were tempted by this sin which, as Paul pointed out in his letter to the Colossians, also encompassed "fornication, uncleanness . . . , and covetousness"—that is, any and all moral behavior at odds with the ethics of "mercies" and "meekness" he extolled in the same epistle (Col. 3:5, 12). Hence the imperative to realign worship with Scripture and initiate a moral or spiritual cleansing of self and community. In Strasbourg and Geneva, the first part of this program prompted a radical reorganization of Sunday services around sermons, prayer, the communal singing of psalms and hymns, and a sharply revised mode of participating in the sacraments of baptism and Holy Communion. Argument persisted on the meaning of Holy Communion, with moderates wanting to sustain the spiritual presence of Christ and others arguing for a "memorialist" understanding of the sacrament.[23]

> 2. *An understanding of divine revelation as fixed or constant,* and therefore a reverence for the Bible as a "completely reliable" record of sacred history and God's plans for humankind. The Word was always "plain and infallible," its purity impossible to corrupt, whereas history or tradition were virtually synonymous with "innovation" and decline. The authority of the Bible (or "the Word") encompassed not only matters of faith or belief but also worship, ministry, and church order. Granted, the Bible mixed specific rules with more general principles that the church on earth had to interpret. Nonetheless, Scripture was normative. No other rules or traditions had any merit: "no doctrine, no ceremony, no discipline can be attributed to Christ the King and to his Kingdom . . . except what has been instituted and come forth from the Holy Spirit," a point reiterated by the Scottish reformer John Knox, who identified idolatry as the willful refusal to obey Scripture: "Vaine religion and idolatrie I call whatsoever is done in Goddes service or honour, without the expresse commaundement of his owne Worde." This argument empowered the reformers to renounce the authority of tradition that Catholics claimed for themselves.[24]

The importance of Scripture to the reformers was strengthened by its connections with the Holy Spirit, which pulsated through the Word. No mere printed book, Scripture came to life thanks to the presence of the Spirit. Joined together, Word and Spirit could overturn any kind of oppression. This was a lesson the reformers learned from the apostolic letters, which provided example after example of the Spirit at work within the earliest communities of

Christians. The stories of suffering and deliverance in the Old Testament also confirmed the master narrative on which Protestants depended to justify the rupture with Catholicism. Like the people in ancient Israel and the earliest communities of Christians, they were overturning oppression and tyranny for the sake of free access to the Word.[25]

3. *High praise for the church on earth*—the "visible" church—as God's instrument of grace and His means of bringing Christians together in a special kind of community where they would sustain each other. So important was the church as means of grace that no one could be saved who remained outside it; in Calvin's telling phrase, the church was "Mother" of all the faithful, an assertion directed against the much more stringent practice of the Anabaptists, who substituted a visible church of adults who had been properly baptized for the territorial or inclusive church that Calvin was endorsing. Now, with the Reformation, the church was reclaiming the authority it received directly from Christ—and, in the eyes of the Reformed, reclaiming something almost as important: the rules that could be found in the apostolic letters of the New Testament, seconded by the Gospels and portions of the Old Testament.[26]

Searching these texts, the leaders of the Reformed came upon a form of ministry they regarded as Christ's own counsel to the church: no longer the "extraordinary" offices of apostle and prophet but an "ordinary" ministry of pastors and teachers ("doctors," charged with defending true doctrine), together with those of elder and deacon, an argument grounded on Ephesians 4:11–13 and other references in the New Testament.[27] This cluster of ministries received its authority from the Holy Spirit and secondarily from the people of God, not, as in Catholicism, from an apostolic succession. Once the concept of the priesthood as a sacred order was abandoned, the reformers were free to eliminate a cluster of Catholic practices: ordination ceased to be a sacrament, clerical celibacy fell by the wayside, and congregations "consented" to the naming of their ministers.[28]

The organizers of the Reformed tradition also did away with most aspects of hierarchy in church governance. Their reading of Scripture taught them that no civil or ecclesiastical office rivaled Christ's authority as "king" of the visible church. This assumption disposed of the tyranny that Protestants attributed to the papacy. Another principle known as "parity" got rid of differences of rank and thus of bishops, although Calvin acknowledged the role that bishops of a certain kind had played in church councils of the post-apostolic centuries.[29] Simultaneously, the Reformed introduced a system of collective responsibility centered on inter-parish synods, assemblies, and eventually local associations known, in late sixteenth-century Scotland, as presbyteries—hence the term "presbyterian." Partly to guard against an overly authoritarian leadership and partly out of sympathy for the visible church as a community of the faithful, the leaders of the Reformed encouraged congregational participation in church government. But Calvin and Bullinger did not want laypeople to go off on their own and create quasi-independent congregations, as happened with the Anabaptists. Instead, unity was imperative, a unity sustained by the authority of ministers and the Christian magistrate.

4. *"Discipline" as a necessary feature of the Christian community.* As well as wanting to free the church from Catholic-style tyranny, the leaders of the Reformed aspired to enhance its holiness. Calvin in Geneva, Bucer in Strasbourg, and the makers of the Reformation in Scotland shared what has been termed a "dualist" understanding of the church: open to everyone, but also a righteous or sanctified community not of profane persons but of "saints" who were "citizens of the heavenly Jerusalem."[30] In Bucer's words, the church was "the Kingdom of Christ," where, as indicated in places such as Isaiah 11:4, a "severity of judgment against sins" must be practiced so that all within the church were challenged to repent. Even so, Calvin and Bucer rejected Anabaptist-style exclusivity. For them and the Reformed tradition in general, the visible church was more inclusive than the invisible church of the elect, if only because the earth-bound church would always contain many who, in outward appearance, were Christians. One way of reconciling the "incompatible" goals of exclusion and comprehensiveness was to bar the "scandalous" from Holy Communion, a sacrament reserved in principle for the "worthy" who met certain criteria. Another was to emphasize ecclesiastical discipline, which encompassed the penalties of admonition and excommunication (or being excluded from Christian fellowship) the church could impose on the unrighteous. Calvin took for granted that the progress of reform depended on these penalties and, especially, excommunication, which he regarded as the church's most effective means of preserving a semblance of purity. [31]

Whether discipline should be considered one of the "notes" of the true church was a question some, such as Calvin, answered by saying no and others, such as the leaders of the Scottish Reformation, answered by saying yes. Yet all agreed that discipline had a high importance alongside the two notes on which Lutherans and the Reformed concurred, correct preaching of the Word (i.e., proper doctrine) and proper administration of the sacraments (i.e., not the Catholic version). [32]

Less obviously but of deep importance, the meaning of discipline grew out of the doctrine of election and its consequences for the Christian life. As was argued by all Reformed theologians, God had chosen (elected) some people to be redeemed. Here on earth, the elect were actively pursuing a distinctive phase of their life with Christ, a phase Calvin characterized as an "actual holiness of life," or sanctification. Attempting to define the visible church, the sixteenth-century Scottish minister John Craig responded, "The whole companie of Gods elect called and sanctified," or a people participating in the process of becoming righteous, aided in doing so by the presence of the Holy Spirit, the Word as preached, and the disciplinary consequences of divine law (see chapters 4 and 5). In the most important English catechism of the Elizabethan period, Alexander Nowell also tied the doctrine of election to the being of the visible church as a group of "godly . . . knit together in community of spirit, of faith, . . . and . . . sharing the benefits that God gives his Church through Christ." As Calvin pointed out in the *Institutes*, "the church makes progress from day to day" toward a "holiness [that] is not yet complete." Slowly but surely, a fuller righteousness was emerging within this body, a righteousness expressed in the willingness of the elect to observe the "great commandment" (Matt. 22:36–40) of mutual love and embedded in an apparatus of discipline—which, as John Craig recognized, was the church's means of sustaining the process of sanctification.[33]

5. *An evangelical and social activism* predicated on transforming self, church, and

society into a "new order" approximating the kingdom of Christ. Made in the image of a God ever active in the world, Protestants were employing their newfound freedom to reclaim what had been lost with Adam's fall. This process of renewal and transformation was ongoing, never fully accomplished within church or world or even within the self, but certain to culminate in the renovation of all three, for God was enabling the faithful to emancipate church and society from the corruption introduced by Roman Catholicism. Looking *back* to the perfection of the "first" or apostolic period and imagining a restoration of what had been lost under Catholicism, Calvin and the Reformed also looked *ahead* to the emergence of a community in which coercion gave way to "free" or voluntary practices, with congregations electing their ministers and "equity" or fairness installed as the core principle of social ethics. The benefits of this new order were many—in Calvin's words, "injustice made just, weakness made virtuous, . . . debts paid, labors lightened, . . . division unified." Looking back and looking ahead was also a matter of practicing biblical rules like those found in the Ten Commandments. Even though much of Jewish law was no longer binding, Calvin and many others argued that some moral rules were everlasting, as much a part of the new covenant with Christ as they had been of God's covenant with ancient Israel. Bucer incorporated this emphasis on Old Testament law into a book he completed shortly before his death in 1551, *De Regno Christi* (*On the Kingdom of Christ*). In its pages, he foregrounded an evangelical ministry as the agency that would renovate church and civil society.[34]

For Calvin and Bucer, civil society (or "the world" outside the church) was never going to be as free as the church. Nonetheless, civil governments should serve as allies and agents of a properly reformed church and its program of evangelical and moral reform.[35] As leaders of the Reformed were quick to recognize, any wholesale transformation of church and society was impossible without such support. This was a lesson the two men learned the hard way in the Rhineland city of Strasbourg when the civil elite turned against them, and a lesson Calvin learned anew in Geneva, where a divided and sometimes hostile civil leadership dragged its feet.[36] He believed that rulers were responsible to Christ for seeing that idolatry was suppressed and righteousness enforced, an assumption he validated by citing the Old Testament kings who stamped out idol-worshipping, the Emperor Constantine, and Romans 13:1–2, which described civil officers as commissioned by God. Now, with reform beckoning, leaders of the Reformed called on the Christian ruler to restore "the true, pure, and sincere Christian religion" and to "destroy . . . all false worshipping and superstitions, contrary to the Word of God." Francis I, the ruler of Calvin's native France, was Catholic, yet Calvin appealed to him in the preface of the initial printing of the *Institutes* (1536) to support the Protestant cause. If kings and magistrates respected Scripture or, as Calvin said in his 1535 preface and subsequently in a letter to Edward VI of England, "subject[ed]" themselves "in all humility and reverence under the spiritual scepter of" the "gospel," "there could be no questioning of the ruler's authority."[37]

What a civil state could undertake was also limited. Calvin and his fellow reformers worried about giving the civil state or Christian prince any substantial authority over religion or the church any direct role in affairs of state. Fiercely critical of the papacy in Rome for the claims it was making to authority in the sphere of the state, the reformers wanted to protect civil governments from the church but, above all, the church from the state. Echoing Luther, they endorsed a "two kingdoms" approach to church and state: the new order of the church could not employ "temporal" authority, nor the temporal kingdom the "spiritual" authority of the church. This distinction evolved into a set of rules designed to prevent each from trespassing on the other, one of them a rule prohibiting the civil state from telling the church what doctrines it should teach and another, prohibiting church officers from holding positions in civil government.[38]

Alongside the two-kingdoms framework, Calvin and other Reformed leaders articulated a "constitutional" approach to civil governance. Civil rulers had to acknowledge the superior authority of divine law. The office they held, although of divine origin, was curtailed on its civil side by the imperative of securing the consent of some of the people. Advocated at a moment when civil and ecclesiastical realms were entangled throughout Europe, the constitutionalist implications of two-kingdoms theory were not welcomed by the Protestant rulers of Scotland and England. And, as the more ardently Reformed discovered to their dismay, these same rulers were reluctant to enforce a wide-ranging program of religious and social reform. Conflict was inevitable given the emphasis upon the special freedom of the church, conflict that persisted into the seventeenth century.[39]

6. *Divine providence and apocalypticism* (but not "millenarianism")[40] as ways of understanding the divine-human relationship and the history of the church. Calvin began the *Institutes* with the doctrine of providence, or the principle that God was actively guiding the visible church through stress and storm. Opening the Old Testament, the reformers came upon scene after scene of His interventions among the people of Abraham, sometimes to punish and other times to sustain them. The emergence of Protestantism was another chapter in the recurring drama of divine interventions to punish the disobedient and reward the faithful, or so the reformers believed. When they turned to the prophetic books of Isaiah, Daniel, and Revelation or consulted verses in the Gospels and apostolic letters that seemed of the same tenor, the leaders of the Reformed also encountered a story of ongoing warfare between the "true" followers of Christ and the many hypocrites who, although ostensibly Christians, were aiding the Antichrist or "man of sin" (1 John 2:18, 22; 2 Thess. 2) in his campaigns against the saints. True faith was always under siege from forces allied with the Antichrist, as evidenced by the many episodes in the Old Testament when people had succumbed to idolatry. Now, with reform underway again, the most dangerous enemy of the true church was the papacy, which Protestants regarded as the institutional presence of the Antichrist.[41]

The prophetic books contained a more hopeful message. As had happened in ancient Egypt to the Jews, who awaited deliverance from captivity, the faithful few were awaiting the moment when Christ would return in triumph, release the saints from their suffering, and restore the true church to a state of perfection. At the climax of that event, "Babylon" would give way to "the holy city, [the] new Jerusalem," which descends from the heavens as God declares, "Behold, I make all things new" (Rev. 21:2–5). The church was at the heart of this transformation in the making, a church burdened by the deceptions of the Antichrist yet also "fulfilling itself in a voluntary, harmonious community." John Knox summed up this mixture of militancy and optimism by imagining two armies "betwixt [whom] there continueth a battell, which never shalbe reconciled until the Lord Jesus put a finall ende to the miseries of his Church."[42]

This scenario of ongoing conflict deflected a question Catholics pressed again and again on Protestants. Where were the reformers during the many centuries when Catholicism had flourished? What did Protestants have that matched the antiquity of Rome? The English Protestant John Bale believed he knew the answer to this question. Writing in the 1540s, he argued that the titanic struggle between the saints and the Antichrist, the core narrative of Revelation, was manifested in the conflict between Protestantism and Catholicism. In *The Image of the Two Churches* (1545?) he foregrounded the Christianity that had been preserved by a "saving remnant" that fled into the wilderness (Rev. 12:6) in the fourth century CE at a moment when corruption was beginning to overtake the Church.[43] Bale's concept of two churches, the one true but hiding in the wilderness, the other false but immensely powerful, appealed to English and Scottish Protestants as they began their own struggle against Catholicism. It explained how the true church had survived during the many centuries of Catholic ascendancy, and it linked the Reformation with the scenarios that conclude Revelation and Daniel. John Foxe went further in attempting to align biblical prophecy and the history of the Christian church, using the seven seals mentioned in Revelation 6:1–17 as his starting point. Treating them as symbolic markers of key moments in the history of the world or, as he preferred to say, the history of the church, he argued that the reign of the Antichrist was coming to an end (the breaking of the fifth seal) and the saints were beginning to enjoy the fullness of the Gospel (the sixth seal). He slotted other parts of Revelation into the same general sequence—the seven trumpets, the seven vials, the seven beasts—in ways that allowed him to include both Islam and the papacy as enemies of Christ. One lesson of this exegesis was the great danger of allowing the church to usurp worldly power. Another was a point made by Bale, that Rome and the Antichrist were one and the same. Where Foxe hesitated was in specifying when the seventh trumpet would be sounded and the last judgment take place.[44]

Be it via Foxe and Bale or various Continental writers, the process of interpreting biblical prophecy nourished a great deal of speculation about the New Jerusalem of Revelation 21 and the four monarchies or kingdoms Nebuchadnezzar had seen in a dream (Dan. 2). One after another, the four kingdoms had risen and been destroyed, whereupon God set up a fifth kingdom to "stand for ever" (Dan. 2:44–45). How better to understand the situation of Protestants in the sixteenth century than to represent them as a martyr-like people who, in the larger workings of God's providence, would eventually be raised up as the fifth and final kingdom? And how better to sustain moral activism of the kind that Calvin was expecting of all Protestants? Perpetuated in the *Book of Martyrs* and its many spinoffs, a historical imaginary of the suffering few struggling against the corruption introduced by Catholicism would have long-lasting consequences in Britain, as would the possibility of imagining the visible church as a community of the few, not of the many. Another aspect of Reformed commentary on the Bible, the assertion that God would pour out His wrath on those who violated divine law, would also reemerge as the framework for understanding certain events. The translators of the Geneva Bible turned this premise into the argument that the Catholicism imposed on

England by Mary Tudor was an appropriate punishment of the English people for having allowed such a "horrible backsliding and falling away from Christ to antichrist."[45]

No inventory of Reformed themes and practices is complete if it fails to mention the theological argument that God "predestined" (decided on His own) who would saved or, to use the formal language of theology, who was "elected" to salvation. Based on Romans 8:29–30, "For whom he did foreknow he did predestinate . . . [and] them he also called: and whom he called, them he also justified," the doctrine of election (or predestination) has often been misunderstood or misrepresented. Given the confusion that surrounds the doctrine, I defer this motif to chapter four, which covers theology.

Contingencies and Mediations

Wherever the Reformed tradition emerged and began to flourish, as was happening in Western Europe by the 1550s, its program was controversial. As the chapters that follow will indicate in more detail, the goal of restoring the independence of the church clashed with what monarchs and the nobility or social elites wanted. Rarely, if ever, did those elites welcome a church capable of supervising everyone's moral behavior, their own included. For them, one of the benefits of the new religion was the transfer of authority from Rome to civil governments those of high social rank would control. In parts of Europe as well as in Scotland, rulers and elites also held at arm's length the ferocious anti-Catholicism voiced by so many within the Reformed. Better a de facto tolerance than coercion or a bloodbath, they reasoned, if the country's Catholics remained loyal to the civil state and practiced their religion privately. Most of the time, the same leaders wanted reform to unfold in an orderly manner. The outbursts of popular violence that erupted in the Netherlands and Scotland at mid-century prompted second thoughts among civil leaders about appealing to the people to overthrow false gods.[46]

Thanks to these reactions, what was accomplished often diverged from what Scripture or church history prescribed. Inevitably, hopes for a thoroughgoing transformation of church and society in the name of true religion ran up against the obstacles of local custom, entrenched privilege, and the reluctance of civil governments to forfeit social peace or accept the authority of the clergy. Such was the fate of the Reformation in Scotland and England and especially of the people who wanted a fullblown reformation along Reformed lines.

A major impediment to reform was the economic situation of the Church of England, the Church of Scotland, and the Church of Ireland, where Protestantism was also being introduced in the sixteenth century. Throughout the sixteenth and seventeenth centuries, religious reformers and the civil state in Britain were at odds on the finances of each national church. The reason was simple. Except for Mary Tudor, the sixteenth-century monarchs of England used their powers of office to seize and put to other uses the wealth of monasteries, abbeys, chantries, guilds, parishes, and bishoprics. Appropriating these revenues and church lands was already underway in Catholic Scotland and Ireland, with Catholics participating in the scramble. Although Protestant reformers tried to reverse this process, the gains they made were modest; the *Book of Discipline* (1561) drafted by the reformers in Scotland envisioned redirecting the wealth of the state church to meet the needs of ministers and the poor but, as a Scottish historian has pointed out, "how could they hope to enforce such a transference of wealth" against the wishes of the nobility?[47] Nor was Mary Tudor able to restore properties to the church during her brief reign as head of the English state. In the 1580s, a small group of Puritan-affiliated activists proposed that the Church of England free itself from lay patronage, an argument endorsed by some in the Church of Scotland, but for obvious reasons never acted on by those who benefitted from that system. Hence the reality that monarchies, social elites, and others who aspired to wealth and power controlled much of the revenues that otherwise would have sustained a comprehensive program of evangelical preaching. Although the chapters that follow omit most of the details of this story, it must always be kept in view as an irritant in the relationship between religious reformers and the wealthy or privileged elites on whom they were depending.[48]

International rivalries caused other difficulties. In late sixteenth-century Europe, the great antagonists were Spain and France, each of them predominantly Catholic and far stronger militarily than any Protestant city, state, region, or country. Nonetheless, the two empires formed alliances with Protestant regimes when doing so was to their advantage, and vice versa. England did so with Spain in 1559 at a moment when French troops were supporting a Catholic ruler in Scotland. Simultaneously, the rulers of Spain and France wanted to aid Catholics in England, Scotland, and Ireland, as Spain was hoping to do in 1588 when Philip II dispatched the Armada. Or could local Catholics be encouraged to resist a Protestant government?

One way or another, confessional identity and foreign policy were rarely aligned. The simple rule would have been for Protestants to aid Protestants. Indeed, in the late sixteenth and early seventeenth centuries, England became a player in the wars of religion that pitted Catholics against Protestants on the Continent, doing so indirectly by allowing English soldiers to aid the provinces of the Low Countries in their revolt against Spanish rule and providing financial support for German soldiers aiding the Huguenot during episodes of civil war in France. Subsequently, Scottish soldiers served various masters on the Continent. During the reign of Elizabeth I and in the early stages of the Thirty Years War (1618–1648), which was fought largely along confessional lines, some officers of state and many in Parliament urged the English government to become much more active in behalf of international Protestantism. Instead, James I encouraged one of his sons, the future Charles I, to seek a royal bride in Catholic France, and, at a moment of peacemaking with Spain in 1604, contemplated using English troops *against* Dutch Protestants. These situations—alliances made or broken, invasions expected or deterred, national fervor aroused or blunted—alternately weakened and enhanced the connections between religion and foreign policy. As the historian Anthony Milton has pointed out, "supranational confessionalism" was always at odds with "nationalist pragmatism." When Catholicism was at its most threatening, militant Protestantism became more appealing and therefore more politically successful. When the game of international alliances muted the division between Catholic and Protestant, as it frequently did, militant Protestantism fell out of favor.[49]

All this is to say that civil governments had more pressing concerns than to expend their political capital and financial resources on religious crusades. For the rulers of England and Scotland, the foremost goal was to extend and deepen their own authority, a project aided by the coming of Protestantism, which enabled the English monarchy to expand its role in matters of religion. As these rulers knew better than anyone else, their authority was jeopardized by fractures—between Catholic and Protestant, or within the social and political elite, a feature of Scottish life from the mid-sixteenth-century onward. Thanks to these situations, armed revolts erupted from time to time, as did civil war in Scotland. When a king or queen had no obvious successor or an heir not yet old enough to take charge—Edward VI of England was nine years old when he succeeded his father Henry VIII in 1547, and James VI of Scotland a mere infant when his mother, Mary Stuart, was deposed—the regents or deputies who ran the government were especially vulnerable to plotting by their rivals. Little wonder, then, that the leaders of England and Scotland put their own interests first when the church called on them to promote true religion. This they did under certain circumstances, but only if such a program strengthened their rule. In England, Henry VIII completed the break with Roman Catholicism by having himself declared "Supreme Head" of the Church of England. The Church would do his bidding, not vice versa, a policy favored by Elizabeth I in England and James VI in Scotland. The English Parliament also wanted a role in deciding how the state church was administered. Assertions of this kind were nothing new. Long before the Reformation, church elders and political leaders had disputed their relationship, each claiming an authority of one kind or another over the other. By the early seventeenth century, the policy favored by Henry VIII had become known as "Erastianism" in the wake of assertions by Thomas Erastus (born Lieber; 1524–1583), a Swiss physician and Protestant theologian, that the civil state should administer the process of church discipline. To rulers such as Elizabeth I, a tempered Erastianism was far more appealing than the two-kingdoms theory of the Reformed. Theoretical support for it was also provided by the commonplace that religious unity and nationhood were one and the same.[50]

Monarchs wanted an all-inclusive state church in which *everyone* was required to accept the faith of the sovereign and participate in the same church services. It was no accident that the title page of the English "great bible" of 1540 featured an image of Henry VIII handing a bible to two figures and a group of people exclaiming "Vivat Rex." If the king had his way, Protestantism was going to enhance royal authority. Yet Henry and his successors in England knew that their subjects—Catholics as well as Protestants—were aware of the argument that God summoned them to disobey an unlawful ruler, a scenario enacted numerous times in the Hebrew Bible. Princely rule thus rested on a contradiction, the difference between lawful and unlawful versions of civil authority.

A Protestant country led by a Protestant prince was plagued by other contradictions. Uniformity as a political ideal was never matched by uniformity in practice. It was relatively easy to deny a Catholic minority the freedom to observe its faith in public and execute a handful of dissidents but impossible to enforce any general conversion to Protestantism, and just as impossible to drive the laggards out of the country. Nor could the Protestants who questioned the monarch's version of uniformity—in this book, most of them come under the heading of Puritans or Puritan-Separatists—be suppressed. As the literary historian Debora Shuger has pointed out, the larger issue was as old as Christianity itself, "the problem of the relation between temporal institutions and divine presence." In 1530s Strasbourg, 1540s Geneva, and recurrently in Protestant Scotland and England, tensions became acute when the policies of a would-be Christian prince diverged from the making of true religion as imagined by the more ardently Protestant. To add paradox to paradox, no one believed in the toleration of religious dissent, not even those who were being punished for refusing to conform. Agreement prevailed on the principle that defending the one true religion was a "charitable" means of saving people from heresy. Nonetheless, religious dissent never disappeared from England, Scotland, and especially Ireland, where most people were Catholics. At certain moments, therefore, the authority of a monarch was severely challenged when its agenda in matters of religion became implausible. For the godly who play such a large role in this book, this was both good news and bad, though mostly bad because their program depended on state support to succeed.[51]

One other circumstance qualifies as bad news, the condition of "the people."[52] Could they be counted on to embrace a Reformed-style program bent on imposing moral discipline and high standards of belief and piety? Ardent reformers on the Continent and in Britain were of two minds. On the one hand, many clergy painted an unflattering portrait of widespread illiteracy, fickleness, and amoral behavior. It was disheartening that most of the people in England had acquiesced in the transition from the Protestant Edward VI to the Catholic Mary Tudor and, in Scotland, did so little to encourage the coming of Protestantism. Longer term, it was just as disheartening that they disdained a rigorous Protestantism. A late sixteenth-century English theologian divided laypeople into categories that began with "unbelievers who are both ignorant and unteachable" before moving upward to a somewhat more sympathetic grouping of those who were "teachable, but yet ignorant." About the same time, the ultra-Protestant John Penry disparaged the people of his native Wales for resorting to "southsaiers, and enchanters"; by his (prejudiced) estimate, the Welsh "have *not one* in some score of our parishes, that have a saving knowledge" of Christ.[53] Penry may have overstated the problem, but he was basically correct in suggesting that large numbers of people knew little and seemed to care less about Protestant doctrine and practice. As historians of sixteenth-century England have pointed out, the rapid transition from Protestantism to Catholicism and again to Protestantism within the space of six years (1553–1559) may have convinced lay women and men that the wise course of action was to hedge one's bets and lie low.[54]

Hence the irritation of ministers in England such as Arthur Dent. In his best-selling manual of religious devotion, *The Plain Mans Path-way to Heaven* (1601), he created a fictional character who typified the people of *very* modest expectations. After listening to Dent's description of the new birth, this man responded,

> Tush, tush: what needs all this adoe? If a man say
> his Lord's praier, his ten Commandments, and his Beliefe,
> and keepe them, and say nobodie no harme . . . , and doe as hee would
>   be done too, have a good
> faith to God-ward, and bee a man of Gods beliefe, no doubt
> he shall be saved, without all this running to Sermons
> and pratling of the Scripture.

In numerous towns and villages, people of this temperament overlapped with men and women who preferred the sociability of the alehouse to the more demanding fellowship of their parish church. Meanwhile, Catholicism persisted in part because of the acute regionalism of Scotland, where the Gaelic-speaking Highlands remained Catholic, and a similar regionalism in England, where the northern counties of Yorkshire and Lancashire were much more Catholic than the rest of the country.[55]

Another aspect of the problem of the people concerned social rank and privilege. Did some groups become especially active on behalf of Protestantism (or Puritanism) while others dragged their feet? In sixteenth-century England and Scotland as in Germany, the Protestant message was welcomed by people of middling and upper social status and especially by people living in cities and towns, who appreciated a more participatory form of religion that reduced the distance between clergy and laypeople. This was not the reaction of the people of aristocratic or noble rank whose well-being was linked to owning land and securing favors from the monarch. Once those of this status realized that the reformers were insisting that everyone was subject to social and moral discipline, they recoiled from allowing ordinary people or parish clergy to supervise their behavior. As Alexander Nowell pointed out in his *Catechism*, "the rich and men of power" wanted "impunity and most free liberty to sin" and would not accept an effective mode of "ecclesiastical discipline." Accustomed to deference from others and benefitting from privileges that included membership in the House of Lords (England) or other governing bodies (England and Scotland), men and women of this kind were also unlikely to welcome a more participatory form of religion that curtailed their special status. Nor could they be expected to challenge the policies of the reigning monarch. In a social world marked by entrenched forms of privilege and differences of power, did evangelical Protestantism have a chance?[56]

Yet the leaders of the Reformation in England remained hopeful. Soon after returning from exile in 1558, John Jewell traveled around England as part of a campaign to curtail or eliminate Catholic practices, an experience that led him to believe that "the people everywhere [are] thirsting after religion"—meaning the Protestantism he himself espoused. Reports of this kind were probably flavored by Jewell's debate with an English Catholic about the legitimacy of the English Reformation, a debate in which he argued that "husbandmen and ditchers and herdsmen" could reason more wisely about religion than the Catholic clergy. Others during this period were reporting that a "numerous audience eagerly flocked" to hear them preach, an optimism buttressed by the fact that, during the reign of Mary Tudor, dozens of ordinary women and men had died at the stake because they felt so strongly about their new faith. During those same years, laypeople had formed covert congregations and, as John Knox noted about his homeland, Protestant mobs had ransacked Catholic shrines and churches. Indeed, the process of reform in both countries relied on the fervency of laypeople, as did regional or national reformations on the Continent. By the middle of the sixteenth century in Scotland and England, and continuing into the next century, some laypeople were exceptionally active on behalf of Protestant principles.[57]

The most exciting possibility was the suggestion that, thanks to their simplicity, common people were more discerning of spiritual truth than the Catholic clergy under whom they suffered. Well before the coming of the Reformation, religious reformers had employed the figure of the plowman as "most nearly the servant of God," someone of the same wise innocence as the fishermen who became the earliest of Jesus's disciples. Now, with the coming of Protestantism, the early reformers imagined every plowman perusing the Bible as he worked his fields. A useful fiction, this figure of "the people of God, redeemed by the bloud of his sonne, unto whom the Gospell doth belonge" and therefore with "as great interest and full right" in matters of religion as anyone else, enjoyed a long life within English Protestantism. Foxe, for one, depicted laypeople as wiser than the clergy in "seeing through the corruptions of pop-ery" and therefore the saving remnant who preserved true religion. Women had a place in this story, especially martyrs such as Anne Askew, whose medita-tions became something of a model for proto-Protestants in England. For the moment, no one worried about putting the genie of an activist laity back into the bottle of a state church, perhaps because, by the close of the century, the reform-minded knew that their program was gaining adherents within urban elites, middling social groups, and a portion of the gentry or landed class.[58]

The problem of the people was more than a matter of overcoming custom, illiteracy, and indifference. In Bucer's vision of the kingdom of Christ, the peo-ple could be won over if two conditions were met: the Christian prince gave wholehearted support to preaching as the crucial instrument of evangelization, and the universities began to produce zealous ministers who would do the preaching. What if neither happened? And what if, as he himself recognized, the imperative of securing everyone's repentance was possibly asking more of the people than was realistic. Setting aside coercion, which Bucer regarded as less effective than persuasion, could Protestantism as defined by the Reformed tradition become the faith of a nation as a whole? Or was this project destined to become a Christianity for and of a spiritual elite? There were moments when the makers of the Reformed international and, in England and Scotland, the leaders of the Reformation in those countries, had to wonder which of these alternatives was more likely.[59]

Enacting the Reformed Program

These contingencies and circumstances dogged the reformers in sixteenth-century England and Scotland, and even more so in Ireland, where Protes-tants were a tiny minority. The "gross darkness of popery" was beginning to recede, but Satan was still at work in the world, "sometimes by bloody death and cruel torments, other whiles imprisonments, banishments and other hard usages; as being loath his kingdom should go down, the truth prevail and the churches of God revert to their ancient purity and recover their primitive order, liberty and beauty."[60]

Nonetheless, the influence of the Reformed tradition in sixteenth-century England, Scotland, and, by the early seventeenth century, a few parts of Ire-land, was palpable. Because of local circumstances, this program enjoyed less success in England than in Scotland. In the first of these countries the rupture with Rome began as an affair of state and unfolded as a top-down process or-chestrated by Henry VIII. Via his authority, Protestantism of a limited kind was imposed on the English people, followed by a more emphatic Reformation imposed during the reign of his son Edward VI, followed (after 1558) by a more tempered Reformation that suited the tastes of Elizabeth I, who cared a good deal about outward conformity but distanced herself from the agenda of the

Marian exiles. The rupture with Rome that drove the Scottish Reformation was resisted by James V (1512–1542) and the two queens who succeeded him, Mary of Guise (d. 1560) and Mary Stuart. Consequently, Protestantism became something of a movement from beneath—not a popular movement, since it relied on members of the aristocracy and landed classes, but nonetheless a movement of outsiders who came to power only after having precipitated a civil war and chased Mary Stuart from the throne. This political situation, with monarchs too weak to impose their will on the country, worked in favor of those Protestants who admired the Reformed tradition.[61] Again by way of comparison, uprisings but no sustained warfare linked to confessional and dynastic fault lines broke out in sixteenth-century England. Notably, conflict was averted in 1553 thanks to the collapse of a plot to substitute a Protestant noblewoman for Mary Tudor, who inherited the monarchy after Edward VI died in 1553. Of more significance in the long run was the fact that Protestantism was endorsed by a significant portion of the clerical elite, including the long-serving Archbishop of Canterbury, Thomas Cranmer. Unlike what happened in Scotland, the higher clergy and the monarchy collaborated in the process of reform—or, from the point of view of radical Protestants, thwarted a more comprehensive renovation of the state church.[62]

In summary, the English Reformation sidestepped three accomplishments or principles that were typically Reformed. Instead of shifting to a polity in which all ministers held the same rank, the Church of England preserved a hierarchical structure centered on the office of bishop. Instead of embracing a spare, biblically grounded mode of worship, it preserved some aspects of the Catholic mass and liturgy. And, instead of proclaiming Christ as sole king and ruler of the visible church, the Church of England acknowledged the monarch as its Supreme Head or Supreme Governor, the term Elizabeth I preferred. The leaders of the Scottish Reformation were far more daring. By the 1570s they had embraced each of these principles and aligned the Church of Scotland with the Reformed international.

Yet in neither country did reformation achieve closure or completion; in both, its development was punctuated by spasms of intense feeling about "idolatry" as well as by a process that scholars of Christianity in Western Europe have named "confessionalization." Gradually, the possibilities for compromise between Catholic and Protestant or Lutheran and Reformed that marked the opening phases of the Reformation gave way to a consolidation of doctrine and worship, a process signaled by a burst of Reformed creeds (chap. 4), firmer definitions of church government (chap. 2) and programs for training the right kind of minister (chap. 4). It was symptomatic of this process that the 1570s saw the emergence of "presbyterians" in England and Scotland, with consequences that reverberate in the chapters that follow.[63]

Always, however, the dynamics of reform were checked or contested. By the 1580s, the stability of the Scottish Reformation was being disrupted by divisions within the political elite, most of them unwilling to endorse a full-blown presbyterianism that transferred authority over major aspects of religion from the civil state or nobility to the clergy. Crucially, a Protestant king shared these misgivings, a king too young to exert his authority in the 1570s but, after 1585, insisting on greater control of the church. James VI of Scotland endorsed several aspects of Reformed Protestantism, but he also liked being in charge. Because Elizabeth I was indifferent if not hostile to Reformed principles, in both countries the Reformed ideal was deeply contested—resisted by some, advocated by others. And in both, this struggle persisted well into the seventeenth century, to the point of provoking a civil war that broke out in 1642 among English Protestants, a war touched off by an insurgency in Scotland. Within a few years the promise of a perfect reformation of both national churches gave way to internal divisions and, by the 1650s, to the collapse of the Reformed project.

The planting of Protestantism in New England followed a different path. Leaving England at a moment when the state church was suppressing Reformed-style Protestantism, the emigrants brought with them strong hopes for enacting the reformation that, from Henry VIII onward, had been thwarted in their mother country. Now, in the "free air of the new worlde" (as the Scotch Presbyterian Robert Baillie put it), they could do as they wished. And, since the society they set up was spared the trauma of civil war and the fracturing of Protestantism in mid-seventeenth-century England and Scotland, the colonists were able to sustain a more homogeneous system. Here, on the periphery of the English empire, the principles of the Reformed tradition were fulfilled in both expected and unexpected ways.

These are stories I tell in the rest of this book. They owe some of their richness and complexity to the ever-present difference—as much a part of our world as of theirs—between Christianity as an ideal and Christianity as embodied in an institutional church closely allied with the civil state. Before I tell those stories, it will help to set the stage if I underscore the importance of four dilemmas or predicaments that recurred throughout the longer life of the Puritan movement. The first of these arose out of the Reformed principles of obedience to both divine law *and* the Christian prince. Regarding God as lawgiver and Scripture as a demonstration of what God expected of his true followers, the Reformed counted on civil rulers to observe divine law. As voiced by the English martyr John Rogers, who died at the stake in 1555, "Unto it [God's word] must all men, king and queen, emperor, parliaments and general councils obey—and the word obeyeth no man."[64] Inevitably, this assumption ran afoul of a Catholic ruler such as Mary Tudor who, in Protestant eyes, was defying divine law or a ruler who, although Protestant, disdained much of the Reformed program. These possibilities prompted John Knox, living in exile from his Scottish homeland at midcentury, to pose the question, "Whether obedience is to be rendered to a Magistrate who enforces idolatry and condemns true religion?" to which his answer was, "The history of Daniel, and the express command of God, Matt. 10, and the examples of the apostles in Acts 4 and 5, as also that of many of the martyrs ... teach us that we must not obey the king or magistrates when their commands are opposed to God and his lawful worship, but rather that we should expose our persons, and lives, and fortunes to danger." Well before Knox began to ponder the contradiction between the authority of civil rulers and the authority of the Word, Lutherans in Germany had argued that, although God ordained civil rulers as lesser "gods" and made obedience to them a moral law—a line of reasoning based on Romans 13—this obedience was contingent on whether those rulers supported the Protestant cause. If not, Lutheran political theology acknowledged the possibility of resistance to such persons. Together with the English refugee Christopher Goodman, Knox endorsed this line of argument at a moment when Mary Tudor was on the throne, although the two men shied away from the extremes of "tyranicide" (assassination) or popular revolt. In general, Knox, Goodman, Calvin, and the theologians of Zurich insisted that religious minorities must limit themselves to passive resistance and, within the limits of what was possible, to practicing their own version of Protestantism.[65]

Adhering to this theology tested every Reformed community on the receiving end of state-endorsed violence. An extreme example was the St. Bartholomew Day massacre of 1572. A French Catholic king (or his apologists) justified the massacre on the grounds of self-defense against a presumed Protestant conspiracy. No massacres of this kind occurred in England and Scotland, but their monarchs sometimes used the same argument to justify the repression of the more aggressive Protestants and, after 1570, of Catholics. Situations of this kind made it difficult to reconcile loyalty to divine law with loyalty to civil rulers. Forcefully present within the Huguenot version of the Reformed tradition in a country where no king ever endorsed the Protestant cause[66] and again in England during the reign of Queen Mary, a crisis of authority reemerged in the closing years of the sixteenth century and persisted throughout much of the seventeenth. Christian prince or servant of the Antichrist? Unquestioning loyalty or defiant conscience? Out of these antitheses emerged the quintessential Puritan dilemma, the challenge of reconciling loyalty to the civil state with loyalty to Christ as the true head of the church.[67]

The core principles of the Reformed tradition prompted a second tension, the scope of what was meant by idolatry. A master word among the reformers in Scotland and England, idolatry was ostensibly about *visible* aspects of worship. But what if it signified inward or spiritual idolatry, as when someone turned aside from wholehearted worship of God and listened to Satan?[68] And did some forms of social behavior also qualify as idolatry? The answer to these questions was yes, an answer that made it increasingly difficult to know when the endpoint had been reached—that is, when church, society, and people had actually been purged of corruption, or sanctified. Iconoclasm, with mobs destroying the Catholic apparatus of relics and altars, was a step in the right direction but never sufficient. Witch-hunting was another possibility, a means of exposing a half-hidden version of idolatry. For other Protestants, however, iconoclasm was too extreme a response to a problem that was not all that troubling. Longer term, therefore, the Puritan movement was not of one mind about what it meant to eliminate idolatry.[69]

The principle of obedience to the Word generated a third problem, the question of what Christ had mandated. Did Scripture contain a comprehensive, explicit answer to this question? Early on, Calvin and other early leaders of the Reformed acknowledged that the Bible spoke more clearly on some matters than on others. Moreover, Calvin was willing to acknowledge the merits of local variations: one size did not fit all. For these reasons he refused to denounce the episcopal structure of the Church of England. But how were reformers to know when and how the Word was normative? This was no casual question, for any decision that contradicted the Word was, in effect, a decision tilted toward idolatry—and in the ethos of the Reformed tradition, slippage of this kind was akin to betraying divine law. Reasoning of this kind explains the fervency of the more daring reformers about ending episcopacy and restoring "discipline," a fervency that prompted others to recommend compromise or moderation.

Tension also arose around a fourth aspect of reform, the relationship between the economy of redemption and the boundaries of the church. At the outset of the Reformation, Protestants were akin to a rare species of fish swimming in a vast lake filled with other species. With confessionalization came a sociology of state or territorial churches that, by definition, included everyone: in principle, all fish shared the same religion. The transition from small-scale communities identifying themselves as the "few" who fled into the wilderness to churches defined by territory and political rule was bound to raise questions about the benefits of inclusion versus selectivity. Was Calvin wrong in suggesting that the visible church—the church on earth—should be generously inclusive? For many Protestants, the imperative was to tighten the boundary between the wheat and the chaff. In them, the "latent sectarianism" of Calvin's understanding of the church rose to the surface.[70]

The unfolding of the Reformed tradition in England, Scotland, and New England was deeply marked by these issues. In my telling of this story, I make room for those Protestants more willing than some others to blur the hard edges of reform. Moderation and compromise may not seem as authentically Reformed as the zeal of a John Knox, but in Knox's Scotland as in Elizabethan England and, several decades later, in New England, both were widely practiced. Within the Continental Reformation, Melanchthon had been the quintessential moderate who tried to reconcile different understandings of the Eucharist. He was criticized for doing so, but others followed in his footsteps—men in England who doubted episcopacy but became bishops in the hope of using their office to promote some aspects of reform; men in Scotland who supported the authority of a Christian prince although preferring the two-kingdoms theory of church and state; men and women in New England who relished the purity of the gathered congregation but wanted it to incorporate their children. As these examples suggest, moderation was inherently precarious, its emphasis on unity and compromise threatened by aggressive kings and a fervently evangelical clergy and laypeople. The history of the Reformed or, as I shall begin to say, of Puritanism in England, Scotland, and New England was never free of pressures that worked against the goals of the movement.

CHAPTER TWO

A Movement Emerges

THOMAS SAMPSON WAS APPREHENSIVE. HEARING in 1558 of the death of Mary Tudor and her stepsister Elizabeth's succession to the throne, he rejoiced that Protestantism would return as the state religion of his native England, which he had fled in 1554. Even so, he was anxious about the practice and policies of a newly reborn church. When rumors reached him that a bishopric awaited, he told a leader of the Reformed international that the office had no warrant in Scripture. He objected to the office for another reason, the fact that bishops were not chosen by the consent of the people as happened in the "primitive" churches described in the New Testament. He worried, too, about being asked to wear any of the vestments the Church of England had inherited from Catholicism. Some months later, he told the same friend that, having seen how the new queen was acting, he and others were "afraid lest the truth of religion . . . should either be overturned, or very much darkened," citing Elizabeth's decision to keep a crucifix on the altar in her private chapel. The more he realized that an "entire reformation" aimed at "the right ordering of all things according to the word" was in jeopardy, the more he anticipated a crisis that would pit obedience to the Word, or "conscience," against loyalty to the new queen and the church over which she presided.[1]

Sampson was a nonconformist before there was conformity, someone who knew at the very beginning of Elizabeth's reign that he would have to choose between conscience and state-imposed rules and regulations. A friend and fellow exile, Thomas Humphrey, felt the same way even though he accepted a professorship of divinity at Oxford. Called before the Archbishop of Canterbury in 1564 to answer complaints about their behavior, the two men pleaded "tender consciences" and offered half a loaf: they would stop criticizing the rule about clerical dress but never wear the surplice, the name for a garment associated with Catholic practice.[2] Half-loaves were theirs thanks to vacillation among the bishops and the influence of the two men's lay patrons. Yet was half a loaf what Christ expected of his disciples? For the rest of the queen's reign, the doubts voiced by Sampson in 1558 would trouble the laypeople and clergy who wanted an "entire reformation."

A similar intermingling of high hopes and frustrations characterized the reformation in Scotland. For John Knox, whose vision of thoroughgoing reform had been sharpened during his years as an exile in places like Geneva, the process of reform in his homeland seemed on the verge of eliminating all "idolatry." "There is no realm this day upon the face of the earth, that hath them [the sacraments] in like purity," he declared in the history he wrote of the Scottish Reformation. *This* Knox regarded himself as a prophet of the same kind as those described in the Old Testament. Yet he was almost useless when it came to the day-to-day negotiations on which reform depended. Inevitably, he and like-minded reformers settled for something less, although agitating for more.[3]

With Protestants in power in both countries as of 1560, Knox yearned for bridges between Scotland and England, a truly *British* reformation that would strengthen the Protestant cause in both places. Instead, the Church of Scotland went in one direction and the Church of England in another. How this happened for England is described in this chapter; how reformation unfolded in Scotland in the next.

Elizabeth I and the Puritan Movement

A backward glance at the English Reformation will set the stage for the emergence of the Puritan wing of the state church. After Mary Tudor died in November 1558 and Elizabeth ascended to the throne, England's state religion officially passed overnight from Roman Catholicism to Protestantism. An erratic transition of this kind had already occurred during the reign of Mary and Elizabeth's father, Henry VIII. With the consent of Parliament, Henry had renounced the authority of the papacy over the Church of England and approved or, toward the end of his life opposed, other means of making the state church fully Protestant.[4]

When Henry's nine-year-old son Edward VI succeeded to the throne in January 1547, a government headed by the Duke of Somerset endorsed major changes of the kind Henry had resisted, and the pace of reform quickened anew under the Duke of Northumberland, who came to power in 1549. Between them, these two governments eliminated much of what remained of institutional Catholicism. By mid-1550, a zealous Protestant was exulting that "never before in our time has there been such hope of the advancement of the pure doctrine of the Gospel, and of the complete subversion and rooting up of antichristian ceremonies and traditions." During the first fifteen months of Somerset's regime, the government ordered the destruction of all "shrines, paintings and pictures of saints and all images which had been offered to or had candles burned before them" and forbad the worship of relics, the ritual of pilgrimage, and the celebration of certain traditional ceremonies.[5] Subsequently, Parliament or the bishops recast the theology of the Eucharist, a step that included replacing altars with communion tables, substituting ordinary bread for the wafer, and simplifying the distinctive dress of the clergy who, from 1549 onward, were free to marry. Simultaneously, the government was abolishing guilds and chantries and expropriating their wealth. Once these disappeared, the practice of intercessory prayer for the dead lapsed, deemed no longer necessary since the Catholic concept of purgatory had been abandoned.[6]

Some of these changes, together with much that was carried over from Catholicism, made their way into a liturgical text, the *Book of Common Prayer* (1549)—common in the sense of enabling laypeople to participate in an English-language liturgy. Publicly endorsed by the Crown, it was followed by a second, more vigorously Reformed version (1552) that severed English worship from Catholic practice by emphasizing the place of Scripture in church services, subjecting the church to the same authority, and affirming a more distinctively Reformed understanding of Holy Communion. Even so, some in England regarded it as falling short of "entire perfection," one problem being the rule, too Catholic for someone such as Sampson, that communicants kneel instead of sitting when they received the sacrament. In some printed versions, the 1552 prayer book included a specially inserted "black rubric" denying that the practice of kneeling to receive the sacrament signified the real presence of Christ in the bread and wine.[7] Despite its imperfections, the 1552 version seemed to justify the reputation for Reformed-style Protestantism that Edward was acquiring. In the eyes of his admirers, he was a veritable Josiah, the last of the righteous kings of Judah (sixth century BC). Like his Old Testament predecessor, the boy king was intent on cleansing the church of "all monuments of idolatry."[8] Then, to the dismay of the reformers, Edward died in 1553, leaving Mary Tudor next in line for the throne.

Most of the Edwardian program was unwound once Mary succeeded to the throne in August 1553, for she had guarded her Catholic faith. The wheel turned anew: the Roman mass was restored, the authority of the papacy reaffirmed, and celibacy required of all clergy. We may marvel that a country could pass from Protestantism to Catholicism so rapidly, but it was almost unthinkable to question the legitimacy of Mary's claim to the throne and, in everyday life, the adjustments were not as wrenching as we may suppose. Nonetheless, Mary's regime found plenty of Protestants to pursue, executing nearly three hundred at the stake between February 1555 and the queen's death in late 1558.

Now the fate of the Reformation rested in the hands of Elizabeth and her advisors.[9] Would she take on the mantle of Josiah and resume a vigorous program of reform? This was the counsel of the English exiles who prepared the "Geneva" translation of the Bible. In an opening "Epistle to the Queen," they reminded her of the Old Testament examples of the temple builder Zerubbabel and idol-destroying kings such as Josiah and Asa, who pursued "the utter abolishing of idolatrie." The corrective to idolatry was to "embrace the word" and bind everyone to "obey" it, an argument fleshed out with allusions to Christ as the "cornerstone" of the church and someone who, in Scripture, "left an order . . . for the building up of his body." Other advisors emphasized the difference between "true religion" and any mingling of old and new, Catholic and Protestant.[10]

Elizabeth waited until the first Parliament of her new regime met in early 1559 to solidify her authority over the church and give explicit recognition to Protestantism. Hoping to preserve peace with Spain and anxious to conciliate those who continued to prefer Catholicism, some of them still serving as bishops and clergy, she wanted to move slowly. But the first of her Parliaments was impatient. Not without close votes in the House of Lords on key matters, Parliament reenacted a law from Henry VIII's reign naming the monarch the "only supreme governor of the realm, as well as in all spiritual and ecclesiastical things or causes, as temporal," a modest reworking of Henry's title as Supreme Head that pleased those Protestants who regarded Christ as the true head of the Church. An Act of Uniformity allowed people to receive both bread and wine during the administration of the Eucharist, and another endorsed the prayer book of 1552. When it was reprinted, however, the "black rubric" had been eliminated and language added to the liturgy suggesting something closer to the Catholic doctrine of Christ's presence in the bread and the wine, steps in keeping with the new queen's sympathies. Moreover, ministers in the church were to continue wearing the surplice and other "ornaments," a rule that (apart from the surplice) reversed what had been specified in the 1552 version of the *Book of Common Prayer*. In the aftermath of these measures, Catholic-minded bishops resigned rather than accept the Act of Uniformity. In came a fresh crop of bishops, some of them former exiles who would continue to seek advice from friends within the Reformed international.[11]

The tasks that awaited the new leaders of the state church were many and, without fresh resources of money and personnel, virtually impossible to accomplish. Foremost among them was infusing an evangelical spirit into an institution that encompassed everyone from Catholics to the nominally Protestant. Some of these leaders had a second goal, to resume the process of reform in a church "haunted by its Catholic past."[12] To this end, bishops began to instruct parish councils and local officials known as church wardens to discard the apparatus of Catholic ceremonies and whitewash the inside walls of their churches. Books that taught Protestant doctrine or abetted Protestant-style worship were quickly made available: Sternhold's *The Whole Booke of Psalms*, revised and expanded by John Hopkins and others; an English translation of the Bible known as the Bishops Bible; sermons refuting Catholic doctrine; and by 1570, an official catechism for ministers to use in instructing laypeople.[13] Matthew Parker, who became Archbishop of Canterbury in 1559, called for the destruction of "images and all other monuments of idolatry and superstition" and told church wardens to arrange a "comely and decent table" around which to celebrate Holy Communion. Shortly after moving from a post as bishop of London to the diocese of Yorkshire, a region in which Catholicism was widely favored, Edmund Grindal ordered his church wardens to acquire the *Book of Common Prayer*, the psalter, and the Bible in English, telling them as well that they must "utterly" destroy any altar and prohibit "superstitious ringing" of church bells during funerals. Grindal also emphasized the duty of weekly catechizing and its bearing on access to the sacraments: local clergy and wardens should bar people above the age of twenty from participating if they could not "say by heart" the Ten Commandments and other parts of the catechism.[14]

Meanwhile, steps were being taken to reeducate and strengthen the clergy now that preaching had become a principal means of grace. In the short run, Parker and his fellow bishops endorsed the practice of allowing laymen to read from the prayer book as a substitute for sermons. Ministers deemed unprepared to preach on their own could fall back on an officially endorsed collection of sermons, or *Homilies*. These were pebbles cast into a sea of spiritual darkness. Year after year, church leaders complained that the state church lacked a corps of effective ministers. "Many there are that hear not a sermon in seven years, I might safely say seventeen," a bishop remarked in 1588, adding that "their blood will be required at somebody's hands." What was needed was much better funding and, at Oxford and Cambridge, a stronger commitment to training evangelical preachers. Neither was forthcoming except by fits and starts.[15]

To men of Sampson's temperament, the pace of progress was frustratingly slow. By contrast, the reformers in Scotland were doing much better. "The Scots have made greater progress in true religion in a few months, than we have done in many years," a former Marian exile wrote friends in Europe.[16] What would it look like to further the Gospel in England? This question dominated the first Convocation (1562–63) of church leaders in Elizabeth's reign. Beforehand, a small group drafted a substantial agenda of reform and worked hard to get these proposals adopted. Of uncertain membership, it included Parker, Grindal, Sampson, and other former exiles, all of them expecting that the Elizabethan Settlement was a way station on a journey that would conclude when the state church had become emphatically Protestant. These men and their allies wanted the church to curtail or eliminate the long-established practices of clerical pluralism (allowing a single minister to hold multiple positions) and nonresidency (when a local priest lived elsewhere and delegated his pastoral responsibilities to a person of lesser rank and, often, lesser capacities). Reasoning that, without changes of this kind, no program of evangelization could succeed, the reforming party also recommended several steps to improve the financial situation of the state church. As well, they hoped to dispose of certain residues of Catholicism: ministers were not to wear "vestments, Copes and Surplesses," the sign of the cross in the service of baptism was questioned, kneeling would become optional or "indifferent," church bells would be silenced, the number of holy days curtailed, and "some few imperfections" remedied in the *Book of Common Prayer*.[17]

The tone and the substance of these proposals echoed the politics of some of the Marian exiles and the martyred bishop John Hooper, who, before entering the episcopate in 1550, had objected to the surplice and Catholic phrasing in the liturgy of the Eucharist. When the exiles were organizing congregations of their own in cities such as Frankfurt, Emden, and Geneva, some decided to replace the 1552 version of the *Book of Common Prayer* with an order of worship much closer to what was used in Geneva. Others insisted on keeping the prayer book but seemed willing to consider eliminating the surplice, kneeling at communion, saints' days, the sign of the cross in the liturgy of baptism, and confirmation by bishops. Argument was fierce within the English congregation in Frankfurt, where the more moderate proposals eventually prevailed. In Geneva, which attracted the largest number of exiles, the English church, which included some of the Scottish exiles, agreed to replace the *Book of Common Prayer* with an English translation of the Geneva order of worship. There and elsewhere, the exiles created congregations that enjoyed a de facto autonomy at odds with a bishop-centered state church.[18] This experience, together with what they had learned about Reformed practice and principle, nurtured the ambition of the reformers of 1562–63 to unsettle the Elizabethan Settlement. For the moment, its allies were few and its critics, many.[19]

The Convocation seemed ready to adopt the reforms the group recommended. Indeed, it came close to abolishing the surplice. Some in the Parliament of 1563 were also sympathetic. But Elizabeth was unwilling to go this far. She assented to a statement of doctrine known as the Thirty-Nine Articles (endorsed by Parliament in 1571), most of them copied from an earlier set of articles prepared by Archbishop Cranmer and based on Continental creeds, and she may not have noticed a few changes in the *Book of Common Prayer*.[20] Otherwise, she dug in her heels. Had she sided with the reformers of 1563 or, in the next decade, supported Grindal after he became Archbishop of Canterbury, she might have helped fashion a broad-reaching consensus about the scope and nature of reform.[21] Famously, the queen said no to the men who wanted to marry her. The no that resonates in this book is hers to a further reformation. From the moment Elizabeth ascended to the throne until her death some forty-five years later in early 1603, she rejected every plea, petition, and motion on its behalf whether broached in the Convocation, urged by some of her bishops, or endorsed by members of the Privy Council and the House of Commons.[22]

Enter the Puritan movement. No specific date was stamped on its birth certificate and no single manifesto spelled out its goals, most of which had already been voiced during the reign of Edward VI, with others emerging after

1558 in response to circumstances at home and abroad.[23] Any summary description of the movement in the mid-1560s, when the word "puritan" was introduced by English Catholics, is of little value, for it cannot do justice to the complexities of a coalition that encompassed reformers who agreed on some matters and disagreed on others. Hindsight, too, is misleading, for it tempts us to focus on the more outspoken members of the movement but ignore those who hesitated to endorse every aspect of the program of 1562–63.[24]

The most serious mistake we can make is to accept what was said about the reformers by nineteenth-century "Anglicans" (a word that did not exist in the sixteenth and seventeenth centuries) who regarded Puritanism as a sickness that threatened an otherwise healthy state church, a sickness signaled by its "sectarian" understanding of the church and "seditious" refusal to abide by the authority of church leaders and the monarchy. In reality, all but a very few of those who criticized the Elizabethan Settlement endorsed the model of a comprehensive state church and a ministry-magistracy alliance. At its heart, the Puritan movement was as magisterial and corporate as its parent, the Reformed tradition. Thanks to these commitments, it was situated within a broad consensus on matters of doctrine and the responsibility of the Christian monarch to support true religion, to which it added a forceful emphasis on anti-Catholic evangelization, the visible church as a site of discipline, the authority of Scripture, and the insidious presence of idolatry, all of them arguments or themes that many within the state church were willing to endorse in the 1560s.[25]

What was wrong with things as they were? A much-reiterated complaint arose in response to the realities of 1560—and of 1600, for change was slow in coming. The state church had far too few ministers of any real competence as preachers at a moment when the doorway to salvation was shifting from a sacrament-centered theology to a theology of the Word. From parish to parish, financial resources were badly distributed, bunched in some places, virtually absent in others. Until this situation was remedied, the "dark corners" of the country would never be adequately evangelized. From parish to parish, moreover, the work of guarding the two sacraments of baptism and Holy Communion from the "unworthy," a task endorsed by the *Book of Common Prayer*, was incomplete or ineffective. The heart of the matter was pastoral, the church's betrayal of the people of God. Likening these people to "sheep" who, for want of proper food, were soul-starved, critics pleaded for action: something must be done, and done quickly, to weed out ineffective clergy and replace them with a cadre of *real* preachers. Who could disagree? All wings of the movement, together with many others who recognized the plight of the state church, wanted the queen and her bishops to undertake a program of this kind even though it would require her to overlook the disobedience or "non-conformity" of men such as Thomas Sampson. As a bishop pointed out to a member of the Privy Council at a moment when Sampson and others of his kind were being suspended, things could go from bad to worse—"many places . . . destitute of preachers"—if punishing Sampson-like dissidents pushed "worthy" ministers out of the church.[26]

Some men of high status endorsed this complaint, especially, perhaps, Henry Hastings, the third Earl of Huntingdon (d. 1595), who owed his Protestantism to his father but on a deeper level to the time he spent as one of the "young gentlemen surrounding Edward VI," whose tutors vied to ensure that the boy king and his circle of friends added a firm knowledge of Scripture and Reformed theology to their training in Latin and Greek. From that point on, Huntingdon labored to ensure that Protestantism prevailed against its enemies, most especially those in England who continued to profess the old religion. A good many of the ministers he supported became nonconformists, and some had been among the most emphatic of the Marian exiles. At his domestic seat in the town of Ashby de la Zouch, he installed the former exile Anthony Gilby as the town preacher. Gilby honored his patron by including him in the title of a translation (1570) of Calvin's commentaries on the book of Daniel, done (according to the title) *especially for the use of the family of the right honourable Earl of Huntingdon, to set forth as in a glass, how one may profitably read the scriptures, by . . . mediating the sense thereof, and by prayer.* Ten years later Gilby dedicated his translation of *The psalms of David truly opened and explained by Theodore Beza* to the Countess of Huntingdon, a book Beza had already given the earl in its Latin version. Others who entered Huntingdon's circle included the Bible translator William Whittingham and Sampson; after losing his post within the state church in the mid-1560s, Sampson accepted the office of master of the local hospital in a town over which Huntingdon had considerable authority. Huntingdon reached out to Walter Travers (see below) in the mid-1580s, befriended the perennial nonconformist Arthur Hildersham, and sent his younger brother Francis Hastings to Geneva to study with Beza, a step in keeping with his strong support for Reformed Protestantism on the Continent. Thereafter, the younger Hastings remained close to Thomas Cartwright. As President of the Council of the North (1572–1595) the earl used his authority in five English counties to encourage godly preaching whenever and wherever he could, a goal Grindal endorsed while serving as Archbishop of York. In Parliament, the two brothers sided with the faction that complained of pluralism and nonresidency and called for stricter enforcement of the laws against Catholic recusancy. The third earl also aspired to fulfill the role of godly magistrate, an aspect of his Puritanism described more fully in chapter 5.[27]

For a smaller group, evangelism took second place to the story in Foxe's *Book of Martyrs* of the faithful few at war with the many who succumbed to idolatry. According to this story, the purpose of Protestantism was to restore what had been lost during the centuries of Catholic domination, the simplicity of the "first times" when the earliest Christian communities adhered to the

Word as divine law. To accomplish this mission of recovery and restoration, the faithful few would have to identify and eliminate every vestige of anti-Christian idolatry. Doing so would allow the true church to reemerge in all its glory.

Sampson, Humphrey, and many others also regarded the true church as endowed with a singular "liberty" rooted in the presence of the Holy Spirit and made manifest in the loving relationship shared by everyone in God's household. Another way of describing this kind of church employed the analogy between church and house or temple and, taking this one step further, between temple and Christ's body. Via this reading of Scripture, "edification," a word St. Paul had used to describe the goal of his evangelism (1 Cor. 3:14; 2 Cor. 13:10) became important to the reformers. To them it denoted the church as "a living, growing thing," a house or building constructed out of "living stones" made so by the Holy Spirit. Reading Paul's words in Ephesians 4 and his letters to the Corinthians through the lens of Reformed theology, Sampson and his fellow reformers argued that, left untouched, the residues of corruption would "impede . . . edification" and thwart "our Christian liberty." The liturgy of the state church failed this test, as did the argument of things indifferent (see below).[28]

Generously defined, these were themes that a surprising number of English Protestants could endorse. During his years as Archbishop of York, Grindal attempted a wide-ranging program of reform and, in private correspondence, indicated his affection for "some godly brethren, which do wish that such things as are amiss were reformed." In the mid-1560s, most of the bishops continued to support aspects of the reform program of 1562–63, doing so notably during the Parliament of late 1566, which considered a series of bills relating to the Articles of Religion, Catholic nonconformity, nonresidence, the abuse of church property, and the capacity (or lack thereof) of the country's clergy. The first of these bills, known as "A," passed through the House of Commons and probably would been accepted by the House of Lords, where it was favored by the bishops, only to be halted by the queen.[29]

All the while, these efforts were accompanied by argument about the prevalence of idolatry and the implications of divine law. How precise was the Bible in describing the structure and practices of the true church? And was the Church of England really tainted with corruption? To men such as Sampson, the answers were obvious: the church of circa 1559 remained imperfect, still too close to Catholicism in certain respects and falling short of the biblical standard in others. As divisions began to emerge, the more radical ministers turned the rhetoric of Christian primitivism into a cry for immediate action: "The whole scriptures are for destroying idolatry, and every thing belonging unto it." As Gilby would complain in the mid-1570s, the compromises of the Settlement of 1559 were akin to what the prophet Elijah had characterized (1 Kings 18:21), as a "crooked halting betwyxe two religions." For the more zealous laypeople and clergy, therefore, it was imperative that the church undo the compromises of the Settlement of 1559.[30]

Conflict was inevitable. It was the queen who forced the issue. What aroused her to act in the mid-1560s was her preference for uniformity in matters of religion. When Elizabeth learned that Sampson and other ministers were refusing to wear the surplice, she was dismayed.[31] Here was visible evidence of *nonconformity* among *Protestant* clergy alongside *Catholic* nonconformity of the kind that prompted the Act of Uniformity of 1559. Moreover, Protestant dissent was on the rise, becoming a source of much "contention." Accordingly, she instructed Parker in January 1565 to apply the principle of uniformity to Protestants. He responded by issuing "Advertisements" requiring every minister in the church to acknowledge the legitimacy of the Thirty-Nine Articles, the *Book of Common Prayer*, and the surplice, and threatening those who refused to do so with suspension or dismissal. In 1567 he summoned the parish clergy in London to meet with him and, on the spot, asked them to accept the Advertisements. Many conformed, but thirty-seven refused, as did others elsewhere in the country.[32]

The "vestarian controversy" was about conformity and who had the nerve to enforce or defy it. For those balked at agreeing to the Advertisements, the dispute turned on whether the church would accept "Gods holy word" as the only "rule . . . to measure his religion by." Fully observed, this rule would mean eliminating all "traditions" stemming from Catholicism up to and including the surplice, which implied a Catholic understanding of the Eucharist. William Axton used a syllogism to drive home this point: "that which was consecrated by antichrist, and constantly worn by the priests of antichrist, in their idolatrous service, was one of the garments of antichrist. But the surplice was consecrated by antichrist, and . . . therefore, the surplice is a garment of antichrist."[33]

In the same breath, critics of the surplice applied this reasoning about Catholicism and the Antichrist to the sign of the cross and other features of the *Book of Common Prayer* and, more tellingly, to the episcopal structure of the church. Sampson had already questioned the office of bishop. Critics asked if the office was lawful—that is, designated in Scripture—when, from their point of view, the churches described in the New Testament practiced a ministry of equals. A close reading of the apostolic letters suggested that "bishop" was a generic name for ministers who served a single congregation. Objections of this kind flowed from the men who were being pressured to accept the Advertisements, questions that struck at the very heart of the compromises the church was making. Ultimately, the issue was the Second Commandment and the prohibition of idolatry. Had the time come to take a stand against every example of the "superstitious invention[s] of men"? If England was sinking into "corruption," should "Gods people" mobilize to ensure that its faults were "utterlie abolished"?[34]

And what about the royal supremacy? If the authority of the state was being used to *prevent* the church from cleansing itself of corruption, were faithful Christians entitled to act on their own? Did loyalty to Christ come before loyalty to the Crown? In an undated "Supplication" of circa 1561 detailing the miseries of the church, the queen was warned that, unless she acted promptly to provide the right kind of ministers, she could not expect people to obey her. As their response to the rule about wearing the surplice became more emphatic, some of the radicals began to dismiss Romans 13:2 and other biblical texts that enjoined obedience to rulers. For them, the authority of the Christian prince was trumped by the New Testament rule of "called unto liberty" (Galatians 5:13) and, at a deeper level, by the Word and the imperative of "edification" in the sense of ensuring that "Christ's little ones" have their faith strengthened. Framing the conflict of circa 1565–67 in terms of "God" versus "man," the radicals found it easy to justify their rejection of "Popish trash" no matter who—queen or bishop—commanded them to act otherwise.[35]

Language this stark was alarming, for it seemed to rule out any compromise. In response, Parker tried to change the terms of debate. To those who evoked the unwavering authority of Scripture, he responded by differentiating what the Bible *explicitly* authorized and the many topics on which it was silent or contained general rules the church was empowered to interpret. Hence his conclusion: "we deny there may be nothing in the Church which is not named expresslie in the Scriptures. . . . We deny that whatsoever the Apostles did not, we must not do." For Parker and his allies, the principle of things indifferent (in Latin, *adiaphora*) was important because it validated the authority of the state church to decide how to interpret Scripture. Or, to say this differently, it endorsed the intervention of the queen in religious affairs in her role as arbiter of religious policy. To buttress this insistence on things indifferent, Parker cited letters from Reformed theologians who used the same concept at various moments. His ace in the hole was not these arguments but the royal supremacy itself. To challenge the authority of a bishop was to challenge the authority of the queen. Unlike Sampson and his colleagues, who invoked *adiaphora* on behalf of their liberty to dissent, Parker used it to affirm the authority of the state church and the monarchy in matters of religious policy.[36]

The holdouts countered by playing the card of conscience. If the surplice was truly a thing indifferent, then the church should allow clergy to practice what their conscience was telling them about idolatry. Conscience came first to men of the prestige of Sampson and Humphrey. And if conscience were recognized as authoritative, what basis was there for the queen's role as governor of the church? Anthony Gilby asked this question as part of a more general critique of the deficiencies of the church: who should "do evil at the magistrate's command"? To command acts of this kind was to betray the Old Testament example of Josiah and emulate a bad king such as Nebuchadnezzar: "You think it dangerous for subjects to restrain the prince's authorities to bounds and limits. We think it as dangerous to enlarge the prince's authority beyond the bounds and limits of holy Scripture."[37]

Eventually, both sides gave way. Some of the thirty-seven London dissidents signed the Advertisements, a few bishops never enforced them and, pressed by high-placed civil leaders, several bishops, and local groups, Parker allowed several of the holdouts to preach after they had been suspended. Not long thereafter, troubles at home and abroad—a Catholic uprising in 1569, the pope's excommunication of Elizabeth I in 1570—distracted the queen and her government. The initiative shifted to the other side, with Parliament as its focus because the Convocation was controlled by Parker and his fellow bishops. Some members of the Parliament of 1571–72 wanted to go much further in the direction of Reformed style ecclesiology, although willing to keep the office of bishop. The more daring proposals, one of them a bill calling for revision of the *Book of Common Prayer*, were dropped after others pointed out that the queen alone could decide such matters. Parker responded to this hostility toward his leadership by resuming the push for uniformity. After Parliament reconvened in the spring of 1572 and dissidents in the House of Commons proposed to legalize "the service used in the Dutch and French Church" as a way of exempting Protestant nonconformists from what was expected of Catholics—"conformity [is] not always necessary," was how one member of the House justified the measure—the queen abruptly halted debate on such measures.[38]

Elizabeth intervened a second time in the mid-1570s to suppress a form of clerical training known as prophesying. She did so in the aftermath of a surge of arguments for reform by a new generation of activists linked with Cambridge University. For the first time, episcopacy was explicitly put in play in Parliament and, more daringly, in the court of public opinion. The opening salvo in this campaign was a brief book published in June 1572, *An Admonition to the Parliament*, followed some months later by *A Second Admonition to the Parliament*, each of them printed surreptitiously. The texts brought together in the first *Admonition* were the doing of two young Cambridge graduates, John Field and Thomas Wilcox, with help from others who may have included a layman, Job Throckmorton.[39] The "first popular manifesto of English Presbyterianism," which was quickly reprinted despite attempts to halt its distribution, the *Admonition* called on Parliament to abet the "abandoning [of] al popish remnants" in worship, ministry, and church discipline and ensure that they were replaced by "those things only, which the Lord himself in his word commandeth." A reply was forthcoming, followed in turn by counterarguments and other manifesto-like statements. Collectively, these texts and the response of the authorities constitute the Admonition Controversy, an event that deserves close attention for what it tells us about a program contemporaries were beginning to characterize as "puritan."[40]

The young Turks who launched the controversy were weary of hearing from their elders that anyone who wanted an "entire reformation" must "beare with the weaknes of certaine for a time." For Field and Wilcox, the Catholic uprising of 1569 and the ineffectiveness of Parliament signaled the failure of a strategy of persuasion. "We have used gentle words to[o] long, and ... the wound groweth desperate," Field declared in defending the uncompromising language of the *Admonition*. Although there was a price to pay for speaking so bluntly, he and his collaborators agreed that the time had come to say what had not been said at the time of the Elizabethan Settlement: the Church of England should abandon episcopacy and adopt the system of governance and style of worship of the Reformed international. The two men were forcefully critical of the *Book of Common Prayer*, bemoaning its collection of liturgies as "culled & picked out of that popishe dunghil, the Masse booke full of all abhominations [*sic*]." What Field, Wilcox, and their allies wanted by way of a positive program was "a thorow reformation both of doctrine, ceremonies, and regiment [polity or governance]" as evidenced both in "the Word of God and example of the primitive Church, as also of Geneva, France, Scotland, and all other Churches rightly reformed," a program—tied to the forming of parish-centered "consistories"—described in more detail in the *Second Admonition*. Compared with renewal and recovery in those countries, the progess in England was deplorable.[41]

Arrested and questioned repeatedly during the summer and fall of 1572, Field and Wilcox remained in prison until the following spring. Thereafter, the controversy expanded to include a long-running (1572–77) debate between John Whitgift, master of one of the colleges at Cambridge, who defended the church, and Thomas Cartwright, who argued on behalf of a "thorow Reformation." Both had studied and taught at Cambridge. Too young to have caught the eye of Catholic authorities in the mid-1550s, Cartwright was in Ireland during the vestarian controversy. Returning in 1567 to Cambridge, where he became Lady Margaret Professor of Divinity in 1570, Cartwright relied on the framework of Christian primitivism in the inaugural lectures he gave that year. Unable to find the office of bishop in the New Testament, Cartwright called for major changes in the structure of the Church of England: bishops, although still permitted, should no longer appoint and ordain ministers (which, according to the rules of the Church of England, no one else could do), parishes should elect their officers, and local churches should be governed by a collective of ministers, or "presbytery." By the close of the year, his outspokenness cost him his professorship. Leaving for the Continent in 1571, Cartwright spent some months in Geneva in the company of another Cambridge academic, Walter Travers; as well, he came to know Andrew Melville (see chap. 3) and Theodore Beza before returning to England in 1572. Five years later he was back in Europe, where he arranged to minister to an English mercantile group in Antwerp and secured the printing of his replies to Whitgift and a book by a fellow reformer.[42]

The emergence of a group so critical of episcopacy and the *Book of Common Prayer* altered the coalition of circa 1565 in ways that had long-term consequences for the meaning of the term "puritan." Thereafter, the line between reformers and conformists or churchmen began to harden as new issues came to the fore. The back-and-forth between Cartwright and Whitgift is significant, for it revealed differences of opinion about six matters: (1) the authority of the Bible and its bearing on ecclesiology (church governance) and worship; (2) the understanding of "bishop" in Scripture and the earliest centuries of Christian history; (3) the "notes" of the true church and, beyond this, the nature of the church as a body of worshipping believers; (4) the validity of "things indifferent" to justify retaining certain Catholic practices, tempering the imperative of the Word, and allowing the monarchy a role in religious affairs; (5) the relationship between the royal supremacy and two-kingdoms principles; and (6) the form of worship. What the two men said in response to each other on these topics became an important moment of definition for the parties that were emerging within the state church.

Were we to rank these topics by their importance, worship would come first, as it did for the authors of the *Admonition*, who devoted a third of their manifesto to the faults of the *Book of Common Prayer*. For Field, Wilcox, and Cartwright, the ceremonies retained from the Catholic past were either innovations that contradicted Scripture or too evocative of Catholic doctrine and practice. Kneeling to receive Holy Communion was one such practice (at the Last Supper, the apostles had sat around a table), as was administering it without a sermon beforehand. Holy days, private baptisms, the sign of the cross in that rite, and prayers for the dead were other examples of idolatry or bad practice. The alternative to the *Book of Prayer*'s formality was preaching-centered worship and something closer to free-form prayer; instead of using "prayers invented by men," prayer should be spoken by ministers "as the spirit moved them." Relying on the benchmark of Christian primitivism, the radicals also called for eliminating church music other than psalmody. Moreover, the state church erred in allowing someone in the pulpit to substitute "bare reading" of printed homilies for lively preaching of the Word. The substance of right worship was the Genevan model as practiced by the Marian exiles in that city and favored by the radical party in 1550s Frankfurt, a sequence of practices centered on prayer, the singing of psalms, and sermons. In his response, Whitgift insisted on a genealogy of holy days and other rituals that pushed their origins back to the beginnings of Christianity and early church councils, to which he added examples of how worship was handled in some corners of the Reformed international. He also argued that preaching could include reading.[43]

What each side said about the authority of Scripture may seem similar, for Whitgift acknowledged its importance almost as fervently as his opponent. Yet he insisted that, at best, it provided "general" rules, to which he added an insistence on the principle of things indifferent, which he used to buttress the argument that God had empowered the civil magistrate "to govern the church" and guide the process of deciding how Scripture should be interpreted: "surely the magistrate hath authority . . . to appoint what shall be thought . . . most convenient, so that it be not repugnant to the word of God." Whitgift had Calvin and Heinrich Bullinger of Zurich in his corner, citing them to good effect on the latitude that Protestants enjoyed (or wrestled with). Via such arguments, he and other apologists for the state church tempered the regulative principle or Scripture as law that Cartwright, Field, and others evoked to validate the authority of their scheme.[44]

Where the substance and rhetoric of the radicals' agenda clashed with the Elizabethan Settlement most dramatically was twofold: the nature of the church and the royal supremacy. Field and Wilcox tied their understanding of the true church to three "notes"—sound doctrine, proper administration of the sacraments, and a Word-based ecclesiology or "discipline." All three, but especially discipline, were seriously impaired—or absent!—in the Church of England to the point of jeopardizing its capacity to serve as the visible body of Christ. In effect, the church in England had crossed the line that divided the lawful from the unlawful. Ministry, too, was impaired in ways that called into question any role as evangelical heralds of the Gospel promise. The faults of the state church also included its failure to guard the sacraments from the unworthy and advance the process of edification among the faithful. Cartwright was outspoken: a church that lacked an effective discipline could not provide what was "necessary to salvation, and of faith."[45]

Whitgift was shocked. To impugn the validity of the Church of England as a means of redemption was to play into the hands of Catholics who challenged the legitimacy of the English Reformation. In response, he cited the official position of the Reformed international: the validity of a church was solely a matter of the two "notes" of "true preaching of the word of God" and the "right administration of the sacraments," both of which were present in the state church. Not only did he say, with some warrant, that Cartwright and company were venturing beyond the boundaries of the Reformed tradition by adding discipline or church structure as a third note of the true church, he also painted them as Anabaptist-like because they blurred the difference between the visible and invisible church. As he pointed out, the visible church that encompassed an entire nation would inevitably include people of faith and others who seemed insufficiently Christian.[46]

Cartwright and his fellow reformers conceded that, here on earth, the church was not the same as the invisible church of the elect; theologically, the visible church was different from the community of the saints known only to Christ. Yet all of them wanted the church on earth to resemble the kingdom of God, an assumption these men owed to John Foxe's emphasis on the faithful few, the Pauline concept of the church as continually advancing in edification, and Reformed theologians such as Calvin and Bucer. The authors of the *Admonition* insisted that, within a church that was properly organized, people grew in faith or were edified. As they put it, the visible church was a "company or congregatione of the faythfull called and gathered out of the worlde by the preachinge of the Gospell, who following and embracinge true religione, do in one unitie of Spirite strengthen and comforte one another, daylie growinge and increasinge in true faythe." Cartwright amplified this description by citing St. Peter on the connections between Christ's spiritual body and the "temple" constructed out of "living stones" transformed by grace and participating in the process of edification (1 Peter 2:5). Only through lively, unfettered, Spirit-touched preaching of the Word and a more effective system of discipline would parish churches become akin to Christ's kingdom. Any such process depended as well on stricter rules about who could participate in Holy Communion, which should be offered only to those who "have made confession of their faith and submitted" to the "discipline" of the church. Another aspect of edification was structural. Every minister should serve a single parish, the reason being (aside from many others) that this would enable him to differentiate the worthy from the unworthy.[47]

A sanctified church would also entrust the power of the keys to each parish and, in some manner, share this power with laypeople. A fundamental text was Matthew 18:17, where Jesus seemed to describe how a congregation should deal with those who sinned. In Matthew 16:19, the word "keys" (as in keys of the kingdom) became a metaphor for the means of excluding people from the church or judging them worthy of remaining. Interpreting this term to signify the empowering of *each parish church* to supervise its members, the group associated with the *Admonition* defended an emphatically communal or collective understanding of church discipline, to the point of insisting that the "power of the keys" was shared in some manner between ministers and laypeople—only the worthy, however, not those who had never accepted the discipline of the Word.[48]

The twin principles of biblical authority and the church as community ever advancing in edification dictated a third, that Christ was the sole head (or king) of the visible church. Within English Protestantism this point had already served to justify the rupture with papal authority. Now Cartwright turned it against the authority of the queen. Sincere in professing his loyalty to Elizabeth I in her role as head of state and re-affirming her God-given mandate to protect the church from its enemies, Cartwright was no less earnest in reiterating the two-kingdoms theory of church and state proposed by Calvin and other Reformed theologians: "the godly magistrate is the head of the commonwealth, but not of the church." Thanks to its singular relationship with Christ, the visible church could appoint ministers, decide all matters of doctrine, and administer the process of discipline. Although granted a role as "nursing fathers" (Isa. 49:23) of the church, the civil state had to observe "the rules of God prescribed in His word." According to another reformer, William Fulke, the Christian prince was obliged to accept the advice of a council of clergy or, alternatively, receive instruction "by the word of God through the ministry of the preaching of the same," a principle supported by more mainstream ministers on the basis of biblical examples. Using stronger language, Cartwright called on all civil magistrates "to subject themselves unto the Church to submit their scepters, to throw down their crowns before the Church." Pointedly, he insisted that no Christian prince (meaning the queen) could be "excepted from ecclesiastical discipline."[49]

His intention was not to subordinate civil to religious authority but to validate the autonomy of the church, which was "divine in a sense not applicable to the state." As Fulke pointed out in *A Brief and Plain Declaration*, "The church of God was perfect in all her regiment before there was any Christian prince. . . . By which it is manifest that the . . . government thereof dependeth not upon the authority of princes but upon the ordinance of God." The real difference between church and civil state (or magistrate) arose out of the relationship between the visible church and the history of redemption. Unlike any other institution, the church was awaiting the return of Christ and the ingathering of the elect, at which point it would be enfolded into Christ's spiritual kingdom. This Christ-centered identity entitled the church to a distinctive freedom that no "prince" could impair. According to the *Second Admonition to Parliament,* "None is so high in the church as Christe, none to doe anything . . . but as it is appointed in his woorde." Despite the many ways in which Cartwright and his fellow reformers emphasized the close connections between church and state, their real goal was to limit the reach of the royal supremacy. In a passage as striking to read today as it must have been to its readers in the mid-1580s, Fulke characterized the royal supremacy as "a mist to dazzle the eyes of ignorant persons, that they think all things in the ecclesiastical state ought to be disposed by . . . the absolute power of the civil magistrate." Echoing Cartwright, Travers insisted in his *Ecclesiasticae Disciplineae, et Anglicanae Ecclesiae* (1574) that civil magistrates "must as well as the rest submit themselves and be obedient to the iust and lawfull authoritie off the Officers off the churche."[50]

No other aspect of the two-kingdoms framework would be as irritating to the political elite in England and Scotland, where the leaders of the state church were also insisting on this principle. Whitgift seems to have sensed that the experience of dealing with hostile bishops and an obdurate queen was pushing the radicals to imagine the church as sharply different from and threatened by the civil state.[51] Responding to the assertion that certain aspects of the liturgy were tainted by their Catholic past, he reasoned that this genealogy became irrelevant when any such practices were put to Protestant ends. The more dubious genealogy was that of the reformers themselves. Were they not reenacting the errors of the fourth-century CE "Cathari" (in English, the "pure" or the "puritans") and of sixteenth-century Anabaptists, who, as Whitgift rightly pointed out, had adopted a strongly literal version of *sola scriptura:* "This name Puritan is very aptly given to these men; not because they be pure . . . but because they think themselves to be 'more pure than others,' as

Cathari did, and separate themselves from all other churches and congrega-tions." Whitgift backed up this statement by citing a single sentence in the *Admonition*: the assertion that the Church of England was "so far off, from having a church rightly reformed, accordying to the prescript of Gods worde, that as yet we are not come to the outward face of the same."[52]

Defending the royal supremacy was easier. From Whitgift's perspective and undoubtedly from that of Elizabeth I, the two-kingdoms framework "utterly" overthrew "her authority in ecclesiastical matters." Possibly the church that was yet to be—that is, a church enjoying a unique spiritual freedom—might exist. At the present moment, however, church and civil state remained coextensive, a "Constantinian" position based on the premise that the Christian common-wealth was more or less identical with the church of Christ: "I make no differ-ence betwixt a christian commonwealth and the church of Christ." Responding to the reformers' objections to the principle of things indifferent, he used it to justify the policies of Elizabeth and her bishops on behalf of conformity: the church was entitled to resolve any and all disputes about liturgy or governance because its authority overlapped with the royal supremacy or, as he put it, the "christian magistrate."[53] Like Parker before him, Whitgift reiterated Elizabeth's uneasiness about any mobilizing of "the people," doing so by associating the reformers' scheme of church governance with "popularity." In a section entitled "Elections by the multitude for the most part disordered," he characterized the people as lacking "judgement and discretion" and therefore incapable of a role in preserving "peace and good government." Because the reformers ignored this reality and "despise[d] authoritie" (that is, the royal supremacy), they were rightly characterized as seditious, an epithet that implied their sympathy for the theorizing of John Knox and Christopher Goodman (see chap. 1) about resistance to ungodly rulers.[54]

He was onto something. As the twentieth-century historian A. F. Scott Pearson has pointed out, "the notion of an absolute sovereign State was alien to the mind of Cartwright," for whom God (or Christ) came first. The reformers were almost as emphatic about the evils of allowing power within the church to be concentrated in one person's hands. Cartwright made it clear that he wanted significant authority to be transferred from a centralized hierarchy to each parish, where power would be shared by clergy and laity alike. As he put it, "the consent of all" was imperative in situations where the common interest was involved. Papal "tyranny" was the extreme example of what could go wrong, but not far behind was the "imperious and pompous dominion" of bish-ops, and a Constantine-like monarchy. Within the scheme of the reformers, any such abuse of authority was checked by the rule of parity (all ministers having the same rank), an "eldership" that included ministers, deacons, and ruling elders, and the practice of "popular Election," or empowering laypeople to participate in the "choosing and deposing" of their ministers and elders. Whether these rules amounted to a "republican" mode of governance, as historians have occasionally suggested, seems doubtful. True, the reformers insisted on the capacities of ordinary people, extolling them, in Cartwright's words, as "wise as serpents in the wisdom especially which is to salvation." In the same breath, however, they reiterated the truism that laypeople would need advice and supervision from the officers of the church.[55]

Meanwhile, Travers, Cartwright, and the authors of the two *Admonitions* were amplifying their conception of a fully reformed church, Travers doing so in *Ecclesiasticae Disciplinae . . . Explicatio*, which appeared in an English translation in Heidelberg in 1574. In the early 1580s, it was supplemented by a much briefer "Book of Discipline" that circulated in manuscript copies until printed in 1644 under the title *A Directory of Church-Government*. Never finalized, the text was reviewed and discussed by county-based or "classis" groups of ministers as late as 1589, when Travers was still attempting to incorporate various changes into the text.[56] It may have been easy to agree on this book's description of ministry, for it reiterated the Reformed model of that office as inherently collective, a "consisterie" in each parish of a pastor (responsible for administering the sacraments, and for connecting doctrine to the experience of redemption), a teacher (to handle doctrine), and the two lay offices of elder and deacon, the first charged with managing the process of discipline, the second with caring for the poor and managing parish finances. Bishops had no place in this system, which eliminated nonresidency and pluralism by requiring *every* minister to serve a single parish or congregation, an argument dating from the 1560s.[57]

In keeping with Reformed-style presbyterianism, the *Directory* outlined a system of "conferences" or national bodies to which all congregations were in some manner subordinate. Here, it seems certain that debate was vigorous and the outcome something well short of a hierarchical system of synods and assemblies empowered to supervise local parishes, for the *Directory* specified that "no particular Church [i.e., parish] hath power over another," a statement modestly qualified by the assertion that "every particular Church of the same resort, meeting and counsel, ought to obey the opinion of more Churches with whom they communicate." This emphasis on the strictly local may have prompted a rule prohibiting a minister chosen by and ordained within the context of a single parish from exercising his office elsewhere except for a limited time, and only if his home parish assented. Otherwise, the workings of a synod and presbytery-centered system of the kind that would emerge in the Church of Scotland (see chap. 3) remained vague. Cartwright seems to have wavered between two different interpretations of the word "church" in Matthew 18:17, taking it to signify the eldership or ministry but also open to the possibility that it referred to "the people." What was said in the *Admonition* about the election of ministers requiring the "consent by the people" was subsequently rephrased as "election was made by the elders, with the common consent of the whole church." Questions or uncertainties of this kind persisted throughout the 1580s, although usually voiced in private.[58]

What *did* matter to the young Turks of these years was making their case to the queen and her principal advisors and, beyond them, to a broader public.[59] Hoping that a face-to-face encounter with Elizabeth or getting her to read their manifestos would convert her to the cause of a "thorough" reformation, the radicals had to settle for the support of a network of like-minded ministers and high-ranking laypeople—for Walter Travers, it was William Cecil (Lord Burghley), the most important member of the Privy Council, who employed him as a chaplain in 1581 and, a year later, arranged for his appointment to Temple Church in London. Addressing Burghley in an undated (c. 1574) letter, Sampson reminded him of a truism of Reformed political theology: he must exercise "the sword, which God hath put in the hand of Christian magistrates." In December 1584 Burghley and other members of the Privy Council attended a disputation at Lambeth Palace at which Whitgift and Travers squared off alongside others.[60] As well, strong words were spoken in the presence of the queen. When the young minister Edward Dering preached before her in 1570, he spoke bluntly of the "greatest duty" of the Christian prince "to maintain the gospel, to teach the people knowledge, and build his whole government with faithfulness." Lest the queen miss his point, he called on her to emulate the "godly rulers and princes of Israel" who had kept "the sanctuary undefiled." Dering wanted her to rid the state church of incompetent and nonresident clergy and replace them with a ministry committed to teaching "the difference between the holy and profane." To ignore this agenda and persist in being "careless" would put all of England in danger from the workings of God's providence: "We have fearful examples before our eyes to take heed of God's judgments when we abuse his graces." The aging John Foxe weighed in as well, tempering in later editions what he had written about Elizabeth in the dedication of the *Acts and Monuments* to indicate his dismay at her recalcitrance.[61]

Not that the authorities sat by and did nothing. Despite important friendships and family connections, Dering was suspended from preaching after he told the Privy Council that he favored the presbyterian program up to and including the principle that Christ, not the queen, was head of the church. Others, too, were suspended, deprived, or imprisoned unless, like Cartwright, they returned to Europe, where he remained until 1585.[62] Yet in 1578 the *Admonition* was reprinted, and Gilby published a terse summary of *A View of Antichrist, his Laws and Ceremonies in our English Church, unreformed.* Three years later, Field became a lecturer in a London church. Using his connections with the book trades, he secured the printing of partisan texts, including a letter by Calvin's successor in Geneva, Theodore Beza, denouncing the office of bishop. Field also masterminded a national census of the state of the clergy designed to embarrass the bishops by showing how many "dumb dogges" (Isa.

56:10) were ministers, a document published in 1593, five years after his death, in *A parte of a register, contayninge sundrie memorable matters, written by divers godly and learned in our time, which stande for, the reformation of our church*; a parallel collection remained unpublished until the early twentieth century.[63]

Equally remarkable was Field's success in nurturing local and national attempts to create the semblance of presbyterian-like practices within the church, as though an alternative to episcopacy could be constructed from beneath. Building on informal meetings of "ministers of the brotherhood" in 1570s London, events of this kind began to occur elsewhere by the early 1580s. By mid-decade, clergy and college fellows at Cambridge were getting together in conferences in several Sussex and Essex towns and also in Warwick, where Cartwright lived after returning from Europe. In September 1587 and again in 1588 and 1589, many of these activists gathered in or near Cambridge to discuss draft versions of the "Book of Discipline" and other matters. Of these conferences, one is well known thanks to the chance survival of its records, the Dedham "classis" of ministers and Cambridge University fellows (but apparently no lay elders) that met for several years to fast, hear sermons or lectures on the Bible, debate matters of pastoral policy, scrutinize draft versions of the "Book of Discipline," offer counsel to one another about employment, and debate how they should respond to the campaign to suppress nonconformity that Whitgift, newly elevated to the post of Archbishop of Canterbury, initiated in 1584. Ever the organizer, Field advised the Dedhamites to "use what meanes yow can" to resist this campaign.[64]

Field's greatest achievement may have been to pursue the tasks of "propaganda and organization" with such effectiveness that he transformed "the somewhat incoherent dissent" of the Cambridge radicals into "a purposeful and militant movement."[65] Notably, he had a hand in arranging petitions to Parliament and, when elections to that body were scheduled, in mobilizing votes for certain candidates. Although Elizabeth continued to insist that Parliament not address matters of religion, some members of the House of Commons attempted to do so in response to petitions that emphasized the importance of a preaching ministry. From one Parliament to the next, members of the House of Commons called on the church to overlook nonconformity in matters of dress and liturgy lest it lose some of its ablest preachers. Proposals of this kind had broad support that became almost universal whenever the House was considering stronger measures against English Catholics and, especially, against the priests who were filtering into the country. Still another tactic was to exploit an ever-present anticlericalism by introducing measures to curb the bishops' privileges.[66]

Nonetheless, in 1584 it looked as though Whitgift held the winning hand. To help him in his campaign against Protestant nonconformity, he resurrected Parker's "Advertisements" and demanded that every minister in the church assent to them. To intimidate those who were more radical, he began to employ a Court of High Commission or "prerogative" court (i.e., deriving its authority from the monarch) charged with enforcing the authority of the state in religious affairs and controversial for this and other reasons. Even so, the outcome was something of a standoff. Not only had the agitation of the 'seventies increased the number of ministers who refused to conform—in all, some three or four hundred ministers did so initially—but Parliament and the Privy Council had other priorities than those of the archbishop. In places such as Essex, where the support for a presbyterian-like program was unusually vigorous, Whitgift suspended as many as forty-three local clergy. When the dust had settled, all but one returned not only to preaching but, almost certainly, to some degree of nonconformity.[67]

Satisfying as this standoff may have been, the reformers inside and outside of Parliament wanted much more. Throughout the 1580s, bills were introduced in the House of Commons lamenting the "infamous" behavior of many of the clergy and the plight of laypeople who, because of Whitgift's campaign against nonconformity, "have none who do break the bread of life unto us." Urging the authorities to restore everyone who had been suspended, and encouraged by a series of tracts calling for changes so extensive as to be "revolutionary,"[68] the session of 1586–87 was notably aggressive. Thanks to the networks Field had helped build, petitions and partisan documents poured in, all of them underscoring the shortage of zealous ministers and requesting that no one of this caliber be punished. In February 1587, a small group of Parliamentarians took the daring step of introducing a bill that would have required the church to replace episcopacy with "presbyteries" of pastors, doctors, and elders, adopt an alternative to the *Book of Common Prayer* based on the "Geneva Liturgie," curtail the queen's authority in matters of religion, and restore certain properties to the church. Simultaneously, Peter Wentworth argued that the House of Commons was entitled to review and correct what the bishops were doing. As happened whenever the state church was criticized, someone reminded the House of Commons that the queen interpreted the royal supremacy to mean that she but not Parliament was entitled to regulate affairs of religion. Nonetheless, some members of the House continued to complain that the state church was defective.[69]

One of the sponsors of the bill of 1587, a country gentleman named Job Throckmorton, had sided with Field and Wilcox during the Admonition Controversy and may have written the *Second Admonition*. Angered by the impasse of 1586–87 and back in the safety of his home to avoid being imprisoned for his outspokenness, he added his voice to a literary campaign that had been in full swing for several years thanks to Travers, Gilby, Dudley Fenner, John Udall, and Cartwright and, on the other side, to bishops and other high-ranking clergy, one of them the ponderous John Bridge, who spoke out on behalf of the policies of Whitgift. In substance and tone, these exchanges covered familiar ground: the meaning of "bishop" in the New Testament, the plight of a church that suppressed its best ministers, the benefits of stricter discipline, the proper handling of excommunication—a key issue because of its role in maintaining the church as a sanctified community—and, on the side of the presbyterians, the insinuation that Whitgift's policies were enabling Catholicism to persist in England.[70]

The tone of these exchanges suddenly intensified when, in October 1588, the London printer and Puritan sympathizer Robert Waldegrave issued the pamphlet-length *O Read Over D. Bridges*, followed shortly thereafter by a second tract and, by the summer of 1589, five more, each with a false imprint and authored by the pseudonymous "Martin Mar-prelate." Throckmorton was principally responsible for the series and his impatience the driving force behind them; as he remarked in *Hay any Worke for Cooper* (1589), "I saw the cause of Christ's government, and of the Bishops' antichristian dealing, to be hidden. The most part of men could not be gotten to read anything written in the defence of the one and against the other. I bethought me therefore of a way whereby men might be drawn to do both."[71] Conventional in how they referenced the presbyterian program, the Mar-prelate tracts were suffused with apocalyptic overtones and unprecedented in their sarcasm—most of it directed at the bishops and certain bishops in particular, all of them characterized as hungering for wealth and privilege and ignoring the pastoral needs of the people.[72]

The excitement was short-lived. Replies poured forth and, in the summer of 1589, the authorities hunted high and low for the press on which the tracts had been printed. From these investigations, Whitgift learned of the networks Field had helped create. The archbishop seized the moment. Knowing of the queen's disdain for nonconformity and emboldened by changes within her circle of advisors that included his own entry to the Privy Council in 1586 and the disappearance of advocates of reform—a telling loss was the death in 1588 (the same year in which John Field died) of the queen's sometime favorite Robert Dudley, the Earl of Leicester, who worked behind the scenes to abet the presbyterian program—he initiated a new campaign against the radicals fueled by the accusation that their network of "conferences" was the staging ground for a conspiracy against the state. He had an ally in the ambitious clergyman Richard Bancroft, who rummaged through confiscated letters and manuscript treatises seeking evidence of the presbyterians' disloyalty, much of which he publicized in *Dangerous Positions and Proceedings* (1593). Bancroft had already narrated a genealogy of the Puritan movement in *A Survay of the Pretended Holy Discipline* (1593) and savaged its politics in *A Sermon Preached at Paules Crosse . . . 1588* (1589), in which he insisted that monarchy and presbyterianism were incompatible.[73]

Polemics of this kind marked a new stage in the making of anti-puritanism, to which English Catholics had also contributed. Stigmatized as "sedicious and factious persons in the commonwealth" who "seeke the overthrowe of Civill Magistrates" and encourage people to "frequent private Conventicles," would-be presbyterians and well-known nonconformists such as Cartwright were questioned, deprived, or imprisoned. A telling sign of the authorities' paranoia was their assertion that Cartwright was conspiring to subvert the authority of the queen "by force and arms."[74] Released in 1592, Cartwright waited a few years before defending himself. But the clock could not be turned back. The meeting book of the Dedham "classis" ended abruptly in 1588, as did general meetings of the kind Field had been able to organize. Simultaneously, the church acquired a new group of defenders—Bancroft for one, Richard Hooker for another—who insisted that episcopacy was what the church fathers had intended.[75] The Protestantism of these men was, in some general sense of the term, Reformed and therefore anti-Catholic in its contours, but the arguments they set in motion would have unexpected consequences in the next century, as would the pleas of Cartwright and company that the Church of England align itself with the Reformed international.

Defeat and Its Contradictions

When Whitgift and his allies reckoned up the score after two decades of contestation, the outcome was exhilarating: victory seemed theirs, with Parliament rebuffed, the compromises of the Church of England justified, Puritanism tagged as seditious, and episcopacy given a fuller rationale as apostolic if not biblically mandated. Moreover, the bishops who had gone abroad during the 1550s were being "replaced by a different species: more rigidly authoritarian conformists" who had little in common with the moderates of the 1560s.[76] The queen, too, was pleased. Caring little about personal belief but a great deal about conformity, she acquired a compliant archbishop in Whitgift, but only after punishing his predecessor. Hearing in 1576 of disorders connected with the exercise known as prophesying,[77] the queen had ordered Grindal to suppress it. Although he offered to curtail abuses of the practice, the archbishop rejected her request, telling her in a letter that conscience prevented him from doing so. Defiance of this kind was unacceptable to Elizabeth. On her orders he was sequestered, whereupon the work of running the church fell to others. Forewarned by this episode, Whitgift did Elizabeth's bidding. He and Bancroft, who became archbishop in 1604 after Whitgift's death, threw themselves into suppressing nonconformists and erstwhile presbyterians, a program paralleled in the realm of political philosophy by their "imperial" version of royal power and the royal supremacy.[78]

Among the men and women whose hopes ran high in 1559 that the church would align itself with the Reformed international, the mood was one of deep discouragement. According to a veteran of the struggle for a "thorough" reformation, "these thirty years we have neither added any thing which might further, nor took away anything which might hinder, the building of God's Temple among us: but that our proceeding therein is like to the journeys of the Israelites in the wilderness, which went but eleven days' journey in forty years."[79] To be sure, the church was Protestant in its understanding of salvation and the Eucharist. Yet the twin tasks of reforming an imperfect Reformation and launching a broad-based program of evangelization remained undone. What had gone wrong? And why had some reformers turned so strongly against episcopacy when doing so alienated them from the queen and many others?

The imperative to evangelize and the practical difficulties in the way of such a program underscored the failings of episcopacy. Called to account by the bishop of London in 1578 for refusing to conform, a young minister named Francis Marbury minced no words: the bishop and others of his kind were "guiltie of the death of as manie soules as have perished by the ignoraunce" of those parish clergy unable to preach the Word in the manner Christ and St. Paul had mandated. Edward Dering said something of the same kind to Elizabeth's chief administrator, Lord Burghley; without sermons that taught the "horror of sin," "we can never have faith." John Udall summed up this and other shortcomings in a fiery statement printed surreptitiously in 1588. Allied with the Antichrist and Rome, the bishops were soul killers who deprived common people of the promise of free grace because they refused to eliminate pluralism and suppressed godly preaching.[80] Documented in Puritan-sponsored county-by-county "calendars" identifying hundreds of parishes without regular preaching or controlled by pluralists, this critique was echoed in sessions of Parliament, as when Job Throckmorton told the House of Commons in 1586 that, "If I were asked what is the bane of the Church and commonwealth, answer make, 'The dumb ministry, the dumb ministry'; yea, if I were asked a thousand times, I must say, 'the dumb ministry.'"[81]

Whenever the reformers exploited the weaknesses of the church as an evangelical institution, their movement aroused broad support. Notably, some of Elizabeth's bishops ignored the rules about conformity if doing so enabled them to retain the most effective ministers in their dioceses. High-placed civil leaders followed suit, reasoning that zealous preachers were "far too useful and necessary to be persecuted," an argument the Privy Council acknowledged when it intervened to provide evangelical preachers for one of the "dark corners of the land," the Catholic-tilting county of Lancashire, knowing that such men would "instruct the people the better to know their duty towards God and Her Majesty's laws." It helped, as well, that several members of the council used their powers of patronage to secure bishoprics and other offices for the more resolute of the Marian exiles. In the 1580s and 1590s, Lord Burghley tried to blunt Whitgift's anti-puritan policy, as did the Earl of Leicester, the Earl of Huntington, and Robert Rich, the second Baron Rich. Local gentry, church wardens, and justices of the peace also favored the reformers. This willingness to befriend nonconformists and evangelizing ministers enabled the movement to survive and flourish in towns, parishes, and a handful of colleges at Oxford and Cambridge. In Parliament as well, some in the House of Commons could be counted on to complain about the "greevous abuses" of the bishops. As the historian Alan Cromartie has pointed out, "In every single parliamentary session from 1566 to 1593, there was some attempt to bring in legislation . . . to remedy what were seen as clerical abuses." On high and from beneath, the reformers were assured of a voice in church and civil politics.[82]

The dynamics of reform persisted for another reason, the ability of the fervently Protestant to play upon popular fears that Catholicism might return as the state religion by conquest or conspiracy. Within the country itself, no one knew for sure if high-ranking Catholics would put loyalty to Elizabeth ahead of loyalty to their faith. Some did not. Although a Catholic-led insurrection in 1569 was quickly crushed, Pope Pius V's decision to excommunicate the queen brought into being a militant group that aspired to remove her from the throne and make Catholicism the religion of the land. Militant Catholicism spawned a militant Protestantism that spilled over into foreign policy. By the mid-1580s, the firmly Protestant members of Parliament and the Privy Council had persuaded Elizabeth to support the anti-Catholic, anti-Habsburg insurgency underway in the Low Countries, although she turned a deaf ear to pleas that robust preaching would prevent a resurgence of Catholicism in England itself, an argument tied to assertions that the defects of the church were responsible for the "abounding increase" in domestic Catholicism. For good reason, a foreign policy directed against Spain seemed urgent in the 1590s. Domestically, Parliament continued to press for stronger laws against Catholic recusancy and stricter enforcement of laws already on the books.[83]

The question remains, why did militant reformers become so vocal in the 1570s and 1580s about episcopacy and the *Book of Common Prayer*? Matthew Hutton, the future Archbishop of York, posed this very question to Lord Burghley in 1573: "at the Begynninge, it was but a Capp and a Surplice . . . but now it is growen to Bishopps . . . and (to speake Plaine) to the Queene Maiestie's Authoritie in Causes ecclesiasticall."[84] We must look to the Continent and ongoing connections with the Reformed international for a significant part of the answer. From the late 1550s onward, Reformed churches in Europe were engaging in a process of self-definition signaled by the emergence of creeds or confessions alongside schemes of church governance or polity. All this was happening at a moment when, in the context of the Counter-Reformation, the Council of Trent was summoning lay Catholics to "exterminate" the heretics in their midst. The first of these developments ended any possibility of rapprochement with Lutheranism.[85] The second made it much less likely that the Reformed international would tolerate episcopacy. In France, the Huguenot community formalized a version of presbyterianism in the 1560s and early 1570s. The Dutch Reformed followed suit in 1586, and the Church of Scotland in 1578–81, after several years of argument.[86] As the historian Andrew Pettegree has pointed out, these events, together with insurgencies or civil war in the Netherlands, France, and Scotland between Catholics and Protestants, signaled a new mood of militancy within the Reformed about worship, church structure, and the errors of Catholicism, a militancy more than matched on the Catholic side. This was also the period when a new kind of minister came onto the stage, a cadre formed at the academy Calvin set up in Geneva and, in Britain, at a handful of colleges at Cambridge and Oxford and others both old and newly founded in Scotland. What happened in France, Geneva, the Low Countries, and Scotland was being transmitted to England via publications and personal connections; notably, Travers spent four years (1571–75) in Geneva, where he became good friends with Beza and met Andrew Melville (see chap. 3).[87]

It seems more than accidental, therefore, that a group of university-trained ministers began to agitate against episcopacy in the 1570s. For these young men, the advantages of something akin to presbyterianism were sixfold: (1) as was argued in the opening sentence of the *Directory of Church-Government*, such a scheme was warranted by Scripture; (2) it contained multiple safeguards against Catholic-style "tyranny" while guarding the "liberties" of ordinary people to participate in the choosing of their ministers; (3) it provided a rigorous set of procedures for protecting the sacraments from the unworthy and advancing the imperative of edification; (4) it disposed of nonresidency and pluralism by the rule that all clergy serve a single parish; (5) it safeguarded the church from an imperious monarchy; and (6) it supported a sermon-centered mode of worship. The sum of these advantages made it everything the Church of England was not, a church cleansed of "idolatry," capable of evangelizing the entire country, and fostering edification.[88]

Of these advantages, two had a special importance in the English context, the possibility that presbyterian-style discipline would enable the state church to become a sanctified community and the emphasis on a more participatory style of governance. In Cartwright's exchanges with Whitgift as well as in the *Admonition* and other critiques, a picture was painted of local churches allowing the wrong kinds of people to receive Holy Communion and bring their children to be baptized. Of the "hundred pointes of poperie" listed in the undated (c. 1575) "Viewe of Antichrist . . . in our English Church unreformed," two were "the want of examination before the receiving of the Lords Supper" and "the wante of true Discipline for the whole congregation." The remedies were obvious: improve the workings of discipline and expand the privileges of the worthy, who deserved a better reputation than what was implied by the trope of laypeople as ignorant, illiterate, and unstable. As was said from time to time by English presbyterians, the people were spiritually capable of great things: "although they be called sheep in respect of their simplicity . . . yet are they also for their circumspection wise as serpents in the wisdom especially which is to salvation . . . they are the people of God, and therefore . . . those of whom St. Paul saith, 'The spiritual can discerneth all things.'" Hoping that a cadre of such people would emerge around them, the makers of the presbyterian program also knew that many of their countrymen would not welcome godly discipline.[89]

Eventually, all roads led to the question of authority: where it resided, what gave it legitimacy, and how it was being thwarted or sustained. Well before Bancroft came on the scene, the Puritan movement had tied the lawfulness of worship and church government to the authority of Scripture and the "primitive" phase of Christian history. The movement did so having absorbed the rule of *sola scriptura* from the makers of the Reformed tradition, who also passed on the message that true (or lawful) religion was the very opposite of Catholic-style "tyranny." From day one, therefore, the more daring wing of the movement endorsed a version of authority at odds with the royal supremacy and a strong version of episcopacy. With his customary astuteness, Sampson posed the crucial question in 1566: "Whether any thing of a ceremonial nature may be prescribed to the church by the sovereign, without the assent and free concurrence of churchmen?" The "troubles" in Frankfurt arose out of a division of opinion about the absolute authority of Scripture, moderates insisting that the policies of the Edwardian state church should be respected and radicals insisting that those policies must be revised to align them more fully with what Christ had prescribed. The same division of opinion, although overlaid with problems posed by the royal supremacy, marked the vestarian controversy of the 1560s, the disputes provoked by the emergence of the presbyterians, and the agitation in the House of Commons about reform. At these moments, the reformers evoked the authority of "conscience," which registered what was *really* lawful, or tied the legitimacy of ministers to a congregation's affirmation of them or, in Parliament, questioned the scope of the royal prerogative in matters of religion; as was argued in a statement of 1586, subscription to Whitgift's "Advertisements" should be "left free to the full perswasion and resolution of a good conscience" instead of being threatened with "menacing" penalties. Sampson saw what was coming, a politico-religious crisis that pitted religion as endorsed by the civil state against religion as endorsed by Scripture and conscience.[90]

Not that every critic of the state church shared his perspective. By the 1580s and early 1590s, contradictions abounded within the movement thanks to mediations and circumstances of several kinds. From the start, it encompassed laypeople and clergy who hesitated to transform their discontent into a program of the kind that Field, Travers, and Cartwright were proposing. Such half-hearted Puritans—or half-hearted conformists—were much less likely to question the principle of things indifferent, the royal supremacy in matters of religion, and the office of bishop if some of its Catholic aspects were eliminated. Cartwright himself climbed down from a strong version of presbyterianism after he was criticized by Richard Bancroft from one side and more radical Puritans from another. Responding to Bancroft's assertion that he "intended" a "seditious and rebellious disorder," Cartwright insisted that the presbyterian party had always stayed within the bounds of what was "lawfull and godly" as judged by "the law of this land." In his more moderate guise, Cartwright was willing to play the card of institutional authority, as were others who reasoned that the royal supremacy was how national unity was preserved and the English Reformation legitimized, a line of argument most Protestants welcomed as a means of refuting Catholic assertions that Protestantism was an illegitimate and disruptive novelty.[91]

Supporting the royal supremacy in the context of anti-Catholic polemics may have been easier to do given the fact that Elizabeth I did not have a free hand in matters of religion. From the earliest moments of the Elizabethan Settlement, it was being said that civil rulers must defer to divine law and that sacerdotal power—as in being able to administer the sacraments—was singular to ordained clergy. As bishops and ministers pointed out, matters of doctrine and worship came within the jurisdiction of the church and its leaders. Richard Hooker, whose credentials as an anti-puritan were impeccable, insisted in *Laws of ecclesiastical polity* (1594 and beyond) that the monarch, although entitled to enforce the rules of the church, should leave the fashioning of these to "pastors and bishops." Hezekiah was the great exemplar, the godly king who restored true religion but called upon the priests to regulate religious affairs. Exercising this principle in practice was no simple matter. Yet its presence buffered the royal supremacy.[92]

Another constraint on the royal supremacy—on paper if not necessarily in fact—was Parliament's role in matters of religion. From its point of view, the history of the English Reformation vindicated this argument. Had Parliament not shaped the government's anti-Catholic program and, at various moments, urged Elizabeth to pursue a foreign policy that favored international Protestantism? As well, from the mid-1560s onward, bills were being introduced and sometimes approved that touched on worship, the plight of nonconformists, the economic problems of the Church, and the bishops' authority to grant dispensations from penalties imposed by the church courts. Yet the queen herself and those who spoke on her behalf in Parliament were quick to deny that institution any real authority over matters of religion. As Christopher Hatton, a loyal supporter of the queen, said in February 1586 in response to assertions within the House of Commons of Parliament's privileges, "It overthroweth her Majestie's supremacie."[93]

Disputes of this kind explain why the agenda of a thorough reformation could become entangled in its own contradictions. What Parliament wanted was not a two-kingdoms system but a role for itself that was as imperious or "Erastian" as the queen's.[94] When it came to core principles, these could also be ambiguous or uncertain. Things indifferent or *adiophra*, which Whitgift used to such effect in the 1570s, had a respectable genealogy within the Reformed tradition. Tone also mattered. Martin Mar-prelate alienated moderates within the Puritan movement who preferred a go-slow process of reform instead of the more sweeping program endorsed by Sampson and others. Inevitably, therefore, a spectrum emerged, some chafing at any compromises and others, like Cartwright by the late 1580s, retreating from his initial insistence on a church aligned with divine law.

Yet the questions that John Foxe tried to finesse in the *Book of Martyrs* refused to disappear. Were the faithful entitled to act on their own if their ruler disobeyed divine law? Did the true church consist of the faithful and ever-suffering few, or was it a national institution headed by another Constantine? And if a church of the few, did this point toward a congregation-centered polity?[95] Summing up the tension between these two possibilities, a historian of the Puritan movement in England has described the presbyterians as "torn between an actual state of schism and their devotion to the Calvinist ideal of a Christian society."[96] Time would tell whether this and other contradictions would overwhelm the possibilities for compromise and moderation, as in fact they did for the handful of Puritans who chose the path of Separatism.

Separatism

When Whitgift and Bancroft began their assaults on John Field-style dissidents in the early 1590s, the hardest blows fell on a different kind of Puritan, the people who became known as "Brownists" or Separatists.[97] Tiny in numbers but vocal about a state church they regarded as suffused with "Idolatry" and in "bondage" to the "invention[s] of man," Separatists inserted themselves into the story of the faithful few Foxe narrated in the *Book of Martyrs*. They owed other themes to the authors of the *Admonition*, including the imperative to never "goe backeward" but always "labour or contend for perfection." Scorning compromises of the kind that enabled Cartwright and his allies to argue that the state church was lawful, Separatists formed congregations of their own.[98] In doing so, they sidestepped the two dilemmas that dogged English Puritans and, more intermittently, the reformers in Scotland. The first of these was how to reconcile an inclusive state church with the church as a sanctified community, and the second, how to remain loyal to a Christian prince while acknowledging the authority of divine law. Separatists solved the first by reimagining the visible church as a cluster of small-scale voluntary communities, each of them empowered to exclude the unworthy, and the second by withdrawing from the magistracy-ministry alliance so dear to the Reformed international. Aware of how Cartwright and company had trimmed their sails in response to the argument of things indifferent, Separatists reaffirmed the regulative principle and its corollary, Christian primitivism.[99]

What counts as Separatism has perplexed every historian of these people, for some continued to acknowledge the state church but abstained from its patterns of worship.[100] Any long-lasting stability was hard-won; debate persisted about the details of what was lawful, as did quarrels of the kind that so often disrupt projects aimed at achieving absolute purity. People came and went, some so alienated from their fellow Separatists that they washed the dirty linen of these communities in print or returned to the church they had repudiated. Caution is in order, therefore, in labeling the men and women who make their appearance in the rest of this chapter, especially if we keep in mind the informal meetings of laypeople and clergy that arose alongside presbyterian-style reform, the virulent anti-popery of this period, and the dismay among so many of the godly with compromise and accommodation.[101]

Something akin to Separatism emerged during the reign of Mary Tudor, when "zealous professors of the gospel" in London and southeastern England stopped attending Catholic services and formed covert fellowships where they worshipped in a Protestant manner.[102] Writing of one of these groups after it emerged into the open in 1558, Thomas Lever, a former Marian exile, spoke admiringly of how it had barred anyone with a reputation for "evil conduct" or "popery" from participating in Holy Communion and sustained a "godly mode of worship," language that suggests the group was using either the 1552 *Book of Common Prayer* (possibly with changes) or an order of worship closer to what was being practiced by the exiles in Geneva. Foxe was also impressed, marveling in the *Book of Martyrs* at the "preservation of a congregation" in London that, at its height, may have numbered two hundred people and citing the "godly multitude" that gathered at Smithfield to support seven persons about to die at the stake, "meeting and embracing, and kissing them" and, as fire engulfed the martyrs, declaring "Almighty god, for Christ's sake, strengthen them!" One of those martyrs was John Rough, who fled his native Scotland after converting to Protestantism and became a minister in England, only to flee again after the accession of Mary Tudor. Returning to London in late 1557, he became the minister of a "secret" congregation until he was captured, condemned as a heretic, and executed. Thanks to Foxe, who included Rough in the *Book of Martyrs*, the London congregation became a legendary presence among Elizabethan Separatists. [103]

Then came the vestarian controversy and, with it, Archbishop Parker's insistence on uniformity. This situation prompted several new communities of laypeople to emerge as the controversy was winding down. The most substantial was probably the Plumbers' Hall congregation, so named because of where it met in London. Discovered by the authorities in 1567, its members were interrogated by Grindal in his capacity as bishop of the city. They responded to his inquiries by invoking the Marian martyrs, the English congregation in Geneva, and the vestarian controversy to justify their independence; as one of the group told him, "We remembered that there was a congregation of us in this city, in the days of Queen Mary; and a congregation at Geneva, which used a book and order of preaching, ministering the sacraments and discipline, most agreeable to the word of God . . . which book and order we now hold," a reference to the *Forme of Prayers* published in Geneva in 1556. Possibly not hostile to episcopacy but certain that the Church of England was infected with "idolatrous trash," the group characterized "the whole religion of papistry" as "filthy Idolatry," a judgment that encompassed the surplice. Simultaneously, these people cited the apocalyptic scenario of warfare between the few and the many in Revelation: the state church bore the "markes of the Romanish beast," whereas their community exemplified "the pure unmingled and sincere worshipping of God" shorn of "all traditions and inventions of men."[104]

Try though the government did to suppress such groups, people of this temperament continued to choose resistance over accommodation, a process fed by the sympathies of nonconforming clergy such as Lever but fed above all by the compromises of the Elizabethan Settlement. John Coppin (or Copping) of Bury St Edmunds was among the more intransigent. In 1578 he refused to have a newborn child baptized and, during his time in prison, complained of parts of the *Book of Common Prayer* and the queen's supremacy in matters of religion.[105] In the early 1580s Robert Browne (d. 1633) became the architect of a more theorized Separatism that acquired the nickname of "Brownisme." After graduating from Cambridge in 1572, Browne turned to school teaching, unable to enter the ministry because he refused to acknowledge the authority of the local bishop. At some point he decided that episcopacy was an "antichristian" legacy from Catholicism, an argument he expanded into an uncompromising rejection not only of that office but also of the men who held it and those they had ordained. In his alternative, the lawful route to becoming a minister was congregation or parish-centered, which was where Christ had placed the authority to call and appoint someone to that office. Browne was just as scathing about the surplice and worship. Echoing what was said in the *Admonition*, he lamented the "worshipping [of] Idols." It was imperative, therefore, that ministers and laypeople throw off the "yoake laid upon [true Christians] by antichrist."[106]

Browne's enduring contributions were twofold: the case he made against nonconformity and his understanding of the true church. In *A True and Short Declaration*, he rehearsed the back-and-forth he had with Robert Harrison, a disaffected minister who clung to the possibility that the Church of England was lawful. In response, Browne insisted that the "open wickedness" of parish churches and the anti-Christian nature of episcopacy nullified the customary marks of a true church. Hence the imperative to "leave such parishes"—an imperative he also justified by his understanding of the "liberty" of Christians and the true church to act without the assent of the monarch. Browne accepted a Moses-like role for civil rulers, a role limited to protecting the "outward" being of the church (or religion). Otherwise, the church did not need to "tarrie" for the magistrate to endorse reform. Turning to church membership, he argued that "the kingdom off God was not to be begun by whole parishes, but rather off the worthiest, Were they never so fewe," a position he justified by citing the parable of the mustard seed (Matt. 13). Via this argument, Browne abandoned the premise—dear to presbyterians and conformists alike—of the church as an inclusive institution. The alternative was a network of small-scale congregations limited to the "worthy" and organized around a "covenant" requiring those who accepted it to "keep & seek agreement under [Christ's] lawes & government." Arguably, Browne's "emphasis on the voluntary church and the unforced conscience went beyond the thinking of any other English religious leader of his time," to the point of making "Brownisme" "synonymous with popular governance."[107]

Together with Harrison, who, at Browne's urging, had rejected ordination by a bishop, he organized a covenanted fellowship in the city of Norwich in early 1581. Wanting to further the process of edification or, in their words, to ensure that the "clean" were not mingled with the "unclean," the two men empowered the congregation to "protest, appeale, complaine, exhort, dispute, reprove, &c," and allowed "men which had the guift" to exhort, practices sanctioned by Browne's assertion that the church as the body of Christ was "the voice of God." In his exegesis of Matthew 18:17, he altered how this verse was usually understood in Puritan circles by insisting that "the church" referred to the congregation, not, as presbyterians assumed, to officers or elders. When the authorities caught up with him that spring, Browne was also preaching in "private houses and conventicles" in nearby towns such as Bury St Edmunds, aided in doing so by "some gentlemen" in the region.[108] Released from prison a short while later, he persuaded a few dozen people to follow him to the town of Middelburg in Zeeland, a province of the Netherlands.

There, with access to a local printer, Browne and Harrison began to publish books in which they explained why, on the grounds of conscience, the faithful must leave the Church of England. Before the end of 1582 a Middelburg printer had issued *A Booke which sheweth the life and manners of all true Christians, and how unlike they are unto Turkes and Papistes and Heathen folke*. What Browne meant by "true Christians" was spelled out in a related publication, *A Treatise of reformation without tarrying for anie*. Tempted by the ideal of the Christian prince and the two-kingdoms understanding of church and state and, in one of his treatises, acknowledging that the godly magistrate "may reforme the Church and commaunde things expedient for the same,"[109] Browne preferred to empower the faithful few who adhered to Christ and "presse[d] unto his kingdome" even if doing so was accomplished by "violence" (Luke 16:16). In exile, he also assailed the presbyterians for counseling their followers to "wait" for the queen or Parliament to act. For him the alternative to Christ was simply the Antichrist.[110]

Before and after Browne moved to the Netherlands, his message appealed to laypeople elsewhere in Suffolk, most notably in Bury St Edmunds, where "a hundred at a tyme" gathered to hear him speak and, some time later, began to read the books he and Harrison were writing. When the government learned that these were trickling into the country, it issued an order in June 1583 demanding that copies be "burned or utterly defaced." Coppin and another man arrested for distributing them were hanged in Bury in July and some forty books committed to a bonfire. Despite another execution in a nearby town, local expressions of Separatism managed to persist.[111] Browne's own revolt was short-lived. After leaving Middelburg and returning to England via Scotland, he wrote one more defense of Separatism, *An Answere to Master Cartwright* (1585), before beginning a process of reconciliation with the state church that ended in his ordination in 1591.

Others proved more resilient. By 1587 the authorities were aware of small groups of Separatists in London who ordained their own ministers and celebrated Holy Communion. One or more of these groups had also employed a simple covenant in which the signers pledged to "walk in the way of the lord and as far as might be warranted by the word of God."[112] That year, the authorities seized and imprisoned some twenty members of such a fellowship led by Henry Barrow, a Cambridge graduate and, at one point, a lawyer in training in London, and John Greenwood, another Cambridge graduate and ordained minister who subsequently repudiated his ordination. Both men denied having any connections with Robert Browne. In the same breath, however, both reiterated his insistence on the freedom of the church to adhere to divine law if the civil magistrate was unwilling to do so.[113]

During their nearly six years of imprisonment, punctuated for Greenwood by his release in July 1592, whereupon he helped organize a new congregation which he served as pastor until he was rearrested in December, the two men found printers willing to publish tracts in which they denounced the Church of England as unlawful, basing this argument on the regulative principle and its corollary, the imperative to separate from idolatrous worship. Echoing a theme of *An Admonition to the Parliament*, Barrow complained of the laxness that enabled the "profane and ungodly" to have their children baptized and allowed others to participate in Holy Communion. The larger problem arose out of the abrupt transition in 1558 from Catholicism to Protestantism. That the state church was so accepting of people who were never summoned to repent their errors had filled it with "prophane ungodly multitudes." The alternative was virtually identical with what Field and Wilcox wanted, a "people called and separated from the . . . worlde." But Barrow transformed the presbyterians' "faithfull people" into "a select peculiar people" who "voluntarily make a true profession of faith and vowe of their obedience." Only those who repented and in some public manner acknowledged divine law could become church members. In *A true description out of the worde of God, of the visible church* (1589), the two men incorporated the biblical and Reformed concept of edification into their understanding of the true (visible) church, characterizing its members as "a most humble, meeke, obedient, faithfull, and loving people, everie stone livinge, elect and precious . . . All bound to edifie one another," language that came close to associating membership with being among the elect. A covenanted church of the worthy was also a church in which "only the children of such . . . are to be baptized," a point on which Barrow and Greenwood agreed with Robert Browne. Likewise, they described the power of the keys as held by ministers and lay members alike, although Barrow withheld the privilege of choosing ministers from the membership, assigning it, instead, to a select group of lay officers. Nor did he want laymen administering the sacraments.[114]

The daring of Barrow and Greenwood extended to the figure of the Christian prince. Declaring themselves loyal to the queen as their Protestant ruler and endorsing the magistrate's authority to order the external features of the church, Barrow and Greenwood rejected the royal supremacy in matters of religion. Moreover, conscience as a register of divine law trumped the authority of the Christian ruler: "we are not bound to obey the prince's law for conscience sake, because only God's laws do bind men's consciences." Questioned by the authorities, who challenged Barrow's assumption that the church could proceed on its own to reform abuses, he replied "that it might and ought, though al the Princes of the world should prohibit the same upon paine of death." Moreover, the authority of each covenanted congregation was such that Elizabeth I in her capacity (wholly hypothetical!) as a member of such a group was subject to discipline. Not, however, to discipline as practiced in the official church, for Barrow insisted that excommunication, the most severe of the spiritual penalties that a gathered church could impose, should not have civil penalties added to it.[115]

Charged with sedition for refusing to accept the authority of the queen, the same accusation used to justify the execution of John Coppin, Barrow and Greenwood were hanged in 1593; a few months later, the Oxford-educated Welshman John Penry—who, after living in Scotland, became involved in the making of the Mar-prelate tracts and in 1592 joined the Greenwood-Barrow congregation—met the same fate. It was also in 1593 that Parliament approved the repression of "seditious sectaries" who refused to attend church services, a measure aimed at radical Puritans.[116] The survivors of the Barrow-Greenwood community had already acquired a new leader in the person of Francis Johnson, a Cambridge-educated minister who was expelled from that university in 1589 after preaching a university sermon on behalf of presbyterianism. Johnson then moved to Middelburg in the Netherlands and ministered to the same English congregation that had welcomed Thomas Cartwright. There, he also encountered the congregation that Browne and Harrison had created. When this group arranged a local printing of a book by Henry Barrow, Johnson secured the town government's consent to destroy the edition except for a few copies he retained and read. Convinced by Barrow's critiques of the state church, he became a Separatist, returned to London, and in late 1592 began to minister to the Barrow-Greenwood group. Arrested and imprisoned but finally released in 1597, he and two "elders" made their way to Amsterdam, where they met up with others of the London congregation who had arrived in 1593. Subsequently, they were joined by the Cambridge-educated Henry Ainsworth, a noted biblical scholar and translator whose version of the Psalms was adopted by the "Pilgrims" of Leiden and new-world Plymouth fame.[117]

Separatism had no creed or catechism, although individual congregations published documents of this kind. At best it was a fragile movement, persecuted in England, disparaged in Scotland, and scorned in the Netherlands by the leaders of the Dutch Reformed Church, who regarded the exiles as schismatic.[118] Within its own sphere it was prone to disagreements and secessions; as happened with Robert Browne, people who became Separatists sometimes returned to the state church. Nonetheless it acquired a remarkable energy thanks to the personalities of a few leaders and the power of certain themes. One of these was the biblical injunction (2 Cor. 6:17) to quit the company of the unclean; another was a contempt for bishops as virulent as Throckmorton's in the Mar-prelate tracts. A third theme concerned the "true minister of Christ," who must oppose the "corruptions of Religion" even if doing so cost him his place in the church.[119] More unusual, perhaps, was an emphasis on the free movement of the Spirit and its corollary, the "Lords Kingdom" as a place where nothing happened by "force." Simultaneously, the radicals were emphasizing the spiritual capacities of the "Lords people." It may have been the last of these themes, together with Browne's insistence on their freedom to act, that prompted some of the townspeople in Norwich to listen so intently to him. For sure, the laymen and laywomen who gathered around Barrow and Greenwood shared an unusual self-confidence. Thomas Cartwright's sister-in law Anne Stubbe, whose second husband was the lawyer and member of Parliament John Stubbe, lived and breathed this confidence, telling Cartwright in a letter of c. 1590 that she was "Commaunded by the lorde to Come out from amongst them that weare not the churche of God." Unmoved by his suggestion that some ministers in the Church of England were lawful because they had been chosen for their post by their congregations, she played her trump card, the imperative to "obey the lorde accordinge to his worde." When Cartwright criticized the exegetical capacities of lay Separatists, she retorted that persons of her way of thinking had been "taught" by Christ and the Apostles. "It must needes be Christ or Antichrist," was her final response to the compromises she discerned among the presbyterians.[120]

Reflections in a Mirror

A tiny number of people acted on the imperative to quit the state church. Why did others who wanted reform or reformation not follow their example? As often happened in early modern Europe, outbursts of radicalism prompted a reaction in favor of more moderate or even conservative principles or goals. The first of these was the ambition to take over and refashion a state church with the help of the civil magistrate. In 1558 hopes ran high for Elizabeth—and, some years later, in Scotland, for James VI—to play this role. In the eyes of English and Scottish presbyterians, magisterial Protestantism—that is, church and state working together to impose and protect a certain version of Protestantism—was justified by biblical precept and political theology. Moreover, this kind of Protestantism preserved a strong role for the clergy over against the "Brownistical" or "democratic" implications of Separatism. At a moment when the rhetorical strategy of anti-puritans such as Bancroft was to emphasize the "Anabaptisticall" aspects of the movement (i.e., nullifying the authority of the magistrate and favoring a sectarian or schismatic kind of church), a third goal was political, to deflect the force of that rhetoric by insisting on the benefits of a national church and some version of the royal supremacy.[121]

These contexts explain why Cartwright and the English minister George Gifford went on the attack. Dipping into the grab bag of anti-puritan rhetoric, Gifford pulled out Whitgift's complaint that the English presbyterians were akin to the fourth-century CE Donatists in their understanding of the visible church and turned it against the Separatists. He backed this critique by citing the Calvinist principle of comprehension intermixed with discipline; the Church of England remained true despite the "presence of sinners," for the purpose of the church on earth was "to redeem, not abandon." Job Throckmorton weighed in as well; the radicals were not the bitter fruit of the movement for reform but people with a wholly different genealogy.[122]

Nonetheless, apologists for the Church of England continued to tie the tin can of "Brownisme" to the tail of every Puritan they encountered. Were they onto something? Whitgift had already detected Anabaptist-like elements in the presbyterian impulse to strengthen the practice of discipline in each parish church. Refusing to "tarie for anie" may be understood as a more emphatic version of what the presbyterians were saying about the liberty of the church, and Separatist-style "congregationalism" as in keeping with the imperative of purging the church of those deemed unworthy. Moreover, assertions that ministers who accepted ordination from a bishop were illegitimate servants of the Antichrist was already being voiced by the more radical presbyterians.[123]

These continuities can tempt us to embrace the Separatists as authentically Puritan because they acted out the principles of liberty, edification, and a "thorough reformation." Any such gesture is useful up to a point, for the Separatist insurgency can be likened to a mirror that reflects certain tendencies the broader movement was struggling to contain. Here, yet again, the dynamics of reform in France and Scotland illuminate the situation in England. Never allowed to worship freely by that country's Catholic rulers, the French Reformed had to accept the fact that theirs was substantially a congregation-centered church. Not so in Scotland, where neither "congregational"-style reform nor Separatism emerged in the sixteenth century, thanks to the fact that John Knox and his fellow reformers took over the state church. Nonetheless, the Separatist presence in late sixteenth-century England forewarns us that something akin to its principles and tactics was likely to emerge whenever moderate reformers found themselves confronted by an alliance of monarchy and ministry advocating a definition of true religion at odds with their own. For that phase of Puritan history, we must wait for chapters 7 and 8.

CHAPTER THREE

Reformation in Scotland

IDOLATRY VERSUS TRUE RELIGION: FROM the moment John Knox gave up on Catholicism and joined the beleaguered Protestant community in his native Scotland, he framed his preaching around the difference between the truth as he understood it and the idolatry he imputed to Catholicism. In an early sermon (1547), he drew on the book of Daniel to explain what was wrong with Rome. No Catholic could be trusted, since all were allied with the Antichrist. Nor was Catholicism capable of adhering to the commandment that declared, "Thou shalt have no other gods before me." Placing himself in the lineage of Old Testament prophets who warned their people to dispense with idols and worship the one true God, Knox evoked this ancestry to justify his outbursts against a Catholicism he deemed "Anti-christian." I teach "all men to hate sin," he wrote the Scottish nobility in 1558, adding that "vaine religion and idolatrie I call whatsoever is done in Goddes service . . . without the expresse commaundement of his own Worde." These assertions stemmed from the goal he set himself after experiencing the powerful ministry of the martyred George Wishart and living as a Marian exile in the Geneva of John Calvin. The time had come for Scotland to emulate the Swiss city he esteemed as "the most perfect school of Christ that ever was on the earth since the days of the Apostles."[1]

Like his Old Testament predecessors, Knox knew that the process of reform was easily disrupted. England's reformation was a case in point, an unfinished reformation compromised, in his words, by "Diabolicall inventions" such as "crossing in baptism, kneeling at the Lord's table," and "singing of the Litany." He wanted Scotland to do better—*much* better, if it were to enjoy a "perfect reformation" that recovered "the grave and godly face of the primitive Church." The missing element in England was discipline in the double sense of purging "superstition" from worship and reworking church structures (economic and ecclesiastical) to ensure the presence of an evangelical ministry. En route from Geneva to his homeland in 1559, he wrote an English friend that God was

mustering an army to assault the great "adversary" Satan and release true religion from every "dreg of Papistry."[2]

Such a reformation was within reach if the transformation of religious life
in the towns of Dundee, Perth, and St. Andrews could be replicated elsewhere.[3]
In each place, spasms of iconoclasm eliminated the material presence of Catholicism. As the ecclesiastical capital of the country, St. Andrews had a cathedral, important monasteries, and the oldest of the Scottish universities. Militant Protestants arrived in mid-June 1559, as did Knox, who preached on
Sunday, June 11, in Holy Trinity, the town church, on the theme of Christ's
cleansing of the temple. Taking this theme to heart, the vigilantes purged Holy
Trinity and the cathedral of statues of the saints, rood screens, altars, and the
gold and silver dishes used for communion. Overnight, this day of "Reformation" undid the Catholic presence in St. Andrews.[4]

Nothing this violent occurred in England during the early years of Elizabeth I's reign or of Edward VI's before her, and the gap between the two reformations began to widen because of Elizabeth I's indifference to the "thorough
reformation" Thomas Sampson and John Field were advocating. Fortunately
for Knox and his allies, the weakness of the Scottish monarchy enabled a resolute Protestantism to emerge *against* the wishes of a Catholic queen regent,
Mary of Guise. Much more tellingly, a coalition of Protestants and those with
other grievances overthrew her successor, Mary Stuart. After 1559, no English
Parliament had an effective voice in deciding religious practice, but the leaders
of the Reformation in Scotland secured the approval of an irregular Scottish
Parliament in 1560 and, more convincingly, of another in 1567 for a firmly
Reformed model of worship and a Reformed statement of doctrine. Unlike the
coming of reform to England, the Scottish reformation owed almost nothing
to the church's bishops. Despite many moments of contact, exchange, and
cross-border politics dating from the late 1540s, the two reformations diverged
in ways that had far-reaching consequences.

Before Mary Stuart took the throne in 1561, reformers and courtiers on
both sides of the border had pondered the possibility of a fuller union between
Scotland and England. This project went nowhere. Thereafter, the question
the reformers in Scotland had to ask themselves was akin to the question answered in an unsatisfactory manner by the settlement of 1559 in England.
Would the Protestantism Knox and other exiles had introduced in Frankfurt
and enjoyed in Geneva—a Protestantism foregrounding the absolute authority
of the Word of God and the imperative to liberate religious practice from
idolatry—prevail or become diluted, as was happening in England? In the
1560s and more explicitly by the late sixteenth century, this question had been
answered in a way that would have satisfied Thomas Sampson. Compromises
of various kinds emerged, but in general the Church of Scotland had aligned
itself with the high standards of the Reformed tradition.[5]

This circumstance explains why, in this chapter and elsewhere, the term "puritan" is attached to the Scottish reformers and the Protestant culture they created. Doing so is at odds with the practice of most historians of early modern Scotland, who regard this word as signifying an insurgency that mutated into nonconformity and de facto "congregationalism." If this is what "puritan" means, it is ill-suited to a country where the state church came into the hands of Protestants who jettisoned every aspect of Catholic worship and, for this reason, a church without Thomas Sampson–like militants brooding over whether to wear the surplice. In Scotland, however (always ignoring those who remained Catholic), the makers of the Reformation shared the same understanding of worship and doctrine. Scottish historians may also want to avoid the negative connotations that accumulated around the term in the late sixteenth century and again in the nineteenth. In these pages, however, I use the word to designate the strong connections between the Protestant program in post-1560 Britain and the goals of the Reformed international. From this perspective, Scotland's Reformation was fully "puritan" or Reformed: installing moral discipline in practice as well as in principle, aligning worship, doctrine, and ministry with Reformed models, and aspiring to implement the two-kingdoms understanding of church and state.[6]

These accomplishments were the envy of Thomas Cartwright's generation in England. At various moments, each side reached out to the other, the leadership in Scotland doing so in response to the vestarian controversy and Knox honored during a visit to London in 1567 by people who remembered him from their days together in Geneva and Frankfurt. On this same trip, he met with members of the Plumbers' Hall congregation (see chap. 2), who told him of their admiration for Geneva-style worship and suggested that he urge Christopher Goodman to write something against "Antichrists clothing." A little later, some of these quasi-Separatists visited Scotland to see for themselves what a true church looked like. Much later (mid-1580s), a handful of radical ministers decamped to London, where they enjoyed the hospitality of that city's "presbyterians."[7] Simultaneously, ministers on both sides of the border were fashioning the "practical divinity" (see chap. 4). On the other hand, the rhetoric of anti-puritanism that emerged in England in the mid-1560s was absent from Scotland until circa 1600, when James VI used it in *Basilikon Doron* (1599). By the 1630s, a presbyterian minister could complain that any "man that professed the power of religion" was "ridiculed and mocked as a Puritan." In this chapter, therefore, a a story of differences is punctuated by intriguing moments of convergence.[8]

The Coming of Reform

Catholic in faith and practice before the coming of the Reformation, Scotland in the early sixteenth century had a national church closely intertwined with the workings of the civil state, the privileges of the aristocracy, and the Catholic rulers of France. Connections with that country, or the "auld alliance," dated from the late thirteenth century and were strengthened in the sixteenth by marriages that linked the French and Scottish royal dynasties: the second wife of James V (1513–42) was the Frenchwoman Mary of Guise, and in 1548 their only child, Mary Stuart, was betrothed to the dauphin of France, the future Francis II, whereupon she moved to France when she was five. Henry II of France, the father-in-law-to-be of Mary Stuart, knew she had a strong claim to the English throne. But he welcomed the marriage mainly because of his country's rivalries with Spain and its then ally, England.

As news circulated within academic and elite circles of the stirrings of Protestantism in Europe, and as copies of the Bible in English became available, townspeople in the southwestern region of the country began to practice the new religion. They did so in the context of a Catholic church that acknowledged the importance of reform but lacked the will and resources to change.[9] Its weaknesses enabled the movement to gain the support of some of the nobility and landed classes, although these people may have been more "evangelical" or humanist than emphatically Protestant. To these stirrings James V responded erratically, mingling severe repression in the late 1530s with gestures of support. When he died unexpectedly in December 1542, six days after the birth of Mary Stuart, the government came into the hands of the Earl of Arran, whose claims to the throne were second only to hers. He sided with England in the ongoing contest over Scotland's international allies and, whether out of conviction or to please the English government, "briefly pursued a program of evangelical reform" that, for the first time, sanctioned the reading of the Bible in English, a practice the Catholic hierarchy had forbidden.[10]

The year 1543 promised great things for Protestantism. Evangelicals were preaching openly and, in the fall, the more intransigent staged anti-Catholic riots. Violence of this kind was not what Arran had expected or what he and the leaders of the state church could accept. English troops moved north, only to be checked by the arrival of French forces. Facing a hostile government, Protestantism subsided into household communities and kinship networks where people shared what they were learning from the Bible and sang psalms; some may have listened to sermons preached by former priests who became Protestants. The most impressive of these men was George Wishart. Fleeing to England once he converted and, while he was there, translating a Reformed confession into Scots, Wishart returned in 1543 or, more likely, in 1544 and began a preaching tour that ended with his arrest and execution in early 1546.[11] Shortly thereafter, a group of high-ranking Scots murdered the senior Catholic clergyman, Cardinal Beaton, and seized the castle of St. Andrews, where they were joined by Knox, himself a former friar. Later that year the castle fell to a French force, and Knox was taken to France as a prisoner of the state. But the leaders of the state church refused to follow the example of Mary Tudor. A handful of Protestants were executed, though far fewer than in England. Nor did many of Scotland's earliest Protestants become refugees.

The situation of the country's Protestants began to change dramatically in 1557, the year in which several of the landed elite, a self-styled "Lords of the Congregation," signed a "band" or covenant to promote the Protestant cause. Until Mary Stuart came of age and returned from France, Mary of Guise was head of state, or regent, a title she assumed in 1554. She was never going to abandon the Catholicism she shared with her powerful and intensely political family in France. In contrast to theirs, however, her authority was much weaker, hampered by the defects of the state church, a sharply divided nobility, and an uneasy relationship with England after Elizabeth I became head of state. Determined to secure Mary Stuart's succession to the throne, Mary of Guise negotiated with the Lords of the Congregation, who pledged their loyalty to the government if she would allow Protestants to practice "lawfully" their own ways of worship. Mary assented to this compromise, as did the Scottish Parliament. For a moment, therefore, Protestants could worship as they pleased in the setting of "privy kirks" or "congregations of the faithful gathering in private," doing so at the urging of preachers such as Knox, who had emphasized the "unlawfulness of communion with Papists" during a preaching tour of parts of his homeland in late 1555 and early 1556.[12]

Neither party was satisfied with these arrangements, and when Knox returned to the country for the third time in May 1559 he summoned Scottish Protestants to confront and overthrow "idolatry." As Scots in greater numbers began to avoid the mass and outbursts of iconoclasm swept through a handful of communities, Knox and other leaders justified this fervency as a necessary means of repudiating "the servants of sin in their filthy corruptions." Simultaneously (1559), he was telling the "communaltie" or "people" of Scotland that, because they were the spiritual "equall" of "Kinges, Rulers, Judges, Nobils," God was calling on them to ignore their traditional deference to leaders of higher rank and, on their own, deliver Scotland from "bondage."[13]

This gesture toward the people had few immediate consequences. For Protestantism to prevail, the reformers would have to secure the support of a significant group of the nobility and the head of state. The second was not going to happen. Instead, civil war broke out once Mary Tudor's death in 1558 and the accession of Elizabeth I eliminated the threat of an alliance between Catholic England and Catholic Spain directed against Protestants in Scotland. Heartened by this turn of events and the possibility of English troops crossing the border to help Protestants defeat French forces, a group of nobles pledged at the end of May 1559 to "set forward the Reformation of Religion according to God's Word," although, for political reasons, they emphasized a civic program of recovering "ancient freedoms and liberties." The most important member of this group was the fifth Earl of Argyll, who in 1558 succeeded his father, himself an early convert to Protestantism and head of Clan Campbell. At his dying father's bedside, the young earl was charged to "set forward the public and true preaching of the Evangel of Jesus Christ, and to suppress all superstition and idolatry, to the utmost of his power." Argyll recruited the troops that carried out the "Day of Reformation" in St. Andrews. Several months later (February 1560), he "personally secured" a treaty with England that Elizabeth reluctantly endorsed; wary of radicals such as Knox but not wanting France to gain control of Scotland, she finally agreed to send troops to aid the Lords of the Congregation.[14] Mary died suddenly in June 1560, a treaty between France and England in July brought fighting to a close, French and English soldiers withdrew, and Scotland became a Protestant country, affirmed as such by an irregular Parliament in August 1560. This year too, the first "General Assembly" met in December; ten or twelve ministers turned up, as did a larger number of laymen.

Seen through the eyes of any European ruler, the accomplishments of 1560 did not mean much until the relationship between civil authority and the state church had been clarified. For the moment, the Reformation in Scotland was anomalous.[15] Nowhere else had Protestants defied a legitimate ruler and taken over the state church, and nowhere else, except in France and the Netherlands, did Reformed-style Protestantism advance without the support of a local ruler. And anomalous the decisions of 1560 remained once Mary Stuart returned in 1561 after the death of her husband in 1560 (the two were married in 1558), for she was fervently Catholic. Within days of her arrival, John Knox was "inveighing against idolatry" and threatening "terrible plagues" if the nobility allowed her to observe the Catholic Mass—which some were willing to do.[16]

The confusion associated with her presence was echoed elsewhere. Catholicism was still being practiced in some regions of the country, and the newly reformed church included a few bishops who had changed sides, with Mary appointing more. At best, only a minority of the Scottish people were enthusiastic about any wholesale process of change; as was true in much of Europe and England, the process of turning ordinary people into full-fledged Protestants would extend well beyond the sixteenth century and never encompass everyone.[17] Many within the landed and political class may have been glad to see French troops removed and Mary of Guise in the grave, but in the presence of a legitimate monarch they fell back on a traditional respect for that office. Doing so was consistent with their reasons for resisting Mary of Guise—not Knox's evocation of a holy covenant between nation and God but a secular politics of "common weal." As with the Elizabethan Settlement of 1559, therefore, the pace and extent of change remained in doubt. Indeed, the Parliament of 1560 had decided nothing about ministry and discipline, topics addressed in a "Book of Discipline" (usually known as the *First Book of Discipline*, to differentiate it from the second of 1578) drawn up by a group of clergy and finalized in early 1561.[18]

To the dismay of Knox and Argyll, an elegant and willful Mary continued to attend the mass. Nor did she endorse the *First Book of Discipline*.[19] Otherwise, she deferred to the Protestant nobility until, in early 1565, her engagement and marriage with Henry Stuart, Lord Darnley prompted some of them to become her allies after she promised to support the kirk. Out of favor, Argyll and his allies schemed to kidnap the queen, a plot that, instead of aiding Argyll, gained Mary Stuart more support among the Scottish magnates—even, for a moment, Argyll himself, who switched sides and joined the queen's party. Fortunately for the Protestant cause, she conducted her private life in ways that undermined her public role. These missteps and ever-present political rivalries encouraged an uprising that pitted a "King's Party" (supporting Mary's infant son) against a "Queen's Party." When the two forces confronted each other at Carbury Hill in 1567, hers was defeated. Some months later she escaped, only to be defeated again at the battle of Langside. In its aftermath, she fled to England. Small-scale civil war finally ended once a group of Protestant and Catholic nobles accepted the "Pacification of Perth" (1573), which stipulated that Mary could not reclaim her throne and that her son James become monarch. In exile, encouraged by Catholics who aspired to place her on the English throne, she flirted with conspiracies against Elizabeth I (a politics greatly exaggerated by an English Parliament terrified that she would succeed a childless Elizabeth) to such an extent that she was executed in 1587.

Amid the confusion of civil war, the situation of the country's Protestants was changing for the better. In December 1567, a new Parliament granted the General Assembly much of what it wanted: ratifying the votes of 1560, limiting the holding of public office to Protestants, assuring the kirk of its authority to supervise all appointments to benefices (endowed positions within the state church) and shifting certain revenues from the Crown to the church. That same month, James VI, although acknowledged as Scotland's monarch, was not named supreme head of the church in deference to the General Assembly's preference for a two-kingdoms model of church and state that barred the "spiritual" and "temporal" kingdoms from having authority over the other. Looking back on this sequence of events, the General Assembly of 1567 celebrated a "most miraculous victory": "Our enemies, praised be God, are dashed; religion established; sufficient provision made for ministers; order taken, and penalty appointed for all sorts of transgression and transgressors; and, above all, a godly magistrate, whom God of His eternal and heavenly providence has reserved to this age; to put into execution whatsoever He by His law commands."[20]

Exciting though it was to dispose of Mary Stuart, the practical workings of the state church, and especially the authority of general assemblies, remained in doubt for more than two decades. Year after year, those who disagreed with the particulars of a Knox-style perfect reformation clashed with others who wanted religious practice in Scotland to duplicate the model Calvin and Bucer had established in Geneva and elsewhere. In a much-divided country where church and state had been entangled for many generations, rearranging this relationship was never going to be easy. The most significant parties to this process were James VI and the regents who headed the government until he came of age; the political classes headed by the nobility; the clergy, who were not of one mind; and the European regimes, especially England, with a stake in the outcome. As for any hopes that the people could be evangelized, the geography of Scotland—economic, linguistic, and social—posed a host of difficulties.

James VI was Scotland's first Protestant monarch. Unlike England's queen, he enjoyed listening to sermons and practicing his skills as biblical exegete and theologian. His tutors, one of them the Scottish humanist George Buchanan, saw to his acquiring a command of Latin and other languages and an appetite for reading; later, and especially in the 1590s, James used his learnedness to translate some of the psalms, compose poetry, engage in anti-Catholic biblical commentary, write a treatise on the nature of monarchy, and in *Basilikon Doron* advise his eldest son Henry on how to govern an unruly Scotland. To these interests James added a passion for hunting and other amusements. As monarch, he inherited a position that none of his sixteenth-century predecessors had employed with skill or persistence. Authority was widely dispersed, so much so that James could not count on the obedience that Henry VIII and Elizabeth enjoyed as a function of their office. Initially, he ruled only in name, with regents doing the real work until he turned eighteen. Thereafter, he relied on a coterie of courtiers or favorites. Being close to the king was risky, for it threatened the ambitions of other magnates for access to power and the wealth it could provide. The governments of Spain, France, and England also meddled with James's government, England in particular, for Elizabeth and her advisors wanted certain things of a Scottish king—agreement on how to bring order to the "Borders" between the two countries, an alliance with England rather than one with France or Spain, and, in the context of a formal treaty with England in 1586, James's willingness to accept the execution of Mary Stuart. Of the benefits he gained from this concession, one seems to have been the reassurance that he was first in line to succeed Elizabeth.[21]

James was reared a Protestant, and a Protestant he remained despite having had a Catholic mother. Yet for him, the meaning of true religion differed from what Knox and his allies wanted. By the time he came of age in 1578, he had decided that their version contradicted his quest for greater authority as king, a decision that haunted the Scottish church for the rest of his reign. James may have been at his best in navigating the troubled waters of diplomacy. Perennially short of funds, he preferred peace to warfare and, at an opportune moment, secured a treaty with England that boded well for Protestants. Ever vulnerable to the talents and charm of certain courtiers, in the 1580s and 1590s the king included French-educated and possibly

Catholic-tilting Scots among his closest friends and officers of state. One of these men, James Stuart, became regent in 1584 and received the title of Earl of Arran. Another, George Gordon, the sixth Earl of Huntly and leader of Clan Gordon, was repeatedly in trouble with the state church, which wanted him excommunicated for his closeness to Catholicism. Despite outbursts of militancy that included a battle between Catholic Gordons and Protestant Campbells in 1594 and a period of exile in France, Huntly managed to retain the king's favor.

The weakness of the Scottish monarchy was intertwined with the character and circumstances of the Scottish nobility and landed classes that monopolized the government's administrative offices. The nobility were one of three "estates" (the others being officers of the church and the lesser landholders, or lairds) in the Scottish Parliament. Accustomed to appropriating the property of the church for their own benefit, the higher nobility spurned every plea to disgorge the income they were receiving. The most spectacular prize in this scramble for personal gain was the revenue attached to bishoprics; whenever possible, the great families claimed this office and the benefits associated with it. Religious affiliation, much less religious commitment, took second place to the competition for wealth, political office (which could be economically beneficial), and access to regents or the king, and second place as well to an intricate game of alliance making among the major families in the context of interclan conflict. Allies came and went; betrayals, double-dealing, and coups d'état were everyday affairs; and vengeance, up to and including assassination, was an acceptable means of settling disputes. As James VI observed in *Basilikon Doron*, the nobility had a "feckless arrogant conceit of their greatness and power." From almost any perspective, and certainly that of the Crown, the rule of law was tenuous. A nobleman called to account by a judicial court or the government was likely to arrive in Edinburgh or elsewhere accompanied by a retinue of armed men, a show of force the government was not always able to withstand. Tellingly, the nobility spurned the authority of the state church to call them to account for their moral behavior.[22]

People of this kind were not the best material on which to base a church bent on upholding a strict moral code and eliminating Catholicism, which a significant fraction of the nobility continued to prefer. According to the *First Book of Discipline*, everyone was accountable to the church and social rank was irrelevant; "to discipline must all the estates within this Realm be subject, as well the Rulers, as they that are ruled," a rule the kirk struggled to enforce. Nor did rank offer any protection from the message that God expected great things of kings and the nobility. Knox made this point in his *Appellation . . . from the Cruell and Most Unjust Sentence Pronounced against Him by the False Bishops and Cleargie of Scotland* (Geneva, 1558). Addressing "the Nobilitie and Estats" of his homeland and quoting Romans 13:1–2, he summoned them to exercise their God-given authority to "promote true religion." To this message he attached the prophet-like warning that, were they to neglect this role, they could not "escape God's judgements." Year after year, Knox and his successors reiterated this message, usually in the context of disputing the politics of religion pursued by various regents and, eventually, James VI. Knox also knew that, without the support of some of the nobility, neither his preaching tour of 1555 nor the overthrow of Mary of Guise would have been possible. Wavering or inconsistent in their alliances among each other and in their allegiance to the king, the nobility and lairds were, in the telling words of one Scottish historian, unable to "deliver the type of religious revolution which the ministers sought." Nonetheless, an important group continued to prefer a Protestant-style state church.[23]

Where else did the Protestant program find substantial support? As was true in Germany and England, urban merchants, the lesser nobility, craftsmen, and tenant farmers were more likely to be Protestant. Support also came from townsmen and "burgesses" who met annually to debate affairs of state that impinged on the "royal burghs" in which some burgesses held office.[24] John Knox owed his invitation (1559) to become minister of a key church in Edinburgh to men of this status. They turned up by the dozens in 1560 for the informal Parliament of that year and, as the century progressed, staffed the church courts or kirk sessions (see below). Quantifying the growth of the merchant class in sixteenth-century Scotland is difficult, but grow it did in wealth, numbers, and political influence. Despite their prominence, these Protestants of middling rank or status never created the versions of "voluntary religion" (see chap. 6) that became a significant feature of religious life in England; to cite one example, the Church of Scotland had no locally supported lecturers of the kind that emerged in England. Well into the seventeenth century, the sociology of Protestantism in Scotland was parish centered, with none of the flavor of the "congregationalism" that historians detect in the program of Cartwright and Travers. And, although generalizing about the texture of everyday or popular Protestantism is a questionable enterprise, it seems certain that Knox's vision of an embattled few who repudiated all aspects of Catholicism ignored the many in Scotland who preferred a more relaxed version of Protestantism.[25]

Other headwinds in the face of the Protestant reformers arose out of the economic and cultural geography of Scotland. Much more so than England, it was a rural society of landless peasants and tenant farmers, some of them quite prosperous, with Edinburgh the only town of any real size (possibly some 12,000 inhabitants in 1560, at a time when the overall population may have approached 700,000; by the 1620s, the city's population had doubled). This social and economic geography overlapped with the division of the country into the Gaelic-speaking and, after 1560, substantially Catholic Highlands and the Scots-English–speaking and more fully Protestant Lowlands. The "Borders" (where England and Scotland met) was a region unto itself, an area dominated by the sixteenth-century equivalent of gangsters who defied all attempts at establishing law and order. Planting a Protestant ministry in the Highlands was virtually impossible, and as late as 1609, only a minority of parishes in that region employed a professional clergyman. A minister charged with introducing churches to the area complained in 1567 and again in 1572 that he was "not able to travel" in "the north" and collect church rents for the benefit of Protestant missionaries after he provoked a local magnate with little sympathy for Protestantism. Planting one in the Lowlands was hampered by a shortage of university-trained ministers and the low level of their stipends, so low in the early decades that some ministers gave up their vocation. Thanks to a multitude of such circumstances, turning Scotland into a Protestant country along Reformed lines would happen slowly and, in some regions, incompletely.[26]

Headwinds notwithstanding, a group of ministers in the 1560s held fast to the vision of a perfect reformation they had inherited from the example of Geneva and the Huguenot movement in France and passed this vision on to their successors. This vision rested on a concept of a covenant between God and a Protestant Scotland, a concept central to Knox's preaching and the theological rationale for the fast days he wanted his fellow Scots to observe. At a perilous moment in 1565, Knox collaborated with another minister of the same thinking, John Craig, to write *The Ordure and Doctrine of the General Fast*, which they fashioned as an appeal to Scotland's faithful Protestants to employ "prayer, fasting and repentance" as weapons against the queen and her allies.[27] The self-confidence of these men may make us uneasy, and in sixteenth-century Scotland it irritated Mary Stuart, James VI, and some of the nobility; to a modern ear, although not to anyone who knew of Knox's practice in the 1550s and 1560s, it seems unimaginable that a minister could admonish the noble house of Anstruther for collecting revenues that should have gone to the church, a message James Melville (1556–1614) reinforced by adding "a curse and malediction from God upon whosoever shall intervene and draw away the commodities thereof from the right use of sustaining of the ministry."[28]

Always tense,[29] the relationship between ministers and the country's magnates was eased by the social status of some first- and second-generation ministers; men such as Robert Bruce, Robert Rollock, and John Craig were the sons of lairds or connected with the nobility, and John Erskine of Dun, a member of the Lords of the Congregation and akin to a minister in the role he would play as a superintendent (see below), was a laird with strong connections to those of "the nobility and gentry" to whom "he was related." Thanks to their personal piety, some of these men acquired an authority as "especiall instrument[s] of God" in the work of evangelization. Questioned at the ceremony in 1561 admitting him to the office of superintendent, John Spottiswood cited his indifference to "worldly commodity, riches or glory," pledging at the same moment to "profess, instruct, and mentain the purity of the doctrine, conteaned in the sacred word of God" against all attempts to introduce "men's inventions." Men such as Spottiswood, Bruce, James Lawson, and John Davidson had a high understanding of their office as the "especiall instrument of God" in the work of evangelization.[30]

In the 1560s, enough well-qualified ministers were on hand to staff the three major churches in Edinburgh and those in university towns such as St. Andrews and Glasgow. Elsewhere, such men were scarce; as the historian John McCallum has shown for the region of Fife, two or three parishes shared the same minister until near the end of the century or made do with "readers." As in England, moreover, the state church continued to rely on men who had been priests or monks before the coming of the Reformation, a transition eased by the decision of the Scottish Parliament to allow these men to retain two-thirds of the income from their benefices. Keeping an eye on them, and especially on the credentials of readers, became a special concern of the General Assembly. Longer term, it was not these men but the dozens of students at one or another of the Scottish universities who implemented the new religion.[31]

Another challenge was arranging for a supply of service books and Bibles. A local printer issued an edition of Calvin's *Catechism* in 1564, and John Craig's *A Shorte Summe of the Whole Catechisme* (1581) had several local printings, but many other books were imported, especially Bibles and psalters; not until 1579 did a Glasgow printer publish a local edition of the Geneva Bible, which the Church of Scotland officially endorsed.[32] Well beyond 1600, churches and people in Scotland depended on Dutch-printed Bibles and other books for most of their needs. The first book printed in Gaelic arose out of the ambition of the Earl of Argyll and the earliest superintendent in his part of the country, John Carswell. Hoping to evangelize the western Highlands, Carswell translated the worship guide known as the *Book of Common Order* (see below) into classic common Gaelic (an elite version of the vernacular) in 1567. He and Argyll talked of doing a Gaelic version of the Bible, a project thwarted by Carswell's death in 1572 and the earl's in 1573. Nonetheless, the way was open to introducing Protestantism to the Highlands.[33]

Toward a Presbyterian System

The measures accepted by the parliaments of 1560 and 1567 were steps along the way to the reformation Knox aspired to accomplish. Of the objections that process was certain to include, four became contentious: the workings of discipline; the king's authority in religious affairs or, if not the king's, that of the regents serving in his stead; the administrative structure of the church; and the place clergy should have in the country's Parliament. Reserving the politics and practice of church discipline for chapter 5, this chapter follows the up-and-down relationship between general assemblies and the country's leaders to the end of the century and beyond.[34]

Theirs was not a simple relationship, and the details that follow may obscure the role of theological principles in the making of religious politics. One of these was the regulative principle, or the singular authority of the Word. Eventually, one wing of the Church of Scotland resorted to the argument of "things indifferent," but for most of the sixteenth century the kirk insisted on a strong version of the Word as law. Another was the imperative to rid the church of idolatry, an imperative cloaked in a ferociously apocalyptic anti-Catholicism that some in civil society did not share, most notably James VI. But the brightest thread that wound its way through the tapestry of religious politics concerned the visible church and its place in the grand scheme of redemption. Ensuring the welfare of the church as a divine institution was the rock on which all other reforms were based—reform of ministry, an office or vocation of the highest importance and therefore open only to certain kinds of men; of worship, from which all idolatry should be removed; and of discipline, for the holiness of the church depended on its capacity to punish the immoral and the unworthy. Then and only then would the church become a veritable city upon a hill (Matt. 5:14); then and only then would it justify its identity as the "best" and purest church in all of Christendom. In the eyes of the more daring reformers, such a church was what the Reformation had brought into being, a church notably superior to its English counterpart and, as signaled by divine portents and providences, especially dear to God.[35]

In the 1560s, the kirk had achieved the impossible, a transition from Catholicism to Protestantism against the wishes of the country's ruler. The price of doing so had been civil war and a severely divided nobility. Now, with the coming of peace, where did the civil magistrate figure in the country's newfound Protestantism? Taking for granted that church and state "were two aspects of the one Christian commonwealth," a Christendom headed by magistrates as well as ministers, each of them holding offices that God had ordained, the church's new leaders also wanted to protect the distinctive freedom of the church. James VI welcomed the role of Christian prince because it seemed to confirm his authority in matters of religion. And, as was true in England, the clergy and their more immediate supporters needed a Christian prince to uphold their own authority and keep Catholicism at bay. On the other hand, the ministers valued the autonomy that the church was promised within the two-kingdoms framework. Tension was inevitable, one party wanting the officers of the church to defer to the magistrate and another insisting on the ministers' independence alongside a strong role for a Christian prince.[36]

There was less reason to be anxious about worship or the lawfulness of the state church. On these there was broad agreement, so much so that English-style nonconformity was conspicuous by its absence, as were any flickerings of Separatism. In 1561 the General Assembly accepted a revised and expanded version of the *First Book of Discipline*. Affirming that "Gods written and revealed word" was normative, it created procedures for admitting persons to the ministry of local congregations (the longest section of the book); endorsed the practice of having congregations "elect" their pastors, elders, and deacons, for Knox a key aspect of a minister's "call";[37] and reiterated the importance of supervising moral behavior, a task assigned to church officers known as elders, who wielded punishments of several kinds, most notably excommunication. Nothing was said of episcopacy, although Knox had previously inveighed against the "wicked, slanderous and detestable life of prelates," contrasting their lust for "riches and possessions" with the simplicity of "able and true ministers." During the back-and-forth with Mary of Guise, the Protestant leadership had insinuated that the Scottish bishops were tyrants in league with the Antichrist and therefore not "true ministers of Christ's Church."[38] As of that moment, therefore, any English-style system of diocesan episcopacy was out of the question.

Unlike Calvin, the Scots made discipline a mark or "note" of the true church, a premise included in the Confession of 1560 on the grounds that discipline and "Christ's Kingdome" rose and fell together. According to the *First Book of Discipline*, it was imperative that the church distinguish between "men of eveill conversation" and "God's children" and just as imperative that some sort of barrier keep the godly from being "infected" with evil, a premise linked to Paul's injunction to the Corinthians to expel evil doers (1 Cor. 5:6–7, 9–12). Both were means of sustaining the process of "edification" or mutual watch among church members and the ideal of the church as "more purely governed" than civil society. The ultimate remedy for corruption was to excommunicate anyone who remained unrepentant, a step elaborated on in an "Ordour of Excommunication" (1569).[39]

Simultaneously, the leaders of the church were redefining the substance of worship. An ideal version was readily at hand, the stringently anti-Catholic *Forme of prayers and ministration of the Sacraments*, the service book prepared by the Genevan community of Marian exiles (1556).[40] Printed in Edinburgh in 1562, the year it was endorsed by the General Assembly, and reprinted many times thereafter, it was commonly referred to as the *Book of Common Order*. This text and its companion, the *First Book of Discipline*, contained a strongly Protestant understanding of baptism and Holy Communion that eliminated the sign of the cross in the first of these sacraments; specified that sitting at a table was the appropriate means of receiving the elements of bread and wine, for which ordinary bread was used; and eliminated all holy days "commanded by men" and "those that the Papists have invented," a list that included Christmas.[41] Holy days gave way to two services on Sunday, each centered on preaching, prayer, and the congregational singing of metrical psalms. Holy Communion would be celebrated four times a year (a schedule local churches rarely sustained), and procedures were put in place to prepare those who wanted to participate—in particular, "preparation" sermons preached a week or so before the sacrament was administered. Private baptism of newborn children was proscribed and rules spelled out for weddings and funerals, usually in a manner that disrupted Catholic or popular custom. Catholic vestments also vanished, for Knox agreed with those in England who denounced these garments as "badges of idolaters." In their place, ministers in the kirk wore the scholars' gown, a practice favored by Reformed communities on the continent.[42]

This pattern of worship validated the assertion that the Church of Scotland had purged itself of all "inventions." Not in England, however, which was why the General Assembly sympathized with the ministers on the losing side of the vestarian controversy. Hearing of that dispute, the leaders of the assembly sent a letter of advice to Elizabeth and the English bishops. Its point was to underscore the imperative of eliminating idolatry, an imperative accomplished in Scotland but not in England now that vestments were being re-imposed. Opening with a rhetorical question, "What has darkness to do with light?" the assembly characterized "surplices, cornet cap and tippet" as "badges of idolaters," adding that the wise course of action would be to jettison "the dregs of that Romish beast; yea, what is he that ought not to fear either to take in his hand or forehand, the print and mark of that odious beast?" To Elizabeth herself the assembly spoke in strong terms. She should not use her authority "against God," but "oppose" herself "boldly . . . against all such as dare burden the consciences of the faithful further than God chargeth them in his own word." For the kirk as for the protestors in London, conscience trumped "worldly wisdom," a coded allusion to the queen's willingness to ignore divine law.[43]

Meanwhile, the assembly was improvising an administrative structure for the kirk and casting about for ways to improve the financial situation of the clergy. Some parts of this process were easily accomplished—for example, curtailing Catholic-style church courts headed by bishops or their appointees and replacing a cathedral-centered system with an emphasis on the local parish. Measures of this kind ensured that episcopacy in any strong sense of the term had been eliminated. Actual bishops were not, however, for the state church inherited several men who converted to Protestantism. As would gradually become apparent, the Scottish bishops resembled a cat with nine lives—diminished or seemingly eliminated, yet somehow reappearing. Although the English and, even more so, the Catholic version of episcopacy contradicted the principle of ministerial equality, the reformers knew that Bucer and Calvin had entertained the possibility of a "reformed episcopate" justified by its administrative functions. With three Protestant bishops on hand, the authors of the *First Book of Discipline* settled on differentiating good from bad bishops, the former able to be "preachers themselves," the latter, "idle Bishops" who had little or no role in the economy of salvation. An easy way to underscore the difference between the two was to order every minister to live in a single parish, a step that also had the benefit of curtailing nonresidency.[44]

With bishops sidelined, the General Assembly devised the office of super-intendent, assigning the men who held this post the responsibility for oversee-ing regional clusters of local churches and giving them the task of staffing new parishes. A short-lived experiment with precedents in European practice, su-perintendency had nothing in common with bishops in the Church of England. Longer term, the leaders of the kirk wanted to control the process by which ministers were appointed to a parish, a goal frustrated by the privileges of magnates and others who owned church property.[45] These steps taken, the leaders of the General Assembly turned to reforming the Scottish universities. A purge of Catholic faculty from the University of Aberdeen in 1569 was fol-lowed by the appointment of new leaders for Glasgow and St. Andrews, where Andrew Melville (1545–1622) moved in 1580 after spending several years as principal in Glasgow. Thanks to the expertise he gained in Europe, Melville became "the dominant figure in the education of Scottish divines," although his influence as a theologian was less than that of Robert Rollock, who became the first head (1583) of a newly founded college in Edinburgh.[46] As a practical step, the kirk endorsed the exercise of ministerial education known as proph-esying, and the *First Book of Discipline* added a request that masters of fami-lies instruct their households in matters of religion.

Establishing an effective regulation of morals, manners, and access to the Lord's Supper would take another four or five decades. The rules may have been in place—the *First Book of Discipline* called on ministers to exert a "sharp examination" to ensure that no one was admitted to the Lord's Supper who "can not formally say the Lord's prayer, the Articles of the Beliefe and declare the summe of the Law"—but it was another matter to find the men who, as elders, would do the hard work of supervising everyday behavior.[47] The good news was the presence of an institution with no direct counterpart in England, the kirk session or church court (see chap. 5). These were up and running in a handful of places as early as the 1560s and functioning throughout most of Lowland Scotland by the turn of the century. Thanks to their effectiveness, the disciplining aspects of the country's Protestant culture were gradually incor-porated into popular practice.[48]

The final part of the reformers' program concerned the relationship be-tween church and state. Aware of the two-kingdoms framework so important to the English "presbyterians" but also knowing that the Zurich theologians assigned a strong role to the magistrate or Christian prince, the leaders of the kirk could not do much by way of reform while Scotland was ruled by a Catho-lic queen. Nonetheless, in 1559 the Lords of the Congregation called on Mary of Guise to act in keeping with her duties as "Christian Prince" and "put away idolatry." (She and her allies, and subsequently Mary Stuart in the 1560s, re-plied by accusing the Lords of the Congregation of fomenting "sedition.") For the rest of the century and beyond, the leaders of the state church pushed and prodded regents, nobility, and James VI to live up to the role of Christian prince. Simultaneously, the assembly wanted to protect the freedom of the state church to regulate most aspects of religion—doctrine for one, discipline and the penalty of excommunication for another. It was easy to agree that ministers and superintendents should not hold civil office or serve in the Scottish Parliament, a rule contradicted by the few bishops who retained their place in that body.[49] Far from withdrawing from civil life, however, the reformers insisted that the kirk play a major role in the life of the country. As God's "watchmen of the people," its leaders were entitled to summon the Scottish elite—kings, regents, and magnates—to remedy "all vices commanded by the law of God to be punished" and to threaten them in the name of God if they refused to do so. Simultaneously, assemblies evoked the concept of a "mutual bond" uniting king, people, and God, a contract that required the Christian prince to "maintain . . . the true religion of Jesus Christ."[50]

With James VI too young to rule in person, the politics of religion revolved around the men who became regents. The first of these, James Stewart (first Earl of Moray), the deposed queen's illegitimate brother, was sympathetic to the needs of the kirk. After he was assassinated in 1570 by allies of Mary Stuart, his successors, two of whom also died at the hands of assassins, began to appoint high-placed Protestants as bishops without seeking the consent of the General Assembly. Amid these difficulties, a compromise was struck in 1572 when a group of nobles and state officers commissioned by the current regent, James Douglas, the Earl of Morton, met in the town of Leith with a delegation of ministers. Erskine of Dun, an early supporter of reform among the nobility and gifted at crafting compromises, sketched a framework of rules aimed at reclaiming some of the property attached to bishoprics and requiring anyone of this rank to serve a parish. His scheme paved the way for an agreement to acknowledge an episcopate appointed by the Crown and empowered to ordain men to the ministry but in other respects "subject . . . to the general assembly." For its part, the government agreed that, in theory, the role of these bishops was the same as that of superintendents, who would continue to be appointed. (In point of fact, this office gradually vanished.) The government also agreed that, each time the government named a new bishop, he would be vetted by the assembly, take up pastoral responsibilities, and accept the guidance of a "chapter of learned ministers." The Convention of Leith was of the mix-and-match variety, each side getting something of what it wanted. The clauses about church revenues and adding more clergy epitomized this process; on the one hand they preserved lay patronage (ownership) of church property, but on the other they gave the church a greater role in managing its revenues and strengthened the funding of students at the several universities.[51]

As often happens with compromises of this kind, the convention disappointed the more emphatically Reformed, who sniped at the oddity of bishoprics shorn of most of their revenue.[52] In August 1572, the General Assembly insisted that the names of "archibishop archdeacon" and the like had the "sound of papistry" and urged the government to regard the agreement reached at Leith as provisional or interim, which in fact it was, since no assembly had approved its provisions. In October, disaffection made its way into a fast-day proclamation that singled out the "reformation of the nobility" as of special importance, noting their "wrongful use of the patrimony of the Kirk" and "their great negligence in times past" in punishing "vice."[53] The more significant reaction to Leith was the decision to begin work on a new book of discipline that would define the relationship between church and state; decide, once and for all, the status of episcopacy; and clarify other aspects of church structure.

Little is known about this process or who within the assembly and the nobility led the way. What seems certain is that such a step was envisioned as early as 1571 and others were being taken as of February 1574, when the assembly appointed a committee to prepare articles "which conerne the jurisdictioun of the kirk," a process that gained fresh importance once the regent Morton, who wanted some version of episcopacy, began to tamper with the boundaries between church and state. Parliament having voted to endorse this project, the assembly returned to the question of bishops, past, present, and future. In 1576, Chancellor Glamis, a Protestant nobleman, sought the advice of Theodore Beza about church order at a moment when, in Glamis's words, the "hindrances" of "internal strife" had been succeeded by "peace." Hoping for consensus on "the form of government" for the state church, he told Beza that, as yet, "adequate agreement has not yet been reached among us on matters of government and constitution." From Geneva, Beza responded by recommending that the state church avoid an institution he identified with tyranny, those "bastard bishops, the relicts of the Papacie." Almost certainly aware of Travers's *Ecclesiasticae Disciplinae* (1574) and the French Reformed discipline of 1571, which Beza had helped write, and armed with copies of his *De Triplici Episcopatum*, the assembly voted in 1575 to entrust a small group of ministers with the task of revising "all Books that are printed and published"; a year later, it authorized a committee to prepare what became known as the *Second Book of Discipline*. That year, too, the status of episcopacy as a divine office was debated, with Andrew Melville and John Craig, among others, arguing that the "name of Bishop is common to every one of them that hath a particular flock." According to a later account, Melville was also saying "that the corruptions crept into the estate of Bishops were so great, as unlesse the same were removed, it could not go well with the Church, nor could Religion be long preserved in purity."[54]

By late fall of 1578, the new book of discipline had advanced to the point where, at the king's request, a draft was reviewed and amended by a committee of thirteen men, four of them important ministers in the kirk and another, Erskine of Dun. What is known of these deliberations suggests that the group was clarifying how magistrate and minister would work together in practice and how, going forward, episcopacy would be dealt with and the office of ruling elder introduced. Some details may have remained unclear, including, it seems, the situation of the existing bishops, and in 1578 Parliament was unwilling to ratify the document, but in 1580 the assembly resolved that the office of bishop "had no sure . . . ground out of the Scriptures, but was brought in by the folly and corruption of men's invention to the great overthrow of the true Kirk." Singling out the four bishops who remained, the assembly ordered them to "quit, and leave" the office.[55]

Now, at long last, the kirk acquired a presbyterian system of church government, although still burdened with an ambiguously situated office of bishop, which the government never agreed to abolish. According to the *Second Book of Discipline*, one great benefit of the new system was its capacity to prevent "all occasion of tyranny" given the principle (p. 74) that ministers must "rule with mutuall consent of brethren, and equalitie of power"—that is, parity among themselves, with laypeople empowered to assent to (not make) the selection of their parish minister. Curtailed in this regard, ministry was nonetheless an office that Christ brought into being and one to which he assigned a distinctive authority, doing so "immediately," that is, without it passing from church to office (p. 71). Another branch of ministry, the office of elder, also came into its own as having near-clerical status (chap. 6). Taking up the vexed question of how to ensure adequate supervision of local churches and ministers, the assembly assigned most of this responsibility to provincial synods. Simultaneously, it affirmed a strong version of its own authority (chap. 7), which included the privilege of vetting and supervising any bishops. Another sign of the kirk's newfound freedom was the decision to invite Thomas Cartwright and Walter Travers to join the faculty of St. Andrews, although neither did so.

Other details were in keeping with Reformed practice. As in the plans of the English presbyterians, so in Scotland each local church was to be governed by a "consistory" of pastors, elders, and deacons complemented by intercongregational structures of presbyteries and synods, with the General Assembly acting as the final court of appeals for cases of discipline, the appointment of clergy to parish churches, and matters of larger policy. All ministers were barred from holding political office, a principle of two-kingdoms theory, and bishops were wished away by a rule that they must serve as pastors of a parish church (chap. 11). The post of reader, a leftover from the 1560s, disappeared although lingering in practice. As had been true since 1560, assemblies, synods, and presbyteries continued to include a substantial bloc of lay members, some of them holding office as elders in local churches, others elected or appointed, and still others participating by virtue of their social or political rank.[56]

In other sections, the *Second Book of Discipline* contained what may best be described as a wish list of hopes and expectations. This was notably the case with chapter 12, which insisted on "the libertie of the election of persons called to the Ecclesiasticall functions," a liberty juxtaposed with a statement condemning any appointing of ministers "either by the prince or any inferiour person[s]." The same chapter included a critique of patronage in the hands of the nobility because it put the selection of parish ministers into the hands of the wrong people. Likening "patronages and presentation to benefices used in the Popes kirk," the *Second Book of Discipline* "desire[d] all them, that truly fear God earnestly" to recognize that the popish "manner of proceeding has no ground in the word of God, but is contrary to the same, and to the said liberty of Election," that is, the liberty of local churches to play a meaningful role in naming their ministers (pp. 89–90).

When it came to the relationship between church and state (chapters 10 and 11), the tone hardened. On the one hand, the *Second Book of Discipline* reiterated the customary wisdom about the Christian prince as "nourisher" of the church, an assertion embedded in the Confession of 1560. On the other, it combined this truism with a quite different principle drawn from two-kingdoms theory, the magistrate's responsibility to "maintain the present liberty . . . God hath granted by the preaching of his Word." To this assertion it added a ban on "usurping any thing that perteins not to the civil sword, but belongs to the offices that are merely Ecclesiasticall" (p. 85). Strong words about the jurisdiction of the church followed in chapter 12, which spelled out an autonomy vis-à-vis the Christian prince: "The Nationall Assemblies of this Countrey, called commonly the Generall Assemblies, ought alwayes to be retained in their own liberty, and have their own place. With power to the kirk to appoint times and places convenient for the same, & all men, as well Magistrates as inferiors, to be subject to the judgement of the same in Ecclesiasticall causes, without any reclamation or appellation to any Judge, civill or ecclesiasticall, within the Realm" (p. 89). Via language of this kind, the *Second Book of Discipline* aspired to curtail the authority of regents, kings, and parliaments to intervene beyond a certain point in the workings of the state church.

The deeper point—too easily overlooked—was the implication that the General Assembly derived its legitimacy not from the monarchy or civil state but from God. At the General Assembly of 1581, the delegates insisted anew that the national church's "power ecclesiastical flows immediately from God and the mediator Jesus Christ, and is spiritual, not having a temporal head on earth, but only Christ." With aggressive regents in mind as well as James VI, the assembly also resolved that "it is a title falsely usurped by the anti-Christ, to call himself head of the Kirk," a title deserved by neither "angel or . . . man, of what estate soever he be."[57] To be sure, everyone knew that assemblies had repeatedly negotiated the details of certain policies with regents and the Scottish Parliament or depended on their being endorsed by the government— witness the Parliament of 1560 and, in 1578, a willingness born of political necessity to negotiate with the regent Morton about certain aspects of the *Second Book of Discipline*. More negotiations lay ahead over presbyteries, which did not fully emerge until the mid-1580s after being formally introduced in

1581, and more as well about the handling of excommunication and the presence of bishops (or any clergy) in the Scottish Parliament. Another task was to clarify the relationship between clergy and lay elders—in the case of lay elders, ensuring they were outnumbered by ordained ministers in presbyteries and synods. Nonetheless, the *Second Book of Discipline* asserted a strong version of autonomy against the wishes of Esme Stewart, a former Catholic, cousin of the king, and regent as of 1581.[58]

Many years later, it was said by supporters of episcopacy in Scotland that the presbyterianism of the *Second Book of Discipline* was the doing of Andrew Melville. Perhaps they knew of his nickname (as reported much later by his nephew James) as "the flinger out of bishops." Melville was in Geneva when the impulse to rewrite the first *Book of Discipline* emerged within the kirk.[59] Leaving Scotland for France in the 1560s, he studied in Paris and Poitiers before moving to Geneva, where he met Cartwright and Travers, acquired a copy of Travers's *Ecclesiasticae disciplinae*, and worked alongside Beza at a moment when he was helping the Huguenot complete their structure of governance. These experiences and his academic training were immediately acknowledged in Scotland as helpful to the country's colleges and the General Assembly, which he served as moderator in 1578 and a few of its successors. It may also have been at his initiative that Cartwright and Travers were invited to Scotland.[60]

A convincing victory by the presbyterians would be theirs only when the government endorsed the decisions of the assembly. After Morton's regency ended in March 1578, the political situation became remarkably unstable even by Scottish standards, with coups d'état unfolding in rapid succession—six of them by September 1585, when the current regent James Stewart was overthrown, a series of events that also included the Ruthven raid (1582), a plot by several Protestant members of the nobility to seize the king and exclude the regent and counselors he was favoring. That James VI was trespassing on the liberties of the kirk had already been noted by the General Assembly in 1582, at a moment when the young king was hearing from anti-presbyterians that a "free" monarchy was incompatible with that system. Heartened by this coup, some of the clergy urged James to approve several measures to improve the economic situation of the church and sustain its independence. As so often happened in Scottish politics, extreme views—in this instance, those of the "Protestant zealots" who endorsed the Ruthven raid—provoked a counterreaction led by courtiers and Catholic nobility, one of them the ever-troubling George Gordon, the Earl of Huntly. With the king's support and seconded by Patrick Adamson as archbishop, James Stewart encouraged the Parliament of 1584 to enact the so-called "Black Acts." Unflinchingly royalist, the new rules assigned an unlimited or "absolute" power to the king in matters of religion. The most telling was the second act ("confirming the king's majesty's royal power"), which nullified what was said in chapter 8 of the *Second Book of Dis-*

cipline. In an accompanying "Declaration," Adamson emphasized Romans 13:2 on the God-given authority of kings. Perhaps with the hope of deflecting criticism, the first of the Black Acts endorsed the liberty of the clergy to preach and administer the sacraments, although dropping any reference to discipline. Otherwise, the provisions of the *Second Book of Discipline* went by the boards: no general assembly or "conventions" could meet without the king's approval and "the new pretended presbyteries" were suppressed, a step justified by the possibility that presbyterianism would mutate into an "Ecclesiasticall tyrannie." The government also demanded that all clergy agree to the acts or lose their stipends, an "unprecedented" step in Scottish history.[61]

These measures, together with rumors of a conspiracy to restore Mary Stuart to the throne and the possibility of being convicted of sedition for refusing to subscribe to the Black Acts, prompted the nobility who led the Ruthven raid or participated in an assault on the royal castle at Stirling in 1584 to flee to England, as did some twenty ministers, including James Lawson, Melville, and Melville's nephew James; when Lawson died in London, local presbyterians honored him at a funeral they arranged. Others in Scotland rejected the acts as ungodly, but acquiesced once the king allowed them to add the phrase "so far as they agree with the Word of God" when they pledged to obey "all . . . laws and acts of Parliament."[62] Before many months passed, a fresh wave of conspiracies against the rapacious Stewart drove him and his clique from office, a change of regimes encouraged by the English government. In came a new chancellor, John Maitland, who seems to have advised the king to pursue a policy of compromise with the kirk. When members of the assembly of 1586 met with James VI, he denied that he had "made defection from the true religion," words he backed with a promise to "establish" the "discipline" which, "by conference amongst them, should be found most agreeable to the word of God." Nonetheless, he insisted on the privilege of deciding when and where the General Assembly would meet. Presbyteries reappeared, and in negotiations between the king's representatives and leaders of the kirk, it was decided to allow a diminished version of bishops. That crosscurrents persisted within the assembly itself was implied by a decision to discuss, behind closed doors, whether "there was any man of other judgement but that the discipline . . . , was according to the word of God."[63]

The twists and turns of these years are singularly visible in the career of the first Protestant to become Archbishop of the (Protestant) Church of Scotland. Patrick Adamson (1527–1592) graduated from St. Andrews in 1558. Studies in France and a phase as a lawyer intervened before he gained access to the highest political circles in the country as chaplain to the regent Morton. With his backing, Adamson became Archbishop of St. Andrews in 1576, although previously (1572) he had questioned the legitimacy of that office. Called to account by various synods and assemblies and professing to accept the authority of one of them (1578), he may have conceded that bishops were not superior to other pastors. Two years later, he accepted a post as parish minister in St. Andrews and worked alongside Andrew Melville on various committees charged with implementing the *Second Book of Discipline*. With the arrival of James Stewart as regent in 1583, Adamson switched sides and began to advocate for episcopacy. During a visit to London (1583–84), where he met John Whitgift, he let it be known that he admired the English liturgy and English-style bishops. What he said in London and to the young king after he returned to Edinburgh matched the currents of royal and parliamentary policy, so much so that one of the Black Acts ratified his authority to summon synods and appoint ministers. Unbending when it came to the guilt of the clergy involved in the "late attempted rebellion" (the Ruthven raid) and freshly enthused about James VI, Adamson extolled him as the most important member of the church and a worthy successor to Old Testament kings and Christian emperors such as Constantine.[64]

With the fall of Stewart and the return from exile of the Ruthven raiders, the wheel turned anew. Urged on by James Melville, the synod of Fife excommunicated Adamson a second time. The General Assembly of 1586 noted his "submission" in which he "denied" having ever "professed" a supremacy" over "other pastors." For the time being, he avoided the penalty of excommunication, thanks to the intervention of the king. But in 1589 a string of penalties imposed by another assembly culminated in a decision to confirm his excommunication. Two years later, at a moment when he was suffering from the illness that concluded with his death in February 1592, he appealed to the presbytery of St. Andrews to release him from this censure, which it agreed to do after he acknowledged his mistakes. Shortly thereafter, he reversed himself on the question of bishops, declaring that the office "hath no warrant of the word of God, but is grounded upon the policie of the invention of man," language akin to what he had said about presbyteries. He apologized as well for defending the authority of the king over the church when, in his words, "the power of the word is to be extolled above the power of princes."[65]

Adamson's about-face may have affected James VI, who became more forbearing of the presbyterians. Even so, he refused to allow the kirk to punish any officer of state or to excommunicate Huntly at a moment when leaders of the church were sounding the alarm about the Counter-Reformation militancy of Jesuit missionaries, the converts they were making, the threat of a Spanish invasion, and a Huntly-led insurrection in 1589, the same year in which James promised the leaders of the assembly he would "uphold discipline."[66] When the coronation of James's new wife, Anne of Denmark, was celebrated in Edinburgh in 1590, Andrew Melville and another ardent presbyterian, Robert Bruce, participated in the ceremony. Learning that Richard Bancroft had lambasted Scottish presbyterianism as "an introduction to . . . popularitie" and "tended to the overthrow" of the Crown," the king professed dismay and, in August 1590, criticized the *Book of Common Prayer* ("their service is an ill-mumbled Mess"), spoke of his delight at being "King, in such a Kirk, the sincerest Kirk in the world"—better even than the church in Geneva—and "charge[d]" the General Assembly "to stand to your purity." Beforehand (1589), the leaders of the church denounced Bancroft's portrait of presbyterianism as incompatible with the authority of the monarch, a response notable for its firm evocation of two-kingdoms principles, affirming, on the one hand, that magistrates whether "heathen" or "Christian" must be obeyed, and on the other, that "church officers . . . are appointed of God, to execute all ecclesiastical matters."[67]

James's warm words were followed by a parliamentary session in late May 1592 that met at a moment of intense conflict among the nobility and dismay within the state church with Huntly for his role in the murder of James Stewart, the Earl of Moray. Beforehand, the General Assembly agreed to ask the king and the new Parliament to annul the Black Acts of 1584 and restore certain properties to the church, adding, as well, a request that bishops be excluded from sitting in Parliament. James endorsed most of these requests, as did Parliament, which granted official recognition to a system of presbyteries and synods and repealed some of the Black Acts. In principle, the king also agreed that assemblies should meet every year "at the least." The most crucial of the Black Acts, the second, which awarded James supreme power in matters spiritual and temporal, was not repealed but softened by glossing it in a way that upheld the "privilege" of the kirk to decide the "heads of religion" and excommunicate and otherwise punish ministers and laypeople who misbehaved. As historians have pointed out, the wording of the "golden acts" was deceptively satisfying. Much remained unclear, for their wording did not specify who should judge which censures were "essential" or define the scope of the "privilege . . . god has given" the kirk. Nor did the new rules seriously curtail the role of the king in religious affairs or say anything about episcopacy, a silence that could be interpreted in different ways. Nonetheless, some of the men who had been alienated from the king in the mid-1580s were telling each other that "the Kirk of Scotland was now come to her perfection." On paper, perhaps, but not consistently in practice, for assemblies continued to remind the government that it was not always adhering to the new rules.[68]

When James intervened in late 1596 and 1597 against the presbyterians, the situation of Andrew and James Melville and their allies took a sharp turn for the worse. Alarmed by the resurgence of Catholicism and the king's willingness to pardon high-ranking Catholics who had been exiled, a party of ministers persuaded the General Assembly that met in March 1596 to accuse the king of "swearing" and other moral faults, and the people around him, including the queen, of bad behavior and indifference to true religion. Implicitly if not to his face, the kirk was threatening the king with excommunication. As had happened under similar circumstances in 1580–81 and the year of the Spanish Armada (1588), the assembly appealed to the Scottish people to "join

[themselves] to the Lord in a perpetual covenant that shall not be forgotten."
On his own, Andrew Melville confronted the king directly. Included in a deputation that met with James to complain about his handling of Huntly's excommunication, Melville was "unable to restrain himself" (in the words of an admiring nineteenth-century biographer) after hearing the king denounce a
special meeting of the ministers as "illegal and seditious." Taking James by the
sleeve, Melville told him to his face that he was "but God's silly vassal," adding
that "there is two kings and two Kingdoms, in Scotland. There is Christ Jesus
the King, and his kingdom the kirk, whose subject James the Sixth is, of whose
kingdom not a king, nor a lord, nor a head, but a member."[69]

Thus was set in motion the parting of the ways between James and those
who insisted on the autonomy of the state church, a process linked to the
deaths of the great Protestant "magnates" of the 1580s and earlier. The king
had already reprimanded the clergy for their comments about him and in 1596
confronted David Black, a minister in St. Andrews, for using "undecent" language in a sermon that touched on the behavior of the king and Queen Anne.
A hard-liner, Black refused to acknowledge the king's jurisdiction in "spiritual"
matters. In the aftermath of an attempted coup (or more likely, a riot) in Edinburgh in December 1596 fed by rumors of "plots" against the kirk,[70] the king
exploited his powers under the "Black Acts" to bypass Edinburgh and fix on
Perth as the site of the General Assembly of 1597. This time around, the king
not only convened the assembly but decided its agenda. Doing so made it more
likely that the ministers and laypeople who attended were out from under the
influence of the Melvilles—Andrew was banned from attending—and their
fellow presbyterians. The Perth Assembly was not as complacent as he may
have expected. Nonetheless, it endorsed most of what he wanted, agreeing, for
example, to allow bishops to vote in parliaments and the king a role in the appointment of ministers. In exchange, James promised better revenues for the
kirk and a military campaign against extremist Catholics in the Highlands. As
well, the Perth Assembly accepted the king's suggestion that, between sessions
of the assembly, fourteen "commissioners" manage its business. Knowing he
could influence the naming of these men, James may have thought of them as
de facto bishops.[71]

Here, for the moment, we must conclude the story of the Reformation in
Scotland. Buffeted though it was by the twists and turns of regional, national,
dynastic, and international politics, the reforming party had turned Scotland
into a Protestant country despite the presence of Catholic-leaning clans. By
1600, James was imposing the rule of law on some of the Scottish nobility and
clarifying his authority over a church that aspired to be independent. Knowing
he was likely to succeed Elizabeth as monarch of England, he may have taken
to heart the warning he received from her in 1590: "There is risen, both in your
realm and mine, a sect of perilous consequence, such as would have no kings
but a presbytery."[72] James tucked this counsel into *Basilikon Doron*. There, he

defended a theory of kingship as hereditary and criticized any and every attempt by Catholics and "puritans" alike to differentiate a king's authority in "spiritual" affairs from his authority in the realm of the civil or secular. Retracing the history of the Scottish Reformation, he likened it to a "popular tumult and rebellion" that, unlike the reformation in England, had not been initiated by a "Princes order" but by "some fierie spirited men in the ministerie" who "fantasie[d] to themselves a Democraticke forme of gouernment." With Andrew Melville and others of his temperament in mind, James was especially contemptuous of ministers who "breath . . . nothing but sedition and calumnies" against the country's rulers. What made their preaching seditious? The message that "all Kings and Princes were naturally enemies to the libertie of the Church, and could never patiently beare the yoke of Christ: with such sound doctrine fed they their flockes." In a companion treatise, *The Trew Law of Free Monarchies* (1598), he repudiated the "resistance" theorizing of John Knox and others on the grounds that kings were "Gods Lieutenant in earth" who could be "judged onely by God." By the early seventeenth century, he wanted nothing to do with such a system and its principle of ministerial parity. As he put it, parity was "the mother of confusion and enemy to Unity, which is the mother of order."[73]

In the new century as well as previously, James benefitted from the presence of ministers or statesmen who wavered in their commitments, as Erskine of Dun and John Craig (d. 1600) had done during their many years of service to the state church. George Gledstanes (d. 1622) was already known as a moderate when, probably at the king's behest, he replaced David Black in St. Andrews in 1597. At the Perth Assembly, he supported the proposal to reinstate bishops as voting members of Parliament, a step approved by the assembly of 1600, the year he became a bishop and, four years later, Archbishop of St. Andrews—possibly a reluctant archbishop, for he told his local presbytery that he claimed "no superiority" over other ministers and promised "to behave himself in . . . great humility."[74] Gledstanes, Andrew Boyd (who also became a bishop), and Robert Rollock, who served as moderator of the Perth Assembly of 1597, were among those who had wearied of conflict between kirk and king. Attracted to James because he seemed to promise unity and peace, they admired him for pushing back against the lawlessness of the nobility. It mattered, too, that he was promising to strengthen the financial situation of the clergy. Moreover, James was committed to Protestant doctrine. Late in life, Rollock extolled him for having "walled round religion with sound discipline" and "protected it by his person," adding that he himself had "laboured heart and soul" that church and state "should mutually assist each other," an alliance grounded on James's self-proclaimed identity as a Christian prince. Another moderate and future bishop, David Lindsay, counseled his fellow ministers that they did more harm than good when they confronted the king. Not that moderates approved of the king's fondness for some of the Catholic nobility or welcomed his aggressive handling of the General Assembly. Nonetheless, he did not deserve the harsh words spoken by a David Black or John Davidson, harsh words they may possibly have owed to the theorizing of George Buchanan about the origins of monarchy.[75]

To a group that included Davidson, Bruce, and the Melvilles, anything short of outspokenness would allow James to become another Jeroboam (1 Kings 12), who endorsed idolatry and persecuted the faithful.[76] A story the king's critics learned from the Old Testament, it overlapped with a theme inherited from the *Book of Martyrs*, the ever-present menace of the Antichrist in the form of Catholicism. Melville and his allies liked to recall the moment when church leaders, nobility, and the young king had endorsed the "King's" or "Negative Confession" of 1581, a forcefully anti-Catholic "band" that came into being in response to a resurgence of Catholicism in the country. Then and there, James had acted in keeping with a model of godly kingship.[77] Now, some two or three decades later, the church under his leadership was becoming corrupt. James Melville, who waited until 1604 to go into opposition, poured his frustration into "A True Narratioune of The Declyning Aige of the Kirk of Scotland; From M.D.XCVI to M.CD.X." Beginning with the General Assembly of March 1596, which vowed to eliminate all "corruption" by renewing the covenant between God and Scotland, and concluding in 1610 with the reestablishing of episcopacy, the "True Narration" was premised on the "incomparable" or "full perfection" of the Scottish church in its infancy, a church "without any mixture from Babylon" thanks to a reformation that surpassed what had happened "in all the kingdoms of Europe," a reformation "faire as the morning, clear as the moon." Thereafter, the "True Narration" became a story of betrayal by "Judases" who toppled the kirk from its heights of purity to a situation of being "oppressed by authority, circumvented with craft, and kept in thralldom, against God's word, [and] her own constitutions and custom."[78]

Events in 1606 (see below, chap. 6) reinforced the worldview of men such as Melville and like-minded ministers. Forty-two such men signed a protest delivered to the Scottish Parliament in 1606, and a single theme dominated their version of recent history: the "decline" of the kirk. Once upon a time, the kirk had truly been the "House of God," a house built according to the specifications prescribed in the Word. There was no choice in this matter, for the true king of the church was Christ. "All other authority" was secondary or subordinate to his. Neither Parliament or James VI could therefore command the kirk to adopt a "form of divine service which God in his word hath not before allowed." Yet this is exactly what the king was doing when he reintroduced the English-style office of bishop. Drawing on the same vocabulary of apocalypticism that English Separatists had used, the protestors of 1606 referred to bishops as the fruit of the "man of sin," the Antichrist or "monster" that was Rome. A turning point had been reached, they warned, a moment when the kirk would either reclaim the truth or follow the path of decline to its endpoint, the plight of being cursed by God. How could this be happening when "the Noble-men and Estates of this realm" and the king himself had sworn in 1581 to preserve the kirk from Catholicism?[79]

Even though men of this worldview complained of betrayal from within, the presbyterians could point with pride to two projects of great significance in the longer history of Scottish Protestantism. One of these was structural and social, the development of a system of disciplinary courts responsible for over-seeing social and moral behavior. The other was religious and cultural, an iden-tity for the Scottish church based on Bale and Foxe's narrative of the few who remained faithful to their covenant with God, a faithfulness tested by the siren song of idolatry but never giving way to corruption. Instead of tying that iden-tity to the apostolic age, which was where Foxe had begun his narrative in the *Book of Martyrs*, the presbyterians evoked a more immediate past, the events of circa 1560–1567 that had transformed the Church of Scotland into its glori-ous identity as the most perfectly reformed church in all of Protestant Europe. So Knox had insisted in the opening pages of his *History*: "We are bold to af-firm that there is no realm this day upon the face of the earth" with "greater purity" in how the sacraments were administered and doctrine taught; "yea (we must speak the truth whomsoever we offend), there is none that hath them in the like purity." Assertions of this kind were commonplace, voiced by James VI himself in the early 1590s, incorporated into the Scottish Confession of 1616, where the state church was characterized in somewhat tempered language as "one of the purest kirks under heaven to this day," and evoked in 1621 by a radi-cal of the next generation, David Calderwood. "Was there ever any realme since Christ's incarnation that professed Christian religion so universally . . . in such puritie, discipline, and publike worship, with such liberties," was how Calder-wood understood the significance of the Church of Scotland, a significance borne out by the testimony of divine providence. Writing in the wake of what Knox had said about the providential blessings God poured out on a cove-nanted people, Calderwood and James Melville filled their narratives with ex-ample after example of providential interventions against the kirk's many enemies.[80]

This was the good news. The bad was Melville's tale of woe. Paradoxically, this was good news, for God was certain to befriend the Scottish church when and if prophet-like leaders aroused Scottish Protestants and, especially, the nobility, to reaffirm their covenant with God. A ritual process was available for doing so, the fast day, as were ministers eager to resume the role played by Jeremiah and Hosea in ancient Israel and relished by Knox in the 1550s and 1560s. Covenant making on behalf of Protestantism dated to the 1550s. What may be regarded as the archetypal fast happened in December 1565 when, at the urging of Knox and John Craig, the General Assembly summoned Scottish Protestants to repent their sins in the context of anxieties about the nobility and its support for Mary Stuart. A political as well as a spiritual event, the fast of 1565 promised a double deliverance: from the "angry wrath" of the God who had "come upon us for our sins" and from a Catholic queen. Covenant making and covenant renewal took on a fresh importance in 1581 in the context of the Negative Confession, which committed the country's leaders to defend "the Doctrine and Discipline of this Kirk . . . according to our vocation and power" against the errors of Rome. For those who fashioned this "touchstone to try and discern Papists from Protestants" and oversaw its renewal in 1588, 1590, and 1595, it promised to protect kirk and country from Catholic missionaries aspiring to "corrupt and subvert secretly God's true religion." Be it in 1581 or 1595, covenants and the repentance that preceded them were understood by the more ardent Presbyterians as ensuring that idolatry never reemerged, or could be overcome if it did. Covenants were also making it possible to incorporate the apocalyptic scenario of true religion contending against the anti-Christ into opposition to the king's politics of religion.[81]

Where did Scotland's monarchs fit into this story of a true church warding off its enemies? On the one hand, an unequivocal affirmation of their authority was impossible thanks to the origins of the Reformation as an insurgency against two rulers deemed "idolaters" by Knox. Out of that process emerged the premise, articulated in the 1550s and 1560s by Knox, Craig, and others, that a Christian prince who flouted divine law must be resisted, to the point of "execut[ing] God's law against" such a person. The context for this argument included the assertion at the General Assembly of 1567 that "all kings, rulers, magistrats, at their installing in their office, shall sweare to defend the true religion, and set forward the work of reformation" and, some thirty years later, the story of Gideon, who refused to become king after liberating ancient Israel, which a group of insurgents cited in December 1596 to justify their objections to the policies of James VI.[82]

Such statements were not as daring as they may seem, for they never dislodged the Reformed assumption that God had empowered the Christian prince to protect the church. As Knox liked to point out, Moses the civil leader, not Aaron the priest, had brought true religion to the people of ancient Israel. Nonetheless, he also knew from reading the Old Testament that kings could mutate into tyrants who turned against God. In a sermon he preached on Isaiah 26:13–21 (1565) in the presence of the queen's husband, Knox tied the authority of any earthly ruler (specifying judges and kings) to their service as "lieutenants" of God, who charged them with "put[ting] in execution suche things as [are . . .] commanded in divine law, without declying eyther to the right or left hande." Faithful kings could expect to be obeyed. A monarch who betrayed Scotland's covenant was another matter, a possibility that may account for the wording of a sentence in the Negative, or King's, Confession: "we perceive that the quietness and stability of our religion and church depends upon the safety and *good behavior* [emphasis added] of the king's majesty . . . for the maintaining of his church." Via assertions of this kind, obedience became contingent on the meaning of lawfulness. Hence the conclusion of a modern historian that "the legitimacy of the Scottish Reformation impugned the legitimacy of the Scottish crown," to the point of seriously "circumscrib[ing] James VI's authority as monarch." That James felt the sting of this possibility is apparent from his hostility to the makers of the Scottish Reformation,[83] for he sensed that anti-monarchical themes were in the air. When and where they were being voiced remains unclear, although a good starting point would surely be the Confession of 1581, which asserted that "the cause of God's true religion and His Highness' authority are so joined as the hurt of the one is common to both" and conflated loyalty to "true religion" with loyalty to James VI.[84]

Going forward, the mythic vision of a purified and God-centered church made any lasting alliance with James and the Scottish nobility less likely. Not only did the "purity via covenant" paradigm seem to exclude compromise of any kind, it also incorporated a ferocious anti-Catholicism at odds with James's willingness to include Catholics in his government. Moreover, the concept of a covenanted society included a role for latter-day prophets that Knox and his successors played to the hilt. The struggle for true religion in Scotland thus assumed the same shape as the struggle for true religion in ancient Israel— encompassing the same covenant, the same obligation to obey divine law, and the same role for truth-speaking prophets. In the 1560s, Knox had confronted Mary Stuart in this manner. By the early seventeenth century, another confrontation of this kind was becoming inevitable. In the presence of a king visibly irritated by the theme of kings experiencing divine judgment, Melville had insisted that ministers were entitled to describe the judgments God inflicted on bad rulers. He softened this message by insisting on his loyalty to James. Yet he made it clear that God came first and kings and the nobility, second. James may have been a godly king, but in Scotland, the church belonged to God (or Christ). As was said at the assembly of 1583, God had entrusted its purity to those who served in Christ's stead as His ministers and "watchmen" and empowered them to pronounce "fearful" warnings in His name against anyone one "who neglects to execute faithfully every part of their charge."[85]

Did the true church include everyone in Scotland, or only the faithful few? In principle, the Church of Scotland was all-encompassing, an assertion embedded in the description of the visible church in the Scottish Confession of 1560. In practice, it was as well; kirk sessions took for granted a near-universal system of parishes equipped with the machinery of discipline. Yet there was also the possibility of imagining the true church as a "little flock," the few who, when called upon to repent, did so from the "heart," an image or idea Knox had embraced in the 1550s and reaffirmed in the fast-day order of 1565. Or was every covenant inclusive or corporate in one dimension but limited to the faithful in another? The series of covenants or "bonds" out of which the reformation of the late 1550s had emerged were mainly the doing of the few, but the

Negative Confession of 1581 was ostensibly a national document, as were fast days that began to be practiced in that decade. For the time being, the sectarian alternative of "the few" was pushed aside in favor of a more encompassing program. In England, stalemate or defeat and the ever-pressing question of "lawfulness" had fostered the alternatives of Separatism and nonconformity. Neither of these tendencies existed in Scotland, where Protestants had no basis for questioning the lawfulness of ministers ordained by their peers. No diocesan bishops, no Catholic-style liturgy, and no issues of doctrine alongside an emphasis on discipline, this triad precluded anything akin to the restlessness of the Puritan movement in England. Not until this triad was replaced by practices akin to those of the Church of England did nonconformity emerge and, eventually, a popular insurgency. For the moment, events of this kind remained implicit in the rhetoric of the presbyterian party.

To recognize that certain possibilities were implicit is not to say that they were without consequences. Andrew Melville was eventually banished, and John Knox had died in 1572, but others resumed the role of prophet: the ministers who secured the Negative Confession; John Davidson, who fled his homeland in 1574 but returned in 1579 and participated in an attempt in 1589–1590 to renew that Confession; James Melville, who in 1584 told the nobles who had fled with him to England that God expected them to repent of their sinfulness; and a long line of others in the next century. These men were willing to use biblically grounded prophecy against the powers that be because doing so would preserve the accomplishments of 1560–61 and 1592: a pattern of worship that, unlike the *Book of Common Prayer*, discarded all aspects of Catholic practice and installed a structure of church government that protected the kirk from bishops as ambitious "for power as ever the Papisticall Prelates" alongside a two-kingdoms framework that curtailed the scope of royal or state authority. They also looked to "bands" or covenants as the means of restoring the greatness of the Church of Scotland. By 1600 and even more so by 1610, it seemed unlikely that covenanting, fast days, and prophecy could thwart James VI. Yet a Protestant imaginary that fused kirk, covenant, and anti-Catholicism with a critique of imperial kingship, a synthesis grounded in "Calvinist anti-monarchical constitutionalism" and its appropriation of Old Testament examples of evil kings being overturned, was not going to disappear, for its core elements were preserved in sermons and histories of the church. Only time would tell if this version of the past would provoke a second reformation marked, in the words of James Melville, by a "spirit of action, zeal, and courage" among "a few from every presbytery and province" with the courage to "censure" all "corrupters of the kirk to the uttermost."[86]

CHAPTER FOUR

The Practical Divinity

SENT TO OXFORD IN 1604 by his wealthy, puritan-hating father, John Harrington was drawn to a way of being religious his family had expected him to ignore. In a prayer he wrote some years later, he asked God to "work" in him "a thorough humiliation in the sight and sence of that boundles and bottomless sea of corruption and wretchedness wherein I am overwhelmed that I may rightly value and prize and long after the salvation purchased for me by the death and passion of Jesus Christ." In this single sentence, Harrington summarized the message of the sermons that moved him to embrace humiliation: those who turn away from God are lost, but those who repent and believe will participate in the gift of grace made possible by the cross. Some thirty or forty years before Harrington put pen to paper, the same message prompted a woman in York to repent "her former life, idly spent and evil." As remembered by a minister, Margaret Metcalfe was "superstitiously and popishly bent in times past" until, in response to evangelical Protestantism, she became "devout and godly."[1]

With this version of Puritanism we set aside disputes about an unfinished Reformation and take up the question put to St. Paul by his jailor in Philippi: "What must I do to be saved?" (Acts 16:30).[2] Provocative because of its simplicity, the jailor's query drew from preachers and theologians a "practical divinity" animated by the imperative to translate doctrine into faith as something "experimentall" or "inward" and manifested in outward "watchfulness."[3] Summing up the essence of theology, the early seventeenth-century English theologian William Ames described it as "living to God," or in such a way that the divine-human connection became visible. Well before Ames was emphasizing the interplay of piety and practice, the sixteenth-century humanist Desiderus Erasmus had advised clergy to avoid "intricate syllogisms" and focus on the "gospel life." Theology of this kind had a special importance given the assumption that ordinary people must be prodded to repent their sinfulness lest they content themselves with the assumption that, "because they are baptized and live in the church . . . they are in God's favour." To people who made this argument, the Cambridge-based Elizabethan theologian William Perkins retorted that they "never knew what sin was" and consequently were "never yet reconciled to God." The makers of the practical divinity wanted to convert Catholics into Protestants and to stabilize the contours of orthodoxy, but a more telling goal was to raise the bar for all those who contented themselves with the vernacular wisdom summed up in the saying, "the God that made me, save me." Nothing this simple would do.[4]

Simultaneously, the bar was being raised for those who became ministers. In the 1560s, few British clergy were versed in Protestant theology or could preach in an evangelical manner, if only because so many of them had been formed within the Catholic system.[5] Replacing these clergy with evangelical preachers paralleled the project of turning the British people into committed Christians. Then and only then would the truth be "miraculously and mightily propagated, enlarged, and governed by the true ministry of . . . word and sacraments," the visionary hope of the Marian martyr John Bradford (d. 1555) and his successors for another century.[6]

To these goals, the makers of the practical divinity added another, its value as an instrument of social and moral reformation (see chap. 5). In a state church such as England's, preaching that emphasized repentance and restitution could supplant the discipline supervised by ecclesiastical courts, which never seemed effective. The same was true of access to the sacraments. Sermons of the right kind could nurture a scrupulosity that would keep the unworthy from participating in the Lord's Supper or bringing their children to be baptized. Evangelical and disciplinarian at one and the same time, the practical divinity was also a means of sustaining theological orthodoxy as it was defined within the Reformed tradition.[7]

The substance of such a reformation emerged in England during Edward VI's brief reign, as evidenced by the letters, translations from Scripture, and testimonies Foxe preserved in the *Book of Martyrs*.[8] Not until midway through the reign of Elizabeth I, however, did the practical divinity begin to blossom with the publishing of Bradford's devotional writings, which Thomas Sampson edited, and the ministries of Edward Dering, George Gifford, Richard Greenham, and Henry Smith, among others. By the turn of the century, another cadre of ministers and university teachers, a fully British group that included Perkins, Richard Rogers, Arthur Hildersham, and in Scotland, Robert Bruce, John Craig, and Robert Rollock, added greatly to what Greenham and Dering had accomplished. Their successors, many of whom will turn up in these pages, continued to publish books that were widely read.[9] Before long, this evangelism was mobilizing large numbers of people to advocate on behalf of ministers or lecturers who preached its core themes, its reach demonstrated by the runaway sales of such books as Arthur Dent's *Plain Mans Path-way to Heaven* (1601). As a historian of "church and people" in England has observed, "Where there had been one zealous lay promoter of Protestantism in 1560, forty years on there might well be four." In the early years of the Elizabethan regime, a newcomer to London went eight years without hearing a sermon he liked, but by 1600 or a little beyond, godly ministers were thick on the ground.[10]

Beginning with a description of theological motifs and their sources, this chapter encompasses the themes and technologies of devotion, the idea and practice of a Word-centered ministry, and the emergence of alternative theologies of grace. The bearing of the practical divinity on social and moral reform is deferred to chapter 5.

A Theology of Affective Experience

The practical divinity rested on premises that were classically Protestant and, in most respects, aligned with Reformed practice and doctrine.[11] Several of these premises were affirmed in the Thirty-Nine Articles and the Scots Confession of 1560. Both contained the doctrine of free grace that Martin Luther had endorsed, together with the kindred doctrines of justification by faith, original sin, and the primacy of Scripture, juxtaposing them with another principle of great importance in Reformed theology: predestination (article 17), a term replaced by the word "election" in chapter 8 of the Scots Confession. Twenty-five years later, John Whitgift sought to clarify these doctrines at a moment when dissidents were questioning some of them. At his behest, the Lambeth Articles (1595) strengthened article 17 by introducing the concept of reprobation—"God has from eternity predestined certain men to life, and some he has reprobated to death"—and underlined the certainty of assurance. These assertions reappeared in the Irish Articles of Faith (1615) and the Aberdeen (Scotland) Confession of Faith (1616). A translation of Reformed creeds and catechisms assembled by the French Huguenot Simon Goulart and arranged topically, *An Harmony of the Confessions of the . . . Christian and Reformed Churches* (1586), to which John Field or someone else added the Scottish Negative Confession of 1581, embodied a consensus on matters of doctrine that all but a few evangelicals in England and Scotland would endeavor to sustain.[12]

Challenged after 1590 by Catholic and Protestant "Arminians" of various stripes, certain parts of this system were reaffirmed by an international synod that met in 1618–19 in the Dutch city of Dordt. Thereafter, the synod's "five points" were incorporated into most versions of Reformed orthodoxy.[13] The English lawyer-polemicist William Prynne drew on Dordt and a host of minister-theologians dating from the origins of Christianity in Britain to validate *The Church of England's Old Antithesis to New Arminianism* (1630).[14] He had history on his side, a history that justifies a modern historian's assertion that "the characteristic theology of English Protestant sainthood" was "Calvinism." Allowing for the presence of "moderate" or "soft" Calvinists, something akin to a consensus of this kind prevailed in Scotland and, after 1630, the newly founded colonies in New England—to be sure, a consensus never as crisply defined as some may have preferred.[15]

Convincing on the face of it, this argument must not obscure the debates that persisted within the Reformed tradition and its British offspring or the importance of local contexts in shaping what was actually being preached or published. Moreover, it runs the risk of converting a *sympathy* for several aspects of Reformed theology—a sympathy shared by general assemblies and every Archbishop of Canterbury from Thomas Cranmer to George Abbott (d. 1633)—into a hard-and-fast allegiance to certain principles. Generalizations about Calvinism may also lead us down an ever-narrowing corridor in search of "true" Calvinism, usually identified as what John Calvin of Geneva had said, and, via such a journey, to puzzling over when and where the preacher-theologians of Britain and New England sustained or departed from his thinking. (Actual citations to his treatises and sermons were few.) All too often, such an inquiry focuses on the doctrine of predestination as if it were the heart of the matter. And, all too often, such an inquiry overlooks the differences between theology as debated within the universities or the highest levels of the church and theology as summarized in catechisms or calibrated in response to pastoral situations.[16]

Hence the importance of sketching wider contexts and sources for the practical divinity. The most important of these contexts was the Bible. Not the quest for "primitive" rules about the church but what the Scriptures said about being saved and the practice of devotion drew ministers and laypeople to Paul's letters and those ascribed to Peter, James, and John. Seeking to understand the workings of the Holy Spirit, these people turned to passages that spoke of Christians being filled with the Spirit (Eph. 5:18) and reborn through its workings. So Paul declared in Romans 8:14, "For as many as are led by the Spirit of God, they are the sons of God," followed by a verse contrasting the "spirit of bondage" with the "spirit of adoption" and, in verse 16, affirming that "the Spirit itself beareth witness with our spirit, that we are the children of God," a theme reiterated in Ephesians 1:13–14 and 1 John 5:6–10. Romans 8 was crucial for another reason, the apostle's assertion (v. 29) that "for whom he did foreknow, he also did predestinate to be conformed to the image of his Son." Important, too, were passages associating the gospel promise with self-examination and righteousness, notably 2 Corinthians 13:5, "Examine yourselves, whether ye be in the faith"; Philippians 2:12, "work out your own salvation with fear and trembling"; and the much-cited 2 Peter 1:10, "Wherefore the rather, brethren, give diligence to make your calling and election sure," which the 1560 edition of the Geneva Bible glossed to signify that "we must confirm it in our selves, by the fruites of the Spirit." That faith and works were necessarily joined was asserted in James 2:17: "faith, if it hath not works, is dead." Other parts of Scripture, but especially the Psalms, modeled how the faithful should meditate, pray, repent, and give thanks to a God who promised them consolation. Song of Songs (Canticles), the most lyrical and erotic of the Scriptures, prompted commentaries that emphasized the loving, affective relationship between God and humankind.[17]

The ministers who endorsed the practical divinity based everything they preached and wrote on the Bible, most commonly by organizing their sermons around a text and anchoring systematic statements in Scripture.[18] Perkins cited Calvin and Luther once each and Augustine a dozen times in one of his treatises but used Scripture more than 150 times. Richard Rogers filled the margins of his much-read *Seven Treatises* (1601) with references to the Bible, and although the margins of John Norton's *The Orthodox Evangelist* (1657) contain a multitude of references to Continental Reformed theologians, the text itself drew heavily on Scripture.[19]

Every sermon series or work of devotion associated with the practical divinity took for granted that the Old Testament foreshadowed the story of redemption narrated in the New. A principle of interpretation known as typology treated Adam, Abraham, and David as "figures" of the Christ who would be more fully revealed in the New Testament. In another version of typology, God's promise to Abraham (Gen. 17:7) and his "seed" validated the sacrament of infant baptism. Armed with this method of interpretation and its near neighbors—the literary devices of allegory, analogy, and example—the makers of the practical divinity ranged widely within the Bible for models of religious experience and arguments in behalf of various doctrines.[20]

Less commonly, the makers of the practical divinity cited the Church Fathers and philosophers such as Aristotle.[21] By far the most influential of the Fathers was Augustine, evoked time and again because of the stand he took against assertions attributed to the fourth century CE British monk Pelagius (hence Pelagianism), who questioned original sin and proposed that humans were free to behave morally or to sin. For Augustine, Pelagianism became the assertion that humankind could save itself. In response, he insisted that a sovereign God acted solely for His own glory in electing some to salvation, an argument based on Romans 8:29. This was the Augustine on whom the Reformers relied whenever they defended the doctrines of free grace and salvation by faith alone against a Catholic theology that blended divine mercy with human effort (penance). In doing so, they frequently amplified his version of predestination to include the reprobate who would never receive saving grace, that is, a *double* predestination of those who were saved and those forever excluded from salvation. Their Augustine also insisted upon the total corruption of human nature.[22] From antiquity came other categories that fleshed out God's way of working in the world: the four causes described by Aristotle (the final, formal, efficient or instrumental, and material); the assertion that humans were "rational," that is, active in contrast to the inert qualities of nature; and possibly a much-employed distinction between the "order of time," when the work of grace happened "all in one instant," and the "order of nature," when redemption unfolded as a sequence of stages.[23]

This "Augustinianism" was supplemented by productive connections with sixteenth- and early seventeenth-century Continental Reformed theologians such as Martin Bucer, Peter Martyr Vermigli, Heinrich Bullinger, Theodore Beza, and their academic allies and successors, a group that included Johann Piscator and Girolamo Zanchi, among others.[24] After Calvin died in 1564, Beza became the leader of the Protestant community in Geneva and an important presence in France. He was also a presence in Britain, where three of his books were translated into English and part of another incorporated into a treatise by Perkins. In 1586 Archbishop Whitgift ordered Church of England clergy awaiting an official license to use the sermons in Bullinger's *Fifty Godly and Learned Sermons* (in English, 1584) in their Sunday services. Certain Reformed creeds were also influential: the widely translated Heidelberg Catechism of 1563, its teachings reiterated in a commentary by Zacharias Ursinus, a professor at Heidelberg who helped draft the catechism; the firmly predestinarian Second Helvetic Confession (1566), approved by several Reformed churches, including the Church of Scotland; a catechism by Calvin, together with his commentaries on the Bible.[25]

The traffic in texts between Britain and the Continent was accompanied by traffic in people, thanks to invitations issued by Thomas Cranmer and the Continental experiences of English and Scottish exiles (see chap. 1). By the early seventeenth century, Robert Boyd (d. 1627) and John Cameron (d. 1625) were among the Scottish minister-academics who taught in Huguenot seminaries or in Geneva, where Andrew Melville lived for several years before returning to Scotland in 1574. Other British clergy taught in the Netherlands, where William Ames went after being forced out of Cambridge University. Two of Ames's books, *De Conscientia* (1630 in Latin, 1639 in English) and *The Marrow of Sacred Theology* (1627 in Latin, 1638 in English, 1656 in Dutch) enjoyed a long life in Scotland and the New England colonies. Traffic in the other direction included the "method" of the French Huguenot Pierre de la Ramee (Ramus), which Melville introduced into Scotland, Perkins utilized in England, and Ames incorporated into his textbooks. Any reckoning of sixteenth- and early seventeenth-century influences must also include humanism, although its main contribution may have been to social ethics.[26]

To these influences must be added a surprising source of ideas and practices: Catholicism and its expertise in devotion. Richard Rogers was prompted to write his *Seven Treatises* by the competition he was feeling in his ministry from Catholic manuals of devotion, especially the English Jesuit Robert Parsons's *First booke of the Christian exercise*, much reprinted (at least thirty times before 1630) in a version prepared by a *Protestant* clergyman for Protestant readers. An English version of another book that originated within Catholicism, Thomas à Kempis's *Imitation of Christ*, enjoyed a similar popularity.[27]

Other continuities with Catholicism were unspoken: the recycling of medieval exempla into a Protestant lore of wonders, the expectation that the sacrament of baptism was efficacious (i.e., enabling parents to assume that their children were encompassed within the doctrine of election), an understanding of death and dying as akin to a theater where Christ and the Devil contended for someone's soul, a lingering affection for Christmas and saint's days, the texture of certain prayers. The deeper continuity may have been the emphasis on interiority that emerged within medieval Catholicism and became such a feature of the practical divinity.[28]

This multitude of sources provided five overlapping themes or languages. One of these was the possibility of representing the history of redemption as a series of covenants. Foreshadowed in Calvin, elaborated among his Continental successors, becoming prominent in Scotland and England around the beginning of the seventeenth century and incorporated into the Westminster Confession (1647), the covenant or "federal" theology represented the history of redemption as a sequence of covenants: the first of these between God and Christ, followed by a covenant of "works" God made with Adam, a covenant of grace reestablished with the Second Adam (Christ) but already visible in the Abrahamic covenant, and finally a "new covenant" with the saints (or elect) made possible by Christ's death on the cross.[29] This framework had several benefits. It supported an understanding of the Christian life as grounded in obedience to Old Testament law and buttressed the argument, itself classically Reformed, that law and grace were always intermingled, the law serving as a means of preparing for grace and a framework for the righteousness that the elect were obliged to practice. Moreover, it endeavored to reconcile divine sovereignty with the "liberty" or freedom humankind enjoyed as "rational" beings. In this regard, the covenant of grace could be characterized as both "absolute" and "conditional," absolute because it conveyed an unmerited promise of salvation to the elect but conditional in the sense of expecting the godly to "performe" certain duties.[30]

This fusing of divine initiative with human obligations depended as well on scholastic assumptions about the role of "second causes," or what humans contributed to the divine-human relationship; as a modern historian of this idiom has pointed out, the covenant was "dispensed under a conditional form because God freely elects . . . to respect the integrity of second causes, including the human mind and will." By this reasoning, the motif of covenant authorized a space for "consent." Finally, it reinforced the message, already embedded in the doctrine of election, that God was certain to extend redeeming love to (some of) humankind.[31]

Intertwined with the language of covenant was a second framework that likened the unfolding of redemption to a "chain," or what was "ordained." Employed by Perkins in one of the best-known of his treatises, *A Golden Chaine, or the Description of Theologie, containing the Order of the Causes of Salvation and Damnation, accordeing to Gods Woord* (1590 in Latin, 1591 in English, and enlarged in 1592),[32] this figure of speech became a convenient shorthand for the several stages of redemption. The key stages were those Paul had speci-fied in Romans 8:30: "whom he did predestinate, them he also called; and whom he called, them he also justified; and whom he justified, them he also glorified," a sequence commonly restated as effectual call or vocation, justifica-tion, and sanctification. By the early seventeenth century, these categories were being supplemented by a stage referred to as "preparation" under the "law." Whether drawn from Romans 8 or amplified by British Protestants, every description of this sequence made the point that "the conversion of a sinner is not wrought all at one instance, but in continuance of time and that by certain measures and degrees." In general, laypeople on the receiving end of the practical divinity did not experience the shattering rebirth that became characteristic in eighteenth- and nineteenth-century Anglo-American revival-ism. Instead, conversion was a lifelong process. Hence the gloss on Romans 8:30 in the Geneva Bible: conversion happens "by degrees, [the Holy Spirit] carrying saints toward the perfection that would become theirs in heaven not on earth."[33]

Here, as with covenants and their conditions, a space emerged in which sinners could respond to the gospel promise via the "means of grace" included in the chain, a repertory that included the Word (preaching), sacraments, and visible church. As the English layman William Prynne pointed out, "When God doth offer grace unto us, we must know that he doth not immediately infuse this grace into us, but he works it in us by the use of means." The point was simple. Although the doctrine of election could be described as an unmediated expression of divine sovereignty, Reformed theologians emphasized God's will-ingness to accommodate His will to human capacities by using human inter-mediaries that included preaching and the sacraments. Seeking to illustrate the concept of means of grace, a late sixteenth-century writer resorted to an analogy between a candle and humankind to make this point: "For as wax is not melted without heat . . . so God useth means . . . to draw those close unto himself whom he hath appointed unto salvation."[34]

A third language or framework concerned the law. Not, of course, the law that figured in the covenant of works God had fashioned with Adam, for this had been superseded by the covenant of grace. Nor was it the law imposed on Ancient Israel as a condition of its covenant with God, for most of this was irrelevant to Christians. To be sure, the moral rules spelled out in the Ten Com-mandments were "perpetual," as binding now as they were before the coming of Christ. Otherwise, what persisted was the law as sign or instrument of God the lawgiver whose glory was acknowledged by all who obeyed Him. Con-versely, to disobey the law was the essence of sin.[35] Given that humankind *as sinners* turned away from God and "brought guilt upon themselves" for doing so, the law had a special role to play in the drama of redemption. In the grand scheme of things, the imputation of the righteousness of Christ, or "justification," overcame this guilt, but as John Harrington had realized, a crucial aspect of the process of redemption was a sinner's repentance for being so prideful and therefore so alienated from God. A simple way of illustrating this assumption was to compare the workings of a mirror to the workings of the law. In the words of Richard Rogers, the law "serveth to set forth (as in a glasse) many secret and deceivable corruptions of mans heart; and to helpe us to finde out what swarmes of noisome, dangerous, vaine, wicked, and worldly lusts doe lurke and lodge therein . . . and to make us wearie and ashamed of them." Or, as emphasized by the English minister Alexander Nowell in a rephrasing of Galatians 3:24, the law was a "schoolmaster" that pushed sinners into "knowing of ourselves, and . . . repentance and faith." Theologically, the law established beyond any shadow of a doubt that humankind could do nothing to earn or merit grace. At the same time, it prepared the way for sinners to encounter the gospel promise of free grace.[36]

This sequence—law before grace in a preparatory role as the "spirit of bondage" (Rom. 8:15) and, at a deeper level of theological argument, the law as part of an evangelical economy of grace—was a prominent feature of British Protestantism from Nowell, Perkins, and Greenham to Robert Bolton and Thomas Hooker and beyond (see chap. 9). In the words of the mid-seventeenth-century Scottish theologian William Guthrie, "the most ordinary way by which many are brought to Christ, is by a clear and discernible work of the law, and humiliation, which we generally call the spirit of bondage." "Set before thine eyes the curse that is due unto sin," Perkins advised readers of *A Golden Chaine*, "that thus bewailing thy misery and despairing utterly of thine own power to attain . . . happiness, thou mayest renounce thyself and be provoked to feel and sue unto Christ Jesus." Predicate to becoming a faithful pilgrim, the law enabled the earnest Christian to break away from Satan and initiate a lifelong process of repentance for continuing to sin.[37]

A fourth framework concerned divine providence. Relying on this doctrine as well as on a Christianized folklore of "wonders" and portents, British theologians evoked a world suffused with signs of God's overarching supervision of humankind. This was not the God represented by some eighteenth-century philosopher-theologians as a distant watchmaker. On the contrary, a wonder-working God was continually intervening to sustain the faithful and punish the wicked. Acts of divine providence were also His way of goading sinners into acknowledging the hidden recesses of sin. Alternatively, portents and wonders could reinforce someone's sense of God's supportive presence in their lives. A devastating fire in a town where the Sabbath was not being properly observed was an example of divine wrath. But a spider detected in a "bowl of porridge before the children . . . had eaten of it," an event the layman John Winthrop thought worthy of preserving in a notebook, was the doing of a God who protected the faithful. Day after day, people such as Winthrop took for granted that portents were attuned to their own spiritual situations—reassuring in the case of the spider but often construed as a rebuke.[38]

A fifth approach to the workings of redemption stemmed from the doctrine of predestination, an assertion of God's omniscience and His "electing" (choosing) those who would enter the kingdom. The concept of election appealed to Perkins and his contemporaries for the same reason it appealed to Calvin, its imperviousness to arguments that God expected sinners to earn their way to grace, a position Reformed Protestants attributed to Catholicism, with its emphasis on penance. John Bradford knew of people who regarded the concept of election as antithetical to human freedom and too severe in limiting the scope of the Atonement to the elect. The men who preached the practical divinity disagreed with this point of view. Bradford extolled God's "loving-kindness" and "gracious goodness" that enabled sinners to be redeemed, adding (in the context of assertions that the doctrine nurtured libertinism) that, since none of the elect would ever be repudiated, "God's eternal and immutable decree bindeth not our hands . . . but rather provoketh us thereunto mightily." Here, in a nutshell, was what a long line of ministers said in response to the possibility that the elect would be indifferent to the moral law. Even though God would never disenfranchise the elect, a premise known as the perseverance of the saints, His true children would always use their "liberty" to bear the "fruit" of love, joy, peace, [and] longsuffering" (Gal. 5:13–22) made possible by this great gift.[39]

Who were His true children? The orthodox answer to this question was straightforward: God knew, but otherwise His decisions remained a "mystery" to humankind. This assertion had several important consequences. For one, it ensured that the visible church (the church on earth) would always include "hypocrites" who, despite their outward righteousness, were not among the elect. For another, the premise of "mystery" allowed evangelical preachers to offer the gospel promise of salvation to everyone and insist that they act on this possibility. To do nothing, as though God did everything, was to misread what God intended by predestination. Summing up William Ames's approach to the doctrine, the historian John Eusden has pointed out that, for Ames and others like him, "predestination is an invitation to begin one's spiritual pilgrimage—with the implicit warning that the certainty of God's decree shall not be known until one does begin."[40]

This combination of law and grace, or divine sovereignty and human striving, may seem puzzling and, to some ministers and laypeople in the 1630s and 1640s (see chap. 9), it came close to compromising the gospel promise of free grace. Nonetheless, it gave British evangelicalism a distinctive place within the Reformed international—a muted distinctiveness, since the makers of the practical divinity regarded themselves as members of a theological tradition initiated by Calvin, Bucer, and the authors of the Heidelberg Catechism, with Bullinger somewhere in the mix.[41] Three of its themes or assumptions made it unusual: a covenant-centered understanding of redemption and, closely connected to this framework, a strong version of an accommodating God who allowed the workings of divine sovereignty to incorporate human initiative or freedom; an emphasis on interiority or "the heart" as the location of real or "sincere" faith; and the role of the law in the making of righteousness or moral behavior. The first rested on the concepts of chain, covenant, and means of grace, or the assumption that God approached sinners through the ministry in a manner that respected their free will. The second had Catholic sources that British Protestants began to amplify in the sixteenth century. The third descended directly from Calvin's understanding of the Christian life and acquired a fresh importance in the British context. The outcome was a mode of preaching that tied together preparation under the law, the sinner's self-perception as (in Perkins's words) "vile, wretched and miserable [and] . . . unable to do any good," self-discipline or what was often characterized as "watchfulness," and the joy of encountering the risen Christ. That this mixture resolved the relationship between law and grace or divine sovereignty and free will seems doubtful. Yet it excelled in its close attention to the textures of personal piety.[42]

The experience-centered texture of the practical divinity enabled it to play a significant role in the making of the "Further Reformation" in Dutch and German Reformed churches. As translations into Dutch, German, and Latin of devotional texts by Ames, Perkins, Lewis Bayley (at least fifty-three editions of his *The Practice of Piety*), the Scottish minister Samuel Rutherford (whose letters of spiritual consolation were eventually published some fifteen times in Dutch), and many others multiplied in the course of the seventeenth century, Dutch and German Protestants absorbed and made their own this model of affective experience. The founders of the practical divinity had no way of knowing that their emphasis on heart-centered piety and outward righteousness would have such consequences. Nor could they have foreseen that these aspects of their preaching would survive the decline of Reformed orthodoxy.[43]

The long-lasting influence of the practical divinity is worth emphasizing for another reason: the recognition it enjoyed in English and Scottish Protestantism. The motifs that made it distinctive were warmly received by bishops of the stature of Bayley, Joseph Hall, James Ussher, and in Scotland, William Cowper. This catholicity contradicts the argument that the practical divinity was a perverse cancer infecting an otherwise healthy system of divinity, as anti-puritan historians of the Church of England have sometimes suggested.[44] For sure, its repertory of themes overlooked or intentionally omitted aspects of Christian spirituality that occur within Lutheranism and Catholicism. Lutheran devotion had less to do with the law and more with experiencing the crucified Christ. Johann Sebastian Bach was characteristically Lutheran in the "St. Matthew Passion," which evokes a sensate relationship with Jesus as he underwent the Passion. Catholicism made grace and the healing powers of the saints accessible through the intermediaries of relics, holy sites, and sacraments, all of which the makers of the Reformed tradition had eliminated alongside Catholic rituals of confession and absolution. Much within the broader stream of Christian spirituality had been lost or minimized, but as the stories that follow indicate, much also had been reappropriated or reimagined.

The Practice of Piety: Devotion and the Quest for Assurance

Devotion was the beating heart of the practical divinity, the space where its pastoral and incorporating aspects met and sometimes clashed with the intermingling of joy, suffering, and uncertainty that marked the pilgrim's pathway to heaven. Devotion was the answer to the question posed by Greenham, Dent, and Rogers: how do people become "real" or "sincere" in their faith and practice? The answer, because devotion encompassed a panoply of rituals or routines from psalm singing, prayer, meditation, reading Scripture, and fasting to sermon-going and small-group testimony. In his version of this repertory, John Preston cited "constant & conscionable hearing, reading, prayer, meditation, receiving the sacrament, holy conference, and watching over thy heart."[45] Each of these entailed more than mere outward show. As Perkins pointed out, being a Christian depended on an "experimental knowledge" of God. As well, worship and devotion were connected to righteousness or, in Perkins's words, the "reformation and amendment of life." In and through the several layers of devotion, laypeople aligned their bodies, minds, and souls with divine law and the redemptive power of the Holy Spirit.[46]

In its more private or inward aspects, devotion was about the joy of experiencing the presence of a loving Christ. According to an exegetical commonplace (see John 3:23), the saints on earth were united with Christ as their bridegroom, a marriage or "love-knot" Samuel Rutherford evoked in his letters of spiritual counsel. Craving reassurance at a difficult moment, he turned to the Christ who showered those he loved with "soft and sweet kisses" (Song of Songs 1:2) and washed away their tears (Rev. 21:4, here described as God's doing).[47] The Massachusetts-based Thomas Shepard knew the same Christ, someone to "lie by [beside]" and "roll upon" at moments the young minister likened to being "ravished." Language of this kind reminds us that the law-centered aspects of the practical divinity were paired with evocations of intimate communion with the risen Christ. This was the Christ who appealed so strongly to Richard Sibbes, a Christ "full of love . . . to humankind," an assertion Sibbes grounded in part on Song of Songs, which manifested "the mutual joys and mutual praises of Christ and his church."[48]

Laypeople responded in kind. "What hart can conceave or tounge of men or angels express the vastnes of this unlimited depth of love and goodness which is without bottome or bancke," an English friend wrote John Winthrop

Jr. in 1631. Together with deeply felt moments of repentance, encounters with a tender-hearted Christ brought people to the verge of weeping. For the English devotional writer Nicholas Byfield, the "teares" that "trickle[d] down" someone's face signaled a "heart" that "melt[ed]" in response to the sensate presence of a forgiving God. In one of his sermons, the Scottish minister-theologian Robert Rollock said something similar: "sobs and sighs" were how people expressed the "joy" of knowing that the Holy Spirit had entered their hearts. Sternly outward in its emphasis on self-discipline, the practical divinity also nurtured a remarkable depth of feeling.[49]

Devotional writers evoked a quite different mode of spiritual experience when they transposed the figure of the martyr who died for his or her faith into the Christian who, pilgrim-like, traveled through the "wilderness" of the world. The moral was as old as the warning in Ecclesiastes 12:8 that "all is vanity" and as recent as Calvin's insistence that the Christian remain "constantly watchful . . . against becoming involved in a vain and excessive love of this earth." The good pilgrim knew it was imperative to live "in the world but not be of the world," a rule captured in a Protestant emblem of the early seventeenth century showing such a person, staff in hand, crossing a maze with his gaze fixed on heaven. Here as in countless prose versions of the same message, the lesson was obvious: remain vigilant lest you succumb to "any inward or outward evil," a lesson underscored by Richard Rogers in a diary entry recording his pledge "to come nearer to the practice of godliness and . . . endeavour after a more continual watch from thing to thing."[50]

Hence the likening of pilgrim to soldier, each engaged in combat with an enemy bent on their destruction. One version of this drama was the ongoing presence of "spirituall enemies," especially Satan, for the "old feud" between his agents and the "followers" of Christ was ongoing. In his massive *The Christian Warfare against the Devil World and Flesh* (1604), John Downame itemized the multitude of "temptations" that "Satan and his assistants" deployed against the saints. As he and others pointed out, another aspect of the saint's journey was the interplay between flesh and spirit, flesh ever vulnerable to Satan's seductive voice and a metaphor for the allure of false gods (see Gal. 5:17).[51]

Taking these struggles for granted, devotion was about learning to accept and benefit from a "suffering life," which was how Rollock described the Christian's journey in sermons he preached on the Passion. That suffering was inevitable was a truth all too real to the martyred John Bradford, and one to which Rutherford returned again and again in his pastoral letters of the 1630s. The makers of the practical divinity agreed, to the point of eschewing any "easie way to heaven." As "silver-tongued" Henry Smith was apt to remark, a little "groaning and sighing" was to be expected among those with their "hearts" in turmoil. Perkins added another layer to this advice, that the godly would constantly be "exercised, turmoiled, and tempted with the inborne corruptions and rebellions" of their "hearts." The word that conveyed this message most succinctly was "affliction." It denoted misfortune or bad luck God was using to reawaken anyone who had become too casual or worldly in his or her devotion. Misfortune was therefore to be understood and acted on as spiritually beneficial. Margaret Winthrop made this point to her husband John in 1628 when she reminded him that God chooses to "exercise us with one affliction after another in love, lest wee should forget our selves and love this world to[o] much, and not set our affections on heaven wheare all true hapines is." Hence the spiritual significance of the Marian martyrs, whose faith was tested by the ultimate affliction.[52]

Was it possible to become overwhelmed by a sense of one's sinfulness and lose sight of the gospel promise of mercy? The answer was yes, for a concatenation of misfortunes—sickness, unexpected deaths, spiritual emptiness—could make people doubt the existence of a merciful God. And what if someone was more aware of God's absence than of His presence? In new-world Massachusetts, the spiritually adept Thomas Shepard endured this moment time and again. Writing to someone who, in the words of her counselor, was wrestling with the reality that God "withdraweth that from you which he imparteth to others," the English minister (and future colonist) Ezekiel Rogers acknowledged the possibility of being discouraged. His remedy was classic: revitalize "humility" and wait patiently for Him to return.[53]

Hence the injunction to sustain unrelenting activity. To remain idle was to play into the hands of Satan. The motto of the Christian soldier was constancy in devotional practice, a motto reinforced by the rule that "every day" mattered, each of them summoning the faithful to practice spiritual exercises—eight in all, according to the list Richard Rogers provided in his *Seven Treatises*, where he warned that these "may not be omitted any day at all without sin: nor carelessly and wittingly without great sin." Outwardly as well as inwardly, the true saint framed his or her life around the routines of moral and spiritual duties.[54]

The point of departure was self-examination, to the end of gaining a "true sight of [the] sin" that held every Christian in bondage or, as Perkins noted, of being "pricked" in the "heart" with "grief" for being such a sinner.[55] A solitary practice, self-examination was embedded in the ritual structure of Sunday worship. As had been the rule in Calvin's Geneva and elsewhere within the Reformed international, the ministers in Scotland and England connected self-examination to Holy Communion. The *Book of Common Order* was emphatic: "the danger [is] great, if we receive the same unworthily . . . : we kindle Gods wrath against us, and provoke him to plague us with diverse diseases and sundry kinds of death." According to the *Book of Common Prayer*, no one without a "lively faith in God's mercy through Christ" could take part in the ceremony, a rule reiterated by the godly minister William Bradshaw in his much-reprinted *A Preparation to the receiving of Christs Body and Blood* (1609), "shewing what a dangerous sin it is to receive this Sacrament unworthily."[56]

Bradshaw's proof text was Paul's sobering message to the Christian community in Corinth (1 Cor. 11:27–29) that anyone who eludes self-scrutiny and repentance "drinketh damnation to himself," a passage cited in the *Book of Common Order* and manuals such as Bradshaw's. For the scrupulous or fainthearted, some of whom hesitated to participate in the ritual, this was a discomforting text. So a minister preaching on it in the 1620s acknowledged, adding that he had "knowne some, who have abstained seven yeeeres, because they were afraid they should eate unworthily."[57] Yet for those who came to the table, the benefits were substantial: the bread and wine, although outward "signs" and "seals" of the covenant of grace, made Christ "neerly and visibly to the soule" in ways that few other aspects of devotion were able to do. As was often said, Christ was more fully present in the sacrament than elsewhere.[58]

To judge from the sales of manuals of devotion, a great many people took the counsel of self-examination seriously and built their spiritual lives around it. We learn of their practice from the chance survival of a handful of diaries and what was said in letters and biographies, a genre used by godly writers to provide models for the less adept.[59] Of the Marian martyr John Bradford, a biographer noted that he wrote out a "catalogue of all the grossest and most enorme sins which in his life of ignorance he had committed" and laid "the same before his eyes when he went to private prayer," to the end of offering God a "contrite heart." For him, the crux of devotion was learning to "hate sin" and simultaneously to accept his dependence on Christ. Bradford also used "an ephemeris, or a journal" to decipher "the signs of his smitten heart," a text that prompted him to pray for "mercy" and the "grace to amend."[60] Lady Brilliana Harley (c. 1598–1643) practiced meditation according to the timetable she found in Nathaniel Cole's *The Godly Mans Assurance: or A Christian's Certain Resolution of his Owne Salvation* (1615): "1. every night and morning. 2. in the time of judgement. 3. upon our death bed. 4. before the sacrament."[61]

Constancy of this kind mattered a great deal to Margaret Hoby (d. 1633), a woman of wealth and high rank who spent part of every day in prayer, making notes in her Bible, "examin[ing]" herself, and meditating, much of it done in "private," although she also attended two services on Sunday and, some evenings, listened to others read aloud from the *Book of Martyrs* and the writings of Richard Greenham (a favorite), Perkins, and George Gifford. In her quest for constancy, she turned back to what she written in her journal some years earlier, hoping to "finde some profit" from a "Course" she was neglecting. When she could not attend a Sunday service or was away from home in London, she relied on sermon notes others had taken. Sometimes she took such notes herself, which she used to reflect on "the pointes of the sermon." As well, she depended on meditation to remind herself that ill health was God's means of thwarting the "temptations" Satan placed in her way.[62]

In a spiritual diary he kept in the 1630s, the young Scots lawyer Archibald Johnston recounted an almost daily sequence of two experiences: the first, an overwhelming sense of guilt for his sinfulness; and the second, the rapture of drawing close to a loving Christ. For guidance on how to pass from one to the other, Johnston relied on sermons he was hearing and a carefully plotted reading of manuals of devotion. The lesson he gained from these books was the imperative to seek God consistently through the means of grace, a message driven home by a sermon that taught him "if thou would seek the Lord aright and find him, thou must first seek him wisely, to wit, in earnest prayer, frequent meditation, hearing and reading of the word, communicating at his table, and keeping conference with good Christians." Ever dutiful, Johnston sought out church services and, especially, celebrations of the Lord's Supper, from which he gained so strong a sense of comfort that he often wept with joy. In keeping with Scottish practice, he usually attended a service of "preparation" before he came to the table. Fasting was another ritual that prompted him to remember his sins. At home, he staged family "exercises" in the hope of including his wife and children within the scope of divine grace, sometimes sharing advice from Scripture and the books by English Puritans he was reading—John Dod on the commandments, Downame's *The Christian Warfare*, and Nicholas Byfield's *The Marrow of the Oracles of God* (1620 and ante). Communal singing also figured in his practice.

Year after year, Johnston's was a spiritual life dominated by the paired sensations of "terror," as though Satan were on the verge of conquering his soul, and a "heavenly assurance and confidence that God the Father Son and Holy Ghost . . . had delivered me from the greatest evil of damnation." In a single day he frequently passed from one to the other, sometimes doing so as he read the Bible or a collection of psalms. Opening a psalter and lighting on Psalm 103:9, he felt as though he "received as ane oracle from heaven assuring me that God was wonderfully mynded for to delyver me and to blisse me." Turning back to Scripture, he identified with the "David" who experienced God's presence as he was confessing his sinfulness. The same relationship with Scripture marked Johnston's encounter with Deuteronomy 4:7 ("For what nation . . . , hath God so nigh unto them, as the Lord our God is in all things that we call upon him for?"), which elicited "many tears" and prompted him to assemble seven passages from Scripture that strengthened his sense of comfort. His ability to insert himself into the Bible was paralleled by the ease with which he discerned the significance of providential events. Both taught him the rule that sinners must place themselves entirely in the hands of an all-powerful God who provides "salvation and consolation." Ever in search of regularities, yet aware of his own imperfections, Johnston used the occasion of sacramental services to renew his covenant with a God who expected a great deal of the "fittest."[63]

For Nehemiah Wallington (1598–1658), a London artisan and committed Puritan, devotional practices became all-absorbing. From an early age he accepted the imperative of self-examination: "As it is also God's command to examine myself, so also in examining myself I see much of God, which doth abound much to the glory of God." These practices were recorded in fifty or so notebooks (an estimated twenty thousand pages of handwritten prose) filled with meditations, notes on sermons, examples of portents and providences, commentaries on the practical divinity, and extracts from his reading. Attending a sermon preached by Hugh Peter in 1643, Wallington recorded Peter's advice to "keep your day book; write down your sins on one side, and on the other side God's little mercies." Already, Wallington had created a list of thirty rules he gradually expanded to seventy-seven, each of them a means of reinforcing the discipline of resisting sin and practicing "watchfulness." Ever aware of a spiritualized Satan, he found that the Lord's Supper strengthened his sense of "spiritual" connection with Christ. From time to time, he renewed the "covenant" between himself and a loving God, a covenant in which he pledged to practice unending "obedience." That he would falter and fall short was certain. Yet it was just as certain that, were he to repent, God would reach out to him again.[64]

Devotion could be a private matter, as it usually was at some moments of the day. Yet several of the more important practices were communal, as when people gathered around deathbeds to pray for and console the dying or, as Margaret Hoby was doing, shared sermon notes with a group of "good" women. In prayer, the "I" and the "we" were intermingled, the transition from one to the other almost unnoticed.[65] Sermon-going was always a social experience, and especially so when those in search of evangelical preaching left their local church and went elsewhere for one of the Sunday services, a practice known as "gadding."[66] Participating in the Lord's Supper was social, as were fasts and feast days that punctuated the yearly calendar in Scotland. Fast days in England were usually arranged by godly magistrates and town councils, with others observed in households or voluntary communities where the godly gathered to pray and reflect. Something of their importance is indicated by the organizing of weekly fasts in the town of Dorchester, England, in the early seventeenth century and the frequency of the household fasts attended by the minister Samuel Rogers during his time as a lecturer in Wethersfield. Private or public, godly fasts were ritually akin to the Lord's Supper. As Thomas Cartwright indicated in a careful description of the rite, it summoned everyone to repent and make a "solemne confession" of their "unworthiness" as sinners, a process with great benefits if this were done "inwardly," for God would forgive the "evilles tending to our destruction." In Puritan circles, "sympathy" for others crowned this cluster of practices, the sympathy emphasized by Rollock in his summary of how assurance of salvation was made apparent: "love to the brethren, hospitality of love, and Christian sympathy to the saints in their afflictions."[67]

Baptism was another social practice and, theologically, an important means of grace. No godly minister in England or presbyterian in Scotland wanted to perform the sign of the cross during the ceremony, which the English liturgy included. Nor did these ministers sanction the practice of private baptism (with women possibly performing the rite), which the Church of England allowed in situations where a newborn child was at risk of dying before a minister could perform the rite in a parish church. The easy objection to this practice was to cite the possibility that women would depart from their biblically assigned role; the more serious, that such urgency implied the Catholic and Lutheran understanding of the sacrament as conferring regeneration. The rule in Scotland was that baptism should always occur in the context of Word-centered worship. Rightly administered, and in keeping with the covenant between God and Abraham (Gen. 17:7) which encompassed all of Abraham's "seed," baptism by water was much more than a "naked and bare" sign. According to article 21 of the Scots Confession of 1560, "by baptism we are ingrafted into Christ Jesus, to be made partakers of his righteousness, by which our sins are covered, and remitted." This was a strong version of the sacrament, more emphatic than what Calvin and other leaders of the Reformed were saying about its "efficacy" in the context of the doctrine of election. Possibly from knowing what was said in the *Book of Common Prayer* or the Scottish confessions, or perhaps from hearing ministers extol the "singular comfort" parents would experience once their children were "received into the bosome of Christes congregation," the godly took for granted the high importance of baptism and the burden it imposed on parents of being "diligent and carefull" in teaching their children about God.[68]

The practice of teaching children and young people the contents of a catechism was explicitly inclusive, regarded as such by bishops and general assemblies and a topic of concern in episcopal visitations in England.[69] Unglamorous and likely to bore some of the people who, Sunday after Sunday or on weekdays, rehearsed what they were learning, this practice was widely regarded as the doorway to the rest of the Christian life.[70] The best evidence of its role in the making of devotion is the quantity of printed catechisms. Dozens were published in the late sixteenth and early seventeenth centuries, and many more thereafter. Some editions of the Geneva Bible included Calvin's catechism, which may have been the text most widely used in sixteenth-century Scotland, where sacramental services were preceded by instruction from a catechism. In England, the catechism of choice was often Alexander Nowell's "official" catechism of 1570, printed in various formats more than fifty times by the 1640s and sometimes included in editions of the *Book of Common Prayer*.[71]

This ensemble of practices sustained a vigorous sociability at odds with the assertion by the early twentieth-century sociologist of religion Max Weber and repeated by some modern scholars that the practical divinity isolated the godly in an unhealthy "individualism."[72] Of the sites where sociability and devotion intersected, several others merit emphasizing. In some places in Scotland and England, the godly gathered in "conventicles" (a red flag to the official church) and, less tendentiously, in fellowship of the kind John Winthrop helped organize among his neighbors, a gathering of people to pray "every one of us each Friday . . . to be mindefull one of another in desiring God to grante the petitions that were made to him that daye." As did many such groups, Winthrop's sang psalms together. In the late 1630s, Robert Woodford was attending house-based conventicles in Northampton where "god's people" prayed and, using notes some of them had taken, studied anew the meaning of sermons they were hearing. More unusually, perhaps, Woodford went to a "nearby town" to participate in spiritual exercises at the bedside of a man who was dying; "now he had but a step to heaven, and desired us to helpe lift him up by our prayers." There is evidence of similar conferencing in Herefordshire, Shropshire, Cheshire, Lincolnshire, Essex, Lancashire, and London, where the ever-obsessive Nehemiah Wallington participated in gatherings of this kind. In some parishes, a self-selected group of the "godly" entered into a covenant with one another to "yield . . . subjection to the gospel of Christ," a procedure John Cotton introduced in the Lincolnshire town of Boston. The deeper meaning of these social moments was the unique "love" or "charity" that united the "people of God." Hence the advice to seek out the company of fellow saints.[73]

Within households, piety was firmly social, for the strongest bond between children and their parents was spiritual, the covenanted faith that they were extending to their children. Families were also where women came into their own, celebrated by husbands for their spiritual vitality and assigned a major role in preparing children to become Christians, a premise English readers encountered in Dorothy Leigh's *The mothers blessing: or, the godly counsaile of a gentle-woman* (1616), reprinted some twenty-two times in the course of the century, and Elizabeth Joscelin's *The Mother's Legacie to Her Unborne Children* (1624).[74] Fathers, too, had responsibilities, for a well-ordered household was the rock upon which church and commonwealth were built; without the one, the other would be undone. Two Puritan-affiliated ministers, John Dod and Robert Cleaver, collaborated on an important manual about household obligations, *A Godly Forme of Household Government* (1598; much reprinted), and William Gouge provided more advice in *Of domesticall duties* (1622). Many other ministers endorsed the central theme of these books, that fathers and mothers must introduce their children to Scripture and other godly books and, by personal example, prepare them for the pilgrim's life of self-discipline.[75]

Caught up in a thickening of devotional practices, laypeople were unlikely to undergo rapid-fire conversions. Instead, laypeople took for granted a life-long process initiated by a "first conversion" and developing out of "weake" beginnings to something "great."[76] Conversion as process rather than time-specific moment accounts for the many assertions that fullness of faith was achieved over time. As Perkins, Richard Rogers, and John Downame insisted, "weak faith" (Rom. 4:19, 14:1) was the point of departure in everyone's spiritual journey, a stage that customarily ripened into a more robust relationship with Christ. In *The Summe of Christian Divinity* (1625), Downame likened the earliest moments of "apprehending Christ" by faith to an "Infancie" that matures "according as our Faith doth grow." Others compared the growth of faith to the maturing of wheat: in the one as in the other, growth that was "fast" was unlikely to be well rooted, but that which "goeth on faire and softly . . . and doeth constantly proceed, in renewing the worke of faith and repentance" was the real thing.[77]

The real thing was, however, also problematic, for how would someone whose faith was weak know that she or he were among the saints? According to the English minister John Preston, "those who have but a weak faith" have "the weaker assurance." Or, as ministers and laypeople were alike in acknowledging, confidence or certainty about being among the elect could be undermined by seasons of spiritual "deadness" or having a "barren heart"—in other words, seasons when God (or the Holy Spirit) seemed to withdraw. The deeper point, which the Synod of Dordt endorsed, was that assurance, though "unchangeable" as an aspect of "election to salvation," was "given to the chosen in due time, *though in various stages and in differing measure* (emphasis added)."[78]

The tenuous relationship between weak faith and assurance—surely a prime example of assurance "in differing measure"—helps to explain why the makers of the practical divinity wrote so much about assurance and how it could be fortified or regained. They did so knowing that people "who are touched by the Spirit, and begin to come on in Religion, are much troubled with feare that they are not Gods children." To this situation the response on the part of the clergy was straightforward: anyone with "faith" could be "certain" he or she was saved. So Calvin had declared, and so the architects of the practical divinity reaffirmed in their turn.[79] Indeed, "full" or "sound" or "infallible" assurance was what Perkins and Richard Rogers promised those with faith, an assurance arising out of the doctrine of election and justification by faith alone but also out of an "especial" or "inward persuasion" planted in the heart by the Holy Spirit or, for Rogers, of being truly humbled. Likewise, Arthur Dent insisted that "he, that hath the spirit of God, knoweth certainly hee hath it; and hee that hath faith, knoweth that he . . . shall be saved." For Bradford, Perkins, Dent, and the authors of the Lambeth Articles, the message was loud and clear: assurance was available to all those who had experienced the inward workings of the Spirit and responded in faith.[80]

Only by listening carefully to these assertions of "full" or "sound" or "infallible" assurance do we grasp that Perkins, Dent, Richard Rogers, and a host of others were adding other layers to them. Always in the air was predestination of both the elect and the reprobate, a decision that to everyone but God was a "mystery."[81] A mystery this may have been, yet it was inevitable that some would not make their way to heaven. What could be said to curtail uncertainty and enable laypeople to perceive their relationship to the gospel promise? And what if the cycle of ups and downs that characterized the spiritual journey of someone such as Archibald Johnston stalled at its low point, the moment when the godly acknowledged how unworthy they were of forgiveness and how great the distance was between them and divine love? How could someone differentiate a productive emptying of self-confidence from an anxiety so paralyzing that all hope of redemption seemed to vanish?

This was not a hypothetical scenario, for it darkened the lives of many of the godly. The men who published major sermon series on faith and salvation repeatedly acknowledged the presence of people who questioned whether they were included within the covenant of grace. Letters of consolation sent to those in need of advice mention the same question and its corollary, the suffering that was coded as affliction. As well, sermon series and personal writings report a sense of unworthiness that kept laypeople from coming to the Lord's Supper or pursuing the "duty" of spiritual exercises. In a worse-case situation usually described as "melancholy," some people reasoned that God would *never* extend his mercy to them. Everyone had encountered or heard stories of such people, Lady Harley from one of her maids, who experienced "grievous agony of conscience and despair"; the English minister Thomas Hooker from knowing Joan Drake, who felt she was beyond the reach of divine grace; the congregation in new-world Boston from witnessing the plight of a fellow church-member, who "grew into utter desperation, and could not endure to hear of any comfort." The readers of *The last conflicts and death of M. Thomas Peacock* (1646) encountered another example, a man who, on his deathbed, "suffered Satan to winnow him" and abandoned any hope of mercy.[82]

Acute or tempered, emotional situations of this kind prompted two different responses, one spiritual or devotion-related, the other more theological. On the side of the spiritual and devotional, the makers of the practical divinity asked laypeople to reflect on whether they were truly sincere in their professions of faith or going through the motions—that is, engaging in hypocrisy. Self-deception and, almost as bad, an outward show of godliness, was a principal theme of Perkins's *A treatise Tending unto a Declaration Whether a Man be in the Estate of Damnation, or in the Estate of Grace* (1588), from which readers learned "that a reprobate might (in appearance) attain to as much as" the true saint. Hence the imperative—pressed on people such as Nehemiah Wallington—to discern whether their faith was seated in the "heart."

Alternatively, the imperative was to discern whether they had pursued preparation under the law to its "painful" end of self-recognition as hopelessly entrapped in sin. Here, the strategy endorsed by some godly ministers was to use the weapon known as "terror." The contemporary argument on behalf of terror was straightforward: because sinners had "stony" hearts hardened by pride, terror was a weapon of last resort for breaking through the barriers to repentance. It followed, therefore, that ministers should "rip up" the heart, counsel that John Rogers of Dedham (and nephew of Richard Rogers) transformed into a dramatic style of preaching. His antics included "roaring hideously, to represent the torments of the damned" and possibly "frisk[ing] on the floor" from "joy" after hearing "sad stories" of a woman's despair, which he took as a sign that she had been touched by the Word. Like many others, Perkins called on sinners to visualize "how little a step there is" between salvation and damnation, a point he illustrated by describing life as a "frail bridge" beneath which lay "the craggy rock and hell the gaping gulf under it." At its core, preaching of this kind relied on the argument that only a small fraction of humankind would be saved, a fraction sometimes expressed as one out of a thousand. Whatever the context, the ministers and popular writers who brandished the weapon of terror took for granted the merits of doing so.[83]

Others disagreed. The ever-present possibilities of weak faith and the reluctance of some ministers to use terror animated a debate among the makers of the practical divinity about the sources of assurance, the emotional costs of emphasizing preparation under the law, and—possibly in response to complaints about the limiting of salvation to the few who were the elect—to the scope of the Atonement. By the 1620s, a few minister-theologians, foremost among them Sibbes and more daringly, the "Antinomian" John Eaton, were sketching an alternative model of the work of grace (see chap. 9). In some of Sibbes's sermon series, he reached out to people of "weak faith," the group he addressed in his exegesis of Matthew 12:20, "A bruised read shall he not break, and smoking flax shall he not quench, till he send forth judgment unto victory." In a prefatory "To the Christian Reader," Sibbes extolled divine love: "We are saved by a way of love. . . . It is love in duties that God regards, more than duties themselves. This is the true and evangelical disposition arising from Christ's love to us, and our love to him again. . . . It is almost a fundamental mistake, to think that God delights in slavish fears, whenas the fruits of Christ's kingdom are peace and joy in the Holy Ghost." From diagnosis he turned to remedy. Those who doubted must be told again and again of how much they were loved by Christ and how, in the grand scheme of things, Christ's mission was to communicate love, not fear. Sibbes touched on the merits of the "law" as a means of preparing sinners to receive the Gospel, but he preferred to encourage those in whom "there is but a little measure of grace," telling them how greatly they were valued by Christ and how, with his assistance, they would strengthen their faith. Seemingly in response to the preaching of other ministers, he counseled "moderation": set aside any list of conditions or "terms" and imitate the Christ who "stooped down" to those in need. Sibbes may have been at his most astute in warning against excessive scrupulosity. Granted, scrupulosity could be a "sign of a godly soul, as some weeds are of a good soil." Yet it was also a "heavy affliction." Hence his insistence that the "end of Christ's coming is to free us from all such groundless fears."[84]

Someone Sibbes admired, the contemporary Suffolk, England, minister Ezekiel Culverwell, was also questioning law-centered preaching. As he pointed out in *A Treatise of Faith* (1623; much reprinted), his purpose was to "strengthen the weake in faith." What worried him was the possibility that the practical divinity was undermining—even contradicting—the doctrine of free grace by making the gospel promise not "absolut, but (as it is commonly said to be) conditionall, which is, when God declareth his will, what he will doe if we doe our part, els not." Although he granted that "this conditionall promise well understood may be borne," he warned that it could also destroy "the free and gracious promise of the Gospell." Law and Gospel or "Covenant of works" and "covenant of grace" must never be confounded; in the second of these, "Faith" was not a condition. Nor was "obedience." Again with those of weak faith or doubting their assurance in mind, he insisted that the promise of salvation was offered to everyone, although effective only for the elect.[85]

The same emphasis on the God who made the gospel promise available to everyone—truly, everyone—flavored the sermons of John Preston. In his sermon series *The Brest-plate of Faith and Love* (1628), he reminded its readers that the promise was "given to every man, *there is not a man excepted* [emphasis added]." Assertions of this kind lay at the heart of Preston's "hypothetical universalism," hypothetical because, in his eyes, it did not contradict the doctrine that God had elected the few, not the many, to salvation. Preston acknowledged the work of the law and the difficulties of overcoming human sinfulness; like many of his contemporaries, he endorsed preparation under the law. But as his two editors remarked in a brief preface, his purpose was to prevent the "weake Christian" from "los[ing] the comfort of his faith, through want of evidence." Elsewhere, he taught that "the true believer hath such a light going on with his faith that he comes to know, though not perfectly, yet truly and infallibly, that God hath chosen, adopted, and sanctified him." For Simonds D'Ewes, an exceptionally engaged lay reader in 1620s and 1630s England, Preston's insistence that "God's children may ... ordinarily in this life attain to the Assurance of their own salvation" enabled him to believe that he was among God's chosen.[86]

Sibbes, Culverwell, and Preston were insiders who tweaked the practical divinity without altering its core assumptions. Others who shared the observation that assurance seemed hard to come by were having second thoughts, a possibility hinted at in sermons of the early 1630s by the future congregationalist Thomas Goodwin.[87] In the context of this chapter, however, it is important to note that, from Perkins onward, mainstream ministers never strayed from a forceful insistence on routines of devotion or from advising those of weak faith that doubt was inevitable. The trick was to turn doubt into a positive sign and to attribute anxiety to the presence of the Devil, who, as described by Perkins, Preston, Dent, Downame, and many others, relished making people doubt the message of the Gospel. Or, as indicated in some of the penitential psalms of David and the example of Thomas in the New Testament, the ministers emphasized the inevitability of doubt and did their best to turn it into a positive sign.

Beyond these explanations (which were also intended as aids to reflection and props for the overly anxious) lay advice that almost everyone who preached the practical divinity articulated, the possibility of using sanctification or righteousness as a source of assurance. Advice with deep roots in Reformed theology, its starting point was known in Reformed circles as the practical syllogism: "he that repenteth and beleeveth the Gospel shall be saved / But I repent and believe the Gospel / therefore I shall be saved," a structure validated by 2 Peter 1:10: "give diligence to make your calling and election sure: for if ye do these things, ye shall never fail." Some Reformed theologians treated the syllogism cautiously but ended up saying something very similar, as Calvin did.[88] Indeed, to reason from effects to cause or from works back to faith was fully in keeping with Reformed confessions and the concept of the golden chain. In chapter 6 of the "Bohemian" Confession of 1575, good works were described as "signes and testimonies, and exercises of a livelie faith, even of that faith, which lieth hidden in the heart" and, with 2 Peter 1:10 in mind, as how Christians "confirme and build up their Election and vocation in themselves." In the catechism attributed to Thomas Cartwright, the answer to the question, "How do we knowe that wee have true faithe?" is "By the frutes thereof." Evoking the false wisdom of "carnall professors" who comforted themselves with saying, "If I be elected, however I live I shall be saved," the Scottish evangelical William Cowper reaffirmed the connections between human activity and election: "it is impossible that the elect man effectually called, can reason after this manner; yea the more hee heares of Election, the more he endeavours to make sure by well doing [an allusion to 2 Peter 1:10], knowing that no man can attaine to the end of our Faith . . . but by the lawfull and oredinary meanes." Hence the phrasing of Richard Greenham's catechism when he turned to the topic of "works." Spurning "good works" as inherently "imperfect" and of no merit in the larger economy of salvation, he reintroduced them as the consequence of saving faith and therefore valid evidence of "faith & election."[89]

This emphasis on sanctification or what looks like moral activism troubles those historians who prefer Calvin's emphasis on faith or Luther's doubts about the law.[90] Whenever a minister in England or Scotland declared that faith was real if it resulted in righteousness, he did so knowing that this advice was aligned with Scripture and sanctioned by his predecessors in the Reformed international. Long before Perkins began to teach at Cambridge, the makers of the Scots Confession had asserted (chap. 13) that "the cause of good works . . . is . . . the Spirit of the Lord Jesus, who . . . brings forth such works as God has prepared for us to walk in." In confessions of this kind, as in the practical divinity, faith was construed as an active or transformative force manifesting itself in righteous or godly behavior. So, of course, was the Word as preached and "discipline" as practiced by the visible church.[91]

Doctrinally, the path most ministers took was to remind everyone that faith preceded justification and the law preceded faith. Scholastic categories made it possible to attach the word "instrumental" to faith and to imply (or assert) that assurance was conditional on certain actions. To protect themselves from critics who regarded these arguments as tilting toward works-righteousness, the ministers who argued in this manner always added that God worked the conditions (see chap. 9). For some of their contemporaries, this was to make more of the law as an instrument of repentance and self-denial than Calvin did, and *much* more of the experiential aspects of election. Yet in their own eyes, these men retained the core principles of unmerited grace, the transformative power of the Holy Spirit, and faith as always and everywhere associated with righteousness.[92]

Richard Sibbes and Samuel Rutherford deserve the final word on the quest for assurance. For Sibbes, it was important that the godly recognize that joy and tribulation were always and everywhere commingled in the Christian life. In his words, "God often works by contraries: when he means to give victory, he will suffer us to be foiled at first." What made this wisdom pertinent was its bearing on assurance, which he described as beset by doubts and difficulties. Writing to a woman of high status who was ill and sensing her mortality, Rutherford urged her to cultivate a "holy fear of the loss of your Christ." Aware of the alternating of confidence and self-doubt, he brought them together in a single sentence: let "the Spirit of God . . . hold your soul's feet in the golden mid-line, betwixt confident resting in the arms of Christ, and presumptuous and drowsy sleeping in the bed of fleshly security." Here, as with the conditionality of the covenant of grace and the role of the law as preparation, the practical divinity embraced what may seem paradoxical or ambiguous.[93]

Ministry and People

People "abhorre and loath" us, people crave our preaching: this stark duality was inescapable to those of the godly who became ministers in Tudor-Stuart Britain.[94] Inescapable because an evangelical mode of ministry brought peace to some but troubled many others; as was candidly acknowledged by a committee of the House of Commons in 1643, "too many" people in the pews were "loath to come under a powerful ministry." Inescapable because strong claims to being Christ's "ambassadors," a title stemming from one of Paul's letters to the Corinthians (2 Cor. 5:20) irritated other groups in a social world rife with competition for authority. Superior though they may have been to the many "idle, unsound, unprofitable, and scandalous Ministers" the state churches in England and Scotland continued to employ, those who preached the practical divinity could never shake off popular criticism and elite disdain.[95]

No easy fix to the adversarial relationship between ministry and people was available because that relationship had so many layers—conformity for some ministers, nonconformity for others; competition with missionary priests who insisted on the superiority of Catholicism;[96] employment arranged by patrons who controlled a large share of the church's revenues; an ever-present anxiety in England about rituals in the *Book of Common Prayer* that some parishioners valued and others preferred to avoid.

The most common response to a tension-filled relationship was to insist on an identity as faithful shepherds who gave fully of themselves to the twin tasks of awakening sinners to their plight and leading them to Christ. At the core of this self-understanding was a framework these men owed to the Reformed tradition and especially to Calvin, who wanted to bring into being a ministry that "would have the kind of moral authority that is worth more than any quantity of formal rights." Given the realism that a highly trained and self-disciplined ministry was "the *sine qua non* of good order and even of the survival of a reformed church," he provided extensive instructions on how ministers should be recruited, trained, and supervised. The same realism prompted the authors of the *First Book of Discipline* to linger on the making of ministers and the English presbyterians to protest the presence of so many ill-prepared "dumb dogges." What the church needed and what Christ expected of all who entered this vocation was something quite different, a ministry devoted to its role as means of grace in the economy of redemption.[97]

First things first, a Dent or a Perkins may have reasoned when the moment came to justify their authority: let us make clear what God intended by our office. Knowing that Catholic priests in Britain described themselves as divinely consecrated intermediaries between Christ and humankind, the makers of the practical divinity insisted that, on the contrary, ministers were God's true messengers, an argument stemming from the Reformed premise that "ministers of the Word" were "ambassadors of God, who must be heard as we would hear God himself," to which Calvin added the assertion that all true ministers had been directly "commissioned." John Preston was blunt-spoken in sermons he preached in the 1620s: "we that preach the Gospel are Messengers sent from the Father," adding that, "if you refuse" the Gospel, "the Lord . . . will have you brought and slaine before his face." Here, in theory, was everything a godly minister needed to affirm his authority, a concept of vocation that differentiated his office from all other versions of rank in a society, a point emphasized within the Reformed tradition by the rule that only ordained pastors could administer the sacraments of baptism and Holy Communion.[98]

Christ-like authority flowed from another aspect of ministry, the significance of preaching. Rightly taught and communicated, the Word was the vehicle God had appointed as His means of communicating the gospel promise, an argument the makers of the practical divinity based on Romans 10:14–17, which concludes with the statement, "Faith cometh by hearing, and hearing by the Word of God." This verse prompted Arthur Dent to construct a syllogism-like statement: "No preaching, no faith, no faith, no Christ: no eternall life." Many others echoed him, as George Downame did in asserting that, without the presence of preaching, "ordinarily men cannot attain to salvation no nor yet to any degree of salvation."[99] The Word was just as crucial when it came to curtailing sin and advancing the process of edification. As advocates of reform liked to say, "bare reading" from a printed homily or the *Book of Common Prayer* was ineffective. In a world overflowing with "sinne and iniquitie" and blighted with "superstition," the one sure means of enacting moral reform was evangelical, law-centered preaching. Thus construed, the Word would cleanse church *and* society of sin and corruption. On a grander scale, preaching of the right kind would enable the visible church to approximate the "Sion" that awaited the return of Christ in triumph.[100]

So the founders of the Reformed tradition had argued, and so the makers of the practical divinity insisted in their turn. From humanism and the Reformed tradition came still another justification for ministry in general and Puritan-style ministry in particular: the importance of learnedness in the on-going struggle to comprehend the exact meaning of Scripture and rebut Catholic objections to Protestant theology. Learnedness in early modern Britain was a version of literacy available only to the few who attended one of the British colleges. In a society where a great many people were illiterate or, in Scotland and Ireland, knew Gaelic, a university education equipped young men with the ability to read, write, and possibly converse in Latin, together with a more limited knowledge of Greek and Hebrew. Just as significant was a facility in the "arts" of logic and rhetoric, which enabled would-be ministers to handle cases of conscience, or casuistry. Finally, learnedness provided ministers-to-be with the means of defending the truth against its enemies.[101]

For the makers of the practical divinity, the skills associated with learnedness had a special importance in the context of understanding Scripture. It was all well and good to affirm the ability of everyone with the "eye of faith" to determine the meaning of the dark places in Scripture, but learning was called for when the time came to defend Protestant theology. Mary Stuart pounced on a related problem in one of her confrontations with John Knox, telling him that the Bible was too variable to serve as the basis of the true church. In her presence, Knox was willing to acknowledge the "obscurity" of certain passages, a realism he shared with the early sixteenth-century translator of the Bible into English, William Tyndale, who agreed that in the Old Testament "Christ was "figured . . . in riddles, and parables, and in dark prophecies." Knox made up for this concession by insisting that obscurity in any "one place" was clarified by the "Holy Ghost" somewhere else. For Perkins, who dealt with biblical exegesis in *The Arte of Prophecy,* and Richard Bernard, who devoted several chapters of *The Faithfull Shepherd* (1607) to the same topic, the academic remedy for the queen's complaint was learnedness of specific kinds: knowing the languages in which Scripture had been transmitted and using "grammatical, rhetorical and logical" modes of analysis, which everyone with a college education had acquired.[102]

What may surprise modern readers who assume that Puritan-style Protestants relied on a "literal" sense of the bible is how persistently they did the opposite.[103] To be sure, British Protestants condemned the fourfold hermeneutics that was customary among Catholics, which they replaced with the "plaine and natural sense" of the text. As the historian Andrew Crome has observed, the point of this assertion was to sustain the authority of Scripture over the Catholic emphasis on tradition or history. Meanwhile, the godly were relying on figural and allegorical readings of Scripture as long as these could be aligned with "faith." There was nothing "plain" about godly prose and poetry, and certainly nothing that coincided with the understanding of "literal" that emerged among Protestant conservatives at the end of the nineteenth century and continues to the present day.[104]

A learned ministry was a ministry associated with hierarchy. Yet the right kind of ministry also undermined some versions of rank and office. Perkins, Bernard, and other makers of the practical divinity never wanted to sanction the hierarchies embedded in an episcopal system, much less the hierarchies within civil society. Hence the populist flavor of so much anti-episcopal rhetoric, a case in point being the anticlericalism Job Throckmorton recycled in the Martin Mar-prelate tracts. The fictive Martin assailed the bishops of circa 1585 as time-servers more interested in acquiring wealth than in being pastors of the people. Before and after him, godly ministers employed the image of bishop as wolf or serpent set loose among the "sheep," the point being to highlight their own identity as shepherds who served unselfishly. The rhetoric of shepherd versus wolf validated godly complaints about the greed that sustained pluralism, nonresidency, and the scramble for high office in the state church. The same rhetoric underscored the difference between the "tyranny" embodied in the rank of bishop and the Christ-like demeanor of the good shepherd.

Zeal was another marker of difference, an aspect of ministry that figured in biographies of Scottish clergy and of English ministers dating from the early years of the seventeenth century,[105] all of them emphasizing these men's tireless service to church and community. The writers who honored Greenham described him as preaching twice on Sundays and once each weekday, with a single exception. Simultaneously, he was counseling his parishioners in their homes, catechizing the young people of the parish, and conversing with the young men who attended his household seminary in Dry Drayton. Panegyrics of this kind were commonplace, as were descriptions of the "good death" someone had experienced. Or, as was sometimes implied, the self-sacrificing zeal of the ideal minister became the spiritual equivalent of martyrdom.[106]

The Christ-like aura and authority of the faithful shepherd depended, as well, on a mode of preaching characterized as "plain" or "humble," the same

words the godly used to describe the speech of Jesus.[107] The substance of plainness was threefold. The social imperative was for ministers to "accommodate"
their preaching to "those of the meanest Capacity" so that everyone—literate
or illiterate—could understand. The literary-cum-theological imperative was
to translate theological principles into "applications" or "uses" that "pierce[d]"
the inner self and aroused "godly affections." As Perkins insisted in a treatise
on right worship, the preached Word must be made "special by application."
This, too, required plainness.[108] The third was spiritual-literary, the assumption that ministers must preach from the heart or inner self if Word and Spirit
were to meld. As was said in every description of effective preaching, the exemplary minister had been St. Paul, who preached "not with enticing words of
man's wisdom, but in demonstration of the Spirit and of power" (1 Cor. 2:2–4).
His example prompted Perkins and other makers of the practical divinity to
argue that the evangelical minister must be "inwardly taught by the spiritual
School-master the holy Ghost." Knowing of Calvin's assertion in the *Institutes*
that, without the presence of the Spirit, the Word was ineffective, Perkins insisted in *Of the Calling of the Ministry* (1607) that "the true Minister must "first
be godly affected himself, who would stir up godly affections in other men."
This precept, which in other hands in the 1640s would undermine the prestige
of learnedness, did double duty before that period. On the one hand, it figured
in all descriptions of plain-speaking (i.e., bible-centered) and "affective"
preaching. On the other, it underscored the distinctive authority that accompanied a Spirit-driven ministry.[109]

Distinctive it may have been, but a ministry of this kind still had to contend
with a social world in which every version of authority was contested and high
claims for the Word as preached were frequently ignored. High claims to authority may have been most openly contradicted whenever the preachers' message of free grace encompassed (as it always did) the warning that, unless
sinners speedily repented or began to practice righteousness, God would exclude them from the community of the redeemed. Everyone who preached the
practical divinity took for granted the imperative to denounce the presence of
sin. But everyone also knew that bold speaking could backfire. Instead of repenting, people in the pews could repudiate a faithful shepherd.[110]

Nonetheless, plain speaking appealed to some ministers. During Edward
VI's reign, Thomas Lever, John Knox, and John Bradford became "famous for
their plain and bold preaching" in the presence of courtiers and others of high
social rank; as remembered by someone who heard them speak, "they
ripped . . . deeply in[to] the galled Backs of the great Men of the Court," to the
end of purging "them of . . . insatiable Covetousness, filthy Carnality, and . . .
intolerable Ambition and Pride." Outbursts of this kind in Scotland were
the norm in late sixteenth-century Scotland, a practice so irritating to James
VI that he pressured the clergy closest to his court to stop preaching in this
manner. In early seventeenth-century England, ministers associated with the

Puritan movement or, for other reasons, unhappy with the policies of James I and Charles I, continued to rebuke the two monarchs, doing so openly as well as indirectly. In their everyday preaching, they were just as emphatic. The practical divinity was a "precise way," and those who resisted it should be targeted with "keen arrows of truth and terror" sharpened with "great indignation."[111]

One context in which plain speaking seemed important was the ever-frustrating practice of controlling access to the Lord's Table. This was a double-sided task, requiring ministers (or in Scotland, lay elders) to find out whether people knew a catechism or lived in peace with their neighbors and, on the other hand, obligating church wardens to pursue those who did not turn up for the sacrament at least once a year, as the Church of England required. In Scotland, the oversight of laypeople by elders and kirk sessions made it more likely that the Lord's Table would be protected, although it seems doubtful that much was done in practice. This may explain why most of the men who preached the practical divinity relied on generalized warnings of the kind that appear in manuals such as Bradshaw's *A Preparation to the receiving of Christs Body and Blood*, all of them based on 1 Corinthians 11:27–30.[112]

Generalized warnings were prudent because plain speaking could have unfortunate consequences. Early in Elizabeth I's reign, Alexander Nowell made a point of saying that pastors "ought not" to admit the "unworthy" to the Eucharist. In the same breath, however, he added a telling qualification: no minister should ever mention someone of this kind "by name" in a "public" sermon but do so "privately," leaving the actual work of exclusion to "elders" or "ecclesiastical magistrates." This was a lesson the young zealot Roger Williams never learned. Confident of his authority as an "eagle-eyed, fayfull and observant" counselor to Lady Joan Barrington, Williams told her in a letter of early 1629 that "afflictions" she had recently experienced, one of them the death of her husband, were God's way of indicating that He "hath a quarrel" with her for not allowing Christ into her heart. No letter from Barrington to Williams survives, but she seems to have ignored him for several months. Plain speaking got Williams in trouble, whereas a minister who, the same year, urged her to "goe on . . . chearfully" in "confidence of your hope" secured her services as godparent of his first child.[113]

John Vicars chose the path of confrontation and paid a heavy price for doing so. According to witnesses who testified before the London-based Court of High Commission in 1632, Vicars used his pulpit in Stamford, Lincolnshire, to denounce the misbehavior of some of the townspeople, telling those who avoided the second service on Sundays that they were going to hell. Simultaneously, he drew close to a small group of the godly who were meeting each week in his house to pray and enjoy other spiritual exercises; in some unspecified manner, six of his female admirers formed themselves into a "nunnery." A ministry this divisive cost Vicars his post.[114] William Pemble, who died in his early thirties in 1623, never left Cambridge University for a parish living. Nonetheless, in one of his treatises he evoked the situation of a minister who, having applied "the censure of the Word in . . . direct reproofe" of the "sinnes" of his parish, aroused "an "unmerciful fury" and "fiery opposition . . . at the hands . . . of the people." Itemizing what to expect in situations of this kind, Pemble evoked the "uproar" of an entire parish "once they have been touched where they would not be medled with. Straitway . . . dirt and scorn is hurl'd in the face of the Minister and his doctrine, all forward courses taken to work him woe and shame, and all this done by those that will yet be counted obedient and believing Christians."[115]

The troubles that befell John Vicars confirm this picture, although his downfall also involved the government. So do the many moments in Scotland when James VI or some of the nobility turned against ministers as outspoken as David Black and John Davidson—the latter so vehement that Andrew Melville advised him to lower the pitch of his rhetoric.[116] On the other hand, when Arthur Hildersham preached an aggressive assize-day sermon that aroused the "anger and displeasure" of a local judge, calm returned once Hildersham spoke "some words unto him with ministerial authority, [and] he stayed till the Sermon was done." Here, the conflict between two different strategies and two different versions of authority ended with godliness coming out on top.[117]

Situations of this kind remind us that the authority of godly ministers was constantly being mediated by social and cultural circumstances. That their status was precarious had something to do with a structural feature of ministry as practiced alike by the godly and their rivals, the systems on which they depended for employment. When many of these men went looking for parishes they could serve, they learned anew the lesson that church "livings" belonged in large part to members of the gentry. Finding a patron among the gentry was thus a crucial step, so much so that, in the words of a historian of seventeenth-century Sussex, "gentry patronage" became "the lifeblood of Sussex Puritanism," an assertion just as true of some other counties. Early in the reign of Elizabeth I, the Earl of Huntington was using his authority to plant "good preachers . . . in the market towns" of Lancashire. Francis Hastings followed in his brother's footsteps, noting in 1602 the "bond of duty" he felt to enable "a longing people to hear . . . a laboring, speaking minister." By the beginning of the seventeenth century, a network of aristocratic families in various parts of England was providing posts as house chaplains,[118] lecturers, and parish ministers for men who otherwise would have been suspended or deprived. No one was more indebted to patrons and the bishops they influenced than Hildersham. Silenced several times for refusing to conform, he kept reappearing thanks to "the connivance and favour" of church leaders and patrons in high places. He and others also benefitted from town corporations and parishes that acquired the right to name their own ministers or promised to supplement a minister's stipend in order to make an appointment more appealing. According to a careful study of lay patronage in the diocese of Cheshire (England), merchants, tradesmen, and women with the wealth to do so busied themselves in both ways.[119]

Dependence on lay patrons was as old as the hills, as much a feature of Catholic Britain as of Protestant. Now, however, the high expectations for ministry as a vocation clashed with ancient practices, as witnessed by the attempts in late sixteenth-century Scotland to curtail the prerogatives of lay patrons, a campaign resumed by general assemblies in the 1640s.[120] In England, a more satisfactory alternative emerged by the close of the sixteenth century, a position as lecturer. Lectureships arose as a way for corporations and parishes to employ a better quality of preacher-pastor—often but not always a godly minister—than was possible in parishes where the incumbent minister was uninspiring or lay owners had siphoned off the revenues. Or it could be that in London, where 90 percent of its parishes were employing a lecturer by 1630, the wealthier used this kind of position to add more men to their staff. The crucial piece in this puzzle was money, be it voluntary contributions from a parish or the patronage of a smaller group or the income from an endowment someone had set up. The business of a lecturer was to preach two or three times a week, leaving the liturgical or sacramental aspects of worship to another person. The downside of these appointments was their brevity—lecturers were appointed for as little time as a year—and although some men lingered in these positions, most appointments of this kind were way stations on the road to the permanence of a parish living.[121]

Way stations or safe havens they may have been and would remain in some parts of England, but at various moments in the early seventeenth century the leadership of the state church intervened to make them less attractive to nonconformists, a story touched on in chapters 6 and 7. Looking for ways of providing positions for the right kind of minister, a group of Puritan-affiliated merchants and ministers in mid-1620s London created a new version of lay patronage, a treasury (investments) producing income that could be used to buy vacant livings or impropriations. The organization created for this purpose, the Feoffees for Impropriations or "collectors of St. Antholin's," a London church active in employing lecturers, acquired properties in some twenty-six parishes before being suppressed by the government in 1633. Although the Feoffees came and went, town corporations and county aristocracies that made space for lecturers were a fixture of English society.[122]

The sum of these circumstances was the situation evoked at the beginning of this section—on the one hand, assertions of a singular authority; and on the other, popular indifference or political resistance to those claims intermixed with affection, respect, financial support, and, to be fair, confusion. Throughout these decades, the godly version of ministry continued to be framed by contradictions: preaching to the many, yet converting the few; denouncing sin, yet wary of being too outspoken; declaring themselves loyal to a country's rulers, yet seen by Elizabeth and James VI and I as agents of sedition; peacemakers in their parishes, but also regarded as troublemakers. From the standpoint of the ministers themselves, the practical divinity was akin to a musical score, with rhythms and tonalities that varied from one performer to the next. As Hildersham, Richard Rogers, and Hooker learned from their life work as pastors, some of these variations were a sensible response to a parish that included people at several different stages of knowledge and practice. In the "uses" of a sermon series as lengthy as Rogers's *Seven Treatises*, what was said to one group differed from what was said to another. Perkins sketched the same challenge in *The Arte of Prophesying*, where he specified seven different categories of people a minister must address.[123]

These circumstances underscore a paradox: despite the tensions it aroused, the practical divinity was a remarkable success as measured by the enthusiasm of the London book trade for books by Perkins, Dent, and other godly writers. By the early seventeenth century, vast quantities of catechisms, psalters, sermon series, and books of devotion were being printed by booksellers who knew that "religious" books were highly "vendible." The makers of "cheap print" exploited a parallel market for ballads and tales of remarkable providences, the stranger the better. In Britain as a whole, tens of thousands of people were reading these books.[124]

"He giveth me to see light in His light . . . Oh, I lived in and loved darkness . . . yet God had mercy on me. O the riches of His mercy!" These words of an English country gentleman named Oliver Cromwell remind us of the joy felt by the many who spoke openly of being among the elect or assumed that their pilgrimage would conclude with a "free and comfortable passage" into eternal life. Joan Drake, who suffered from acute spiritual despair, linked her recovery to practicing the "meanes" of grace: prayer, catechizing, expounding and reading of the word, and "singing of Psalms constantly" in her "family." During the revival-like excitement at Stewarton in Scotland (1625–1630), hundreds of people responded to the preaching of David Dickson and others by passing from "great terrors and deep exercise of conscience" to "sweet peace and strong consolation." As recorded by an eyewitness at the Cambridge, Massachusetts, deathbed of Thomas Shepard's wife Joanna (1636), she "broke out into a most heavenly, heart-breaking prayer after Christ, her dear Redeemer . . . and so continued praying, to the last hour of her death, 'Lord though I am unworthy, one word—one word,' &c. and so gave up the ghost."[125]

This melding of heart-felt repentance with the sensate presence of the living Christ marks Dickson's *True Christian Love* (1634), a meditation on the theme of love in Colossians 3:14–16. As in so much of the practical divinity, *True Christian Love* acknowledged the reality of divine absence even as it affirmed a vibrant sense of divine presence: Christ is truly at the writer's side who sings this poem with "thankfulness" in his "heart" (Col. 3:16). Challenging though it must have been to undergo the ever-recurring alternation of absence and presence, and challenging, as well, to sustain the "certainty of hope," the evidence suggests that a substantial number of people in Britain aligned themselves with this model of the spiritual life.[126]

Controversy

Never without its Catholic critics or internal dissent, the practical divinity came under pressure from an alternative version of Reformed Protestant doctrine in the late sixteenth and early seventeen centuries. For the moment this alternative was held in check, but by the mid-1620s "Arminianism," which owed its name to the Dutch theologian Jacob Arminius (d. 1609), was becoming a divisive presence in England. Arminius was a professor at Leiden University and, in his self-estimation, loyal to the Reformed tradition even though he revised the doctrines of election, the irresistibility of divine grace, and the perseverance of the saints. Wanting to make more of free will and broaden the meaning of divine justice, Arminius proposed that the decree of election took account of God's foreknowledge of whether some people would have faith in Jesus Christ and live righteously. As was argued in a remonstrance (1610), predestination was conditional upon faith. Arminius was not a full-fledged Pelagian, that is, someone who attributed salvation to a sinner's own efforts. Yet he and the Dutch theologians who shared his point of view were challenging the argument that redemption was solely the doing of irresistible grace. Controversy erupted in the Netherlands and, with the support of the Dutch government, Arminius's critics convened an international "synod" of Reformed theologians in 1618–19. After protracted debate, it endorsed a list of five "points" in opposition to Arminianism: (1) the total depravity of humankind, (2) unconditional election by divine sovereignty, (3) the atonement limited to the elect rather than being universal in some manner; (4) irresistible grace, or grace overriding any agency on the part of humankind; and (5) the perseverance of the saints—that is, once elected, always saved.[127]

Well before debate in the Netherlands became a crisis in that country, a few academic theologians in England were revisiting certain aspects of Reformed orthodoxy. In the mid-1580s, the French Huguenot Peter Baro (1544–1599), the Lady Margaret Professor of Divinity at Cambridge, challenged the doctrines of election and a limited atonement. Baro had an ally in another Cambridge fellow, William Barrett, who in 1595 repudiated certainty of assurance in a public sermon laced with hostile allusions to Calvin, Beza, and Reformed scholastics. He did so at a moment when William Whitaker, who became professor of divinity at Cambridge in 1579, was vigorously defending a repertory of Reformed principles. Whitaker told Whitgift and Lord Burghley about Barrett and, in Oxford itself, encouraged the university authorities to denounce what Whitaker regarded as Arminianism. Barrett backpedaled, left the university in 1597, and after moving to the Continent, seems to have become a Catholic.

Informed of these disputes, Whitgift set in motion the drafting of the Lambeth Articles. Nine years later, the sense among some clergy in the Church that Arminianism was gaining ground prompted the Puritan delegates to the Hampton Court conference (1604; see chap. 6) to propose that Lambeth be combined with the Thirty-Nine Articles as a means of strengthening what it said about the doctrine of election and the perseverance of the saints.[128] Fast-forward again to the 1620s and beyond, and "Arminian" objections to orthodox doctrine continued to worry ministers and lay theologians such as John Cotton. When Cotton arrived in Boston, Lincolnshire, as the town's parish minister, he encountered an "Arminian" faction and responded to their questions by "clear[ing] the orthodox doctrine of predestination from such harsh consequences, as are wonted to be derived from absolute reprobation." In the words of a modern scholar, Cotton was assuring the local Arminians that God "would not arbitrarily sentence a human being to damnation without that being's prior transgression." When a manuscript copy of his musings came into the hands of the forcefully anti-Arminian English theologian William Twisse, he pounced on them in comments that remained in manuscript until 1646.[129]

This episode was among the many signs that, within the world of British Calvinism, the practical divinity was coming under pressure from criticism of several kinds that included the objections of an "Antinomian" underground to the role of the law in the practical divinity. Tensions flared up anew in the 1640s and 1650s and, among the people who settled in New England in the 1630s, in the so-called "Antinomian controversy" of 1636–37. The story of how the practical divinity fared in New England and, after 1640, in England and Scotland, follows in chapter 9.

CHAPTER FIVE

A Reformation of Manners

JOHN DAVIDSON (D. 1604) WAS worried—and angry. Why were ministers in his Scottish homeland unfaithful servants of Christ, speaking "so coldlie that their flocks were consumed with hunger"? And why were they allowing the people of Scotland to decline into "grosse sinnes"? Invited to address the General Assembly that met in March 1596, Davidson detailed "the cheefe offences and corruptiouns in all estats." His strong words were approved a little later by the assembly, which fashioned them into a catalogue that "spared no sin and mitigated no offence," from tavern keeping and "filthie gain" in commercial transactions to misconduct among the clergy, the worst of these their failure to denounce public sins. As the assembly was ending, Davidson urged his colleagues to emulate Ezekiel, the prophet instructed by God to warn the "house of Israel" of its "wickedness" (Ezek. 3–4). Moved by these sermons, to which he added another on the parable of the faithful steward, the assembly accepted Davidson's advice to enter "into a new league with God," a covenant committing them "to walke more warily in their ways and more diligentlie in their charges."[1]

Davidson was singing a familiar tune. As those who signed the Covenant of 1596 surely knew, perceptions of "decline" had prompted fast days in Scotland ever since the 1560s. Several of these exercises in repentance and covenanting were means to the end of a firmer alliance between a Protestant state church and a monarchy (or civil state) susceptible to Catholic or more moderate tendencies. This was the purpose of the Negative, or King's, Confession of 1580/81, when the young James VI and most of the political class pledged never to allow "the usurped tyranny of the Roman Antichrist" to return to Scotland. John Knox had organized a similar event in 1565 at a moment when the political fortunes of Mary Stuart were on the mend. Akin to what Davidson was recommending in 1596, Knox had called on the General Assembly to institute a countrywide fast directed against "idolatry," with the queen as its implied target. Responding to Knox's sense of crisis, *this* assembly endorsed a "reformation of manners" and "public fast" as the means of "avoiding of the plagues and scourges of God, which appeared to come upon the people for their sins and ingratitude." Simultaneously, it urged the queen to suppress "the Mass" and other "such idolatry and Papistical ceremonies."[2]

Forty-three years after Davidson's fiery words of 1596, an English correspondent of Archbishop Ussher in Ireland warned him that England was in an irrevocable situation of decline, "this being the last and worst age of the world, and surely for all crying and notorious sins, as whoredom, lying, swearing, and drunkenness." John King, the man who wrote these words, was "persuaded that . . . our own nation is become the very worst of any in the Christian world." Hence the certainty that God would enact "some heavy judgment" on England if it persisted in its sinfulness. Venturing to imagine what this judgment might look like, King singled out the possibility of an invasion by Spanish troops aided by "English papists, whereof the kingdom is too well stored." "All things concur very untowardly against us," he concluded.[3]

These assertions took for granted a covenant God had established with the people of Scotland and those of England, each of them paralleling the covenant He had fashioned with ancient Israel. Unlike the covenant of grace, a national covenant was contractual and inclusive; freighted with conditions, it encompassed everyone.[4] The essential condition was resolute, heart-centered obedience of divine law. Otherwise, the God who promised to sustain a covenanted people would turn on them in anger, an assumption based on the many examples of covenants broken and covenants renewed in the Old Testament. Both versions of divine action appear in Psalm 78, which summarized what would happen when a "generation" charged with keeping God's commandments became "stubborn and rebellious" or, as noted by the psalmist, "forgot" what God had done for them. Provoked in this manner, a "wrathful God " (v. 21) "delivered" these covenant breakers to "captivity" (v. 61). Yet God was also "full of compassion" (v. 38) and enabled David, when he emerged as Israel's leader, to reclaim the covenant his people had come close to rejecting.

How were a covenanted people to know if they had ignored its obligations? The answer was obvious. God spoke to them through wonders or portents as well as through ministers who acted as His "watchmen," a role undertaken in ancient Israel by Hosea, Nehemiah, Jeremiah, and many others. Discerning the meaning of wonders was something almost anyone could attempt thanks to books such as Thomas Beard's *The Theatre of Divine Judgments*, a vast collection of stories about supernatural (or "preternatural") signs of God's wrath—comets, voices, apparitions, people who fell down dead after uttering a curse, corpses bleeding in the presence of a murderer, Catholic persecutors of the faithful choking on their own blood. Many other stories of this kind circulated via Stephen Batman's *The doome warning all men to the iudgemente* (1581) and cheap pamphlets publicizing "wonders."

In general, portents signaled God's dismay and possibly an impending crisis. Hence their importance to the genre of preaching known as the jeremiad. The English minister Laurence Chaderton used the occasion of a sermon he preached in London in 1579 to cite a host of "signs and forerunners of God's wrath" (floods, earthquakes, plague) He was using to summon England and especially its clergy to reform their behavior. Some forty years later, John Preston discerned a similar crisis for England and the Reformed international at a moment when French Protestants and English soldiers sent to help them were overwhelmed by Catholic troops. Preston interpreted these defeats as a sign of God's determination to punish the English people for betraying their covenant. Worse would follow, Preston warned, unless his countrymen repented: "Are not our allies wasted? Are not many branches of the Church [a reference to the Thirty Years War raging in Germany] cut off already, and more in hazard. . . . Are not these cracks to give warning before the fall of the House?"[5]

A narrative shaped around covenant, decline, and rebuke was double-edged. A nation or church that disobeyed divine law would be punished, but righteous monarchs and a faithful people could expect great blessings—the downfall of Mary Stuart, the defeat of the Spanish Armada, the failure of the Gunpowder Plot of 1605. The greatest of these blessings was the arrival of Protestantism, which had released Britain from the "tyranny" Knox and his heirs associated with Catholicism. More often, however, this narrative reiterated the scenario of decline or disobedience, a narrative played out in ceremonies of covenant renewal. As was said at the General Assembly of 1565, this ritual was God's means of "straitlie command[ing] reformation of maners in all estates."[6]

A process of this kind was widely endorsed. As historians of social discipline have reminded us, campaigns directed against "moral transgressions" occurred within the whole of "western Christendom" during the early modern period and (leaving aside the Inquisition), were especially important to societies where the Reformed international had a strong presence. In this chapter, however, the focus is on England and Scotland. At every level of governance in these two countries, officeholders acknowledged their responsibility for the well-being of families, towns, and nation. Ministers recognized a role for themselves as watchmen, and laypeople lobbied for reform as a means of warding off epidemics or devastating fires. This agenda was never a Puritan program in any strong sense of the term, or singular to British Protestants. Catholicism had its moral reformers and, in the Late Middle Ages, prophets such as Savonarola. For this reason, my narrative begins with a description of the common wisdom about decline and renewal, followed by a description of a more specifically Puritan version of this politics.[7]

Common Wisdom and the Moral Imagination

Moralists agreed.[8] Britain was in "decline," its moral and social health undermined by multiple versions of corruption. Long before Elizabeth I came to the throne, but resonating in her reign and continuing into the seventeenth century, high-pitched complaints about declension filled countless sermons, fast-day proclamations, collections of wonder stories, and sessions of the General Assembly in Scotland and of Parliament in England. According to the English homily "Against Whoredom and Uncleanness," England was beset by an "outrageous sea of adultery, whoredom, fornication, and uncleanness," all of them "grown into such an height that in a manner among many it is counted no sin at all." Nowhere was decline evoked more dramatically than in Philip Stubbes's *The Anatomie of Abuses: Containing A Discoverie, or Brief Summarie of . . . Notable Vices and Corruptions* (1583). Stubbes sounded the alarm about everything from stage plays to dancing and much else; in his overheated imagination, dancing was a "quagmire or puddle of all abomination" and a "preparative to wantonness" that "sprang from the teats of the Devils brest, from whence all mischeer els dooth flow." A prolific writer of inexpensive tracts about portents, Stubbes employed the same exaggerated language in his description of a covetous woman who, refusing to excuse a dying man for the debt she was owed, was stricken by the Devil, whereupon her body became "as black as pitch" and spewed "fesses most fettulent." Decline or decay was also occurring in the natural world, "dame Nature herself . . . "sending foorth . . . untimely births" and "monsters . . . both in man & beast." Hence the imperative that people repent, for "The day of the Lord cannot be farre of[f]."[9]

Extreme but not unique, Stubbes's litany of complaints serves as a useful point of entry into commonplaces about decline and its remedies. As in his publications, so elsewhere the conventional wisdom about decay, corruption, and disorder relied on a stock of truisms dating from Scripture, Late Antiquity, and the Middle Ages.[10] Some of this wisdom evoked the "sea of troubles" experienced by Shakespeare's Hamlet; his were inward or spiritual, but moralists discerned a sea of troubles everywhere they looked. Spiritual decay and social disorder had their counterpart in nature—the stars misaligned, the weather punctuated by storms and droughts, the birth of shockingly deformed fetuses. "Many are the wonders which have lately happened," declared the compiler of *A Miracle of Miracles* (1614) "as of sodaine and strange death upon perjured persons, strange sights in the Ayre, strainge births on the Earth, Earthquakes Commets, and fierie Impressions, with the execution of God himself from his holy fire [lightning] in heaven, on the wretched man and his wife, at Holnhurst." Portents of this kind confirmed the moral decay so shockingly apparent in the "overflow[ing]" of "adulteries, incests . . . robberies . . . and savage cruelty."[11]

Moralists likened this process of decay to the "plague," an all-too-familiar reality thanks to the presence of the bubonic plague in early modern Britain but even more alarming because of the biblical plagues God had inflicted on a disobedient people, first and foremost the plague of Exodus 32:35 that struck everyone who worshipped the golden calf, but also the seven plagues forecast in Revelation, a sequence culminating in an outbreak of disease as Babylon was being overthrown (Rev. 21:9). For other moralists, deformed births and similar corruptions of nature, all of them characterized as "monsters" or "monstrous," were telling signs of disorder. Or perhaps the appropriate term was an unstoppable "gangrene," which is how the mid-seventeenth-century English minister Thomas Edwards represented the religious turbulence of the 1640s.[12]

Taking this master narrative of decline for granted—"every day groweth worse & worse," Beard declared in *A Theatre of Divine Judgements*—moralists agreed on its causes. Chief among them was the immorality associated with a craving for alcohol ("drunkenness") and sex out of marriage. The first led to brawling and violence, the second, to unwed mothers whose illicit children burdened local systems of welfare and threatened the sanctity of marriage.[13] Sex between adults who were married to someone else—adultery—violated the seventh commandment and, in Jewish law, was considered a crime punishable by death, a penalty some Puritans wanted to revive. Incest, sodomy, and buggery (sex with an animal), were just as troublesome. Alongside sex, alcohol consumption, and a generalized "intemperance," church leaders and local magistrates placed "Sabbath-breaking," the practice of avoiding church services or, more commonly, of merrymaking on Sundays. In the Elizabethan *Second Book of Homilies*, moralizing about the Sabbath expanded into a Stubbes-like denunciation of people who "rest in ungodliness and in filthiness, prancing in their pride . . . painting themselves to be gorgeous and gay; . . . they rest in wantonness, . . . in filthy fleshliness; so that it doth too evidently appear that . . . the devil [is] better serviced on the Sunday than upon all the days in the week beside." Sabbath breaking was rivaled by a much-publicized site of disorder, the local inn or alehouse. Its role in moral decline figured in an archbishop's insistence that parish officials in Yorkshire make sure "that no innkeeper, alehouse-keeper, victualler, or tippler . . . admit or suffer any person or persons . . . to eat, drink, or play at cards, bowls, or other games in time of . . . preachings, or reading of homilies, on the Sundays or holy days." Like most of his fellow bishops, Edmund Grindal wanted to protect the sanctity of "holy" time by prohibiting shops from being open or allowing "fairs or common markets" during morning services. Beard agreed. In one of the chapters of *A Theatre of Divine Judgements*, he asserted that the Sunday Sabbath had been turned into a "day for tipling houses and taverns to be fullest fraught with ruffians" who pass the time singing "lecherous and baudie songs." This too was "the day when . . . blasphemies flie thickest and fastest: this is the day when dicing, dauncing, whoring, and . . . hatred" rise to the surface.[14]

More signs of decline emerged from the intersection of the marketplace and moral values. The world of commerce was overrun with "oppression," a word denoting self-serving or dishonest practices—inflated prices, mislabeled goods, the abuse associated with money lending, the government's practice of granting lucrative monopolies. Hence Richard Greenham's gloss on the eighth commandment ("Thou shalt not steal"), which he interpreted as obligating tradespeople and artisans never to deceive, extort, or oppress anyone. Self-interest contradicted the moral imperative of neighborliness and its near-synonym, social peace. Valuing peace, moralists complained of people who uttered curses (itself a violation of the third commandment), or shouted insults at others. Peace and peacemaking were high on the list of positive values, as was the golden rule (Matt. 7:12). Speaking as a good Elizabethan, William Perkins reminded his readers that "the office of love is to pour out again the same goodness that it hath received of God upon her neighbor, to be to him as it feeleth Christ to be to himself." For him and many others, peace was also about "equity" or fairness or "justice." Indeed, "public equity" was the "glory of all Christian commonwealths."[15]

As moralists pointed out, time, gender, and the body were deeply complicit in the making of disorder. The wrong kinds of people thronged the everyday world, people characterized as "brawlers" and "masterless" or as the "wicked, wandring, idle people of the Land" (beggars, thieves, vagrants, ex-soldiers, the unemployed). Their behavior threatened every aspect of social and moral order. As the conforming minister George Herbert complained, "idleness" was "great in itselfe and great in consequence; for when men have nothing to do, then they fall to drink, to steal, to whore, to scoffe, to revile."[16] The visible evidence of idleness included locations or practices as diverse as the London theater and dancing around maypoles. Commonplaces about the misuse of time flowed into representations of women as always and everywhere overly sexualized because of their "painted faces, resembling Jezebel," whose flagrant behavior aroused God to order that she be fed to dogs (1 Kings 16:31; 21:23). The opposite of the painted lady was the witch. Adding fuel to the flames of village conflict wherever she appeared, the witch overturned every moral rule by allying with the Devil and using her tongue to poison a community.[17] Books could also be frightening if they encouraged people to turn away from the moral discipline associated with the *right* kinds of reading. Hence the objections of William Tyndale to the appeal of "Robin Hood, and Bevis of Hampton . . . with a thousand histories and fables of love and wantonness, and of ribaldry, as filthy as heart can think," an outburst he concluded by citing St. Paul's criticism (1 Cor. 6) of "fornication, and all uncleanness, or covetousness."[18]

Other moralists focused on real-life enemies of British Protestants—the Catholic regimes in Europe and the presence of Catholics in Britain itself—for they threatened every aspect of moral order and civil authority. Catholicism had its own array of martyrs and wonders to rival the evidence assembled by

Beard and John Foxe, a repertoire that included modes of spiritual healing that British Protestants had rejected. Above all, the presence of Catholicism contradicted the premise that the social health of a nation depended on unity, or a common confession and a common set of values. A house divided against itself cannot stand (Mark 3:25): mindful of this precept, moralists took for granted that deep fractures around religion—not only Catholic/Protestant but also conformist/Puritan—weakened moral order and the authority of the state. Looking back on the unprecedented *disunity* of the Civil War period in British history, a minister underscored its consequences: "envy, malice, seditions, factions, rebellions, contempt of Superiors." Hence the many ritual occasions during which unity as an ideal was evoked, one of these the ceremonial opening of new Parliaments in England, when the Speaker of the House of Commons reminded everyone of the harmony that existed (or should exist) between the values of Parliamentarians and those of the monarchy.[19]

Across the Protestant spectrum, moralists agreed on the moral, social, and political alternative to a world so filled with disorder. In the aftermath of the Catholic uprising of 1569 in England, the Church of England homily (1571) "Against Disobedience and Wilful Rebellion" characterized Lucifer as "the great captain and father of all rebels" and rebellion itself as "the first and principal cause both of all worldly and bodily miseries" and the "very cause of death and damnation eternal." Hierarchy made its way into this argument because God had "ordained" the subordination of wives to husbands and children to parents, and "people" to the "governors and rulers" commissioned to serve in His stead, a principle based on Romans 13:1–2, which begins with the assertion, "Let every soul be subject unto the higher powers." Hence the imperative to bear the "yoke of subjection" willingly. The alternative was "confusion" that, disease-like, would destroy every benefit of authority. As the forceful Scottish minister Robert Bruce pointed out in sermons he was preaching in the 1580s, without such restraints no kirk "could be gathered" or "society" persist. When Elizabeth I complained to Archbishop Parker about the politics of a book she had read, he found himself imagining the disorder that was likely to erupt in England if the book was not suppressed, a disorder he likened to the Anabaptist "commonwealth" in 1530s Münster. For many moralists, "Münster" served as shorthand for a world turned upside, the kind of world likely to emerge from an insurrection. Little wonder, then, that memories of the recent past and ongoing Protestant-Catholic conflict fed the "obsession" of monarchs and moralists with the scenario of subversion from beneath.[20]

Social theorists valued authority for another reason, its role in the making of "common weal" or "common wealth." Popularized during the reign of Edward VI and a central theme of humanist social theory, this image and ideal took for granted that the right kind of leadership could restore social health to society. As was said in an English tract of 1542, "A king is anointed, to be a defense unto the people, that they be not oppressed nor overyoked, but by all godly and politic means to seek the common wealth of his people." In popular politics as well as within the discourse of common weal, a country's leader would use his or her authority to aid those most in need. Scripture was one source of this ethical-social program and its bearing on leadership. Thomas Sternhold's translation of Psalm 41 included the counsel that "The Lord will help that man again, / that helpeth poor and weak," and his paraphrasing of the Hebrew of Psalm 49 included a strikingly forceful lament about the "rich men" who "oppress the poor" and because of "vainly trusting in their goods," will "perish evermore." The "Book of Orders" issued by the government of Charles I in 1631 addressed these broad objectives by way of "orders" aimed at employing the poor, suppressing alehouses, and curtailing vagrancy—an agenda so encompassing that, in the words of a twentieth-century historian, "it is difficult to distinguish" the king's version of "social regulation" from that of the "Puritans."[21] Guided by these ethics, theorists of common weal called upon the Christian prince to enact policies that would remedy the grievances of the people. Speaking to the queen in 1570, Edward Dering advised her to "defend the fatherless and widow[ed], relieve the oppressed, and have no respect of persons in judgment."[22]

This was the high road, the path taken by an exemplary magistrate. The high road mattered to the governments of England and Scotland. In England, Henry VIII and his chief advisor, Thomas Cromwell, undertook a remarkable program of "renewal and reform" under the aegis of "commonweal." Slowly but surely, the civil state strengthened its means of regulating popular behavior and intervening at times of social and economic crisis. The Elizabethan Poor Law of 1601 and, in the late sixteenth and early seventeenth centuries, measures to suppress vagrancy were the doing of a reinvigorated administrative state—as it happened, a state gripped by a "paranoia" about disorder. In Scotland, James VI did his best to shut down interclan violence. In both countries, the administrative state wanted to regularize the rules that governed marriage. And in both, moralists supported an alliance of magistrates and ministers in behalf of order. Their cooperation epitomized the benefits of unity and hierarchy. Working together, judges and ministers could reestablish peace and order.[23]

Where civil governments led in the making of moral and social reform, state churches followed. Their principal mission may have been saving souls, but every parish church was also responsible for maintaining peace and order. What was special to the church was its responsibility for making everyone aware of moral rules God Himself had prescribed. Chief among these was the imperative to obey parents, superiors, ministers, monarchs, and God. When Grindal tried to persuade Elizabeth to tolerate the exercise of "prophesying" (see chap. 2), he emphasized the church's role in abetting obedience, using sermons as his example: "By preaching," he reminded the queen, "due obedience to Christian princes and magistrates is planted in the hearts of subjects:

for obedience proceedeth of conscience, conscience is grounded upon the word of God, and the word of God worketh this effect by preaching." Godly critics of the Church of England made the same point whenever they complained of nonresidency and pluralism; without ministers on hand to provide "publick instruction," the "multitude" would lapse into "wicked and traitorous practices" and become ungovernable.[24]

An ethics of obedience was pervasive in the collections titled *Homilies* (1562, 1571), which included sermons on topics such as "idleness," "drunkenness," "strife and contention," "swearing and perjurie," and "whooredome and adulterie," all of them preceded by the assertion that sermons were "the principal guide and leader unto al godlinesse and virtue" and the means by which "the people . . . may . . . learne their duety towards God, their prince, and their neighbours." The same connection between moral order and institutional religion threaded its way through visitation articles. Typically, Archbishop Parker used his visitations of the 1560s to ask if ministers in his diocese were "peace-makers [who] . . . exhort the people to obedience to their prince, and to all others that be in authority." Hence the importance of the well-ordered family or "little commonwealth," for it nurtured the practice and ethics of obedience. Summing up this wisdom, a minister of Puritan inclinations described the family as a "school wherein the first principles and grounds of government are learned."[25]

Ritual processes implemented what was said in sermons. Fast days tied to situations of the plague or other crises were the church's way of reincorporating laypeople into a community practicing peace and love.[26] Never staged with the same frequency in England as in Scotland, government and church-ordered fasts were usually a way of responding to unexpected disasters—a crippling fire, an outbreak of the bubonic plague—or to moments when social and political conflict seemed to worsen. As the literary historian Timothy Rosedale has pointed out, the rituals included in the *Book of Common Prayer* and, for that matter, the book itself abetted the common good. Instead of separating clergy from laity and those who knew Latin from those who conversed in the vernacular, the liturgy presumed an entire nation united around a pattern of worship. Moreover, its origins under Edward VI and its rebirth under Elizabeth I as a mandatory scheme of worship made it a sign and instrument of an "Erastian" state committed to hegemony in matters of religion.[27]

Baptism and, especially, Holy Communion were other means of sustaining peace and an ethics of "charity" or mutual love. In the Scottish *Book of Common Order*, the frightening language of 1 Corinthians 11:27–29 (see chap. 4) justified the assertion that "any" person who was "a blasphemer of God, an hinderer or slaunder of his worde, an adulterer, or be in malice or envie" could not participate in the sacrament. According to the 1552 version of the *Book of Common Prayer*, anyone who wanted to receive the bread and wine had to reconcile beforehand with neighbors, share with those in need, and practice an ethics of "charity with all men." In his much-reprinted catechism, Alexander

Nowell parsed the sacrament as enabling "brotherly love to our neighbours, that is, to all men, without any evil will or hatred."[28] More expansively, Nowell and his fellow clergy emphasized both parts of the "great commandment" (Matt. 26:36–40): love God and love your neighbor. Behind such injunctions lay the premise of interdependence, which Philip Stubbes translated into the moral imperative of generosity toward to others so "that all may live jointly together." In an England and Scotland experiencing fractures of many kinds— religious, social, economic, political—love and/or generosity to others were antidotes to decline. So was mercy. An English Protestant urged the readers of a funeral sermon he preached in 1601 to practice the traditional "six works of mercy" relating to the soul and "seven" relating to the social body: "To visit them which be sicke: to give drinke to them which be thirstie: to feed them which be hungry: to rdeeme the captives: to cloath the naked: to lodge the harbourlesse: and to bury the dead." On the eve of immigrating to Massachusetts in 1630, the layman John Winthrop reiterated this wisdom in a "Charitie Discourse" he shared with some of his fellow immigrants and others in England. Its message was simple. A people "knit together" by a "bond of love" would care for those in need. At his most eloquent, Winthrop imagined a community in which people lived "together in all meekness, gentleness, patience and liberality," to the point of being able to "mourn together, labor, and suffer together . . . as members of the same body," a passage he based in part on Ephesians 4:3.[29]

For sheer repetition of moral rules, however, nothing matched the weekly exercise of learning a catechism. The Ten Commandments had a prominent place in every such book, their importance underscored by how broadly they were interpreted. In a typical exegesis, an English catechism transposed the prohibition of murder in the sixth commandment into an indictment of quarreling and other versions of anger, an exegesis sanctioned by Jesus's words about anger in Matthew 5:21–22. An expansive reading of the seventh commandment, which prohibited adultery, described it as encompassing "lust" of many kinds—excesses of food and drink as well as "uncleannes with our neighbors wyffe" or the mere "desire" of such pleasures. An equally expansive reading of the eighth, "thou shalt not steal," turned it into a critique of marketplace ethics by emphasizing that the true Christian never sold something for more than it was actually worth or used "deceitful mesure or waightes." The same commandment also bound the godly to "be liberall to the poor" and "labor" in a "lawfull calling."[30]

The state churches had one other means of social discipline, a system of ecclesiastical courts. Delaying a description of the Scottish kirk session (see below, sec. 3), church courts in England were responsible for regulating marriage, divorce, inheritances, church attendance, Sabbath breaking, drunkenness, defamation, children born by unmarried women, adultery, and the alehouse. As well, these courts handled cases of nonconformity by both Catholics and Protestants, together with complaints about the behavior of parish clergy. The hard work was done by local church wardens who, year after year, "presented" people who had misbehaved. Penance was the most common punishment, with excommunication—that is, barring someone from coming to church, receiving the Eucharist, and being buried in consecrated ground—imposed in exceptional cases. Exceptional, because the goal was really reconciliation and reform. The ideal outcome was getting some one to confess and commit to (self-) reform. Whenever this happened, a local court customarily responded by welcoming lawbreakers back into the church. Often reconciliation broke down, perhaps because people failed to show up or courts bent over backwards to favor the more privileged or, in Puritan eyes, abused their authority to excommunicate laypeople. Nonetheless, they enclosed many local people within a framework of moral discipline.[31]

Alongside these rituals lay a set of rules that originated within Christian humanism. Relying on sources as diverse as the moralists of ancient Greece and Rome and the Christian tradition, humanists fashioned an ethics of self-discipline that foregrounded the contrast between idleness and work, the first a source of disorder, the second a means of strengthening the whole of society. Idleness and poverty were two sides of the same coin, a relationship the humanists wanted to alter in the context of a larger project of social and moral improvement. For them, a crucial means of doing so was education—for most people, a practical education aimed at equipping the poor to become productive workers. The making of a good society also depended on leaders and citizens who actively promoted a life of virtue centered on the humanist version of "moderation."[32]

The outcome of these perceptions and proposals was a widely endorsed reformation of manners[33]—endorsed, but never actually accomplished, or so it seemed to the moralists who lamented decline. Moral reform was the stone that constantly rolled back down the hill, thwarted by the reluctance of kings, nobles, and magistrates to do their part; the presence of so many ineffective ministers; and the resistance of sinners to the twin imperatives of repentance and self-regulating "watchfulness." Or was the problem the great mischief-maker Satan? As depicted by Nowell in his *Catechism*, "that subtle, guileful, and old wily serpent" was "like a ravening lion," ever active in exploiting "our own lusts" and "enticements of this world." Like his fellow moralists, Nowell ascribed "vices and offences" or more simply, "sin," to the Devil's cunning. Necessarily, most people would disobey divine law at some moment in their lives. Whatever the reason, year after year, church courts in England and kirk sessions in Scotland admonished unmarried men and women for having sex; year after year, church wardens and justices of the peace complained of Sabbath breaking.[34]

From a more recent perspective, the ineffectiveness of reform had social and economic sources. Twentieth-century social historians with no interest in churches or theology have proposed that programs of moral and social reform were thwarted by the demographic and social history of Tudor-Stuart Britain, a period in England that saw the rise of "a market society" and its consequences, one of them the "gradual separation of economic activity from social morality." More telling, perhaps, was the intersection of population growth and inflation. In England, many of the people who owned no land or other property wandered in search of work as servants or day laborers. Never fully incorporated into the routines of religious practice and social discipline, such people (most of them unmarried) were more likely to haunt a local alehouse or defy the village constable. Toward the end of the sixteenth century, their numbers were increasing while the cost of living was on the rise. Add in the social and economic disruptions caused by episodes of the plague and it seems inevitable that social practice among a very large share of the British people would contradict what churches and moralists were prescribing.[35]

Decline as perceived and perhaps as actual persisted for an entirely different reason, the confusion that accumulated around the meanings of authority and obedience.[36] In principle, authority was seamless. In practice, it was deployed in erratic or contradictory ways in towns, boroughs, and villages. Edinburgh was a case in point, for the burgesses who administered town affairs remained wary of James VI and I's attempts to dictate who could hold civil or religious office. Here as in London and elsewhere, a culture of "civic republicanism" (to borrow a phrase from the German historian Heinz Schilling) blunted the efforts of the civil state and state churches to curtail the "burgher elites" that dominated civic office. Something deeper was also involved, a suspicion of rules and values imposed from outside, a point of view that favored localism—that is, putting local values and communal peace ahead of instructions originating elsewhere.[37]

Since towns were where campaigns for reform can be most fully analyzed, it is crucial to recognize that these communities had their own means of sustaining social and religious harmony, one of them a realism about the consequences for social and family networks of punishing Catholics and nonconformists. Why fan the flames of difference when, in places such as Edinburgh, Aberdeen, and London, social peace endured thanks to the agility of Catholic and Protestant artisans and merchants to sidestep controversies about religion. As for sex between unmarried adults, was it all that dangerous given the likelihood that most of the men and women summoned before a church court for premarital sex would end up marrying each other? Irrevocable evidence of disorder to some, premarital pregnancies were more matter-of-fact events for others. Taverns, too, could be valued for the sociability they fostered.[38]

Thanks to popular wisdom of this kind, the authority of civil courts, kirk sessions, and orders emanating from afar was blunted.[39] Just as telling was the disarray at the highest levels of government. In theory, an ethics centered on unity and obedience was sustained by hierarchies that were God's making. At every turn, however, political rivalries and the indifference of rulers to a strong version of common weal principles contradicted this assumption. Conflict extended into the very heart of civil government thanks to competition for the prizes of office, a process overlaid in Scotland with the antagonism between clans and the nobility who led them. Another enduring source of tension was the reluctance of privileged groups to submit to church courts, a practice James VI endorsed when he told the General Assembly that no member of the nobility in Scotland could be excommunicated without his approval. Simultaneously, the workings of a nascent public sphere were undermining the aura of authority in high places. By the close of the sixteenth century and continuing into the seventeenth, the disarray at the highest levels of the English government was being publicized in manuscripts that passed from hand to hand or in printed pamphlets and books. No version of censorship halted the flow of gossip and criticism.[40]

The news was not all bad. According to another set of commonplaces, too much authority in the wrong hands was dangerous. By the early seventeenth century, the French social philosopher Jean Bodin was advocating a strong version of monarchical authority. Traces of this "absolutism" appeared in how James VI and I described himself and, more emphatically, in his son Charles I's self-understanding. For most British moralists, however, absolutism was dangerous given the tragic history of ancient Rome and Greece and the biblical record of God's response to evil kings. What happened again and again in the classical world and the Old Testament was frightening, the mutation of good kings and Christian bishops into "tyrants" who abused the "liberties" of the people or flouted divine law. Stories of this kind filled a section of *The Theatre of Divine Judgments*, which included a remarkable warning about the culpability of "great men" who "are more guilty and culpable of sin than any other." Reminding his readers that "there is a God that judgeth the earth," Beard singled out those who "are in the highest places of account, who being more hardened and bold to sin, do as boldly exempt themselves from all corrections and punishments due unto them, being altogether unwilling to be subject to any order of justice or law whatsoever." He was voicing a widely held disenchantment registered elsewhere in a Puritan-linked funeral sermon of 1602 where, having introduced the "works of Princes," the minister characterized these works as "done foolishly, rashly, and unjustly." In a commentary on parts of the Book of Revelation (1628), the English minister Henry Burton noted that a "lawful good King" could easily become a "usurping Tyrant." In another commentary on Revelation dating from circa 1640, the Massachusetts-based John Cotton observed that where "transcendent power is given," it "will certainly over-run those that give it." The corollary was obvious: "all power that is on earth [must] be limited."[41]

With institutions wavering in their zeal for enforcing the rules and vested interests intervening to protect their privileges, it should not surprise us that the response to decline and decay was spasmodic and the consequences of any action—a fast day or proclamation, a bishop's visitation, a harsh sentence by an ecclesiastical court—short-lived. Moral panics came and went, their arrival signaled by a flurry of new laws and/or an outpouring of complaints about the failure to enforce the laws that already existed. Simultaneously, witch-hunting surged, portent-mongering flourished, and the Antichrist raged more furiously against the faithful—or so it was alleged from dozens of pulpits. No historian has charted these spasms, but it seems likely that the enthusiasm for reform at the beginning of Elizabeth I's reign, the flurry of fast days accompanying Protestant objections to Mary Stuart, the surge of witch-hunting in some parts of lowland Scotland in the late 1590s, and another phase of it in mid-1640s England and Scotland fall into this category. Or moral panics could emerge in response to the plague, bad harvests, and a resurgence of Catholicism of the kind that seemed to be happening in late sixteenth-century Scotland and again in the 1620s. As night follows day, these seasons of moral fervor were succeeded by a sense of exhaustion and a slackening of rigor—to give way, at some point in time, to a fresh sense of crisis.[42]

The circumstances that impeded any national or collective reformation of manners also impeded the godly version of moral and social reform. We turn now to this version and its singularities. What made a godly reformation of manners unusual was how it was aligned with Martin Bucer's summary of Reformed themes and practices in *De Regno Christi*, the book he wrote for the eyes of Edward VI. Together with the practical divinity, Bucer's manifesto nurtured the hope that England and Scotland could be transformed into sanctified societies.

The Godly and the Good Society

A reformation of manners was immensely important to the advocates of a perfect reformation in Scotland and England. From the earliest days of Elizabeth I's reign, the godly in England were identified with this very program. When Job Throckmorton rose to speak on behalf of "puritans" in the English Parliament of 1585–86, he itemized practices he regarded as singular to Puritan-style reform: "To reprove a man for swearing, it is Puritanisme. To banishe an adulterer out of the house, it is Puritanisme. To make humble sute to Her Majestie and the high courte of Parliament for a learned ministery, it is Puritanisme." In 1621, a bill to strengthen the Sunday Sabbath was described by someone in the House of Commons (England) as "savour[ing] of the spirit of a Puritan."[43]

What was obvious to contemporaries should be just as obvious to us. Although "civic godliness" was widely endorsed, it had a special importance to a movement that envisioned a sanctified society, a sanctified church, and, among laypeople, a faith-centered commitment to living righteously. Armed with

these legacies from Calvin, Bullinger, and Bucer, Puritan-influenced presbyteries, synods, general assemblies, ministers, justices of the peace, magistrates,
and laypeople pressured church and state to accomplish more by way of reform. Simultaneously, moral vigilantes insisted that ministers denounce sin
and sinning wherever they discerned it.[44]

Puritan-style moral reform is dogged by stereotypes and half-truths. A few
of these date from the sixteenth and early seventeenth centuries, but the stereotypes that abound in modern Britain and America were mainly the doing
of liberal Protestants and secular cultural critics who propagated the image of
the Puritan as hostile to the arts, intolerant of dissent, and hyper-legalistic, a
paradigm closely tied to a narrative of modernity freeing itself from unnecessary restraints. Independently of this rhetoric, sociologists have attached the
Puritan movement to a "disciplinary revolution." By the middle of the twentieth
century, the assumption that social change and social discipline were parallel
processes was endorsed by those historians who turned Puritanism into a project of a "middling" social group that aspired to control those beneath them.
More recently, another generation of social historians has discounted every
aspect of this argument. Simultaneously, theologians, social theorists, and
historians have invalidated any strong version of the "Weber thesis," the
argument—already noted in chapter 4—that a new version of asceticism (the
"Protestant ethic"), driven by deep anxiety about the doctrine of predestination, abetted the rise of capitalism.[45]

Setting aside grand theory, what does Puritan-style reform look like when
it is situated in the contexts of Scripture, the Reformed international's emphasis on discipline as means to the end of a sanctified church, and the practical
divinity? In outline, this program becomes an array of themes and practices
that included the following:

> —having a broad definition of idolatry that melded the inward or "spiri-
> tuall" with the outward or "bodily" aspects of idol worship from "monu-
> ment" to tavern haunting on Sundays. Idolatry infected churches, local
> communities and the hearts and minds of every Christian;[46]
> —recognizing that sin is omnipresent and, unless held in check, certain
> to overwhelm love, justice, mercy, and righteousness in both the church
> and the commonwealth;
> —accepting divine law as binding on civil society and the church;[47]
> —adding the judicial laws of Moses, including those about adultery and
> the Sabbath, to British law. The Church of England wanted to protect
> holy time, but the Puritan movement went much further by purging the
> Christian year of holy days and festivities and expanding "rest" to in-
> clude all of Sunday, a day Richard Greenham characterized as "the
> school of all the other commandments";[48]
> —insisting that civil governments and monarchs endorse "wholesome

Lawes" and rebuking them in God's name when they ignored this responsibility;

—relying on a Word-based ministry to carry out the process of social and moral transformation, and being confident (in the words of the English minister Richard Baxter) that "the People would certainly be reformed" by such men, a premise reiterated in the 1620s by Samuel Ward of Ipswich: "where God hath raised up zealous Preachers, in such townes this Serpent [of drunkenness] hath no nestling." In godly circles, stories circulated of how the right kind of preaching had altered the behavior of a town, family, or person—stories without any counterpart among conformists;[49]

—embedding reform in descriptions of repentance and sanctification. According to the firmest of commonplaces within the practical divinity, being "sanctified" or walking "uprightly before God" was linked to assurance of salvation, an argument grounded on biblical verses such as 2 Peter 1:10 and Hebrews 12:1–14. Conversely, those who "doe noe good works declare that they neyther are justified nor sanctified," an argument reiterated in the Scottish Confession (1560), which described everyone from murderers and oppressors to drunkards and idolaters as having "neither true faith, neither any portion of the Spirit of the Lord Jesus," the proof of this being their "wickedness." In his English sermons, Thomas Hooker was emphatic: people who "will not . . . forsake their lewd practices . . . cannot . . . obtaine" grace. On the other hand, it was never too late to repent and return to God. Collective and personal repentance was the real driver of this process, as Bucer recognized by emphasizing the ritual of the fast day;[50]

—making discipline a mark of the true church, relocating supervision of moral and social behavior to local parishes, introducing the office of elder, and extolling the possibility of a "most perfect and absolute order" purged of "unbridled license of ungodly living";[51]

—tightening access to the sacraments of baptism and Holy Communion to strengthen the identity of the church as a sanctified community, a goal more within reach and, in fact, more important than achieving a sanctified society;[52]

—emphasizing the special relationship among the godly in their symbolic identity as the body of Christ, an identity manifested in peace, mutuality, and "love of the brethren" (1 John 3:14) and particular covenants to keep "lives and hearts in good order." Arguing in favor of gathered churches (see chap. 8), an English minister extolled the spiritual temper of such communities: "there is, or can be, the like love one to another; the like care one for another; the like spiritual watchfulness one over another; the like union and communion of members in one mystical body, in a sympathy of affections . . . as is described, Psalm. Cxxxiii."

Sympathy or "compassion" was also how the godly should respond to
the suffering of others;[53]

—attaching a reformation of manners to the workings of divine providence and the covenantal relationship between God and those He favored. Providentialism, or the practice of deciphering signs from
heaven deemed of God's doing, was not unique to Puritans but, as Alexandra Walsham acknowledges in her acute history of this way of thinking, the godly were drawn to it more than others;[54]

—nurturing literacy among ordinary people as a means of expanding
their knowledge of Scripture and therefore of divine law;

—regarding "oppression" and poverty as morally wrong and hoping to
undo their consequences for as many people as possible, although favoring the worthy poor;[55]

—evoking "equity" and "justice" as key aspects of "righteousness," and, in
their name, calling for reform of English civil and criminal law;[56]

—accepting coercion by the civil state and state church as part of any
comprehensive program of reform, but hoping that people would participate voluntarily via oaths, covenants, and a heartfelt response to the
Word;

—urging restraint or "moderation" in appetites for worldly goods, and
condemning "popular" customs such as card playing and dancing. Like
everyone else, Puritan moralists were troubled by women's sexuality
and dress.[57]

A single book spelled out this agenda and may have influenced its British
advocates. When Martin Bucer was in England (1549–51), he drafted a blue-
print for transforming the state church and country into sanctified communities. He addressed the document to the young king Edward VI, the person he
was counting on to "restore the Kingdom of Christ in your realm."[58] In the first
and longer section of *De Regno Christi* (kingdom of the Son of God), Bucer
described a church restored to the purity of the apostolic period because it
adhered to Scripture in determining doctrine, discipline, and worship. Such a
church would be a "communion, not of profane persons, but of saints," made
so by the authority of Scripture and the power of the Holy Spirit. Via these
instruments, it would undertake a process of sanctification, doing so voluntarily because Christians are "a free and voluntary community, serving God not
out of constraint but willingly, as if there were no laws to compel us." Such a
church needed a corps of ministers who taught the reality of God's "unbearable
anger" with those who disobeyed divine law. Although Bucer hinted at
Anabaptist-style exclusivity in his understanding of a sanctified church, he
acknowledged that it would continue to include "hypocrites" but also bar them
from the Lord's Supper, which he wanted to restrict to those who could demonstrate "true repentance for sin." The point of having lay elders was to ensure

each church had officers who kept everyone but the "worthy" from the sacrament. (Deacons would look after the poor.) Access to baptism was also restricted. These steps taken, the church would emulate the church described in Acts 4:32, a group of people who "embrace each other . . . with supreme love and have a most attentive mutual concern for each other" or, as Bucer also said, fulfill the obligation (Matt. 7:12) of love of one's neighbor.[59]

In the second part of *De Regno Christi*, Bucer described the ideal Christian commonwealth and the responsibilities of the Christian prince, Parliament, and other civil institutions. Reiterating a core premise of Reformed political theology, Bucer called on Edward VI and England's godly magistrates to fulfill the role of "Christian prince" modeled by certain kings in the Old Testament. Thereafter, he outlined fourteen policies the king should pursue. Much of what he said about education, idleness, luxury, and poverty echoed humanist teachings. When it came to the legal system, however, Bucer's biblicism took over. The moral rules spelled out in the Ten Commandments were everlasting, as much a part of the new covenant with Christ as they were of God's covenant with ancient Israel. Hence the recommendation that capital crimes include Old Testament rules about adulterers and children who rebelled against their parents. Both should be put to death, as should those who blasphemed. On the other hand, Bucer disapproved of English laws that made theft of property above a certain amount a capital crime. In a godly commonwealth, thieves would not be executed but, in keeping with biblical rules, make restitution. Marriage should become a matter of civil law and divorce permitted. In general, Bucer emphasized repentance and reconciliation as what the law should encourage. He also endorsed the importance of fast days as means to the same end.[60]

It may seem audacious to attribute the making of a Puritan-style reformation of manners to a book that was not printed in English in the sixteenth century—in fact, it was not printed in its entirety in English until the mid-twentieth century. Yet it shaped the *First Book of Discipline* (1561) and the second of 1578, and a case has been made for its importance to Matthew Parker and Edmund Grindal, who made notations in his personal copy. That other Elizabethans admired the book is apparent from a letter Thomas Sampson sent William Burghley (undated, c. 1573) urging him to "apply" himself to a Bucer-like program of ecclesiastical reform.[61] Many years later (1641), a group of Puritan clergy writing under the pen name of Smectymnuus cited it, as did John Milton, who incorporated Bucer's comments on divorce into a brief tract, *The Judgement of Martin Bucer, concerning Divorce* (1644), to bolster the case he was making for its legality, in the same decade in which Scottish Presbyterians were citing *De Regno Christi*. And, in the 1650s, Richard Baxter came under its spell.[62]

Like other schemes of reform, the Bucer-Puritan version was dogged by the indifference of local people and, in Scotland especially, of the privileged few. In

that country, assembly after assembly rebuked the nobility for their "great negligence in the punishing of vices" as diverse as "adultery, blood shedding and
sorcery." Everywhere, as well, strong words about protecting the Lord's Supper
did not prompt systematic efforts to exclude the unworthy, and in towns
such as Aberdeen the magistrates were reluctant to enforce the letter of the
law when it came to "horning" (banishing) vagrants. Godly reform was also
dogged by the contradiction between its aspirations for peacemaking and the
conflict it aroused. Where there was smoke—the many assertions that the Puritan movement was divisive or seditious—there was fire. Time and again,
godly ministers emphasized the gulf between the worthy few and the many
who were servants of Satan. In Chelmsford, where the blunt-spoken Thomas
Hooker preached in the 1620s, he characterized most of the townspeople as
members of "the Devils camp." In his vision of the town's culture, the godly
were at war "with the drunkard, with the profane swearer, with the maypole
dancer." Others were just as confrontational—Davidson in Scotland, Samuel
Ward in Ipswich—even as some urged the importance of peacemaking.[63]

Covenant making involved other contradictions, as did any evocation of
conscience. Was a covenant meaningless if people were coerced into taking it?
Theologically, the correct answer was yes, for covenanting presumed the workings of repentance and the presence of faith. Nonetheless, the political importance of broad-based covenanting seemed to have justified coercion (see chaps.
7–8). And, although endorsing the injunction to obey rulers even if they were
tyrants, the movement wrestled with the question of how to behave in the presence of a ruler who violated divine law. [64]

Despite an enduring confusion about means and ends, the agenda of the
godly became a significant presence in certain parts of England and informed
the activism of political leaders such as Henry Huntington (see chap. 2). In
keeping with what was said in *De Regno Christi* about men of his rank as leaders of a reformation of manners, Huntington founded schools, subsidized the
distribution of coal to poor people in Leicester, set up a workshop to train cloth
workers, and helped the unemployed during an epidemic of the plague. These
many services were summed up in an inscription on his tomb that read, "To
poor and to needy, to high and to low, / Lord Hastings was friendly, all people
doth know; His gates were still open the stranger to feed, And comfort the
succourless, always in need."[65]

What Huntington attempted in his part of England others were attempting
in towns and villages in the southeast and the west.[66] The three Suffolk County
towns of Bury St Edmunds, Kedington, and Dedham are among the best-
documented examples of this process. In Bury St Edmunds, a change of leadership in the mid-1580s enabled "godly townsmen" to begin a local version of
"lectures by combination" staffed by ministers who took turns preaching on
market days. With town government in the hands of the godly, the leadership
"set out in meticulous detail their vision of the godly borough" in an elaborate

list of bylaws. Typically, one of these was about idleness and how to curtail it. As a first step, the town council told the overseers of the poor to prepare an accurate census of the able-bodied poor and place them in a local industry. In other bylaws, the new leadership took aim at alehouses, telling constables to inspect these places at least once a week so that fines could be levied on anyone who played "unlawful games" or drank too much. Knowing that these activities distracted people from observing the Sunday Sabbath, the leadership added rules prohibiting alehouse keepers and others from hosting stage plays, comedies, and other forms of entertainment. In Kedington, the townspeople were "very ignorant and prophane, being generally aliens and strangers from the commonwealth of Israel." Or so they seemed to Samuel Fairclough when he arrived as the parish minister in the late 1620s. Before long, his sermons (four a week, it seems) and catechizing had persuaded hundreds of people to undertake a more disciplined way of life. Fairclough owed some of his success to the support of the local magnate and staunch parliamentary Puritan Nathaniel Barnardiston, who helped him persuade "the substantial men of the town" to enforce the "attendance" of entire households at the exercise of catechizing. Another goal, also apparently a success, was getting the townspeople to accept tighter rules for access to the Eucharist. Fairclough's was a notable experiment in what could be accomplished when ministry and magistracy collaborated.[67]

In Dedham, a town where the godly had a strong presence, a group of men drafted fifteen "orders" in 1585 to abet the securing of "Christian order." A mixture of the social and the moral, and "imprinted" throughout "with the earnest godliness" of the men who drafted the document, it opened with an emphasis on "the right use of the lordes daie." Thereafter, parents were told to make sure their children were catechized, a schedule was set up for examining anyone who wanted to participate in the monthly Eucharist (a key criterion being if they lived "charitablie with all their neighbors"), and householders ("as many as may be spared" from work) were summoned to attend twice-weekly lectures. As in Bury St Edmunds, the makers of this document wanted all children in the town to learn how to read. More unusual was the decision to meet the expense of teaching "pore mens children" by a special offering at each month's service of Communion. The town officers added other means of bringing order to the lives of the poor, one of them a scheme of household visits aimed at identifying the "disordered" and urging them to leave the town, information the officers also used to discern certain needs and remedy them. As well, the Orders of 1585 touched on premarital sex, or "filthines before . . . marriage," which the town minister was asked to denounce in ways that would "terrify" anyone who committed this sin. The most significant of the orders was akin to a covenant. Limited to townspeople deemed worthy of participating in Holy Communion, the document asked them to "settle" any "discord" privately before turning to civil or ecclesiastical courts. More unusually, the social ethics embedded in the orders touched on the relationship between people deemed "of habilitie" and their "poore neighbors" who aspired to godliness, with the first group encouraged to invite the second to dine with them. Via this practice, the orders endorsed the goal of reconciliation or unifying fellowship emphasized in *De Regno Christi* and the ethics attached to Holy Communion.[68]

One other well-studied project of reform, this time in the Dorset county town of Dorchester, was exemplary. There, some of the townspeople were accustomed to mocking the godly as a "Counterfeit Company and pack of Puritans." The situation began to change with the arrival in 1605 of John White, a conforming but resolutely evangelical minister. When a fire in 1613 destroyed half of the town, White and his allies seized on the disaster as a warning sign from heaven. A decade later, with "puritan reformers" dominating its membership, the town council undertook a remarkable array of initiatives: a new hospital (akin to what we would characterize as a workhouse) "for the setting of poor children on work," a "vast increase in poor relief," "improved care for the sick and elderly," and better opportunities for becoming literate. Simultaneously, magistrates and constables were doing their best to clear streets and taverns of vagrants and curtailing disorder on Sundays. Soon, the success of this program was evident in higher attendance at church services, substantial donations of money to charitable causes, and fewer pregnancies among unmarried women.[69]

In the early 1630s or a little earlier (the dating is uncertain), White summed up his aspirations for Dorchester in a list of "Ten Vows." The first of these, which called on everyone to "cleave unto the true and pure worship of God" and oppose "all ways of innovation or corruption," referenced the anti-puritan policies of Charles I that prompted the Parliament of 1628–29 to warn against "innovations" (see chap. 7). The same politics of religion accounted for the eighth and ninth vows, which singled out "the gospel at home and abroad" as needing support—that is, support for Protestants who were refugees from the Thirty Years War. As in other programs of reform, however, the central themes emerged directly out of the practical divinity and its emphasis on sanctification. Hence the importance of devotional exercises as a means to the end of sustaining "Christian peace" and overcoming selfishness: children learning a catechism, adults "watch[ing]" themselves "daily" and acknowledging their "failings," the practices of "reading hearing and meditating Gods word," humbling of "hearts," being willing to accept "brotherly admonitions," abandoning "groundless suspicions, slanders, and contentions," reconciling with neighbors, avoiding "all ways of gain" that were "scandalous," attending church services, "using time wisely for spiritual ends," and "work[ing] out" their "salvation with fear and trembling" (a reference to Phil. 2:12).

In a preamble White attached to the Ten Vows, he placed his vision of Christian fellowship or community in the context of decline. The punishments God was inflicting on "neighbor" churches—another reference to the Thirty

Years War—were judgments He was entitled to make of Dorchester, which had its share of sinners. The signs of decline were obvious: "security" and "deadness of heart," "pride and self love," "love of the world," "contention and envying one another," and a cooling of "love and affection towards our brethren." All these were signs of mutual affection gone sour, as was another word he used, "luke-warmness" in "zeal for God's honour and unto his truth." Most of those who read or listened to the vows would have recognized the reference to Laodicia (Rev. 3:15-16), the "luke-warm" city that God threatens to disown, a verse the English Puritan minister Thomas Brightman had recently interpreted as an allusion to the Church of England (see chap. 7).

From diagnosis White turned to the antidote of "love" or mutuality that Christ had endorsed and the apostle John reiterated in 1 John 3:14. For White, a love-centered ethics should characterize the relationship of the godly with those who were experiencing duress. "Take nearer" to your "hearts" our "afflicted Brethrens distresses," he urged the townspeople, and provide them the necessities of food and clothing. Did White ask the town council to adopt these vows or expect the people who were attending church services to enter into covenant? This seems likely given his recommendation that the townspeople "bind" themselves "by a solemn vow, and covenant with the Lord our God to endeavor . . . the practice" of the ten duties he had listed.[70]

The town records say nothing about how the vows were publicized or enforced. Presumably, White incorporated their spirit and substance into his everyday preaching. Like the vows themselves, he owed his understanding of the Word as an agent of transformation to the practical divinity and the example of men such as Edward Dering, the minister who spoke so forcefully in the presence of Elizabeth I. White wanted Dorchester's town officers to do everything they could to align social behavior with moral and ethical values, yet he took for granted that outward or merely institutional-driven changes would never be as effective as a grace-driven righteousness or sanctification. In a very real sense, the making of a sanctified society and sanctified church depended on both. An agenda of social reform from one perspective, the Ten Vows was also deeply rooted in the practical divinity.

To understand the connections between social reform and spiritual renewal or rebirth, it may help if we glance again at Arthur Dent's *Plain Mans Pathway to Heaven* and a text of the next generation, Henry Scudder's *The Christians Daily Walke* (1631). Dent was unrelentingly moralistic in his description of the true "pathway" to heaven. As he pointed out repeatedly, the quest for grace was also a quest for self-discipline and unstinting watchfulness. Without these, no one would be included among the redeemed. In the early pages of *The Plain Mans Path-way to Heaven*, he characterized the people who fell outside the economy of grace as infected with "plague sores," his evocative phrase for moral and social faults that included pride, whoredom, covetousness, swearing, lying, drunkenness, idleness, and oppression. Personal and collective at the same time, these were "Deadly venome . . . to the Soul" and also the sins of an entire "Nation"—that is, a nation guilty of flouting divine law, as England most certainly was. In passages of this kind, *The Plain Mans Pathway* became a warning cry to Dent's countrymen to repent. Returning to assurance of salvation in the book's closing pages, Dent argued that, next to the inward "work of God's grace" apparent in the soul, the surest evidence of knowing who was saved and who was among the reprobate was social ethics, or behavior. The reprobate were amoral in every possible way—Sabbath breakers for sure, but also the kinds of people Dent addressed collectively as "you": "You break out sometimes into horrible Oaths and cursings. . . . Your wife is Irreligious, your children dissolute and ungracious, your servants profane and careless. You are an example in your own house of all Atheism and conscienceless behavior. You are a . . . spend-thrift, a drinker, a common Ale-house haunter . . . and, to conclude, given to all Vice and naughtiness." On the other hand, the elect were known for "Keeping of . . . Sabbaths. Truth. Sobriety. Industry. Compassion. Humility. Chastity. Contentation," "temperance" and "Brotherly kindness," all of these practiced in response to the imperative to "subdue" the body, "dye to sin, and live to righteousness." Turning, once again, to England as a whole, Dent credited godly ministers and the godly themselves with preserving it from the wrath of God, the godly doing so by forming a "bond" with civil magistrates obligating them to uphold divine law.[71]

Scudder's *The Christians Daily Walke* brings us even closer to the social ethics embedded within the practical divinity. Writing three decades after Dent, he was more confident that Protestantism had overtaken Catholicism as the faith of the English people. Even so, he was realistic about popular indifference to rule-bound moralism. He worried, too, that some of the godly were not practicing the pilgrim-style "duties" he regarded as normative. His description of the spiritual life included ecstatic experience and a social ethics of "equity" and "affection toward others" (chap. 9), but his principal theme was "strictnesse" in how time was used, the "frugall" appearance of the clothes someone wore, and the day-long observance of Sunday Sabbath. Preparing for the Lord's Supper was another means of implanting a "constant and . . . unfained endeavor to perform all duties." Crucial, too, was the moral and social distance between the godly and those who "yet remain mere worldlings" or were "lukewarme professours." From Scudder's perspective, such people were little better than the "drunkards" and "whore-masters" who thwarted every attempt at a reformation of manners. Like Dent before him, he invited his readers to compare their own "watchfulness" with those who were undisciplined.[72]

In *De Regno Christi*, Bucer had emphasized the institutional means of accomplishing a reformation of manners: church, ministry, magistrates, education, measures to alleviate poverty. All these, plus the family, continued to figure in local programs of civic godliness. Yet by 1600 and increasingly thereafter, the practical divinity and a reformation of manners were two sides of the same coin. Everyone seeking assurance of salvation knew that this process entailed doing the hard work of self-examination, repenting for sins both small and large, and reordering everyday life around the imperatives of watchfulness and edification. Heart-centered piety and outward behavior (or social ethics) were really one and the same.

Godly Reform in Scotland

A reformation of manners was high on the agenda of the earliest Scottish reformers. At the very debut of the Scottish reformation, they incorporated this goal into the *First Book of Discipline* and the Confession of 1560, which underscored the "wickedness" of humankind as evidenced in "murderers, oppressors, . . . adulterers," and "filthy persons." By the close of the 1560s, John Knox and his allies had added two other texts to this repertory, an "Order for a Fast" (1565) followed in 1569 by an "Order of Excommunication and of Public Repentance." According to the *First Book of Discipline*, "No Commonwealth can flourish or long indure without good lawes and sharpe execution of the same, so neither can the Kirk . . . be brought to purity . . . without . . . ecclesiastical discipline." The list of sins the church should punish began with "drunkenness" and extended to "fornication, oppressing of the poore," and "slander." Nearly two decades later, the General Assembly of 1588 reported an appalling array of practices among "the poor," most of them apparently practicing "filthy adultery, incest [and] fornication, [their] children unbaptized, and they themselves never" attending services or participating "in the sacraments." Apart from recommending another general fast, the assembly urged that alms be withheld from such people until they proved their own baptisms and had any children baptized. This year, too, the kirk reported that, contrary to law, people were attempting to bury corpses within a parish church, a practice that signaled the persistence of Catholic teachings about consecrated ground. Progress must have seemed impossibly slow, a perception that may account for the stern tone of the Order of Excommunication: "all crymes that be [against] the law of God deserve death, deserve also Excommunicatioun from the societie of Christis Church." Yet the records show that statements of this kind existed alongside others affirming an ethics of "equitie, justice" and "compassion upone the poore."[73]

Despite the headwinds of civil war in the late 1560s and early 1570s, general assemblies continued to reiterate this agenda and strengthen the apparatus for carrying it out. Described in the *Book of Discipline*, lay elders and the kirk session (the Scottish equivalent of English ecclesiastical courts) were incorporated into the more hierarchical structure outlined in the *Second* of 1578, which emphasized the role of presbyteries and synods. Up and running in a few towns by the 1570s, kirk sessions gradually spread through lowland

Scotland.[74] Where the kirk led, Parliament was quick to follow. As early as 1563 it singled out witchcraft and adultery as capital crimes. Fornication and incest were condemned in 1567, adultery again in 1581, and the Sunday Sabbath repeatedly protected (1579, 1593 and 1594). Before long, the list of public and private sins had expanded to include drinking, "oppressing of the poor," contentious speech ("slander"), celebrations of Christmas, usury, and the reprise of Catholic-style burials. The moralizers' agenda also encompassed several of the priorities Bucer had borrowed from humanism—in particular, overcoming illiteracy and limiting poverty. At a moment (1596) when the assembly was convulsed by a sense of moral decline, it expanded this list to include the presence of "idle persons without lawfull calling" whose children were unbaptized, unlawful marriages that local judges were ignoring, "cruell oppression" of "poore tenants," idolatry (as evidenced in pilgrimages and carol singing at Christmas), and the decay of family religion.[75]

As in England, the advocates of moral discipline incorporated the Lord's Supper into the process of parish discipline, a principle insisted upon in the *Book of Common Order*. In "preparation" sermons for the sacrament, Robert Bruce was marvelously evocative about the importance of being "in love and charity" with neighbors," insisting that, without love of this kind, "you are not a member of His [Christ's] Body." On the other hand, John Craig was prompted to write his *Shorte Catechisme* by the apparent indifference of the "great multitude" to the requirement that anyone wanting to participate in the sacrament know the "Principal Heads of our Christian Faith." Subsequently, Craig prepared a much briefer version, *Ane Form of Examination before the Communion* that ministers were urged to buy in "bulk" and distribute to every family in their parish.[76]

Strong words from the General Assembly and local initiatives to impose social discipline became a prominent aspect of Scotland's Protestant culture. As the historian Michael Graham has emphasized, the leaders of the kirk became adept at refining the substance of reform in response to political circumstances, as happened in the 1590s when Catholicism seemed so menacing and James VI stepped out of line. Yet in ways that paralleled the campaign for social discipline in England, the Scottish version was hampered by the reluctance of judges, burgh leaders, magistrates, and parliaments to come down hard on offenders or do so consistently. Nonetheless, detecting and (it was hoped) suppressing sex out of marriage, adultery, cursing, violations of the Sunday Sabbath, and the like kept kirk sessions busy. Human nature being what it was, success in any grand sense of the term was elusive, as evidenced by the complaints of a kirk session in early seventeenth-century Glasgow about the women who entered "the Kirk dore . . . with their plaids upon their heads" and, faces covered, slept during most of the service. Or perhaps it was the habit among some people of leaving church services early or not attending at all.[77]

Nonetheless, kirk sessions were where, in real life, thousands of Scottish men and women repented their misdeeds. The workings of these courts overlapped with the workings of the civil government. Careful studies of who served on them has revealed close ties between elders and those who served in town governments. (Parish ministers were also involved.) At this level, the two-kingdoms theory was overtaken by a common concern for moral discipline and social peace and, more tellingly, overtaken by the assumption that civil authorities should do the actual work of punishing the people convicted of adultery, witchcraft, or other major faults. For sure, kirk sessions were never "of the people" or their members democratically elected by the parish. Nonetheless, they were no respecters of persons. As John Knox and others repeatedly emphasized, Scots of high status and low were equally under the watch and care of these groups.[78]

In the main, kirk sessions wanted the people brought before them to repent, as many in fact did, for this process opened the door to reconciliation with that person's parish church and civil community. A ritual thus came into being, a carefully scripted process of shaming wrongdoers. Customarily, the women and men caught having premarital sex or violating the rules about the Sunday Sabbath were asked whether they were willing to confess their misdeeds and acknowledge the authority of the church. As part of this procedure, some of these people were required to attend church services wearing a white robe and sitting on a "stool of repentance" in full view of everyone. The "Ourder of Repentance" (1569) specified the "feare and terrour . . . of God's Judgments . . . and dolour for the same" that the repentant person should experience and, if these emotions were deemed "unfeigned," the rite would conclude with "reconciliation" between the "Penitent" and the congregation. In a dozen years in Perth (1577–1590), a substantial majority of the people who came before the court acknowledged their faults—commonly, sex out of marriage—and were fined, shamed by having to sit on the stool of repentance, briefly imprisoned, or threatened with banishment. In the longer workings of this system, very few people were excommunicated, a penalty local courts seem to have avoided because it was too severe.[79]

Another ritual the kirk sessions endorsed was the sacrament of baptism. Not, of course, baptism as it happened within intact families, but as a means of incorporating abandoned children or those born to unmarried women into the church by providing them with the equivalent of godparents. Doing so was so important that kirk sessions sought out parents who would sponsor abandoned children and orphans for the rite.[80] Yet rigor could rise to the surface, as it did in 1585 when Perth was experiencing a severe epidemic of the plague and a man and woman convicted of adultery were executed. With sermons ringing in their ears about the relationship between plagues and public sins, the kirk sessions enforced the parliamentary statute that otherwise it preferred to ignore.[81]

Failure and Success

Accomplishing a reformation of manners was as unlikely in England and Scotland as the aspiration to turn everyone into the piously repentant. These two goals were inseparable but, from another point of view quite different, for church courts or the state could coerce the unruly into behaving and remedy the situation of the poor. On the other hand, heart-centered repentance could not be coerced, and as Hooker's lecture-day sermons in Chelmsford indicate, Puritan-style evangelism took for granted that many people would not become sincere Christians. Moral reform was potentially inclusive, but the practical divinity was shadowed by the possibility that a sanctified church would be limited to the faithful few.

Like the ocean, moral reform rose and fell, energized at some moments and subsiding at others. Each spasm illuminated inconsistencies or contradictions in the workings of moral reform. What the moral laws of the Old Testament prescribed was different from what kirk sessions and local churches or governments practiced. Instead of handing cases of sex out of marriage or adultery over to the civil state, kirk sessions resorted to shame and similar penalties. In England, a "godly" Parliament made adultery a capital crime in 1650. But the statute was crafted to exempt members of Parliament from its penalties and was rarely enforced. Much was said in sermons and manuals of devotion about keeping the unworthy from the Lord's Supper, but as the Scottish minister George Gillespie suggested in his defense of Presbyterianism (see chap. 8), local churches and ministers hesitated to do so knowing the outcome could be severe conflict.[82] In early New England, the capital crimes that seem so abusive to a modern eye—children disobeying parents, for example, or adultery—were rarely (or never) enforced. And, as the historian Philip Benedict has shown in his comparative study of Reformed churches, the same inconsistency and inefficiency dogged every attempt to install disciplinary religion.[83]

To these thickets of ideology, representation, mythmaking, and actual history, theology contributed the assumption that the church on earth, although always imperfect because it contained both tares and wheat, was moving toward greater purity in keeping with God's grand design and Christ's vision of the coming kingdom. On the one hand, therefore, it was imperative that the church have the means of doing so. This was why the church as an institution needed the right kind of minister and why church discipline should be transferred from ecclesiastical courts to local churches themselves. Just as important was ensuring that local churches excluded unrepentant or uninformed people from the sacraments. Scripture and theology validated two other aspects of this program, the presence of a Christian magistrate who protected the church from its enemies and the enforcing of laws God had given the children of Israel.

Another basic premise was the reality of human sinfulness. Because sin and sinning were so omnipresent, the means of keeping them at bay had to combine discipline within the church with state-sponsored policies aimed at quelling disorder. Keeping sin at bay was why godly people joined together in "bands" and covenants. The prevalence of sin and sinning also meant that the visible church was never coeval with civil society—institutionally for the time being, perhaps, but as the kingdom neared, the saints would withdraw from the "world."

The punitive or disciplining aspects of Puritan-style moral reform were real, but they coexisted with an insistence on the "liberty" God was restoring to the saints. Thanks to the workings of the Holy Spirit, some people passed out of bondage to sin and became "free" in a special way. Hence the emphasis in the Scottish kirk sessions and descriptions of fast days and covenants on repentance, for it enabled sinners to reclaim their place at the table (as it were) and communities or nations to reclaim God's trust. At such moments, openness or possibility overcame restraint or condemnation. Liberty and obedience (or human freedom and divine sovereignty) existed side by side in this story, each tightly intertwined with the other. Here, especially, the underpinnings of a Puritan-style reformation of manners mirrored what was said about becoming a "new creature." To be liberated from sin was never to be liberated from sinning; to experience the terrors of the law or "deadness" was never to forfeit the joyous experience of union with Christ. Conjunctions of this kind became less plausible once western culture moved toward "individualism." But their presence in early modern England and Scotland (and as well, early New England) go far toward explaining the substance of a Puritan-style reformation of manners.

CHAPTER SIX

Royal Policies, Local Alternatives

JAMES I WAS THE FIRST truly British monarch. When he succeeded Elizabeth I in 1603 and added England, Wales, and Ireland to his native Scotland,
the hopeful and the admiring outnumbered the detractors, for the godly knew
that in 1592 he had endorsed presbyterianism in Scotland and, more recently,
had disparaged Catholicism and Dutch Arminianism.[1] Their hopes aroused, a
small group of English activists initiated a petition the king received as he
made his way to London. The "Millenary Petition," so named because of the
assertion it was endorsed by a thousand ministers, complained of pluralism
and nonresidency, singled out bishops as pluralists although otherwise saying
nothing about episcopacy, and called for higher standards in admitting men to
the work of ministry. It also urged the king to relax the rule about wearing the
surplice, ensure that neither women nor men could baptize infants in private,
and reform the process of excommunication. As well, the petition recommended "that examination may go before the communion" and a sermon precede it. The most explicitly political request was that no minister be "suspended, silenced, disgraced, [or] imprisoned for men's traditions."[2]

The Millenary Petition signaled the persistence of Puritan sympathies in
England despite the damage done to the movement in the 1590s. Locally and
in Parliaments of the early seventeenth century, laypeople continued to demand a better quality of minister and defend the practice of nonconformity.
The "classis movement" so dear to John Field had vanished, but not an uneasiness with the *Book of Common Prayer*. Behind the self-professed moderation
of the petitioners—we are "neither . . . factious men affecting a popular parity
in the Church, nor . . . schismatics, aiming at the dissolution of the state
ecclesiastical"—lay forceful complaints about aspects of worship and discipline
deemed "simply evil and such as cannot be yielded to without sinne." In a
follow-up petition the king received in late 1605, a group of ministers in the

diocese of Lincoln echoed what had been said in the 1560s and 1570s about abolishing "idolatry and superstition." For this group as for Cartwright's gen- eration, the second commandment made it imperative to eliminate "not only all Idols but also all the ceremonys & instruments of idolatry," to the point of "root[ing] out the very memory of them." Kings as well as leaders of the state church were responsible for sustaining divine law and at fault if it was ig- nored; in the words of the petition, no monarch could "appoint to the Church, what rites and orders he thinks good, but he is bound to serve them in those rules, which God . . . hath presented." In another gesture to the past, the peti- tioners cited Reformed churches on the Continent as exemplary in "both the doctrine and discipline, as it was delivered by our Saviour Christ, and his holy Apostells."[3]

Would James acknowledge this argument and undo the compromises of the Elizabethan Settlement? This seemed unlikely given the breakdown in his relationship with the Melvillian party in Scotland. Looking around him from the perspective of London, James realized that each of his three kingdoms (the third being Ireland) had its own version of Protestantism. Scotland's national church was the outlier, made so by a weak version of episcopacy, the feistiness of the General Assembly, and the persistence of Genevan-style worship. Relish- ing the royal supremacy he inherited once he arrived in London, James con- templated changes in the kirk that would align it more closely with the Church of England. During his reign as James I and James VI, he went partway down this road, leaving it to Charles I, who came to the throne in 1625, to complete the project of imposing Church of England–style Protestantism on Scotland and Ireland.

It was not to be. When and why this project failed and what happened in the aftermath of its collapse are questions that inform this and the next two chapters (7 and 8). Here, in chapter 6, the story begins with the king's attempts to bring a measure of peace to the Church of England—peace on his terms, yet a peace that encompassed the less aggressive wing of the Puritan movement. On the other hand, the politics of religion in Scotland darkened once the king decided to alter the pattern of worship practiced by the state church and to do so by royal fiat. After Charles I assumed the throne, he abandoned any pretense of moderation and pursued a program of uniformity aimed at disrupting the connections between British Protestantism and the Reformed international. Suddenly, much more was at stake than the surplice or a few ceremonies.

"All's well," declares the captain of the ship of state. James could say these words with conviction a decade or more into his reign as monarch of three countries. "All's well," declares a captain unaware of how the ship of state is endangered by his piloting. Charles was that kind of king, someone whose policies contradicted the unspoken rules that enabled uniformity to co-exist with nonconformity.[4] By the close of 1640, his version of uniformity was col- lapsing, overturned in Scotland by a popular uprising and about to be thwarted in England by a new Parliament that met in November 1640. Beforehand, thousands of the godly had voted against Charles's policies by moving to the New World, some to the Caribbean and the Chesapeake and many others to the region known as New England. The story of these decades begins with what James wanted. Thereafter, this chapter touches on the religious situation in Ireland before turning back to England, Scotland, and the Netherlands, where the British presence in the early seventeenth century encompassed refugee ministers and laypeople, some of them Separatists, some of them not. The story of his son's program, the insurgency in Scotland, and the exodus to New England follows in chapter 7.

The Royal Program

James arrived in London in 1603 hoping to unite the kingdoms of Scotland and England, a goal he failed to achieve. He also wanted to align the Church of Scotland with the Church of England, a project that would require the consent of the Scottish bishops and a general assembly. This too he failed to achieve.[5] Singular to England was a third goal, the taming of nonconformity. Here, James could count on the support of Richard Bancroft, who became Archbishop of Canterbury in 1604. Bancroft agreed with James that the church should crack down on religious extremists and especially "Puritans," the name James had used in *Basilikon Doron* for those in Scotland who challenged his authority over the church and used again in his speech (March 1604) to the first of his English Parliaments. Extrapolating from his experiences in the 1590s, the king believed he could rally most of the clergy in England to his side—and, for that matter, most English Catholics—once he made clear the benefits of conforming. In a proclamation of July 1604, he "admonish[ed]" the clergy in the state church to conform. To Protestants, he reiterated the disdain for "Puritanes and Novelists" he had voiced in 1598; now as in the past, he regarded them as "ever discontented with the present government, & impatient to suffer any superiority, which maketh their sect unable to be suffred in any wel governed Commonwealth." To Catholics, he offered the assurance that he was not an "enemie" to Rome, but only to its "corruption." By his own description he was someone "free from persecution, or thralling of my Subiects in matters of Conscience," meaning, he would let private belief alone. At its most expansive, this politics prompted an invitation to the Pope in Rome to discuss the possibility of reunifying a divided Christendom.[6]

James also realized that unity among Protestants in England would mean doing more to eliminate "unlearned, un-preaching, scandalous" ministers (to quote a Puritan-sponsored petition of 1604). He spoke sympathetically of the financial plight of the clergy and, to the surprise of the leaders of the state church, acknowledged the "many seeming zealous" who questioned some aspects of the *Book of Common Prayer*. But in October 1603, James endorsed episcopacy as the form of church government most "agreeable to God's word, and near to the condition of the primitive church." Hoping to win over the moderate wing of the Puritan movement or, as he put it, willing to listen to those who regarded "some things amiss in ecclesiastical matters," he invited several of the bishops and four men he regarded as Puritans to meet with him at the royal palace of Hampton Court. There, in January 1604, he declared that his goals were to "settle an uniforme order through the whole Church," encourage unity, and "amend abuses," adding that, for "kings to take the first course for the establishing of the church, both in doctrine and policy" was "according to the example of all Christian princes."[7]

Except for Laurence Chaderton, the long-time master of Emmanuel College, the three others speaking on behalf of reform were sympathetic to conformity.[8] The most vocal was John Rainolds, the master of Corpus Christi College, Cambridge. Aware of the stirrings of Arminianism at Oxford (see chap. 4), he proposed that the Thirty-Nine Articles expand to include the Lambeth Articles of 1595 and that the government suppress "popish opinion," a code word for the anti-Calvinism that worried him. This proposal went nowhere, as did Rainolds's objections to kneeling to receive the Eucharist and the sign of the cross in the service of baptism. Nor did James welcome the suggestion that bishops be required to associate themselves with "a Presbiterie of . . . pastors and Ministers of the Churche," a possibility the king ridiculed; in his words, it "as well agreeth with a Monarchy, as God and the Divell." On the other hand, he agreed to ask the bishops to improve the workings of the ecclesiastical courts and recommended a few minor corrections in worship, ordering, for example, that private baptisms come under the jurisdiction of clergy. Possibly because he disliked some of the marginal annotations in the Geneva Bible, he welcomed the proposal that the state church undertake a fresh translation of the Bible and spoke of doing more to protect the Sunday Sabbath, but spurned the suggestion that ministers not be required to acknowledge the *Book of Common Prayer*. A little later, he met with thirty-two ministers of "Puritan" inclinations to hear their concerns about the shortage of well-educated clergy. Afterwards, he urged the bishops to do more by way of planting ministers in unserved regions of England, Scotland, and Ireland. Otherwise, the Hampton Court conference reaffirmed the practices and policies of the state church.[9]

James had a high view of monarchy and its role in the workings of the state church. In the aftermath of Hampton Court, he cited the "supreme power resting" in his office to preserve the church and pledged to use that "authority" to subdue the "authors of divisions and sects." Think better of disobeying me, he advised those who had a "zeal of reformation." In statements to the English Parliament as well as in what he wrote about kingship, he declared that monarchs acquired their authority directly from God, who empowered them to rule both church and state. Never comfortable with Parliament in Scotland or, after 1603, with what its counterpart in England saw as its due in the political process, he advised his son to "hold no Parliaments, but for necessitie of new Lawes, which would be but seldome." Seldom is the right word, for James did without a new Parliament in England for almost seven years (1614–21) and told the Parliaments of 1610 and 1614 he could impose the subsidies he needed to finance his government.[10]

Thanks to the nature of the Elizabethan Settlement, James was liberated from the two-kingdoms model of church and state and the principle of ministerial parity so dear to the Scottish reformers. During the Hampton Court conference, he insisted that parity was incompatible with kingship. "If once you were out," he reportedly said to the bishops, "and they [i.e., extremist presbyterians] in place, I knowe what would become of my Supremacie. No bishop, no king." When he was told that the campaign against nonconformists was undermining the spiritual well-being of thousands of people, he "most bitterly inveyed against the puritans" and reminded the Privy Council that "his mother and he from their cradles had bene haunted with a puritan diviell." Spurning every plea that he ease the punishing of nonconformists, he equated their repudiation of "things indifferent" with a repudiation of his own authority. Such men were no better than "troublesome spirits" or "seditious schismatics." On the other hand, his appreciation of episcopacy led him to appoint seven bishops to the Privy Council (Elizabeth had appointed only one), and support the Court of High Commission against its common-law critics.[11]

Perhaps out of deference to James's professed moderation in affairs of religion, the Parliaments that met infrequently during the early years of his reign limited themselves to questioning the government's handling of nonconformity, pluralism, nonresidency, and Catholic recusancy. Bills to minimize the impact of the canons of 1604 (see below), which the House of Commons was denouncing as late as 1610, never made their way through the House of Lords. Nor did others aimed at tightening the restrictions on Catholics and protecting the Sunday Sabbath. As had happened during the reign of Elizabeth I, the House of Commons continued to assert a voice in matters of foreign policy and insist on its own privileges, especially freedom of speech. Even though no one introduced bills as daring as those Job Throckmorton had endorsed in the mid-1580s, the king's pleas for additional revenue were usually deflected, in part because, in the words of a member of the House of Commons in 1614, "If the King may impose by his absolute power then no man [is] certain what he has, for it shall be subject to the King's pleasure." In a foretaste of tensions during the reign of Charles, the Parliament of 1610 censored a legal theorist who asserted the king's supremacy over Parliament.[12]

Catholics as well as nonconformists could be dangerous, a possibility underscored by a plot in 1605 to blow up the building in which Parliament was about to meet, with James present. Five years later, he was dismayed when a radical Catholic assassinated Henry IV of France, another king who was attempting to ease interconfessional tensions. Yet at neither moment did James endorse the virulent anti-Catholicism favored by some within the House of Commons. He included a Catholic aristocrat among his principal counselors and, in foreign policy, ended the long-standing state of war with Spain (1604–5). Once the Thirty Years War (1618–48) began, he was reluctant to provide soldiers and money to any of the Protestant regimes on the Continent, a policy that irritated many in the House of Commons. Diplomacy was preferable to warfare—the one an inexpensive means of keeping the peace; the other, costly and frustrating.[13]

Meanwhile, James was supporting a fresh campaign against ministers who continued to avoid some of the ceremonies or refused to wear the surplice. At the earliest Convocation of the new regime (1604), the bishops secured the passage of 141 canons (rules) covering worship, organization, and the behavior of the clergy. The great majority of these rules repeated or were based on existing canons and "advertisements." Some were mildly reformist in attempting, yet again, to curtail the practices of nonresidency and pluralism. Canon 82, which required "prophesyings" to be licensed by a bishop, indirectly authorized the practice. Several justified the rituals and ceremonies singled out in the Millenary Petition, characterizing them as cleansed of "popish superstition." A dozen concerned the errors of Separatism. Others required lecturers to wear the surplice and administer the Eucharist twice a year. From Archbishop Bancroft's point of view, the most important was the thirty-sixth. Based on the Advertisements John Whitgift had issued in 1583, it required clergy to subscribe—that is, to formally acknowledge—the Thirty-Nine Articles, the authority of the monarch in religious affairs, and the validity of the *Book of Common Prayer*. Anyone who refused to do so was threatened with the penalty of deprivation. Another canon (the second) provided for the excommunication of anyone who questioned the royal supremacy, and the sixth dismissed any argument from conscience against this rule. Within the Convocation, one of the bishops warned that conscience remained an issue for some clergy. Others supported the suggestion that the Convocation acknowledge a limited version of nonconformity. But for Bancroft and James, the time had come to pressure nonconformists to fall in line.[14]

When the deadline (November 30, 1604) arrived to subscribe and conform, the main response had been a raft of petitions emphasizing the unfortunate consequences of depriving godly ministers and urging something akin to toleration for nonconformity.[15] Thereafter, each bishop became responsible for pursuing everyone who defied the canons. Several did so, but when enforcement petered out by 1606, no more than eighty ministers had been deprived. Patronage and local foot-dragging tempered any rigor, as did a long-standing reluctance on the part of some bishops to dismiss the more effective preachers and lecturers in their dioceses. In the northern province of Yorkshire, to which the canons did not apply and where well-trained ministers were in short supply, Matthew Hutton, the archbishop until 1606, did almost nothing to end nonconformity; in his estimation, "Puritans" could be tolerated because "they agree with us in the substance of religion; and . . . love his Majestie." Or, enforcement faltered because clergy who were temporarily suspended or deprived moved to other dioceses or parishes. Tellingly, some subscribed without intending to conform, or said they would conform but never subscribed.[16] In the long run, the canons may have had some real consequences, for subscription to number 36 was required of every new minister in the church. Even so, "moderate" nonconformity remained alive and well, sustained by its patrons and endorsed by many in the House of Commons.

The new canons were irrelevant to the Church of Ireland. Here, in the third of James's kingdoms, the state church was fragile and its leadership preoccupied with the menace of Catholicism. A reformation imposed during the reign of Henry VIII, a coercive, top-down "political" reformation of the kind Henry had initiated in England, never gained much of a footing among the bulk of the country's population, the Gaelic-speaking Irish who clung to their traditional faith. So, for the most part, did the Anglo-Irish or "Old English," whose ancestors had arrived in the country in the twelfth century.[17] Expectations that either group would gradually tilt toward Protestantism were thwarted by a religious identity of deep social and political significance. Moreover, the Catholic presence was being reinforced at the turn of the century by missionary priests and an apparatus of bishops and dioceses. Among the Protestant "New English" who arrived as colonists in the sixteenth century, the "godly" were few and far between, a situation that helps to explain the ineffective Protestantism of the clergy, many of them (before 1590) with a background as priests or as members of a family system that included Catholics. From the standpoint of the authorities in London, the remedy was to dispatch more English clergy to Ireland, the downside being the inability of these men to preach in Gaelic. Primers and other basic books in that language were also few and far between.

Only in Dublin, where military officers, merchants, and administrators gathered, did Protestantism acquire much of a presence. Here, the government established Trinity College (1592), the first Protestant college in the country, for the purpose of fashioning a suitable, that is, zealously anti-Catholic, clergy. After William Temple (d. 1627) became provost in 1609, he allowed the college fellows to ignore the surplice. Out of necessity, church leaders continued to recruit ministers from England and Scotland, which is why, after Walter Travers was forced out of his position at the Inns of Court in London, he turned up in Dublin as Provost of Trinity College (1594–98).[18]

A massive uprising against English rule that erupted in 1595 became a watershed in Irish social, political, and religious history. After it was suppressed and the power of the leading Irish clans severely curtailed, James and his advisors changed course and adopted a policy of creating "plantations" colonized by Protestants drawn from Scotland and England. Soon, these enterprises were attracting thousands of Scots to the region known as Ulster. With the Scots came theological and cultural presbyterianism and ministers who had been formed within that system, the likes of John Ridge, John Livingston, and Robert Blair. Once they arrived, these men encountered fellow Scots who held office as bishops and possibly bent the rules for the newcomers—for example, allowing Blair to preserve the Scottish tradition of receiving the Eucharist seated at a table and Scottish congregations to dispense with set prayers. As well, several of the ministers became involved in sacramental feasts of unusual intensity. To describe the Church of Ireland as leavened with a Puritan spirit may be going too far, but as Charles I and the advocates of a distinctly anti-puritan program would discover in the mid-1630s, many of the newcomers and some of the bishops sympathized with Reformed orthodoxy and put evangelism ahead of conformity.[19]

Another difference between London-based and local policies concerned Catholicism. The resolute anti-Catholicism of the bishops and especially of James Ussher, who in 1625 became Primate (Archbishop) of the Church of Ireland, put them at odds with the more irenic approach of James and Charles I. In response to James's attempts to promote the "Spanish match" (Charles marrying a Spanish princess) and its political corollary, an alliance with Catholic Spain, Ussher reiterated the argument that Catholicism bore the mark of the beast. Suspecting that a marriage treaty with the Spanish government would require the government in London to relax the civil penalties imposed on English and Irish Catholics, Ussher insisted that no Catholic could be trusted. "If true religion is already established according to Gods word," one of Ussher's colleagues remarked about this time, toleration was unacceptable. When Charles I began to bargain with the local Irish in 1626, the country's bishops responded by denouncing Catholicism as "superstitious and idolatrous" and any "toleration" of them as a "grievous sin."[20]

These sympathies help to explain why, in 1615, the state church created its own articles of theology, a step akin to a declaration of independence—necessarily incomplete—from the Church of England. Who drafted the Articles remains uncertain, although traditionally they are ascribed to Ussher. A well-informed student of early Christianity, his projects included *A Discourse of the Religion Anciently Professed by the Irish and British* (1622; expanded in 1631), a highly political interpretation of Irish church history keyed to Ussher's discovery of Protestant-like practices and doctrines in the earliest years of Irish Christianity, a phase of history that, John Foxe–like, he described as giving way to "corruptions . . . creep[ing] in little by little." Within court circles in London, it was murmured that he was a "puritan," perhaps because he was close to ministers such as Ezekiel Culverwell, Richard Sibbes, John Preston (who turned down an appointment as professor of theology at Trinity), and Samuel Ward of Cambridge, or perhaps because he favored Reformed orthodoxy as defined by the Lambeth Articles.[21]

Ussher really was a "committed anti-Arminian" who made sure that the Irish Articles incorporated the Lambeth Articles virtually word for word.

Unlike the Thirty-Nine Articles, the Irish affirmed the perseverance of the saints and their assurance of salvation. On the other hand, the Irish eliminated the argument that baptism was a "sign of regeneration." Except for references to the pope, who in article 80 was described as the Antichrist, nothing was said about the form of church government aside from the general rule (carried over from article 20 of the Thirty Nine Articles) that no church on earth could "ordaine anything that is contrary to Gods word." It may be significant that article 36 of the English creed, which specified the role of bishops in ordaining ministers, was omitted and that article 68 recognized as true the "many" churches in which "the word of God is taught" and the sacraments properly administered, a nod in the direction of the Reformed international. In 1631, at a moment when the leadership of the Church of England was disparaging Reformed orthodoxy, Ussher defended the continuities between "the religion professed" by the earliest Christians in Ireland and the creed as "now by public authority maintained" (i.e., the Irish Articles), his way of criticizing the policies of Charles I and William Laud.[22]

The "Old Non-Conformity"

Canons and the pressure to conform aside, the situation of the godly in early seventeenth-century England seemed promising. More towns were implementing programs of civic godliness, and more people were buying (and presumably reading) printed sermon series and manuals of devotion linked to the practical divinity. Arthur Dent's *Plain Mans Path-way to Heaven* and the layman Michael Sparks's *Crumbs of Comfort, the valley of tears, and the Hill of Joy* (1623) were steady sellers before 1640, and the "remarkable popularity" of books by the ambiguously Puritan William Perkins was demonstrated in what the university press at Cambridge was publishing. By the 1620s, new writers were emerging alongside older favorites—Robert Bolton for one, John Preston for another." And, although not specifically the doing of godly writers, editions of the psalms and other parts of the Bible remained popular.[23]

The thickening presence of godly books and their readers suggests that something akin to a "Puritan" culture had come into being, a culture centered on certain practices and a strong sense among the godly of being different.[24] Both figured in the identity of Richard Baxter's father. In the Shropshire town where Baxter was born in 1615, the people who shouted "puritan" at his father did so because, on Sundays, they were making merry in the streets while he remained indoors reading his Bible. As the high-status Robert Harley indicated in a "Character" of the Puritan he wrote in 1621/22, he and his wife were aware of being different because they combined "discretion with zeal" or picked their way between speaking truth about "idolatry" and subservience to the king. The Harleys teetered on the edge of nonconformity in how they worshipped, but like many others in the early seventeenth century, they focused their religious politics on the plight of Protestants on the Continent, where Catholic forces were gaining ground, and on the situation of English Protestants who were being denied the presence of an evangelical clergy.[25]

In the years after 1610, people such as the Harleys were also participating in a broader culture they shared with most of their fellow Protestants. Anti-popery was a case in point. Featured in yearly celebrations of the defeat of the Spanish Armada in 1588 and the failure of the Gunpowder Plot in 1605, the rhetoric of anti-popery lay at the heart of English popular Protestantism, winding its way through the lore of portents and surfacing whenever someone complained about the menacing presence of lay Catholics and their priests.[26] This worldview was on the upswing in the 1620s in response to Catholic victories in the early stages of the Thirty Years War, one of these the battle of White Mountain (1620) in Bohemia—a defeat experienced with special intensity in England because of its consequences for the king's son-in-law Frederick, the Elector Palatine, who had accepted the crown of that country but was quickly driven out by Habsburg troops and subsequently driven from the Palatinate.[27] As narrative or rhetoric, anti-popery depended on the premise of unending warfare between the Antichrist (understood as the papacy) and the saints—an unusual version of conflict, because the Antichrist was relying on deception and deceit as weapons in a campaign to dismantle a Protestant monarchy and Protestant state church.

As had been true since the middle of the sixteenth century, anti-popery aligned the contemporary situation of Protestants with the struggle against idolatry in ancient Israel, the Babylonian captivity of the children of Israel, and the apocalyptic scenario of the suffering few who fled into the wilderness, Babylon being to Israel what the papacy was to Protestants in England, Ireland, and Scotland. Merely to utter the word "Babylon" or "Beast" or "tyranny" was to evoke the scenario of the end times when true religion would face one more moment of immense struggle. As understood by most English Protestants, this struggle was alarming because the Antichrist was using deception to wend its way into the very heart of state and church. That enemies were not far off but working *within* the system precipitated spasms of anxiety about who was scheming to betray true religion.[28]

This anxiety explains the exuberant celebrations that broke out in late 1623 when news arrived of the failure of the "Spanish match." Ever since rumors of the king's intentions (1617) began to spread, a sense of alarm dogged his government, and feelings hardened once it was learned that, in his negotiations with the Spanish government, James had been asked to cancel or suspend the laws against Catholics in England as part of a marriage contract. Hoping to forestall this project, Thomas Scott, a former royal chaplain, denounced the marriage in an anonymous pamphlet purporting to reveal the Spanish side of the story—bribes being offered to courtiers close to James alongside other attempts to influence the government. The moderate bishop Joseph Hall was almost as outspoken in a sermon he preached at the opening of the 1624 Convocation. Urging the government to "destroy this . . . Monster (Popery, I meane)," he asked James and his advisors to halt their censuring of "puritans." For Hall, James Ussher, and Archbishop George Abbott, anti-popery signaled the "fundamental agreement" of Puritans and conformists on the Protestant identity of the British state churches.[29]

Agreement on anti-popery was seconded by agreement on matters of doctrine. Here, the good news was that James I wanted to sustain the connections between the Church of England and the Reformed international. Right doctrine mattered to the king, so much so that he intervened personally to condemn the theological speculations of a Dutch theologian and dispatched a delegation to the Synod of Dordt (1618–19). The good news included his naming of George Abbott (d. 1633) to succeed Bancroft. Abbott and his brother Robert, a fellow bishop who taught at Oxford, were known for being robustly anti-Catholic and supporters of Reformed orthodoxy.[30] Some of the bishops James was appointing were critical of that system. Nonetheless, Laurence Chaderton remained the master of Emmanuel College until his death in 1625, Samuel Ward continued to preside over Sidney Sussex until the 1640s, Richard Sibbes, who subscribed to the canons of 1604 after hesitating for a moment, became master of Katharine Hall, Cambridge in 1626, and Preston succeeded Chaderton in 1626.[31] Preston's career was telling. The intellectual flair he displayed in an academic exercise attended by the king gained him the backing of a "Puritan faction" within the aristocracy. Subsequently, he acquired a patron in the Duke of Buckingham, an alliance that led to Preston's appointment as one of the chaplains to the king's son Charles and, via an intricate politics, to his post at Emmanuel. All the while, he enjoyed strong connections with bishops such as Ussher as well as with nonconformists such as John Dod.[32]

When these features move to the center of early Stuart Protestantism, the godly seem much less singular. Yet singular they remained to some of their enemies, who painted them as cranky, hypocritical, and seditious. Not this rhetoric but the practices and values known as "voluntary religion" had a special importance to the godly. The prophesyings that irritated Elizabeth I vanished, but in the late sixteenth century something similar came into being, an exercise known as "lectures by combination," a weekly or monthly lecture preached by ministers who held regular positions in the state church. Common in market towns in southeastern England and a frequent event in Yorkshire during the years (1606–1628) when Tobie Matthews was Archbishop of the Northern Province, lectures by combination (or "exercises") emerged as a means of training apprentice ministers and promoting evangelical Protestantism. Worried by the practice, Bancroft and the makers of the canons of 1604 ordered local bishops to regulate these events. Yet they continued to thrive among the godly.[33]

Another aspect of voluntary religion was the clerical post known as a lectureship. Never uniquely Puritan, it came into being as a means of providing evangelical preachers for towns or parishes without them (see chap. 4). More specific to the godly were other examples of voluntary religion. As Nehemiah Wallington sometimes did in London, like-minded people would travel to another parish to hear the afternoon sermon on Sundays. Other lay Puritans were gathering together in private meetings, a practice noted again and again in the testimonies of laypeople in 1630s new-world Cambridge. In a handful of places laypeople and ministers formed covenanted communities, one of them the doing of Richard Rogers (of *Seven Treatises* fame), who gathered together those in his parish who "as far exceed the common sort of them that profess the Gospel, as the common professors do exceed them in religion which know not the Gospel." Some of these temporary communities were akin to a halfway house between conformity and Separatism.[34]

Always, of course, the godly were associating with each other via an informal sociability of the kind enjoyed by Wallington, the schoolmaster-clergyman Thomas Dugard, and the sometime attorney Robert Woodford. Never much of a traveler outside his own London parish, Wallington participated in a community fashioned around the transmission of news by printed and handwritten letters. Thanks to these, he knew what was happening in faraway New England and not-so-distant Scotland. Advising a correspondent to get "acquainted with those that they call puritans," he also relied on attending services in other parishes to sustain his sense of fellowship. Dugard, who departed Cambridge for Warwick and a job as master of a local school in 1633, inherited connections with the godly from his family and formed others during his student years at Sidney Sussex, Cambridge, a "puritan" college. In his new county, Dugard became close to ministers who shared his understanding of good religion. Dining with Lord Brooke, the principal aristocrat of the region, he met political figures such as John Pym and Richard Knightly, the latter an important patron of nonconforming ministers and, like Pym, a persistent voice in Parliaments of the 1620s on behalf of Reformed-style religion. Thanks to his own services as a supply preacher and willing critic or editor of his friends' manuscripts, Dugard enjoyed a robust social life virtually untouched by campaigns against nonconformity. In Woodford's Northampton, the interval between Sunday services became a moment for sociability among ministers and "substantial townsmen" he supplemented by participating in weekday meetings at which "God's people" shared sermon notes and spiritual counsel. In Northampton as in London and elsewhere, godliness flourished in households, special Sunday services, and informal politics of the kind that involved Lord Brooke.[35]

Regarding circumstances and ceremonies: had the Puritan movement really weaned itself from Cartwright-style objections to episcopacy and the *Book of Common Prayer*? Abbott was confident it had, a confidence based on the waning of agitation about the bishops and the royal supremacy. He may also have sensed that the sectarian phase of the movement was in retreat. Other evidence supports this reading of the situation: the posthumous reputation of that quintessential moderate William Perkins, Preston's career within the state church, and the numerous ministers and laypeople who, although privately identifying themselves as "puritans," wanted nothing to do with the "seditious" Separatists.[36] Circumstances such as these have prompted historians of early Stuart Britain to attribute the intensity of religious politics in the 1620s and 1630s not to the heirs of Cartwright and Field but to a radicalized "Anglicanism" fashioned by a small group of bishops and theologians (see chap. 7).

Any reckoning with the temper of the Puritan movement circa 1620 must include what was being said about this period some two decades later. In the mid-1640s, the Puritan wing of English Protestantism experienced a time of crisis when any pretense of unity gave way to factions—Presbyterians, Baptists, Independents, and others—each claiming to represent a perfect reformation (see chap. 8). To moderates, the years before 1640 became a nostalgic alternative to the confusion unfolding around them, an alternative that deserved its own name: the "good old non-conformity," the "old conformity," or the "old Puritanism." This terminology took for granted that the movement had abandoned Separatist-style disdain for the state church and become more accommodating—or better, a movement centered on evangelism and moral reform rather than on contesting the structure of the state church or the royal supremacy.[37]

The poster child for the old nonconformity may have been Chaderton, the long-serving master of Emmanuel College. In the context of the Hampton Court conference, Chaderton reiterated one premise of this perspective, the importance of pastoral ministry, reasoning in a private note that "We may and ought to use them [the ceremonies] to purchase and procure liberty by preaching the Gospel."[38] With Elizabeth I in mind, the master of Sidney Sussex, Cambridge, Samuel Ward, reminded himself in 1597 of this and related arguments as the reasons why he should make peace with the state church, the presence of "notes" that characterized the true church and the enduring Protestantism of the country's monarch: "the not considering of the great benefites we enjoy under the raigne of ouir Soveraigne, as also here in the University, having the word truly preached and the Sacramentes duely administered." Walter Bedell, an evangelical bishop in the Church of Ireland who questioned the legitimacy of the surplice, agreed with Ward. Writing him in 1604, Bedell endorsed a policy of "swallow[ing] all inexpediences" so long as "nothing impious be required at our hands." Bedell also endorsed the "authority of the magistrate" to sustain "canonical obedience." The aging Walter Travers added his voice to this chorus. Now, instead of criticizing the *Book of Common Prayer*, he endorsed it as adequately apostolic, doing so in response to Catholic-inflected arguments on behalf of the intercession of the saints as well as to Separatist-style assertions of free-form prayer.[39]

Chaderton's friend John Davenport was also negotiating his way through the thickets of religious politics with a certain ease. Davenport drew on the principle of things indifferent in his response (1624) to someone who confronted him about the practice of kneeling to receive the sacrament, the same year in which the vestry of St. Stephens, London, elected him vicar of the church—and, as he pointed out to an aristocratic patron, the votes in his favor were *not* from "a puritannicall faction." In his previous post, Davenport had worn the surplice, administered the Eucharist only to those who knelt, and used the *Book of Common Prayer* "as is appointed by the church." For him "puritanical" signified being "opposite to the present government," whereas he had "perswaded many to Conformity." When the Scottish radical Alexander Leighton (see chap. 7) challenged Davenport to acknowledge that kneeling to receive the sacrament was a practice initiated by the Antichrist, he retorted that the ceremony was not an "essentiall part of Worshi[i]p" and therefore could be "Commanded by Authorye." Simultaneously, Davenport was supporting political initiatives that were "puritan" in a broad sense of the term: joining with several other ministers in 1627 in an appeal for donations to provide "reliefe" for refugees from the Palatinate, editing the sermons of Preston after his death in 1628, serving as one of the Feoffees for Impropriations (see chap. 4), and becoming a member of the Massachusetts Bay Company. To these activities he added a plea on behalf of unity among the godly at a moment when state church and kingdom were threatened by "Atheisme, Libertinisme, papisme, and Arminianisme."[40]

Davenport's practice was in keeping with the "old Puritanism." So was the understanding of ministry promoted by Nicholas Byfield, the devotional writer of such importance to Archibald Johnston. Byfield was willing to speak out against rulers who willfully interfered in religious affairs, but he preferred to emphasize the principle of things indifferent and its practical consequences as defined by the government. In his own ministry, Byfield seems to have spurned nonconformity.[41] Voices such as his and Joseph Hall's weighed on a great many of the men who took up the work of ministry after 1610.

Despite its merits, this commitment to ministry as a means of moral reform and broad-based evangelicalism was dogged by the persistence of objections to the "ceremonies" and high claims for the authority of "conscience." Chaderton's fuller reflections on conformity are a case in point. At the close of the Hampton Court conference, he joined the other three Puritan delegates in agreeing "to bee quiet and obedient, now that they knew it to be the Kinges mind, to have it so." Being quiet and obedient had immediate implications for the college he headed. Its fellows had never worn the surplice during services in the college chapel. Now, with the college master having agreed to accept the rules of the state church, they were told to conform, a requirement Chaderton defended by citing the concept of things indifferent that a Christian magistrate (the king) had endorsed. Weighing the alternatives, he concluded that conformity was better than nonconformity if it kept a valuable minister from being deprived. Alongside these private reflections, however, he added others in which he rejected episcopacy as "no ministrie ordayned by christ" and assailed the sign of the cross in the service of baptism as an "abuse" without warrant in Scripture. Moreover, he wanted local churches to have an important role in the naming of their ministers. Even more telling of his doubts about the state church were his strong words about conscience. Again, he reminded himself in private that no royal command "reacheth . . . to conscience." Reflections of this kind tilted Chaderton closer to a more emphatic Puritanism defined by its strong objections to the liturgy, the surplice, and episcopacy.[42]

Conscience was an issue that would not die, its tenderness among the godly kept alive by the imperative (voiced in the *First Book of Discipline*) that nothing can be "imposed upon the consciences of men, without the expressed commandment of God's word," Perkins's observation that "a subjection of conscience to mens laws, I deny," and the high-minded protests preserved in *A Parte of a Register* and the *Book of Martyrs*. Near the end of the sixteenth century, the tug of war between compromise and conscience had been dramatized in the person of Arthur Hildersham after he was confronted about his nonconformity. Hildersham admitted that he found himself "between two straights [straits]," one of them to "seeke" the approval of his bishop, the other, to "speake plainlie and flatlie." Pondering these alternatives, he concluded that he must listen to what was "inward . . . whereof God is [the] onely . . . witness," that is, the workings of his conscience: "I would use some ceremonies, and stay from speaking against some abuses," he reported, but only "so farre forth as I might not hurte my conscience, or give offence to others." Aware of how the government was representing nonconformity as "sedition," Hildersham protested that he was a "loyall subject to the Prince," adding, however, a citation to Calvin's assertion that human laws cannot overrule the teachings of conscience. The price he paid for these life rules was high, to be deprived or suspended for long periods of time. Yet he never chose the path of Separatism and, when clergy sought his counsel, may have urged them to remain within the state church.[43]

A good many young men heeded this advice, but only after tuning out what a handful of the godly were saying about the evils of the state church. For these holdouts, the surplice was most definitely *not* a thing indifferent and subscription or conformity impossible to accept, given the idolatry that clung to the English liturgy. The premise of three books by William Bradshaw—*English Puritanism* (1605), *A Treatise of the Nature and Use of Things Indifferent* (1605), and *A Treatise of Divine Worship, seeking to prove the Ceremonies, imposed on the Ministers of the Gospel . . . are in their use unlawful* (Amsterdam, 1604)—was the regulative principle, which Greenham had also invoked. For

Bradshaw, conscience would not allow him to "subscribe to any thing but to the worde of God, and things manifestlie gathered out of the worde of God." Nothing with a Catholic past met that test, since any mingling of "the Beast" and true Christianity ended up favoring the Antichrist. Bradshaw implied that godly ministers who came too close to the "Beast" would alienate their parishioners.[44] Robert Parker made the same point in *An scholasticall discourse against symbolizing with Antichrist in ceremonies: especially in the signe of the crosse* (Middleburg, 1607), a pedantic defense of nonconformity no matter what the cost; the alternative, to wear the surplice and practice the sign of the cross, was to side with the devil. William Ames, who joined his friend Parker in the Netherlands after being forced out of Christ's College, Cambridge, in 1609, reiterated these objections to "unlawful" ceremonies or practices—the surplice, the sign of the cross in the liturgy of baptism, kneeling to receive the Eucharist—in tracts published in the 1620s and early 1630s. In a preface to Ames's posthumous *A Fresh Suit Against Human Ceremonies in Gods Worship* ([Amsterdam], 1633), Thomas Hooker, a former lecturer and nonconformist, rejected out of hand any defense of the ceremonies as matters "indifferent" on the grounds that "no worship . . . is legitimate unless it has God as its author and ordainer." The real import of conscience was its God-given authority: "he alone is Lord of the conscience." To these principles Hooker added harsh words about "temporizing" among the would-be godly, or what he characterized as "wink[ing] at the sins of men . . . though with reluctance of conscience."[45]

Henry Jacob agreed. One of the organizers of the Millenary Petition and, for other reasons, arrested and imprisoned for nonconformity, Jacob told the bishop of London in or around 1605 that he was not a "schismatic" but merely someone who listened to his conscience: "We have consciences desirous to serve God," he declared, adding that it pointed him back to the Word as the source of truth and, behind the Word, to Christ, the "sole teacher in all matters of the Church." Otherwise, corruption would ensue, a corruption visible in the "Ecclesiasticall Traditions or inventions of men" that plagued the Church of England. Radicals such as John Row in Scotland were of the same mind. In Row's opinion, only those clergy with "sleeping, senseless, seared consciences" put up with the changes James I was introducing in Scotland after 1606, since anyone with a "tender" conscience would regard Catholic-tilting practices as too great a "burden" to bear. Men of this way of thinking were also evoking the imperative of communal edification. Like Cartwright and Travers before them, they believed that a state church burdened with unlawful practices would never be able to edify British Protestants.[46]

This back-and-forth about conformity and conscience was very real to would-be ministers in the Church of England. John Reyner was one of these young men, a Cambridge graduate appointed to a lectureship circa 1627. Worrying about the right course of action, he shared his anxieties with the veteran minister John Cotton. The sticking point for Reyner was whether he should perform any of the "ceremonies." Outlining his dilemma, he spoke of wanting to rely on the Bible: "I must search the Scripture for a Ground of doing or refusing them." He worried that this process would leave him unsettled. "I enter this way with a trembling foote," he added, asking in the final sentence of his letter that Cotton pray for him. Within the same period (1627–28), Charles Chauncy, an older man who left the comfortable setting of Cambridge University for a parish post, was sharing a similar dilemma with Cotton. Unhappy with some aspects of worship, Chauncy wanted to know if he should accept the canons of 1604 or hold out against them. More letters of this kind reached Cotton, one of them from a Dutch minister who came to London in 1629 to care for a congregation of his countrymen. Realizing that he would be asked to accept the canons, he wrote of being "troubled much" about the contradiction between an oath of this kind and the Third Commandment. Are we "bound in Conscience" not to take such an oath, he asked?[47]

The man on the receiving end of these letters was no stranger to these questions. Staying on as a fellow of a Cambridge college after finishing his studies, Cotton became a candidate for the post of rector of the town church in Boston, Lincolnshire, in 1612. As sometimes happened elsewhere, the town council found itself at an impasse until the mayor broke a deadlock by voting for Cotton. In the aftermath of his ordination at the hands of the local bishop, he presented himself as someone capable of bringing peace to a divided town and parish. In sermons, he lamented "the heat of fallinge out among the brethren" and counseled the more radical to forgo "Offensive carriage." Prefacing a book by Hildersham, he dismissed Separatism as sinful, an opinion he juxtaposed with the principle that "good Kings" must sustain "the purity of Religion."[48]

Even so, unity in Boston remained elusive. Several years after Cotton arrived in the town, a group of zealous townspeople removed the statue of St. Botolph that adorned the spire of the town church. Adding insult to injury, some of them also defaced the iconography of the two maces that town officials carried in processions. Investigators came from London, a conforming minister arrived to restore peace, the church wardens were questioned, and Cotton was called before his bishop, who suspended him for a year (mid-1621 to mid-1622) for nonconformity. In his role as peacemaker Robert Sanderson rebuked both sides, the "popishly-affected . . . that make it their sport upon their Alebenches to rail and scoff at *Puritans*; as if it were warrant enough to . . . talk bawdy, swear and stare, or do anything without control, because forsooth they are no *Puritans*," and the godly for being too "scrupulous," as instanced by the practice of "appropriating to themselves the names of *Brethren*, *Professors*, Good men. . . as differences betwixt them and those they call *Formalists*." Was it not fair to call such people "*Puritans*," he asked, given their claim to "have a Brotherhood . . . of their own, freer and purer from Superstition and Idolatry, than others have"?[49]

The reverberations of this question for Cotton were both personal and professional. At some point in his ministry (the exact date is not known), he encouraged a group of the townspeople to meet on their own while also attending
regular services. Meanwhile, he was avoiding some aspects of the liturgy, which
explains why he was suspended in 1619 and why John Preston asked James
Ussher if Cotton could resume his ministry in Ireland. Earlier, too (1614), he
preached about ministry in a way that offended his diocesan bishop.[50] Facing
the possibility of being suspended anew, Cotton wrote an evasive letter in September 1622 to the bishop-to-be of Lincolnshire, John Williams. Employing
the voice of a moderate, Cotton cited his "support" for the Thirty-Nine Articles
and his reverence for "all authority, whether ecclesiastical, or civil, or both
united in our common head, the most serene prince James." Adding a dig at
Separatism, he backtracked; for the moment he could not "embrace "the ceremonies" with "a confident . . . spirit"—some of the ceremonies, however, not
all of them, without saying which ones he rejected. In trouble a little later
(January 1625), he described himself as confused about the relationship between conformity and conscience, specifying the requirement that people kneel
to receive the Eucharist as something he found hard to accept—as it happened,
the same rule that was arousing bitter conflict within the Church of Scotland.
Using "doubt" as his shield, Cotton begged Williams for more time to explore
the reasons for administering the sacrament in this manner: "I see by often
Experience, the shallownesse of mine owne Iudgement."[51]

The bishop was forgiving, so much so that Cotton remained the town minister, although he may have delegated the liturgical aspects of each Sunday's
service to a curate. Some twenty years later, accused by a Scottish Presbyterian
of having conformed, he denied having done so. Passing by the question of
whether he had conformed or not, his effusive professions of loyalty and a self-
representation as humble or inadequately informed expose the disarray he was
feeling. Could a tender conscience be placated by these evasions, and could
bishops, kings, and local conformists find them plausible? In the 1620s, it
seemed possible to answer these two questions with a muted yes. A case in
point was the lecturer Hugh Peter's "subscription" in 1627. Called to account
in 1626 by the bishop of London for remarks he made about the Catholic wife
of Charles I and her "idolatry," Peter was asked if he "diligently" conformed to
the ceremonies, accepted the office of bishop, and would "subscribe to the Book
of Common Prayer." He agreed to do so, although tempering the significance
of his "yes" by adding that he would gladly practice whatever in the *Book of
Common Prayer* was "agreeable unto the Word of God." This was conformity
by evasion or outward show, a strategy coinciding with the now-you-see it-
now-you-don't nonconformity that some bishops and local officials were willing to overlook. Others, too, were parties to that strategy—in Cotton's Boston
the church wardens, who refused to report the irregularities they were witnessing, and elsewhere, gentry such as Robert Harley who, in his home parish,

protected a rector from being punished for ignoring the surplice and the sign of the cross.[52]

These case histories complicate the argument for Puritanism as a culture, but not if we allow that term to encompass a recurrent tension between conformity and lawfulness or conscience. To conform was to participate in ceremonies or practices tagged as corrupt or idolatrous, but to heed the demands of conscience was likely to end in schism, which Calvin and the Scottish Puritans had never sanctioned. Between these two extremes, as it were, a spectrum emerged that was framed, at one end, by the daring nonconformity of Henry Jacob (see sec. 3 of this chapter) and, at the other, by the conservatism of John Davenant, who combined Reformed orthodoxy and anti-popery with a willingness to acknowledge a tempered version of episcopacy. Or, a middle ground existed where people such as Davenport, Chaderton, and the Harleys situated themselves, a space also occupied by Stephen Marshall, a minister in the strongly Puritan town of Braintree, Essex, who conformed "some times but not always."[53]

As is true of any such middle ground, theirs was precarious. For the moment, it seemed invulnerable to the tirades of Ames, Hooker, and Parker against the ceremonies, but as the career of John Cotton would quickly demonstrate—in 1632–33, he renounced the "old non-conformity" (see chap. 7)— the assumptions on which it rested were about to be overturned by a party of bishops the king was beginning to support. It was also James who reshaped the term "moderate" into a synonym for anti-puritanism. In letters prefacing the Bible of 1611, which the translators dedicated to him, he was extolled for preserving the Church of England from "self-conceited brethren, who run their owne ways" and engage in "bitter censures, and uncharitable imputations," that is, preserving the state church from those who deserved the epithet of Puritan. In a second preface addressed to the book's readers, the translators situated the book between Catholics and the "scrupulosity of the Puritanes" who insert "Congregation in stead of Church" in their versions of Scripture. Here, in as in James's own pronouncements, moderation excluded any serious critique of the state church or royal policies.[54]

This was not the case in Scotland, however, where James I's interventions in the life of the state church were arousing a new generation of "fiery and turbulent spirits."

James I and the Church of Scotland

Two circumstances shaped the religious history of Scotland between 1603 and 1638: the ambition of two British kings to align worship and structure in the Church of Scotland with worship and structure in the Church of England, and the mobilizing of resistance to this program. The king who had praised the kirk in 1592 changed his tune once he began to rule all of Britain. Now it was the Church of England that James VI and I admired and the Church of Scotland that needed amending. For the moment, James revealed his larger program in bits and pieces, professing all the while that he intended no "innovations." As soon as he departed for London, however, several of the synods in Scotland began to worry about the implications of uniting England and Scotland. For them, the immediate remedy was a special meeting of the General Assembly to sit alongside the session of Parliament (1604) as it debated this possibility. The more daring of the ministers and laypeople wanted such a meeting even if the king said no. Within Parliament itself, a motion was made that the commissioners sent to London to discuss the project of unification preserve "the estate of religion, both of doctrine and discipline" in Scotland.

Once in England, James used various excuses to postpone the General Assembly of 1604 even though he had agreed in 1602 to having annual assemblies; unusually, no assembly had met in 1603. In the short run, he brushed aside the argument that an assembly was needed to advise the Scottish Parliament about the project of unification and, in early 1605, he delayed the next assembly to 1606. When word reached him in June 1605 that, without his consent, delegates from fourteen presbyteries had agreed to meet in Aberdeen, he told the Scottish Privy Council to command them to desist. Holding fast to the principle that general assemblies could decide on their own to convene, the men who gathered in Aberdeen elected a moderator and adjourned *sine die*, that is, as though intending to reconvene at some future moment. James was not amused. Orders went out to arrest and put on trial for treason several of the more prominent ministers who attended; afterwards, most were banished from Scotland or "warded" to distant parishes.[55]

Hoping to overcome the recalcitrance of Andrew and James Melville, who attended the Aberdeen assembly, James summoned them and a handful of other ministers to London in 1606, the year in which a new General Assembly reluctantly agreed to re-create something akin to a pre-Reformation version of episcopacy, with bishops returned to their place in Parliament. Parliament followed suit by approving the restoration of bishops with "all their ancient and accustomed honors," noting in the preface to this act that the king was "absolute prince, judge, and governor over all persons, estates, and causes, both spiritual and temporal." Anticipating a decision of this kind, the two Melvilles and some thirty other ministers had submitted a "Protestation" centered on the theme of "darkness" descending anew upon the state church, or the reemergence of the Antichrist in the person of the new bishops.[56] In London, the king held all the cards, to the point of requiring the two Melvilles and their colleagues to listen to various bishops lecture them on the merits of episcopacy. The price of holding their ground, as Andrew and James did, was never to live in Scotland again; Andrew returned to France after being confined for several years in the Tower of London, and James retired to an English town near the Scottish border, where he died in 1614.[57] Another outcome of the protest associated with Aberdeen was a fresh determination on James's part to forgo annual meetings of the General Assembly, a policy repeated by Charles I. Between 1603 and 1618 it met only six times, and thereafter not until 1638, when it defied the royal supremacy to do so.

The king's project in 1606 was straightforward: to resolve the ambiguous situation of the Scottish episcopacy and curtail the autonomy of the General Assembly. As he remarked in *A Premonition to all Most Mightie Monarches, Kings, Free Princes, and States of Christendome* (1609) a text directed mainly against Catholic political theory, he was "ever an enemie to the confused Anaarchie or paritie of the Puritanes," adding that, in Scotland, he had been "persecuted by Puritans there, not only from my birth onely, but even since foure monthes before my birth." Separately, he insisted that bishops be recognized as "perpetual moderators" of local synods, a step that eliminated the practice of electing a moderator each time a synod met. Soon he was insisting that bishops also preside over the General Assembly. For him, episcopacy was valuable not only in and of itself but also as a means of buttressing his own claims to authority. Hence the phrase he used in 1604, "no bishop, no king," and his assertion that presbyterianism "can not agree with a Monarchie."[58]

The more James invested his kingship in altering the structure of the state church and, before long, in changing its mode of worship, the more he relied on political tactics at odds with customary practice: ending annual general assemblies, enabling members of the nobility to attend them as voting members even though they had not been selected as such by a presbytery, intervening in the workings of Parliament and political society, appointing bishops to the Council of State and, in 1609, creating a Court of High Commission (similar to the court established in England in 1584) for handling breaches of ecclesiastical law. Tensions persisted within the General Assembly of 1609, but without serious consequences for the king's program, to which James attached a pleasing show of anti-Catholicism. A year later, he arranged for three of the Scottish bishops to be consecrated by bishops in the Church of England. Parliament having authorized an oath in 1612 requiring ministers in the church to affirm that "the only lawful supreme governor of this realm, as well in matters spiritual and ecclesiastical as in things temporal," was the king, James could safely ignore the Golden Acts of 1592 and the *Second Book of Discipline*. Now he had a church with *real* bishops whose office descended from the early church—real on paper, but still not quite the same as their English counterparts, for most of these men were mindful of anti-Catholic sentiment among the Scottish people. A telling sign of the bishops' anxieties on this score was Archbishop John Spottiswood's decision to dress in Scottish fashion when he was in London to attend the coronation of Charles I. For the moment, the Scottish bishops also remained faithful to Reformed orthodoxy and, in their everyday administration of the church, relied on the apparatus of synods and presbyteries.[59]

After several years of inactivity, James began to unveil the changes in worship he would pursue for another decade and Charles I would impose in the 1630s. As both kings would discover, worship mattered far more to Scottish Protestants than whether their church had bishops or a presbyterian structure. Why true worship, Catholicism, and idolatry remained so closely associated had much to do with what Knox had said in the 1560s about the mass, a message reiterated in the Negative Confession of 1581, which railed against the "bastard sacraments" and "ceremonies" of the "Roman Antichrist." At that moment in Scottish history, the young king and the political and religious leadership had pledged to resist a Catholicism stigmatized as mere "idolatry and superstition." Now, however, a king bent on uniformity with England was asking that the *Book of Common Order* give way to a new "Liturgie . . . and Form of divine Service" aligned in some manner with the *Book of Common Prayer*.[60]

The steps James took in this direction included a royal proclamation (1614) ordering clergy to celebrate Holy Communion at Easter. Two years later, he required university chapels to observe four holy days (Easter, Christmas, Ascension, and Whitsunday) the kirk had always avoided. He also asked the General Assembly to prepare a "uniform order of liturgy . . . to be read in all kirks," a project that remained incomplete until the mid-1630s. (Without controversy, the assembly of 1616 approved a new confession of faith.) In 1617, James came in person to Scotland and instructed the assembly of that year to accept five new practices, all of them regarded by the more ardently presbyterian as "disagreeing in many . . . points from the purity of the word." These five included feasts and saints days (which, as one of the bishops noted at the time, was something "hitherto we have been frie" from); private services of Holy Communion and baptism, a practice at odds with the rule that these two sacraments must always be preceded by a sermon; the rite of confirmation at the hands of a bishop, which may have been less contentious; and requiring people to kneel when they received the Eucharist, a practice John Knox had opposed as early as 1552 and the Church of Scotland had never practiced.[61]

This was asking too much of the assembly of 1617, which insisted that changes of this scope required its consent. Privately, a group of ministers forwarded a "Protestation" to the king disputing his interpretation of the royal supremacy. It evoked the 'puritie' of the church and the "perfection" of the Scottish Reformation. Infuriated by the "disgrace offered unto Us" and reminding the bishops that he had "once fully resolved" never to authorize another assembly, the king told them that he regarded this defiance as a challenge to his "innate power . . . to dispose of things externall in the Church" and would impose the articles if a new "national assembly" did not approve his program.[62] Already, the Privy Council had voted (January 1618) in favor of celebrating the new list of holy days. Thanks to the king's stage-managing of an assembly that met in Perth in August 1618, it endorsed the articles, although a substantial minority of the delegates voted against the five articles after hearing

Archbishop Spottiswood apologize for being unable to dissuade the king from introducing "innovations." The Scottish Parliament followed suit in 1621, again with significant dissent. These victories in hand, the king seems to have assured the Parliament of 1621 that he would go no further. Having gotten what he wanted, he withdrew from any direct involvement in church affairs, although insisting (in the context of resistance to the Articles of Perth) that members of the Privy Council and other officers of state observe the new rules. Thereafter, these were variously honored or, as was said by hardline critics of Perth, "never practiced" in "the most part" of local parishes. Tellingly, the Scottish bishops were reluctant to enforce them.[63]

Enforced or defied, the Five Articles of Perth became the equivalent of the vestarian controversy in 1560s England, a turning point for ministers and laypeople who found themselves having to decide between obeying Parliament and the king or becoming nonconformists. In 1617, the immediate response had included a flurry of meetings, petitions, and printed pamphlets aimed at thwarting any favorable action at the assembly of 1618. In its aftermath, and especially after 1621, the articles and the assembly were denounced anew alongside the earliest stirrings of nonconformity within the Church of Scotland.[64] Robert Blair, who taught at the University of Glasgow, was among the disaffected. Remembering, many years later, a time in his life when he "had not laid to heart the controversy about Church government" or fretted about bishops who "took little upon them," Blair had been present when some "ancient worthy men" contended that moderators must be elected and condemned the "innovations" introduced at Perth. Then and there, he became politically active. He was joined by two outspoken critics of the articles, the ministers David Calderwood (d. 1650) and John Row (d. 1646), each incensed by what happened at the assemblies of 1617 and 1618 and the actions of Parliament in 1621.[65]

Of those who fought the good fight, Calderwood was the most intransigent. Deprived of his position as a minister and banished in 1617 for denying that the king could override a general assembly, he poured out his rage in a series of Dutch-printed books that included *Perth Assembly: Containing 1 The proceedings thereof; 2 the proofe of the nullitie thereof* (Leiden, 1619), a tell-all account of machinations that, from his perspective, nullified the legitimacy of the Five Articles, and *A defence of our arguments against kneeling in the act of receiving the sacramental elements of bread and wine* (1620). Subsequently, Calderwood oversaw the printing of the two sixteenth-century books of discipline, to which he added extracts from assembly and parliamentary records and a fiercely anti-Catholic preface, to the end of demonstrating that the Articles of Perth contradicted "the Oath of the whole State of the land," a reference to the Negative Confession of 1581. This same year (1621), an English printer in the Netherlands brought out another forceful critique of James's policies, *The Altar of Damascus; or, The Patern of the English Hierarchie, And*

Church Policie obtruded upon the Church of Scotland, a text stuffed with references drawn from Theodore Beza, Thomas Cartwright, Henry Barrow, and other hard-core Puritans to simony (the sale of church offices) and parishes deprived of "liberty of election."[66]

As had happened during the agitation about the surplice and the ceremonies in Elizabethan England, the radicals blamed the doings at Perth on the bishops. Blair, for one, came to feel that "Prelacy itself was the worst of all corrupt ceremonies." What Row said in a manuscript history that remained unpublished until the mid-nineteenth-century and Calderwood said in various places echoed Martin Mar-prelate: the Scottish bishops were false shepherds whose craving for power confirmed the apocalyptic message (Rev. 13) that the "beasts" allied with the Antichrist would betray the true church. The two men were just as scathing about the manipulation of assemblies, synods, and conventions. Reminding their readers that assemblies, local kirks, and parliaments in Scotland had once been "free"—general assemblies meeting annually and electing their moderators, and parliaments enjoying open debate from which bishops had been excluded, a privilege James I had overridden—Calderwood and Row underscored the parallels between his policies and the evils of Roman Catholicism. Simultaneously, Calderwood and others around him reemphasized two-kingdoms principles that limited the authority of the monarch over religious affairs. The alternative to the policies of James I and the bishops was simple: to reclaim the "primitive" or apostolic perfection of the Church of Scotland. As well, Calderwood and his allies revisited the argument of things indifferent, which bishops such as David Lindsay were evoking to justify the new rules.[67]

Here, refreshed in response to new circumstances for a new audience of readers, was the story James Melville had told in his narrative of decline.[68] This rhetoric was not heeded by the many ministers and bishops who, after hearing the king distinguish the essentials of doctrine from matters of form and practice, stood by him. In the words of David Lindsay, who became a bishop in the church in 1619, James was "the matchless mirror of all kings, the nursing-father of his church," a man "so wise . . . so religious, so learned" that he should be obeyed. Reasoning of this kind enabled William Cowper and Patrick Galloway to align themselves with the king. In their judgment, sustaining the king's authority mattered in a Scotland that had experienced civil war and an abortive attempt (1600) on the king's life, the so-called Gowrie conspiracy. Tensions may also have been eased by the anti-Catholicism of the bishops and their willingness to retain some aspects of presbyterian-style worship and structure.[69] Another means of defending the king was to revisit the history of the Scottish Reformation. As represented by some of the new bishops, the reformers of 1560–61 had never endorsed presbyterianism. According to Cowper, the kirk "had no government but episcopal" during its first twenty years. Hence the legitimacy of the events of 1606 and 1610, which denoted the recovery of an earlier, more moderate reformation that had never rejected the office of bishop, a story from which John Knox was largely absent, given the role he played in the deprivation of Mary Guise. So Archbishop Spottiswood argued in a history of the Church of Scotland he wrote at the behest of James. Earlier, in response to Calderwood, he pointed out that episcopacy was not condemned in the Negative Confession of 1580/81.[70] As happened so often among nonconformists in England, the disaffected had to ask themselves whether holding out against king, bishops, and Parliament outweighed the consequences of being suspended or deprived. The numbers are telling: of the fifty-four ministers called before the Court of High Commission in the early 1620s for refusing to accept some of the new practices, most recanted. Others were suspended or, after being deprived, were restored, leaving a mere eight who were permanently dismissed.[71] Even so, protest persisted. In one of its versions, people avoided services of Holy Communion if they knew they would be required to kneel. In another, they formed "conventicles" (the name used by the authorities for unauthorized meetings) where they could enjoy the company of like-minded dissidents and, it seems, practice a freer form of prayer.[72] Hindsight teaches us that the real import of these years of controversy was the revitalizing of prophetic testimony against Catholic-style corruption and a similar revitalizing of the idea or image of national covenants as an instrument for restoring purity to the state church. When Charles I ascended to the throne (1625), the question that would dominate his reign was not which version of the past he endorsed but whether the one he most certainly opposed would blossom into a forceful reassertion of Scotland's covenanted perfection.

Puritanism in the Netherlands

The geography of the Puritan movement had encompassed the Netherlands ever since the 1570s, when Cartwright and Walter Travers ministered to a church organized under the auspices of a cloth traders' company known as the Merchant Adventurers; in 1582 this congregation moved from Antwerp to Middelburg. Robert Browne's short-lived congregation settled in the same town in 1581, and members of the Francis Johnson–led community known as the "Ancient Church" (the adjective signaled its fidelity to Scripture) made their way to Amsterdam in the 1590s after briefly attempting to relocate to North America. Any Separatist-style communities were outnumbered by those brought into being by the thousands of English and Scottish who staffed military garrisons, worked for trading companies, or were students at a Dutch university. When the time came to recruit chaplains for a garrison or ministers to lead a merchants' congregation, nonconforming clergy and disaffected Scots were usually available, a group that included Thomas Scott (d. 1628), who fled to the Netherlands after he denounced the Spanish match; there, he was assassinated in 1628. Some of these churches or chaplaincies—twenty-two of them were named in a survey made for the English government in 1633, alongside three Separatist congregations—ordained their own ministers and discarded the *Book of Common Prayer* or used a Dutch liturgy in translation. For a decade (1622–31) most of them participated in a loosely organized "English" synod, a means of preserving their distance from the Dutch Reformed Church. The English church in Amsterdam (1607), which served that city's English merchants, was the exception, abetted by the city's leaders, welcomed by the state church, and becoming part of the local Reformed classis. John Paget, its first minister, though of Puritan sympathies, was critical of Separatism and turned his congregation into a haven for people wearied of the disarray within the Ancient Church of Johnson and Ainsworth.[73]

It is tempting to describe the practice of these garrison and merchant-centered churches as a significant link between Robert Browne and modern congregationalism. It is just as tempting to expand this genealogy to include the theorizing of a few English ministers who repudiated Separatism but endorsed the concept of self-governing congregations.[74] As is true of most denominational genealogies, such projects distort the workings of "Dutch Puritanism." The categories of Separatist, non-Separatist, semi-Separatist, congregationalist, and presbyterian are ill-suited to the handful of ministers who set aside the project of taking over a state church and situated themselves somewhere between the Separatism of Barrow and Browne and the moderation of a Preston, a space more explicitly congregation-centered than what Cartwright, Travers, and Fulke had sketched, but also a space that implied a certain degree of interchange with the state church.[75]

Meanwhile, printers in the Netherlands were actively publicizing the worldview and politics of English and Scottish exiles and their Elizabethan forerunners. In the early seventeenth century, Dutch-printed books rehearsed the merits and demerits of Separatism and the quarrels that flared up in local Separatist communities. Of more importance, printers in the Netherlands—a group that included the Separatist John Canne, who took over the church of Ainsworth and Johnson in the early 1620s and operated a press in the late 1630s and early 1640s—were issuing controversial books by more recent dissidents: the first edition in English of Thomas Brightman's *A Revelation of the Revelation* (1615), several books by William Bradshaw, William Ames's *A Fresh Suit Against Human Ceremonies*, a handful of David Calderwood's tell-all attacks on the Scottish bishops, three tracts by John Davenport's critic, Alexander Leighton (1624–25), and Samuel Hieron's *A defence of the ministers reasons, for refusal of subscription to the Book of common prayer* (1607–8). Canne, who returned to England by 1640, where he moved in Baptist circles and eventually became a Fifth Monarchist (see chap. 8), survived the attempts of the English government to shut him down and, with the support of the Dutch printer Jan Stam, published some of the most outspoken critiques of the policies of Charles I, including Leighton's *Sions Plea against the Prelacie* (1629) and others written by Henry Burton and William Prynne (see chap. 7). Separatist-owned presses also reached back to the late sixteenth and early seventeenth-centuries, printing or reprinting texts by Cartwright, Travers, Robert Harrison, Laurence Chaderton, and John Spring's *True, Modest, and Just Defence* (1618) in support of the Lincolnshire petition of 1604. Far from being forgotten, the rhetoric and principles of the Elizabethan movement remained an important resource for these displaced English and Scottish. Only in minor ways was their radicalism directed against Cartwright-style presbyterianism, to which they owed the argument that congregations or parishes had a special authority of their own.[76]

The new century also saw the arrival of men and women who started out as nonconformists before moving on to Separatism. In Nottinghamshire, the Cambridge-educated layman William Brewster was in trouble in 1598 for "repeating sermons publicly in church without authority." A bishop's visitation had uncovered nonconforming ministers in the same region in 1590, and more were detected a few years later, one of them the minister Richard Clifton. In the aftermath of the canons of 1604, any nonconformist of Brewster's temperament had to choose between hard times in England and the freedom he would gain by moving to the Netherlands. Facing the same predicament, John Robinson (d. 1625) and John Smythe (d. 1611) resolved it by choosing exile over nonconformity. Both men were graduates of Cambridge who briefly served the state church, Smythe as lecturer in the town of Lincoln until he was dismissed for preaching "erroneous doctrine." Thereafter, he continued to preach and may have gained a license to do so before losing it again. Robinson was associated with a church in Norwich until he ran afoul of the canons and was deprived in 1606.[77]

Both men decided to leave the Church of England after listening to arguments for and against such a step; among those urging them to remain were the much-punished Hildersham and John Dod. By the close of 1606 or perhaps the following spring, laypeople and ministers, a group that included Clifton, had formed two covenanted congregations or "fellowship[s] of the gospel," one of them with Smythe as its minister, the other led by Robinson and Clifton. A year later, the two communities fled to the Netherlands, although Clifton and some others did not arrive until 1608. Their reasons for leaving the state church included the regulative principle, which guided their reading of Scripture as a description of what Christ "hath commanded," to which they added a yearning for the company of "Christ's faithfull and obedient servants."[78]

Soon after reaching Amsterdam, Smythe began quarreling with Francis Johnson and Henry Ainsworth about the role of laypeople in church affairs and, by 1609, decided that baptism within the Church of England was invalid. Although he was not the first Separatist to question infant baptism, he turned idea into action by rebaptizing himself and several laypeople in his congregation, one of them the well-to-do merchant Thomas Helwys (d. 1616?), who came with him from England. A year later, Smythe challenged the doctrines of original sin and election. Before he died in 1611, the evolution of his quest for the true church and a valid form of adult baptism led him and a fraction of the congregation to join a Mennonite church in Amsterdam. (Mennonites owed their name to Menno Simons, a former Anabaptist who adopted pacifism.) Helwys shared Smythe's disdain for orthodox Calvinism. When he returned to England in 1612, he became one of the founders of the Arminian Baptist tradition (see chap. 8), an honor he shares with Smythe in Baptist historiography. By this time he had written *A Short Declaration of the Mystery of Iniquity* (1612). An excited reader of Daniel and Revelation, Helwys discerned four scriptural "prophecies" about the relationship between divine judgment and the history of England. The third of these foresaw "the brightness of his [Christ's] coming [2 Thess. 2:8] for the consuming and abolishing . . . the man of sin" (i.e., the bishops), and the fourth, "Christ's coming in judgment." As many others had done before him, he employed this apocalypticism to "awaken" England from a "dead security and spiritual slumber." Wanting, as well, to free himself and his fellow Separatists from the slur of being "sower[s] of sedition," he extolled the authority of James I and pleaded his loyalty to the king's "power" in "all earthly things." On the other hand, he spurned the bishops, contrasting the "bondage" they imposed on "the disciples of Christ" with communities that emancipated themselves from the "man of sin" and "edif[ied] one another in the liberty of the spirit." He also argued that the civil state should stop punishing the faithful few who wanted to practice what the New Testament taught; if they offended in doing so, they "should be punished only with the spiritual sword and censures." Assertions of this kind enable modern Baptists to hail him as the first Englishman to call for unqualified religious freedom.[79]

John Robinson was cut from a different cloth, as was his congregation, which left Amsterdam in 1609 and resettled in Leiden. Always an orthodox Calvinist, he intervened during the dispute about Arminianism that split the Dutch Reformed Church. His reflections on the nature of the church became the benchmark of a congregation-centered polity he discussed with several nonconforming but not Separatist ministers who arrived in the Netherlands after having gotten into trouble in England. The most impressive of these men was Ames, who turned up in 1610 accompanied by Robert Parker and became the chaplain of an English garrison. Soon, the two men met Henry Jacob, who moved to the Netherlands in 1606. William Bradshaw, who remained in England, came to know Cartwright in the 1590s when both were living in Gurnsey; that he referred to himself as a "Presbyterian" at one point may have been a consequence of this friendship. Never taking up the work of ministry, he endorsed a congregation-centered polity in *English Puritanisme*, which Ames enlarged and translated into Latin in 1610. Paul Baynes (d. 1617), another friend of Ames's who stayed in England, theorized about congregational autonomy in a book Ames saw through the press, *The Diocesans Tryall* (1618).[80]

Except for Jacob and, after 1630, a few others, none of these men brought into being an actual congregation, and Jacob's was a singular version of proto-congregationalism or, as was said in the 1640s, "semi-Separatism." What Ames had to say of church order after 1620 was an incidental feature of his academic theology, and the garrison church he served was not organized along congregational lines. Moreover, these men were constantly rubbing shoulders with Scottish dissidents such as John Forbes, who ministered to a congregation in Delft and was the principal architect of the local English classis. In the free-floating world of what has been characterized as Dutch Puritanism, lines were constantly being crossed and identities rearranged in ways that defy neat classifications; for example, Hugh Peter, who is considered a congregationalist because he emigrated to Massachusetts after spending several years in the Netherlands, initially wanted to work with John Paget, who remained on good terms with Parker and accepted the jurisdiction of the Dutch Reformed (state) church. Well into the 1640s, Ames was being cited by British presbyterians, as was Parker. In turn, Separatist printers republished texts dating from the movement associated with Cartwright and Travers.[81]

Passing by Jacob, Ames, and John Robinson for a moment, another phase of Dutch Puritanism unfolded in the 1630s with the founding or refounding of two "gathered" congregations. The first of these experiments occurred in 1633 in Rotterdam under the auspices of Hugh Peter and the second in Arnheim, where a group of affluent English exiles formed a church in 1637. Imprisoned from time to time and his license to preach suspended in 1627, Peter went back and forth between England and the Netherlands, where in 1629 he became the chaplain of an English regiment. Four years later, after receiving an invitation to minister to the English church in Rotterdam, he agreed to take up the post if the congregation accepted a covenant he seems to have drafted. Only about a third of congregation did so, possibly because others objected to the provision that anyone who wanted to become a member would have to undergo a "meet trial" for their "fitness." Thereafter, no one who had previously belonged was admitted to the Lord's Supper unless this happened. The Arnheim congregation was situated somewhere between nonconformity and Henry Jacob-style semi-Separatism, a space defined, in part, by the decision of John Bridge and John Ward, its ministers, to renounce their ordinations in the Church of England and reordain each other. Theirs became a troubled community, some favoring and others opposing the practice of allowing laymen to prophesy. The outcome was schism, whereupon the discontented minority moved to Amsterdam. As the historian Keith Sprunger has emphasized, the Arnheim congregation had strong ties to godly members of the English nobility. When the authority of Charles I began to collapse in 1640–41, the ministers who founded it returned to England, where several of them played an important role in the making of English Independency (see chap. 8).[82]

Well before either of these churches came into being, Henry Jacob had organized a "free congregation independent" in London. As early as 1604–5, Jacob was arguing that the visible church existed in the form of "particular ordinary" congregations, each of them entrusted with the power of the keys (Matt.18:17) and exempt from the authority of any "synod." As outlined in *Anno Domini 1616: A confession and protestation of the faith of certaine Christians in England* (Amsterdam, 1616), his was a project predicated on Christ as king of the true church and Scripture as the source of its form, assertions he used to nullify the principle of things indifferent. As well, these rules justified the decision to eliminate bishops and a "provinciall" or "diocesan" form of church, that is, any version of centralized authority, for Jacob rejected the concept of a visible universal or "catholic" (in the root sense of this word) church that existed apart from local congregations. Like Browne before him, Jacob emphasized the "liberty" of "true visible Christians" to participate in governing their congregations, a liberty exercised by men but not by women to choose and ordain a minister. Church discipline was handled by the same group, and men were entitled to prophesy (speak) during services. Jacob expanded the "voluntarie" aspects of church order to a minister's maintenance; instead of any fixed version (as in tithes), he extolled free-will offerings. Worship was also free in the sense of jettisoning set prayer.[83]

Like the Separatists of the 1580s and early 1590s before him, Jacob tied together soteriology, or the possibility of being saved, to church order. In *Reasons taken out of Gods word* (1604), he argued that the right kind of church order was essential to securing "the safety of our souls," using the much-cited 2 Peter 1:10 as his proof text for the argument that obeying divine law was part and parcel of being a true believer. Like Separatists as well, he wanted to prevent "prophane and scandalous" people from entering the church, which was open only to "true visible Christians," the wording used in the Confession of 1616. Assertions of this kind harkened back to the practical divinity and its emphasis on sanctification as a reliable sign of the work of grace as well as to Calvin's insistence on the church as a sanctified community. Otherwise, the Confession was relatively conventional in what it said about two-kingdoms theory, the duty to obey the civil magistrate, and the role of the state in protecting true religion.[84]

Jacob's was a project that eludes quick-and-easy labeling.[85] Even though he accepted reordination after having renounced the ordination he received in the Church of England, he insisted on maintaining fellowship with local parishes in England, to the point of allowing his followers to have their children baptized in that setting. Earlier, in 1605, he had petitioned James I to "tolerate" an autonomous "assembly," a request he sweetened by offering to have everyone in the group take the oath of supremacy and "keepe brotherly communion with the rest of our English Churches." Reiterated in a subsequent petition, these proposals suggest that Jacob may have been thinking of his congregation of circa 1616 as akin to the "stranger" churches that continued to exist in London. Internal tensions, together with an eventual crackdown by the authorities, prompted Jacob and a portion of the congregation to immigrate in 1622 to Virginia, where he seems to have died by 1624. After a period of lay leadership, the congregation recruited John Lothrop, a nonconforming minister who also renounced his ordination. At a moment when the congregation was coming under severe pressure from the government, Lothrop moved in 1634 to Massachusetts, where the people who came with him founded the town of Scituate within the boundaries of Plymouth Colony. By this time, the London congregation had become a site of free-floating speculation about ministerial authority and other aspects of church order, with infant baptism favored by some and rejected by others.[86]

Aspects of what Jacob, Robinson, Ames, and Bradshaw were saying seem to echo Robert Browne's concept of the church. Yet it is doubtful that Separatist manifestos of the 1580s had directly influenced any of these men. Although their efforts to avoid the taint of "Brownisme" may have been self-serving, it seems likely that they owed a good deal to Cartwright and the cohort of "presbyterians" that included Travers and Fulke. It is easy to overlook the insistence of an earlier generation of reformers that ministers in the Church of England serve a single parish, each of them charged with administering church discipline. As well, that generation had emphasized every congregation's privilege of consent and the close connections between ecclesiology and soteriology.[87] Some forty years later, preferences of this kind were ripening into a stronger version of congregational autonomy. Given the date of Bradshaw's *English Puritanisme* and Jacob's musings of 1604 and 1605 on the authority of every "particular ordinary Congregation," neither man could have been influenced by Robinson. Nonetheless, Jacob sharpened his understanding of congregational autonomy and the structure of ministry during the conversations he and Robinson had in 1610. So, perhaps, did Ames, even though he and Jacob disagreed with Robinson's repudiation of the Church of England and may have persuaded him to acknowledge the possibility of "private" communion with parishes in England, a step he took by 1618 when he endorsed the possibility of hearing sermons that were preached in the state church.[88]

The master word in the ecclesiology of this group was "edification," which Ames regarded as the most important purpose of ministry: "The duty of an ordinary preacher is to set forth the will of God out of the word for the edification of the hearers." For Robinson, edification was impossible in a state church that retained close connections with the civil state and used a corrupt liturgy. For him, it was also the most reliable evidence that congregations could use in admitting persons to the covenant—indeed, the only evidence given the premise that the visible church was unable to identify the elect and therefore remained imperfect. Nonetheless, Robinson evoked the image and idea of church members as "spiritually hewn and lively stones . . . purchased with the blood of Christ . . . elect, redeemed, sanctified, justified."[89]

Circumstances transformed the Leiden Separatists into a fabled identity as "fathers" or "founders" of the new American nation. Learning of the English settlements in Virginia and the Caribbean, the community began to ponder the benefits of quitting the Netherlands and, in 1617, agreed to immigrate to North America, a decision linked to the impending resumption of war between Spain and the Netherlands and the older members' dismay that their children were being assimilated into Dutch culture. To this end the Leiden community sent a carefully worded statement to the Privy Council acknowledging the authority of the king "in all causes, and over all persons," to which it added the qualification that "in all things obedience is due unto him either active, if the thing commanded be not against God's Word, or passive if it be, except pardon can be obtained." As well, the group acknowledged episcopacy insofar as it was "derived from" the monarchy—that is, not based on Scripture—and tempered their Separatism by agreeing that the state church was responsible for saving "thousands in the land."[90] After a brief flirtation with the Dutch colonizers of New Amsterdam, the group secured the financial support of a few English merchants, a patent from the Virginia Company of London, hired a ship, and recruited specialists like the soldier Miles Standish. In September 1620, a hundred people crammed on board the *Mayflower*. (Robinson stayed in Leiden, where he died in 1625, but others from the Leiden community continued to arrive.) Reaching Cape Cod in November, well to the north of the region specified in the patent from the Virginia Company, the group went ashore in present-day Massachusetts. Before leaving the *Mayflower*, the leaders of the venture responded to "mutinous speeches" among some of the "strangers" (passengers who had not been part of the Leiden congregation) by creating a document known ever since as the "Mayflower Compact." The forty-one men who signed it agreed to "covenant . . . together into a civil body politic" capable of enacting "just and equal laws," a government to which they pledged "all due submission." On land, the colonists suffered a horrific rate of death during the winter and early spring of 1620–21. Nonetheless, more people continued to arrive, some of them Separatists, others not. Until the early 1630s, when the church in Plymouth finally acquired a minister, William Brewster, the ruling elder of the Leiden community, preached, although never able to administer the sacraments in keeping with the principle that these must be performed by a duly ordained minister.[91]

Among the English congregations in the Netherlands, controversy persisted about aspects of church order and their relationship with the Dutch Reformed Church. In the early 1630s, Paget's church in Amsterdam underwent a time of troubles after some of its members urged their aging minister to accept a colleague. Thomas Hooker, the first to be considered, was admired by the congregation's lay leadership but not by Paget, who handed him twenty questions about worship, church governance, Separatism, and the practical divinity. In his response, Hooker straddled the Separatist/non-Separatist divide: church members could attend a Separatist congregation; free-form prayer was as acceptable as fixed forms; new members should be admitted by the congregation but also approved by the leadership. On one point, however, he was emphatic. Congregations could choose their ministers without seeking the consent of the Dutch Classis, a practice justified by the principle that "particular congregation[s] hath complete power by Christ's institution to give a . . . call . . . without any derived power from a Classis." Hooker underscored this "congregationalist" stance by citing objections by Ames, Parker, and Baynes to a "superior ecclesiastical power."[92] Paget rejected this argument and, against the wishes of the church, persuaded the local authorities to prevent Hooker's appointment. Other candidates also came and went, one of them John Davenport, who began to preach informally to the congregation in 1632 or early 1633 while Paget was ill. Although some in the congregation wanted him to remain, he was politically unacceptable to local representatives of the English government and, on the issue of baptism, at odds with Paget. By the mid-1630s, moreover, Davenport was citing Ames and Parker on the limited authority of synods, a strong sign of an emerging sympathy for a decentered church system. This turn of affairs accounts for his removal to Rotterdam, where he became Peter's co-pastor, remaining there until 1637 when, like Peter before him, he left for Massachusetts.[93]

The Old Order Changeth

Narrating the debates in the Netherlands has carried us beyond the reign of James I, who died in early 1625. In the final years of his life, the king drew closer to a group of English bishops who encouraged him to distrust any and all "puritans." The most influential of these men was Richard Neile, though in matters of theology Lancelot Andrewes (d. 1626) led the way in extolling the importance of the sacraments as means of grace and objecting to the practical divinity as too preaching-centered. Andrewes and Neile regretted a key aspect of the Elizabethan Settlement: the destruction of altars and the transfer of the communion table to the lower end of the chancel or the middle of the church. Acting cautiously, the two men intervened in a few parishes to relocate the table to about the same place where altars had been when the Church of England adhered to Rome.

What the king thought of these efforts is uncertain, but by the early 1620s he was no longer the James of 1618. Everything he wanted by way of alliances was being undone by the Thirty Years War. Moreover, a new favorite had entered his life, the young George Villiers whose ascent to the rank of Duke of Buckingham (1616) happened with amazing swiftness. Neither fish nor fowl religiously, Buckingham broke with the old nonconformity in the mid-1620s. His master had already begun to detach himself from what he characterized as a "popular" movement and, by the early 1620s, was also moving away from Reformed orthodoxy. In the context of agitation about the "Spanish match," he told Archbishop Abbott in 1622 to instruct clergy in the church to stop meddling in "matters of state." In 1624 the king refused to punish the minister Richard Montagu, who derided the Calvinist affinities of the Church of England in *A New Gagg for an Old Goose* (1623) and a sequel, *Appello Caesarem* (1625). Angered by its themes, the House of Commons voted to censure Montagu on the grounds that his "Arminianism" was a stalking horse for Catholicism, coupling this gesture with a petition to the king warning him that popery was gaining ground in England. James ignored the petition and, when one of the bishops reintroduced images into his diocese, defended him against his critics.[94]

Suddenly worship, anti-Catholicism, Reformed orthodoxy, and the royal supremacy were all in play, issues that simultaneously were arousing popular anxieties in Scotland. The more Charles expanded on what his father had begun, the more he undermined each of the assumptions that had enabled moderates in three state churches to downplay "conscience" and endorse the "old non-conformity." Would a crisis in the new king's relationship with that version of Puritanism rejuvenate the more daring wing of the movement in England and revive the agenda of circa 1580—that is, no *Book of Common Prayer*, no episcopacy, and sharp limits on the royal supremacy? And what would happen if the king's program utterly overturned Scottish assumptions about covenant, church, and nation?

CHAPTER SEVEN

A New Sion?
Reform, Rebellion, and
Colonization c. 1625–1640

THE "PILGRIMAGE" THAT, toward the end of his life, Robert Blair (1593–1666) recalled in "some notes concerning" its "chief passages" carried him from his native Scotland to Ireland and, thereafter (1636), to passage on a ship heading to newly founded Massachusetts, a voyage thwarted by bad weather. That he left Scotland had everything to do with the Articles of Perth, which turned him into a critic of the state church. After losing his post at the University of Glasgow, he went to Ireland and ministered to fellow Scots who had emigrated to Ulster. A decade later, after being forbidden to preach (1634), he looked around for another haven—possibly in Massachusetts, having listened to John Winthrop Jr. describe the new colony. Almost overnight, this quest came to an end when an insurgency against the policies of Charles I erupted in Edinburgh. In its wake, Blair became one of the leaders of a newly reformed state church and chaplain in a Scottish army that repelled the king's attempt to restore his authority (1639–40). For a man who remembered being indifferent to the politics of religion at the outset of his career, this sequence of events was unimaginable: the insurgency and civil war, followed by a far-reaching purge of the innovations forced upon the kirk by James I and Charles I. The repercussions in England were almost as remarkable. There, in the aftermath of his failure to subdue the Scottish insurgency by military means, Charles I authorized the election of two new Parliaments, the "short" of April 1640 and the second, of November, which eventually became known as the "Long Parliament." Its policies were so at odds with Charles I's understanding of monarchy and the true church that the outcome was civil war in England between supporters of the king and supporters of Parliament.[1]

Explaining this sequence of events tests every historian of 1630s and 1640s Britain. The puzzles are many. In the context of this book, the most significant of these is the relationship between civil politics and the politics of religion. Intertwined throughout the history of the English and Scottish reformations, their relationship tightened in the practice and rhetoric of Charles I and the party he favored, here known as the Laudians. Like his immediate predecessors, the young king took for granted that opposition to his version of true religion was equivalent to challenging his authority as king. At once, the religious and the political (and especially the royal supremacy) become inseparable. Before 1640, the political and the religious in Scotland had also become intertwined, but in a quite different manner. There, it was being argued that a monarch's policies were corrupting a perfect church. And there, as registered in the life of Robert Blair, a unique event in British history unfolded.[2]

Beginning with Charles I's agenda and the reactions it aroused in the 1620s and 1630s, this chapter takes up the experiment of godly rule in New England and, thereafter, the remarkable turn of events in Scotland.

The Carolinian Program

Robert Blair was already in Ireland when James I's reign ended in early 1625 and Charles ascended to the throne. A change of monarchs could provoke fresh debate about which version of religion should prevail. Not in 1625, however, for Charles shared his father's preference for a rapprochement with Catholicism abroad and at home, although he briefly (1624–27) allied himself with a "patriot" or "war" party in Parliament eager to intervene on the side of European Protestants caught up in the Thirty Years War. By the close of 1625, he had concluded the negotiations with France begun by his father and married Henrietta Maria, the youngest daughter of Henry IV. With her came a retinue of Catholic priests who staffed the private chapel she was allowed to have in London. Before long, the Catholic presence at the Court or nearby in London included papal agents, a Jesuit "house," and high-ranking converts.[3]

Meanwhile, Charles was indicating that he preferred a sacrament-centered worship and a strong version of episcopacy. By the decade's end, the king was supporting a group of bishops and clergy who brushed aside the themes of "idolatry" and "primitive perfection" that had been of such importance in the making of the English and Scottish Reformations. Dubbed by some historians the "avant-garde conformists" but in these pages referred to as "Laudians" after William Laud (d. 1645), who in 1626 became the king's most important advisor on matters of religion, this group included Richard Neile, Lancelot Andrewes, John Cosin, George Montaigne, and Matthew Wren. By the 1630s it also included a few bishops in Scotland, where they acquired the nickname of "Canterburians." In Ireland, John Bramhall, who arrived in 1633 and was made bishop the next year, would advocate Laudian-style churchmanship. The Duke of Buckingham (d. 1628), had his finger in church affairs and, after allying himself with Neile and others, did everything he could to impede the Archbishop of Canterbury, George Abbott, who ended up being sequestered, that is, relieved of most of his authority, in 1627. Abbott had already been eclipsed by Laud, who became bishop of London in 1628 and archbishop in 1633, two days after Abbot's death.[4]

Charles was no theologian and Laud no Dutch-style Arminian.[5] Where the king led and Laud followed or the clergyman led and the king followed is a question that can tax the best of historians.[6] Broadly speaking, Laud, Andrewes, and Bramhall preferred a more positive view of human nature and its capacities for good than the practical divinity endorsed. The doctrine of double predestination was their bête noire, as was the Reformed premise of a limited (not universal) atonement. As Protestants, Laud and his allies agreed that divine (free) grace remained the ultimate source of salvation. Otherwise, they exploited the ambiguities of the Thirty-Nine Articles vis-à-vis high Calvinism. Uncomfortable with the nexus of preaching and "experimental" piety nurtured by the practical divinity, the Laudians extolled the sacraments, the ceremonies, and the visible church as an institution, or what Laud regarded as the "external" means of divine grace. Assumptions of this kind prompted the resumption of practices and artifacts the state church had curtailed under Edward VI and Elizabeth: baptismal fonts, chalices (the cup containing the communion wine), a full array of clerical vestments, standing when the creed was read and bowing at the name of Jesus. For many in England, the most troubling of these changes was how the celebration of the Lord's Supper was rearranged. At a moment when parish churches were administering the sacrament at a table situated in the middle of the chancel or perhaps in the main aisle of the church, Laud and his allies decided to make this setting more altar-like. The remedy they chose was to restore the table to the upper end of the chancel and enclose it within rails. Thereafter, no one could participate in the sacrament without kneeling to do so.[7]

Like the king, the Laudians regarded unity or uniformity as foundational. No evasive subscriptions by erstwhile nonconformists would do. Nor could dissidents appeal to the principle of things indifferent that had been the church's response to Puritan complaints about the ceremonies. Instead, the Laudians justified kneeling in particular and the ceremonies in general as apostolically sanctioned and therefore crucial to the very being of a *jure divino* church. Just as provocative was the argument that the unity of the church depended on episcopacy, which Laud regarded as sanctioned by Christ, existing in an unbroken sequence since the origins of Christianity, and grounded in a higher authority than that of the apostles. Most of his predecessors had emphasized the fidelity of the church to Scripture as the reason why Protestantism was superior to Catholicism, but Laud relied on the Church Fathers to validate his understanding of bishops and the ceremonies. For those who shared his understanding of Christianity and its political implications, the theme that unified the several parts of this program was the presence of the sacred in monarchy, state church, bishops, and worship, all of them seamlessly linked in a divinely instituted economy of grace.[8]

In keeping with this program, Laud had a more positive view of Roman Catholicism than was customary among English Protestants. Rome was a true church, he insisted, although erring in some respects. It followed that the apocalypticism of John Foxe and so many others was simply wrong: the pope was *not* the Antichrist despite the presence of this commonplace in the Irish Articles of 1615, the *Book of Martyrs*, a treatise on Revelation written by James I during his tenure in Scotland, and countless expressions of popular and academic Protestantism. So was idolatry when it was broadly defined, that is, applied in some blanket manner to Catholicism. Wanting reconciliation but not reunion with Rome, the Laudians followed the lead of James and Charles and, at home and abroad, attempted to ease the anti-Catholic rhetoric so prevalent in religious politics.[9]

Implementing these assumptions in Ireland became one of Laud's priorities in the 1630s. Like Charles, the archbishop wanted uniformity throughout the whole of Britain at a moment when the Church of Scotland continued to preserve some aspects of presbyterianism and the Church of Ireland much of Reformed orthodoxy, together with a posture of independence from the Church of England. Never going there in person, Laud worked through surrogates, most importantly the imperious Thomas Wentworth, who became the highest civil official in the country in 1633. Aided by Bramhall, who became bishop of Derry in 1634, Wentworth undertook to curtail the autonomy of the Church of Ireland and eliminate nonconformity. Bramhall was dismayed by what he found in those dioceses where Scottish-style preaching and worship persisted, reporting to Laud in 1634 that "it would trouble a man to find twelve Common Prayer Books in all their churches, and those not only cast behind the altar because they have none, but in place of it a table . . . where they sit and receive the sacrament together." He and Wentworth put their mark on the state church by tightening up the rules for uniformity and revising its official statement of doctrine. At a Convocation of church leaders and clergy in October 1634, Bramhall insisted on the adoption of the Thirty-Nine Articles, although foot-dragging by James Ussher and some of the other Irish clergy kept the Articles of 1615 from being formally repudiated. At the next Convocation (1635), however, a set of canons was adopted after much give-and-take between Bramhall's insistence on Laudian norms and Ussher's strong feelings about the autonomy of the Irish church.[10]

The new regime also targeted the Scottish families and their ministers in Ulster, driving out most of the ministers who had come over from Scotland and, when news arrived of the National Covenant (see below), requiring the

Scottish community to abjure (deny) that covenant and swear never to take up arms against the king. What seems to have survived was an underground network of prayer meetings not unlike the "privy kirk" of the 1550s. It seems certain, too, that in parish churches, some laypeople avoided the rules about kneeling and other ceremonies by staying away. What also survived among these Protestants were memories of the fervent spirituality that erupted during sacramental feasts and monthly lectures from the early 1620s onward, a spirituality some in western Scotland were beginning to experience thanks to the presence of ministers who returned to their homeland after being forced out of Ireland.

Of the measures taken by Laud, Charles, and some of the bishops to impose similar policies in England, several deserve special notice. At each of the two English universities, college fellows and presidents began to speak out against doctrines characterized as "Calvinist" or Reformed. Any such attempts had been punished in the 1590s and continued to be controversial throughout the 1620s. But by the 1630s, the more ardent defenders of Calvinism (moderate or otherwise) were being dismissed or falling silent in the face of censorship, real or threatened.[11] In 1626 and again in 1629, fresh versions of James I's 1622 "Instructions" specified that ministers in the church were not to preach "new inventions or opinions," language that, in the coded discourse of these years, referred to aspects of Reformed orthodoxy. As well, the "Instructions" were designed to minimize the role of preaching in the economy of grace. Continuing what Richard Bancroft had begun, in 1633 Laud required all lecturers—in his eyes, "the people's creatures" who "blow the bellows of sedition"—to take up a second appointment. The archbishop also ordered that clergy limit themselves to the exercise of catechizing at the afternoon services on Sunday. In 1633, Charles reissued a proclamation his father had previously endorsed (1618), the Book of Sports, which pushed back against any strong version of the Sunday Sabbath by authorizing certain "lawful" recreations—archery, other exercises, dancing (including Morris dances), maypoles, and church ales. Unlike James's version, which not been enforced, the proclamation of 1633 commanded every bishop to ensure that it was read aloud in each parish and to punish any minister who refused to do so. The same year, the Privy Council, on which Laud and other bishops served, resolved a dispute about the location of the communion table in an important London church in favor of those who wanted it "placed altar-wise."[12]

The year 1633 was also when Laud oversaw the dissolution of the Feoffees for Impropriations (see chap. 4), an organization condemned by the government's lawyer as "a Confederacy or Conspiracy, and this against the Church" and described by Laud himself as one of "the main instruments for the Puritan faction to undo the Church." In his own diocese of London, which included parts of East Anglia as well as in other regions where like-minded bishops had been installed, a fresh campaign against nonconformists and, especially, lecturers, unfolded. During a "draconian" visitation led by Matthew Wren in his diocese of Norwich in 1637, he ordered local church wardens to move the communion table to the upper end of the church and build rails around it; thereafter, he expected clergy to face the altar during some of the service. Wren also instructed ministers to limit the scope and substance of their sermons to what was laid out in documents like the prayer book catechism and use the sign of the cross in the ritual of baptism. Here and elsewhere, efforts were underway to suppress the versions of voluntary religion that the godly were accustomed to practicing.[13]

The final project of the Laudians was a fresh set of canons. Ratified by a Convocation in the spring of 1640 after the "Short Parliament" had been dismissed by the king, these opened with a dubious interpretation of the English Reformation: the emphasis on "rites and ceremonies" was not new but had been approved during the reign of Edward VI and practiced during the reign of Elizabeth I. More telling of the king's mood at a moment when his authority in Scotland had collapsed was the assertion that complaints about the ceremonies were really "aim[ed] at our own royal person, and would fain have our good subjects imagine . . . that we intend to bring in some alteration of the religion here established." This awareness of anti-popery and the damage it was doing to the king's authority prompted the first canon, which required every minister in the church to read aloud four times a year a statement extolling divine right monarchy. Canon 6 required clergy and certain others to swear an oath approving "the doctrine, and discipline, or government" of the church and promising never to "alter" its episcopal structure, an oath known as the "et-caetera oath" because "&c." followed the statement about episcopacy. The liturgy—or, as was commonly said, the "ceremonies"—was the subject of canon 7, which, among other rules, called for people to bow toward the altar when they entered and left a church, a gesture justified by its being a "most ancient custom of the primitive church in the purest times."[14]

Step by step, measures of this kind alienated the many clergy and laypeople who preferred a toned-down version of prayer book worship and took for granted the connections between English Protestantism and the Reformed tradition. Or perhaps their alienation had to do with rumors of a "popish plot" in which Laud and some of his fellow bishops were implicated—a plot directed at the political system (or "liberty") as well as at Protestantism. None of this resistance made sense to Laud despite the historic importance of anti-Catholicism in the making of popular Protestantism. His supporters justified their program not only on its own terms but also politically. They did so at a moment when Parliament and the young king were increasingly at odds over his authority to impose certain levies he needed to finance the government—so much at odds over "constitutional" issues that, after dissolving the Parliament of 1628–29, Charles governed on his own until 1640, when the crisis in Scotland forced him to authorize a new Parliament. Lacking his father's astuteness about compromise, Charles absorbed the argument that nonconformity, presbyterian schemes of church government, and Calvinist theology were, at bottom, anti-monarchical. Left unchecked, they would subvert the royal supremacy in religion and the authority of the monarchy in general. Laud saw any discontent through the same glasses, declaring in 1637 that those who disagreed with his program were bent on "rais[ing] a sedition, being as great incendiaries in the state (where they get power) as they have ever been in the Church." The king's steadfastness was repeatedly praised by men such as Samuel Brooke of Cambridge University, who warned him in 1630 that Puritanism was "the roote of all rebellions and disobedient intractableness in parliaments etc and all schisme and sauciness in the countrey, nay in the Church itself."[15]

Almost as telling as the actual program of the Laudians was the high pitch of their rhetoric. By the mid-1630s, with no Parliament to worry about, ministers such as Edmund Reeve in *The Communion Booke Catechisme Expounded* (1635) and Peter Heylyn in a series of books were praising the new emphasis on the altar, defending the Book of Sports, and mocking lectureships and Puritan-style sabbatarianism. Many years later, the ever-aggrieved Heylyn revisited the origins of the English Reformation and blamed much of what had gone wrong—in particular, the repudiation of Catholic-style worship—on sixteenth-century Edwardians who had fallen under the spell of John Calvin.[16] Meanwhile, English Catholics were heartened by the Laudian program and its beneficial consequences, including a "calme . . . from the violence of persecution" and a "good disposition . . . in many principall statesmen," as one Catholic noted in a letter of mid-1633. In the same circles, it was whispered that Charles was leaning toward their faith and that Laud was exchanging letters with the pope.[17]

Rumors of this kind were not what the Laudians were expecting once they endorsed a rigid version of uniformity. Yet as others before them had learned to their dismay, nonconformity always seemed to survive the campaigns directed against it. As had been true since the Elizabethan Settlement, bishops, church wardens, laypeople, and clergy variously embraced, ignored, or resisted aspects of official policy, avoiding it to such an extent in some counties or dioceses that a historian of religion and politics in Hampshire describes avant-garde conformity as a "failure," an assertion notably true of the Book of Sports.[18] Even though no one could criticize the monarchy, moderates within the church defended the traditional location of the communion table or documented the historic ties between the Church of England and the Reformed international. Others urged the government to align its foreign policy with the "Protestant cause" in a wartorn Europe. John Williams, the bishop who allowed John Cotton to drag out his nonconformity, was among the few of his rank who challenged the very heart of the Laudian program, which he did by questioning the new emphasis on the altar in a book published anonymously in 1637. Williams's politics prompted the government to fine and imprison him.[19]

As his protest indicated, the Laudian agenda was alienating some who favored episcopacy and the *Book of Common Prayer* or were at the moderate end of the Puritan spectrum. The onslaught on what many English Protestants had taken for granted—anti-popery, for one—drew a critical response from someone as well placed as Samuel Ward, the longtime master of Christ's College, Cambridge, and one of the delegates to the Synod of Dordt, who balked at labeling Reformed orthodoxy as distinctively "Puritan." As he put it, "Why that should now be esteemed puritane doctrine which those held who have done our Church the greatest service in beating down Puritanism, or why men should be restrained from teaching that Doctrine herafter, which . . . has been generally . . . maintained . . . I cannot understand." On the third day of the Short Parliament (April 17), a member of the House of Commons revisited the overtones of the same word, tying its abuse to "the divell" and, more immediately, to a popish plot. Another possibility was to insist anew on the connections between the papacy and the Antichrist, as the venerable Thomas Beard did in *Antichrist the Pope of Rome* (1625), a project abetted by a Puritan-managed reprinting of the *Book of Martyrs* (1632), and Beard's *Theatre of Divine Judgments* (1631).[20]

Locally, church wardens and magistrates in towns where the godly were a significant presence dragged their feet when told to move the communion table and rail it in, possibly because they recognized in Laud and his allies a clericalism that threatened every local elite. In All Saints, Northampton, where the wardens refused to do so, they filed suit after suit with various agencies in the hope of delaying any action. Once the rails were installed, they remained in place for a few months until someone moved the communion table back to its traditional location (1638). Other people were adding their weight to this resistance by refusing to take communion in the new manner.[21] It was telling that neither Laud nor local justices of the peace could prevent these expressions of defiance. Nor were they able to rein in lectureships and the workings of voluntary religion. All this we learn from sources that include Thomas Dugard's diary, which documents the persistence of "a quasi-presbyterian clerical community" and the "practical failure" of the Laudian program in the second half of the 1630s.[22]

By the close of the 1620s, the Laudians were being dogged by something far more serious than foot-dragging or surreptitious publications, a rhetoric akin to anti-popery but more extreme in the sense of identifying a conspiracy aimed at undoing Protestantism and English liberties.[23] One place where this rhetoric flourished was the House of Commons, which enjoyed a freedom of speech that could not be exercised elsewhere. The agitation in 1621 about the "Spanish match" and James's attempts to relax the pressure on English Catholics were fresh in the memories of Charles's first Parliament (1625), and although he enjoyed a better relationship with that body than his father had, the new king never understood that the rhetoric of anti-puritanism made little sense to many in the House of Commons and a smaller group in the House of Lords. Slowly, but with a growing assurance that they were right, a handful of parliamentarians began to argue that liberties that everyone took for granted were being betrayed by a faction of church leaders and courtiers. A name for this faction was easily at hand: "Arminian." Using this word loosely, critics of the policies of Laud and Charles I combined their several discontents into an alternative version of conspiracy, in this case a plot organized and led by a cabal bent on altering not only the historic identity of the Church of England but also the constitutional system.[24]

An important moment in the making of this social imaginary came in 1624, when John Pym, a member of the House of Commons, warned that "Arminianism" threatened the very foundations of English Protestantism and civil liberty. Speaking in Parliament for the first time in 1621, Pym had criticized James I's "lenity" toward Catholics and any relaxing of the laws against Catholic recusancy on the grounds that a domino-like sequence would unfold: "after toleration they [Catholics] will look for equality, after equality for superiority, and having superiority they will seek the suppression of that religion which is contrary to theirs." Thereafter, Pym drew on anti-popery and the apocalyptic tradition, with its bifurcating of Christ and the faithful few against an ever-threatening Antichrist, to incorporate the whole of the Laudian program into a story of deceit and deception. For men of this mindset, the rhetoric of anti-puritanism had been devised to weaken the unity of the Church of England and make it more vulnerable to subversion. Politically, the implications were just as alarming, for a "popish and malignant party" was using this rhetoric to alienate the king from Parliament and its role in governance.[25]

No one paid Pym much attention in 1621, but by the mid-1620s the mood in Parliament was changing as more was learned of Charles's sympathies and speculation rose about the connections between current events and the apocalypse. Stories circulated of who had his ear in Court circles—not only his Catholic wife, but also agents of the papacy and the entourage of priests she had been allowed to bring from France. Telling, too, was his indifference to the plight of Protestants on the Continent. Like his father, Charles ignored this crisis until deciding abruptly—and recklessly—to declare war first on France and then on Spain, episodes that culminated in embarrassing defeats, one of them inflicted on forces sent to relieve the siege of the Huguenot stronghold of La Rochelle.

The full force of these anxieties was felt in the Parliament that met in 1628 and reconvened in early 1629. In a June 1628 "remonstrance," the House of Commons singled out Neile and Laud as agents of an Arminian conspiracy, and that same month, both houses endorsed a "petition of right" protesting the king's breach of constitutional privileges. In November, the Commons resolved that "Whosoever shall bring in innovation in Religion, or by favour or countenance, seek to extend or introduce Popery or Arminianism or other opinion disagreeing from the true and orthodox Church, shall be reputed a capital enemy to this Kingdom and Commonwealth." What Charles said in return—

affirming his own authority as "supreme Governor" of the church, endorsing the Thirty-Nine Articles, and characterizing the anxiety about Arminianism as nothing more than "disputes" about "curious points" (i.e., inconsequential)—prompted a committee of the House of Commons to warn in 1629 of the "unfaithfulness and carelessness" of some of the king's "ministers" who were jeopardizing "the preservation of God's religion, in great peril now to be lost." Pointedly, the same committee linked the "extraordinary growth of popery" to "the Queen's Court" and "the subtle and pernicious spreading of the Arminian [i.e., Laudian] faction," to which it added a list of parliamentary and other statements on behalf of Reformed orthodoxy. As Pym had done in 1621, the authors of the report asserted that pro-Catholic groups were behind the government's anti-puritan rhetoric.[26]

The most striking of these outbursts may have been a speech by Pym's brother-in-law Francis Rous, a lay theologian who took for granted a Catholic conspiracy against English religious and political liberties. Characterizing Catholicism as "the whore of Babylon" and conflating it with Arminianism, Rous urged the House of Commons to "look into the belly and bowels of this Trojan horse, to see if there be not men in it ready to open the gates to Romish tyranny and Spanish monarchy." The taxes being levied by the government, taxes the House had repeatedly protested, were part of this conspiracy, as were other tactics aimed at weakening the role of Parliament in the making of state policy. But for Rous, the real challenge was to thwart a project that tied together the religious and the political in ways that corrupted both. If the one fell, the other was sure to suffer the same fate: "when the soul of a Commonwealth is dead, the body cannot long overlive it." Hence his concluding appeal to the House (and the nation): avert a decline into tyranny by "mak[ing] a vow and covenant . . . to hold fast our God and our religion."[27]

The day would come when the people of England and Scotland were summoned en masse to sign such a covenant. In the 1630s, with no Parliaments meeting in England and seemingly no effective avenues of dissent in Scotland, a handful of individuals came forward to dramatize the polarizing of good and bad religion and the specter of tyranny. These men acted at a moment when an updated apocalypticism was reinforcing the scenario of a popish plot. Ever protean, the biblical symbolism of trumpets, seals, vials, whore, and beasts had tempted sixteenth-century Protestants to align the narratives of apostasy, divine judgment, and restoration with the end times as described in Revelation 20: Babylon overthrown, the Devil sealed in a pit, the saints and martyrs reigning with Christ for a thousand years. Uncertainty about the dating and substance of this "millennium" (a "mystery" to John Bale and others in the sixteenth century) persisted, but in the 1590s and continuing thereafter, a fresh group of commentators began to link the symbolism of beasts and vials with history as they knew it and, using various methods, to redate the turning point when renewal or restoration would overtake apostasy—or if not the millennium itself, a millennium-like phase when the visible church would enjoy a distinctive purity. These attempts to decipher Revelation were paralleled by attempts to situate in current history the four kingdoms Daniel discerned in a dream (Dan. 2) and the four beasts he evoked in Daniel 7. Doing so would make it possible to foresee when the fourth kingdom would give way to the rule of the saints in a fifth and final kingdom.

Of the Protestants who struggled to untangle the chronologies embedded in this symbolism, the fiercely anti-Catholic John Napier, a Scottish mathematician, was especially influential. In *A Plaine Discovery of the whole Revelation of Saint John* (1593), Napier calculated that the final battle against the Antichrist would begin in 1639 and the Last Judgment happen by the end of the century. Foreseeing a period of well-being for the church on earth as it awaited "the sudden coming of the Lord and bridegroom, Christ Jesus"—a church without any need for another Constantine—Napier may have been the earliest British writer to connect current and future history to the coming kingdom.[28] Arthur Dent was much less specific in *The ruine of Rome, or An Exposition upon the Revelation* (1603), although he predicted that "even in this life" Rome would fall: "What can be more ioyfull or comfortable to all the people of God, then to know afore-hand that Babylon shall fall: Rome shall downe: Antichrist the great persecutor of the Church, shalbe utterly confounded and consumed in this world." The worsening situation of Protestants in the early stages of the Thirty Years War prompted the important Continental Reformed educator Johann Alsted, whose prodigiously inclusive *Encyclopaedia* had made him famous, to fix on 1694 as the beginning of the thousand-year rule of the saints, an argument he made in his *Diatribe de mille annis apocalypticis* (Frankfurt, 1627; translated as *The beloved city; or, The saints reign upon earth a thousand years* [1643]). In this as in earlier work, he insisted that the sequencing of vials and trumpets encompassed his own era. The English churchman Joseph Mede introduced a new method of aligning prophecy and contemporary events in *Clavis Apocalyptica* (1627 in Latin, 1643 in English). Although a loyal churchman, he maintained the connections between the papacy and the Christ in the course of arguing that the millennium was not something already accomplished but could be expected at some point in the future.[29]

For evangelical Protestants in Britain, Thomas Brightman was the most persuasive of these commentators. Like so many others who passed through late sixteenth-century Cambridge University, he became a nonconformist and, in the aftermath of the canons of 1604, was suspended for making "divers bitter invectives against" the state church. After he died in 1607, a Frankfurt bookseller published *Apocalypsis Apocalypseos* (1609), followed by an English version, *A revelation of the apocalypse* (Amsterdam, 1611), which, when reprinted in 1615, bore the title *A Revelation of the Revelation*. Brightman also wrote a Latin commentary on Song of Songs (Basel, 1614) and another on the Book of Daniel (Basel, 1614). Much of his exegesis concerned the dating of the conversion of Jews to Christianity, which he regarded as a necessary prelude to the return of Christ, an assumption grounded on Romans 11:26. [30] The more specifically Puritan aspects of his commentary—which drew heavily on Foxe, Bale, and more recent interpreters such as Napier and Hugh Broughton—was the perilous situation of the "whole Christian world" and especially the Church of England, a veritable "Laodicia" (Rev. 3:15) or "lukewarm" church that God would eventually "spew out of his mouth." What made it lukewarm was the "contagion of the Romist regime" and the absence of effective church discipline. No friend of episcopacy and, like Napier, critical of Constantine although continuing to appeal to the figure of the Christian prince, he interpreted the reference to "Philadelphia," the *most* favored of the churches singled out in Revelation (3:7–13) and certain to be included in the "new Jerusalem" to come, as a reference to Reformed-style churches in Scotland, France, and the Netherlands. Using language that harkened back to Thomas Sampson, Brightman warned his own church that it was "far off from coming to a full and due reformation" and would experience the "fury" of Christ unless it altered its pattern of worship.[31]

That dramatic change *would* occur was certain, in part because spiritual blindness was gradually giving way to a fuller awareness of divine truth. Taking for granted the progressive unfolding of sacred history, Brightman shared with other interpreters the assumption that, as the return of Christ neared— signaled, among other signs or portents, by the blasts sounded by seven successive trumpets (Rev. 8–9) and the conversion of the Jews—the visible church would experience a second millennium. The first having already occurred, the next phase was a "Middle Advent" or "Brightness of his Coming" (2 Thess. 2:8) when Christ would rule *spiritually* and the visible church achieve a remarkable purity. Brightman repeated another of the themes of Revelation, that conflict and suffering would intensify as Protestants approached the Middle Advent. A decade or more after he wrote, an English minister influenced by Brightman's analysis was among the many who corroborated this scenario by citing the Thirty Years War and the rise of the English "Arminians," both of them interpreted as signs that "Babylon" was continuing to ascend and the papacy to gain ground.[32]

How it happened that Brightman's analysis became so well known remains unclear, but it was immediately acknowledged by moderates and radicals in Scotland, England, and the Netherlands: James Melville in a letter of 1609; Separatists in the Netherlands; Robert Parker in *An exposition of the powring out of the fourth vial*, a brief tract (1616) that circulated in manuscript before being printed in 1650; Richard Bernard in *A Key of Knowledge For the opening of the secret mysteries of St Johns mysticall Revelation* (1617); David Calderwood in 1619 and 1621; Alsted in his treatise of 1627; Henry Burton in his apocalyptic *The Seven Vials; Or a briefe and plaine Exposition upon the 15: and 16: Chapters of the Revelation* (1628). Tellingly, the conformist minister

Robert Sanderson remarked in a sermon he preached in 1619 in Boston, Lincolnshire (possibly as a guest of John Cotton), that Brightman was the "great admired [by Puritans] opener of the Revelation." Summing up one version of his message, Sanderson complained that he "maketh our Church the linsey-woolsey Laodicean Church."[33]

Whether Brightman's doing or, more likely, in response to a wider array of arguments about the impending conversion of the Jews and other events, speculation about the approach of the end times made its way into godly culture on the heels of anti-popery. John White, the godly minister in Dorchester, tucked a reference to the conversion of the Jews into *A Planters Plea* (1630), as did John Wheelwright in his incendiary fast-day sermon of January 1637 (see below). In April 1639, Brilliana Harley reminded her son Edward, then living at Oxford as a student, that "this year 1639, is the yeare in which maney are of the opinion that Antichrist must begine to falle," adding that, "if this be not the year, yet shure it shall be, in its due time." Her afterthought may be as telling as her ability to repeat Napier's dating, for it suggests that she and her fellow godly were deeply engaged with the scenario of the true church at war with the Antichrist, a process unfolding as she wrote, for English troops were being mobilized to attack Scotland. At about the same moment, Robert Woodford was discerning "the whore of Rome the mother of fornicacon and all the abominacons that are in the earth" in the Laudian program and asking himself "why should not Babilon fall and be cast . . . into the botome of the sea like a milstone"?[34]

Enter the suffering few who defied church and state in order to expose the malice of the Antichrist. The resolve to become a martyr-like figure came easily to Alexander Leighton (d. 1649), the Scottish minister-turned-doctor who had challenged John Davenport's conformity in the mid-1620s. At the same moment, he was sounding the alarm about Catholicism in a book of 1624 and did so again in *An appeal to Parliament; or Sions plea against the prelacy* (1628; printed in Amsterdam with a title page that included a prophetic allusion to the defeat of English troops sent to relieve the siege of the Protestant stronghold of La Rochelle). Warning that the true church was in danger and highlighting the duplicities of bishops in the Church of England, he characterized them and "Arminians" in general as agents of a Catholic conspiracy.

The corporal punishment and life imprisonment he suffered in 1630 for his outspokenness were inflicted anew in 1634 and 1637 on three English critics of the regime. Henry Burton, a former royal chaplain who pushed back against the rhetoric of anti-puritanism in the mid-1620s, poured his complaints about Laudian "innovation" into *For God and the King* (1636) and a "collection of sundry memorable examples of Gods judgements upon Sabbath-breakers" (1636; a direct attack on the Book of Sports); politically, he tied Arminianism to assertions of the divine right of kings. The lawyer and lay theologian William Prynne had already insisted in *Anti-Arminianisme* (1630) that "Arminians swarme like Locusts in our Church of late," instancing Richard Montagu and others and characterizing all such men as "Traitors to our Church, our State, our selves." By the early 1630s, he was arguing in strongly worded books and pamphlets that "Arminianism" was really Catholicism in disguise and, like Burton, singled out Laud as the person responsible for destroying true religion. Prynne was also fiercely critical of the Laudians' *jure divino* argument for episcopacy. John Bastwick, a physician, was criticizing the policies of Charles and Laud by 1634 and became more outspoken by 1637, when a Leiden printer published his denunciation of the bishops, "the very offspring of antichrist," as power-hungry and persecuting tyrants. All three drew on the fusion of Christian primitivism and apocalypticism that Brightman had consolidated at the beginning of the new century, and all three exulted when the moment came for them to withstand the Antichrist in the person of Laud.[35] Burton was in trouble by the end of the 1620s and Bastwick by 1634, when he was heavily fined, the same year Prynne lost his ears for publishing what the Star Chamber (a royal court of which Laud was a member) classified as a "libel" against the monarchy.

On the same day in June 1637, the lives of the three became irrevocably intertwined when they were publicly punished after having been convicted in Star Chamber: imprisoned for life, heavily fined, the rest of Prynne's ears cut off, his forehead branded with the initials "SL" (for seditious libeler), with Burton and Bastwick losing their ears as well. "Many thousands of people" gathered at the site of the humiliation of the three men, a scene transformed by the response of an immense crowd "clapping and shouting for joy to see so great courage and comfort and undauntedness in each of them." As the victims of this violence made their way across the countryside to places of imprisonment, others cheered them on. Likening this process to a "pilgrimage," an observer reported that "the Puritans" were treating "the bloody sponges and handkerchiefs that did the hangman service in the cutting off their ears" as the "relics of martyrs."[36]

For the thousands who applauded the three men as well as for those who gathered up relics of their brutal treatment, a narrative familiar to every English Protestant had sprung to life. What happened so often in Foxe's *Book of Martyrs* was happening before their very eyes, the transformation of Burton, Bastwick, and Prynne into suffering servants of Christ. At that moment, everything Laud and Charles were hoping to accomplish began to unravel. Now, enemies of the state were really God's agents on earth and those in power were ungodly tyrants. Or did the treatment of the three martyrs replicate the persecution of the "witnesses" described in Revelation? This was what young John Lilburn assumed at the debut of his career as an outspoken critic of oppression by churches and governments. For Nehemiah Wallington, the government's handling of Burton, Bastwick, and Prynne was another episode in the overarching story of "the wicked . . . hat[ing] the godly and plot[ing] against them."

"What had these men don that they must suffer so much misery to the sheding of their blood with perpetual imprisonment[?] All was but for preaching and wrighting of the trueth of the word of God. In which their [*sic*] was a terror to the prelets false prophets Idolatry and profainors of the Lords day." Echoing Pym and many others, Wallington concluded that forces in England were conspiring to "corrupt" the true church."[37]

Several weeks later, a more far-reaching process of reversal erupted in Scotland when a crowd of women attending a Sunday service in Edinburgh shouted down a minister who began to read aloud from a new prayer book. For Laud and the king, this prayer book was the capstone of their program to align the Church of Scotland with a reimagined Church of England. The protests in Edinburgh and, by early 1638, throughout Lowland Scotland, had exactly the opposite outcome, the return of presbyterianism and the abolition of episcopacy. Across the Atlantic in the region known as New England, a similar process was unfolding. There, too, every aspect of the Laudian program gave way to a reformation that surpassed what the presbyterians of Cartwright's generation had imagined.

Kingdom Come: Visible Saints and Godly Rule

Several years before Burton, Bastwick, and Prynne were mutilated, thousands of English men and women were crossing the Atlantic and colonizing a region the explorer John Smith had named New England. At about the same time, many others from Scotland and England were moving to Ireland or creating communities in the Caribbean, Nova Scotia, and the Chesapeake. The earliest of the mainland ventures in North America, the doing of the Virginia Company of London, led to the founding of Jamestown in 1607. Some investors in this project were Puritans of one kind or another, but it was the Virginia Company's financial difficulties that caused it to assign a patent of land to the Leiden Separatists, who ended up on the north side of Cape Cod, where they founded the town of Plymouth in December 1620. The founders of the Somers Island Company (1612; known today as Bermuda) included Puritan-affiliated investors, one of them Robert Rich, the Earl of Warwick, who also promoted the founding of Providence Island (1630), which he envisioned as a base for raiding Spanish settlements and possibly as a refuge for political opponents of the king. Of the clergy who came to Bermuda and Virginia, several had been nonconformists in England or presbyterians in Scotland and, in the absence of bishops and church wardens to hold them accountable, did pretty much as they pleased. In the early 1640s, a few of the ministers in Massachusetts went to the Chesapeake at the invitation of preaching-starved colonists in Virginia, a mission terminated by the colony's royal governor after civil war broke out in England. Thereafter, the two regions diverged, leaving Massachusetts and three other jurisdictions (Connecticut, New Haven, and Plymouth) as the only places in mainland North America with a resolutely Puritan culture.[38]

The Massachusetts phase of this story began in 1628 when a group of investors, most of them London merchants known for their Puritan sympathies, formed the New England Company for the purpose of establishing a settlement along the coast. A year later, the company enlisted prominent ministers and gentry from East Anglia and renamed itself the Massachusetts Bay Company. Several of these London merchants had participated in the Feoffees for Impropriations and, in the 1640s, became "pre-eminent among the financiers and organizers of the parliamentary cause."[39] Despite being at odds with the policies of Charles I, the company's leaders secured a royal charter to the land between Cape Cod and a few miles beyond the Merrimack River to the north. Charter in hand, the company voted in October 1629 to transfer its leadership (or "government of persons") and the actual charter to Massachusetts, a decision paired with the naming of John Winthrop, who owned a manor in Groton (Suffolk), as the company's governor after he agreed to participate in the venture. A frenetic several months devoted to recruiting ministers, colonists, supplies, and ships enabled Winthrop and many others to leave England in March 1630. The venture hung in the balance for the next year or so, but by 1633 fresh waves of immigrants began to arrive, some of them organized in "companies" made up of parishioners of a minister or of families that knew one another. Separately, several Puritan-affiliated English aristocrats and gentry created the Saybrook Company (1632) and acquired the rights to territory along the coast and upriver in present-day Connecticut as well as to the north of Massachusetts. In trouble with the government of Charles I because of their connections with the Scottish insurgency (see below, sec. 3), some of the Saybrook organizers considered moving to Connecticut or elsewhere in the New World but stayed put once Charles I summoned the Parliament that met in November 1640.[40]

By the end of the decade, the colonists had dispersed along the coast or moved inland, migrations that ended up adding two more colonies—Connecticut and New Haven—to Plymouth and Massachusetts. Another cluster of settlements on Aquidneck Island and the nearby mainland evolved into the colony of Rhode Island (1644), which became a haven for people such as Roger Williams. From the start, and in sharp contrast to early Virginia, the four orthodox colonies attracted intergenerational families bent on remaining in their new home and, by the time immigration ceased in 1639/40 in response to political turmoil in England, several dozen men who had previously been ordained in the Church of England had arrived and resumed their profession.[41]

Only a small fraction of the godly crossed the Atlantic in the 1630s. The decision to do so came easily to some. For others, it emerged out of careful consideration of the merits and risks of an ever-more-threatened "old nonconformity" versus the merits and risks embedded in the project of colonization. As recalled by one of the colonists before he changed his mind, it seemed better to remain in England and "suffer than to cast himself upon dangers in flying [fleeing]." Seeking more advice, John Sill exposed his dilemma to "many ministers" who "sought God and could not tell [him] what" to do. For those who made up their minds more quickly, worship was the heart of the matter. In entries in a notebook he began to keep in the 1640s, John Brock recalled having been taught by his parents and others to "see the Evil of the Idolitrous Worship & Ceremonies of the Church of England." Brock had avoided ministers who adhered to the rules of the state church, a practice that made it easier to immigrate. Another incentive was the "love" he felt for "the Saints that were called Puritans" and the possibility of entering "the Society of a beloved Christian." The laymen Nathaniel Sparrowhawk and Edward Collins also cited the difference between the "superstitions" that "clouded God in ordinances" and the "purity" of worship in New England as their main reason for leaving England; according to Collins, he had been unable to "find God's presence in ordinances, being full of mixtures" and welcomed the "liberties" he had gained by immigrating. Writing from Massachusetts in October 1635 to his brother in England, the layman Edward Trelawny contrasted the "abominations and wickedness" he had witnessed in his homeland with the "pure worship of God" he found in Massachusetts, a difference he "account[ed] the greatest happiness" he had ever known. Summing up these aspirations and his own as of 1630, John Winthrop noted that the purpose of the migration was to secure "a place upon the earth" where the church could be "better preserved from the Common corruptions of this evill world" and the "Ordinances" would regain their "purity."[42]

For most of the ministers who left England, the decision to immigrate grew out of tensions between conscience and conformity that the Laudian program was exacerbating. As several pointed out in a collaborative letter (1637 or 1638) explaining why they gave up on the old nonconformity, the turning point had been the decision to regard certain practices or rules in the state church as "unlawful" and therefore too much for "conscience" to bear. John Davenport made the similar point in a letter of 1633: "in matters of conformity to the ceremonies established . . . I cannot practice them as formerly I have done." With compromises a thing of the past, most of the ministers and many of the colonists were eager to use their newfound "libertie" to achieve familiar ends: eliminating every trace of idolatry, protecting the sacraments from the unworthy, and asserting the authority of the church to act on its own. No longer bound by the principle of things indifferent associated with the old nonconformity, ministers and laypeople imagined Massachusetts (and more broadly, New England) as a place where they could restore church, worship, and ministry to their primitive perfection.[43]

A reformation of this kind looked back to what Thomas Sampson and John Knox had attempted in the 1560s, and forward to the Middle Advent. In Winthrop's letters as well as in those he received on the eve of immigrating, references abound to the "worke" of "establishing of a true church" and right worship. Writing from Massachusetts in 1634, John Cotton told a friend that "our people here desire to worship God in spirit, & in trueth," adding that the principal reason he and others had for leaving their homeland was "that we mighte enjoy the libertye, not of some ordinances of god, but of all, & all in Purity." Two years later, he told another correspondent that the colonists "doe in generall professe, the reason of their coming over to us was, that they might be freed from the bondage of such humane inventions and ordinances as their soules groaned under." A prominent layman echoed these words in a letter of 1634 to an English correspondent: "I account it an excellent mercy that the Lord has brought me to see that which my forefathers desired to see but could not: to see so many churches walking in the way and order of the gospel, enjoying that Christian liberty that Christ has purchased for us." For Thomas Weld, freedom of this kind was reason to rejoice. In a rapturous letter of mid-1632 to the godly of Terling, Essex, where he had been a lecturer in the 1620s, Weld reported that in his new homeland, "all things are done in the form and pattern showed in the mount [Exod. 25:40] members provided church officers elected and ordained sacrament administered . . . fast days and holy feast days and all such things . . . performed according to the precise rule," adding, a sentence later, that "all things [are] so righteously so religiously and impartially carried, I am already fully paid for my voyage." Echoing what Brightman had prophesied about the immanence of the kingdom, Cotton exulted in a letter to John Davenport, then in the Netherlands, that "the Order of the Churches and of the Commonwealth was so settled in New England, by common Consent, that it brought to his mind, the New Heaven and New Earth, wherein dwells Righteousness." A journey to Massachusetts thus became a journey down a road that very few English Puritans had traveled, a journey driven by "the Spirit of God" and destined to "set a patterne of holiness to those that shall succeed us."44

Simultaneously, the founders of Massachusetts embarked on an experiment in civil governance. According to the provisions of the Massachusetts Bay Company charter, "freemen" were stockholders in the company. Only a handful were present by the fall of 1630, a circumstance these men amended by admitting 116 men to the status of freemen and, the following spring, tying the status of freeman to church membership. At once, this step eliminated the criteria of wealth and rank that, for the most part, determined who could vote in England. Several years later (1635), a small group of ministers articulated a rationale for this rule and its corollary, that anyone holding *office* in the colony must also be a church member. Citing, among other biblical passages, Proverbs 29:2, "Where the righteous are in authority, the people rejoice," they gave two reasons for requiring "that all free men . . . be only Church-members." The first was the possibility that, without such a rule, "others besides Church members" would become part of the government and turn it against the project of reform.

The second combined the biblical and the political, the imperative of adhering to "the pattern of Israel, where none had power to choose but only Israel, or such as were joined to the people of God."[45]

Some months later, John Cotton defended the law in response to Lord Say and Sele, an English aristocrat of Puritan sympathies who wrote Winthrop asking for political privileges consistent with his rank if he came to the new colony. At Winthrop's urging, Cotton replied that the law was a "divine ordinance" based on (among others) Exodus 18:21 and could not be compromised. Cotton also emphasized its benefits in a colony that was assigning so much authority to church members and conferring significant "liberties" on everyone. Stability hinged on giving some group an "interest" in supporting the new version of church government. As Cotton noted, "Purity, preserved in the church, will preserve well-ordered liberty in the people." Doing so was also in keeping with godly rule, or the moment—tied to the rhythms of prophetic time—when the "saints" would finally come into their own as rulers.[46]

Left unsaid at this moment but discernible in hindsight were three circumstances that enabled the colonists to travel as far as they did down the path of reformation. Of these three, the most crucial was being on the other side of the Atlantic. Had Charles I been able to defeat the Scots in 1639/40, it seems certain that his government would have curtailed the colonists' autonomy. In 1636, it demanded that the colony return the Massachusetts Bay Company charter, which the leadership in Massachusetts refused to do. A year later, there was talk in London of sending a royal governor. Instead, Charles found himself dealing with the Scottish insurgency and, by the end of 1640, contending with a Parliament that would not have agreed to undo what was happening in New England. The reformers in Scotland came close to having a similar freedom, but Massachusetts was the first place where the godly could act without having to worry about the royal supremacy, a Court of High Commission, and a state church with its apparatus of canons, *Book of Common Prayer*, and parishes. As the minister Thomas Allen observed to John Cotton in 1642, the "dangerous" aspects of the royal supremacy had given way to a situation where the colonists could proceed without "such burdens as the churches [in England] were not able to bear." Thanks to being on the other side of the Atlantic, the colonists also avoided the clash between Presbyterians and Independents that disrupted the Westminster Assembly, the Long Parliament, and the alliance formed in 1643 between the Long Parliament and the Scottish government (see chap. 8).[47]

Immigration dispensed with another obstacle to reform. Although the people who arrived by the thousands in the 1630s were never of one mind, few of them resembled the "swearers" and "sons of Belial" who abused the godly in England. Of more importance in the short run, none of the grandees or aristocrats who participated in the Puritan movement turned up and remained. It is telling of Lord Say and Sele's perspective that, in Providence Island, the colony off the coast of South America he helped create, political authority was vested in a small group of officers appointed from afar, whereas in Massachusetts (as of 1634) the governor, deputy governor, magistrates, and deputies who represented each town were being elected annually by a substantial group of "freemen." Policies of the kind Cotton defended in his letter to Say and Sele ensured that Massachusetts and its sister colonies attracted only a tiny number of landed gentry and very few others, such as lawyers, who enjoyed special privileges in England. This shortening of the social scale and curtailing of socio-legal privilege had immense consequences: long-stalled demands for reform of the legal system became feasible, and popular participation in churches and civil governments expanded well beyond what was customary in England and Scotland. Because no town or colony awarded local congregations any property and tithes had disappeared, the crazy-quilt system of financing the state churches in England and Scotland vanished. No layperson in early New England would ever own church property, profit from church tithes, or in some manner "own" the privilege of choosing a local minister.[48]

One other circumstance is often overlooked—and, in the present-day rush to discover "diversity" among the colonists, overlooked without any awareness of what diversity looked like in Ireland, Scotland, and England. In two of those countries, Catholicism remained the religion of a significant number of people; and in Ireland, of nearly all the native Irish. Decade after decade, governments and state churches pressured these people into becoming Protestants and executed the militantly Catholic. In all three countries, therefore, coercion was a fact of life for Catholics, with persecution an ever-present possibility, although Catholics and others deemed heretics, like the tiny sect known as "Familists," became adept at blending in. Spared any such Catholic presence, Massachusetts and the other orthodox colonies were not spared the presence of Protestants who questioned this or that policy. But as commonly happened in Scotland, the typical response to criticism from within, as it were, was to banish these people.

At the outset, the organizers of the Massachusetts Bay Company remained silent about their understanding of the true church. Aware of rumors that the company was a Trojan horse filled with Separatists, its leaders initiated a literary campaign (1630) that included John White of Dorchester's *A Planters Plea: Or the grounds of plantations examined*, another text by John Cotton, and a brief statement issued just before Winthrop set sail in which he and six others professed their affection for "our deare Mother" the Church of England, a statement White (who may have written it) quoted in his own text.[49] In the other, a letter by John Cotton that circulated in handwritten copies, he complained about an event in the town of Salem, where an advance group of colonists had organized a church in 1629 and, shortly thereafter, installed two ministers hired by the company, Francis Higginson and Samuel Skelton. The newly formed congregation was "gathered" or selective, omitting two-thirds of the settlers and bringing the other third together in a covenant. A year later, as this group was preparing to celebrate the Lord's Supper, Winthrop and a handful of others who arrived at Salem with him asked if they could participate. Another newcomer wanted the two ministers to baptize one of his children. To each request the answer was no, the reason being that the two sacraments were reserved to those who were joined in covenant. On the other hand, the congregation welcomed a member of the semi-Separatist Jacob-Lothrop community "upon sight of his testimony from his church" and agreed to baptize his child. Hearing of this event, Cotton wrote at once to express his dismay, for the rebuff of Winthrop seemed to signal a Separatist-like policy of rejecting the parish churches in England because they lacked "the essentiall forme of a church," that is, a covenant and some means of disciplining the many who were "scandalous gospellers." Cotton thought he knew what had happened. "You went hence of another judgment," he told the two ministers, adding that "your chaunge hath sprung from new-Plimmouth-men."[50]

Seen through Cotton's letter, the events at Salem imply a fast-paced process of improvisation, as though the earliest people to arrive were reaching into the grab bag of Puritan ideas about the true church and emerging with several akin to Separatist principles. The more apt comparison may be with the "unsettled" Elizabethan Settlement. As in that long-ago period, so in early 1630s Massachusetts hopes ran high for an unflinching process of reform that would eliminate anti-Christian "tyranny" and Catholic style 'idolatry." Turning these hopes into rules and practices tested the civil leadership of Massachusetts and the cadre of ministers who participated in the migration. As late as 1635–36, the situation remained fluid in places such as Salem. There, the presence of Separatist-like tremors had much to do with the volatile Roger Williams. After he arrived in the colony in February 1631, he refused to "joyne with the Congregation at Boston because they would not make a public declaration of their repentance for haveing Communion with the Churches of England." Two years later, he asserted that Charles I was guilty of "blasphemy" and, as a "friend of the Beast," had "committed Fornication with the whore." He also complained that the colonists had no right to the lands they were occupying. In Salem, where he preached from time to time and eventually was chosen by the congregation as its "teacher," he declared that all the "churches of England" were "Antichristian." The following spring (1635), after the government required every man in the new colony to take an oath of loyalty, Williams preached that no magistrate should "tender an oath to an unregenerate man" or ministers "pray with such though wife child etc." He disagreed as well with the Old Testament model of righteous kings who enforced divine law, which his fellow ministers endorsed. In these early moments of his long life in New England, Williams was true to one strand of the Puritan movement in placing so much emphasis on the difference—for him, almost impossible to bridge in the everyday world—between purity and corruption in both churches and civil life.[51]

Elements of this purism turned up elsewhere, as when George Phillips, about to be named minister of the congregation in newly founded Watertown in 1630 and previously a minister in England, told his prospective congregation that "if they will have him stand minister by that calling which he had received from the prelates in England, he will leave them"—troubling because a stance of this kind echoed Separatist practice and threatened to divide congregations from ministers and ministers from each other. (Williams was also a critic of "unlawful" callings.) Simultaneously, some of the colonists were saying harsh things about the Church of England in letters that became widely known. A correspondent alerted Winthrop to rumors of "a too palpable separation of your people from our church gouernement" and, in a follow-up letter, that "you count all men in England, yea all out of your church . . . in the state of damnation." The tremors also included an act of iconoclasm. In November 1634, with warm support from Williams, John Endicott, who had headed the new colony until Winthrop arrived, sliced the St. George's cross out of the English flag the militia in Salem was using.[52]

These gestures drew a strong response from civil and religious leaders. Learning that an unidentified person had accused certain congregations of "mak[ing] whores and drunkards visible Christians," Winthrop offered a measured defense of people of "weake" faith and their nurture by the church. He had an ally in John Wilson. Elected minister of the congregation in Boston in 1630, he told the group that, although he gladly accepted reordination, he would not "renounce his ministrye he received in Englande." In another riposte to Separatist-style purity, the leadership of the colony censured Endicott and enlisted Thomas Hooker to defend the proposition that the flag was "no . . . danger" to the program of reform. (Two years later, the government eliminated the St. George's cross except in the flag at the fort which guarded the harbor.) Although Cotton sided with Endicott, he told Williams that the colonists were bent on "walk[ing] with an even foote betweene two extreames; so that we neither defile our selves with the remnant of pollutions in other churches, nor doe wee . . . renounce the Churches [in England] themselves, nor the holy ordinances of God amongst them," a stance he characterized as "moderation." The decisive step came in December 1635 when the magistrates ordered Williams to leave the colony. After a brief stop in Plymouth, he reemerged as one of the founders of the town of Providence in what subsequently became Rhode Island.[53]

Amid these crosscurrents,[54] a consensus was emerging on several key aspects of church order. Winthrop signaled this process in a letter to an English friend in September 1633 noting the concurrence of Cotton and Hooker, who traveled together to Massachusetts that year. Agreement on a two-kingdoms framework happened easily, abetted by the willingness of the civil leaders of Massachusetts to forgo any role in the process of church discipline and the colonists' determination to dispense with the heavy hand of the civil state in religious affairs. A conference among the ministers held in 1635 produced "A Model of Church and Civil Power." Reiterating the difference between spiritual and temporal forms of authority that so many Reformed Protestants (and Luther!) had articulated, the authors of the "Model" described Christ as head of the visible church, and Scripture ("the pattern in his Word") as authoritative in all matters of church order. Thereafter, it empowered congregations to choose their ministers, admit members, and carry out the process of church discipline in local churches, to encompass everyone regardless of rank or social status. Conversely, the "Model" barred churches from "erecting or altering forms of Civil Government" and ministers from holding civil office. The purpose of these strictures was to ensure that "the civil state and the church may dispense their several governments without infringement . . . of the power and honor of the one or the other." The boundaries between the two were sacred, the doing of a sovereign God. The point was also to disprove the commonplace that two-kingdoms theory threatened the authority of the civil state. Not so, the authors of the "Model" insisted, as long as the church stayed within the confines of the "ecclesiastical and spiritual." Ultimately, the significance of the "Model" was its understanding of the church. Instead of reproducing a Christendom in which church and nation or empire were indistinguishable, it took for granted that the true church was akin to the church of the earliest Christian centuries: possibly persecuted, never itself an instrument of persecution, and "free" in the sense of embracing voluntary membership and divine law. As John Cotton had been wont to say, "Christianity fell asleep in Constantine's bosom." Now, among a newly awakened group of the colonists, a postimperial church was coming into its own.[55]

The making of church and state extended into the 1640s, when the substance of the "Model" was incorporated into the "Body of Liberties," a text drafted in the late 1630s and circulated among all the towns before being endorsed by the colony's General Court in 1641. Among the "liberties" pertaining to the church was the "full liberty" of godly people to "gather themselves into a Church estate," followed by a liberty from "injunctions" by the state "in point of Doctrine, worship or Discipline." Simultaneously, the "Body of Liberties" conceded to "Civil Authority" the "power and liberty to see the peace, ordinances and Rules of Christ observed in every church according to his word so it be done in a Civil and not in an Ecclesiastical way."[56]

When John Davenport arrived in the colony in 1637, he reemphasized these principles in a text that remained in manuscript until the 1660s, "A Discourse about Civil Government in a New Plantation Whose Design Is Religion." Starting from the premise that church and state were "co-ordinate States" working together to promote the "spiritual good of men and the glory of God," Davenport warned against any confounding of these two spheres, "1. . . . either by giving the Spiritual Power into the hand of the Civil Magistrate . . . or 2. By giving Civil Power to Church-Officers." Davenport's "Discourse" and the ministers' "Model" are striking for what was *not* said. When Cartwright endorsed the same principles during the Admonition Controversy, he was pressed by Whitgift to acknowledge the royal supremacy. Nothing akin to the equivocations in Cartwright's response appear in the two Massachusetts statements and nothing, as well, of the tortured deliberations of the General Assembly in Scotland about clerical representation in the Scottish Parliament. Instead, the "Model" affirmed a policy that had been signaled in 1632 when the ruling elder of the Boston Church resigned his post as secretary of the government rather than hold these two posts at the same time. Thereafter, no minister or ruling elder held civil office of any kind in Massachusetts and its sister colonies. When asked by English moderates if the churches in Massachusetts could act without the approval of the head of state, the ministers answered, Robert Browne-like, that there was no need to wait for such support, one sign, among many, that the colonists had put the royal supremacy and the tempered Erastianism of English Parliaments out to pasture.[57]

Agreement also came easily on what form of church government the new colony would adopt. By the close of the 1630s a few "presbyterians" had arrived in Massachusetts and set up town churches. Yet they were far outnumbered by ministers and lay colonists who preferred a congregation-centered system. No document survives from discussions of circa 1631–1634 about the merits of a congregational polity, and we cannot make much of the example of Salem. However, Cotton's insistence mid-voyage in 1633 that he would not baptize a ship-born son because his ministry had lapsed clearly pointed in this direction, as did the presence of Thomas Hooker on the same ship. In 1631, Hooker had told John Paget, the minister of the English church in Amsterdam, that he favored the reasoning of William Ames about the capacity of a "particular congregation" to choose its own minister. In their back-and-forth, Hooker also cited the theorizing of Ames, Robert Parker, and Paul Baynes on the autonomy of each church in other respects. John Davenport had taken the same stand during *his* dealings with Paget.[58] Another straw in the wind was the arrival in 1635 of Hugh Peter who, in England, had helped raise funds for the Feoffees for Impropriations before leaving for the Netherlands, where he reorganized the English church in Rotterdam in accordance with the theorizing of Ames, who died just as he was about to join the Rotterdam congregation. Plan or no plan on the part of the Massachusetts Bay Company, it is striking that Peter and Ames had been approached in 1629 about becoming ministers in the new colony; after Ames died, his wife and family arrived in 1636. Knowing little about the politics of most of the ministers who reached Massachusetts by 1635, we can credit Cotton, Hooker, and a few others with extraordinary influence (which may have been the case) or acknowledge that long-existing possibilities rooted in the hybrid program of Cartwright, Travers, and their fellow presbyterians were springing into life. In May 1634, Winthrop told someone in England that "our Churches are governed by Pastors, Teachers ruling Elders and

Deacons, yet the power lies in the wholl Congregation and not in the Presbitrye further then for order and precedencye," a clear indication that agreement been reached on a de-centralized structure—soon to acquire the name of "Congregational Way"—akin to what Henry Jacob had attempted in London and others in the Netherlands.[59]

To Cartwright and, for that matter, John Calvin, several aspects of this polity would have seemed appropriate and others, unsettling. Every minister was to reside in a parish—or more precisely, was attached to the town-based congregation that elected him to office. In keeping with what was said in Travers's *Full and Plaine Declaration of Ecclesiastical Discipline*, the "office" of these men could not be exercised outside the boundaries of that congregation. More unusual was the principle, which Robert Browne had emphasized and Ames endorsed, that congregations should be founded on a covenant. Covenants of this kind were welcomed by most of the ministers in Massachusetts as a means of committing church members to mutual "edification," and symbolically as a means of differentiating Christ's spiritual kingdom from the profane or fallen world. Tradition reappeared in the structure of ministry, for the colonists reaffirmed what was said in the Scottish books of discipline: corporate or collective and incorporating the rule of "parity," it retained the familiar titles of teacher, pastor, elders (in Massachusetts, a single person), and deacons. Left unsaid, yet telling in light of what would happen in England in the 1640s, was the assumption that ministers held a distinctive office entitling them but not laymen to administer the sacraments.

To these principles and practices, the ministers and lay leaders were adding others that would have bothered Cartwright and, in the 1630s, were criticized by more conservative godly in England. One red flag to moderates was the decision to empower lay church members (the men, that is) to select their minister and ordain him without outside supervision. Congregations also held the "power of the keys," a principle that allowed them to debate and vote on matters of church discipline. Telling, too, was the willingness to let laymen "prophesy" (by asking questions, or perhaps by commenting on Scripture) during church services. From a presbyterian perspective, the decision to do away with centralized structures to which congregations were accountable was troubling. So was the shift toward lay governance. Both clashed with the assumption that parish churches should be supervised by a collectivity of ministers and, more tellingly, by synods.

Any such structures were melting away in the hothouse atmosphere of 1630s Massachusetts, their place taken by a robust understanding of each congregation's liberties. Always with episcopacy and Catholic "tyranny" as reference points, Cotton underscored the importance of safeguarding the churches from unlimited power in sermons he was preaching on Revelation 13 in the late 1630s. These were notable for his pessimism about the tendency of "transcendent power . . . [to] certainly over-run those that give it, and those that receive it." Everyone in Massachusetts and, for that matter, every Puritan in Britain, knew of real-life examples of this process—Catholicism, of course, and the royal prerogative in the hands of Charles I and church leadership in the hands of William Laud. For Cotton, a system of autonomous, self-governing congregations was the ideal means of protecting laypeople from a relentless appetite for power.[60]

About the same time as Cotton was describing the perils of unlimited authority, two of his fellow ministers were justifying the experiment with lay-centered governance. Responding to English critics who complained that the new system was empowering "illiterate" people, Richard Mather altered the meaning of literacy by locating it in the "hearts" of those who "have learned the Doctrine of the holy Scripture in the fundamentall points thereof." Thomas Hooker was explicit in *A Survey of the Summe of Church-Discipline* (1648; written several years earlier). There, he argued that "these are the times when people shall be fitted" to "receive and practice" much greater privileges. Like Mather before him, he deployed the scenario of the end times to subvert the cultural trope of "the people" as ignorant and unskillful and therefore "not fit to share" authority with those who were their superiors. Citing Brightman and evoking the new day that was dawning, Hooker insisted that God was enacting a great reversal: those of low rank or status were being raised up and made "fit," for "the Lord hath promised: To take away the vail from all faces in the mountain, the weak shall be as David, and . . . the light of the Moon shall be as the Sun."[61]

This newfound confidence in the people prompted other aspects of the new system. With state-mandated tithes and lay patronage dispensed with, congregations shifted to voluntary contributions. Justifying this practice to English critics, Mather evoked the framework of Christian primitivism: the "poison" of "settled endowments" had not entered the Christian church until the fourth century CE.[62] What happened with maintenance was also happening with worship, which the colonists wanted to liberate from structures that impeded the free movement of the Spirit. Stray copies of the *Book of Common Prayer* made their way to Massachusetts, but local congregations preferred the pattern of worship used in Scotland and endorsed by English presbyterians, a Sunday service consisting of Scripture readings, the singing of psalms, Word-centered sermons, and several times a year, the Lord's Supper. More daringly, the ministers insisted on free-form prayer, which they defended as in keeping with the "liberty wherewith Christ hath made us free" and the "Primitive patterns of . . . the Churches of God in their best times." There may have been some restlessness with singing a fixed text, as the psalms most certainly were, and argument arose about allowing laymen to ask questions during church service. Yet these disputes never became divisive, perhaps because what Cotton said on behalf of text-based singing was persuasive. As in Scotland and as Cartwright had proposed in the 1570s, marriages and funerals became civil events.[63]

The culminating feature of the Congregational Way was its version of church membership. What mattered most was to replace the "mixt multitude" of the typical English parish with churches "of saints . . . called by god into the fellowship of Christ" where they would "edify themselves." Complaints about inclusive churches filled with the unworthy had figured in the *Admonition to the Parliament* and the presbyterian program of the 1570s and 1580s. At that moment, the remedy was twofold: bar them and their children from the sacraments of baptism and Holy Communion and transfer the workings of church discipline from ecclesiastical courts to each parish. Now, in Massachusetts, this project acquired a fresh importance in the context of the colonists' aspirations for purity. No longer constrained by the parish system, and remembering how they had grieved in their homeland "when . . . profane persons" participated in the Lord's Supper, ministers and laypeople concurred on limiting membership to "Saints by calling" or "visible saints," the phrase used by the organizers of a congregation in the newly founded town of Dedham, Massachusetts.[64]

A step of this kind had been anticipated in Separatist or semi-Separatist ventures dating from the 1580s and hinted at in the Admonition Controversy. At those moments, the more "forward" Puritans had narrowed the distance between the visible and invisible churches and tied the validity of the church as a spiritual community to the ongoing presence of edification, or growth in grace as expressed in mutual love. Without using this word, John Winthrop endorsed the goal of edification in his "Charitie Discourse" of 1630. There, he outlined an ethics of "sympathy" or "love" for one another that visible saints were uniquely able to practice. Soon after he arrived in Massachusetts, Cotton was extolling the same ethics of love he discerned among those who had passed into membership. In the earliest of his manifestos about church order, Cotton echoed Paul's counsel to the initial Christian churches, calling on the saints to practice "brotherly love . . . and the fruits thereof, brotherly unity" and "brotherly equality." By unity he meant a congregation "perfectly joined together in one mind and one judgment . . . not provoking or envying one another . . . but forbearing and forgiving." By equality he meant a version of the golden rule, Christians "preferring others before ourselves . . . and seeking one anothers welfare . . . and feeling their estates, as our owne," playing here on the double meaning of estate as worldly wealth and spiritual condition.[65]

The unity of the local church and its commitment to the golden rule were ideals embedded in the covenants adopted by most New England congregations. In 1639 the founders of the congregation in Branford agreed to "deny ourselves . . . all ungodliness and worldly lusts, and all corruptions and pollutions wherein in any sort we have walked" and, looking ahead, to "walk together . . . in all brotherly Love and holy Watchfulness to the mutuall building up one another in Faythe and Love." Woburn's covenant affirmed a commitment to "mutual aid," adding a rejection of "the ordinate love and seeking after the things of the world." In Concord, the covenant opened with a backward glance at the "yoke and burdening of mens traditions" of the colonists' English years and the "precious liberty of the ordinances" they were enjoying in New England. Agreeing to subject themselves to Christ as king, the church members spoke with unusual realism about the possibility of "devour[ing] one another" and giving way to "self-love." Their way of thwarting such self-love was to promise to "avoid all oppression . . . and hard dealing, and [to] walk in peace, love, mercy, and equity . . . doing to others as we would they should do to us."[66] In 1647, the congregation in Windsor, Connecticut, renewed its commitment to a social ethics it shared with many other local churches, an ethics encompassing "love, humility, peacefulness, meekness, inoffensiveness, mercy, charity, spiritual helpfulness, watchfulness, chastity, justice, truth, self-denial," and mutual encouragement in the form of "counsel, admonition, comfort, oversight."[67]

A similar fervency flavored the process of organizing the congregation in Dedham, Massachusetts, in 1637–38. The handful of men who led the way began by agreeing that "the proper matter of" a church was "visible believers or saints," by which they meant people "who ought to make their faith and holynes visible not only by ther baptism" and "a civillle restrained life and some other religious duties . . . but such as by a *profession of an inward worke of faith & grace declared by an holy life sutable therto* [emphasis added]" made them capable of expressing "brotherly love" to others. This step accomplished, the next was to join in a covenant or "band of love" requiring everyone to preserve the "ordinances . . . in purity" and practice "all [the] duties of brother love especially faithfulnes to the soules of one an other in watching over each other."[68]

What happened in Dedham was also happening elsewhere. The founding of a congregation in Newtown (soon to be renamed Cambridge) in February 1636 seems to have been regarded as an example that other communities should emulate. Accepting the advice of colleagues who were present that seven persons were needed to "make a Churche," Thomas Shepard and six or seven men of the town "declare[d] what worke of Grace the Lord had wroughte in them" and "gave a solemne assent" to the church covenant. That the sermon text he chose for his sermon this day was Ephesians 5:27 indicates how fervently Shepard wanted the new congregation to be "a glorious church . . . holy and without blemish."[69] Thereafter, the women and men who became members in the 1630s and 1640s described their spiritual histories in "relations," a practice in other churches as well, although not in all of them and not always in the same manner. In sermons Shepard preached on the parable of the ten virgins (Matt. 25:1–13) soon after the congregation had been organized, he spoke rapturously about "virgin churches, not . . . defiled with the company of evil men; pure ordinances, pure people, pure churches," evoking, as he did so, the "brightness of his coming" prophesied in Daniel and Revelation when, awaiting the second coming of Christ, churches would "make themselves ready" by admitting only those who seemed "visible saints, visible believers, virgins espoused to Christ, escaping the pollutions of idolatry and the world."[70]

We may find it perplexing that the colonists raised the bar for church membership, and we may also wonder what was meant by "visible saint" and whether the bar was so high in practice. These are three quite different questions, of which only the first and second can be answered with reasonable precision. Setting the bar as high as possible was in keeping with the dynamics of reform in new-world Massachusetts. The meaning of "visible saint" drew on what ministers such as Shepard, Mather, and (with some reservations) Cotton were saying in the mid-1630s in the context of the practical divinity. Explaining to Mather why the gathering of a church in Roxbury, where he was about to become minister, was thwarted several months after the church in Cambridge came into being, Shepard emphasized the imperative to "build . . . a temple, not of stones, but of saints elect and precious." After listening to the 'profession[s] of faith" by laymen in that town, Shepard had decided that these were lacking in "evidences" of "gracious hearts." The same emphasis on interiority figures in a letter of circa 1637 from a group of Massachusetts clergy to English friends: "We heare them [i.e., candidates] speake concerning the Gift and Grace of Justifying Faith in their soules, and the manner of Gods dealing with them in working it in their hearts." That local churches wanted to hear about the inward workings of grace was underscored by what was said about infant baptism. As Richard Mather pointed out in *Church-Government and Church-Covenant Discussed*, a text dating from the late 1630s, allowing baptized adults to become church members could mean admitting someone who was a "drunkard" or "adulterer." This was a rhetorical flourish. Mather's real point was that people baptized as infants in the new colony would still need to make a "personal profession of Faith . . . when they come to yeares," a rule he likened to the practice in Reformed churches of examining people who wanted access to the Lord's Supper.[71]

Statements of this kind seem unimpeachable evidence of how the colonists understood the term "visible saint." These were people known for their capacity to practice edification and who were able to describe heartfelt "repentance" and encounters with a loving Christ. All too often, historians of this process have relied on "conversion" to encapsulate what was being described or expected. When this word was used in 1630s Massachusetts, it referred to a lifelong process. More commonly, people spoke of making a "profession." This term may seem formulaic, but in 1630s Massachusetts it signified the same combination of qualities Winthrop singled out in his lay sermon of 1630: profession as ethical practice (mutual love) that stemmed from the workings of the Holy Spirit on the heart. According to a spiritual autobiography written some years later by a woman who had been turned down for membership in Roxbury in the mid-1630s, that church was counting on her to describe a "particular promise made . . . in power" to her, or knowing "experimentally what it was to have . . . grace in my heart." It seems safe to conclude, therefore, that references to profession took for granted a combination of "inward" or "experimental" and outward evidence or righteousness, which is exactly what happened in Dedham.[72]

By 1640, a healthy share of the colonists had made their way into church membership.[73] Nonetheless, the Newtown-Dedham model excluded people who felt that being a member in good standing in England should entitle them to the same status in Massachusetts. One such person was Mary Oliver of Salem, who "plead[ed] her right" to "be admitted to the Lord's supper without giving public satisfaction to the church of her faith," a statement that must be read alongside what she said a little later to John Winthrop, "that all who dwell in the same town, and will profess their faith in Jesus Christ, ought to be received to the sacraments there." In Shepard's Cambridge, a high-status woman was remarking about the same time that the congregation was "too strict in examining of members." Already, too, people who had become church members were beginning to worry about the status of their children, who were not considered real members of a church until, as adults, they satisfied the requirements of circa 1636. Were they condemned to ecclesiastical limbo if they could not do so? A decade after the model of gathered churches had been formalized in Dedham and Newtown (Cambridge), pressure was growing to strengthen the significance of baptism, a story narrated in chapter 9.[74]

Amid tensions of this kind, the founders of Massachusetts and its sister colonies were implementing an innovative array of rules and practices in social and economic life. In a step with far-reaching consequences, the Massachusetts government distributed the land assigned to the Massachusetts Bay Company by the charter of 1629 to towns to dispose of as they wished. In turn, they distributed it as freehold (rent-free) to the firstcomers or founding families.[75] Amazing in and of itself, this process was accompanied by the near-universal practice of allowing all "admitted inhabitants" (i.e., heads of households) to vote in town meetings on how other distributions should be arranged. Commonly, townspeople evoked "equity" or "fairness" alongside the rule of proportionality (those with more received more) as these distributions were being made. The outcome was a system that ensured the economic independence of the great majority of households. In civil affairs, the colonists were almost as daring as they were with their churches. By 1634, the structure of governance described in the Massachusetts Bay Company charter had mutated into a system of deputies from each town meeting alongside magistrates in a "General Court," with freemen voting annually for governor and magistrates. In Connecticut, the founders of Hartford, Wethersfield, and Windsor were not constrained by a charter and could do whatever they wished. Hostile to Stuart-style monarchy, these towns arranged for the annual election of colony governors and the magistrates (or "Assistants") who served alongside them. No governor could succeed himself, and the assembly could call itself into session if the governor refused to do so.[76]

Another forward-looking aspect of governance was visible in the altering of legal procedures and the substance of civil and criminal law. Beginning with a statement titled "How Far Moses [His] Judicials Bind Mass[achusetts]" and another of uncertain title that John Cotton drafted in the mid-1630s, a small group of colonists, none of them lawyers by profession in England, revised practice and principle. Out went law French. In came a cluster of rights and privileges for plaintiffs and defendants: no one could be imprisoned "before the Law hath sentenced him," bail in all but exceptional cases, the right of appeal to a higher court, allowing plaintiffs and defendants to represent themselves. As well, in came a relocating of courts to towns and counties, with capital cases or those involving banishment reserved for the colony government to decide. Out went torture, high fees, and long delays. In Massachusetts, these reforms were incorporated into the provisional code known as the "Body of Liberties" (1641), which gave way to a Cambridge, Massachusetts–printed compilation of all the laws in force, *The Book of the General Lawes and Libertyes* (1648). The earliest book of its kind in British culture, the *Lawes and Libertyes* reaffirmed the revisions in legal procedure already spelled out in the "Body of Liberties." Theft ceased to be a felony punishable by death and became tied to restitution, and crimes deemed "capital" shrank to a short list of Old Testament rules about adultery, witchcraft, blasphemy, and the like—laws that, with few exceptions, no court enforced. The other orthodox colonies followed suit. Overnight, the cruelties of the English law and the abuses of power and money it sanctioned gave way to the values of peace, "mutual love," and equity.[77]

Unexpectedly, unity broke down in Massachusetts in the mid-1630s. The proximate cause was the preaching of John Cotton. By 1636, he was having second thoughts about the procedures for admitting new members and the customary wisdom about assurance of salvation. In Cotton's home congregation of Boston, a laywoman named Anne Hutchinson shared his apprehensions about what people understood as assurance and whether churches were being misled. For her as for Roger Williams, congregations were admitting too many who were hypocrites, a complaint she and Williams owed to their Separatist-like anxiety about who had been a true Christian in England. More emphatically, she objected to the preaching of the colony's other ministers. Except for John Cotton and John Wheelwright, who had recently arrived, she regarded everyone else as preaching a "covenant of works" instead of "free grace."[78] These assertions touched off a wave of anti-ministerial sentiment that flooded local congregations—Boston's in particular, where a dispute broke out about the authority of the church members to chastise or dismiss John Wilson, Cotton's older colleague. "Now the faithfull Ministers of Christ must have dung cast on their faces, and be no better then Legall Preachers, Baalls Priests, Popish Factors," was how a witness to these events recalled the turmoil of circa 1636–37.[79]

John Wheelwright added fuel to these fires in a fast-day sermon he preached in Boston in mid-January 1637. The purpose of the fast was to restore peace to a community that was becoming badly divided. Instead of urging peace, Wheelwright evoked the scenario of the faithful few at war with the "many" allied with the Antichrist. Massachusetts, he warned, had its false Christians or "hypocrites," the people who were saying that "sanctification" was reliable evidence of justification. Evoking a phrase dear to John Knox and many others, Wheelwright characterized the "saints of God" as "few, they are but a little flocke, and those that are enimyes to the Lord . . . are very strong." To this message he added the ultimate imperative of apocalypticism, the mandate to "kill" the enemies of Christ "with the word of the Lord." You may lose everything you own, he told those he was characterizing as true "saints," yet waging war against the Antichrist would only strengthen their relationship with Christ. "Therefore let the saints of god rejoice, that they have the Lord Jesus Christ, and their names written in the book of life."[80]

The response on the part of the magistrates and other ministers was unequivocal. Recognizing that Wheelwright's evocation of "spirituall" warfare threatened to derail any magistracy-ministry–led project of reformation, the government voted him guilty of sedition in March and, in November, banished him from the colony. (He moved to the region that became known as New Hampshire and, by the early 1640s, was beginning to reconcile with Cotton and others.) Thereafter, the magistrates, ministers, and most of the deputies to the General Court closed ranks and initiated a "cure" for what they termed an "infection." In September, a "synod" of ministers identified eighty-two "errors" and five "unsavory speeches," doing so in the presence of laypeople who participated in some of the discussion. The final day of reckoning came in November, when the General Court fined, disfranchised, and disarmed dozens of men on various grounds; simultaneously, it banished Hutchinson and men in several congregations. In March 1638, having spent the winter in Roxbury under the watchful care of a minister, Hutchinson was excommunicated by the Boston church for lying about her theological commitments. Later that year, she and her family moved to Rhode Island and subsequently to the Dutch colony of New Netherland, where she and some of her family were killed by Native Americans in 1643.

No one knew this in 1637, but the "Antinomian controversy" anticipated the confusion that overtook the Puritan movement in 1640s England, where the dawning of a new age of the Spirit spurred some of the godly to repudiate the principles of mainstream Puritanism (see chaps. 8 and 9). No such disruption occurred in Massachusetts, for the crackdown on Hutchinson and her allies renewed the alliance of ministers and civil leaders. As the response to Roger

Williams had indicated, that alliance was in good shape *before* the controversy broke out. Amid political unrest about the accountability of the colony's highest officers, Winthrop and his allies had voted in April 1634 to require every male above the age of sixteen to take an oath of loyalty, adding, a month later, a second oath for the colony's freemen, a step akin to what the leaders of the "pilgrims" had accomplished with the "Mayflower compact" of 1620. The same year, the government urged ministers and church members to devise a "uniform order of discipline" for the churches, and "to consider how far the magistrates are bound to interpose for the preservation of that uniformity." The mere hint of an "order" that would include interchurch cooperation aroused Williams and Samuel Skelton, the minister in Salem, to protest that such a step "might grow in time to a Presbiterye or Superintendancye, to the prejudice of the Churches Libertyes." Brushing aside their complaint, in 1635 the government called on all householders and single men to live within half a mile of a meetinghouse, a response—never of any practical significance—to the untidy dispersal of the immigrants across the landscape, but also a means of preserving moral supervision of the colonists.[81]

More telling was a step the government took in March 1636, when it ordered that any group intending to organize a new church must "acquaint the magistrates and the elders of the greater part of the churches in their jurisdiction, with their intentions, and have their approbation herein." Subsequently, the government welcomed the "synod" of September 1637 and, in the "Body of Liberties," authorized ministers and "brethren" to meet and discuss "doctrine or worship or government," to the end of "preventing and removeing of errour and offence." Hearing that the system of voluntary maintenance was causing problems, the government ordered in 1638 that every household in each town contribute to a minister's income. This year too, the government added civil penalties onto the ecclesiastical penalty of excommunication, a step justified by the presence of people who had not repented within six months of being condemned by their congregations.[82]

These steps suggest that that a more corporate and state-driven church was emerging within the outer husk of the "Congregational Way." Something akin to this was happening, although curtailed by the structure already put in place and the fervency of certain ministers and congregations for the freedom and purity of circa 1635–36. Learning of the law of 1636 just as Dedham was beginning to organize a congregation of its own, the people involved in that process asked the government to clarify its practical significance, effectively a shot across the bow of encroaching state control—and a salutary one, for the government quickly acknowledged the liberties of the church. Cotton spoke out against the new law about maintenance and insisted that his own church continue to rely on voluntary contributions. He intervened more emphatically in 1639 when, aroused by the law of 1638 imposing civil penalties on people who had been excommunicated, his strong words about it as an anti-Christian exercise of state power and possibly other protests prompted the government to repeal the measure.[83]

Nonetheless, the insurgency of 1636–37 was altering the priorities of many ministers and lay leaders. Salem had been a hotbed of dissent while Williams was there, for the congregation included a "separatist" faction. Some of these people left before Hugh Peter arrived in December 1636 as the church's new minister. Acting quickly to calm things down, Peter gained the congregation's assent to a covenant that bound church members to spurn "irregularities" and "carrye our selves in all lawfull obedience to those that are set over us in Church and Common wealth." The Boston congregation also renewed its covenant, vowing as it did so to "submit our selves to the discipline and government of Christ in his Church." Possibly at the urging of Winthrop, Thomas Shepard preached a sermon in May 1638 on "election day," when most of the freemen in Massachusetts gathered in one place to cast their votes for governor and other magistrates. Shepard used the occasion to contrast "discontent" and the misuse of "popular election" with "the strict government of god" upheld by the magistrates. From his point of view, the first would result in a politics of "divide and rule" and the second in "peace," with "public" needs replacing those that were "private." Perhaps because he knew of restlessness with the rule of 1631 tying the status of freeman to church membership, he warned that those who were "shut out of the fellowship of churches" were certain to be "an enemy unto the strictnes of churches," adding that, "to "ruine church you ruine state."[84]

Another way of preventing future difficulties was to reemphasize catechesis, as the Boston church did in 1636. At his ordination in 1641, Ezekiel Rogers spoke "somewhat earnestly about Catechizing, which (if God mean us good) must be a maine help." Its benefits were social as well as religious, benefits he regarded as imperative because of the "many Anabaptisticall Spiritts among us." By the close of the 1640s, thirteen different ministers had written catechisms for their congregations, some doing so in response to a recommendation of the government in 1641 that they resume the practice of instructing their congregations. Founding a college belongs in this sequence of events. The initial steps in this direction were taken in 1636. Two years later, a generous bequest from John Harvard, a Cambridge graduate and minister who died soon after arriving in the colony, prompted the organizers to attach his name to the new institution. Brushing aside any doubts about the importance of formal learning in the formation of ministers, the founders reproduced as closely as they could the curriculum at Oxford and Cambridge. As was said in *New Englands First Fruits* (1643), which publicized the college and the earliest stirrings of missionary outreach to the Native Americans, the purpose of Harvard was to produce a *learned* ministry.[85]

All this while, the godly community in Britain had been watching and wondering as news trickled in of Williams's outbursts, the "Antinomian" insurgency of 1636–37 associated with Anne Hutchinson, and the making of the "Congregational Way." Much of this news was alarming to men of the stature of Richard Bernard and John Dod. What made them anxious was the possibility—signaled in John Cotton's letter of 1630 to the ministers of Salem—that the colonists had veered too close to Separatism. In a letter of 1637 signed by Dod and twelve other ministers, the group expressed its dismay with the colonists' aversion to "stinted" prayer and the empowering of a majority of church members to decide matters of discipline, "though the pastours & governers & part of the asssemblie be of another minde." These men also worried that church membership had become effectively Separatist, given the rule that membership in the Church of England did not qualify someone for church membership in New England. The deeper issue was theological. How could congregations be confident of knowing the difference between the worthy and the unworthy? And why were the ministers rejecting the concept of a universal visible church that encompassed all who were Christians? Turning to church governance and the power of the keys, Dod and his colleagues warned that the new system was unduly "popular." In what sense was ministry a divine "calling" if everyone in this office received his authority from the congregation and was ordained by laymen? Wary of "popularity" at a moment when it was synonymous with "Brownisme," the letter writers urged the ministers in Massachusetts to hold on to the authority that was rightfully theirs—indeed, necessarily theirs given the sorry consequences of popularity. Concluding, Dod and his colleagues pleaded with the ministers to reconsider what they had done and "speedily reforme what is out of order."[86]

Queries of this kind suggest that, from afar, no one understood that a dynamic process of reform had preserved as much as had been altered. When the dust began to settle, the outcome—unplanned but fortuitous—was a "parochial" or "diocesan congregationalism" of covenanted churches, each of them the *only* church in a town and each therefore responsible for every member of the community. This double identity and the practices associated with it—limiting who was admitted but including every young adult or child in the exercise of catechesis—was unlike any of the Separatist experiments in the Netherlands or Jacob's congregation in London. Nor had any of those experiments included a magistracy-ministry alliance of the kind that existed in Massachusetts, an alliance shorn of the Erastianism of the royal supremacy and the daunting presence of nobility and royal commissioners, as in Scotland. Somehow, the colonists had managed to combine high claims for purity and a strong version of local liberties with something more corporate or collective, a mixture impossible to replicate in Scotland and attempted in England only in the informal setting of conventicles.

Scotland: To the National Covenant and Beyond

Eight years (1633) after his coronation in England, Charles returned to his native Scotland to be crowned as monarch of that country, a ritual occasion he used to display his indifference to the Scottish Parliament and the customary privileges of the nobles. With Laud at his side, Charles wanted to complete the project of religious uniformity his father had initiated. As part of that process, he had begun to appoint bishops who disdained all aspects of presbyterianism. Nicknamed the "Canterburians" because of their sympathy for Laud's agenda, this group included James Wedderburn, John Maxwell (who seems to have endorsed a *jure divino* understanding of episcopacy), and William Forbes (d. 1634), possibly the first person of this rank in Scotland to question some aspects of Reformed orthodoxy and advocate a closer relationship with Rome.[87]

All was not well when Charles reached Edinburgh, for grievances of several kinds had been accumulating from the moment he succeeded his father. As was true of discontent in England, these encompassed social, economic, political, and religious aspects of his rule—such as much higher taxes than usual, a project of "revocation" that disquieted the Scottish elite, the same group's resentment of the bishops who were holding offices of state, the king's indifference to petitions and local styles of governance, and rumors of "innovations" he was contemplating.[88] The "coronation Parliament," which included all of the Scottish bishops, saw in Charles the same king whose high understanding of the royal prerogative had prompted the "Petition of Right" in England. Tellingly, he told the Scots that his authority in matters of religion was indistinguishable from his authority in general, to the point of allowing him to command changes in worship without consulting a general assembly or any branch of civil society. The king's rough handling of Parliament, which was given a single day to vote on various measures without being able to review them ahead of time, alienated most of the gentry and burgesses.[89]

Then and later, Charles bet the house on the royal prerogative. He did so without heeding anyone who protested his policies, as William Haig (c. 1586–1639) did in a "Supplication" the king might never have read. Speaking on behalf of a group of men who recruited him to publicize their opposition to royal policy, Haig singled out a mode of taxation that violated the unwritten rules of the Scottish system. He complained, too, of the king's disdain for parliamentary procedures. Haig knew of the "anti-popery" voiced by John Pym and the assertion that "Arminianism" was a stepping stone to tyranny. He gave this argument a Scottish twist: bishops were instruments of the king's authority and should be excluded from parliaments, an argument reiterated in a separate petition signed by Thomas Hogge, a minister who had been deprived for refusing to acknowledge the Articles of Perth. Summing up "the grievances of the Presbyterian party," his petition cited the suppression of general assemblics (none had met since 1618) and the silencing of ministers who rejected the modes of worship prescribed at Perth. The master theme of both texts was being "free": once upon a time Scotland had enjoyed free assemblies and free Parliaments where people could speak without having to fear the Scottish version of the Court of High Commission or be accused of sedition, as happened to Haig and, after he fled the country, to John Elphoinstone, Lord Balmerino. An opponent of the Articles of Perth who, in 1633, voted against some of the king's program, Balmerino was convicted of treason after a copy of the "Supplication" was found in his house. Although the sentence was suspended, the king's pursuit of Balmerino gave the Scottish political elite an additional reason for distrusting Charles.[90]

The Church of Scotland saw another side of the king, his determination to align worship in Scotland with worship in the Church of England. The religious services Charles attended in Edinburgh were startling for their pomp, as was the coronation. Privately, he and Laud informed the Scottish bishops that the time had come to prepare a new service book for their church, a task Laud entrusted to a few of these men, although intending to review and, if necessary, edit any text that came his way. At an earlier moment (1616–19), when James I was urging a similar step, it seemed likely that the *Book of Common Prayer* would be melded with some of the peculiarities of Scottish Protestantism. This project lapsed, in part because of opposition to the Articles of Perth. In the end, the book that reached the bishops largely reproduced the English mode of worship, although closer to the more conservative (that is, more Catholic) prayer book of 1549 in how the Eucharist was described.[91] That it came with the king's personal endorsement and therefore the authority that was his as head of the church was underscored by the language of a new set of canons imposed by fiat in early 1636. The most immediately political of these may have been the requirement that every minister use the new service book, which no one had seen, or be deprived. Others reaffirmed the Articles of Perth, treated private meetings (conventicles) for prayer or discussions of Scripture as illegal, placed discipline in the hands of the bishops, called for moving the communion table to the upper end of the chancel, assigned the king the authority to summon a general assembly, and imposed an oath of supremacy (i.e., acknowledging that "the king's majesty hath . . . the same authority in causes ecclesiastical" as "Christian emperors in the primitive church") on all of the clergy.[92]

Learning in the spring of 1637 that Scotland's Privy Council and the bishops had done little more than require ministers or local kirks to purchase a copy of the just-published prayer book, the king imposed a deadline: bishops were to use the book in the cathedral church in Edinburgh at once. Thereupon the bishop of Edinburgh ordered the churches in and near that city to do so on Sunday, July 23. What happened on that date has become legendary in Scottish popular Protestantism. At St. Giles, with most of the Privy Council, the city magistrates, and a delegation of bishops on hand, a group of women shouted insults at the minister who rose to read from the book, tacking on abusive language addressed to the bishops: "Sorrow sorrow for this doolefull day, that they are bringing in poperie among us," was reputedly among the milder complaints. According to another report, a stool was thrown at the head of one of the bishops, a gesture accompanied by "out cries, rapping at the Doors, throwing in of Stones at the Windows by the Multitude without, who cry'd a Pope, a Pope, Antichrist, pull him down." When the bishop of Edinburgh chose the path of least resistance and walked out, he was stoned. Rioting erupted elsewhere in the city, with crowds assaulting bishops and other officials.[93]

These were not the spontaneous protests of an undisciplined rabble. Beforehand, letters and conversations had linked a "wide circle" of ministers and civil leaders hoping to thwart the imposing of a text deemed nearer to "Rome" than to authentic Protestantism. A letter of this kind reached the minister Samuel Rutherford at the beginning of 1634, whereupon he promptly dispatched copies to his circle of friends. The message was simple: from being a "glorious church" in "doctrine, sacrament, and discipline," the kirk of Scotland was in decline thanks to the "bastard porters" who ruled it. Prompted by this rhetoric of decline into apostasy, a loosely structured "underground" formed by early 1637, a process abetted by a small group of nobility and clergy aware of and probably encouraged by the conventicles and prayer meetings that emerged in the aftermath of Perth. Almost certainly, the group was also in touch with some of Charles's critics in England, who passed on news of the political situation in that country; and some were familiar with what David Calderwood and a newcomer to religious politics, the young minister George Gillespie, were saying about the fate of true religion in their homeland, Gillespie in the Dutch-printed *A Dispute against the English Popish Ceremonies Intruded upon the Church of Scotland* (1637). Hence the legitimacy of associating their cause with criticism of Laud's program in England; the grievances in Scotland were British grievances and the militant response to the new prayer book was warranted by a British-wide conspiracy aimed at true religion.[94]

The events of 1636—the new canons and, in November, the announcement that the new prayer book was being printed—accelerated the organizing of discontent. By June 1637, the leaders of the movement included two important ministers, Alexander Henderson and David Dickson. At St. Andrews, where he studied, Henderson had been among the "episcopal party" headed by George Gledstanes. Early in his ministry, however, he heard the sometime exile and fiery presbyterian Robert Bruce preach on the theme of the robber who enters the sheepfold (John 10:1) and switched sides, to the point of opposing the Articles of Perth in the assembly of 1618. Never actually suspended, he remained a parish minister until the insurgency thrust him into a public role he retained until his death in 1646. From his seat as moderator of the assembly of 1638 (see below), Henderson recalled the situation of ministers who, like himself, "entered" their office "unlawfully and with an ill conscience," thereafter doing little to "repair the injury" to God. The purpose of this self-criticism was to underscore the imperative to realign conscience and divine law, the same imperative felt by so many of the ministers and laypeople who went to New England. Awaiting the arrival of the new prayer book, the group pondered how to thwart it. In the aftermath of the riots of late July, Henderson and his allies began to insist that the moment had arrived for obeying God, not man, a theme leavened with apocalyptic allusions to the challenge of "rebuilding Gods house, and casting doune the Kingdome of Antichryst." What gave this assertion its political significance was the backing it received from nobles such as Lord Balmerino and John Rothes.[95]

Perhaps to their surprise, the organizers of the turmoil of July 23 were rapidly joined by other members of the nobility who objected to the prayer book, episcopacy, and how Scotland was being governed. (The "most powerful noble" in the country, Archibald Campbell, had to wait until his father, a royalist sympathizer, died in October 1638 before he could join the insurgency. Once he did so in his capacity as the eighth Earl of Argyll and chief of Clan Campbell, he became de facto leader of its political wing.) As the historian Laura Stewart has pointed out, the breadth of support in Edinburgh and elsewhere arose out of a "deep sense of alienation from the king and his Scottish government."[96] Hearing of the riots, Charles I told the Privy Council to punish those who were responsible for the disturbances, telling them also to impose the new liturgy, which he described as something he had personally "seen and approved." "Continue as you have begun . . . till the work be fully settled," he told the bishops. Powerless to do so because of the insurrection and of different minds themselves about the right course of action, the council was hearing from local kirks and members of the nobility that the time had come to oppose all "innovations" in religion. Tellingly, a substantial number of the nobility added their names to a "Supplication" justifying the revolt, a document critical not only of the prayer book but also of the canons of 1636 and the behavior of the Scottish bishops.[97] By December, the insurgents were demanding that the government abolish the Scottish version of the Court of High Commission and remove bishops from the Scottish Parliament and other civil offices. As the year was ending, they put together a structure of "Estates" to serve as an alternative to a Privy Council paralyzed by the intransigence of Charles I and its own internal politics. A little later (February 1638), when it became obvious that the king was unwilling to compromise, the leaders of the protest decided to draw the entirety of the Scottish people into a ceremony of covenant renewal tied to a document known as the Scottish National Covenant or "confession of faith," the phrase used in its opening sentence.[98]

As with any text of this kind, negotiations about the final wording softened some of its language; for example, "innovations" were mentioned but not specified. Yet there was no mistaking the core message of the text. To the "noblemen, barons, gentlemen, burgesses, ministers, and commons" who, beginning on

February 28, added their names to the covenant, it represented the insurgency as an act of conscience tied to the difference between "true and false religion" and justified by the imperative to eliminate all "papistry and superstition." Pointedly, the document cited a plot to "corrupt and subvert" God's true religion and "our liberties, laws and estates." Doing so was intentional, for it linked the insurgency in Scotland to the uneasiness in England with Charles's quest for revenue and his indifference to the customary role of that country's Parliament. Yet the centerpiece of the document was the version of Scottish church history fashioned by ardent presbyterians in the late sixteenth century, a history centered on the argument—evoked in late 1637 in the presence of the Privy Council by John Campbell, the first Earl of Loudon—that "ancestors" had entrusted the current generation in Scotland with a Protestantism "without mixture of human inventions" and incorporated into "the oath and covenant of the whole land." In keeping with this version of the past, the National Covenant included the entire text of the Negative Confession of 1581, to which it added a long list of parliamentary measures from the sixteenth and early seventeenth centuries directed at maintaining "true religion, and His Majesty's authority." Doing so was forcefully political, for these documents validated the capacity of "free" parliaments, presbyteries, and general assemblies to decide matters of religion.[99]

To its makers, the National Covenant was primarily a theological text. In the context of divine providence, the Scottish people were being summoned to throw off idolatry and reclaim the true church that had once been theirs, a church clothed in the aura of the myth so carefully nurtured by the Melvilles and David Calderwood, among others. As was said in the opening paragraph, the "true Christian faith and religion," although "believed and defended" elsewhere in the world, was "chiefly" visible in the "Kirk of Scotland," an assertion reiterated via a quotation from a statute that characterized Scottish-style Protestantism as "Christ's true religion, the true and Christian religion, and a perfect religion." To this assertion, the young Edinburgh lawyer Archibald Johnston, who drafted the text, added an apocalyptic overlay: the covenant signaled "the Lords merciful end so to perfect this reformation of ours" as part of the "work of destroying . . . Antichrist in the world." The covenant also evoked the story of decline from the high standards set by the "Golden Acts" of 1592. In effect, its purpose was to justify a wholesale unwinding of all that two Stuart kings had imposed on the church—an unwinding that necessarily extended to the royal supremacy. The covenant papered over the chasm between true religion and the king's policies by pledging to uphold "the majesty of our king." Yet it was unmistakable that the policies of Charles I had turned him into "an enemy" of what the Covenanters "considered to be the true faith."[100]

No mere piece of paper, the covenant was sanctified by fast days, appeals to repent and renew the historic covenant between kirk and God, and the fervor unleashed at these moments. Beginning on February 28 in Edinburgh and throughout the country in the weeks that followed, parishes, the nobility, burgesses, and many others added their names to the text or affirmed it with "uplifted hand," doing so after listening to a sermon and a public reading of the covenant. Describing one of these services in Edinburgh on April 1, 1638, Archibald Johnston noted that the minister used Exodus 19:5–8 (on keeping God's covenant) and Jeremiah 3:1 (where an unfaithful Israel is likened to a prostitute) as springboards for arguing that the covenant was God's means of "recalling and reclaiming his people" from their "former whoredomes and idolatries." As recorded by Johnston, "thereafter he desyred the nobles . . . to hold up thair hands and swear by the naime of the living God, and desyred al the people to hold up thairs in the lyk manner; at the which instant . . . thair rose such . . . abundance of tears, such a heavenly harmony of sighs and sobbes . . . as the lyk was never seen nor heard of." Ever mindful of divine providence, Johnston took this emotional outburst as a sign of God's "immediat presence, and inexpressable influence of his Spirit upon the whol congregation, testifying from heaven that he directed the work." "Taking the covenant" thus became a moment of collective and individual purification, tears flowing as repentance gave way to a powerful sense of God's sanctifying presence. At long last, the kirk was regaining "the greatest purity that ever any enjoyed . . . since the apostles' days."[101]

Samuel Rutherford shared this elation, to which he added an apocalyptic gloss. In 1636 the Court of High Commission had ordered him to leave his usual place of ministry and move to distant Aberdeen. There, he continued to counsel the people who sought him out, telling them that, despite the country's many sins, God was on the verge of doing something great for Scotland. In his reading of divine providence, signs of the times included Catholic victories in the Thirty Years War and the animus against "Puritans" in his homeland, all of them evidence that the ancient "feud" between the "dragon" and "the Lamb and his followers" was ripening to a climax. In his gloss on the National Covenant, Rutherford melded biblical references to the escape from Egypt and the end times foreseen in Revelation into a celebration of a Scotland that had taken Christ as its bridegroom: "For the Lord is rejoicing over us in this land, as the bridegroom rejoiceth over the bride: and the Lord hath changed the name of Scotland. They call us now no more 'forsaken,' nor 'desolate'; but our land is called 'Hephzibah' and 'Beulah'" (Isa. 62:4). Turning prophet, Rutherford predicted that the end times were fast approaching. The conversion of the Jews was in sight, and God was "fetching a blow upon the Beast, and the scarlet-coloured Whore." Writing in 1639 to his countryman, the imprisoned Alexander Leighton, he remained confident that the "kingdoms of the earth" were about to "become Christ's."[102]

Rutherford did not speak for everyone, for others felt that the covenant went too far in curtailing the king's authority. In a fast-day sermon preached in April, Henderson acknowledged that some of his countrymen were reluctant to act "against our superiors" but brushed such "scruples" aside. The covenant was not directed against the king; "on the contrary," everyone who signed the document was promising to "stand to the defence of our dread Sovereign the King's Majesty . . . in the preservation of . . . true religion." As the leaders of the Covenanter movement surely knew, the stipulation "true religion" altered the meaning of what was said about the king, as did the rest of this sentence, which committed those who signed it to "the mutual defence and assistance every one of us of another . . . against all sorts of persons whatsoever." Mutual defense against whom, a contemporary reader may have wondered, to which the implicit answer was, the king and those of the nobility who sided with him, that is, "all sorts of persons whatsoever" who opposed the document.[103]

Some modern scholars ignore this wording and question the radicalism of the Scottish National Covenant, pointing out, for example, the role of a disaffected nobility in the revolt of 1637–38, a circumstance they regard as a sign of business as usual, that is, reform or protest as a top-down process the nobility was expecting to control. Or it has been suggested that the Covenanters were depending on concepts of "fundamental" law they owed to an English tradition and were imagining a pan-British process of renewal.[104] For sure, the "covenanting movement was never completely homogeneous."[105] Yet in the context of what was happening (and in England, *not* happening), the radicalism of the insurgency that brought it into being is unmistakable. In the wake of the covenant and hints that Charles I might be willing to relax his policy, the leaders of the insurgency specified eight demands that were quickly made public, a list that included the elimination of the Court of High Commission, holding of general assemblies once a year, allowing a new Parliament to endorse what a forthcoming assembly would decide, and no appointments of ministers unless these were approved by the local parish and presbytery. The insistence on free assemblies and parliaments implied something much closer to a constitutional monarchy, as did the covenant itself, which was "distinctly unorthodox" in how it represented the relationship between king and people. Framing itself as an "unconditional" pact between God and the Scottish people, it was explicitly *conditional* with respect to the monarch's authority: were a king to introduce corruption, the people were empowered to purge church and state on their own. As David Dickson said in August 1638, "Better to obey God than man; where he proved that disobedience to God could not be disobedience to authority."[106] According to the covenant and what was being articulated in its aftermath, the true "lieutenants of God" were the Scottish people, together with the institutions of assembly, parliament, and a ministry Henderson described as blessed with "a seal from heaven" to pursue "with all diligence and faithfulness" the cause of reform. In fast-day and communion sermons he preached in 1638, Henderson attributed great things to the document. It was liberating Scotland from a "slavery" akin to what ancient Israel had experienced during *its* "captivity," and enabling the kirk to reclaim its identity as a "Sion" unlike any other in being so fully committed to "the Word of God."[107]

That Presbyterianism was the sole alternative to anti-Christian innovations became clear when a "free" General Assembly met in Glasgow in late November 1638. The question that haunted the two hundred ministers and lay delegates—the same question that has haunted every revolution in modern Europe—was how to ensure the legitimacy of a newly renovated institution. According to a rule laid down in the 1580s, no general assembly could meet without the approval of the king. On the eve of the assembly, a group of Scottish bishops underscored the precarious legality of the assembly-to-be in an angry "Declinotor and Protestation": the "pretended" assembly was usurping the king's authority and their own, without which it was unlawful. Already, however, the leaders of the insurgency were evoking an alternative understanding of authority. In a "Protestation" justifying their insistence on a free assembly—free in the sense of debating and deciding without any "limitation[s]"—they argued that it was warranted without the king's approval thanks to an "authority" God had entrusted to the kirk so it could best serve the "salvation of the peoples Soules."[108] Via assertions of this kind, a line Charles I regarded as sacrosanct was about to be transgressed.

For the moment, the king acceded to the advice of his principal advisor in Scotland, the Marquis of Hamilton, and allowed him to attend the assembly in the role of the king's "Commissioner." In the opening moments, with Hamilton nodding his approval, Henderson endorsed the concept of the godly monarch as guardian of the church: "it hath been the glorie of the reformed Churches, and we accompt it our glorie after a speciall maner, to give unto Kings and Christian Magistrates, what belongs to their places." Hamilton may have assumed that the assembly would refrain from rejecting episcopacy—abjure, perhaps, but not abolish. Any hopes of a more moderate outcome ended once the assembly approved the presence of lay elders chosen by local presbyteries, whereupon Hamilton walked out. In his absence, Henderson sang a different tune: Christ "hath given divine warrants to convocat assemblies whether Magistrates consent or not," adding that the kirk was subject to the authority of God and entitled to act on its own if need be.[109] With virtually no dissent (none of the bishops were on hand, and local elections of delegates had been dominated by the covenanting party), the assembly nullified each of the six assemblies that had met since 1606 and repealed the Articles of Perth. Simultaneously, it dismissed the canons of 1636 and the new prayer book; declared null and void the oath required of newly ordained ministers to accept the Articles of Perth; and overturned all suspensions or deprivations of ministers under the old regime. As well, it prohibited any blurring of civil and ecclesiastical offices, insisted on annual sessions of the General Assembly, and restored the "Powers and Jurisdictions" of presbyteries, synods, and assemblies. Last but not least, it voted to excommunicate most of the bishops, a few of whom had already recanted their office, with episcopacy itself "abjured, never hereafter to be established," a step it took after listening to the minister Robert Baillie read "A Discourse anent Episcopacy," which retraced the biblical and post-apostolic evidence for and against a "perpetuall superioritie" and "divine institution" of this office.[110]

This package made it certain that Charles I would try to intervene and quash the insurrection by force of arms and just as certain that some in Scotland would support him or look for ways of combining royal authority with free parliaments. As Charles noted in a statement of February 1639, the issue was "whether he were king or not," a point underscored in a royal proclamation of May 14 referring to the insurgents as "Rebells" and specifying the king's determination to "destroy" them.[111] By this time, a "committee of estates" comprised of gentry, ministry, and nobles was running the country alongside the customary institutions of governance. Its immediate task was to prepare for what was coming, an invasion by English troops in mid-1639. The deeper question arose out of the extraordinary fervor of March 1638. Could the covenant become a truly national or unifying document? In 1638, a near miracle had occurred, an upwelling of support that included most of the nobility and, with a few significant exceptions, the whole of the ministry and virtually the whole of Scottish Protestants. Anyone who knew Scottish history was aware of other moments of popular fervor—the Negative Confession of early 1581 and the covenant of 1596—that, in the long run, had not impeded James VI. Was there something different about the National Covenant that would give it an enduring presence?

Scotland being Scotland, some people were never going to acknowledge the covenant—Catholics, most obviously, but as it turned out, also the theological faculty in Aberdeen, a group known as the "Aberdeen doctors," who protested the theological and political implications of the covenant, with the backing of the town's lay leaders. As the "doctors" pointed out, the Negative Confession of 1581 had not condemned episcopacy, and the Articles of Perth had been ratified by a Parliament and a "national assembly." A delegation of ministers from Edinburgh having failed to convince them otherwise, the new government undertook military action against the town and other dissidents in the Highlands where, as usual, rivalries among the clans were intertwined with religious and political affiliations.[112]

That force or something close to it would be necessary to bring about the semblance of unity was demonstrated when the next General Assembly asked the government to impose the covenant on everyone, a step the Scottish Parliament, meeting for the first time since the insurgency, took in August 1639. Simultaneously, it endorsed the abolition of episcopacy. A year later (August 1640), the assembly voted to deprive or excommunicate any ministers who had subscribed to the covenant but were "speak[ing] against the same"; in a separate action it excluded any minister who refused to sign from serving in the church or one of the universities. Via actions of this kind, a revolution initiated in the name of conscience, true religion, and "free" institutions came to depend on central state authority. In March 1638, covenant taking had been a religious exercise, framed as such by Henderson and others as a gesture of repentance that would repair the relationship between the Church of Scotland and its God. In retrospect, it seems inevitable that a covenant that presumed the unity of church and nation under God would become a divisive force in Scottish politics.[113]

When the two armies met at the Scottish border in June 1639, the outcome was a truce or "pacification" preceded by negotiations that, on the Scottish side, centered on the lawfulness of the assembly of 1638. The leaders of the insurgency made it clear that peace would depend on the king accepting the independence of that assembly, which Johnston and his colleagues justified by using two-kingdoms theory. Charles gave way and agreed to authorize another "free assembly" and a new Parliament.[114] When the assembly met in August, it endorsed the decisions of 1638 up and including the eliminating of bishops as a third estate in the Scottish Parliament. For reasons having to do with an increasingly complex if not dysfunctional relationship between the two governments, Hamilton accepted these actions and signed the covenant. Some months later (June 1640), with Charles still bent on a military solution at the urging of Thomas Wentworth, who promised to provide Irish soldiers to stiffen the army Charles was trying to assemble, the Scottish Parliament met without his approval, a step it took after another commissioner prorogued (postponed) it in 1639. With no representative of the king on hand to say yea or nay, the new Parliament terminated clergy representation by voting to substitute "barons" (or lairds) for the bishops' "estate." Simultaneously, it redefined the representation of boroughs or shires in such a way that, thereafter, burgesses and their ilk would be present in far greater numbers than before. The long-term consequences of this step were immense. In the context of 1640, the most daring step was to eliminate the king's role in deciding when parliaments met or were dissolved. Hereafter, a free Parliament would meet at least once every three years. Simultaneously, Parliament altered its own procedures, replacing a system of committees the nobility had dominated with a much broader process of participation. In matters of religion, the acts of the 1639 assembly were endorsed and became official. Still hoping for national unity, Parliament also authorized military expeditions against clans or magnates who remained loyal to the king and instructed the Scottish army to invade England.[115]

In August 1640, the second Bishops' War ended ingloriously for Charles, with a Scottish army encamped in his country. At long last, the reformers in both countries could take a deep breath. Unable to pay off the invaders, Charles summoned a Parliament that met for the first time on November 4, 1640. At once, both Houses took on the challenge of interrogating the "innovations" Francis Rous had lamented in 1629, innovations at once constitutional and religious. That this Parliament was bent on curtailing the royal prerogative was not said in so many words—not yet, at least. But as inquiries set afoot by the House of Commons about Bastwick, Burton, and Prynne and the sheltering of Jesuits signaled, all roads led to Charles I—an unhappy Charles, who resented what the insurgency of 1637–38 had done to his authority. Now, in his other main kingdom, it was about to be challenged as forcefully as in Covenanter Scotland.

CHAPTER EIGHT

The End of the Beginning,
1640–1660

THE YEAR 1640 BEGAN BADLY for Nehemiah Wallington, as his hopes for a newly summoned Parliament, the first in eleven years, were dashed when Charles I sent it packing three weeks after it convened in April. By midsummer, the situation of the godly was worsening in the aftermath of the canons adopted at a Convocation in May (see chap. 7) and the king's insistence on using military means to suppress the Covenanters in Scotland. Rumor ran rife that, in Ireland, Thomas Wentworth was colluding with local Catholics to add Irish troops to the king's forces. Little wonder, then, that "the poore people of God" took for granted that "papists and Malicious Enemies of God" were plotting against them. Wallington would have agreed with an illicit broadside of 1639 that characterized the king's hostility to the Covenanters as "part of a full-fledged attempt to bring in popery." At moments such as this, he envied the friends who had gone to Massachusetts. Writing to one of them in 1638, he characterized his homeland as so "overrunne with Idoletry and popery and all manner of abominations" that God was on the verge of sending "heavy Judgments among us which many of you did [foresee] which did make you fly to new England as to a city of refuge for to preserve yourselves."[1]

Then came news of a Scottish army entering England in August 1640 and seizing the town of Newcastle. The second Bishops' War having ended in defeat, Charles was advised by a council of peers to summon another Parliament, which met at the beginning of November. Among the earliest actions of the House of Commons was to order Laud imprisoned on charges of treason. Simultaneously, it demanded the release of Bastwick, Burton, and Prynne from their places of imprisonment, a step Wallington regarded as a sign that freedom would be regained by those of "Gods children that have bin persecuted." Several months later, he was among the thousands who gathered outside

Westminster Hall to clamor "with one voice" for "justice" to be done to Wentworth. Hearing about the same time that a picture of the Virgin Mary in his parish church had been destroyed and an "idol" dismantled, he vowed to preserve a shard of stained glass as a remembrance "to shew to the generation to come what God hath don for us to give us such a reformation that our fathers never saw."[2]

What had happened in Scotland between 1637 and 1640 and New England in the 1630s seemed underway in England, "darkness" and tyranny giving way to a "light" that foreshadowed the return of Christ in judgment. In fast-day sermons preached at the request of the new Parliament, ministers reiterated the tried-and-true theme of deliverance: God was enabling England's faithful Protestants to emerge out of spiritual darkness and restore the nation's covenant with divine law.[3] A theme built into Foxe's *Book of Martyrs* and illustrated on the title page of the Geneva Bible, its revival in 1640–41 implied the possibility of eliminating every trace of popish idolatry. As Wallington may have realized, the disruptions rippling throughout the king's three kingdoms—his authority in Scotland impaired, the House of Commons contesting it in England, and imperial rule in Ireland threatened by the emergence of a Catholic-centered confederation with ties to Catholic powers on the Continent—were strengthening the hand of the godly in England. Was the reformation Elizabeth I and two Stuart kings had frustrated about to unfold?

In *A Glimpse of Sions Glory* (1641), an ecstatic evocation of the new day that was dawning, the anonymous author, possibly the Puritan-affiliated minister Thomas Goodwin, reminded his readers of Thomas Brightman's prediction that the pouring out of the final vial upon "the beast" and the beginning of a millennium-like "middle advent" would happen in the 1640s. Now, as prophesied in Revelation 19:6, "And I heard as it were the voice of a great multitude," Goodwin praised the "common people" for demanding that "Babylon" be overthrown. The outcome would be a "pure church," the "most pure" that anyone could imagine, a community in which the "people of God" would triumph over those—unnamed, but clearly a reference to Laud and Charles I—who regarded them as "schismatics, and Puritans." The work of the new day was to purge everything deemed idolatrous and initiate a dynamic process of spiritual enlightenment: "Glorious truths shall be revealed, and above all the mystery of the Gospel . . . shall be discovered."[4]

The high hopes of *A Glimpse of Sions Glory* and kindred texts such as Henry Burton's *The sounding of the two last trumpets* (1641), a narrative, in part, of his personal deliverance from "Babylon," were still resonating when the Scotch Presbyterian George Gillespie preached a fast-day sermon in March 1644. Unhappy with the pace of reform, Gillespie wondered out loud whether Parliament intended to fulfill God's plan for England and Scotland. Were its members unaware that they were witnessing the "last times" when the "beast" of Rome would be overthrown, the Jews converted to Christianity, and both state churches transformed into a glorious "Zion"? "The work is upon the wheel" (an allusion to Ezek. 1:16), he insisted. Hence the imperative that Parliament act with "zeal" to "build a more excellent and glorious temple than former generations have seen."[5]

Four years later, Gillespie was dead and his fellow Covenanters in despair, as was Wallington. Instead of a new Zion, the years between 1641 and 1648 had spawned a "Flood of Errors and sinnes." Even worse, in 1648 "Brother" had gone "to war against Brother" in a phase of civil war that pitted a parliamentary army against a Scottish government allied with Charles I. Turning, as he so often did, to divine providence as the key to discovering what "these seven yeers" signified, Wallington discerned "windings and turneings and overturninges," the doing of a God who "walkes in the darke" and hides "his ways from our eyes."[6]

The "windings and . . . overturninges" of the 1640s and early 1650s were unprecedented in British history. For the Puritan movement, they were devastating. At the debut of the 1640s, the godly in England seemed on the verge of securing the reformation they had sought since the 1570s. As late as 1646 or possibly 1647, the classic goals of the movement still seemed within reach. Yet by 1650 the principles of a comprehensive state church and magistracy-ministry alliance had been displaced by voluntary versions of Protestantism and state support for liberty of conscience. Not in name but in practice, moral discipline had virtually collapsed. Doctrine, too, had become unhinged, although blasphemy remained a civil crime. Order of a quite different kind returned in 1660–62 with the restoration of the monarchy. With it came episcopacy throughout Britain and a line drawn in the sand (1662) about conformity. Some 1,600 ministers were unwilling to conform and, thereafter, became Dissenters (as did some of their congregations) who could not worship openly..

What accounts for the excitement of the early 1640s and the collapse of consensus in the same decade? The answers are twofold. Even before the mechanisms for controlling opinion and practice broke down, long-lasting contradictions within the Puritan movement were springing to life. In the decades leading up to the 1630s, the tug-of-war between conscience and conformity had gradually been muted. Something similar happened with the tension between lawfulness and "things indifferent." Nonconformity of various kinds persisted, as did complaints about worship, but many of the godly preferred to emphasize what Puritans and the more moderate conformists shared— consensus on most matters of theological doctrine, a reformation of manners, the repression of British Catholics, and some sort of magistracy-ministry alliance. By the mid-1620s, this middle ground was beginning to erode as James I turned toward clergy who rejected the consensus of circa 1620, a policy repeated by his son and successor, Charles I. Reaction in one direction prompted reaction in another. In Scotland, nonconformity emerged in the 1620s and, in England, the old nonconformity began to implode. As indicated by the three martyrs of 1637, the fierce response to "Arminianism" by the Parliament of 1628–29, and the re-emerging of Separatist-like communities (see below, sec. 3) the space for compromise was diminishing. Simultaneously, the colonists in New England were creating gathered congregations and empowering laypeople in ways that seemed akin to Separatist policies. There, as in Scotland, the royal supremacy had been dismantled and the compromises endorsed by the old nonconformity replaced with a fervor for aligning church and state with divine law.

The tipping point was the Scottish insurgency, which Charles I and his advisors denounced as a rebellion. His freedom to act acutely limited by defeat and financial crisis, momentum shifted to the new Parliament of November 1640. Though ill-equipped to rethink the constitutional foundations of government and what God mandated by way of true religion, it was thrust into this role by the king's insistence on his privileges, an upwelling of objections to episcopacy, acute anxiety about a royal coup (spring 1641) to suppress the government's critics, and paranoia about a popish plot that intensified in the aftermath of a Catholic rebellion (October 1641) in Ireland. The stakes were already high in May 1641 when a majority in the House of Commons endorsed a Protestation that, like the National Covenant in Scotland, differentiated loyalty to English Protestantism from loyalty to the Crown.[7] Abruptly, constitutional politics (the capacity of Parliament to curtail the royal prerogative) and the politics of true religion coalesced, an explosive combination that in Scotland had all but eliminated the royal supremacy. With other moments of crisis adding to the confusion, Charles I decided to solve the question of his authority by military means. In the absence of compromises the king and his supporters would accept, the Long Parliament of 1640 elevated the Puritan wing of the state church into a place of privilege. Doing so had seemed to work in Covenanter Scotland. Yet there, as in England, authority began to fracture in the mid-1640s, a process that intensified after royalists and moderates allied with Charles I took control of the government in late 1647. By the 1650s, the outcome was a policy of toleration imposed by the government of Oliver Cromwell.[8]

In 1640, no one foresaw the conflicts and confusion that lay ahead. We begin with the promise of the new Parliament, saving the collapse of the Puritan program for subsequent sections of this chapter. One by one, the major players come on stage—John Pym and a House of Commons zealously unwinding a popish plot; the Westminster Assembly, which Parliament summoned into being in 1643; the advocates of toleration and the "sectaries" who benefitted from that argument; the Scottish advocates of *jure divino* Presbyterianism and their English allies; and the king.

Reform or Revolution?

The Parliament that met in November 1640 was restless and resentful. So were the thousands of men and women who rioted in London in May 1640 after the "Short Parliament" had been dissolved, spilling out into the streets in response to a placard urging the city's apprentices to attack Lambeth Palace, the place where Laud lived in his capacity as archbishop. In 1628–29, tensions between Charles I and Parliament had prompted the Petition of Right and a strong statement about the dangers of religious innovation. Now, in the aftermath of the king's personal rule, the House of Commons wanted to curtail the scope of royal authority or "prerogative" and reclaim its own privileges. Angered by the collection of "ship money," Commons voted to abolish this form of taxation and resolved in December that Parliaments should meet every three years (the Triennial Act). A few months later, it protected itself from dissolution by ordering that any attempt of this kind, a privilege Charles I and his predecessors had taken for granted, would require the approval of Parliament itself. Another vote (June 1641) did away with the "prerogative" courts of Star Chamber and High Commission. A united House of Commons and House of Lords endorsed these measures, which Charles reluctantly approved. Simultaneously, the Commons reaffirmed the privileges of free speech and freedom for its members from imprisonment. Suddenly, the substance of monarchy as Charles I understood it was shrinking and the authority of Parliament beginning to expand.

These steps left unanswered the larger question of how Parliament and the king would share the work of governance. Before 1641, no English Parliament had enacted laws on its own or overturned the monarch's "negative voice" (veto). Moreover, it was widely acknowledged that foreign policy, governance of the state church, and most aspects of taxation were the king's to regulate or decide. By early 1641, some of these restrictions were unraveling thanks to the insistence of the Scottish government that negotiations to settle the second Bishops' War involve the new Parliament. The traditional structure of governance was breaking down for another reason, the outcry about a "popish plot" to subvert Parliament and the state church. In his opening speech (November 7, 1640) to the House of Commons, John Pym repeated his prediction that a "designe to alter the Kingdome both in religion and government" was unfolding. Others shared his sense of alarm—the London crowd clamoring for Thomas Wentworth to be punished; the Scots, who distrusted Wentworth because he had encouraged the king to wage the two Bishops' Wars; and the many who knew that he had run Ireland with an iron hand. Summoned back to London in 1639, Wentworth seems to have offered Charles the services of an Irish army dominated by Catholics. Remarks he may have made about using this army against the king's *English* critics persuaded a majority in the House of Commons that he should be executed as an enemy of the state (May

1641). The hysteria about a popish plot had claimed its first Protestant victim.[9]

Not until the late fall of 1641, however, did more evidence emerge of Irish or possibly Continental Catholic troops being mobilized. Rumor overtook fact, a process abetted by Pym and his allies, who relied on a sense of crisis to keep the House of Commons in line. Learning of two plots by officers of the army to intervene on Charles's behalf, the earliest of these exposed in May 1641, and alarmed by an uprising of Irish Catholics that began in late October, the House of Commons resolved that officers of their choosing should command the army being formed to subdue the rebellion. As well, the House used the fiction that Charles I had been misled by advisors implicated in the popish plot to insist on its authority to approve anyone he wanted to appoint to the Privy Council or other high offices of state. That bishops were voting members of the House of Lords was another bone in the throat of those who discerned a plot against true religion. To Pym and his allies, the remedy was obvious. The House of Lords should exclude the bishops from voting, a proposal that expanded into an insistence that they give up their seats in that body. In general, the distrust of Charles and those who were closest to him, a group that included his Catholic wife Henrietta Maria, was palpable.[10]

Seeking to rally support for his program at a moment of disarray in the Commons (late November 1641) and foot-dragging by an obstinate House of Lords, which was reluctant to alter the royal prerogative or exclude the bishops from their place in that chamber, Pym orchestrated the publication of the *Grand Remonstrance*, a massive list of complaints tied to the specter of a popish plot. Narrowly endorsed by the Commons, where many of the gentry did not welcome its overheated rhetoric, the *Remonstrance* reiterated the argument that "divers Bishops" and some of the king's advisors had formed a "malignant" party aspiring to alter "religion and government." Hence the importance of "abridging" the "immoderate power" in secular affairs of the bishops, an imperative best fulfilled by denying them their seats in the House of Lords. Simultaneously, the *Remonstrance* called for removing untrustworthy men from the king's presence, a step that trespassed on the royal prerogative. These assertions gave way to a lengthy description of events in recent English history—unjust taxes, the two Bishops' Wars, the canons of 1640, the presence of a papal nuncio in London, the workings of the Court of High Commission—that confirmed the existence of a Catholic-tilting conspiracy.[11]

As is often pointed out by historians of this period, Charles could have rallied moderates to his side had two events not intervened, one of these his attempt in early January 1642 to arrest several members of the Commons and the second, the Catholic revolt in Ireland. Both worked to the advantage of the faction that wanted to curtail the king's prerogative.[12] Trust came close to vanishing, as did the possibility of a workable compromise. In January 1642, both houses of Parliament finally agreed to exclude bishops from their place in the

House of Lords, a measure the king accepted in February. In March, both also endorsed a bill giving Parliament the authority to appoint commanders of the militia, a measure the king promptly rejected. In response, the House of Commons asserted its legislative authority and, by April, began to enact "ordinances" (de facto laws) the king refused to approve.

Had agreement been reached on the "Nineteen Propositions" the king was given in June 1642, the English government might have mutated into a "king-in-Parliament" structure, with each granted a significant role, but not what Charles regarded as rightfully his.[13] By midsummer if not earlier, he had decided that raising an army to fight on his behalf would serve him better than negotiating with a Parliament dominated by Pym and like-minded members of the nobility and gentry. Negotiations aimed at restoring peace continued even as the country slid into civil war. In the early going, the generals who led the parliamentary armies were ineffective and, in the judgment of what may be termed a "war party," too bent on reconciliation with the king. Gradually, the temper of Parliament changed as royalists left to join Charles or, for other reasons, withdrew from politics. A "hardening of the parliamentary cause" was noticeable by mid-1643, if not earlier, evidenced by the enacting (June 1643) of a "sacred Vow and Covenant" justifying armed conflict as a means of preserving "the true Protestant Religion."[14] The death of Pym in December 1643 prompted a struggle between different factions in the Commons, one of them determined to defeat the king even if this goal forced them into an alliance with the Scottish government, another hoping to bring the war to a close by persuading Charles to accept a package of reforms. In mid-1644, with victory in the civil war still in doubt, the faction that favored war was able to arrange a reorganization of the parliamentary army. Before the "New Model Army" came into action, a regional force crushed the king's troops at the battle of Marston Moor (July 1644). The following June, the New Model Army defeated the king at the battle of Naseby, a victory that effectively ended the conflict, although sieges and skirmishes continued for several more months.[15]

What came next? Even in defeat, Charles clung to episcopacy and the royal prerogative. Nor had he given up on the possibility that an Irish Catholic army or possibly French soldiers recruited by his wife would turn the tide, or that Scottish, English, and Irish royalists would reemerge as a political and military force. For the next three years (1646 to the end of 1648), his agents in Ireland tried to patch together a coalition of Irish Catholics, Old English, and some elements of the New English, an uphill task, given the distrust each had of the other. On the other hand, the Scottish situation seemed more promising. With his defeat, the military alliance formed in 1643 between the Long Parliament and the Covenanter government was no longer necessary. Nor, by this time, were many in Parliament willing to endorse the model of a single state church implied by the Covenant of 1643 (see below, secs. 2–4). When Parliament initiated another attempt in mid-1646 at negotiating a settlement of constitutional and religious questions, the Scots welcomed the provision in the "Newcastle Propositions" that Charles sign the "Solemn League and Covenant," agree to replace episcopacy with presbyterianism, and support a crackdown on Catholic recusants. Other proposals called for Parliament to control the army and militia for twenty years before this authority reverted to the Crown and have a voice in the naming of officers of state. Nothing was said, however, of a limited union between Scotland and England, as the Scots had previously proposed.

Hoping to capitalize on Scottish disaffection with a Parliament tilting toward liberty of conscience, Charles negotiated secretly in late 1647 with moderates who had gained control of the Scottish government (see below, sec. 4). The embers of war flared up anew, royalists in England engaging in local uprisings and a Scottish army marching into England in what became known as the Second Civil War—a short-lived war, for this army was routed at the battle of Preston (August 1648). His allies defeated or dispersed, the king had no chance of returning to power unless he acceded to the demands of the House of Commons. Momentarily, the peace party regained control of the House, but in December 1648 an army-led event known as "Pride's Purge" drove them out, at which point negotiations with the king ceased and he was indicted for treason.[16]

Well before this turn of events, the more moderate or "presbyterian" faction in the House of Commons had been wrestling with the politics of the army it had created. In 1644–45, no one anticipated that the New Model Army would become a key player in religious and constitutional politics or, in the aftermath of victory, would refuse to heed requests that some regiments disband and others move to Ireland, where fighting continued. To the dismay of those who favored uniformity of religion, large parts of the army wanted something closer to toleration or liberty of conscience. A group of "political Independents" in the House of Commons favored the same policy. By this time, the king's intransigence was prompting some in and outside of Parliament to propose that monarchy was unnecessary. The years 1647 and 1648 were filled with the unexpected: the mobilizing of "presbyterians" in London and elsewhere, the New Model Army entering the city and shaking off its parliamentarian masters, a last-ditch attempt to negotiate with the king, "Pride's Purge," and (in January 1649) the king's execution. In May, the "Rump" of the Long Parliament transferred authority in England and Ireland to a Council of State. England was on its way to becoming a commonwealth or republic, with Oliver Cromwell, the generals of the New Model Army, and the Rump sharing in its governance until 1653, when Cromwell abolished the Rump and his government mutated into a Protectorate. The repercussions in Scotland were immense and in Ireland, no less so. There, in 1649, Cromwell and the New Model Army crushed the forces arrayed against the new government, doing so with unusual brutality.

This summary of the circumstances that led to civil war, the king's execution, and the collapse of the Church of England as an effective institution must suffice, for the details of the religious side of the story beckon. As we turn to that story, it is imperative to keep in mind that the projects of reforming the Church of England and preserving the Covenanter revolution were inherently political.[17] Already, the revolution in Scotland had revealed how daring this politics could become—Presbyterianism replacing episcopacy, the royal supremacy radically curtailed, a restructuring of the institutions of civil governance. Would a similar politics emerge in England and the visionary rhetoric of "deliverance" become state policy?

A "Perfect Reformation"

Religion was high on the list of problems the new Parliament would face. The "Short" Parliament, which met for three weeks in April 1640, had been deluged with petitions protesting Laudian "innovations." Come November, the first session of the new House of Commons heard John Pym declare that "the last and greatest grievance" (of the many he cited) concerned "the throne of God." Some in a more divided House of Lords agreed. In September 1640 a group of nobles had told Charles I that "innovations in matters of religion" were among the most pressing of the "evils and dangers" affecting the country. In Commons as well as among the general public, many took for granted the popish plot that Pym and Francis Rous regarded as the real purpose of the Laudian program. No one could say so openly, but the king was implicated in that plot, as was his understanding of the royal prerogative. As Pym pointed out, the makers of the plot had insisted on the "divine authority and absolute power in the king to do what he will with us."[18]

Moved by a sense of urgency and generally in agreement on limiting the authority of the bishops, Parliament began to dismantle rules and practices associated with the Laudians or the king's own doing.[19] The Book of Sports was an easy although belated target, nullified in May 1643 by the House of Commons. Well before this (December 1640) the same House repudiated the canons of May 1640. Their authority vanished once it was decided that these contradicted the "right of parliaments." With the canons suspended and fines levied on those who participated in the Convocation that endorsed them, the Commons voted in December to prosecute Laud for treason. The Laud-hunting hounds unleashed in the mid-1630s by William Prynne and John Bastwick began to bay as soon as the Long Parliament convened. Prynne returned to the fray with two brief pamphlets, and in the House of Commons, Harbottle Grimston assailed Laud and his allies as "the Authors and Causes of all the Ruines Miseries, and Calamities, we now groane under."[20]

Subsequently, the House voted to bar clergy from serving on courts of any kind, a measure justified by the assertion—emphasized in a petition from the county of Kent—that "government . . . by . . . bishops" was "very dangerous both to the Church and Commonwealth," as instanced by their "lordly power," harsh treatment of "godly preachers," and the "claim" they were making to "Divine right for their office." The scholar and temperate Puritan Simonds D'Ewes added his voice to the furor when he underscored the contradiction between the role of the bishops in spiritual affairs and the power they had acquired in the workings of the civil state. The broader point, which a substantial majority in the House of Commons endorsed, was that clergy should be excluded from "secular Affaires."[21]

Should episcopacy be replaced by another structure? In December 1640, Parliament was handed a petition signed by some 15,000 Londoners demanding that it suppress episcopacy and the *Book of Common Prayer*. Procedurally, the "root and branch" petition became a hot potato—some members in the House of Commons insisting that it be rejected and others urging that it be referred to a committee. In January, nineteen county-based petitions voicing a similar politics arrived, one of them signed by "above 2800 persons" who endorsed "the abolishing of Episcopacie." Simultaneously, a substantial group of ministers solicited signatures on behalf of a revamped version of episcopal office.[22] For the moment, the "root and branch" petitions said nothing about what should replace episcopacy. Nor did anti-Laudians in the House of Commons have a plan up their sleeves. Amid much uncertainty, the House of Lords, which continued to include the bishops, sought the advice of James Ussher, John Williams (newly released from prison after being punished by Star Chamber), and other moderate bishops on what to do about "Innovations in the Doctrine and Discipline of the Church of England." In the 1630s, Williams had vigorously objected to the transformation of communion tables into altars. Now, he and others agreed to characterize that practice as an innovation. When it came to episcopacy itself, Williams, Ussher, and Joseph Hall recommended a "limited" or "reduced" or "primitive" version that walked the office back from Laudian-style *jure divino* status and barred those holding it from serving on the Privy Council.[23]

Despite the best efforts of Hall and his colleagues and the sympathy of many in the House of Lords, this scheme never had a chance. As soon as it became public, a coalition that included the bishop-hating Prynne, a youthful John Milton making his first appearance as a political writer, Henry Vane Jr., and five ministers using the pen name "Smectymnuus" assailed episcopacy on various grounds. Several of the Scottish commissioners who arrived in London in late 1640 to participate in negotiations about a treaty of peace added their voices to the outcry against episcopacy, doing so not only because of its troubled history in Scotland but because they knew that Charles's commitment to the principle of "no bishop, no king" contradicted the Covenanter revolution. Common sense told them that, until bishops were replaced with a presbyterian system in England, the Covenanter regime would never be secure. The outcry also included a book by Robert Greville, Lord Brooke, a Puritan-affiliated nobleman. By the close of *A Discourse opening The Nature of that Episcopacie, which is exercised in England* (1641), Greville had mocked the logic of "no bishop, no king," a point Milton transposed into the argument that episcopacy was the real threat to monarchy. More unusually, Grenville urged the civil state to forgo suppressing religious dissent.[24]

For the individuals grouped together as Smectymnuus, the case against episcopacy was political, the bishops' role in nurturing a popish plot. Backdating this plot to the middle of the sixteenth century, they described it as a design to "maintain, propagate, and much increase the burden of human ceremonies; to keep out and beat down the preaching of the word; and to silence the faithfull preachers of it"—in short, a plot against the essence of Puritan-style religion. To these ministers, the *Book of Common Prayer* was also unacceptable because of the damage it did to a true preaching ministry.[25] On the sidelines, as it were, Robert Baillie and Alexander Henderson added their fuel to the firestorm ignited by the "root and branch" petition. Baillie oversaw the London printing of a much-expanded version of a diatribe against Laudianism he had previously published in the Netherlands. Fresh from Scotland, Henderson weighed in with *The Unlawfullnes and Danger of Limited Prelacie, or Perpetuall Presidencie in the Church, Briefly discovered* (1641). His objections were twofold: episcopacy was an unlawful "invention" that should be "removed root and branch"; and the current crop of bishops had abused their power to such an extent that nothing they said or did could be trusted. To these strong words, he added an allusion to "the changes, and revolutions . . . in other kingdoms" (i.e., Scotland), which he hailed as signs that "divine Providence is about some greate worke" on behalf of "the Kingdome of Christ."[26]

On paper, episcopacy remained the structure of the state church, but in practice it was faltering by mid-1641. That it survived on paper was largely the doing of the House of Lords, conservatives in the House of Commons, and especially Charles I, who drew a line in the sand in early 1641 when he told the new Parliament that he would never allow it to be abolished; to "reformation" he could say yes, but not to an "Alteration" that threatened the "Fundamental Constitutions of this Kingdom." A king who sometimes concealed his real feelings remained unequivocal on this point, citing conscience, his coronation oath, and the antiquity of the office as reasons for preserving it. "I am constant for the doctrine and discipline of the Church of England, as it was established by Queen Elizabeth and my father," he remarked in 1642, "and resolve (by the Grace of God) to live and die in the maintenance of it." In mid-1644, after receiving Holy Communion at a service in Oxford, he reasserted his support for "the establishment of the true Reformed Protestant religion, as it stood in its beauty in the happy days of Queen Elizabeth, without any connivance at Popery."[27]

Even though the system he favored was not officially abolished until 1646, its fate was being affected by other events and policies.[28] Desperate for revenue to cover the costs of civil war, Parliament began to seize and sell church properties of various kinds, a process lasting into the early 1650s that, before it came to a close, did serious damage to the financial basis of episcopacy. The petitions of circa 1641 had underscored the plight of local churches staffed by pluralists, Laudians, or ministers who, for other reasons, were unappealing. In a fast-day sermon (December 1640) addressed to the Long Parliament, the future congregationalist Cornelius Burgess evoked the "thousands and millions" who "miserably perish" from spiritual starvation. He exaggerated the situation, but not by much, for complaints were pouring into Parliament and reaching county magnates such as Robert Harley. In his home county of Hertfordshire, godly people in the town of Walford begged him for assistance in getting rid of their "drunken, debauched" vicar. The signers of a petition to Parliament from Oxfordshire were blunt. By their reckoning, the whole of the diocese contained "not above thirty Ministers" who were "constant preachers." By 1643, with civil war forcing ministers to take sides, Parliament was also being urged to dismiss "malignant" clergy who favored the king.[29]

A host of such testimonies prompted the House of Commons in January 1641 to take a leaf out of John Field's program of the 1570s and urge local groups to identify ministers deemed "scandalous." A month later, it endorsed a bill to suppress pluralism and nonresidency that was not adopted by both houses until mid-1642. Meanwhile, Commons had set up a committee to oversee a purge of incompetent or politically incorrect clergy, a task resumed by a "Committee on Plundered Ministers," which also found new positions for godly ministers displaced by the tides of war. The publicity that arose around these purges included a person-by-person description of *The First Century of Scandalous Ministers, Malignant Priests Made and Admitted into benefices by the prelates* (1643), which opened with a depiction of "dumb dogs," followed by a case-by-case portrait of parish ministers whose faults encompassed everything from "buggery" to royalism.[30] By the time the ejections ended, nearly 2,800 ministers had been ousted or "harassed." During the Protectorate, another 300 suffered some sort of displacement. All told, these campaigns affected far more ministers than those who suffered for their nonconformity during the previous three-quarters of a century. In Kent, a full half of the ministers in that county were displaced, and in Leicestershire, a third. In Scotland, purges of a more political kind were also unfolding in the second half of the 1640s. Meanwhile, the reformist broom was sweeping dozens of faculty and fellows out of the two English universities.[31]

Simultaneously, another version of reform was unfolding, outbursts of iconoclastic violence directed against the material fabric of Laudian-style Protestantism. The iconoclasm that rippled through London in 1640 and 1641 was mainly directed at altar rails but also included other décor in Westminster Abbey. In response (February 1641), a House of Commons committee began to consider a bill that would empower local groups to "abolish all idolatrie." The first real step in this direction, an "Order for the Suppression of Innovations"

(September 1641), authorized church wardens and local clergy to initiate the systematic destruction of crucifixes, images, and pictures and prohibited the use of candlesticks on communion tables, among other practices. A more conservative House of Lords demurred, but the issue was revived in February 1642 when Commons debated a similar measure that both houses eventually approved in November. In April 1643, Commons revisited this program and empowered a "Committee for the Demolition of Monuments of Superstition and Idolatry" in London's churches and especially its cathedrals. Down came Cheapside Cross and other markers of the city's Catholic past. In August, Parliament expanded the scope of this crusade by an ordinance authorizing the "utter demolishing, removing, and taking away of all Monuments of Superstition and Idolatry" and extending it to the entire country. The "all" included whatever remained of Catholic or Laudian-style structures: altar rails, candlesticks, and the like, with communion tables restored to their traditional location. Several months later (May 1644), the final bill in this sequence included sterner language: images, statues, and the like were to be "utterly defaced" or "taken away, defaced and utterly demolished."[32]

A forceful purge of stained glass and the like unfolded in Suffolk in 1643–44 after the Earl of Manchester, the military-political leader of the region, appointed the layman William Dowsing to serve as "Commissioner for the destruction of monuments of idolatry and superstition." As reconstructed by the historian John Morrill, the sources of Dowsing's iconoclastic fervor included his close reading of Foxe's *Book of Martyrs*, from which he learned of an episode in English military history that coincided with an outburst of iconoclasm in late 1540s London, a story repeated in a fast-day sermon Dowsing owned and read in 1643. Starting that December and continuing for a year or so, Dowsing visited dozens of churches in search of objects to destroy. In one of these, his crew tore down "about an hundred superstitious Pictures" and "beat down a great . . . cross on the top of the church." Elsewhere, others were carrying out similar campaigns.[33]

Neither of these processes resolved the problem that the Long Parliament had yet to confront head-on: the task of replacing episcopal governance and the *Book of Common Prayer*.[34] Leaving aside differences of opinion within Parliament about episcopacy and the constitutional problem posed by Charles I, the obstacles in the way of simple elimination were practical and conceptual—practical in the sense that a good many people remained on the fence or continued to prefer episcopacy and the prayer book, and conceptual when it came to choosing a new version of church, worship, and ministry. As of 1642–43, three options were in play. One of these had deep roots within the English Reformation and the Reformed international, the idea and ideal of the nation worshipping in the same manner. That church and commonweal were a unity or, as was often said, a single "body," was a commonplace John Whitgift had deployed against John Field–style presbyterians. Apologists for the state church had reiterated it ever since, as had James VI and I and, even more emphatically, the Laudians. During James's reign, the moderate wing of the Puritan movement conceded this point, as did the authors of the *Grand Remonstrance* (November 1641), who agreed that "there should be throughout the whole realm a conformity to that order which the laws enjoin according to the Word of God." Implicitly, this statement also nodded at the importance of edification as an ongoing process sustained by church discipline.[35]

Uniformity had a special significance in Scottish theology. The radicals in that country had never questioned the lawfulness of the kirk even when its integrity was compromised by the "Black Acts" or other measures. For the Covenanters, therefore, any gestures toward voluntary religion or Separatist-style purity were out-of-bounds. In a paper written by Alexander Henderson and printed in London (1641), where Henderson and his fellow commissioners were negotiating with Charles I on the terms of a treaty to conclude the second Bishops' War, he emphasized the merits of the Scottish system as the best means of sustaining "truth and unity." For him and his fellow Scots, there were but two alternatives, episcopacy and the newly reinstated Presbyterianism of the kirk, and as he pointed out, the first of these had already been renounced in Scotland. Knowing that Charles had insisted on retaining episcopacy (January 23, 1641), Henderson reassured his readers that the Scottish version of church government was compatible with royal authority. Knowing, too, that any such proposal would be regarded as an example of Scottish imperialism, he insisted that "no kingdom or Church" should dictate to another. In August 1642, the General Assembly reiterated the gist of Henderson's statement in a letter to the Long Parliament, this time employing a rhetorical question to dramatize what Scotland would gain from uniformity: "What hope can the Kingdome and Kirk of Scotland have of a firme and durable Peace, till Prelacie . . . be plucked up, root and branch"?[36]

To the dismay of the Scots and many in and outside of the Long Parliament, alternatives to this policy were suddenly in play. A novel possibility, which Lord Brooke suggested in 1641 and others quickly endorsed, would allow voluntary or gathered congregations to exist alongside a state church, a proposal akin to what Henry Jacob had attempted in London in 1616. In 1641, Henry Burton was also extolling voluntary congregations as a counterweight to the "Antichristian yoke in the Prelacy" and a means of protecting the Lord's Table from the unworthy, a point he reemphasized in *Satisfaction Concerning Mixt Communions Unsatisfactory* (1643), which underscored the "vast difference" between "hypocrites" and visible saints (p. 7). A scheme of this kind—roughly akin to what the colonists in New England had implemented—would quickly become known as Independency. It presumed the possibility of people being able to choose between a simplified state church and voluntary congregations limited to the godly. To add to the confusion, a more radical possibility emerged. Roger Williams, who came to London in 1643 to lobby on behalf of the settlements in Rhode Island, proposed that the state withdraw from policing religion, or matters of "conscience." Williams also took for granted that a state church would disappear. Parliament ordered Williams's *The Bloody Tenet of Persecution* (1644) burned, but others—Baptists, the sociopolitical theorists known as the Levellers, John Milton, and less emphatically, most Independents—endorsed toleration or liberty of conscience, some for tactical reasons and others as a matter of principle.[37]

These were sharply different possibilities, so different that achieving consensus on any one of them was unlikely. Burton's scheme of gathered churches implied the unlawfulness of parishes within the state church and this, in turn, implied Separatism. From the standpoint of Robert Baillie and his fellow Scots, it was incredible that Independents would keep children from being baptized and adults from participating in the Lord's Supper unless they "give . . . satisfactory signes of reall regeneration." Men of Baillie's persuasion wanted to preserve the sacramental and incorporating features of the national church and retain a reformation of manners enforced by state and church alike. Yet beneath their feet the ground was shifting as "sectaries" (as those who wanted to eliminate any version of a state church were nicknamed) began to question every aspect of magisterial Protestantism. On the periphery of the Atlantic world, the outcome was acute conflict. Within Britain itself, a similar politics unfolded, with devastating consequences for what fast-day preachers of circa 1641 had anticipated.[38]

The confusion was troubling to many and exciting to a few, a confusion rooted in differences of opinion that no one in the 1620s could have predicted. How early did these differences emerge? If we include the hostile reaction in mid-1630s England to the polity the colonists were creating in New England, the alternatives were being clarified earlier than most historians have recognized. Another phase of debate arose in response to Scottish Covenanters, who were extolling Presbyterianism as early as 1640.[39]

Already incandescent, the politics of reform found another venue as of 1640–41: fast days arranged by the new Parliament, the first of them held in November 1640 and becoming a monthly event in early 1642. For the most part, the ministers who preached on this occasion spoke in generalities about divine providence, covenant, and the like, some more fervently than others but usually agreeing that the process of reform should be guided by Scripture as the alternative to the "traditions and inventions of men." Thomas Case, who participated in this series in 1642, may have wanted a "pure and perfect reformation," and Edmund Calamy, a process of "reform[ing] the Reformation it selfe," while the much-punished nonconformist Thomas Wilson called for the destruction of episcopacy as thoroughly as had happened with the "mysticall" Babylon of Revelation 18:1, "throwne down" and "found no more at all." Yet slogans of this kind left unclear the meaning of "purer ordinances" and "more refined churches."[40]

Reticence to endorse grand schemes was widespread, a reticence rooted in the compromises of the "old non-conformity" but also in a lingering affection for the *Book of Common Prayer* and a wariness of alternatives that could include "democratical" schemes of church governance. As the tempo of reform began to accelerate, many in England who equated Separatist-style behavior with social unrest were beginning to insist that Parliament should preserve as much as possible of a state church.[41] Another context for this silence about grand schemes was a tacit agreement among most of the clergy in early 1640s London to say as little as possible about the details of church order. Future Independents and Presbyterians concurred on this decision, possibly because they found themselves agreeing that parishes should be given more authority over discipline and a greater role in choosing their ministers than episcopacy had permitted. Within the longer history of the Puritan movement, these were commonplaces that Cartwright's generation had endorsed. Now, they made sense all over again, especially since so few of the London ministers were versed in *jure divino* Presbyterianism. In the early going, it was up to Henderson and his fellow Scots to make the case for that form of church government, Samuel Rutherford weighing in with *A peaceable and temperate plea for Pauls presbyterie in Scotland* (1642) and *The Due Right of Presbyteries; or, a peaceable plea for the Government of the Church of Scotland* (1644), this time comparing it to the colonists' version of church government and its Separatist predecessors.[42]

Unable on its own to resolve this confusion about the substance of reform, the Long Parliament handed the task of redesigning the Church of England to a special "assembly." The history of the Westminster Assembly, so named because of the building in which it met, began with Parliament recognizing that a Synod or Convocation was the appropriate body to resolve the status of the *Book of Common Prayer*, the Thirty-Nine Articles, and episcopacy. Mentioned in petitions as early as January 1641, the concept of a "free Nationall Synod" was endorsed in the *Grand Remonstrance* and fast-day sermons, seriously discussed in Parliament in January 1642, approved by both Houses that June, included in the Nineteen Propositions submitted to the king that same month, and backed by moderate royalists such as the minister Thomas Fuller.[43] Civil war finally made it possible for an assembly to meet in July 1643 without royal consent. No bishops were on hand, although Ussher had been invited, nor any clergy associated with the Laudian program.[44]

The decisions of the Westminster Assembly enjoy a special place in the history of British and American Protestantism thanks to the Confession it produced, the last in a long line of Reformed creeds and catechisms and the most enduring, for the "Articles of Christian Religion" (to quote the formal title of the Confession) and the two catechisms it spawned, the Larger and the more pastoral Shorter, were widely used in eighteenth- and nineteenth-century America and Scotland and, to this day, remain important statements of doctrine for some Protestants. Deferring the theological work of the assembly to chapter 9, what matters here is how this body navigated the politics of reform. At the outset, it was handed the task of preserving an inclusive state church governed in some other manner than by bishops. It was also handed the challenge of working in the shadow of a major political event, an alliance formed in August 1643 between Parliament in England and the Scottish government at a moment when royalists seemed to be winning the civil war.[45]

Spelled out in a document known as the "Solemn League and Covenant," the purpose of this alliance was to "sincerely, really and constantly" collaborate on matters of religion. More concretely, its purpose was to preserve "the Reformed Religion" in Scotland and, in England and Ireland, pursue "the reformation of religion . . . according to the Word of God, and the example of the best reformed Churches." The emphasis on "reformed" signaled that episcopacy was no longer an option. Did the wording of the Covenant also oblige the Long Parliament to endorse Scottish-style Presbyterianism? Not in so many words. Instead, the agreement called for "bring[ing] the Churches of God in these three kingdoms to the *nearest* conjunction and conformity" in "confession of faith, Church government, [and] directory for worship" (emphasis added).[46]

During the negotiations that led to the drafting of this covenant, the Scots ignored the uneasiness of the English negotiators with uniformity along Scottish lines, perhaps because article 2 committed both sides to "endeavor the extirpation of Popery, prelacy . . . and whatsoever shall be found to be contrary to sound doctrine and the power of godliness," a slap at those in England who questioned uniformity of any kind. English anxieties about the constitutional status of Parliament and Scottish support for some version of monarchy account for the promise in article 3 to "preserve the Rights and Priviledges of the Parliaments" and "defend the King's Majesty's person and authority" alongside "true religion and the liberties of the kingdom." That the English negotiators wanted a "civil" alliance and the Scots a "religious" compact, as the Scottish minister Robert Baillie remarked at the time, points to deeper differences. Nonetheless, there was no confusion about the significance of the agreement: episcopacy was on the way out, and a system derived in some manner from the Reformed international on the way in. At long last, the time had come to bypass compromise and, in the words of a modern historian of the assembly, "finish the job" of creating a biblically aligned church.[47]

After the covenant was affirmed by Parliament and the Westminster Assembly in public ceremonies in September, a delegation of Scots headed to London, some to serve on a committee overseeing the war and others— Henderson, Baillie, George Gillespie, and Samuel Rutherford in their capacity as ministers and Archibald Johnston as lay elder—entering the assembly not as voting members but as representatives of the kirk. As Baillie recognized once he arrived in London, the assembly had nothing in common with the general assemblies of the Church of Scotland, which were "free." On this difference, the ordinance of June 1643 was explicit. Characterizing episcopacy as a "great impediment to Reformation and growth of Religion" as well as "very prejudiciall to the state and Government of this kingdome," it authorized the assembly to recommend to Parliament a form of church government "as may be most agreeable to Gods holie word and most apt to procure . . . nearer agreement with the Church of Scotland and other reformed churches abroade." *Recommend* was the operative term, with Parliament assigned the role of proposing what the assembly should discuss, a rule strengthened a little later by the phrase "give their *advice and counsell . . . when and so often as they shall be thereunto required* (emphasis added)." Whatever the assembly decided could be approved or rejected by Parliament; as was said in the concluding sentence of the ordinance, Parliament was *not* granting the assembly "Jurisdiction power or Authoritie Ecclesiasticall whatsoever, or any other Power than is herein particularly expressed." Before it met, the assembly's wings had been clipped by its masters.[48]

With authority resolved to the satisfaction of Parliament, which also chose the 132 ministers and thirty members of Parliament who made up its membership,[49] the assembly began to clarify the more ambiguous of the Thirty-Nine Articles. By October, the Solemn League and Covenant, together with the imperative to ordain clergy who would replace the many being purged, prompted fresh instructions. Now, the assembly was told to "forthwith" decide on "a discipline and government" that would take the place of episcopacy and satisfy the Scots, who were lobbying for their version of church government. In August 1644, doctrine reappeared on the agenda, as did worship. In December, the debates on church order ended with a rough consensus, preceded several months earlier by agreement on a "Directory for Ordination." (Day in and day out, the assembly was examining candidates for ministry; in all, nearly two thousand persons were vetted.)[50] In January 1645, Parliament abolished the statutory status of the *Book of Common Prayer* and replaced it with *A Directory for the Publique Worship of God*. Agreeing on a statement of doctrine dragged on until December 1646. The two catechisms were sent to Parliament in late 1647 and finalized in April 1648. For all intents and purposes, the assembly ceased to meet by the close of February 1649, although it limped along until 1653.[51]

Worship was the easiest of the three projects the assembly undertook. Agreeing on how to administer the Lord's Supper was accomplished by acknowledging different ways of receiving the sacrament. On set prayer versus free-form prayer, the naysayers prevailed, to the point of eliminating all set prayer from the *Directory* except for the Lord's Prayer. Instead of providing actual texts, the *Directory* recommended certain words or subjects ministers could incorporate in their prayers. It also included guidance for what should be said or done at funerals and weddings, the first of these stripped of prayer, singing, sermons, and the encouraging words of the *Book of Common Prayer* about the fate of the deceased. Marriage became essentially secular—legal, although the suggestion that it was "expedient that marriage be solemnized by a lawful minister" and the rubric denoting "the solemnization of marriage" kept it from being entirely so. Much space was given to directions about preaching, the prayer of adoration and confession that preceded the sermon, and the thanksgiving that followed. Much was also made of the reading of Scripture—far more of it on a weekly basis than what the *Book of Common Prayer* required. As in Scottish practice and as recommended by the presbyterians of Cartwright's day, a sermon would precede the administering of Holy Communion, from which "the ignorant and the scandalous" were barred.[52] In retrospect, the most interesting section of the *Directory* was its endorsement of baptism as "a Seale of the Covenant of Grace . . . and of our Union with him, of Remission of sins, Regeneration, Adoption, and Life eternall," assertions tempered by what was said a few sentences later about the "seed . . . of the faithfull" acquiring "the *outward* Priviledges of the Church" (emphasis added) and characterizing the sacrament as "not so necessary" as a means of grace.[53]

When it came to an alternative to episcopacy, debate was punctuated by efforts at "accommodation" between the alternatives of a national church organized along Presbyterian lines and semiautonomous congregations existing alongside a state church. In October 1643, the assembly took up a question that was instantly controversial: did Scripture contain a specific model of church government that everyone could acknowledge as *jure divino*? A handful of members insisted that Scripture validated a congregation-centered version of the true church. Simultaneously, the Scottish delegates and their English allies argued that Scripture favored a Presbyterianism system. Week after week, this premise forced the assembly to rehearse long-standing questions of biblical exegesis and their implications for church structure. Did the word "church" in Matthew 18:17 or "keys" in Matthew 16:19 refer to ministers, as Presbyterians argued, or to both ministers and laypeople, as those of congregational sympathies insisted?[54] The Scottish delegates wanted a collective ministry of teacher, pastor, deacon, and ruling elder but, as others pointed out, the New Testament never specified the last of these offices or differentiated between teacher and pastor. Was the church on earth best understood as "universal catholic visible," as most in the assembly believed, or "particular visible," as a few were insisting? The first of these would make it possible to define ministry as an office directly created by Christ and receiving its authority from him, not from a congregation. It would also elevate the importance of ordination and turn it into a ministry-centered rite. Were interchurch structures of a Presbyterian kind fully Scriptural? The Scots and their English allies insisted that the church in first-century Jerusalem and Ephesus had been several churches, in which case some sort of interchurch structure had been necessary. Summing up the "chief point" that mattered to the assembly's Presbyterians, Baillie described it as establishing "the real authoritie, power, and jurisdiction of Synods and classical Presbyteries over any the members, or the whole of a particular congregation." This is how the assembly eventually voted, over the objections of its Independents.[55]

That Baillie added "the right of ordinarie professors to the sacrament" to this statement signaled the struggle underway over the handling of church discipline and, simultaneously, over the scope of church membership.[56] It was easy to agree that the church should include "Visible saints" or "believers," defined as those who "professed faith in Christ, and obedience unto Christ," together with their children. Yet Independents wanted local churches to "require" not only "a fair profession, and want of scandal" but "such signs of true grace as persuades the whole congregation of their true regeneration," whereas Baillie and his allies wanted churches to encompass "ordinarie professors, though they can give no certaine or satisfactory signes of reall regeneration."[57] Abruptly, debate shifted from membership per se to church discipline and the practice of excommunication. Almost to a person, the assembly acknowledged the importance of protecting the Lord's Supper from the unworthy, doing so soon after it met in July, when it recommended a fast to remedy "the grievous . . . pollution of the Lord's Supper." After listening to speakers complain that this version of discipline was faltering, the assembly wanted to ensure that local ministers were empowered to do whatever was necessary and, in the draft document of December 1644, listed "authoritative suspension from the Lords table" as one of their "power[s]." Nonetheless, debate erupted about the pertinence of Old Testament references to excluding people from the Passover (Num. 9:6–9) and whether someone who was suspended (not excommunicated) could be barred from the sacrament.[58]

Confusion deepened when the biblical scholar John Lightfoot challenged the New Testament basis for excommunication, an argument introduced in January 1644 by the scholar, lay delegate and member of Parliament John Selden (1584–1654), who, like Thomas Erastus before him, viewed excommunication as a civil penalty and rejected the customary proof texts from the Old and New Testaments. Selden wanted the civil magistrate to have the last word on whether church courts—which would reappear in a Presbyterian scheme— had acted fairly. He attached this argument to another, that Scripture did not support a *jure divino* understanding of the true church, an argument that William Prynne was also making outside the walls of Parliament.[59] Within the assembly but not within the House of Commons, Selden's was very much a minority position. What the majority favored became chapter 30 of the Westminster Confession, which described the church's authority in matters of discipline as by direct gift or commission from "Lord Jesus Christ, as King and Head of his Church." In its entirety, this chapter was omitted from the version approved by Parliament and printed at its request. So was a part of chapter 20, which touched on church discipline, and, because it acknowledged the possibility of divorce, chapter 24 on marriage.[60]

Meanwhile, Prynne, John Milton, and Independent ministers such as John Goodwin were fanning the flames of anti-presbyterianism. One tactic was to imply that this system would give too much power to the clergy. In a poem Milton contributed to the campaign against Presbyterianism, he opined that "New Presbyter is but Old Priest writ Large." In response, the Scottish commissioners pointed out that their system included checks and balances wholly absent from the congregation-based scheme of the Independents.[61] Within the assembly itself, Henderson, Baillie, and their fellow delegates continued to oppose any compromise that undercut the church's *jure divino* authority in matters of discipline, an argument made at length by George Gillespie in *Aarons Rod Blossoming: or The divine ordinance of church government vindicated* (1646). Aware of how the government of James VI in Scotland had interfered with discipline, and familiar with the religious politics of Prynne and other "erastians," Gillespie warned that churches were the last resort in situations "where the Magistrate doth not professe and defende the true Religion." To him and his fellow Scots, it was imperative that parishes take "special care . . . that there be not a promiscuous admission of all sorts of persons" to the sacraments.[62]

The back-and-forth was intense and compromise apparently impossible. Anyone familiar with the history of the reformation in Scotland or the struggle in Calvin's Geneva would have recognized what was at stake. Did the church look to Christ as its sole head or "king," as had been said so many times by Reformed and Puritan theorists, or was it subordinate to civil authority, as the Long Parliament assumed when it drafted the ordinance of 1643 that brought the assembly into being? Passing by the details of this struggle,[63] the outcome was a parliamentary ordinance (August 1645) on the membership of church courts that made laymen the majority, and another ordinance (October 20, 1645) laying out its version of "the Rules and Directions concerning Suspension from the Sacrament of the Lord's Supper in cases of Ignorance and Scandal," which the assembly denounced as "contrary to that Way of Government which Christ hath appointed in His Church, in that it giveth a Power to judge of the Fitness of Persons to come to the Sacrament unto such as our Lord Christ hath not given that Power." The smidgeon of good news was that churches and pastors could continue to exclude the scandalous and ignorant from the sacrament; the bad was that Parliament undercut this possibility by allowing anyone "aggrieved" with these decisions to appeal them to other church courts and eventually to Parliament itself, a rule enhanced a few months later (January 1646) by an order assigning lay commissioners to evaluate whether someone had been sufficiently scandalous to warrant being excluded. Protests by the assembly persisted, to the point of declaring that ministers could not in conscience participate in such a system. It had the satisfaction of knowing that, in

March 1646, Parliament endorsed a Presbyterian system shorn of any independent authority and never equipped with anything akin to a general assembly. In June, Parliament also modified the initial plan for handling appeals relating to church discipline; instead of insisting on county-based courts of "Commissioners of Appeals," it endorsed a single Parliamentary committee based in London. That October, the government finally voted to abolish episcopacy, and by midwinter, the Westminster Assembly and its London allies "made a quiet and grudging peace with" what Parliament had adopted.[64]

As these events were unfolding, London-based Presbyterians, the city government (which had come back into Presbyterian hands), the Scots, and others who endorsed uniformity of belief staged a last-ditch campaign on behalf of the alliance of 1643 and the model of a comprehensive state church. Among its weapons were petitions to the Long Parliament, sermons, public demonstrations, and learned treatises, one of them *Jus Divinum Regiminis Ecclesiastici; or, The Divine Right of Church-Government, Asserted and evidenced by the holy Scriptures*, a lifeless defense of the proposition that (as was said on the title page) "The Presbyteriall Government . . . may lay the truest claime to a Divine Right, according to the Scriptures." A response to "erastians" in and outside of Parliament as well as to advocates of toleration, its author(s) reiterated two assumptions of immense importance to these heirs of Cartwright, Knox, and Andrew Melville: Christ as "King" had endowed the church with an authority wholly different from the authority of the civil state, and Scripture dictated the form of church government. Independency was faulted for other reasons, chief among them the perception that a "gathered" church membership contradicted the Reformed understanding of the visible church. [65]

Another product of this campaign was a wave of books, pamphlets, and petitions publicizing the sorry consequences of toleration (see below, sec. 3). In March 1647, a parliamentary ordinance recommending a fast to bewail the prevalence of "errours and blasphemies" was abetted by the anonymous pamphlet *Hell broke loose*, which drew attention to the unorthodox theologizing of the ministers John Goodwin and John Saltmarsh and the New Englander Samuel Gorton (see chap. 9), among others. In December, fifty-two ministers added their names to *A Testimony to the Truth of Jesus Christ*, which specified a long list of "abominable Errours" and named the men responsible for them. Simultaneously, ministers in New England weighed in on the benefits of theological orthodoxy: Thomas Shepard in a letter of 1645 to his former colleague Thomas Weld, and John Cotton in *The bloudy tenant washed and made white with the bloud of the Lambe* (1647), a response to Roger Williams that touched off more back-and-forth. At a popular level, stories proliferated of divine interventions to punish wayward women. After the New Model Army entered London in mid-1647 and parliamentary "Independents" regained control of Parliament, both houses agreed on "giving ease to tender consciences" (but not those of Catholics), to which the riposte in May 1648, after "presbyterians" briefly reclaimed control of the House of Commons, was an ordinance "For the preventing of the growth and spreading of Heresy and Blasphemy" that authorized the execution of anyone who rejected the Trinity, the divine origins of Scripture, the existence of God, and the meritorious benefits of Christ's death on the cross, among others.[66]

Despite these efforts, the state church that limped into being in 1646 was a toothless version of voluntary religion. No national assembly was ever authorized, synods rarely met, protecting the Sunday Sabbath faltered despite various attempts to preserve it,[67] and mandatory attendance at church services gave way to unrestrained movement back and forth between old-style parishes and congregations organized by Independents, Baptists, and others. Nonetheless, the Presbyterian community in London busied itself appointing lay elders and initiating the machinery of associations and synods. The mosaic of belief and practice also included ministers and laypeople who preferred the *Book of Common Prayer* and an unknown fraction of people who withdrew from organized religion in any of its forms.[68]

As had always been the case in post-Reformation England, the new system achieved a certain success wherever ambitious, energetic, and evangelical ministers took over a parish. Richard Baxter in Kidderminster (Worcestershire), and Henry Newcome in several places labored to preserve the shell of a state church, protect the sacraments, and sustain moral order. For Baxter, catechizing every household was the key to making people and parish into a genuine Christian community. With the help of others, he arranged his weekly schedule to include visits of this kind. Simultaneously, he insisted on protecting the Lord's Supper from those without faith, although never requiring the spiritual testimonies that most Independents favored. Looking back on the 1650s, Baxter recalled how the church in Kidderminster had to be expanded five times to accommodate everyone who wanted to attend. He remembered, too, that instead of "disorder" on "the Lord's days," "you might hear an hundred families singing psalms and repeating sermons as you passed through the streets." A few of the local gentry refused to attend his services, but the town had no "private church" or any "sect against sect."[69]

When all was said and done, however, Baxter could not keep "sectaries" from increasing in his part of England. Meanwhile, old-style conformists were also avoiding the Lord's Supper and possibly church services in general.[70] The most obvious index of their resentment was a dramatic decline in the numbers of children being baptized. How social discipline fared remains uncertain, but in the historian Derek Hirst's careful survey of attempts to guard the Lord's Table, protect the Sunday Sabbath, and uphold moral discipline, the evidence assembled from local records, ministers' diaries, and the like suggests the near complete failure of those projects. Likewise, this evidence calls into question the capacity of Presbyterian and Independent ministers in the 1650s to sustain parish-wide catechesis. In his words, "noise" about reform abounded but follow-through or "action" rarely happened. Intermittency of one kind or another was nothing new, but the situation after 1650 in England and Scotland seems much worse, with more people slipping through the cracks by staying away from services, spurning baptism for their children, and giving up on the practice of catechizing.[71]

Baxter's perspective on the 1650s, together with his unsuccessful attempt in 1659–61 to bring together moderates of all persuasions in a reconstructed state church, underscore the impact of those he characterized as "sectaries" on the classic program of moral discipline, a ministry-magistracy alliance, and top-down evangelization. Who were these people and what did they want?[72]

Sectaries and Independents

Of the many disruptions that rippled through the 1640s, the most alarming to mainstream Puritans may have been the emergence of people who repudiated an inclusive state church and of others who jettisoned a learned ministry and orthodox theology. As early as 1641, the presence of these "sectaries" was being publicized in *A Discovery of 29 sects here in London: all of which, except the first [Protestants], are most devilish and damnable* and other pamphlets of the same ilk, several of them the doing of the royalist sympathizer John Taylor, whose contributions to the outcry included *A Swarme of Sectaries, and Schismatiques* (1641) and *A Tale In a Tub, Or a tub Lecture As it was delivered by M-heele Mendsoale, an Inspired Brownist, and a most upright Translator, In a meeting house neere Bedlam* (1642).[73] This publicity, which redoubled in the mid-1640s, painted London as a world turned upside down, the city's bookstalls piled high with unlicensed pamphlets and churches overtaken by illicit conventicles. As reported by the moderate royalist and episcopalian Robert Sanderson, more "new doctrines" sprang up during the opening months of the new decade than in the previous eighty years, a process facilitated by the abolition of Star Chamber and the Court of High Commission, the two most powerful instruments for curtailing heterodoxy and unauthorized versions of voluntary religion.[74]

Simultaneously, a broader reaction against hierarchy and entrenched privilege was unfolding. By January 1642, the elitist and monarchy-favoring aldermen who controlled affairs in London had been displaced by a more openly elected and Puritan-tilting Common Council.[75] This was shocking to conservatives, but the real story was the emergence of a popular politics that mobilized ordinary people to influence public affairs in new ways. Its instruments included a vast increase in petitions, demonstrations or riots outside the walls of Parliament, contested elections, and conventicles mutating into self-administered congregations. As was reported in 1640 of one conventicle, its members were asserting that there was "no true Church but where the Faithful met. That the King could not make a perfect Law, for that he was not a perfect man" and not to be obeyed "but in Civil things." Where the Long Parliament feared to go because of its instinctive conservativism, the sectaries rushed headlong thanks to a liberating awareness of the Holy Spirit, the powerful workings of conscience, and a fresh understanding of Scripture.[76]

Another source of this politics was far greater freedom of expression. With Star Chamber abolished, booksellers and printers could publish anything that came to hand unless they abided by the rules of the Stationers Company, the guild that traditionally cooperated with the government to restrain what was printed. In the main, booksellers wanted it both ways: their "rights to copy" preserved and competition (or "piracy") held in check, yet also profiting from the breakdown of control. Competition won out despite a parliamentary ordinance in June 1643 reinstating a process of licensing. With opinion about true religion beginning to fracture, the book trades began to mirror the shifting relationship between popular politics and the world of print. Before 1640, it was uncommon for petitions to be printed or for disagreements among the elite to be openly publicized. Now, however, appealing to the public became imperative—or seen as such. Hence the amazing increase in the number of books and broadsheets being published, many of them unbound, inexpensive pamphlets and others in the format of newssheets or news books that, before the 1640s, had appeared intermittently as a way of reporting news from overseas. In the 1630s, the annual production of books in Britain or printed elsewhere in the English language averaged 624. In 1641, the number rose to 2,042 and in 1642, 4,038, a trend fattened by wave upon wave of imprints that transgressed the boundaries of what had hitherto been regarded by the government and state church as acceptable.[77] In the words of a Stationers Company remonstrance to Parliament in 1643, the situation was such that "every libeling speritt" was free to "traduce the proceedings of the state, every malicious speritt may then revile whomsoever he pleaseth . . . yea every pernicitious hereticke may . . . poison the minds of good mynded people of wicked errors."[78]

Once unleashed, these "speritt[s]" turned their fire on theological orthodoxy and the church-state axis. The best-known of these assaults, which many in nineteenth- and twentieth-century Britain and the United States celebrated as a sign of moral and political progress, was directed at state-imposed uniformity, which the sectaries wanted to replace with toleration or liberty of conscience. These two should not be regarded as identical; toleration was a means of limiting the authority of the civil state to enforce any single version of Christianity but would preserve a state church and, in most versions, require the state to set limits to what counted as truth. As the historian George Yule has pointed out, advocates of toleration in the 1640s and 1654os did not welcome "anti-religious belief." Any strong version of liberty of conscience severed the connections between the state and religious affiliation, leaving everyone free to choose what form of religion he or she preferred. (In point of fact, arguments on behalf of liberty of conscience excluded Roman Catholics and Mus-

lims or in other ways limited the scope of religious freedom.) Mainstream Puritans opposed each of these possibilities and called on Parliament to reaffirm
the government's control over the marketplace of ideas. Others, like John
Owen (1616–83), wanted toleration for everyone who remained within the
boundaries of theological orthodoxy, a middle-of-the-road position that most
Independents favored because it preserved a place for them if the state church
became Presbyterian.[79]

The sectaries have always had both friends and enemies. Present-day Baptists are excited to see their denomination emerge out of the shadows, while
religious and political liberals hail the advocates of toleration or liberty of conscience.[80] Many others have been critical—for example, most nineteenth-
century Anglicans and, as the mid-century "revolution in print" was unfolding,
the Scottish and English Presbyterians who staged a counterattack on the disruptive and possibly blasphemous doings of the sectaries. The chief architect
of this attack was Thomas Edwards (d. 1647), a nonconforming English min-
ster jolted into print by what he saw happening around him. As early as 1641,
he was predicting that religious liberty would open the way to "libertinisme,
prophaneness, errors, and . . . no religion at all," a refrain he repeated in a
slashing attack (1644) on the authors of *An Apologeticall Narration* (see
below).[81]

Edwards's magnum opus was *Gangraena; or, A Catalogue and Discovery
of many of the Errours, Heresies, Blasphemies and pernicious Practices of the
Sectaries of this time* (1646; reprinted the same year in two larger versions),
which he filled with a biting analysis of dissent and its implications for true
religion. Others, including Prynne, shared this agenda. After being freed by the
Long Parliament and resuming his assault on Laud, he attacked the sectaries
in *A fresh discovery of some prodigious new wandering-blasing stars, *& fire-
brands stilling themselves new lights* (1646). Prynne and Edwards had allies in
the moderate Puritan minister Ephraim Pagitt, who anticipated Edwards in
*Heresiography; or, A description of the hereticks and sectaries of these latter
times* (1645); the Scottish minister Robert Baillie, who filled *A Dissuasive
against the Errours of the Time* (1645) with insinuations about John Cotton's
role in the "Antinomian" crisis in 1630s Massachusetts; and the makers of *A
Discovery of the Most Dangerous and Damnable Tenets That Have Been Spread
Within This Few Weeks* (1647), among others.

The heresiographers wanted to uphold theological orthodoxy, but above all
they wanted to uphold the assumptions and practices associated with state
churches backed by the authority of the civil state. What was happening
around them in 1640s London and elsewhere was upending that possibility.
Edwards and the Scots blamed the tumult on English congregationalists (or
Independents) who were sympathetic to toleration and opposed the model of
an inclusive state church backed by the state; as Baillie remarked in mid-1644,
the "evill of Independency" was "the mother and true fountaine of all the

church distractions here." By 1646, the heresiographers were also blaming Independents and others for the anti-presbyterian politics of the New Model
Army. In the words of a modern scholar, the goal was to fashion "a seamless
connection between the Anabaptists, antinomians, and antitrinitarians [those
who questioned the traditional doctrine of the Trinity]" to the end of
"reestablish[ing] the indispensability of Presbyterianism as the way to ward
off sectaries and heretics."[82]

Today, we value Pagitt, Prynne, and Edwards because they preserved much
of what the sectaries were saying and doing. Edwards was especially detailed,
for he added eyewitness accounts from a network of informants to his own
observations.[83] Out of this mass of evidence, which included alarm bells about
groups that were "utterly fabulous" (i.e., someone's invention) and women taking on a role as preachers and prophetesses, emerged a picture of "confusion
and disorder" as evidenced by the presence of "illiterate mechanic Preachers
yea of Women and Boy Preachers," none of them punished by the government.
It was horrifying when Edwards realized that most were advocating "dangerous and false Doctrines." For readers who wanted to know what these were, he
assembled a nineteen-page "Catalogue of the Errours, Heresies, [and] Blasphemies" for the first version of his book, with more examples added in the
second. From it his readers learned that old bugaboos were reappearing alongside others of more recent origin. Edwards's list included Arminianism, Antinomianism, Socinianism, Familism (the teachings of the sixteenth-century
Dutch "Familist" Hendrik Niclaus, whose ideas had been circulating in England since the late sixteenth century), chiliasm (belief that the end times were
about to happen), mortalism (belief that bodies do not immediately pass to
heaven at the moment of death); and perfectionism (belief that absent sin of
any kind, people could enjoy "worldly delights, begetting many children [i.e,
plenty of scx], eating and drinking"), among others.[84]

That opinions of this kind were being voiced in the 1640s seems certain, but
most of the men and women who throng Edwards's pages were objecting to
core themes of the practical divinity. According to Edwards, some were insisting that "the doctrine of repentance is a soule-destroying doctrine." Others
spurned the concept and practice of the Sunday Sabbath and questioned the
veracity of the Bible. His list also encompassed a strident version of Separatist-
style purity, as evidenced by the argument that " 'tis unlawfull for the Saints to
joyn in receiving the Lords supper, where any wicked men are present, and that
such mixt Communion doth pollute and defile them." The same pairing of
purity and pollution reappeared in the assertion—possibly stemming from
Roger Williams—that no one should pray with someone who was not among
the godly.[85]

The routes by which people arrived at these ideas included the Puritan
movement itself. William Erbury (1604/5–1654), a nonconforming minister
who gave up on institutions and became a "Seeker" (see below), was unusual

in referencing Richard Sibbes and John Preston as teachers of free grace.[86] Separatist-style behavior drew on a long-standing sympathy for John Foxe's story of the faithful few or "remnant" contending against corrupt and oppressive regimes. This narrative reappeared in almost every version of sectarian self-identity, as did the distinction he inscribed between false church and true. As well, sectaries were familiar with the commonplace that Christ spoke in a simple manner that everyone could understand, a proposition easily translated into the argument that those touched by the Spirit could dispense with learned intermediaries altogether.[87]

Another source was the apocalypticism (or "millenarianism") that flourished after 1640. Its sources included the musings of Thomas Brightman and many others about the imminent conversion of the Jews, an outpouring of the Holy Spirit, and Christ's return in judgment. In the 1630s and 1640s, this way of thinking ripened into an understanding of sacred history as a sequence of dispensations: the purity of apostolic times, followed by a descent into darkness, followed by the return of the Holy Spirit and a "new light" that would liberate the worthy few from the coercive authority of a state church and learned ministry. Themes of this kind explain why "illiterate" men and women were asserting a role as prophets after hearing a voice from heaven or claiming to be filled with the Holy Spirit.[88] It explains, as well, the preference for gathered churches fashioned by people who joined them voluntarily. A more daring version of sacred history prompted the emergence of "Seekers." Never a self-acknowledged group or possibly a group at all, these people took for granted the "cessation and departure of the glory of God" from Christianity as currently constituted. It followed that no "true visible . . . Gospel Church" would reappear until God dispatched apostle-like messengers to reveal the truth.[89]

The visionaries and newborn saints who, in the 1650s, acquired the nickname of "Quaker" wanted nothing to do with an inclusive, institutional church of any kind.[90] Familiar with the narrative of true religion succumbing to corruption, these "Friends" or "Children of the Light" situated themselves within a sweeping emancipation from Sion's "long enthralled captivity in Babylon's kingdom," a story they used to justify their rejection of all outward "forms . . . kept by priests." According to the itinerant layman George Fox, the "mixed multitude" of the state church contradicted the New Testament insistence on a church composed of "living stones." Fox centered his own awakening on the immediacy of the Holy Spirit and the simplicity of Scripture, themes he owed to a life-altering encounter with the Gospel of John. For some of the women who joined him in preaching and prophesying, it was the biblical prophecy (Joel 2:28–29 and Acts 2:17–18) of an era when the Spirit would empower women to speak.[91]

When Fox began to speak of an "inner light" that liberated him from outward forms, he found a receptive audience in the north of England among people who were worshipping on their own but uncertain of where the truth lay. The more they learned of Fox's realized eschatology and his emphasis on Spirit-centered prophesying, the more some of these people were moved to share this message with those who lived in darkness. Off went missionaries to Europe, where a few traveled as far as Rome hoping to persuade the pope to acknowledge the new dispensation. Others carried the message of the light to Ireland, the English colonies in the Caribbean, and the mainland of North America. This zeal for witnessing reached something of a climax in the person of James Naylor (1616–1660), who entered Bristol, England, in October 1656 riding a horse and preceded by a group of women hailing him as a Christ-like figure. Naylor's overreaching unnerved the government, which used the provisions of the Blasphemy Act of 1650 to punish him harshly. He and Fox were already at odds and, after Charles II returned to the throne in 1660, Fox and his allies reassured the new government that the Quaker rhetoric of kingdoms being overturned by the Spirit was apolitical. Thereafter, the "peace testimony" became a core theme of Quakerism. Naylor's boldness also pushed the movement into creating methods of self-regulation centered on the all-male London Meeting.[92]

Quakers, Independents, and Baptists were the only survivors of the explosive possibilities of the Civil War period. Independents were the earliest of these three to emerge if we accept the argument of nineteenth-century denominational historians that this way of thinking originated with Robert Browne and Henry Barrow. Baptist sentiments and practice—that is, substituting adult baptism for the baptism of infants—had also cropped up in sixteenth-century England and, in the first decade of the seventeenth, acquired two articulate advocates, the Separatists John Smythe and Thomas Helwys (see chap. 6); after Smythe affiliated with the Mennonites in Amsterdam, Helwys returned to England and spent the final years of his life nurturing half-hidden communities of which little is known. The stringent primitivism of these early Baptists may account for the turmoil inside Henry Jacob's semi-Separatist London congregation, which spawned tiny groups that adopted adult baptism, most of them choosing to do so by immersion rather than by sprinkling. Aware of sixteenth-century Anabaptist opposition to oaths and civil governments, these people usually chose a more moderate path. By 1640–41, they were becoming better known and attracting more adherents. On the other side of the Atlantic, Roger Williams and a few others in Rhode Island rebaptized themselves in 1639 and formed the first Baptist church in British North America, although the ever-restless Williams left the group a few months later.[93]

These steps provoked an outpouring of anti-Baptist propaganda and state action against "Anabaptists" bearing public witness to their faith. As leaders of the new group were quick to realize, it was not in their best interests to be identified with the wildest of the sectaries, a policy reaffirmed in the 1650s in response to Quakers. By 1643, some Baptists were meeting with congregationalists (and vice versa) to discuss their differences, and in late 1644 other discussions unfolded with London-based Presbyterians. In their own words, Baptists undertook these ventures to clear themselves of the "calamy" heaped on them by the heresiographers. As their most careful historian has noted, "all shared the determination of Episcopalians and Presbyterians to outlaw views taken to be blasphemous or undermining of Christianity as a whole," a policy they essayed to combine with a tempered understanding of liberty of conscience— in essence, the liberty for them to practice their own tenets. In the 1650s, the same politics prompted the leading Baptist of the day, John Tombes, to lambast the Quakers in *True Old Light Exalted above Pretended New Light* (1660).[94]

One outcome of this quest for a more moderate identity was a *Confession of Faith*, published in 1644 and endorsed by seven English congregations; two years later a second, slightly revised version was published. Never coupled with any means of enforcing its provisions, the *Confession* (chap. 19) authorized anyone "gifted and enabled by the Spirit" to prophesy and undertake other aspects of ministry. On the other hand, its strictly theological provisions mirrored the five points of the Synod of Dordt and the practical divinity: some were of the elect and would always remain so; the elect "believe" because they have been "effectually called by a special, gracious, and powerful work of his Spirit" (language directed at Arminians who "do maintain a freewill and sufficient ability . . . to believe, and do deny election"); the law remains binding, because Christ "commandeth" the elect to "walk in the way . . . of righteousness" spelled out in the Ten Commandments. The *Confession* also validated the office of magistrate and omitted any argument for "toleration in broad terms." Far from being sectaries bent on turning the world upside down, the makers of the *Confession* represented themselves as a "conscionable, quiet, and harmless people (no ways dangerous or troublesome to human society)."[95] Other small groups of Baptists aligned themselves with an Arminian version of Reformed orthodoxy defined, in part, by Thomas Lambe in *The Fountain of Free Grace Opened* (1644/45) and a statement of doctrine of 1653. Subsequently, some moved on to other affiliations—in the late 1640s with the Levellers, a group that aspired to dismantle every version of privilege in England, and in the early 1650s, to the Fifth Monarchists, who prophesied the impending restoration of Christ's kingdom and urged Cromwell and the first Parliament of the Protectorate (1653) to entrust civil authority to the saints.[96]

Independents (or congregationalists) were the most numerous of the new groups. By the close of the 1650s, something like 250 congregations of this kind had come into being in England, Ireland, Scotland, and Wales, many of them founded after 1649.[97] In general, their organizers echoed what had been said by the colonists to their English critics. Because this scheme encompassed the authority of ministers as well as laypeople, it avoided the democratic excesses of "Brownisme." On the other hand, it also eliminated the centralizing and hierarchical aspects of Presbyterianism, or what was stigmatized as "tyranny."

And, by creating churches limited to the godly, this scheme solved the problem of deciding who was worthy to participate in the sacraments.

The contexts that explain the emergence of Independency resemble those that explain the making of this system in New England. For the five ministers who decamped to the Netherlands in the late 1630s (see chap. 6), a crisis of conscience akin to what John Cotton, John Davenport, and others had experienced led them to abandon the old nonconformity and create covenanted congregations. How much this group owed to the manifestos of Jacob, Bradshaw, Parker, Baynes, Robinson, and Ames is unclear, but Thomas Goodwin and his friends certainly knew of the experiments in church order Thomas Hooker and Hugh Peter had introduced in Rotterdam and elsewhere. Once the political situation in England changed for the better, all five returned and began to publicize their understanding of the true church, a process interrupted in September 1641 when they agreed with London-based Presbyterians to remain silent for the time being—not entirely silent and certainly not invisible, since Robert Baillie knew of them as soon as he arrived in London. On his own, Henry Burton had already begun to advocate for something akin to Independency in *Christ on his Throne; or, Christs Church-government briefly laid downe* (1640) and *The Protestation Protested* (1641), an all-out-assault on prayer-book worship and episcopacy as anti-Christian, combined with a plea to "come out from among them that are unclean" and form gathered churches. His bold words indicated that the fat was in the fire—explicitly so, for someone asks, "How will this stand with a National Church . . . ? This would make for division, and separation," a question Thomas Edwards answered in another tract (1641) detailing the weaknesses of a congregation-centered system. By the mid-1640s, others besides Burton were openly advocating for such a system, some because they had been persuaded of its merits after reading what Cotton, Davenport, Richard Mather, and their colleagues said about the New England version in a string of London-printed books, and still others because it satisfied their Separatist-like disdain for a state church of any kind. John Owen, who became the most important Independent in 1650s England, gladly acknowledged his debt to John Cotton's *The Keyes of the Kingdom of Christ* (1644), which persuaded him that the colonists had tamed their "democratical" polity. Other newcomers to Independency cited the same "non-separating" theorizers—Henry Jacob, Robert Parker, William Ames—that Cotton and his colleagues had also been citing.[98]

In early 1643, the improbable alliance of 1641 among London-based Presbyterians and Independents was still functioning, as witnessed by efforts to prod the House of Commons into restraining lay preaching and "Antinomianism." Yet in the Westminster Assembly, lines were being drawn and issues clarified. The turning point for some English and Scottish moderates was *An Apologeticall Narration, Humbly Submitted to the Honourable Houses of Parliament* (January 1644), signed by the five ministers who had gone to the

Netherlands in the late 1630s. A political text aimed at winning the sympathy of Parliament, it evoked a "clearer light" and a review of "Apostolique directions pattern and examples of . . . Primitive Churches" as the sources of their decision to replace the customary "practice" of "Reformed Churches" with gathered and autonomous congregations. Doing so would truly be a further reformation given the judgment that Continental Reformed churches had not fully purified their membership. Hence the situating of a congregation-centered system as a "middle way" between extremes—not the Scottish version of a middle way, which located Presbyterianism between Catholicism and some sort of anarchy, but a self-promoting version framed by episcopacy and—to the fury of the Presbyterian party in the assembly—their version of the church. What was said about church membership echoed the practice in New England, not a "promiscuous multitude" but only those who "may be supposed to be the least of Christ." It followed that no child could be baptized unless a parent had joined a covenanted congregation. Among the criteria for becoming a member was "the evidences of . . . conversion," a rule enforced in John Goodwin's London-based gathered congregation despite protests from people who had welcomed Goodwin as their *parish* minister. As in New England and among some of the Separatists, the *Narration* also endorsed the free movement of the Spirit and rejected "set" prayer.[99]

The great strength of Independency (a name spurned by the authors of the *Apologeticall Narration*) was its cadre of university-educated ministers, which included men who went to New England in the 1630s but returned once they realized that nonconformity was no longer being punished. Despite his harsh words about the Independents, Thomas Edwards realized that these men did not fit the profile of the prototypical sectary. So should we. On the whole, they were doctrinally orthodox and, when it came to being hired, preferred parish "livings" purged of "scandalous" incumbents or vacant for other reasons, a tendency lamented by some historians of congregationalism. After being entrusted with a congregation gathered out of a parish, many Independents continued to catechize the townspeople or possibly by other means sustain a "parochial congregationalism" akin to what was being practiced in New England. In other parishes, however, conflict erupted once it became apparent that some people were no longer being admitted to the sacraments. Dissidents forced Thomas Larkham out of Tavistock once they encountered this policy, and conflict along the same lines happened in Bermuda and elsewhere.[100]

This church-like congregationalism never rivaled the appeal of Presbyterianism, and its influence was tempered by a Separatist-flavored version led by laypeople and ministers who abandoned a state church corrupted by the Laudian program by withdrawing into conventicles or covenanted communities, a process underway well before the two Bishops' Wars. Wales was one such region, thanks to the missionary outreach of the quasi-Separatist and eventual Baptist Henry Jessey (1603–63), who went there in 1639 to assist local people in forming a congregation of their own. As had already happened with the Jacob-Lothrop group, which Jessey led after Lothrop left for Massachusetts, the congregation he established in Llanvaches began to nurture others. Another hotspot was St. Stephens Parish in London, where the cobbler Samuel How was sharing a Spirit-centered understanding of Scripture that downplayed learnedness.[101]

Emerging from beneath, as it were, this "populist, plebian Puritanism" was enabling certain women to acquire a public presence. Together with her husband Daniel, Katherine Chidley (1616–1653) had participated in conventicles in their home county of Shropshire in the 1620s. Moving to London by 1630 to avoid being punished for nonconformity, she and Daniel joined one of the groups that had withdrawn from the Jacob-Lothrop-Jessey congregation. When Chidley learned of Thomas Edwards's *Reasons against the Independent Government of Particular Congregations*, which included a sneer at "men ignorant and low in parts" setting up their own churches, she insisted in her response (also 1641) that it was "lawfull" to abandon state churches dominated by the Antichrist and replace them with churches based on "Christs true Discipline, grounded and founded in his Word." Authority as traditionally understood was at the heart of Edwards's objections to this practice. Chidley endorsed a quite different version of authority. Citing John Robinson on the privileges of laypeople, she emphasized the empowering consequences of the Holy Spirit on the "whole" of the church and questioned the age-old trope of the "unlearned" who needed guidance from a learned ministry.[102]

Chidley's fiery words on behalf of a decentered church recall the stirrings of lay protests during and after the reign of Mary Tudor. Once underway, the rebirth of this quest for purity became the driving force behind a burst of church foundings. One well-known example is the congregation established in Broadmead (Bristol). There, for several years if not longer, a group of lay women and men had met "together to repeat sermon-notes" while also "fasting and praying . . . frequently." Their disaffection with the state church had everything to do with modes of worship to which Puritans had traditionally objected: kneeling to receive the sacrament, making the sign of the cross in the liturgy of baptism, deploying of "pictures and images" in a church. The alternative was "lively" preaching that communicated a "taste of [Christ's] Spirit" and strengthened their identity as "sanctified" believers who "forsook profaning the Lord's day" and all other "superstitious" practices.[103] The impulse to separate overcame Dorothy Hazard after reading Revelation 14:9–11, a passage warning that anyone who "worship[s] the beast and his image" will kindle the "wrath of God." After forming a covenanted congregation "to worship the Lord more purely," she and a handful of others continued to hear the sermons being preached by her husband in a parish church until John Canne, the sometime Separatist printer-publisher and publicist based in Amsterdam, turned up. According to a history of the group written some years later, Canne "showed them the difference betwixt the church of Christ and antichrist," whereupon Hazard and her allies cast off every minister who did not repudiate anti-Christian worship. "Thus the Lord led them by degrees, and brought them out of popish darkness into his marvelous light of the gospel," a process that culminated in a decision to practice adult baptism by immersion.[104]

Another experiment of this kind came and went in early 1650s Dublin, a Spirit-centered reformation guided by the ardent millenarian John Rogers. A university-trained minister, Rogers (unrelated to John Rogers of Dedham, the minister famous for his preaching of terror) began as a Presbyterian but shifted to a Spirit-centered version of Independency by 1650, when he arrived in Dublin, a city where liberty of conscience had become state policy. There, as well as organizing a covenanted congregation that included both advocates and enemies of infant baptism, he broke with New England–style Independency by allowing women to vote in church affairs and serve as "prophetesses." Knowing of Brightman's argument that 1650 would be a turning point in sacred history and influenced by Fifth Monarchist assertions of impending change, Rogers insisted that "Sion is to be restored" in the form of "gathered churches" liberated from the "mixed multitudes" of the Church of England. No hypocrites would be included (although Rogers admitted that mistakes would be made), for the postapocalyptic church would contain those "in whom . . . the graces of Christ, and the gifts of his Spirit [reside] in some measure." He put this principle into practice by requiring Spirit-centered testimonies of those who wanted to join his congregation. Harkening back to a theme of great importance to John Robinson and others, Rogers also imagined a church of this kind as a community where the "mutual edification of one another" would flourish, with the saints expressing "saint-like" love to each other. All too quickly, Rogers learned the lesson that the goal of purity could be co-opted by groups even more determined than he was to get rid of restrictive structures. Dublin was a hothouse of Baptist sentiments. Before long, most of the congregation abandoned him and went in that direction.[105]

Rogers, Chidley, and the founders of the Broadmead church were exciting figures. Yet most of the makers of Independency tempered their commitment to gathered churches by practicing local versions of "parish" congregationalism. Although their sympathy for toleration was a bone in the throat of Presbyterians, the Independents never welcomed complete religious liberty and, when Presbyterian hegemony vanished in the aftermath of Pride's Purge in December 1648 and the collapse of the alliance with Scotland, a more institutionally minded version came to the fore. Already, Roger Williams had recognized while he was in England in 1643–44 that the "faction" of "so-called Independent[s] . . . though not more fully, yet more explicitly than the Presbyterians, casts down the crown of the Lord Jesus at the feet of the civil magistrate."[106] With Cromwell ascendant after the king's execution, the leaders of Independency could openly celebrate their high hopes for a state church refashioned along congregational lines. Baptists, too, were enthusiastic, to the point of speculating that Christ's kingdom was on the verge of being reestablished.[107] Some of this confidence faded in response to circumstances that included the Quaker assault on ordained ministers, the publicizing of Socinianism (see chap. 9), the disappointing history of the nominated Parliament of mid-1653, which started out as an experiment in "godly rule," and the politics of the Fifth Monarchists. By mid-decade, Quaker and Fifth Monarchist visions of social and religious change were fanning the fears of a "paranoid gentry" that people of their status were being threatened by a "social revolution." Simultaneously, Socinianism and sectarian assaults on institutional religion prompted a coalition of ministers to urge Cromwell to endorse a statement of doctrine his government would enforce, an argument laid out in *The Humble proposals of Mr Owen . . . and Other Ministers for the furtherance and propagation of the Gospel . . . For settling of right constituted churches, and for preventing persons of corrupt judgment, from publishing dangerous errours* (1652). In the fourteenth of these proposals, the group recommended rules against allowing laymen or anyone who disagreed with the basic principles of Christianity to preach. In December, a stronger version of this manifesto specified certain principles the government should uphold, a list that included its obligation to suppress heresy.[108]

Nothing happened along these lines. *The Instrument of Government* (1653) that brought the Protectorate into being had already affirmed the "Christian religion . . . as the public profession of these nations." Language of this kind previously appeared in the "Agreement of the People" (January 1649) fashioned within the New Model Army. Its reappearance may seem almost pointless, perhaps because the policies it endorsed were a curious mixture of new and old. What was new was the provision that the civil state could not coerce anyone in matters of religion. Already (1650), the Rump Parliament had eliminated the requirement that everyone in England attend a parish church. What was old or conventional was the willingness of the Rump to bolster the financial situation of ordained ministers and its recommendation that the civil state employ "able and painful ministers" to confront "error, heresy, and whatever is contrary to sound doctrine." Subsequently, a small group of ministers that included Owen met to devise something like a creed for all English Protestants (see chap. 9), a project that never came to fruition.[109] For conservatives and moderates, a more positive step was the government's decision to regulate the appointment and quality of ministers, initially (March 1654) by setting up "triers" charged with scrutinizing the credentials of candidates for ordination. In August 1654, the government also began to appoint "ejectors" who resumed the process of eliminating "scandalous" or otherwise unacceptable ministers. And, at a moment when Fifth Monarchists and some Independents were urging the government to abolish the tithes that funded many ministers, an unlikely coalition of Independents, Presbyterians, and others blocked this proposal when it came up for debate in the nominated Parliament of 1653. Throughout the 1650s, ministers who straddled the line between congregational and Presbyterian perspectives worked their way to common ground on ministry, a reformation of manners, guarding the sacraments from the unworthy, and protecting orthodox doctrine. Yet in the face of opposition from various quarters and the Lord Protector's unwillingness to curtail liberty of conscience, the institutional consequences were quite limited.[110]

Only after the Lord Protector's death in 1658 did Owen and some of his fellow Independents decide to create a statement of doctrine. Half or more of the congregations in Britain were represented at the "Savoy conference" that met in London in December 1658 and endorsed a statement of faith. In all but a few respects it replicated the Westminster Confession. Despite the ups and downs of the 1650s, it included (chap. 26) a hint of Brightman-like optimism about the future by imagining "that in the latter days, Antichrist being destroyed, the Jews called, and the adversaries of the Kingdom of his dear Son broken, the Churches of Christ" would be "edified through a free and plentiful communication of light and grace."[111] Four years later, the Restoration Parliament voted to exclude from the state church any minister who did not acknowledge episcopacy, the royal supremacy, and the *Book of Common Prayer*. Like hundreds of others, Owen left the church he had worked within his entire life and became a "Dissenter." Independency would persist, as would Baptists and Quakers. Never again, however, would Independents lay their hands on the levers of power in Britain.

From Covenant to Crisis

For Archibald Johnston and other leaders of the insurgency of 1637, the National Covenant of 1638 had been an extraordinary example of divine providence. In its aftermath, more wonders followed in quick succession: the General Assemblies of 1638 and 1639, victory in the second Bishops' War, the "free" Parliament of 1640. In October 1640, the two governments, one of them still unreformed, began to negotiate a treaty of peace that would allow the Scottish army to leave England. To London, therefore, came commissioners to negotiate the terms of that treaty, a group that included Johnston, Robert Blair, Robert Baillie, and Alexander Henderson. Entrusted with eight objectives by the Scottish government, the commissioners secured most of them: no penalties imposed or threatened on those in Scotland who led the insurgency, the royal castle in Edinburgh surrendered to the new regime, suppression of anti-Covenanter propaganda, a promise to never declare war against Scotland (or vice versa) without the approval of each country's parliament, and money to cover the costs of raising and sustaining the Scottish army. The two most significant clauses were constitutional. Charles I agreed to legitimize what the Scottish Parliament of 1640 had enacted, although saying he would do so officially when he visited Scotland, and he accepted a role for that Parliament in naming the king's officers of state, a privilege he was unwilling to concede to the Long Parliament. These were remarkable concessions, yet what the Covenanters really wanted was something no treaty or monarch's good will could provide, a structure (not a document!) that would preserve the revolution of 1638–1640. For the men who had taken over the kirk and civil government, the best means of doing so would be a Church of England organized along Presbyterian lines. To this end, Alexander Henderson drafted and a bookseller published *Arguments Given in by the Commissioners of Scotland unto the Lords of the Treaty perswading Conformity of Church government, as one principall Meanes of a continued peace betweene the two Nations* (1641). Paradoxically, in Scotland itself high hopes for stabilizing the revolution of 1638 were giving way to cracks within the Covenanter movement and, here and there, resistance to the actual Covenant of 1638. It had never been signed by all the nobility or every parish, a fact acknowledged by the Scottish Parliament in 1640 when it ordered every adult to sign, and tensions increased after the government dispatched soldiers to Ireland in 1642 to combat the Catholic rebellion and organized another to join parliamentary forces in England. Warfare was burdensome, felt in higher taxes and the impressment of men to serve as soldiers alongside ongoing reprisals against Catholic or Catholic-tilting nobility.[112]

Nor did the political and social elite of Scotland always welcome the daring of the General Assembly of 1638 and its successors. The royal supremacy was another sticking point, a supremacy the Covenanter government had essentially rejected. Was the institution of monarchy also being undermined, as Charles I had been saying ever since the insurgency of 1637 erupted? Questions of this kind prompted a small group of nobles in 1640 to endorse a "band" that added a royalist tinge to the Covenant of 1638. The most important of the signers was James Graham, Earl of Montrose, the head of Clan Graham. An effective leader of Scottish troops during the two Bishops' Wars, he began to tilt toward the king and, when civil war broke out in England in 1642, sided with Charles.

The king did this group no favors when he visited Edinburgh in late summer of 1641, his second visit as monarch and, as it turned out, his last. Ahead of time, he signaled that he would acknowledge "the Religion, and Church government of Scotland, according to the acts of the late Assembly" (a reference to the assemblies of 1638 and 1640) and respect the authority of Parliament. Privately, he hoped to unwind the extremes of the Scottish revolution and rally local support for his dealings with the Long Parliament. Tense negotiations with Archibald Johnston, Alexander Henderson, the Earl of Argyll, and others ended with the king agreeing to approve what had been voted by the Parliament of 1640 and to exclude opponents of the National Covenant from offices of state. He did so only after his hand was weakened by a plot to remove Argyll and James Hamilton, whose daughter had married Argyll, from the scene.

The good news for Scottish moderates was the willingness of the Covenanter regime to include some of them on the Committee of Estates, an instrument devised by the insurgents to replace the Privy Council and run things between parliaments. In December 1642 the moderates (or, as characterized by a historian of the parliaments of this period, its "pragmatic and conservative" members) actually outvoted the Covenanter faction on a matter relating to the king, only to find that theirs was a short-lived victory once Argyll mobilized his allies and regained control. So matters stood until the summer of 1643, when Parliament reconvened and the government had to decide which side to favor in the English Civil War. By this time, the structure of Parliament had evolved from the days of James VI and I. With bishops eliminated and their place taken by burgesses, the two nonnoble groups (gentry and burgesses) could outvote a divided nobility, some of them jealous of Argyll's prominence or half-hearted Covenanters or, like the current Earl of Huntly who led Clan Gordon, committed to Catholicism. The apparatus for governing the state church also changed when the General Assembly of 1642 authorized a "Commission for the Public Affairs of the Kirk" to serve as an executive committee (to use modern parlance) between sessions of the assembly itself.[113]

Entry into civil war tested every aspect of Covenanter politics and ideology. Initially, this decision seemed the surest means of guaranteeing the revolution of 1638. Monarchy would persist, but Presbyterian-style worship, doctrine, and church government would replace episcopacy in England. In August 1643, enthusiasm for the Solemn League and Covenant blinded the Covenanter party to the possibility that the Long Parliament might not live up to its side of the alliance. Nor did anyone sense the consequences of becoming entangled in the politics of religion in England, a politics that was becoming irretrievably divisive by 1644. At rare moments, as when Robert Baillie returned from London in January 1645 to report to the General Assembly on the workings of the Westminster Assembly, optimism about the alliance overtook what was happening in London, for Baillie told his colleagues that, after long delays, the assembly had approved the directory of worship and a plan of church government. He also reported that "all" of the ministers in London were bestirring themselves on behalf of Presbyterianism. On the other hand, Baillie acknowledged that debate was persisting on a confession of faith. And, as noted above (sec. 2), the Long Parliament was on the verge of unwinding a fundamental premise of the Scottish system: the close relationship between church discipline and ministry-led presbyteries.[114]

A year later, Baillie and his fellow delegates were singing a different tune.[115] The project of uniformity between the two state churches was collapsing, done in by its enemies in the Long Parliament, the politics of the New Model Army, and the king's intransigence. Twice (in 1644 and 1646), the Scots insisted on offering fresh proposals on religious and constitutional issues to the king, the second time after his armies had been defeated. On each of these occasions, the king refused to repudiate episcopacy. The breakdown of these negotiations was bad news for the Covenanters, who had to ask themselves if the advent of peace had turned the Solemn League and Covenant into a meaningless document. All this was happening at a moment when an "ideological revolution" was unfolding under the influence of English apocalypticism. Instead of being perceived as the cutting edge of reformation, Presbyterian Scotland was becoming known as a "Babylonish Beast."[116]

The bad news also included civil war in Scotland itself. In the aftermath of the Solemn League and Covenant, Charles I authorized the Earl of Montrose to organize a royalist counterattack in his homeland. Gathering together Catholic clansmen and Irish Catholics brought over from their home country, Montrose invaded the Highlands in mid-1644. Professing himself a loyal son of the Church of Scotland, he blamed the Covenanter alliance with the Long Parliament for tying Scottish Protestantism to "Brownists and Independents" who rejected Scottish-style Presbyterianism, or what he termed "the middle way of our reformed religion." Soon, his ragtag army, which eventually included some of the Gordons, was defeating every Covenanter force it encountered, and continued to do so after Montrose led it into the Lowlands, where its victories included the capture of Glasgow, the largest town in the southwest. There, he used his newfound authority as the King's Commissioner in Scotland to summon a parliament as a step toward restoring royal rule. Suddenly the wheel turned. Facing Scottish troops withdrawn from England at a moment when his own army was weakened by desertion, he was defeated at the battle of Philiphaugh in September 1645. Montrose escaped, but not most of the Irish, who were butchered by the Covenanters. Fighting continued in the Highlands and elsewhere for another two years before Covenanter forces finally suppressed royalist-tilting clans and stray groups of Irish. Montrose was permitted to live by himself, though he eventually left the country, returning again in 1649 on behalf of Charles II. This time he was quickly defeated and, despite his social rank, hanged in Edinburgh in 1650.[117]

Civil war on Scottish soil and severe episodes of the bubonic plague did immense damage to the fabric of clans, churches, and moral discipline. Wherever Montrose's army looted and those loyal to the Covenanter regime fled, as happened to the Highland Campbells, the state church fell into disarray. Now, for hardliners such as Archibald Johnston, the challenges were twofold: summoning the Scottish people to renew the country's covenant with God and deciding how to punish the "delinquents" who sided with Montrose, a process that began in 1644 and accelerated in 1645. In a "remonstrance" to the Committee of Estates, the Commissioners of the Kirk warned against any overtures of "peace" to the rebels or any slacking of fervor for the Covenant of 1643. Johnston was unyielding when it came to those who had broken with that covenant. When Parliament met in November 1645, he called for a "serious searche and inquiery after suche as wer eares and eyes to the enimies of the commonwealthe." Two months later (January 1646), Parliament approved an "Act of Classes" spelling out the penalties for three different levels of those deemed "malignant." The blood was up; in his absence, Montrose was condemned as a traitor, four of the nobility who had been captured at Philiphaugh were executed; others were fined, banished, or excommunicated; and ministers who had temporized or gone over to the rebels were deprived of their pulpits. Slowly but surely, the revolution in Scotland began to devour itself.[118]

By mid-1646, a deeper crisis was emerging in the wake of the Long Parliament's tempered endorsement of the Westminster Assembly. A theological problem lay at the heart of this crisis, the unwillingness of that Parliament to enforce a covenant that the Covenanters regarded as akin to divine law. With their alliance in doubt, the Covenanter government had few alternatives in 1646 other than to hope for a breakthrough in negotiations with Charles I.[119] In May 1646, when the king voluntarily entrusted himself to the Scottish army after fleeing Oxford, face-to-face debate with him unfolded in Newcastle. To that city came the ministers Robert Blair, Robert Douglass, Andrew Cant, and an ailing Alexander Henderson (who died in August), each of them hoping to persuade Charles to sign the Covenant of 1643 and commit himself to Presbyterianism as the true apostolic system. Charles teased them with the possibility that, if "Episcopacy is unlawful, I doubt not but God will so enlighten mine Eyes." In letters the king exchanged with Henderson, Charles borrowed from his father and the anti-presbyterians of circa 1590–1620 the argument that, because it began from beneath in opposition to the reigning monarch, Presbyterianism was inherently anti-monarchical. Henderson did his best to reassure Charles by citing what James VI had said at the time of the Golden Acts. His main point in these exchanges was to represent Presbyterianism as what Christ had intended for the church and episcopacy as a much later intrusion if not invention, an argument the king deflected by citing the Church Fathers. Neither really listened to the other, for Charles was tone-deaf to the power of the myth that sustained the Covenanters and continued to insist that monarchy was untenable without bishops.[120]

Lacking common ground with Charles and unable to agree with the Long Parliament on the conditions of peace, the government struck a bargain: it would hand over the king and the Scottish army would return to Scotland once the English government initiated the payment of 400,000 pounds to cover its expenses. In November 1646, the Commissioners of the General Assembly tried anew to shame the English government into supporting the alliance and did so again in 1647, citing the many "dangerous errrours in England" and the willingness of some in that country to betray the Covenant of 1643. "Hold fast" to your "profession," the assembly pleaded in 1647, and put "Presbyteriall

Government" into practice. Only if this happened would true religion be rescued from its plight.[121]

Mindful of what was at stake theologically, Samuel Rutherford, Archibald Johnston, George Gillespie, and others hastened to spell out the underlying issues. As early as May 1644, Rutherford had sensed that reformation along Scottish lines was not going to happen in an England still attached to "the remnants of Babylon's pollutions." A vigorous advocate of Presbyterianism within the Westminster Assembly, Rutherford poured his politico-theological militancy into *Lex, Rex, or the Law and the Prince* (1644) and *A Free Disputation Against Pretended Liberty of Conscience* (1649).For him as for Johnston, who articulated his vision of religious politics in addresses in late 1646 to the Long Parliament and the Westminster Assembly, the church possessed an authority in matters of religion greater than that of any civil institution. Both were subject to divine law, but only the church was exclusively governed by principles "established by Christ, the Head and King of his Church." Knowing that this argument had been repudiated by English erastians and that the Long Parliament was tilting toward "conveniency and humane constitutions," Rutherford insisted that "Church Government was "jure divino," that is, "established by Christ" and embedded in "conscience." He warned, too, of the tendency in English negotiations with Charles I to diminish his authority to the point of introducing "confusion." The state was also of God's doing, charged by Him to implement divine law and preserve uniformity of religion and, crucially, to "defend true religion for the salvation of all." Old Testament texts were the basis of this argument, texts that validated the model of a nation in covenant with God and a single state church. Hence the superiority of Presbyterianism vis-à-vis the schismatic consequences of Independency. [122]

For Johnston, the disputes about authority that fractured the Long Parliament and New Model Army were essentially irrelevant. "Christs kingdom" was superior to civil authority: "There is no authority to be balanced with this, nor post to be set up against his post." The conclusion was inevitable. As a sacred text, the Covenant of 1643 remained invulnerable to "civile rights." Only when this argument was recognized would peace and unity return to Britain and a purified Church of Scotland be protected against its enemies. For George Gillespie, writing in *Aarons Rod Blossoming* (1646), the immediate enemy was the Erastianism voiced by William Prynne and others. Insisting on the identity of Christ as the rightful king of the church and, in an aside, disputing the tagline of "Arbitrary" that its enemies had attached to Presbyterianism, he drew on Martin Bucer's *De Regno Christi* and various Reformed confessions to validate an essentially Christendom model of church and state that looked back to the Old Testament.[123]

These high claims for divine law as the framework for state policy resonated with the Commissioners of the kirk, who also reiterated the tried-and-true theme of repentance: at the root of the adversities befalling Scotland was the country's unfaithfulness to the National Covenant and, at a deeper level, its unfaithfulness to the myth of a church shorn of all imperfections and therefore the church most favored by God. In 1637–38, this myth had triumphed over every alternative. Now, however, a weariness with the financial and military burdens of the war was overtaking the drama of doing battle with the Antichrist. This weariness worked to the advantage of James Hamilton, who returned to his homeland in 1646 and patched together a coalition of disaffected nobility, the moderate wing of the Covenanter party, and those who, like Hamilton himself, wanted to come to the aid of the king at a moment when, in their words, he was "in apparent Danger, and environed with Sectaries," a reference to the New Model Army. Politicking in late 1647 was intense, the key issue for some being the king's willingness to take the Covenant of 1643. Had he done so, the hard-core covenanters might have rallied to his side. Instead, the outcome was victory for Hamilton's coalition, which offered the king an alliance against the likes of Cromwell and the sectaries, an "Engagement" that did not commit the king to endorsing Presbyterianism. As his side of this bargain, Charles I promised to implement this system and the Directory for Worship in England for three years but refused to sign the covenant and exempted his practice from worship as defined by the Assembly. As a sop to the more forcefully Presbyterian, he agreed to more "free debate and consultation" with a reconstituted Westminster Assembly that would include twenty persons of his own choosing.[124]

For Hamilton's coalition, it was crucial that the king undertake to suppress the "opinions and practices" of a wide array of sectaries that included "Independents." Nonetheless, hardliners in the kirk, or "Protestors," immediately accused Hamilton of betraying the cause of 1643, the proof being that the new alliance did not provide for the "safety and security of Religion." In July, the General Assembly characterized the Engagement as unlawful.[125] Weakened by divisions of this kind, in July 1648 an "Engager" army crossed the border into Lancashire. Few English royalists came north to reinforce it, for local uprisings had been crushed by parliamentary forces. A month later, the New Model Army and the Engagers clashed in the battle of Preston. The outcome was total defeat for the Scots and, for the Commissioners of the kirk who had objected to the Engagement, another opportunity to run the country.

Even, for a moment, run it in cooperation with Cromwell, who, in the aftermath of his victory, met with Argyll and others to discuss certain common concerns, chief among them ensuring that the remnants of an Engager army would not endanger the new government or threaten the parliamentary regime in England, an event celebrated in *A true Account of the great expressions of Love from the Noblemen . . . of the Kingdom of Scotland* (October 1648). Back in power, the Commissioners of the kirk demanded a far-reaching purge of

Engagers and "malignants." In January 1649, a new Parliament dominated by burgesses and gentry reaffirmed the Covenant of 1643 and endorsed a second "Act of Classes" that defined a range of punishment for those who had sided with Hamilton and the king—fines or exile for some, excommunication for a great many others, a sprinkling of executions, and a ban on "Engager" officers or nobility from participating in political life. In March, a Parliament radicalized by the exclusion of so many of the nobility listened to Johnston (who, after being knighted by Charles I in 1641, became known as Johnston of Wariston) and others insist that it abolish the system of patronage that, for decades, had enabled the nobility to play an outsized role in the appointment of ministers. At long last, this stone rolled over the hill.[126]

By this time, the Argyll government had responded to the execution of Charles I by recognizing his eldest son as Charles II, a step that immediately ended any possibility of collaborating with the Rump in England. The envoys sent to negotiate with the new king in the Netherlands, where he was receiving advice from people of various persuasions, were blunt. Relying on what the Parliament in Edinburgh had laid out as the basis for an alliance, they offered military support aimed at restoring him to the throne provided he took the Covenant of 1643, acknowledged "all parliamentary legislation securing the National Covenant," and agreed to establish "Presbyterian church government in all three kingdoms." He would also have to sustain the immunity of general assemblies from royal control, reject the *Book of Common Prayer*, and acknowledge the "idolatrie of his Mother." Charles demurred, in part because he was counting on an alliance of supporters in Ireland to come to his aid. This possibility vanished once Cromwell took the New Model Army to Ireland (August 1649) and suppressed the royalist and Catholic forces in that country. With no other options, the young king accepted the invitation to come to Scotland.[127]

Nothing was simple about the new alliance.[128] The story of how Charles II was treated and, in turn, treated the Scottish leaders does little credit to either side, with Charles dissembling as he took the covenant and, some months later, was crowned, and Argyll's government keeping up the pretense of unity. Awaiting word of his intentions, Parliament proscribed a group of Scottish nobility from having any contact with the king and, after he arrived, insisted that he exclude some of the supporters he brought with him. Beforehand, the Commissioners of the kirk demanded that anyone associated with the Engagement be dismissed from the army. Not until August 1650 did Charles finally sign the covenant, although he indicated privately that he did not believe in it. He also added his name to a statement lamenting "the idolatry of his mother" and "his fathers opposition to the worke of God, and to the solemne league and covenant."[129]

Now, the challenge was to assemble a fresh army, for the king's presence made it inevitable that the New Model Army would come north. At the battle of Dunbar (September 1650), Cromwell's troops overwhelmed the Scots, a defeat the Commissioners of the kirk blamed on those in Scotland who remained unrepentant—the "malignants" who had accompanied Charles II and, contrary to the advice of the kirk, not been purged, and possibly Charles II, who was asked "to consider if he hes come to the covenant . . . upon politicke interest, for gaining a crowne to himselfe, rather then to advance religioune and righteousness."[130] In early October, Charles slipped the reins placed on him and fled, only to return and reaffirm his commitment to the Covenanter program, which was struggling to survive in midland and highland Scotland in the face of more fractures, one of them the emergence of a group in southwestern Scotland favoring something closer to free-form worship and congregational-style structure, a possibility the kirk had tried to forestall in 1647 by prohibiting the publication of books on behalf of that system.[131]

With another battle looming, royalists and moderates regained a voice in the government and demanded that "Engagers" and "malignants" be included in the government and the army. In June 1651, Parliament agreed to this argument and rescinded the Acts of Classes of 1646 and 1649. Pushed aside, hardline Covenanters turned their fire on Cromwell. Well before this, they had been characterizing him as a "blasphemer" and lamenting his refusal to acknowledge the "perfect" reformation accomplished in Scotland. When he turned up in Glasgow in the spring of 1651, the "lawfulness" of his campaign against the Scottish government was disputed by ministers who told him to his face that he had committed a "breach of covenant" (that is, broken the oath he took in 1643) and was engaging in "sinfull rebellion and murder." Equipped with this rhetoric but enfeebled by the purges it had suffered, a Scottish army entered England, where it was defeated at the battle of Worcester (August 1651). Once again, a Stuart king escaped in disguise, leaving behind a near-decade of agitation by scattered groups of royalists in England, Scotland, and Ireland who fantasized about overthrowing Cromwell's government.[132]

Now all of Scotland came under the sway of English troops. No longer independent, the country was incorporated into a confederation based in London, with toleration as state policy. The final, ineffective General Assembly met in 1653. Ministers continued to preach, spasms of moral discipline erupted, and Independency cropped up here and there, as did a few Baptists. Meanwhile, the quarrels that disrupted the kirk between 1641 and the early 1650s and divided Scottish society—quarrels too many to incorporate into this narrative—were making it difficult for parishes to agree on who should serve as minister or be admitted to the Lord's Supper. On the other hand, the Cromwellian settlement ensured that Scotland had no bishops or prayer book until the wheel turned anew after the Restoration of Charles II, whereupon the tandem of monarchy and episcopacy returned, to be discarded a third time in the aftermath of the "Glorious Revolution" that overthrew James II.[133]

The End of the Beginning

What Charles I had failed to accomplish became a reality in 1651, unity among the three kingdoms in how religion should be practiced. Now, however, unity was more about excluding than including, for the Cromwellian settlement—to give it a name—took for granted that the two alternatives of circa 1640, Presbyterianism and episcopacy, were rejected, as was Catholicism, of course. Nor did England, Scotland, and Ireland have a state church. In retrospect, the pace of change seems astonishing. In the course of several years (c. 1648–52), magisterial religion in Scotland, England, and Ireland had been dismantled, most of the accomplishments of the Westminster Assembly deprived of support, and long-standing ties with the Reformed international effectively broken. In civil society, the constitutional arrangement of circa 1640 had given way to a commonwealth, followed (mid-1653) by the Protectorate.

Of the ironies embedded in this sequence of events, the greatest may be that a Puritan was now the head of state, although only until Cromwell died in 1658. What kind of Puritan was Cromwell? As had become clear by the mid-1640s, he did not share the agenda that John Knox, Walter Travers, and Thomas Cartwright had inherited from the Reformed tradition, which took for granted an inclusive, ministry-centered state church and state-enforced uniformity. On the other hand, his mental world had been shaped by the fervent anti-Catholicism of John Foxe, whose sympathy for the faithful few was among the sources of Cromwell's admiration for "the poor Godly People" who suffered from the oppression of worldly powers. "To love the Lord and His poor despised people, to do for them, and to be ready to suffer with them" was how Cromwell vowed to use his authority as an officer in the New Model Army and subsequently as head of state. From Foxe and many others, including his schoolmaster Thomas Beard, he also acquired a strongly personal understanding of divine providence. Not by his own capacities but by God acting through him was why he and his soldiers were victorious in so many battles, a conviction he retained in the closing moments of his life when he daily "rehearsed the 71 Psalm of David, which hath so near a relation to his Fortune and to his Affairs, as that one would believe it had been a Prophesie purposely dictated by the holy Ghost for him."[134] He owed a good deal, as well, to the practical divinity and its emphasis on an inward experience of divine grace and a reformation of manners. More unusually, he was a "millenarian." Aware of what a long line of commentators on biblical prophecy had said about the conversion of the Jews as a sign of Christ's impending return, he authorized a debate in 1655 about their status and, although never taking official action, his government pursued a de facto toleration of Jews who worshipped openly.[135]

A hypocrite in the eyes of many but a saint-like figure to others,[136] Cromwell's larger goal was to transform religious factionalism into a new version of unity. The alternative to a national covenant based on Old Testament precedents was a spiritual unity among the "saints," a unity he discerned beneath the many differences of opinion about infant baptism, church structure, and matters of doctrine. In a letter of September 1645 celebrating the retaking of Bristol, he commended the "same spirit of faith" in soldiers who were variously Presbyterian and Independent; "they agree here [in the army], and have no names of difference: pity it is it should be otherwise anywhere." In the same letter, he affirmed the principle that "All that believe, have the real unity, which is most glorious; because inward, and spiritual, in the Body, and to the Head" and, in the next sentence, spoke dismissively of "forms, commonly called Uniformity" as meaningless until and unless "conscience" accepted them. As head of state, he attempted an experimental exercise in "light and reason" (light being the Holy Spirit), the Nominated Parliament (1653) of men whose religious sincerity had been validated by certain congregations or churches. Expecting it to agree on an agenda of reform, Cromwell watched in dismay as factionalism thwarted any real progress. Nor was he satisfied with the two elected parliaments that followed, neither of which satisfied his hopes for a fusion of nationhood with godliness.[137]

Nonetheless, Cromwell was willing to use the coercive authority of the state to preserve some aspects of unity, as in being willing to regulate who could enter the ministry. On the other hand, he refused to use his authority as Lord Protector to uphold—or possibly impose—the kind of rules that made sense to the godly in New England and historically had made sense to the Reformed international. That his second Parliament tried to strengthen the barriers against heterodoxy and attempted to punish the Socinian John Biddle was not his doing. Wanting unity but not uniformity, he endorsed religious liberty for almost everyone except Catholics but "connived" at allowing them and prayer-book Protestants a certain freedom. When James Naylor crossed a line by representing himself as Christ when he entered Bristol, pressure from the more moderate or conservative members of his government pushed Cromwell into accepting a response in keeping with the Blasphemy Act of 1650. In the main, however, Cromwell clung to the assumption that unity should not coerced.[138]

The underlying problem was not his doing; an unsettling of authority that accompanied the Protestant Reformation and became more intense once the Puritan movement turned against the Elizabethan Settlement. As historians before me have pointed out, the legitimacy of a Protestant Church of England was denied by English Catholics and, during the reign of Elizabeth I, by more daring Protestants such as John Udall and Robert Browne (see chap. 2). Moreover, the compromises of the Elizabethan Settlement and the crackdown on nonconformity empowered some in the House of Commons to question the integrity of the bishops and assert a voice for Parliament in religious affairs. Thanks to the looseness of social and political authority and ongoing conflict with Catholic Spain, no real crisis occurred until the policies of James I and Charles I alienated some of the nobility and gentry in Scotland and England

and revitalized Puritan objections to episcopacy, the *Book of Common Prayer*, and the royal supremacy.

What no one realized in 1640 was the inability of the Puritan movement to agree on principles of doctrine and church governance. To be sure, Thomas Edwards and others like him grasped that a Separatist-like disdain for an inclusive state church was being reborn in the "Congregational Way" of the colonists and similar experiments in the Netherlands in the late 1630s. Even so, the clergy and laymen who gathered at Westminster Hall in mid-1643 were expecting consensus on doctrine, worship, and governance and achieved the first and second of these. Where agreement became impossible after toleration began to divide the movement was on the role of the state. Once its authority was called into question and someone of Cromwell's temperament began to govern, building a new Sion aligned with Reformed principles became impossible.

The fast-sermons preached before the Long Parliament took for granted that prophetic testimony and the ritual exercise of a fast day would unite the English people around a national covenant founded on divine law. This, too, was what the Covenanters in Scotland believed and, for a year or two, secured. But authority of the kind Johnston and Rutherford outlined in treatises and statements of the mid-1640s did not reappear. Indeed, the two great moments of covenanting—Scotland's in 1638 and Scotland and England's in 1643—fell short of being genuinely popular moments and became divisive. As Lord Protector, Cromwell had to rely on his generals to suppress or exclude Catholics, Royalists, Fifth Monarchists, Quakers, ardent Presbyterians, and the like. On the other hand, his son Henry, the head of the Irish government, turned to local Presbyterians out of dismay with the "many-head monster" of a "popular Protestantism" that in Dublin was undermining orthodoxy and the apparatus of discipline. *This* Cromwell recognized that the key to stability was to broaden the "social basis for his administration" beyond small cells of "visible saints."[139]

In a thoughtful letter to John Winthrop (March 1648), his friend George Downing, who had returned to England from New England, reflected on the "ruine" that succeeded victory in the first Civil War, "the maine ground" of this ruine being "the great divisions among us." One after another, Downing ticked off the goals of the groups that came together to oppose the king, goals so different as to make agreement impossible once the king had been defeated: some opposing "oppression in general" and therefore any form of "Church government" that curtailed liberty of conscience, others content with eliminating the king's "evil counsellors," still others wanting Presbyterianism to replace episcopacy, a handful of republicans questioning the institution of monarchy. Now, with unity no longer imperative in the aftermath of the king's defeat, Downing underscored the reality of unending conflict.[140]

My narrative of the quest for a "thorough" reformation teaches the same lesson from a more theological and biblical perspective. In the 1560s, master words such as idolatry and purity had signified the difference between Catholic practice and Word-centered, Reformed-style worship. Already, however, the scenario in Foxe's *Book of Martyrs* of the few versus the many and the mantra of edification implied that an inclusive state church would never be able to eliminate the unworthy. Apparent in Field and Wilcox, this train of thought became central to the alternative fashioned by Browne, Barrow, Penry, and Robinson and, in the 1630s and 1640s, to the schemes (however defined) of Independents, congregationalists, and Baptists on both sides of the Atlantic. In 1643, the Long Parliament and the Scots who supported the Solemn League and Covenant did not grasp the implications of this scheme, some because they dismissed it out of hand and others because they relied on the traditional ethics of obedience to prevail.

Civil wars have unexpected consequences, as do efforts to mobilize popular resistance. The most telling consequence of 1642–46 was the emergence of arguments on behalf of toleration or liberty of conscience. The more puzzling may be the mobilizing of public opinion in 1641–43 on behalf of "root and branch" reform. As was also true of the Covenanter insurgency in late 1630s Scotland, situations of this kind lured godly ministers and lay leaders into assuming that their program had broad support. This may have been true of a few aspects of that program, but not of those at its core. As a parliamentary military officer posted to Nottingham, John Hutchinson discovered when he undertook to defend the town against local Royalists that the townspeople wanted to sit out the war and did everything they could to thwart his mandate. Or, as happened in Parliament and the wider reaches of agitation about true religion, the lesson taught by civil war was that compromise would give way to more extreme outcomes—the abolishment of episcopacy, outbursts of iconoclasm, elimination of a Christendom understanding of the church, execution of Charles I, emergence of sects centered on the immediacy of the Holy Spirit, and eruptions of significant theological dissent (see chap. 9). In the absence of broad-based consensus, infighting among the godly undermined any semblance of uniformity tied to agreement on the contours of orthodoxy and the figure of a Christian prince who had near-absolute authority.

As in the Greek legend of the dragon's teeth that sprang into life as armed men who began to kill each other, so in mid-century Britain the great themes of the Puritan movement mutated into weapons the godly used to identify and turn against each other and, in spasms of witch-hunting, turn on others.[141] Only in New England were these tensions contained. How this happened after 1640 is described in chapter 9, where we also revisit theological argument and religious practice during the 1640s and 1650s.

CHAPTER NINE

Change and Continuity

THEOLOGY AND SOCIAL PRACTICE,
c. 1640–1660

ALICE STEDMAN ARRIVED IN MASSACHUSETTS in the 1630s, found a husband, and settled in Cambridge, where she was accepted into the church after making the customary "relation" of her spiritual journey. Stedman spoke frankly about the stress of having a godly minister in England describe her spiritual estate as "woeful" unless she reconciled with God. Nor, he had remarked, was she doing enough to "humble" herself. Possibly after reaching her new home, she was hearing sermons that emphasized "the freeness of His love" to those who acknowledged their sinfulness—free but also contingent, for the gospel promise was transmitted through "means" that included her willingness to repent.

This intertwining of divine love, grace, repentance, and the means was reinforced by what Thomas Shepard, her minister in Cambridge, was saying. At one moment, he encouraged her to "believe" that "the Lord" would reach out and help her. At another, something he said led her to conclude that there was "nothing for me" in the gospel promise. She also remembered another minister's message (possibly an echo of the Antinomian controversy; see below) that some people "build upon wrong foundations to close and catch the promise and missed Christ." How long this mixture of messages kept her in suspense is not known, but when she testified to the church, she could report that she had received Jesus. "And so was much confirmed, and many times since the Lord hath spoken to me to help me."[1]

Obadiah Holmes arrived in the same colony in 1638 and, two years later, joined the church in Salem, where he had settled. As children were born, he and his wife had them baptized. Mid-decade, he moved to Rehoboth in Plymouth Colony. There, too, he became a church member—a restless member, for a few years later he affiliated with local Baptists. Narrating a spiritual journey that began with his boyhood in England, he remembered being burdened by "duties," the imperative to repent, and being "left . . . without hopes of any mercy." In retrospect, he blamed his emotional ups and downs on the practical divinity, which stripped him of any "rest in the soul, though I was in a manner as strict as any."

Then came the breakthrough moment when he realized that "all his righteousness" was as "filthy rags" (Is. 64:6) and salvation solely the doing of the "New Covenant" established by Christ. It was a merciful Christ on whom he should depend, not the "means," as he had been told by ministers in England and Massachusetts. Another lesson of this spiritual awakening was that he could "never fully quiet" his "spirit in the most excellent performance." Righteousness or duties paled alongside the grace made possible by Christ's death on the cross. Holmes continued to affirm a Reformed understanding of the Atonement and decree of election, and, as he implicitly signaled in his "Last Will & Testimony," he was no libertine. Yet he found his way to a new understanding of the relationship between faith and works. Summing up that relationship, he declared that an inward "faith in the Son of God" made "works" irrelevant or incidental to the Christian's journey.[2]

Holmes and Stedman were among the many laypeople who, at mid-century, were choosing between two versions of the "new birth," or conversion. Stedman stayed within the contours of the practical divinity. Holmes started out within that framework until he decided that it came too close to endorsing "works." On both sides of the Atlantic, decisions of this kind were propelled by winds of doctrine that threatened the Calvinism of William Perkins and his immediate heirs. Theological controversy had always accompanied the practical divinity, much of it provoked by Catholic and Dutch Arminian alternatives or, more covertly, by "Antinomian" currents in pre–civil war England.[3] Now the whole of the practical divinity was being challenged by tub preachers, itinerant spiritualists, and a handful of university-trained ministers. Catholic and Arminian versions of justification remained a menace, so much so in the case of Arminianism that John Owen addressed it in the first of his many books, *A Display of Arminianisme* (1643). Thomas Hooker did so as well in the revised version of *The Application of Redemption* (1657) that he drafted in Connecticut. The newer enemies included a theological package known as Socinianism. Even though its appeal was limited to a few English ministers and lay intellectuals, the Socinian version of the Trinity threatened the foundations of orthodoxy. By the mid-1640s, a Holy Spirit-centered understanding of conversion and assurance (nicknamed "Antinomianism") had also acquired a new group of advocates who hailed it as an alternative to the practical divinity.

Orthodoxy had constantly spawned renegades and outliers who tested its boundaries.[4] Now, however, originality was becoming more widespread and controversy more intense in response to a mixture of political and intellectual circumstances that included the collapse of censorship. How the practical

divinity was being assailed and defended are topics that lead us to the Antinomians of mid-century, the Westminster Confession, and the reasoning of ministers such as Samuel Rutherford on behalf of orthodoxy. In section 2, this
chapter revisits the Antinomian controversy that roiled mid-1630s Massachusetts. Here, too, debate was prompted by criticism of the practical divinity. A
concluding section describes change and continuity in institutional and cultural practices in the orthodox colonies in New England.

Decline, Persistence, and Alternatives: The Practical Divinity at Mid-Century

Were catechisms our only source for assessing continuity or disruption, continuity would prevail. No matter who wrote them, these were more alike than
different. In New England, Shepard and John Cotton published their versions
of the genre in the 1640s, and Cotton's *Milk for Babes* (1646) would enjoy a
long life as part of a widely used schoolbook. Henry Jessey, the English semi-
Separatist turned Baptist, waited until 1652 to publish his catechism, which
may not have been reprinted. Jessey tilted toward the "spiritualist" end of the
spectrum and the moderate nonconformist John Ball toward the more corporate or institutional in his much-reprinted *A Short Catechism* (c. 1615). Yet no
godly reader of these books seems to have regarded either of them troubling or
controversial. At this level of teaching, consensus prevailed on the basic points
of doctrine.[5]

Catechisms were meant to be conventional in the sense of building on each
other. So were formal creeds. The Lambeth Articles of 1595, which the Church
of England had never endorsed, passed into the Irish Articles of 1615. In turn,
these influenced the making of the Westminster Confession, which became the
principal source of *A Declaration of the Faith and Order Owned and practiced
in the Congregational Churches in England* (1658), or Savoy Declaration. For
that matter, the Baptist confession of 1644/46 was more alike than different
from Westminster and its companions. Despite the battering that Reformed
orthodoxy underwent at the hands of Laudians and, after 1640, from sectaries
of various persuasions, these documents suggest that godly clergy in Britain
and New England (where a local synod endorsed the Westminster Confession)
continued to preach a British version of Reformed orthodoxy.[6]

This was not always articulated in the same manner, however, or with the
same emphases. From day one, the makers of the practical divinity were of
different minds about which system of logic was better, some preferring Aristotle's and others the method of dichotomies introduced by the French Huguenot Peter Ramus. Arminianism in any strict sense of the term was shunned,
yet by 1620 a handful of ministers in Britain favored a "hypothetical universalism" that tempered the doctrine of a limited atonement.[7] More in private than
in public, people were also pondering the relationship between divine sover-

eignty and the effectual call as it was transmitted by the preaching of the Word. Meanwhile, a handful of ministers within the Reformed international were adjusting some aspects of doctrine. The Scottish theologian John Cameron, who taught in Huguenot seminaries in France, was an early advocate of hypothetical universalism. His arguments influenced the Huguenot minister and theologian Moise Amyraut (1596–1664), who, when questioned by the French Reformed church in the 1620s, cloaked himself in quotations from Calvin to keep his critics at bay.[8]

Before 1640, the British side of this story has been characterized as a "series of debates and disputations, carried on in person or through the exchange of position papers and articles," although "London's Antinomian controversy" (c. 1629–33) was a good deal noisier. Aside from this long-running dispute, William Twisse's objections to John Cotton's tinkering with predestination (see chap. 4), and an uneasiness with the hypothetical universalism of ministers such as John Preston, the men who taught or preached the practical divinity seem to have tolerated the second thoughts of Richard Sibbes and Ezekiel Culverwell about some of its themes (see chap. 4). On the other hand, the emergence of anti-Calvinism (see chap. 7) was making many people nervous. When Prynne stumbled on the Marian martyr John Bradford's assertion that "our owne wilfulnesse, sinne, and contemning of Christ, are the causes of Reprobation," he hastened to gloss it as a reference to a "later work this is only a second cause not first cause which is the will of God."[9] A similar anxiety colored Thomas Hooker's preface to John Rogers's *The Doctrine of Faith* (1626). Hooker urged the book's readers to interpret what Rogers said about the "means of faith"—specifically, his assertion that "a saving contribution" happened "before" faith—with "a judicious and fair construction," in which case "it will be found to be beyond exception." Do "not boggle or start" at a "contradiction" between "sorrow" as a "fruit of faith" and its role as a condition, Hooker advised.[10]

The challenges that exploded in the 1640s and 1650s were more aggressively articulated and more threatening, especially once it became clear that the Blasphemy Act of 1648 and its successor of 1650 were ineffective. The English Independent John Goodwin did the unthinkable. In the mid-1640s, he began to advocate an Arminian understanding of redemption and a strong version of liberty of conscience. Worse yet, Socinianism acquired its first English advocates. Others who were characterized as "libertines and Antinomians" seized upon a weak point in the practical divinity, its emphasis on law-driven repentance, and promised to liberate the godly by the message of "free grace." Less noticed, but intriguing from the standpoint of worship and the role of the church as means of grace, Prynne and a few allies began to argue that the Lord's Supper was a "converting" ordinance, Prynne doing so in 1645 in *Foure Serious Questions . . . concerning Excommunication and Suspension from the Sacrament.* Because he favored an inclusive state church supervised by the civil state, he employed this argument to dispute the model endorsed by Independents and sectaries. In the 1650s, John Owen and Richard Baxter came to blows over justification, among other matters. In Scotland, Robert Leighton was voicing his doubts about the theological method favored by his colleagues and their reliance on a covenant-centered theology.[11]

What was so threatening about Socinianism and Antinomianism? Antinomianism as a way of understanding the relationship between grace and the law was nothing new. Martin Luther had encountered it in the publications of his fellow Protestant Johannes Agricola, who insisted that the Gospel made the law and the duties associated with it irrelevant. (Antinomianism derives from the Greek for "against or exempt from the law.") Although strongly favoring free grace, Luther eventually broke with Agricola. In early seventeenth-century England, a tiny "underground" of godly ministers had resurrected this dispute in response to the emphasis within the practical divinity on the pertinence of the law to the elect and the paradox of assigning "duties" or human endeavor a role alongside the divine decree in the order of salvation. For members of this underground such as John Eaton, another weak point was an emphasis on sanctification as evidence of justification. He insisted that justification—the stage of the golden chain in which the righteousness of Christ was "imputed" to the elect—made those people "free from sin in the sight of God."[12] In the 1640s this argument reemerged, its presence promptly publicized by the London minister John Sedgwick in *Antinomianisme Anatomized; Or, A Glasse for the lawlesse, who deny the ruling use of the Morall Law* (1643). Mid-decade, the heresiographers were tagging a handful of writers with this term, a group that included the ministers John Saltmarsh, Tobias Crisp, and William Dell.[13]

These three were all too real to their critics, but the dead or the absent (or the imagined) also colored the polemics aroused by these men and lay sectaries of similar sentiments, especially when London booksellers began to print books by Eaton, Robert Towne, and other members of the "Antinomian" underground of circa 1610–30. Documents from theological controversy in mid-1630s Massachusetts were fuel to this fire once a London bookseller published *A Short Story of the Rise, Reigne, and Ruine of the late Antinomians, Familists and Libertines* (1644). Here, for the first time, English readers learned of Anne Hutchinson's "revelations," the "errours" identified by the synod of 1637, and two monster births, hers and Mary Dyer's. Soon, the radical bookseller Giles Calvert was publishing other documents that originated in New England.[14]

Via the *Short Story* and the publicizing of local examples, a spasm of anxiety about Antinomianism swept through British Protestantism. Detached from precise theological definition and laden with connotations about amoral excess, the term aroused a dismay among the orthodox that Richard Baxter, among others, exploited to the hilt. The actual number of so-called Antinomians was minuscule. But as Thomas Edwards admitted, the more he dramatized the hydra-headed monster of "libertinism" he paired with Antinomianism, the more he aided the cause of those who opposed liberty of conscience.[15] Exaggerating the presence of Socinianism served the same purpose. This term designated the theological speculations of the late sixteenth-century Italian Protestant Fausto Sozzini (Latinized as Socinius), who found a haven in Poland. Socinius was an advocate of human reason as the means for understanding Scripture and the God it revealed. What made him notorious was the assertion that Christ was not created co-equal with God. A formal statement of this anti-Trinitarianism, the *Racovian Catechism* (1609 in Latin), circulated in Europe but not, it seems, in Britain despite being dedicated to James I, who ordered it burned. Thereafter, Socinian-related texts trickled into academic settings via the Dutch Arminian Hugo Grotius, among others.[16]

Noted in fast-day sermons of the early 1640s, this alternative was forcefully denounced by Francis Cheynell, a nonconformist in the 1630s and subsequently a member of the Westminster Assembly, in *The Rise, Growth and Danger of Socinianisme* (1643). Cheynell continued to search for signs of Socinianism and Arminianism throughout the 1640s. He and his fellow heresy hunters cornered their quarry in 1647 when two English anti-Trinitarians, each a university graduate, went public with their ideas. In *Mysteries Discovered* (1647), Paul Best, whose "Blasphemous opinions" had already caught the eye of the Westminster Assembly, characterized orthodox doctrine as a species of mystification. Simultaneously, John Biddle published *Twelve Arguments . . . , Wherein the Deity of the Holy Ghost is Clearly and Fully Refuted.* Biddle may also have arranged the first English printing (1652) of the *Racovian Catechism*, the same year in which John Milton in his role as regulator of the press licensed the printing of a Latin version that alarmed the Rump, which ordered it burned; previously, the Long Parliament had treated Biddle's *Twelve Arguments* in the same manner. Both men were also threatened with execution.[17]

Loosely used, "Socinianism" designated a vein of anti-Calvinism that relied on reason as the means of resolving theological disputes. In the 1630s, speculation along these lines flourished in what became known as the Great Tew Circle, a coterie of university-trained ministers and writers that met at the house of Lucas Cary, Lord Falkland, in Great Tew, a village outside Oxford. A royalist who died at the battle of Newbury in 1643, Falkland was described as someone willing to inquire into "controversies" in religion without regard to what any state church, including his own, regarded as orthodox doctrine. In his own words, he preferred "reason" to "infallibility" as the means of arriving at "Truth." Up to a point, the makers of the practical divinity accepted a role for "reason" in biblical hermeneutics and theological argument. For the Great Tew group, however, the "light of reason" was aligned with a skepticism about the value of grand schemes of theology. In the overheated atmosphere of the 1640s and 1650s, reason also appealed to these men as an alternative to spiritual ecstasy. The name they assigned to ecstatic encounters with the Holy Spirit was "enthusiasm," or mistaking as God-like what was merely natural and therefore a delusion. As well, these men deployed reason to refute the canons of Dordt and especially the doctrine of predestination, which they rejected out of hand.[18]

William Chillingworth (1602–44), a key figure in the Great Tew community and someone Francis Cheynell targeted in his campaign against Socinianism, laid out the case for a simplified, post-Calvinist Protestantism in *The Religion of Protestants: A Safe Way to Salvation* (1637). Famous long after his death for insisting that "the Bible, and the Bible only" was the basis of Protestantism, an argument directed at a Catholic theologian he was debating, Chillingworth endorsed free inquiry in matters of religion. Properly used, it would enable the enlightened to separate mere "fancies" from the essentials of the Christian faith on which all reasonable men could agree. These assumptions validated the "right of private judgment," as contrasted with the coercion he associated with orthodoxy. And, in keeping with Socinianism, Chillingworth and his friends emphasized the ethical aspects of Christianity. In the back-and-forth between conformist and Puritan at mid-century, ministers who, much later, would be characterized as "Anglicans" were voicing a similar understanding of true Christianity as "inward," peace-promoting, and in harmony with a divinely created order.[19]

Socinianism in any of its versions was frightening because it threatened the foundations of orthodoxy. Mid-century Antinomianism was frightening because the men who took it up had previously adhered to the practical divinity. Theirs was a critique from inside, as it were, a critique fashioned out of personal and pastoral experience, a close reading of the Bible, and possibly their encounters with Eaton, Luther, Sibbes, and others. Out of their reflections came an alternative understanding of the law, justification, and assurance of salvation.

The testimony of John Saltmarsh, the most widely read of the mid-century English Antinomians, was typical. A parish minister until, by his own account, a twelve-year time of darkness and a "festering conscience" prompted him to shake off the "legal" aspects of the practical divinity, Saltmarsh put his newfound Antinomianism—a designation he repudiated, as did Crisp—on display in a series of books that included *Free Grace: Or the flowings of Christs blood freely to sinners* (1647) and *Sparkles of Glory; Or, Some Beams of the Morning-Star* (1647). Tobias Crisp (d. 1643) started out as a conventional preacher of the practical divinity but by 1640 was taking a different path. His objections to what he regarded as a law-bound system were not published until the final year of his life, when a London bookseller brought out *Christ Alone Exalted* (1643), reprinted in an expanded version in 1691. The layman Henry Denne also weighed in with *Seven Arguments to prove, that in the order of working God doth justifie his elect, before they doe actually believe* (1643).[20]

If we can trust what Saltmarsh said of his own spiritual history, he turned against the core premises of the practical divinity not because he encountered

Luther or Eaton but because its strictures about repentance in response to the law made him feel hopelessly burdened. Somehow, he found his way to a simple argument: Christ did everything for those to whom he imparted grace, taking on the guilt for their sins and assuring them by his presence that they would never suffer a crisis akin to what he himself had endured. Saltmarsh filled out this argument in several ways. He began by setting aside the Old Testament as too "legal." Contradicting the principle that its core themes of sin, covenant, and the law were included within the covenant of grace, he insisted that a new dispensation of the Holy Spirit was unfolding that made the "law" irrelevant. He and Crisp were also averse to any talk of conditions. As veterans of the practical divinity, both had encountered the rule that the effectual call, or vocation, depended in some way on faith and repentance. Not so, they argued. Christ welcomed everyone to the kingdom, including those who were the worst of sinners and had not prepared themselves to receive the promise. Faith could not be a condition of justification, which was complete in and of itself before faith came along, the doing of Christ without regard to anything in sinners themselves. Another mistake of the practical divinity was the argument that righteousness or sanctification should be used as evidence of justification. The danger in doing so was obvious, the likelihood that sinners would become overly confident and never truly experience the workings of the Holy Spirit.

Saltmarsh reiterated his objections to law-based preaching in a brief letter that Henry Jessey included in *The exceeding Riches of Grace Advanced By the Spirit of Grace, in an Empty Nothing Creature, viz. Mris. Sarah Wight* (1647). An adolescent girl in a pious family, Wight experienced "terrors . . . for sinning against light, against God, and against a parent" and descended into "despair," a condition she eventually overcame thanks to the counseling of visitors such as Jessey and her visionary experiences of a loving Christ. Likening him to a "filling fountain . . . never dry" and insisting that "free Grace" and the "Teaching of the Spirit" were enabling her to find new messages in the Bible, she began to counsel others who were suffering from despair. Her advice to a "Gentlewoman" who could not believe she was justified was to ignore "the means" and receive the Christ who truly "sympathizes with sinners." Summarizing the spiritual freedom Wight attained, Saltmarsh detected "two things very experimentall" in her spiritual history, the first of these a "legall" situation when she had been "in bondage, in blackness, and darkness, and tempest," and the second, "her more Gospel condition," when "God . . . reveales himself in Christ, in his grace and love, [and] the Spirit of the Christian is sweetly . . . cheered." Wight was living proof of what it was like to suffer from a misplaced emphasis on the law and, after being liberated from its grip, of encountering the grace provided by a loving Christ.[21]

This reasoning was nonsense to Samuel Rutherford, whose credentials as a Spirit-centered writer were impeccable. Amid controversy in 1630s Scotland about kneeling at communion, he had counseled someone that "Sanctification will settle you most in the truth." Advice of this kind suited a situation in which outward behavior had become politicized. Now, however, the imperative was to reaffirm the presence of the Spirit and, simultaneously, the importance of a sanctified life. In *The Trial and Triumph of Faith* (1645), he celebrated the loving Christ who, "fountain"-like, poured out grace on unworthy sinners and, in *A Survey of the Spirituall Antichrist* (1648), extolled the "pure and immediate assurances that floweth from the witnesse of the Spirit." Yet in contrast to Crisp and Saltmarsh, he linked free grace with doing or activity. As he remarked in the opening pages of *The Trial and Triumph of Faith*, "Christ's love is liberal, but yet it must be sued." According to another Antinomian-like premise, which he may have come upon in *A Short Story*, "there can be no closing with Christ, in a promise that hath a qualification or condition expressed." Realizing that this argument eliminated preparation for salvation, Rutherford replied that "Christ actually calleth and saveth, but those who are . . . prepared." As well, he counseled "holy walking" and relying on "duties" as remedies for those moments when the elect felt abandoned by God. His central argument concerned the golden chain. Even though nothing done by way of preparation was "deserving" of God's favor, the work of redemption unfolded according to a "way" or system in which divine sovereignty or free grace coexisted with conditions that included repentance and faith. Quoting Scripture, he insisted that "we cannot be justified before we believe."[22] In a follow-up assault on Saltmarsh and others of the same persuasion, Rutherford revisited the writings of Eaton and Luther as well as confronting Saltmarsh directly. According to one of the arguments he was disputing, the elect received a "pure and immediate assurance" via the "witnesse of the Spirit." Not so, he argued, for assurance was always connected to the Word and never exempt from self-doubt.[23]

Of the many who joined Rutherford in denouncing what they took to be Antinomianism, two examples must suffice. In *Prima, The First Things, In reference to the Middle & Last Things: Or, The Doctrine of Regeneration, the New Birth, The very beginning of a Godly life* (1650), Isaac Ambrose directed his description of the new birth at anyone who questioned repentance or "preparation" as a prelude to justification. Ambrose acknowledged Tobias Crisp's objections to "duties" detached in some manner from Christ, but insisted on a "power" from God to perform "gospel-duties," chief among them "watchfulness." Just how much duties mattered for him was clear from his insistence on tying the "new birth" to self-examination guided by the Ten Commandments. Unusually, he quoted Thomas Hooker on "preparation" and Shepard's *Sincere Convert* (1640) for its description of the preparatory stage Shepard had termed "humiliation." To explain why free grace was accompanied by conditions, he resorted to the modalities of time or cause-and-effect-like sequences (including the "order of nature") that mediated the work of redemption. Summarizing this framework, he insisted that "causes which produce an effect, though they be in time together, yet are mutually before one another in order of nature in divers respects to their several causalities. Thus a man must have repentance before he have saving and justifying faith; and yet a man must have faith before the work of repentance be perfect in the soul." Returning to the relationship between repentance and faith a little later in *Prima*, Ambrose agreed that the law "shewes" the sinner "no remedy." Yet he insisted that "we abolish not the Law, in ascribing this comfort to the Gospel onely; though it be no cause of it, yet . . . those doleful terrours, and fears of conscience begotten by the Law . . . are certain occasions of grace."[24]

The most persistent of Saltmarsh's critics was Thomas Gataker, a well-regarded older minister and theologian who served in the Westminster Assembly. When he realized that Saltmarsh had characterized his version of Reformed orthodoxy as implicitly Antinomian, Gataker responded in pithy books that mocked the "short work" Saltmarsh and others were making of belief (or conversion). Singling out the assertion that justification lifted them out of the category of sinner, Gataker reiterated the commonplace that the elect continued to sin and therefore must repent. He insisted, too, that faith was "required" for justification. As so many others were doing, he painted a picture of moral and spiritual chaos that schemes such as Saltmarsh's would permit. In a more personal vein, Gataker complained of the insults Saltmarsh rained on people like himself, chief among them the epithet of "legalist."[25]

Debate about the relationship between law and grace (or Holy Spirit) flared up anew in the 1690s and again during the evangelical revivals of the eighteenth century. Yet in revolutionary Britain there was reason to hope that these matters had been resolved by the Westminster Confession. When the assembly first met in July 1643, its primary task was to ensure that the taint of Arminianism had been scrubbed from the Thirty-Nine Articles. Before long, the willingness of booksellers to print what had previously circulated in manuscript or been suppressed made it imperative to defend orthodoxy from enemies both old and new. As the Scottish General Assembly of 1647 pointed out after the Confession had been completed, it would be "a speciall means for the more effectuall suppressing of the many dangerous errours and heresies of these times."[26]

Of the Confession's thirty-three chapters, the most explicitly political was the twentieth, "Of Christian Liberty, and Liberty of Conscience," which affirmed the legitimacy of "lawful power . . . whether it be civil or ecclesiastical" to preserve the "known principles of Christianity." Liberty of conscience was contingent, not absolute; anyone who turned "liberty" against "the external peace and order" of the church should be "proceed[ed] against, by the censure of the Church, and by the power of the civil magistrate." This point made, the substance of the Confession emphasized the sovereignty of God in a manner that disposed of Arminianism. And, in the sections on the effectual call, assurance, and the law, it reaffirmed the classic teachings of the practical divinity.

The wording of chapter 3 of the Confession ("Of Gods Eternal Decree") echoed the response to Arminianism in the Irish Articles of 1615.[27] What was said about the timing and substance of the decree was in the same vein: enacted "before the foundation of the World was laid" and the doing of God's "free grace and love, without any foresight of faith, or good works ... or any other thing in the creature, as conditions, or causes moving Him thereunto." God had also "foreordained all the means" that accompanied the divine decree. On the other hand, the chapter acknowledged that a decree dating from eternity was situated within the time frame of the "effectual call" when the elect would be "called unto faith in Christ ... in due season." According to chapter 5 ("Of Providence"), "second causes" came into play during God's "ordinary providence" and in the effectual call, when God "maketh use of means." In Protestant scholasticism, "ordinary" signaled an alternative to an unmediated or "absolute" version of God's sovereignty; as had been said for decades (see chap. 4), God of His own free will had chosen to implement the divine decree through "means" or instruments instead of interacting with humankind directly.

Several pages later (chap. 7), the Confession reiterated the idiom of covenant and, in a gesture directed against Antinomian hermeneutics, confirmed the presence of the covenant of grace in both testaments, although more fully effective in the New. As well, the chapter specified that the covenant of grace was "dispensed" via "ordinances" that included the "preaching of the Word" and the sacraments.[28] The door thus opened to the Word and its place within the golden chain, chapter 10 ("Of Effectual Calling") cited the two modes of time noted in chapter 3: eternity, when "God ... predestinated unto life" the elect before the Fall, and "His appointed and accepted time" when the elect were "drawn to Christ," an assertion rephrased in chapter 11.3, where justification was represented as the free act of God existing from "all eternity" but also occurring in "due time" when the Holy Spirit "doth ... *actually apply* Christ" to the elect (emphasis added).[29]

With Arminianism disposed of and space having been made available for preachers of the Word to elicit faith and repentance, the makers of the Confession turned their attention to Antinomian-like themes. In a back-and-forth about justification and preparation (October 1643), members of the Westminster Assembly wrestled with the sequences of the golden chain, one possibility being that "some workes [of preparation] ... goe before Justification and repentance" and that "faith [was] in order to conversion." Or did "vocation" precede justification? There were those—William Twisse among them—who agreed that the "law" was crucial to "preparation for grace" but underscored the importance of characterizing the elect as "merely passive" as this stage was unfolding. On the general point that preparation was not saving, everyone agreed. Yet other members of the assembly insisted that "justification doth follow upon believing." In the text of the Confession (chap. 11), faith became an "instrument" that was "ever accompanied with all other saving graces," a jab at any severing of the divine decree from moral righteousness. A little later (chap. 14), faith and justification were linked again, with faith described as the process of "accepting, receiving, and resting upon Christ alone for justification."[30] In chapter 16, "good works, done in obedience to Gods commands" become "the fruits and evidences of a true and lively faith," although the makers of the Confession emphasized that all such fruits were the work of the Holy Spirit.

When the assembly turned to describing assurance (chap. 18), the several layers of the practical divinity became visible: hypocrites can deceive themselves and assurance itself can be "shaken, diminished, and intermitted" and could entail "many difficulties," yet it was also "infallible," testified to by "inward evidence" and the "testimony of the Spirit of adoption." (That faith could be "weak or strong" was acknowledged in chap. 14.) Although God might withdraw and leave the elect in "darkness," assurance could be regained. All the while, its presence was bound up with "the right use of ordinary means," a proposition tied to 2 Peter 1:10, "give diligence to make your calling and election sure." Another antidote to Antinomian-style perfectionism was the assertion in Philippians 2:12 to "work out your salvation with fear and trembling." The final retort concerned the law (chap. 19), which the Confession endorsed as a means of spurring the elect to humble themselves for sin and regain God's favor—sin, of course, never having vanished from the lives of the elect. Contrary to what Saltmarsh and others were alleging, repentance was imperative, a point underscored in chapter 15, where it was described as "of such necessity . . . that none may expect pardon without it."[31]

Read end to end, the Confession was a pitch-perfect summary of how divine sovereignty and unconditional election were paired with the mediating aspects of its "application"—in human time via the Word as means of grace and, on the part of the elect themselves, via faith, repentance, and sanctification. The crucial words in this synthesis were the words "actually," "apply" and "means." In the Scottish theologian David Dickson's commentary on the Confession, he pointed out that justification remained abstract until, by the agency of Christ through the Word, it was "applied" to the elect. To the question "Are the elect justified, until the Holy Spirit in due time actually apply Christ to them?" his answer was no—based, in his commentary, on Scripture passages indicating that "none are justified until they believe in Christ." In his scheme, faith reappeared as the "instrument" of justification and flowed seamlessly into "all other saving graces."[32]

With an eye on Antinomians who, in his words, were insisting that repentance "ought not to be preached . . . seeing it leads us away from Christ, and is many ways hurtful and dangerous," Dickson tagged it as an "evangelical grace," which Christ and the apostles "preached . . . no less than faith." Where there was faith and (evangelical) repentance, there was also sanctification—an always imperfect sanctification, but nonetheless a Spirit-filled process of "growth in grace." Dickson was emphatic about the irrelevance of "works" to the effectual call. Even so, they remained "fruits and evidences of a true and lively faith" that enabled anyone who "walk[ed] in all good conscience before" Christ to be "certainly assured" of being in a state of grace. He reached back to the Old Testament for verses to validate what he characterized as a "bundle" comprising, on the one hand, Christ's promise to pardon sinners and, on the other, the "new heart" manifested in faith and sanctification. The minister Adam Martindale summed up this bundle in *Divinity-Knots Unloosed* (1649): "Saving faith (though it be not a cause) is a fruit of election, for God hath respect to the means, as well as the end, and conjoyneth them in his decree."[33]

Whether a synthesis of this kind should be labeled "Calvinism," as it often is, may seem appropriate if we single out what the Confession said about divine sovereignty, the Atonement, and unmerited grace.[34] Yet a more encompassing inventory would include themes and arguments that seem less distinctively Calvinistic. The integrity of the divine decree mattered to the makers of the Confession, but so did heart-centered piety and repentance-driven righteousness. For them, true religion was always affective or inward as well as outward or duty-bound. Pattern, not edicts delivered from afar, was how God worked in the world, a pattern that fused the sovereignty of God with the capacity of humans as "rational creatures" to respond voluntarily to the gospel promise of grace. To anyone who objected that the practical divinity was "legal" or deterministic, the response was straightforward: a space existed in the economy of redemption for the "preparatory" workings of the law and the repentance that God expected of the elect. What seemed "legal"—in particular, repentance under the law as a doorway to faith—was really an aspect of the Gospel.

This "bundle" did not satisfy everyone in mid-century Britain who taught the practical divinity or grew up in its shadow. The ink was barely dry on the text before debate resumed about the workings of redemption, the meaning of the sacraments, and much else. That some of its wording was problematic was signaled in 1658 when the Independents responsible for the Savoy Declaration (see chap. 8) approved the Confession but modified aspects of its wording to eliminate "some erroneous opinions" or provide "clearer explanations." The covenantal framework of Westminster survived alongside a modest addition, as did what was said about double predestination, God's "ordinary Providence" and the "Means" or stages—effectual calling, adoption, sanctification and faith—to which, however, the Declaration attached the point that saving faith was always "in the least degree of it" different from "common grace." More substantial interventions occurred in chapter 15 ("Of Repentance unto Life") in order to emphasize the role of "saving Repentance" and the need for "constant preaching" of it. This retort to Antinomianism was followed in chapter 20 by another to Arminian- or Socinian-like arguments on behalf of "mens natural abilities." Perhaps because John Owen was doing battle with Richard

Baxter, this chapter was revised to underscore the "irresistible work of the holy Ghost" (p. 388).[35]

Owen's and Baxter's dispute dated from 1649, when Baxter questioned Owen's high Calvinism in his first book, *Aphorisms of Justification*.[36] The two men confronted each other in person in 1654 when Owen and others arranged a meeting of "able and Godly Divines" to clarify the clauses on religion in the *Instrument of Government* of December 1653. The group included Owen, Stephen Marshall, Francis Cheynell, and Baxter, who was added after James Ussher was unable to attend. As Baxter recalled, Owen wanted a confession of faith to fill out what was meant by "the Christian religion" in article 35 of the Thirty-Nine Articles and "faith in God by Jesus Christ" in article 36. Most of the group agreed with him that the time had come to clarify the boundaries of orthodoxy via a creed. Baxter was the naysayer. In *Aphorismes of Justification*, he had endorsed the "simplicity" of the gospel message as the best means of achieving "concord" or peace among British Protestants, and in *The Saints Everlasting Rest* (1650, rev. 1651), he extolled those who avoided the "extreams in the controverted points of Religion." Now, in 1654, he insisted anew that being too specific on every point of doctrine would fan the flames of discord.[37]

What made agreement between Baxter and Owen less likely was their mutual distrust. Baxter felt that Owen's emphasis on divine sovereignty could mutate into Antinomianism. He also distrusted creed-based orthodoxy because it could impede the goal of Christian unity or "concord," an objective Baxter described in *Christian Concord: or the Agreement of the Associated Pastors and Churches of Worcestershire, With Rich. Baxter's Exposition and Defence of It* (1653). Hence his preference for a Bible-centered faith on which everyone could agree, a stance he owed in part to Chillingworth's *The Religion of Protestants*.[38] On the other hand, Owen had cut his theological teeth as a critic of Arminianism and never stopped emphasizing the sovereignty of God, a sovereignty visible and, at the same time, invisible or mysterious in the work of redemption. In keeping with this understanding of God's action in the world, he insisted that sinners could not resist the offer of free grace and, in his version of the golden chain, put faith after justification whereas Baxter did the opposite. Once Owen turned to curtailing Antinomianism, he extolled the transformative effects of the Holy Spirit and its bearing on assurance of salvation.[39]

Despite Baxter's reputation for being too close to Arminianism,[40] he may have been the better witness to the consequences of the practical divinity. His personal history was living proof that its model of religious experience could make people more anxious, not less. As he noted in a retrospective account of his conversion, the journey he followed did not line up with the conventional language of stages—first this, then that—he had encountered in sermon series by the likes of Thomas Hooker. In his words, "I could not decisively trace the Workings of the Spirit upon my heart in that method which Mr. Bolton, Mr. Hooker, Mr. Rogers, and other Divines describe! Nor knew the Time of my Conversion." Yet Baxter was famously evangelical, an aspect of his ministry that explains the enduring appeal of *The Saints Everlasting Rest*. Asked for advice by someone on what to preach, he responded with a terse summary: "dwell much on the fundamentall truths, about sin, misery, redemption, the nature & way of conversion."[41]

His was not an idiosyncratic history, for others who disdained Antinomianism were complaining that too much importance was being given to "duties." In Robert Blair's autobiography, the Scottish minister described a season of spiritual strain he attributed to this emphasis and, at a later moment, reminded himself that "the diligent use of the means and ordinances" should not be the "object of our faith." Someone else who had second thoughts about duties was John Winthrop. Shaken by what he was hearing in mid-1630s Boston about their irrelevance to assurance of salvation, Winthrop wrote a description of his spiritual history from the time he was a schoolboy in England, a history shaped by his quest for a "sure and settled peace." What he remembered from his youth was the importance of "watchfulness" or, as he noted in retrospect, using "strict observance of all duties" as the doorway to peace. Along the way, he had also absorbed the "doctrine of free justification" and the importance of "love of the brethren" as a sign of inward grace. Possibly the most telling lesson was hearing that "a reprobate might (in appearance) attain to as much as I had done," a Perkinsian point John Cotton was reiterating in new-world Boston. Taken aback by what his own minister was saying, Winthrop wondered if it were "too late to begin anew." The heart of the problem was justification. In his words, the "doctrine of free justification lately taught here [in Massachusetts] took me in as drowsy a condition as I had been . . . these twenty years." Nonetheless, he concluded the narrative by affirming an experimental awareness of divine love.[42]

These testimonies make Saltmarsh's story of despair followed by an awakening to the glories of free grace more understandable, a story amplified in the narratives of two English women who became Baptists, Jane Turner and Anna Trapnel. Each recounted an escape from duty-centered religion in printed books, Turner in *Choice Experiences of The kind dealings of God before, in, and after Conversion . . . Whereunto is added a description of true Experience* (1653) and Trapnel in *A Legacy for Saints; Being Several Experiences of the dealings of God with Anna Trapnel* (1654). Trapnel's book was one of a series of texts rushed into print by allies who knew of the abuse directed at her by the more orthodox, who feasted on the visionary who saw angels and heard God speaking to her, the Trapnel publicized in *The Cry of a Stone* (1654). In *A Legacy*, a more matter-of-fact Trapnel walked her readers through a process of recovery from the burdens of the "law." Early in her spiritual journey, she accepted the argument that the covenant of grace came with conditions. Unable to discern whether she had met these, she "ran from Minister to Minister, from Sermon to Sermon, but . . . could find no rest." Fearing she had been "shut out from Christ" and unware of "the witness of the Spirit," she moved in that direction after realizing that Christ was indifferent to her works, a lesson she absorbed from ministers who "taught . . . the doctrine of free grace." From them she also learned that "there is free grace enough, an ocean, to swallow up [or] . . a fountain open for all manner of sins." Now she understood that the "new Covenant . . . admits of no condition, nor qualification, nor preparation." Soon, she was rejoicing in the presence of the seal of the Spirit and simultaneously insisting that the doctrine of free grace never offered "liberty to sin," a retort to Thomas Edwards and the many others who tagged the message of free grace as a doorway to libertinism.[43]

According to Turner's self-description, she owed a "fear" of sin to her family, which also taught her an understanding of "religion" aligned with the *Book of Common Prayer*. She remembered how, in this phase of her life, she took for granted that "the more I abounded in fasting, book prayer, and . . . mourning and afflicting my self for sin, the better it was." She had not yet learned that "truth" must be "seated in the heart," a lesson Turner absorbed from the preaching of an unnamed minister (seemingly a Puritan) who used "the Law" to convince her of sin. In response, she became "as exact and strict in all my waies (I think I may say) as it was possible for a poor creature to be." Doing so made her miserable until she came under the influence of people who taught her to depend entirely on a loving Christ. Now she understood that the "old covenant" or "Legal righteousnesse . . . is a great obstruction to the carrying on, and perfecting" of "conversion."[44]

These narratives were akin to what others were saying in the 1640s and the 1650s—for example, Obadiah Holmes in New England and the members of John Rogers's short-lived congregation in Dublin. None of the people who testified in Dublin were Antinomians in any meaningful sense of that term. On the other hand, most had moved beyond the traditional framework of the practical divinity, which they regarded as ascribing too much importance to "Forms." According to Thomas Higgins, he had been "formal" to the point of descending into "darkness" and "despair" until a sudden encounter with the Spirit altered his relationship to Christ. Elizabeth Avery had suffered greatly from the deaths of three of her young children, yet was lifted into "full assurance" after "God came in upon my Spirit." Like Higgins, Humphrey Mills had been an exemplary Christian who spent "three years together wounded for sins, and under a sense of my corruptions . . . and I followed Sermons, pursuing the means, and was constant in duties . . . and so precise in all outward formalities" until he realized the insignificance of outward righteousness and began to have a more immediate experience of the living Christ. When Rogers himself testified, he remembered being afraid of hell and the devil until the presence of the Spirit filled him with love.[45]

These stories contradicted the "bundle" so carefully assembled by the makers of the practical divinity and the Westminster Confession, as did the religious histories of the women and men who, in the 1650s, embraced the "inner light" discerned by George Fox.[46] To tens of thousands of others, however, this bundle continued to shape their understanding of the "pathway" to salvation. Blair, for one, returned to it after his season of self-doubt, Archibald Johnston never wavered, and Stedman wrested with its prescriptions in England and Massachusetts. Of the many witnesses to the persistence of this model, the most interesting may be John Bunyan. In *Grace Abounding to the Chief of Sinners* (1666), he recalled how, as a boy and young man, he had ignored the message of "watchfulness" and become something of a rake. Other than the Bible, which he finally began to read, the only books he seems to have owned reached him via his wife's dowry, two chapbook versions of *The Plain Mans Path-way to Heaven* and *The Practice of Piety*. Whether it was hearing sermons, reading the Bible, or learning from the example of godly people he encountered, Bunyan found his way to a sense of himself as "a great and grievous sinner." Later, he began to practice an "outward reformation" that others likened to a conversion, though in his own eyes he remained a "poor painted hypocrite." Much later, hearing of the new birth and the effectual call, he was encouraged by Christ's words "Come to me" and begged him to enact a real conversion. All the while, he had a sense of himself as "more loathsome . . . than a toad." Eventually he found his way to "truth"--crucially, that true faith is utterly different from that which is feigned and that Christ was reaching out in love. The more he pondered Scripture and listened to sermons, the more he realized that God's "severe" ways of dealing with the elect were intermingled with great "kindness and mercy." Unlike Anna Trapnel and the Quakers, however, the Bunyan of *Grace Abounding* never achieved "certitude" or allowed the workings of the Holy Spirit to become detached from the Word. As a modern scholar noted, "Comforting feelings are not the final message" of the book.[47]

Bunyan's may seem an unusually prolonged quest. Yet it becomes less extreme if we remember that the makers of the practical divinity regarded conversion as lifelong. A "first conversion" was merely the starting point for a process of self-examination and attending to "the means of grace." For Rutherford, Ambrose, Gataker and the authors of the Westminster Confession, this process was inherently social and outward. Instead of being averse to "Forms," the pathway to redemption was stuffed with means of grace—the sacraments, the Word as preached, Scripture, catechisms, other holy books, spiritual counsel, the routines of devotion. Churches or congregations of the faithful were also involved as agents of edification. As well, households and especially mothers played a role, a point Ambrose emphasized in his summary of "family du-ties" that included teaching children a catechism and how to practice "watch-fulness." Like his fellow ministers, Ambrose was sanctioning a model of conversion tied to God's instituted (or institutionalized) presence in the means. Doubt figured in this system, and possibly terror and the challenge of decipher-ing the many "signs" of Christ's absence and presence. Above all, however, this *was* a system.[48]

Hence, for Ambrose, Rutherford, Dickson, Gataker, and many others, their confidence in the continuity between the means of grace (Word, sermons, de-votional practices) and the divine decree or, more succinctly, between justifica-tion and sanctification. Baxter incorporated this confidence into *Gildas Salvia-nus, or The Reformed Pastor* (1655), a description of how ministry should be practiced. It opened with the traditional argument that all those who took up the role of ministry should have experienced "the work of saving grace" in their "souls." Just as traditional was the emphasis on providing sinners the "means" of salvation and undertaking their conversion: "The work of conversion is the first and great thing we must drive at; after this we must labour with all our might." Thereafter, the voice of the pastor enters, a pastor who knows that "many of our flock . . . are weak." According to Baxter, this was the "most com-mon condition" in the typical parish, and these, therefore, were the people most in need of the means of grace. Every parish would also include others who had succumbed to "worldliness . . . [or] drunkenness" or fallen into "scandal-ous sin." To them the ideal minister must address strong words that shook "their careless hearts" and prompted them to "repent." Situations of this kind made it imperative that parishes pursue the work of discipline—even, he ad-mitted, the "stool of repentance" employed in Scotland. Comforting, evangeli-cal, and disciplining at one and the same time, Baxter's ideal pastor welcomed family government. "The life of religion and the welfare and glory of Church and State, dependenth much on family government and duty."[49]

Institution builders who incorporate as many people as possible into the church as means to the end of their conversion or purists who create gathered churches of the already converted and relinquish infant baptism—Baxter was firmly on one side of this dichotomy and Trapnel, Turner, Obadiah Holmes, and John Rogers's Dublin congregation on the other.[50] Baptists such as Holmes and Trapnel or Spirit-centered people such as those in Dublin tied their understanding of church, ministry, and conversion to the dynamic pres-ence of the Holy Spirit. In the near future, the Spirit would enable the faithful few who were truly among the elect to withdraw from the presence of those who were not. Baxter's was a quite different understanding of sacred time and sacred presence. Word, sacraments, the exercise of catechesis—all were means by which the visible church functioned as an inclusive and disciplining institu-tion. The political implications were obvious. Civil governments should sustain a learned state-backed ministry vetted by others who were already ordained. And, instead of allowing sectaries to disrupt the cohesion of family, church, and commonwealth, those connections should be reinforced.

Controversy and Continuity in New England

On the other side of the Atlantic, argument about theology was occurring in New England. One focus of debate was liberty of conscience, which Roger Williams was advocating and John Cotton contesting, with others joining in during the 1640s and early 1650s. The well-read entrepreneur and magistrate William Pynchon, who founded the town of Springfield, was a pillar of the establishment until copies arrived from London of *The Meritorious Price of Our Redemption, Iustification, &c* (1650) and his fellow magistrates learned that he questioned the customary understanding of Christ's suffering on the cross. The government ordered the book burned, and Pynchon agreed to meet with a group of ministers who tried to persuade him to recant. Delaying a response to their arguments, he transferred his property in Springfield to a son and returned to England, where he continued to write and publish. About the same time (1650–51) another well-educated layman, Thomas Stoughton of Windsor, Connecticut, was contesting the time frame of the Sunday Sabbath with nearby ministers, doing so in a manuscript that was never printed. Among the ministers themselves, the trade in manuscripts was substantial. The longest-running example of this process may be the correspondence between Cotton and Peter Bulkeley, which they carried on for fifteen years.[51]

The bright light of international publicity touched two of these local debates, the Williams-Cotton exchanges and, because of its repercussions in England, the Antinomian controversy of 1636–37. Not immediately, however, for none of the documents arising out of this event reached English readers until the 1640s, when a London bookseller printed a collection of texts assembled by someone who remains unidentified. No author's name appeared on the title page of *Antinomians and Familists Condemned By the Synod of Elders in New-England, with the Proceedings of the Magistrates against them, And their Apology for the same* (late 1643–early 1644) or on the sequel, a reissue of the same sheets to which a "To the Reader" and "Preface" signed by Thomas Weld was added alongside a new title. Back in London on colony business, Weld had come upon the initial printing and decided it needed "order and sense." With Weld identified but still without an author, the book reappeared as *A Short Story of the Rise, reign, and ruine of the Antinomians, Familists & Libertines, that infected the Churches of New-England* (1644).

Documents uncovered in the mid-twentieth century made it possible to date the rupture between Cotton and his colleagues to the spring or midsummer of 1636, when Thomas Shepard warned the older minister that laypeople in his Boston congregation were voicing "Familist"-like motifs. The allusion to laypeople was something of a ruse, for it was Cotton's own words that troubled Shepard and his allies. Hoping to clarify any differences, in December a group of ministers gave him sixteen questions to answer. The first of these concerned "the Seal of the Spirit" or "witness of the Spirit," which Cotton was endorsing as the only Christ- or grace-centered source of assurance. The most significant was the thirteenth question, which raised the possibility of using "sanctification" as evidence of the work of grace. In the longest of his responses, Cotton accepted it as a "concurrent sign" alongside others, but not when there was "no other ground or evidence," by which he meant the "seale" or "witness of the Spirit." Were the Spirit absent, sanctification turned into a "work" that preceded faith. Thereafter, as Shepard remembered, the "principal . . . seed of all the rest" was whether someone could "take any evidence of God's special grace and love toward him by the sight of any graces or conditional evangelical promises to faith or sanctification." Or was assurance of a wholly different kind, known to the elect via an "immediate revelation in an absolute promise"? Cotton was disputing the first and advocating the second; his colleagues were defending the first and cautioning against the second.[52]

How Cotton reached the point of distrusting sanctification as evidence of justification and therefore a valid means of assurance remains unclear. In his English ministry, he had reiterated the fusion of repentance, duties, watchfulness, conditions, and divine sovereignty typified by the practical divinity and, in one set of his English sermons, listed some forty signs that laypeople could consult if they were anxious about assurance. He had also criticized John Eaton and others he deemed "Familists." Only in a few places do modern readers of these older sermons discern themes that anticipate the Cotton who was beginning to question certain aspects of the practical divinity.[53] Like Thomas Goodwin, however, he may have encountered a more Spirit-centered understanding of conversion in the early 1630s and found it to his liking. Or perhaps he was dismayed by the indecision of the "old non-conformists" as a crisis of conscience loomed in the early 1630s. Did he wonder if some of them were hypocrites and, once he arrived in Massachusetts, begin to second-guess the evidence people were using to qualify for membership? What is certain is that a spiritual deadness he discerned among the colonists seemed akin to hypocrisy. As he noted in a sermon preached in 1636 in Salem, "when Christians come into this Country, though they have been marvelous eminent in our native Countrey, they canot pray fervently, nor hear the word with profit, nor receive the seals with comfort: they wonder what is become of their old prayers," a situation he attributed to their confidence in "holy duties" as a basis of assurance.[54]

Once Cotton started down the path of criticizing duties, it led him to the golden chain. His version emphasized the covenant of grace and the activity of the Holy Spirit. In a sermon series on the covenant, he extolled its "marvelous freedom"—marvelous because God offered it to sinners "without the foresight of Faith, or Works." Unlike his fellow ministers, he assigned faith (to which he attached the adjective "passive") a place after "union" with Christ. Doing so eliminated any possibility of regarding faith or righteousness as "conditions" of justification. Turning to assurance of salvation, he dismissed the value of "sanctification" as the "first evidence of Justification." Not only was it "many times dark to a sincere Christian," sanctification could easily slide into "rank popery" or a "covenant of works," a phrase he attached to the practical syllogism. The Christ-centered alternative was the "witnesse" or "seale of the Spirit" that "reveal[s] Gods thoughts of love . . . in a free promise of grace." Somewhat grudgingly, Cotton acknowledged that the Spirit did not always do so immediately. But he never mentioned "the means" (that is, the Word) except as a minor player in the work of redemption. Responding to a list of questions he was handed in the summer of 1637, he reiterated that "wee doe not know by any other meanes [than the seal of the Spirit], that we are the Children of God."[55]

How it happened that the younger minister John Wheelwright (c. 1592–1679) shared Cotton's point of view remains unclear. In his fast-day sermon of January 1637, Wheelwright divided the colonists into two groups, the many who were "legall" and the few or "little flock" genuinely touched by the Spirit. At that moment, he had severed "knowledge" of justification from "worke" of any kind (that is, sanctification) and characterized the "dutyes . . . pressed" on people as "Burthens." From England, where he returned after a period of exile on the borders of Massachusetts, he revisited the controversy in *A Brief, and Plain Apology* (1658). What he reported of his thinking in 1636–37 overlapped with what Cotton had been saying: "union" with Christ occurred prior to faith and sanctification could not be used as "the first evidence" of justification. Indeed, any evidence antedating "union"—for example, the repentance that meant so much to Hooker and Shepard—he regarded as "legal," the epithet he used in his incendiary fast-day sermon of January 1637 and, if Thomas Weld can be trusted, the master word in the rhetoric of the people who backed Hutchinson and Cotton. In summary, he accused his fellow ministers of abusing the golden chain, for they "beg[in at] workes" and "end at Christ & free grace: I teach . . . to begin at Christ & f[aith] & to end at workes."[56]

The person most responsible for this rhetoric was probably Anne Hutchinson.[57] The daughter of Francis Marbury, who fell afoul of the bishops in 1578 for his nonconformity (see chap. 2), and, as her practice of holding private meetings indicates, someone well-versed in the repertoire of the Puritan movement, Hutchinson arrived in Boston in 1634 with her husband William and their large family. Her entry to the church was delayed for a few months, possibly because of her reputation as a prophetess or because she approved the Separatist-style argument that ministers who accepted ordination at the hands of a bishop were agents of the Antichrist.[58] Already inclined to question the legitimacy of the ministers in Massachusetts, she went much further down this road by reiterating Cotton's assertion that they were preaching a "covenant of

works." What she meant by this insult was their willingness to endorse sanctification (or, as she said, mere "duties") as evidence of justification. Hutchinson
shared her complaints with women awaiting childbirth, and probably did so
as well in the weekly meetings some sixty or seventy women were attending in
her Boston home. What churches were accepting as evidence of being a visible
saint troubled her, and it seems likely that this disdain lies behind two of the
errors listed by the synod of 1637: no. 31, "Such as see any grace of God in
themselves, before they have the assurance of Gods love sealed to them are not
to be received members of Churches," and its companion, no. 24, "The Church
in admitting members is not to looke to holinesse of life, or Testimony of the
same."[59] Because so few of her own words have survived, historians must depend on what Cotton said about her in 1637 and again in the mid-1640s. In his
judgment, she was doing "much good in our Town" because of her forthright-
ness about sanctification and had become the "means" by which "many of the
women (and by them their husbands) were convinced, that they had gone on
in a Covenant of Works . . . and were brought to enquire more seriously after
the Lord Jesus Christ." By way of endorsement, Cotton added that "all this was
well . . . and suited with the publike Ministery, which had gone along in the
same way."[60]

Testifying before the General Court in November 1637, Hutchinson justified her ministry to women by citing Joel 2:28, "I will pour out my spirit on all
flesh; your sons and your daughters shall prophesy." To everyone's astonish-
ment, the following day she evoked a spiritual disarray she had suffered in
England, a disarray that brought her to the verge of "Atheisme." Its source was
a typically Puritan situation: "much troubled at the constitution of the
Churches there [in England], so farre, as I was ready to have joined to the
Separation." Unable to discern true ministers from false, she was rescued from
uncertainty by an "immediate voice"—to her, the voice of God—that resolved
this predicament. "Ever since," she told the court, "I have been confident of
what he hath revealed unto me." To assert such "Revelations" was too much for
the government, which ordered her banished.[61]

Two months earlier, the synod of 1637 busied itself laying out the theological alternative. Its bare bones had been outlined in the *Sixteene Questions of
Serious and Necessary Consequence* (1644) and, after Cotton answered them,
in the "Elders Reply," to which the synod added "Confutations" of eighty-two
"errours." Assurance of salvation was front and center in their response. To
Cotton's insinuation that relying on repentance and duties compromised the
principle of free grace, they insisted that "conditions" had a legitimate place in
the work of redemption, citing, among other Scriptures, Matthew 11:28, "Come
unto me, all ye that labor and are heavy laden"; and Mark 1:15, "Repent ye and
believe." To error 70, which tagged "Frequency or length of holy duties or trouble of conscience for neglect thereof" as a "Covenant of workes," the response
was more references to Scripture, one of them (1 Cor. 13:58) glossed to validate

the rule that Christians are "commanded to abound always in the worke of the Lord, that is, holy duties."[62] This tick-tack-toe gave way to more substantial issues in other parts of the synod's conclusions. Three were especially important: the relationship between faith and justification and, in turn, the relationship between justification and sanctification; the role of repentance in the economy of redemption; and the integrity of the golden chain. Quoting several "unsavoury speeches," which it added to the list of eighty-two errors, the synod rejected the first of these—"To say that we are justified by faith is an unsafe speech"—as at odds with "the constant language" of the Bible and the line St. Paul had drawn between law-based righteousness and the righteousness associated with faith. To the argument that it was a "fundamentall and soule-damning errour to make sanctification an evidence of justification" (error 72; see also errors 45, 60, 77 and the second "unsavoury speech"), the ministers fell back on 2 Peter 1:10. No ground was yielded when it came to repentance. Had King David not admitted his sinfulness and the Gospels tied faith and grace together? And, in response to assertions that anyone who doubted was in serious trouble, they repeated the truism that faith and doubt were always intermingled.[63] The most important of these responses concerned the golden chain. Shepard and his colleagues reiterated the traditional argument that God had designed the order of salvation St. Paul identified in Romans 8:29–30. In doing so, He inserted "bands and ligaments and meanes" into the process of redemption. Hence the possibility of using sanctification, which was situated near the end of the chain, as evidence of justification. As well, faith and righteousness were intrinsically connected.[64]

The pastoral aspects of the give-and-take of 1636–37 and the nuanced meaning of assurance deserve more attention than they usually receive in modern scholarship. Beginning with the *Sixteene Questions*, Shepard and his colleagues foregrounded the situation of those of "weak faith." How were such people to be reassured about their relationship with Christ if their spiritual ups and downs were dismissed as irrelevant? And what if they missed out on the "immediate Witness of the Spirit" that Cotton regarded as the basis of assurance? When it came to hypocrisy, the ministers were also wrestling with the challenge of differentiating hypocrite from visible saint; as Shepard remarked in mid-1636, "we have been generally mistaken in most men and in great professors." Yet in general, they were less dismissive. Their most interesting argument was to attach sanctification to "love" and, more specifically, to "love of the brethren" (1 John 3:14) made possible by the presence of the Holy Spirit. John Winthrop had evoked this same love in his "Charitie Discourse" of 1630 as the most telling quality of the believers. Now, the ministers evoked it anew as a capacity of the saints and only of the saints, centered in the heart. As well, it was a capacity present in the "weake" as well as in the most robust of the saints. As Abram van Engen has pointed out in his telling exegesis of this argument, the ministers acknowledged that "comfort" (i.e., assurance) was experienced in different ways. In their eyes, the "witness of the Spirit" was possible but also apt to be deceiving. Love and the duties that flowed from it were more apparent and therefore more reliable.[65]

Real or imagined, Antinomianism in New England subsided in the aftermath of the controversy once Cotton backed down and Wheelwright and Hutchinson left the colony.[66] Thereafter, it was the English version that drew local ministers into debating Saltmarsh and others. From his home in Concord, Bulkeley reassured the "weake Saints of God" that the "comfort" they received from "fruits" was valid evidence of being included in the covenant of grace. In 1652, the printing office in new-world Cambridge published Richard Mather's commentary on the relationship between faith and justification, *The Summe of Certain Sermons on Genes. 15.6*. Once he established that faith was not a "work" and that Catholics and Arminians got things wrong, he evoked Romans 8:30 as the basis for arguing that justification came after "vocation, or effectuall calling" and was therefore "after faith because faith is wrought in vocation" (p. 13). In John Norton's tediously scholastic *The Orthodox Evangelist, or, a Treatise Wherein many Great Evangelical Truths . . . Are . . . cleared, and confirmed* (1654), he argued that, although justification was both "absolutely, and actually procured before Faith," it did not occur until the elect "doe beleeve."[67]

Thomas Shepard had absorbed scholastic language from his teachers at Cambridge and, in the sermon series published as *The Sound Believer* (1645), he employed some of this terminology to explain how Christ's righteousness was imputed to sinners, and did so again in *Theses Sabbaticae* (1649), where he addressed John Saltmarsh directly.[68] The back-and-forth of 1636–37 and documents dating from the early 1640s show us another Shepard, a spiritual seeker painfully tested during his version of the pilgrim's journey. From Preston and Thomas Hooker, who had been his mentors at Cambridge and remained important to him after he became a lecturer in the village of Earls Colne, he acquired the principle that repentance must precede faith and faith the stage of justification. Only if this sequence were observed would faith be rooted in an honesty about the helplessness of sinners to earn grace for themselves. As the title page of *The Sound Believer* signaled, the sinner was utterly dependent on "the work of Christ's spirit in reconciling" him or her with God. In the early 1640s, Shepard reminded himself of this point in a journal entry that captures one of the paradoxes of his spirituality: "I saw if I laid the evidence of my salvation on my works that it would be various and uncertain . . . and yet on the other side I saw that if I did not walk holily in all things before God I should not, I could not, have assurance of any good estate, so that here I was at some stand."[69]

This was a paradox he brought with him to Massachusetts and revisited in a long-running sermon series on the parable of the ten virgins, which he began to preach in June 1636. According to the parable (Matt. 25:1–13), five of the ten virgins who went out to meet the bridegroom had no oil in their lamps.

Shepard interpreted these five as hypocrites whose identity would be exposed when Christ returned in judgment. For him, this question had an immediate significance. When Anne Hutchinson and Wheelwright began to rail against the presence of hypocrites in local congregations, Shepard was supervising the admission of people to the congregation he had founded in February 1636. That his standards for being a visible saint were high was signaled in mid-1636 by his objections to the "relations" being made by laypeople in Roxbury, where a church was about to be founded. A year or two later, the Cambridge congregation admitted the university-educated Nathaniel Eaton after he made an exemplary "relation" and, because of his family connections and Cambridge training, was named head of Harvard College. Before long, Shepard learned that Eaton was the wrong man for this post. Hypocrites had wormed their way into the most "virgin" of churches![70]

As well as pressures of this kind on his ministry, Shepard was faced with the challenge of supporting everyone who suffered "fears on fears" about assurance of salvation while simultaneously arousing the people in Cambridge from a "deadness" he, like Cotton, was discerning. From his vantage, the source of this deadness was the acute difference between the situation of the godly in England and New England. Speaking to his congregation, he pointed out that "When you went many miles to hear, and had scarce bread at home, O, you thought, if once you had such liberties; but when they are made yours, now what fruit? Doth not plenty of means make thy soul slight means?" Another way of making this point was to cite the spiritual benefits of persecution; it kept people on their toes, but in persecution-free Massachusetts, zeal was slipping away.[71]

Being a pastor who comforts but also chastises was a role Shepard aspired to practice. The pastor who comforts had already been evoked in the back-and-forth initiated in December 1636, for the questions he and his colleagues handed to Cotton emphasized the plight of people "put to sad doubts of their own Estate." Shepard may have penned this part of the "Elders Reply," for he used almost the same language in chapter 9 of the sermon series, which opens with an "exhortation 1. To quicken all those doubting, drooping, yet sincere hearts that much question the love of Christ to them" (p. 77). Several sentences later, he blamed Satan's "wiles" for this situation, a Satan active "here" (that is, in Massachusetts), a not-so-indirect allusion to Hutchinson's attempts to undermine the common wisdom about assurance of salvation. As was customary among preachers of the practical divinity in England, Shepard acknowledged that "very few living Christians have any settled comfortable evidence of God's eternal love to them in his Son, and hence many sad events follow." This may sound abstract, but Shepard was directing these words at people he addresses as "you." Throughout this long passage, he reiterated his concern for those who "rest in uncertain hopes," characterizing theirs as "one of the most dangerous" situations a follower of Christ could tumble into.[72]

In these same pages, Shepard detailed the antidote to uncertainty. Comfort lay in acknowledging the presence of a "tender-hearted" and loving Christ who reaches out to those who suffer and offers everyone the opportunity to accept the gospel promise. "Never any came to him that he cast way," Shepard asserted, citing Matthew 8:17 ("He bore our infirmities"). Telling, too, for those who doubted their spiritual well-being, was the Christ who sympathized with those who suffer from the "miseries" of sin. Allusions of this kind come thick and fast in the sermon series—to the Christ who seeks the "lost sheep," who pities the plight of sinners and "mourn[s] for the hardness of their hearts," who "seek[s] out" those who "reject" the offer of grace no matter how many times this happens. As the literary historian Michael Colacurcio has pointed out, the "parable sermons" continually evoke the "real love" Christ has for sinners, a phrase complemented by allusions to his "fervent, vehement, earnest love," "constant and continual" love, dwelling "with thee as a man must dwell with his wife," and "rejoic[ing] in thee . . . as a bridegroom does over the bride," all of them underscoring the thesis that "the Lord draws a soul by cords of love" and craves everyone's salvation.[73]

Shepard wrote these words at a moment when John Cotton was recommending an "immediate witnesse of the Spirit" as the surest source of comfort. Returning to the practical divinity, he reclaimed the traditional argument that the pathway to Christ began with repentance. Why? Because the "law" remained in force for sinners, the law that sinners were always and everywhere disobeying. Hence the imperative of preparation understood as a means of transforming self-esteem into emptiness. He turned this imperative on its head by emphasizing the commitment of the true saints to sanctification—in one sense, a law-driven, duty-bound sanctification; but in another, a process rooted in their "hearts" and accompanied by an inward spiritual sense that no hypocrite could feign. He summed up this argument by emphasizing the importance of using the "means" to the fullest possible extent. This was why the parable of the ten virgins was so instructive, for it dramatized the benefit of being "prepared." The great danger was "sloth." In effect, Shepard reclaimed a place for duties not as meritorious but as integral to preparation and, in the aftermath of justification, to the sanctified life.

That this message deadened the presence of the Spirit, as Hutchinson and the English Antinomians of the 1620s had suggested, is contradicted by the texture of the journal Shepard was keeping at the outset of the 1640s. On almost every page, he recorded the shifting temper of his heart or inner self. All too often, it was "dead," "dark," "unbelieving," or "self-seeking." Every time this happened, Shepard learned anew the lesson that "Legal duties . . . can never give peace." Alongside statements of this kind, he put his objections to Christians who would "like . . . to have joy and peace always but think their condition woeful if they be left to temptations, fears, and wrestlings." His was a different calculus: the "poor Christian lamenting his wants is the most sincere."

And, it would seem, the most acceptable to God, for Shepard could turn from self-abasement to praising the God who "melted my heart."[74] For him, the lived experience associated with the practical divinity combined moments of spiritual absence and self-doubt with moments of extraordinary joy from feeling close to Christ.

The Christ who reaches out in tenderness to those who are of drooping spirits, the God (speaking through the minister) who demands constant self-searching and sanctions moral behavior as a valid sign of true godliness, a Christ (or God) who withdraws his presence when zeal gives way to deadness—a scenario Shepard described in the parable sermons—a package of this kind may epitomize the "paradoxes" of Puritan divinity. When we turn back to the relations, they too seem paradoxical if we narrow our reading of them to assurance, yes or no? On the contrary, the people who testified in the Cambridge meetinghouse described themselves as beset by ups and downs and, as Alice Stedman reported in her narrative, constantly wanting "signs" they could use to discern their relationship with Christ. In line with what Shepard was saying in the parable sermons, they learned the lesson—central to the practical divinity—that using the "means" was immensely important as an aspect of everyday righteousness and as an avenue to a joyous relationship with Christ. This was a lesson Christopher Cane took to heart: "Hearing . . . it was good to persist in the means," he "resolved to do [so]." On the other hand, by itself this practice did not guarantee some sort of spiritual rapture. After Mary Angier arrived in the colony, "every sermon made her worse and like a block under all means and thought God had left her to a hard hart." Or, if a minister was emphasizing the gospel promise, people "could not lay hold of it," which was Jane Holmes's experience. The paradigmatic testimony may be that of Edward Hall, who told the congregation that the "Lord let him see he was Christless and built upon false foundations and by this text [John 3] he saw himself no new creature but only a mended man." These words may echo Antinomian rhetoric, but it was probably Shepard's voice that accounts for Hall's response to John 5:40: "And here he saw how freely Christ was offered . . . and so was stirred up with more vehemency to seek Christ." Like others, however, the outcome for him was fear as well as its opposite: "And he found his worldliness and this bred many fears of whether ever any work of Christ in him was in truth, and that he was one that might fall short of Christ."[75]

As Shepard told his congregation time and again, nothing was "easie" about the way to salvation. The dark side of "deadness" was a sinner's unwillingness to embark on the pilgrim's journey or, as Shepard put it in his response to Saltmarsh, an unwillngness to acknowledge the imperative of repentance in response to the law. Yet to end the story here would be a misreading of Shepard's message and his ministry and, for that matter, a misreading of the practical divinity. For several decades, the men who adhered to this system had acknowledged the plight of the many who felt that God had abandoned them.[76] Shepard himself struggled with absence and its twin, an unwillingness to "learn the bitterness of sin." Relying in part on prayer and strenuous self-examination to remedy these situations, he was sustained by communion with his fellow saints in Cambridge. In the parable sermons, as in what he said in February 1636 when he and others brought the congregation into being, he idealized the church as a community bound together in love. This was no idle ethic. In everyday practice, church members in Cambridge addressed each other as "brother" and "sister" and, when the economic crisis of 1639–40 hit the town, created a local charity to assist neighbors who had descended into poverty or become disabled. When the scope of baptism was being debated (see below, sec. 3), Shepard sided with those who wanted to incorporate the next generation. Baptism was immensely significant to him as a token and instrument of family continuity. Almost certainly, he was catechizing every young person in Cambridge; as he noted in his journal at the beginning of the 1640s, his "heart . . . was much enlarged to set upon catechizing." Although he decried the townspeople's obsession with stray pigs and their craving for more land, he continued to celebrate the visible church as "almost like heaven." His high hopes for love-based edification alter the meaning of the Cambridge relations, as does the fact that no one who applied for membership seems to have been turned down. Anxiety did not disappear after someone crossed the threshold between world and church. Nonetheless, being part of a loving community was, for Shepard, in keeping with l John 3:14.[77]

Continuity and Change in New England, 1640–1660

The currents of revolution and counterrevolution that swept through England, Scotland, and Ireland in the 1640s and 1650s were felt in Virginia, Maryland (where a Protestant majority engaged in "petty civil war" with the colony's Catholic proprietor), Bermuda, and the Caribbean.[78] The four orthodox colonies in New England were the exception. Never party to the Solemn League and Covenant, the Westminster Assembly, and the execution of Charles I, their governments remained intact, with two post-1660 exceptions: a charter for Connecticut (1663) that brought New Haven Colony into its jurisdiction and, in 1685, the revocation of the Massachusetts charter. The main beneficiary of the Long Parliament was Rhode Island, which secured a charter of its own in 1644 and a second in 1653. When war broke out between England and the Netherlands in 1652, soldiers arrived in Boston and plans were broached to attack New Netherland. Welcomed by the governments in Connecticut and New Haven, this project threatened the commercial interests of Massachusetts and, after sharp debate, the New England Confederation, which the governments of the four orthodox colonies had organized in May

1643, did not support the venture. In the mid-1650s, Cromwell dangled his "western design" to upend the Spanish empire in front of the colonists, a gesture that irritated the leadership in Massachusetts. Otherwise, the authority of the Protectorate in New England was not seriously exercised.[79]

On the other hand, the scuffling between Independents and Presbyterians in mid-1640s England implicated the Congregational Way, which Presbyterians cited as an example of what was wrong with a Separatist-like system. For Robert Baillie, Samuel Rutherford, and others, *A Short Story of the Rise, Reigne, and Ruine of the Late Antinomians* demonstrated the shortcomings of John Cotton. In the 1650s, Baptists and Quakers wrote and published self-justifying narratives of how badly they had been treated in Massachusetts. From the more conservative circle of Dr. Robert Child, who visited Massachusetts in the mid-1640s, came accusations that the government was ignoring English law, and from Roger Williams came more complaints about religious conformity. (The friendship that sprang up between Williams and Baillie, who milked the colonist for gossip he could retell, is among the more curious aspects of the 1640s.) Fending off these critics became a minor industry in the 1640s and 1650s, with Edward Winslow, the sometime governor of Plymouth, doing what he could in London to contradict the self-justifying narratives of Child and the religious radical Samuel Gorton. Once John Eliot began to evangelize among Native Americans (see below), Winslow publicized this project in a series of tracts known as the Eliot Tracts. The benefits were significant. As one of John Winthrop's sons reported from England in 1649, "The conversion of the Indians with you maks New England very Famous, and Mr. Winslow is Labouring hard For you."[80]

Overall, the good news outweighed the bad. The several colonial governments were well on the road to stability and, although squabbling—much of it about boundaries between towns and colonies and, within towns, about transferring land to the next generation or allowing some families to organize their own church and town—was constant. So were efforts to sustain "mutual love" and when it came to initial grants of land, something akin to equality.[81] No one in Britain noticed how the structures of government in New England were evolving or what was being done to reform the legal system. In both respects, the colonists were well ahead of their times. By 1640, the four orthodox colonies were sharing a structure of government that, by European standards, was remarkably democratic. Elections took place annually, with governors, magistrates, and deputies serving a single year before facing the voters again—or, as was the rule in Connecticut, governors waiting at least a year before they could be reelected. Assemblies or "courts" met annually or semiannually. Everywhere, the category of "freemen" (those allowed to vote in colonial affairs) included more than half of the adult men, and in town meetings, which decided how land would be distributed, every adult householder was usually able to participate, although not in Massachusetts until 1647. The political culture of

Rhode Island was singular in being so hostile to centralized authority and so affirming of the terms "democratical" and "democracy." As was said in 1641 by the townsmen in Portsmouth and Newport, they were governed by "a Democracie or Popular Government that is to say It is in the Powre of the Body of freemen . . . or major Part of them to make or Constitute Just Lawes." Not, perhaps, in the same way or with the same enthusiasm, the colonists living elsewhere had acknowledged the same principle.[82]

Just as telling was the fact that every adult (male, female, freeman, nonfreeman) could petition a colonial government for redress of some grievance. Petitions on behalf of someone who had slipped into poverty or was otherwise in need of aid were routinely approved, as were petitions to ease or cancel fines for some misdeed. Longer term, stability was abetted by the practice of allowing adult males and, in some respects, most women certain privileges. In his *Discourse* (1637–38; see chap. 7), John Davenport had specified that, when land was being allocated, non–church members should receive the same share as members of a gathered congregation, a policy favored everywhere. In a statement (1645) responding to Robert Child, who claimed to represent the men left out of church membership, the Massachusetts government underscored the rights or privileges common to everyone: "They [nonfreemen] think it well, that justice is equally administred to them with the freemen; that they have equall share with them in all towne lotts, commons, &c. that they have like libertie of access to the church assemblies . . . as also like freedome of trade and commerce." This list could also have included the fair apportioning of taxes, in contrast to what usually happened in England.[83]

The good news included the economy. When immigration abruptly ceased in 1639–40, the influx of money newcomers brought with them also ceased. Overnight, the colonists were unable to import much by way of clothes, food, tools, and the like. Overnight as well, deflation ended a boom in prices for cattle, labor, and other necessities. Doubts emerged about the region's economic future,[84] and a handful of people decamped to the north shore of Long Island and present-day Delaware. By mid-decade, this crisis was abating as markets emerged in Spain, Portugal, the adjacent Madeira (or Wine) Islands, and the Sugar Islands in the Caribbean for dried fish, horses, foodstuffs, and timber. With boats needed for a coastal trade and longer voyages and plenty of inexpensive timber on hand, shipwrights began to ply their craft. The fur trade had a brief run, and investors from England financed an iron mill in Saugus, Massachusetts, but the Sugar Islands were the main reason why in 1651 the lay historian Edward Johnson celebrated the ways in which "the Lord [hath] been pleased to turn one of the most hideous, boundless, and unknown wildernesses in the world in an instant, as 'twere" to a "mart for merchants" who traded with many parts of an Atlantic economy. By this time, Boston was on its way to becoming a metropolis with two churches, a town library, and a town "house" where merchants met to do business.[85]

Prosperity and the absence of epidemics abetted a startling increase in the population. Overall, the colonists were healthier than their counterparts in England, a blessing they owed to clean water, the nutritional benefits of corn, and the low density of settlement. The best news may have been the disappearance of the bubonic plague. With more children surviving into adulthood, the age ratio of the population began to tilt toward people who had grown up in New England. The downside to this demography was the troubles it caused within older towns about the distribution of land.

Was there room within the "Congregational Way" for the immigrants' children and the burgeoning number of that generation's children? And did ongoing conflict between Presbyterians and Congregationalists in 1640s England illuminate any weaknesses in the "Congregational Way"? In 1643, a synod-like meeting had addressed the complaints of a few "presbyterian"-minded ministers about the empowering of laypeople but made no changes in the rules of circa 1636. Children were another matter, for congregations were beginning to vary in how baptism was administered. Knowing that Presbyterians in England were attacking Independents for allowing congregations to be formed out of (or within) existing parishes and knowing, too, of local "differences of opinion & practice of one church from another," a group of ministers in Massachusetts petitioned the General Court in May 1646 to summon a synod that would articulate the principles of the New England system. In and of itself, the possibility that the government would do so aroused laypeople in Boston and Salem to defend the autonomy of each gathered church. In response, the government withheld an official order and merely expressed its "desire" that churches in the colony meet and agree upon a "forme of government & discipline." A large majority of churches dispatched ministers and lay delegates to the synod, which completed its work in 1648 on a document published by the local printer as *A Platform of Church Discipline Gathered Out of the Word of God* (1649). Known almost immediately as the Cambridge Platform, it was not endorsed by any of the colonial governments, leaving local churches free to say yea or nay to its provisions.[86]

For purists or the more apocalyptically minded, the Cambridge Platform was pleasing because it preserved several of the principles put into practice in the mid-1630s: churches as gathered and autonomous, ministers and laypeople sharing the power of the keys, church and state collaborating within the contours of two-kingdoms theory. Yet in tone and modestly in substance, the text also reflected the countercurrents of the late 1630s (see chap. 7). At that moment, the leadership in Massachusetts had been anxious about Separatist-like tendencies and the ramifications of the Antinomian controversy. Echoes of the controversy lingered into the mid-1640s, which was also when the ministers in New England learned of "sectaries" who were denying the authority of learned ministers and questioning Reformed orthodoxy. In the wake of a successful synod in 1637 and on edge about threats of various kinds to their system, the authors of the platform endorsed (in chap. 15) "the communion of Churches one with another" and, in chapter 16 ("Of Synods"), asserted that "Magistrates have power to call a Synod," a statement seemingly contradicted by the assertion that "the constituting of a Synod, is a church act." The platform also allowed ministers of one congregation to administer the sacraments in another.[87]

More significant were the steps taken to strengthen the authority of ministerial "office," which critics of the Congregational Way had persistently described as insufficient. One way of doing so was to put ordination in the hands of the clergy. Initially and, in some congregations well beyond 1640, laymen in local churches performed this rite.[88] But as described in the Cambridge Platform, the laying on of hands was confined to ministers. Simultaneously, the platform revisited the balancing of lay and clerical authority. In *The Keyes of the Kingdom* (1644), Cotton had made the case for a "binding power . . . proper and peculiar" to the clergy. At the synod, everyone seems to have agreed on providing ministers with a "negative voice" (in modern parlance, a veto) they could use to block lay members from deciding church policy, a provision validated by the concept of an "office-power" intrinsic to the very being of ministry. As some in England were quick to recognize—famously, John Owen, but also Thomas Edwards and some of the Scottish Presbyterians—the *Keyes* and other gestures were dampening down the daring structure of the "Congregational Way."[89]

In other chapters, the synod revisited the relationship between church and state. The back-and-forth between Cotton and Roger Williams made its way into the text via the argument that the civil magistrate was limited to punishing "such things as are acted by the outward man," a rule consistent with Cotton's argument that "private" opinions were beyond the reach of the civil state. But the platform endorsed the argument—overturned by Erastians in England and rejected by Williams on other grounds—that godly kings in the Old Testament had their modern counterparts in magistrates who accepted the "duty . . . to take care of matters of religion." Otherwise, tradition prevailed, with two-kingdoms principles reaffirmed in chapter 17 of the platform. Complaints about the Massachusetts law of 1636 that empowered magistrates and neighboring churches to supervise the founding of new congregations may be responsible for the insistence that local people could "gather themselves into Church state" without "the consent of [the] Magistrate."[90]

Where demography and debates in England left their mark was in in the wording of the two chapters (3 and 12) on church membership. On the one hand, the Cambridge Platform reiterated the rule that candidates for membership must be "Saints by calling" who were "examined" beforehand about their "Repentance from sin, & faith in Jesus" (chap. 12, secs. 1–2). It also reiterated the imperative to "receive none to the Seales [sacraments], but visible saints." In what was said about the rules for becoming a church member, the emphasis fell on making "a personal & publick confession, & declaring of Gods manner of working upon the soul," or, as noted elsewhere, of "shew[ing] repentance from sinn, faith unfaigned; & effectual call." To these statements on behalf of purity, the platform added a recommendation that congregations accept "the weakest measure of faith," a proposal backed up by the assertion that weakness, "if sincere," would do. In chapter 3, congregations were advised to avoid "severity of examination" and practice "charitable discretion" or "the judgment of charity" in evaluating someone, advice coupled with the wisdom that hypocrites would inevitably become members. As a sop to those who hesitated to testify about their "spiritual estate" in the presence of the congregation, the platform (sec. 12.4) authorized the possibility of doing so privately, a procedure that may been especially useful to women. These adjustments left untouched the ministers' objections to the practice—endorsed, it seemed, by British Presbyterians—of allowing the unworthy to become church members and participate in the sacraments.[91]

These rules did not alter the restraints on who could be baptized. These had been questioned as early as 1634, when a grandfather in Massachusetts asked Cotton and the lay leaders of the Boston congregation if a church would baptize his grandchildren should the child's parents not be "full" members, that is, not admitted as visible saints. In principle, the answer was no, a rule Richard Mather defended in 1639, when he argued that "such Children whose father and Mother were neither of them Believers, and sanctified, are . . . not faederally holy, but uncleane . . . And therefore we baptize them not." At that moment, Mather was minimizing the significance of "federal" holiness, the name for the covenantal situation of children who were baptized. Nonetheless, a handful of congregations were beginning to baptize children who did not have a parent or grandparent in full communion, possibly in response to complaints about official policy; as a correspondent of Winthrop's pointed out in 1640, he would have emigrated but for the fact that people of "good judgment and conversation" were being excluded, as were "ther young Children" from baptism. Children were the sticking point given this man's assumption that "Christ would not have such forbidden to be brought to him." And, as the Massachusetts General Court acknowledged in May 1646, congregations were becoming open to the possibility of baptizing children born to parents who had been members of churches in England.[92]

By the time the synod met for its final session in 1648, Mather had decided that continuity along family lines was more important than purity. His draft of the platform included a paragraph justifying the baptism of children whose parents were "not found fit for the Lords Supper" but were free of "scandalls," that is, people who were baptized as infants themselves but never became "full" members. To justify his proposition, he argued that, like their parents, children were included in the "federal" covenant of Genesis 17:7 that God made with Abraham and his "seed" to a "thousand generations." Mather's point was simple. This ever-extending covenant that enabled Sarah to bear children was a means of grace, a point defended at length in Peter Bulkeley's *The Gospel Covenant* (1651) and affirmed by Cotton, who argued in a book published after his death that "the same Covenant which God made with the National Church of Israel and their Seed, It is the very same (for substance) . . . which the Lord maketh with any Congregationall Church and our Seed." Debate broke out and, although Mather's proposal was supported by the majority, any final decision was postponed.[93]

Time was on the side of those who wanted to modify the rules of c. 1636. With Baptist tracts trickling into the colonies, other ministers hastened to endorse the significance of Genesis 17:7. Why baptism was so meaningful to these men is suggested by Shepard's remarks on its importance in *The Sincere Convert* (1645). There, he likened God's "esteem" for the "poorest and most feeble believer" to a father's "double care of his children," adding that "God loves you as sons, as a father doth his sons." Baptism became an expression of this love and a means of ensuring that anyone included within the covenant would "be the Lord's forever." When he reflected on the importance of his own son's baptism, he used words that sound as though they were spoken during the ritual: "God gave thee the ordinance of baptism whereby God is become thy God . . . that whenever thou shalt return to God, he will undoubtedly receive thee—and this is a most high and happy privilege." Mather reiterated these expectations in sermons addressed to his congregation in Dorchester, appealing to parents to do everything they could by way of instruction and counsel for their "poor children . . . to save their soules" and imagining the emotions of parents who hear "their children cry out against" anyone who refused to endorse the sacrament. For Mather and probably for some (not all) of his parishioners, having children baptized became a test of parental love. That others agreed with him is indicated by a letter (1647) from Henry Smith, the minister in Wethersfield, Connecticut, who reported that "our thoughts here are that the promise made to the Seed of Confederates, Gen. 17, takes in all Children of Confederating Parents." By the early 1650s, others were openly advocating that the churches repair their "sinful neglect" of those who had not been baptized. In Ipswich, the congregation voted in 1653 to baptize the children of the "adult children" on the condition that these adults "take the [congregation's] covenant solemnly before our Assembly."[94]

With conflict erupting in congregations and towns about which policy to adopt, the Connecticut government arranged for ministers of three colonies to convene in 1657 and debate twenty-one questions, the most important of them being the theological status of "children of confederate [i.e., covenanted] Parents." Signaling in advance its own preference, the government asked "whether federal holiness or covenant interest be not the proper ground of Baptisme," to which the response was a vigorous yes: "Infants . . . grown up to years of discretion" who "own the Covenant they made with the Parents" and were "not scandalous" could have their children baptized, coupled with a more tentative no to the possibility that "all children of whatever years or conditions" should be included and hesitation when it came to "adopted Children and bond servants."[95] The case for a seamless transmission of spiritual benefits via infant baptism and parents' nurture of their children was reiterated at a synod that met in Massachusetts in 1662. But the synod drew the line at access to the Lord's Supper by reaffirming that "full membership" was required of anyone who approached the table. Even so, this policy was regarded by some laypeople and a few ministers as an "innovation" that undermined the purity so precious to the immigrants of circa 1635. In New Haven, an aging John Davenport lashed out against any weakening of that purity, as did Increase Mather until he swung around to the other side.[96]

As congregations began to include more children alongside their parents, the parochial congregationalism of circa 1640—churches limited to visible saints, but every household expected to attend weekly services (a rule reaffirmed in Massachusetts in 1644) and presumably all children catechized—was turning into a family-centered system. Not always easily and certainly not all at once, families and church membership were being aligned. Women were crucial to this process, women with children or looking ahead to motherhood who renewed their baptismal covenants earlier than men, a pattern apparent as early as 1640 and, by the 1660s visible almost everywhere. Taking for granted the spiritual benefits of being included within the covenant of Genesis 17:7, these women wanted their children to remain (or become) "an holy seed."[97]

The 1640s saw the beginnings of another version of outreach or incorporation, the project of converting Native Americans to Christianity. The Massachusetts Bay Company had cited this project as one of its "Reasons" for founding the new colony and alluded to it in the company's seal, which depicted a Native American uttering the Macedonian cry (Acts 16:9), "Come over and save us." Nothing happened along these lines in the 1620s and 1630s. The delays were due in part to an uneasiness about the colonists' safety, an uneasiness the "pilgrims" of Plymouth acquired from travelers' reports describing Native peoples as "cruel, barbarous and most treacherous" and the news that reached them of the Native uprising in Virginia in 1622. As the historian Jenny Hale Pulsipher has pointed out, the policy in Plymouth was to recognize the authority of local sachems or chiefs in various treaties. Neither side in these transactions could afford to be aggressive, the colonists because they were outnumbered and the Native Americans because the tribes closest to Plymouth and the coastal settlements in Massachusetts had suffered huge losses from epidemics caused by European-based diseases. Nor were the Indians armed with muskets, which they eventually acquired despite attempts to control the trade in weapons. Peace was preferable to war, a rule the governments of Massachusetts and Connecticut broke in 1636–37 when armed parties were sent south to beat back the Pequot who controlled much of the coastline in Connecticut and were threatening nearby tribes and towns along the Connecticut River. Skirmishes of various kinds culminated in an assault in 1637 on a Pequot "fort" near present-day New London. Subsequently, another force attacked the Pequot who retreated to the vicinity of New Haven.[98] In the 1640s and beyond, Massachusetts and its neighbors were drawn into a struggle between the Narragansett and the Mohegan whose sachem, the long-lived Uncas, professed to be a friend of the colonists. Intertribal conflict of various kinds persisted in eastern Connecticut, as did tensions between Natives and the colonists who were founding towns such as New London. Rumor often outran reality and peace became fragile, preserved in part because the New England Confederation was not always able to agree on which "Indian plot" was for real.[99]

The evangelism that sprang into life in 1646 was the doing of John Eliot, the minister in Roxbury. Once underway, he nurtured this project for the rest of his long life. The hurdles were many, one of them the task of learning the local version of Algonquin and turning it into a written language and another, persuading would-be converts to adopt a "civilized" way of life: men instead of women laboring in gardens and fields, marriages based on English rules, men cutting off their long braids, and much else. Theologically, Eliot shunned the Catholic practice of baptizing Natives in a wholesale manner. Instead, conversions had to be voluntary—that is, never coerced. In the early going, Eliot hoped that an "affective" model of conversion, that is, the Native Americans' encounter with the colonists, would persuade some of them to become Christians. As he remarked in *Tears of Repentance* (1653), "the Godly Counsels, and Examples" the Indians "have had in all our Christian Families, have been of great use, both to prepare them for the Gospel, and also to further the Lords work in them."[100] To abet the twin goals of converting and civilizing local people and realizing, too, that proximity to the colonists was not in the best interests of the Native Americans, Eliot persuaded the Massachusetts government to establish a series of "praying towns" on land donated to the Indians, land affirmed in 1652 as theirs by "just right."[101] In Natick, the first of these (1651), he aspired to create a Native-led church. To this end, he arranged a public exercise in 1653 at which several men described their conversions to Christianity. To Eliot's dismay, these testimonies failed to persuade the other ministers on hand that his "converts" were ready for such a step. Finally (1659), Eliot arranged for a small group of Native men to become members of his Roxbury church.[102]

Eliot's project acquired fresh support after the Rump Parliament enacted a bill creating the Society for Propagation of the Gospel in New England, or New England Company (June 1649) and authorized it to collect contributions on behalf of the mission, which it did with some success. Eliot began to be paid, and young Native American men were recruited as potential missionaries. A handful enrolled at Harvard, although Caleb Cheeshahteaumuck of Martha's Vineyard, the only member of this group to complete his studies, died of tuberculosis a year after his 1665 graduation. By the close of the 1650s, the New England Company was also financing the translation of the Bible into Algonquin. A second printer and printing press arrived in Cambridge and, by 1661, the New Testament had been printed, followed in 1663 by the Old Testament. Gradually, Eliot and his co-translators added catechisms, a primer, and devotional books such as Lewis Bayley's *The Practice of Piety*. Elsewhere, Christianity was being introduced to Native Americans who lived on Martha's Vineyard, an island near the Massachusetts coast that became the property of Thomas Mayhew in 1643. After he moved there, his son Thomas (1618–57), although not an ordained minister, began to teach the principles of Christianity to some of the Natives. Among the earliest of the converts was Hiacoomes, who persevered in his new faith despite being threatened by local healers ("powwows") and, in the aftermath of a severe epidemic he and his family survived, began to preach. His son Joel was admitted to Harvard and would have graduated in 1665 but died a few months earlier. By 1671, enough Native Christians were on hand to allow a church to be formed, with Hiacoomes ordained as its minister.[103]

One other challenge during these decades was posed by the presence, real or imagined, of people who rejected Reformed orthodoxy. Tested in 1636–37 by local "Antinomians" and tested in a different way by Roger Williams, the colonists' commitment to orthodoxy was buffeted in the 1640s by the emergence of arguments for toleration or liberty of conscience in England. When news reached Independents in England of "persecution" in Massachusetts, some of them wrote to Winthrop, Cotton, and others to protest colonial practice.[104] In point of fact, dissent within New England after 1640 was not widespread because so many of the more radical colonists had moved to Rhode Island or, like the Baptist Hansard Knollys, returned to England.[105] Of those who remained, the most bothersome was probably Samuel Gorton (1592–1677), a self-educated lay preacher and former clothier in London who arrived in New England in 1637 and quickly made himself unwelcome in several places. Disdaining orthodoxy, the instituted means of grace (which he regarded as "but men's inventions") and "magistracy," Gorton provoked the leadership of Massachusetts into arresting him and his followers in 1643 and bringing them to Boston, where they were briefly imprisoned. For a moment it seemed possible that the government would order Gorton executed as a blasphemer. The "greatest number of the deputies [in the General Court] dissenting," a vote to this effect did not pass. After being released, Gorton and some of his admirers went to England, where they publicized their treatment, secured a safe conduct from the Commissioners for Plantations, returned to New England, and settled on the fringes of Rhode Island.[106]

Apart from Gorton, the main threat in the mid-1640s were Baptists, who were, as heresiographers such as Thomas Edwards described them, as dangerous to moral and political order as early sixteenth-century Anabaptists in Germany had been. Swayed by this image at a moment when local Baptists were few and far between, the Massachusetts government enacted a law in 1644 denouncing them as "infectors of persons" with "errors or heresies" and authorizing their banishment. It was not to everyone's liking, for the government received a petition in which its signers argued that "such as differ from us only in judgment, in point of baptism or some other points of lesse consequence," could live "peaceably" in the colony. About the same time (1645), the Plymouth General Court received a petition urging it to "allow and maintain full and free tollerance of religion to all men that would preserve the Civill peace, and submit unto Government," a petition the leaders of the colony squashed.[107]

Aware of these laws but hearing of Baptists in a Massachusetts town, three Baptists in Rhode Island ventured north in 1651. Arrested soon after they arrived, two of the three paid a fine and departed. Obadiah Holmes refused to do so and was publicly whipped, a martyr-like experience he and his fellow Baptists publicized in *Ill-Newes from New-England; Or, a Narrative of New-Englands Persecution* (1652). When news of his treatment reached John Owen and others in England, they immediately wrote to denounce how Holmes had been treated, a step anticipated by Thomas Goodwin and another ten ministers, who criticized the anti-Baptist law of 1644. Simultaneously, John Winthrop's son Stephen reported from England that "here is great Complaint against us for our severitye against Anabaptist it doth discourage any people from coming to us for feare they should be banished if they discent from us in opinion."[108]

Beginning with Cotton's response to Roger Williams, the ministers who argued on behalf of uniformity articulated the benefits of orthodoxy in treatises and letters. At hand was an argument dating from the earliest centuries of Christianity, the assumption that orthodox doctrine was the doorway to salvation, the corollary being that heresy was equivalent to soul murder. Just as conventional was the ministers' insistence that the voice of conscience condemned the heretic or blasphemer; far from being free or at liberty, conscience was how God enforced obedience to divine law. As Cotton insisted in *The Bloody Tenent, Washed, And made white* (1647), anyone who was punished for violating "Fundamentalls" was not "punished for his Conscience, but for sinning against his owne Conscience." Cotton and his colleagues also differentiated opinions held in private from those made public; the latter were dangerous but not the former, which the state would never attempt to punish. And as Cotton complained in a response to Richard Saltonstall, a former colonist, and others, Protestants of various kinds were being tolerated in Massachusetts. Here, he pointed out in 1651,"wee have tolerated in our churches some Anabaptists some Antinomians, and some Seekers, and do so still to this day", adding that "we have here Presbyterian churches as well as congregationall" and denying that "uniformity" was "required." As though he were recycling Oliver Cromwell, he also endorsed "unity in the foundation of religion" but not in "superstructures."[109]

This unity did not include the Quakers. Their "invasion" commenced in 1656 when two Quaker women arrived in Massachusetts after having been in the Caribbean. Imprisoned, then banished, they triggered an extraordinary sense of alarm about a "cursed sect of heretickes . . . who take upon them to be imediatlie sent of God, & infallibly assisted by the Spirit . . . to speake & write blasphemous opinions," language used to justify the first of the laws (May 1657) enacted to protect the colony from people already known for the troubles they had been causing in "our native land." The easiest means of doing so was to punish the captain of any ship who carried Quakers to Boston and, should members of the sect turn up, to clap them into prison and have them "severely whipt." Books, too, were banned, and anyone who converted would be fined and possibly imprisoned. When these rules proved ineffective, the government voted to execute anyone who returned after being banished and told that, if they did so, the penalty was death. Martyrdom (which is how Quakers in England regarded the outcome) was inevitable, and three men and a woman (Mary Dyer, who had gone to Rhode Island with Anne Hutchinson in 1638) were executed in 1660–61.[110]

No one else was executed for blasphemy or heresy in New England, although Quakers paid a heavy price in 1660s England and again in the 1680s England, when some four hundred of them died from the consequences of being imprisoned. There as well, Baptists—famously, John Bunyan—were imprisoned for long periods. Compared with post-1660 deaths and imprisonments in England and how Catholics had been treated in England before 1610, when dozens of priests were being executed, the response to dissent in New England was tempered. So was the response to accusations of witchcraft. The earliest event to approximate a "witch-hunt" happened in Hartford in 1661–62 when an elderly woman confessed to covenanting with the Devil and implicated several others. Previously, the handful of women and, more rarely, men who had been accused of being witches had not implicated others, and some responded by filing suit for defamation. A minister as well-regarded as John Davenport came to the defense of Elizabeth Goodman in New Haven, and in 1654, Thomas Thacher, the minister in Weymouth, Massachusetts, reassured others in the town and colony that a woman noted for "threatening . . . the judgements of God" was not a witch but someone he characterized as "very unlikely . . . to have known confederacy with divills." In all, ten persons, nine of them women, were executed before 1660, three in Massachusetts and the others in Connecticut.[111]

The outcry in England about the colonists' indifference to toleration had a larger significance. In the 1630s, the immigrant generation had regarded itself as being in the forefront of the quest for something akin to a perfect reformation. Nowhere else were "human inventions" so fully eliminated and the "primitive" perfection of biblical example so rigorously acknowledged. By the mid-1640s, however, the beat had moved on. Now it was England where "Sion" seemed likely to emerge, the scenario Thomas Goodwin had envisioned in *A Glimpse of Sions Glory*, reiterated in dozens of fast-day sermons (see chap. 8) and, in the early days of Cromwell's regime, by English Independents. Impossible to ignore in New England, this situation was acknowledged by the Springfield magistrate William Pynchon after news reached him of the Solemn League and Covenant (1643). In a letter to Winthrop, he reported having "bless[ed] god to see that strict and godly covenant . . . It is the high way of god for their deliverance. I hope it is now the day of Antichrists great overthrow at Armageddon." John Davenport made the same point in a letter to his former patroness Mary Vere. Addressing her in 1647, he evoked a God who "shaketh heaven, earth, and seases, and all hearts" as prelude to "settl[ing] the Kingdom of our Lord Jesus Christ, and bowe all nations under his scepter." England, not New England, was where a "light . . . is now discovered" that would transform how the church was governed. The advent of Cromwell was another sign that England (or Britain) was where the struggle against idolatry was coming to a climax. For anyone who remembered John Cotton's prediction that "about the time 1655, there will be . . . a blow given to" the Antichrist, the Protector seemed destined to advance the kingdom. Cotton implied as much in a letter (1651) extolling him as a servant of God who was "working many and great deliverances for his people" and urging him to meditate on Revelation 17:14: "these shall make war with the Lamb, and the Lamb shall overcome them, for he is Lord of lords, and King of kings." John Eliot was just as effusive in *Tears of Repentance* (1653), where he described Cromwell as the person God had "raised and improved . . . to overthrow Antichrist, and to accomplish, in part, the Prophesies and Promises of the Churches Deliverance from . . . Bondage."[112]

Was Massachusetts (or orthodox New England) still favored by divine providence? Winthrop believed that it was, as did the authors of *New Englands First Fruits*, but others were dismayed by the reverse immigration that began in earnest in the 1640s, a process prompted by the economic crisis of 1639–40 and the political situation in revolutionary England. By the end of the 1650s, a third of the ministers who arrived in the 1630s had returned. The young men who earned an MA at Harvard College left as well, lured to England and Ireland by the promise of well-paid positions as clergy.[113] To those who remained, this exodus was wrenching. "Why do so many come away thence" was a question people in England itself were beginning to ask as early as 1642 or 1643, a question the authors of *New Englands First Fruits* incorporated into a description of Harvard College and a newly formed alliance with a few Native American communities. A few years later, the same question troubled Pynchon, who wrote to Winthrop in 1646 that "the pillars of the land seeme to tremble." Its significance was underscored a year later when Samuel Symonds, a magistrate in Salem, reported that "the irregular departure of some causeth a deeper search of heart wherefore god hath brought his elect here."[114]

The dismay was accompanied by a familiar lament: decline or "declension" was occurring. Anxieties about decline figured in John Robinson's farewell to the people departing on the *Mayflower* and in Winthrop's "Charitie Discourse" of 1630. Like Robinson before him, Winthrop wanted to forestall the self-interest that seemed certin to reemerge. Hence the closing passage in which he evoked the image of the covenanted colony as a "city upon a hill" as reason for guarding against decline, a possibility he emphasized by citing Old Testament jeremiads. All too soon, the implicit covenant of 1630 was giving way to the self-interest he discerned in the exodus of circa 1635–36 of people to Connecticut. William Bradford felt the same way when families in quest of "a great deal of ground [land]" abandoned Plymouth at the beginning of the 1630s and set up towns along the coast. From his perspective, the moral cost of doing so were high, what with "Christian and comfortable fellowship" giving way to "many divisions."[115]

Fast days had already appeared in the ritual calendar of the colonists, although sometimes misfiring, as happened with John Wheelwright's fiery sermon of January 1637 (see chap. 7). When inflation struck the colony two years later, congregations in Massachusetts were summoned in April 1639 to repent "oppression, atheism, excess, superfluity, idleness," and other "troubles." The economic crisis prompted Thomas Hooker to propose that congregations in Massachusetts "make a privy search what have been the courses and sinful carriages," citing "pride and idleness, excess in apparel, building, diet . . . toleration and connivance at extortion and oppression."[116] By the mid-1640s, the government was wrestling with a surge in "unlawful tipling & excesse of drunkenness" linked, in part, to unlicensed selling of "spirits" at a moment when church discipline was faltering. More fast days followed, as did more laments mandated by a ritual process every British Protestant would have recognized. Gradually, the blame for decline was assigned to the "rising generation," a narrative that reached something of a climax in the itemizing of declension in *The Necessity of Reformation* (1679). Within the chronological framework of this book, the rhetorical climax may have been two poems by Michael Wigglesworth (1631–1705), the first of these an evocation of Christ's coming in judgment, *The Day of Doom* (1662), and another of the same date, "God's Controversy with new-England, Written in the time of the great drought." Among his complaints was that "hypocrites" were being admitted to the Lord's Supper, an accusation as old as the Puritan movement that the debate over baptismal policy was revitalizing.[117]

When Charles II returned to the throne in 1660, many of the colonists responded to his presence and, in the mid-1660s, to the arrival of commissioners bearing orders of various kinds, by reaffirming the special significance of their homeland. In petitions to the General Court urging it to remain firmly behind the systems put in place in the 1630s and 1640s, laymen gathered together in town after town to endorse the practice of "liberty." From the outset of colonization, liberty had signified being able to worship in the right manner. It meant this still in the 1660s. Yet the ninety-one men in Hadley, Massachusetts, who signed that town's petition wanted liberty of a more expansive kind. As expressed in the petition, it included "the right from God and man to chuse our own governors, make and live under our own laws." In their eyes, therefore, liberty was at once religious, political, and social. Citing a familiar distinction between slavery and freedom that was a commonplace in Continental humanism, they described themselves as "freemen and not slaves," the difference being that freemen possessed "liberties and privileges." To this assertion they added another that looked back to the Protestation of 1641 and the National Covenant of 1638: "Our privileges herein as Christians in regard of the kingdom, name, glory of our God, is far more precious than our lives."[118]

Religion and politics coalesced anew in the Hadley petition, this time on behalf of an identity rooted in the Puritan past but also in three decades of colonial experience with self-governance in towns, congregations, and colonies. Going forward, the language of the petition would become a legacy to future generations as significant as the covenant of Genesis 17:7 and, if conflict between colony and empire intensified, potentially akin to the Scottish National Covenant of 1638 in its importance.[119]

Legacies

PURITANISM AS A MOVEMENT within the Church of England came to an end in 1662, when some 1,600 ministers who refused to conform were "ejected" and, thereafter, became known as Dissenters (or Dissent). Anyone who accepted the provisions of the Act of Uniformity of May 1662 had to prove that a bishop had ordained him or accept ordination anew. Conformity also required scrupulous adherence to the *Book of Common Prayer*. Understandably, some of the ejected ministers found their way back into the state church or, because of local circumstances, were able to carry on their ministry for a while.[1] After James II fled to France and William III became monarch, plans for reuniting English Protestants were discussed but never enacted. Dissenters remained on the outside for another century and a half—unable to attend the two universities, denied any role in a nascent system of public education, and required to pay taxes to support the state church. In the aftermath of the Restoration, anti-puritanism raged anew, reinforced by the execution of Charles I and the tyranny of Cromwell. In Peter Heylyn's version, he reiterated the argument (1658) that Calvinism was the source of "disobedience and rebellion" and itemized the dreadful mistakes of "Presbyterians" in another book (1670).

The situation in Scotland is less easily summarized. There, episcopacy was restored and the royal supremacy reaffirmed, but no English-style prayer book was reimposed. The Scots who thought of themselves as Presbyterians continued to practice their tradition, although they were harshly criticized for compromising with government of Charles II by countrymen who clung to the covenants of 1638 and 1643. On all sides, the personal tragedies were many. Even after William III agreed to replace episcopal governance with Presbyterian, schisms continued to fracture the kirk in the eighteenth and nineteenth centuries.

Despite the burdens placed on Dissent, it continued to play a role in English society and culture as, in certain ways, did Presbyterianism in Scotland.

Specifying these legacies can be as challenging as specifying the relationship between Calvinism and the practical divinity or the role of the Puritan movement in the run-up to civil war. Most nineteenth- and twentieth-century propositions about the movement's long-term consequences seem overstated. Did seventeenth-century Puritans create a new model of citizen as "radical saint"? Michael Walzer's argument to this effect has been widely discounted, as have Robert Merton's theorizing about the relationship between Puritanism and the rise of modern science and Max Weber's about Puritanism and the work ethic.[2] Were Puritans instrumental in the "rise" of the House of Commons at the expense of the monarchy and the House of Lords? No, according to some historians; yes, according to others.[3] For sure, some seventeenth-century Puritans contributed to arguments in behalf of toleration or liberty of conscience—famously, Roger Williams and John Milton. Yet Williams's way of doing so was peculiar and Milton was a very un-Puritan Puritan. The praising of moral and intellectual progress that animates most histories of toleration excludes (except by way of complaint) the far more numerous Puritans who insisted that blasphemy violated divine law and should be punished by the civil state (see chaps. 8 and 9). Historians of Dissent or nonconformity are on firmer ground in assigning it an important role in the dismantling of privileges tied to membership in the Church of England, a role it played in conjunction with the Whig Party and subsequently with the Liberal Party.[4] As noted in the introduction, Protestant denominations that began to search for founders prompted nineteenth-century Congregationalists to cite Robert Browne and John Robinson and Baptists, Thomas Helwys and John Smythe. Yet, as historians have pointed out, there was no straight line between them and those denominations.[5]

Within the contours of this epilogue, I want to narrow this search for legacies to three aspects of the Puritan movement: its embrace of a reformation of manners, its commitment to Reformed orthodoxy, and its place in the workings of historical "memory," or how past and present are connected.[6] For each, the story is different—long-lasting hopes for moral improvement, on the one hand, but near collapse when it came to doctrine and remarkable examples of mythmaking in the case of memory. By the mid-nineteenth century, British writers such as Walter Scott and Thomas Carlyle had fashioned a politics of memory that the historian Samuel R. Gardiner would revise in his studies of early Stuart politics. In New England, a similar politics unfolded in the aftermath of a schism between Congregationalists and Unitarians and efforts to establish the Puritans as founders of democratic nationalism. Nathaniel Hawthorne's *The Scarlet Letter* (1850) was part of this process, as were orations by Daniel Webster and local histories by scores of antiquarians. My brief resume of this politics concludes with the paradoxical understanding of Puritanism fashioned by the Harvard literary scholar Perry Miller (d. 1963).[7]

Moral Reform

Moral reform as imperative for a nation or people ever on the verge of decline was possibly the most significant legacy of the Puritan movement. The seeds of this possibility had already been planted before 1600 in Scottish and English fast-day sermons and their response to Psalm 78, among other biblical texts. By the early nineteenth century, if not much earlier, fast days were losing their authority. Well before this happened, other aspects of a Puritan-style reformation of manners were being refreshed. A backward glance may be helpful. Within the Puritan movement itself, Lucy Hutchinson (1620–81) is an intriguing witness to Puritanism as a vehicle of self-discipline. In the aftermath of the restoration of Charles II and the death of her husband, a committed Puritan who died in 1663 from the effects of being imprisoned by the new government, she described his character and politics in *Memoirs of the Life of Colonel Hutchinson*. The master word of the *Memoirs* was "puritan." Before the 1640s, this had been a label she and her husband rarely acknowledged. Yet the experience of war and the culture wars associated with that conflict prompted her to embrace it as a name for her husband's ethics. As though Hutchinson were recycling Job Throckmorton's speech in the Parliament of 1586 or Arthur Dent's *Plain Mans Path-way to Heaven* (see chap. 5), she described men of his kind as "zealous for God's glory or worship" and unable to "endure blasphemous oaths, ribald conversation, profane scoffs, Sabbath breaking, derision of the word of God, and the like—whoever could endure a sermon, modest habit or conversation, or anything good—all these were Puritans."[8]

These words were written in the 1670s. Near the end of the same century, anxiety about decline in England spurred the founding of "societies for the reformation of manners," a response in part to the perceived moral excesses of the Restoration. Voluntary and led by laypeople, societies of this kind would become a permanent fixture of moral and social reform on both sides of the Atlantic. In the century that followed, corruption during the administration of Robert Walpole (1721–42) in England was among the contexts for other campaigns in behalf of private and public virtue, campaigns in which the Methodist movement began to play a significant role. Subsequently, the anti-Christian "Jacobinism" associated with the French Revolution prompted spasms of anxiety that Methodists (by now an independent denomination) and "Federalists" in the United States used to mobilize their adherents.[9]

To contemporaries, Puritanism was being reborn in the form of movements to limit the consumption of alcohol, protect the Sunday Sabbath, strengthen the home as a site of moral values, and ensure that prudery prevailed in speech and print.[10] Seen through the eyes of Lyman Beecher (1775–1863), a Yale-educated minister who became the town minister in Litchfield, Connecticut, in 1812 and subsequently brought his agenda to Boston and Cincinnati, the purpose of these groups was to strengthen a "standing order" imperiled by demands that church and state become entirely separate. In response, Beecher looked around for moral causes that would bypass the state but indirectly strengthen the moral authority of a Federalist-Congregationalist alliance. Temperance was one such cause, and the Sunday Sabbath was another. By the 1830s, the repertory of the moralists included a "cult of domesticity" fashioned in part by Beecher's oldest daughter Catharine, who argued that a woman-centered home would restore moral order to the amoral worlds of business and politics.[11]

With remarkable speed, moralizers on both sides of the Atlantic continued to expand this agenda to include Sunday schools for children who might not otherwise be receiving moral instruction, missionary societies to carry the Gospel to ill-served places at home and abroad, tract societies printing "good" tracts in vast quantities, most of them distributed freely, and Bible societies doing the same for that book. Eliminating the slave trade, and eventually slavery itself, became another objective of evangelical Anglicans in Britain and assorted groups in America, though this cause alienated moralizers such as Beecher, who grasped how divisive it would become. Beyond mid-century, several of these campaigns became associated with the Republican Party in the United States and the Liberal Party in England. Near the turn of the century, anxieties about unlicensed sex and licentiousness in the printed word spurred the creation of societies for the prevention of vice—famously in the United States, the New York Society for the Suppression of Vice, founded in 1873 by Anthony Comstock (1844–1915), a former postman who persuaded the United States Congress to adopt a law making it illegal for the post office to transmit "lewd" materials. The ultimate victory on the part of American moralists was adding the Eighteenth Amendment, which prohibited the sale of alcohol, to the Constitution (January 1919).

Advocacy in behalf of moral and social reform is still with us, as is Protestant-based advocacy—dating from the early twentieth century—in behalf of social justice and international peace. Yet the moral universe that sustained "blue laws" in New England, chastity before marriage, and disinterested benevolence has all but disappeared, done in by the hostile reaction to the Eighteenth Amendment, late twentieth-century feminism, and countercultural movements dating from the 1960s, among other circumstances. The moral society that Lyman Beecher and the Methodists aspired to impose on Americans is essentially invisible in many parts of the United States. To cite a local example, in my formerly "dry" Massachusetts town, alcohol can be purchased every day of the week, and Sundays are when people (Christians and otherwise) spend much of the day shopping or watching professional sports.[12]

Doctrine

What happened to doctrine is more complex but also similar. One by one, the canons of Dordt and the arguments enshrined in the Westminster Confession were set aside or simply abandoned.[13] Creeds ceased to matter. In their place, piety, sentiment, or sympathy reigned, as did free agency and reason. Rearguard battles on behalf of "Calvinism" flared up in Scottish, English, and American Presbyterian circles on both sides of the Atlantic, but in 1865 a national conference of American Congregationalists was unwilling to endorse the Confession and, in 1880, the denomination's most stringently orthodox seminary (Andover) reclassified its understanding of Reformed theology as "progressive orthodoxy." Behind this phrase lay a very different understanding of past and present than what was implied in the Confession. Biblical truth or divine law were not fixed or revealed in some timeless manner, for the Andover "liberals" had reached the point of associating truth and religion itself with development over time, a description that required the seminary to practice an ethics of free inquiry.[14]

Well before this worldview became authoritative, certain parts of Reformed doctrine were being questioned. Early in the eighteenth century, Socinianism or possibly the alternative known as Arianism was taken up by some English Presbyterians.[15] Simultaneously, the workings of divine providence were becoming implausible once it was recognized that certain "wonders" were regulated by fixed natural laws. Comets were a case in point, after the English astronomer Edmond Halley realized that the comet that bears his name reappeared in a cycle that never varied. Thereafter, earthquakes, lightning, and much else disappeared from any reckoning of "divine judgments." By this time, too, scholars of the Old Testament were acknowledging that Moses may not have written the books attributed to him. In *The Reasonableness of Christianity* (1695), John Locke retained a place for the miracles performed by Jesus but extolled "reason" as superior to "revelation" in most respects and reimagined Jesus as a teacher of ethics. The most devastating blow may have been the doubts that accumulated around the doctrine of original sin. No moralist ignored the selfish aspects of human nature, but these seemed unrelated to an episode in the Garden of Eden. Instead, with theologians agreeing that humankind was equipped with free will, sin became something that people committed voluntarily. As Nathaniel William Taylor, a theologian at Yale Divinity School, pointed out, "sin is in the sinning."[16]

In mid-nineteenth-century poetry and fiction, doctrine of any kind was giving way to what would come to be characterized as sentimentalism. In the New England poet Henry Wadsworth Longfellow's "The Reaper and the Flowers" (1839), an angry, judgmental God was replaced by a sorrowing Jesus who consoles the mother of a child who has died by comparing her to a flower he will preserve in heaven. Implicitly, the poem denies the doctrines of election and original sin: children are innocent and will not be punished by an angry, unfeeling God. Harriet Beecher Stowe incorporated the same Jesus into *Uncle Tom's Cabin* (1851)—again, a Jesus deeply sympathetic to mothers (slave or free) separated from their children and who ensures that the death of the young Eva (Evangeline, who was herself a stand-in for Jesus) is crisis-free.[17]

It may seem paradoxical that, amid these currents, eighteenth- and nineteenth-century Britain and the United States were experiencing wave after wave of evangelical fervor. Methodists were responsible for much of this fervor in England and the United States, where they were joined by Baptists, Presbyterians, and some Congregationalists. But as John Wesley himself had argued, doctrine was less important than piety or experience, which did not depend on learnedness or creeds. He made this point indirectly by his practice of abridging classic texts of the Reformed/evangelical tradition to use in the library he created for the itinerant preachers who drove the progress of Methodism— when it came to texts by Jonathan Edwards, chopping out the Calvinist bits. Piety or, as is usually said these days, spirituality continues to flourish, although ever more eclectic in its sources.[18]

Doctrine may recede, but life rules persist. Words such as duty or "watchfulness" retained their significance long after the practical divinity and its doctrinal skeleton had evaporated. A case in point is the mid-eighteenth-century English clothier-turned-Unitarian who continued to practice watchfulness after giving up on orthodoxy. Another is the status of Bunyan's *Pilgrim's Progress*, the steadiest of the steady sellers originating in the seventeenth century. In Louisa May Alcott's *Little Women* (1868–69), a novel set in Massachusetts in the early stages of the American Civil War, the four young sisters of the title regard *Pilgrim's Progress* as an admonition to sacrifice worldly (read, fashionable or girlish) desires for the good of family, father (at war), and nation. No traces remain of the burden of sin borne by Bunyan's pilgrim or of the imperative of conversion. At about the same moment, the Harvard-educated Unitarian layman Charles Russell Lowell (d. 1864) responded to the outbreak of civil war in 1861 by committing himself to military service that ended with his death in action, moved to do so by "ambition of the loftiest and strongest kind" that encompassed the ending of slavery. A less intense version of this ethos shaped my behavior as a child and adolescent and, for all I know, may flavor it still. But for many others, it has been replaced by what Lowell (and, long before him, John Winthrop and Thomas Shepard) would have described as self-interest.[19]

Memory

In the early nineteenth century, no one in Britain or the United States remembered the Puritans described in this book. Too much time had passed, and too little was available by way of documents.[20] Nonetheless, antiquarians, orators, and writers of various kinds were busily describing Puritans and Puritanism in ways that come under the heading of mythmaking or "inventions." Like all other aspects of the past, Puritanism lent itself to being reimagined in response to post-Puritan cultural, political, and religious circumstances.

The Scottish side of this story deserves more attention than I can give it, for the kirk continued to replay some of the issues that had troubled it before 1660. Lay patronage, and therefore a role for lay owners of church property to affect church policy, was one of these. Abolished in 1649, it returned after 1660, though protested by the more evangelical wing of the kirk, which finally broke free from the practice by forming the Free Church of Scotland in 1843. Doctrine, too, was hotly contested in the eighteenth and nineteenth centuries, a politics provoked by liberalizing moderates who created the Scottish Enlightenment. Every faction had its hero or martyrs, most especially the Covenanters, who, between 1660 and 1689, had resisted the regimes of Charles II and James II.[21]

Walter Scott (1771–1832), who invented the historical romance, was an Anglican and Tory who regarded the more extreme Presbyterians as "fanatics." Yet as a novelist he grasped the benefits of including sympathetic figures from both sides of that conflict and those of the Middle Ages he also was describing: Saxon and Norman in *Ivanhoe*, Cavalier and Covenanter in *Old Mortality* (1816). The central figure in the latter novel was a young man of good birth who sides with the Covenanters but repudiates the violence they justified in the name of God and, in the end, marries the daughter of a Royalist. As in *Ivanhoe* and other novels, the underlying plot is one of reconciliation, a theme that suited Scott's nationalism but had little to do with the seventeenth century.[22] Almost as important as Scott's novels was the step he took in 1823 to found the Bannatyne Club, which began to print or reprint Puritan or Reformation-related texts along with others from medieval history. The dozens of books sponsored by the club included David Laing's *The Letters and Journals of Robert Baillie* (3 vols., 1841–42), to this day an indispensable source for understanding the 1640s. Laing would become Scotland's foremost editor-antiquarian, whose achievements included a six-volume edition of the works of John Knox.

Clubs or societies of the same kind sprang up in England, the most important of them for sixteenth-century Puritan history the Parker Society (1841–53) founded by clergy and antiquarians to print books and manuscripts demonstrating the firmly Protestant nature of the English Reformation against the claims of Anglo-Catholics. Before 1800, a trickle of nonconformists had returned to a seventeenth century that "haunted" them because of their ancestors' associations with civil war, regicide, and outbursts of "enthusiasm."[23] The tide began to turn when a native Scot, Thomas Carlyle (1795–1881) worked his magic as a writer on Oliver Cromwell. Reared within the boundaries of Scottish Calvinism with ministry as his likely vocation, Carlyle experienced a crisis of faith that undid his commitment to orthodoxy. Thereafter, he fashioned himself into a "seer," an identity he owed in part to the German Romantics who rescued him from the abyss of uncertainty. The seer-like Caryle detested the culture of self-interest emerging around him as the British economy became increasingly commercial and British culture succumbed to the shallow creeds of a nascent bourgeoisie. He vented his dismay in *Past and Present* (1840) via a late medieval monk he fashioned into an exemplary alternative. Looking around him for someone else to appropriate as a foil, he came upon Oliver Cromwell, who had few admirers in early nineteenth-century Britain. The outcome was a three-volume edition of his letters and speeches interspersed with commentary, a genuine example of scholarship but also an assault on the "sham" civilization without real heroes that Carlyle detested. In his hands, Cromwell and indirectly, Puritanism, became "the last of all our Heroisms" because it acknowledged "the Eternal Sacredness" of the "Universe," a sublimity replaced by "Unbelief and our Cant of Belief," just as heroism itself had given way to "Stupidity" and "Dulness." Yet as Carlyle himself acknowledged, his mythmaking did not overcome the gulf between the seventeenth century and his own times. In his words, the passage of time had made the Puritan movement "unintelligible": "we understand not even in imagination . . . what it ever could have meant."[24]

To another historian, the Puritan past was enduringly present. Samuel Rawson Gardiner labored for nearly fifty years on a history of England from 1603 to 1660, a project still admired for his care in using the documentary record. Gardiner's family adhered to an unusual sect-like branch of English Protestantism known as the Catholic Apostolic Church, but Gardiner himself returned to the Church of England in part because the dogmatic aspects of his family's faith were getting in his way as a historian and "liberal nationalist" who, in narrating the run-up to civil war in the 1640s, wanted to transcend Whig and Tory interpretations. The key to doing so was to be impartial or balanced, for he aspired to validate the thesis that the England of his own day "sprang from a union between the Puritanism and the Churchmanship of the seventeenth century." Gardiner combined this thesis with another, that Puritanism had played an important role in the rise of Parliament as "the true representative of a united nation."[25] Here was proof that the movement mattered in the making of modern England, a story historians of Tudor-Stuart England on both sides of the Atlantic endorsed or amplified for most of the twentieth century. Eventually, others revisited the workings of the early Stuart parliaments and staged a counterattack on what they characterized as a "Whig" narrative of unbroken progress. Where that argument rests today is somewhere in the middle. But it seems unlikely that Gardiner's optimism about the relationship between past and present will be renewed.[26]

On the American side, two situations influenced how the Puritan past was being imagined or represented. The first was political and cultural, the challenge of defining the essence of "American." When the United States came into being in 1789 (or 1776), it was a patchwork of regions, each with its own identity. By the 1830s, these regional identities were giving way to "romantic nationalism" that relied on words such as "union" and symbolic figures such as George Washington. For the most part, the political leaders of New England were bystanders to this process, for their federalism had been eclipsed by the "republicanism" of Thomas Jefferson and his southern successors in the presidency. It did not help that during the War of 1812, hard-core federalists met in Hartford, Connecticut in December 1813 to discuss the possibility of withdrawing from the federal union.

Could some version of the Puritan past restore New England's place at the table? When Daniel Webster (1782–1852), a senator from Massachusetts, spoke in Plymouth at the two-hundredth anniversary of the Pilgrims' landing (December 1820), he attempted to transform this event into a founding moment of American "liberty" and unfettered commerce. Other gifts from the Pilgrims or Puritans (a distinction Webster ignored) to the nation-in-the-making were an emphasis on public schools and a strong legal system, both of which he regarded as ballast for a ship of state struggling to survive the storms of an untested democracy. Around him, others in New England were also imagining the Pilgrims and especially the "Mayflower Compact" (see chap. 6) as crucial sources of a democratic America. For these writers and antiquarians, the genealogy of a new, progressive America began not with Jamestown in 1607 but with the arrival of the Pilgrims. Once this myth was launched, it became impervious to criticism.[27] The same could be said of another example of nineteenth-century mythmaking in the service of democratic nationalism, the idealizing of Thomas Hooker as author of the "Fundamental Orders" on which the Connecticut towns based their government. When the outlines of an "election sermon" Hooker had given in 1637 emerged, it added fuel to this fire, for Hooker seemed to be endorsing the sovereignty of the people. Not until the 1930s was this myth questioned and not until quite recently has it been thoroughly discounted; Hooker was not the author of the Fundamental Orders and was never an uncritical advocate of "the people."[28]

The real struggle among those who descended from the Puritans was occurring between Congregationalists and Unitarians after the schism that drove them apart in the 1820s. Theirs was a painful divorce, with each side accusing the other of arrogance and duplicity. A crucial moment for Congregationalists to reassert their theological identity came in June 1865, when the denomination held its first ever national "Council" in Boston. (By then, the denomination had spread to the Upper Midwest and California.) When a committee charged with defining the faith of the denomination submitted a statement that endorsed the Westminster Confession and the Savoy Declaration (see chap. 9), the outcry against anything associated with "Calvinism" forced the council to fall back on a hastily drafted "Declaration" that nodded in the direction of "confessions and platforms" of the seventeenth century but did not describe them as binding. Another telling aspect of the declaration was its emphasis on ethical or social "principles" of the most general kind: "to elevate society . . . to civilize humanity, to purify law . . . and to assert and defend liberty." In the words of the ablest of the denomination's historians then or since, Williston Walker, the declaration was deliberately constructed to satisfy anyone who sided with an undefined Calvinism and the "many, who without being exclusively or even generally Arminian in their sentiments deprecated any party shibboleth." Some three decades later, the German-trained Walker published a scrupulously edited collection of documents, *The Creeds and Platforms of Congregationalism* (1893), that remains authoritative. Himself a liberal Protestant, he attributed the emergence of Congregationalism to the Protestant Reformation—not, however, a reformation centered on free grace and divine law but one undertaking a quest for greater liberty. The significance of his own denomination was the fact that "its creeds are not exclusively binding," a practice in keeping with "the fundamental religious thought" of Luther and his fellow reformers, their "rejection of all authority save that of the Word of God."[29] Left unsaid was the irrelevance of the themes or principles that animated the ancestors of the denomination, chief among them the absolute authority of divine law, a church composed of the worthy few, and a magistracy-ministry alliance on behalf of discipline and obedience.

For the founders of Unitarianism, as for many nineteenth-century Congregationalists, the Puritan past was a burden. The Calvinism of the colonists had been a terrible mistake because the doctrine of predestination eliminated any incentive for moral responsibility, an argument an early leader among the Unitarians, William Ellery Channing, laid out in "The Moral Argument against Calvinism" (1825). There, he argued that anyone who adhered to classic Calvinism was subjecting him- or herself to a despotic God who denied humans any free agency and therefore any capacity to do good in the world. In Channing's words, under the impress of Calvinism, "men's minds and consciences are subdued by terror, so that they dare not confess, even to themselves, the shrinking, which they feel from the unworthy views which this system gives of God." When a Salem-based antiquarian discovered that its Congregational-turned-Unitarian church had required nothing by way of creed in its initial covenant, he took this to validate the denomination's anti-creedal sentiments. (As Williston Walker pointed out, the records told a different story.)[30] Picking through the rubble of the past, Unitarians elevated the "pilgrims" of Plymouth to a place of honor. They were the exception, a people more accustomed to being persecuted than to persecuting others. Ignoring John Robinson's intervention on behalf of Dordtian orthodoxy in the early seventeenth-century crisis provoked by Dutch-style Arminianism, the ex-Congregational-turned-Unitarian church in Plymouth installed a stained-glass portrait of him that included a quotation from a sermon he delivered as the first group of colonists were about to depart:

"I am verily persuaded the Lord hath more truth yet to break forth out of His Holy Word." Unitarianism was most certainly *not* a truth the anti-Arminian Robinson was anticipating, but mythmaking overrode any pretense of theological accuracy.

The surest route to self-vindication was to represent the Puritans as persecutors of well-meaning people. Witches were a case in point. Charles Upham, a minister-antiquarian with a special interest in the Salem witch hunt of 1692, realized from close study of town records that bitter conflict over boundaries and baptismal policy had fueled this epidemic of suspicion and distorted testimony. When push came to shove, Upham blamed the witch hunt on a Satan-obsessed Cotton Mather. Yet again, darkness rather than light radiated from the ranks of the orthodox.[31] A similar anti-puritanism permeated the fiction of the mid-nineteenth-century Unitarian novelist and story writer Nathaniel Hawthorne (1804–64). In the most famous of his novels, *The Scarlet Letter* (1850), the opening pages depict a crowd of grim-faced women wearing "somber" clothes who await the appearance of Hester Prynne and the scarlet letter she bears as punishment for having a child out of wedlock. (Later, we learn that the father was a leading minister in the community.) Hawthorne's narrative juxtaposes the self-sacrificing, sympathetic, heart-centered Prynne with the hard-hearted demeanor of everyone else. According to his narrative, orthodoxy trapped people in the hypocrisy of punishing others' sins but leaving them unable to recognize their own or to forgive. Prynne and her daughter are the innocents, the daughter bathed in light and Hester becoming a lay saint.[32]

That Unitarians could do better than this is suggested by George E. Ellis's *The Puritan Age and Rule in the Colony of the Massachusetts Bay, 1629–1685* (1888). A Unitarian minister and well-read antiquarian, Ellis took from Upham the argument that the Salem witch hunt was actually insignificant. He also characterized Roger Williams as too extreme and therefore justifiably expelled from the colony. Nor did he buy the argument that the colonists had betrayed their demands for liberty of conscience by punishing others; unusually for his time and even for ours, he recognized that this phrase meant something different to them than it did to nineteenth-century liberals. Aware of how harshly the colonists were being condemned for not voicing other "progressive" sentiments of the late nineteenth century, he pointed out that "very little satisfaction or justice" emerges from "visiting our censure or contempt on those who in the light—or the darkness—of their own times were beclouded with delusions and falsehoods."[33]

When it came to theology, however, he found nothing to respect or celebrate. The Calvinism of the colonists was not worth trying to explicate. On this point, he had an ally in Charles Francis Adams Jr., who, as a sideline from business and political affairs, wrote about seventeenth-century New England. In his major book, *Three Episodes of Massachusetts History* (1892), Adams revisited the Antinomian controversy, which he regarded as a perfect example of Puritan-style persecution of dissent. In retrospect, his most telling comment was an aside about Puritan theology as it was being disputed in 1636–37: "Not only were the points in dispute obscure, but the discussion was carried on in a jargon which has become unintelligible; and, from a theological point of view, it is now devoid of interest. At most, it can excite only a faint curiosity as one more example of . . . childish excitement over trifles."[34]

Adams's strong words about the irrelevance of the Puritan past can be likened to a sponge someone uses to erase inappropriate words or an error in arithmetic from a blackboard. The anti-puritanism he shared with so many others in nineteenth-century New England amalgamated the horrors of Calvinism with the horrors of persecution. Notwithstanding dozens of orations that saluted the Pilgrims and the Mayflower Compact, an iconoclastic Adams found nothing of value in his ancestors' culture, a perspective powerfully reinforced in the early decades of the twentieth century by cultural critics who applied the term "Puritan" to the hyper-Victorianism they detested.[35]

To a young scholar coming of age in the 1930s, however, Puritanism had played a crucial role in the origins of American culture—as it turned out, an oddly paradoxical role. Perry Miller (1905–63) was acutely original in small and large ways. Arriving at Harvard in 1932 and eventually appointed to a chair in American literature in the Department of English, he began his scholarly career with an essay repudiating the portrait of Thomas Hooker as democratically inclined and, in *Orthodoxy in Massachusetts, 1630–1650* (1934), challenged the genealogy of modern Congregationalism endorsed by Walker and many others. Miller's greatest feat was to restore intellectual complexity to the colonists' version of Reformed theology, a complexity he detailed in his masterpiece, *The New England Mind: The Seventeenth Century* (1939). Here, he argued that the colonists worked their way around a "rigid" and "arbitrary" Calvinism by fashioning a "federal" or "covenant" theology, although continuing to insist that, on their own terms, they were Calvinists. In an essay published in 1943, he revisited the Antinomian controversy, which Charles Francis Adams had condemned as so much "jargon." In a tour-de-force analysis, Miller insisted that serious topics were in play on which John Cotton disagreed with his colleagues, most especially the role of "preparation for salvation" that Hooker, Thomas Shepard, and others took for granted. Overnight, the controversy sprang to life as a turning point in the intellectual history of early America.

As he worked his way forward and familiarized himself with an almost untouched archive of sermons, treatises, and other documents, Miller began to paint the decades after 1640 as a story of betrayal. Instead of upholding Cotton-style Calvinism, the colonial clergy allowed "preparation for salvation" to evolve into something closer to Arminian-flavored pietism. "Formal creeds" remained authoritative into the early eighteenth century, as did attempts to balance divine sovereignty and free grace with human endeavor. Yet creeds were being eclipsed by assertions of human agency and an emphasis on reason as a natural faculty, trends Miller regarded as culminating in the pathetic "do-good" moralism of John Cotton's step-grandson Cotton Mather (1665–1728), who turned the "engines of piety" into "engines of conformity," an assertion Miller justified by leaping ahead to the early twentieth century. What else was Mather's *Essays to Do Good* (1710) but a "prophecy of Protestant, small-town, Middle Western culture of the nineteenth century" that would culminate in the culture of "Main Street"?[36]

A Midwesterner himself, Miller was evoking that region's most famous novelist, the Nobel Prize–winning Sinclair Lewis and his scathing portrait of middle-class conformity in *Main Street* (1920). The iconoclastic Miller of circa 1935, who was so excited to recapture the intellectual and spiritual complexities of Puritanism, had evolved by 1950 into a cultural critic who, like Carlyle before him, saw nothing but sterility in his own times save for a handful of prophets (he himself being one) who denounced the betrayal of a nation's great promise. The ultimate irony was how this shift in persona affected the significance of American-style Puritanism. Instead of being a resource for modern Americans, it was inherently flawed.

Is there really no means of appropriating the Puritan movement for our own times? Within Anglo-American evangelicalism, a handful of scholars, most significantly the Anglican James I. Packer and those influenced by him, have rediscovered the richness of Puritan spirituality. Yet in the main, the "evangelical" historians who narrate the religious history of the United States begin with the awakenings of the mid-eighteenth century. For them, Puritanism is too magisterial and disciplining and therefore not really the ancestor of a culture that extols human agency and a loving God. Even Jonathan Edwards becomes suspect.[37]

Meanwhile, anti-puritanism remains alive and well, refreshed in present-day America by a sympathy for everyone in the past who was denied full freedom and cultural autonomy—in particular, Native Americans and the Africans brought to this country as slaves, but also dissidents of various kinds, especially women like Anne Hutchinson. Statues of Hutchinson and Mary Dyer adorn the grounds of the Massachusetts State House in Boston. Nowhere, except in the names of streets, a single town, and an undergraduate dormitory at Harvard, is John Winthrop acknowledged. Of Shepard, the visible traces are far fewer and, as I write, the word "puritan" has been eliminated from the official "hymn" of Harvard University. The moral must surely be that misrepresentations outweigh what we have learned from two or three generations of richly informed scholarship about the intellectual, political, ethical, and social aspects of the Puritan movement—scholarship that, in some of its branches, has underscored the vitality of Puritan-style politics and social ethics at a moment in our national history when democracy is failing and a social ethics of "community" is being jeopardized.

ACKNOWLEDGMENTS

THE ASSISTANCE FROM OTHERS that enabled me to write this book includes, first and foremost, a senior fellowship at the Huntington Library in San Marino, California. Thanks to Steve Hindle, the Director of Research, I spent nine months rummaging through the Huntington's inexhaustible collection of early modern printed books. I have depended as well on the Andover-Harvard Library of Harvard Divinity School, a collection admirably comprehensive in its holdings of modern scholarship and blessed with exceptionally helpful reference librarians. I thank Nell Carlson for aiding my access to rare books, Michelle Gautier for promptness in arranging interlibrary loans, and Gloria Korsman for answering a wide range of queries.

The Huntington fellows' weekly workshop responded to a section of chapter 4, and the obligatory senior fellows' lecture was a moment for sharing themes and questions with a broader audience. I am also indebted to faculty at the University of Chicago Divinity School, Notre Dame University, Princeton University, Vanderbilt Divinity School, Washington University (St. Louis), the Center for American Studies, University of Heidelberg, the early Americanists' community in Japan, and Andover-Harvard Library for inviting me to describe the project to informed audiences. I owe a special thanks to the members of the Early Modern History Seminar, Cambridge University, for their response to an early (indeed, premature) description of the project. Jonathan Baddley helped with research as the book was coming to completion, and Jennifer Conforti created the electronic version of the manuscript.

Others who know more than I do about aspects of Puritan history have commented on draft chapters. I thank especially Ann Hughes, Margo Todd, John Coffey, Debora Shuger, and (on apocalypticism) Richard Cogley. The two anonymous readers' reports were also helpful. Any errors that remain are entirely of my doing. Others who have directed me to books and questions I would have overlooked include Lawrence Buell, Matthew Kadane, David Little, Kevin Madigan, Brent Sirota, Roger Thompson, Alexandra Walsham, and Adrian Weimer. My late friend and colleague Francois Bovon passed away before this book was very far along, but his generous enthusiasm sustained me in the early going.

In Hebrews 12:1, Paul speaks of a "great cloud of witnesses" that surround the godly. In my case the secular equivalent has been threefold: students at Harvard and adjacent seminaries and universities who, since the early 1990s, have participated in a seminar on the history of the Puritan movement; the many historians who, since the late nineteenth century, have dedicated themselves to understanding early modern British political, social, and institutional history; and the much smaller group of historians, most of them affiliated with contemporary evangelicalism on both sides of the Atlantic, who in recent years have revisited Reformed/Puritan theology. What I owe to the second and third groups is visible in the many citations to their work.

Yet I should underscore my distance from the debates that animate much of the work on Tudor-Stuart Britain and Reformed theology. To cite two examples of the former, my purpose was never to explain the causes of the civil war that broke out in 1642 or to validate any single interpretation of James VI and I. Instead, I have tried to follow the threads of doctrine, culture, and practice that passed from the Reformed international to early modern Britain. Always controversial, the Puritan movement aspired to evangelize the British people, transform local churches into sanctified communities, introduce godly rule in civil society, and eliminate every "remnant" of Catholicism from worship. Controversy bred confusion and conflict within the movement about this program—as things turned, especially about the nature of the visible church and the relationship between conscience or the regulative principle and the authority of the civil state and/or state church. My deepest regret is that my narrative abbreviates or passes by in silence the many close studies of ideas, situations, and texts historians of Tudor-Stuart Britain and early modern theology have published during the past three decades. The workings of parliaments in England and general assemblies in Scotland are a case in point, as is doctrine. There are no simple doctrines or passages in Scripture, no simple version of the practical divinity, and no simple or unmediated practices, truths I have evoked but not always documented as richly as I would have wished. Such is the price one pays for a book of this kind.

Finally, I thank those at Princeton University Press who endorsed my proposal for a "short" book and, despite the evolution of short into long, have seen it through the process of publication: first and foremost, Brigitta van Rheinberg and Eric Crahan and, on the side of production, Ellen Foos and Molan Goldstein.

Abbreviations

Albro, *Works of Shepard*
>John A. Albro, ed., *The Works of Thomas Shepard*, 3 vols. (Boston 1853)

Ayres, *Works of Whitgift*
>John Ayres, ed., *The Works of John Whitgift*, 3 vols. (Cambridge 1851–53)

Balfour, *Works*
>James Balfour, *The Historical Works of Sir James Balfour*, 4 vols. (Edinburgh, 1824).

Baillie, *Letters and Journals*
>Robert Baillie, *The Letters and Journals of Robert Baillie*, ed. David Laing, 3 vols. (Edinburg, 1841–42)

Breward, *Work of Perkins*
>Ian Breward, ed., *The Work of William Perkins* (Appleford: Sutton Courtenay, 1970)

Burrage, *EED*
>Champlain Burrage, *The Early English Dissenters in the Light of Recent Research*, 2 vols. (Cambridge: Cambridge University Press, 1912)

Calderwood, *History of the Kirk*
>David Calderwood, *The History of the Kirk of Scotland*, 8 vols., ed. Thomas Thomson and David Laing (Edinburgh, 1842–49)

Dickinson, *Knox's History of the Reformation*
>William Croft Dickinson, ed., *John Knox's History of the Reformation in Scotland*, 2 vols. (New York: Philosophical Library, 1950)

Dixhoorn, *Minutes*
>Chad Dixhoorn, ed., *The Minutes and Papers of the Westminster Assembly, 1643–1652*, 5 vols. (Oxford: Oxford University Press, 2012)

Firth and Raitt, *Acts and Ordinances*
>C. H. Firth and R. S. Rait, *Acts and Ordinances of the Interregnum, 1642–1660* (London, 1911)

Foxe, *Book of Martyrs*
> John Foxe, *Acts and Monuments of these latter and perilous days*, ed. Stephen Cattley, 7 vols. (London, 1851)

Gardiner, *Constitutional Documents*
> Samuel Rawson Gardiner, ed., *The Constitutional Documents of the Puritan Revolution, 1625–1660*, 3rd ed. (Oxford, 1906)

Hall, *AC*
> David D. Hall, ed., *The Antinomian Controversy, 1636–1638: A Documentary History* (Middletown, CT: Wesleyan University Press, 1968).

Hall, *ARP*
> David D. Hall, *A Reforming People: Puritanism and the Transformation of Public Life in New England* (New York: Knopf, 2011)

Hall, *FS*
> David D. Hall, *The Faithful Shepherd: A History of the New England Ministry in the Seventeenth Century* (Chapel Hill: University of North Carolina Press, 1972)

HJ
> *Historical Journal*

JEH
> *Journal of Ecclesiastical History*

Kenyon, *Stuart Constitution*
> J. P. Kenyon, *The Stuart Constitution: Documents and Commentary* (Cambridge: Cambridge University Press, 1986)

Laing, *Works of Knox*
> David Laing, ed., *The Works of John Knox*, 6 vols. (Edinburgh, 1846–54)

NEHGR
> *New England Historical and Genealogical Register*

NEQ
> *New England Quarterly*

Peel, *Seconde Parte*
> Albert Peel, ed., *The Seconde Parte of a Register* (Cambridge: Cambridge University Press, 1915)

Peterkin, *Records*
> Alexander Peterkin, ed., *Records of the Kirk of Scotland, containing the Acts and Proceedings of the General Assemblies* (Edinburgh, 1848)

Proc. MHS
> *Proceedings of the Massachusetts Historical Society*

Pub. CSM
> *Publications and Transactions of the*
> *Colonial Society of Massachusetts*

Frere and Douglas, *Puritan Manifestoes*
> W. H. Frere and C. E. Douglas, eds., *Puritan Manifestoes A Study*
> *of the Origins of the Puritan Revolt* (London: SPCK, 1954)

Recs. MBC
> *Records of the Governor and Company of the Massachusetts Bay*
> *in New-England*, ed. N. B. Shurtleff, 5 vols. (Boston, 1853–54)

RSCHS
> *Records of the Scottish Church History Society*

Shaw, *Acts and Proceedings*
> Duncan Shaw, *The Acts and Proceedings of the General*
> *Assemblies of the Church of Scotland, 1560 to 1618*, 3
> vols. (Edinburgh: Scottish Record Society, 2004)

Shaw, *History of the Church*
> William A. Shaw, *A History of the English Church during*
> *the Civil Wars and under the Commonwealth, 1640–*
> *1660*, 2 vols. (New York: Longmans Green, 1900)

Shepard, *Confessions*
> *Thomas Shepard's Confessions*, ed. George Selement
> and Bruce C. Woolley (Boston: Colonial Society
> of Massachusetts Collections, 1981).

Walker, *Creeds and Platforms*
> Williston Walker, *The Creeds and Platforms of*
> *Congregationalism* (New York, 1893)

Winthrop, *Journal*
> John Winthrop, *The Journal of John Winthrop*, ed.
> Richard S. Dunn, James Savage, and Laetitia Yeandle
> (Cambridge, MA: Harvard University Press, 1996)

Winthrop Papers
> John Winthrop, *Winthrop Papers*, 6 vols. (Boston:
> Massachusetts Historical Society, 1929–)

WMQ
> *William and Mary Quarterly*

Zurich Letters
> *The Zurich Letters, comprising The Correspondence of Several English Bishops and Others*, ed. Hastings Robinson, 2 vols. (Cambridge, 1842)

Introduction

1. William Bradford, *Of Plymouth Plantation*, ed. Samuel E. Morison (New York: Knopf, 1952), 7.

2. Alexandra Walsham, *Charitable Hatred: Tolerance and Intolerance in England, 1500–1700* (Manchester: University of Manchester Press, 2006), chap. 2.

3. Gordon Donaldson, "The emergence of schism in seventeenth-century Scotland," in *Schism, Heresy and Religious Protest*, ed. Derek Baker, Studies in Church History 9 (Cambridge: Cambridge University Press, 1972), 277–94.

4. See chaps. 2, 4, and 9.

5. Argument about the adequacy of a thesis or interpretation is an everyday fact of life for academics, but not for many others. Most references to these arguments appear in the endnotes.

6. Ever since the seventeenth century, any assertion that theology within the Church of England was tilted toward "Calvinism" has aroused the ire of certain "Anglican" historians and theologians who call attention to what was *not* said in the Thirty-Nine Articles. For critical analysis of this argument, see Nicholas Tyacke, "Anglican attitudes: War," *Journal of British Studies* 35 (1996): 139–67; Tyacke, *Anti-Calvinists: The Rise of English Arminianism c. 1590–1640* (Oxford: Clarendon, 1987), intro. and chaps. 1–3; Anthony Milton, *The British Delegation and the Synod of Dort (1618–1619)* (Woodbridge: Boydell, 2005), xix–xxi; Peter Lake, "Predestinarian Propositions," *JEH* 46 (1995): 110–23; Lake, "Calvinism and the English Church 1570–1635," *Past & Present* 114 (1987): 32–76, also noting how, within a presumed consensus, significant differences were emerging. Other studies of pertinence include Dewey D. Wallace Jr., *Puritanism and Predestination: Grace in English Protestant Theology, 1525–1695* (Chapel Hill: University of North Carolina Press, 1982), chap. 2; and Daniel J. Steere, "A Calvinist Bishop at the Court of King Charles I," in *Adaptations of Calvinism in Reformation Europe: Essays in Honour of Brian G. Armstrong*, ed. Mack P. Holt (Aldershot: Ashgate, 2007), 193–218; see also Steere, " 'For the Peace of Both, for the Humour of Neither': Bishop Joseph Hall Defends the 'Via Media' in an Age of Extremes, 1601–1656," *Sixteenth Century Journal* 27 (1996): 749–65. Ian Green, who has surveyed more printed sermons, catechisms, and manuals of devotion than any other historian, argues for common ground, an "orthodoxy" that largely negates the practice of contrasting Puritan theology with what "Anglicans" were saying. Green, *Print and Protestantism in Early Modern England* (Oxford: Oxford University Press, 2000), chap. 10.i. See also Sean Hughes, "The Problem of 'Calvinism' in the Elizabethan and Stuart Church of England," in *Belief and Practice: A Tribute to Patrick Collinson from His Students*, ed. Susan Wabuda and Caroline Litzenberger (Aldershot: Ashgate, 1998), 229–49. Other discussions of the term are noted in chapter 1.

7. Richard A. Muller's understanding of Reformed theology is spelled out in "Diversity in the Reformed Tradition," *Drawn into Controversie: Reformed Theological Diversity and Debates within Seventeenth-Century British Puritanism*, ed. Michael A. G. Haykin and Mark Jones (Gottingen: Vandenhoeck & Ruprecht, 2011), 11–30; and *Calvin and the Reformed Tradition on the Work of Christ and the Order of Salvation* (Grand Rapids, MI: Baker Academic, 2012), chaps. 2–3; see also Muller, *Christ and the Decree Christology and*

Predestination in Reformed Theology from Calvin to Perkins (Durham, NC: Labyrinth, 1986; repr., Baker Academic, 2008), with a new preface that is essential reading; and Muller, *Post-Reformation Reformed Dogmatics: The Rise and Development of Reformed Orthodoxy, c. 1520-1725* (Grand Rapids, MI: Baker, 1987), chap. 2. More recently, the literature is reviewed in Irena Backus and Philip Benedict, "Introduction," *Calvin and His Influence, 1509-2009*, ed. Backus and Benedict (Oxford: Oxford University Press, 2011), 12–16. David Hoyle questions sharp dichotomies in the English context in *Reformation and Religious Identity in Cambridge, c. 1590-1644* (Woodbridge: Boydell, 2007), chap. 1. Beza as villain of a Calvin vs. Calvinists framework is challenged in Raymond A. Blacketer, "The Man in the Black Hat: Theodore Beza and the Reorientation of Early Reformed Historiography," in *Church and School in Early Modern Protestantism: Studies in Honor of Richard A. Muller on the Maturation of a Theological Tradition*, ed. Jordan J. Ballor, David S. Sytsma, and Jason Zuidema (Leiden: Brill, 2013), 227–41.

8. Debate over the origins and nature of the covenant theology may be followed in Carl R. Trueman, "The Harvest of Reformation Mythology? Patrick Gillespie and the Covenant of Redemption," in *Scholasticism Reformed: Essays in Honour of Willem J. van Asselt*, ed. Maarten Wisse, Marcel Sarot, and Wiollemien Otten (Leiden: Brill, 2010), 196–214; Lyle D. Bierma, *The Covenant Theology of Caspar Olevanus* (Grand Rapids, MI: Reformation Heritage, 2005); John von Rohr, *The Covenant of Grace in Puritan Thought* (Atlanta: Scholars Press, 1986), with a review of previous scholarship; William G. B. Stoever, *"A Faire and Easie Way to Heaven": Covenant Theology and Antinomianism in Early Massachusetts* (Middletown, CT: Wesleyan University Press, 1978); and Charles Lloyd Cohen, *God's Caress: The Psychology of Puritan Religious Experience* (New York: Oxford University Press, 1986), chap. 2 and p. 52 n. 16. For Scotland, see Arthur H. Williamson, *Scottish National Consciousness in the Age of James VI: The Apocalypse, the Union and the Shaping of Scotland's Public Culture* (Edinburgh: John Donald, 1979), 74–77; David George Mullan, *Scottish Puritanism, 1590-1638* (Oxford: Oxford University Press, 2000), chap. 6 (correcting Williamson on certain points); Richard L. Greaves, *Theology & Revolution in the Scottish Reformation* (Grand Rapids, MI: Christian University Press, 1980, chap. 6; and John Coffey, *Politics, Religion and the British Revolutions: The Mind of Samuel Rutherford* (Cambridge: Cambridge University Press, 1997), 130–38. See also David A. Weir, *The Origins of the Federal Theology in Sixteenth-Century Reformation Thought* (Oxford: Clarendon Press, 1990), with an extensive bibliography. In general, these books overturn the argument, originating in the nineteenth century and reiterated in the mid-twentieth, that the "covenant theology" weakened orthodox Calvinism. Instead, all focus on the covenant as an aspect of redemption.

9. Expecting consistency and rigorous, well-informed engagement with biblical and theological commonplaces and categories, historians of the practical divinity repeatedly encounter what Ernest Kevan characterizes as an "indefiniteness of expression" coupled with a misreading of theological opponents and a capacity to entertain conflicting assumptions. Other historians discern "ambiguity," "ambivalence," and "a process of theological development" as certain themes or topics emerge and others wane; see, e.g., Michael Mc-Giffert, "The Problem of the Covenant in Puritan Thought: Peter Bulkeley's *Gospel-Covenant*," *NEHGR* 130 (1976): 107–29; and Leif Dixon, *Practical Predestinarians in England, c. 1590-1640* (Burlington, VT: Ashgate, 2013). Hence E. Brooks Holifield's remark in regard to sacramental theology that "by selective quotation one could depict most of them [the makers of the practical divinity] as heirs either of Zurich or of Geneva"; he notes, too, "the almost universal tendency of second generation Reformed divines to minimize earlier disagreements." Ernest F. Kevan, *The Grace of Law: A Study in Puritan Theology* (1964; repr., Grand Rapids, MI: Soli Deo Gloria, 1993), 31–33, 147; Holifield, *The Covenant Sealed:*

The Development of Puritan Sacramental Theology in Old and New England, 1570–1720 (New Haven, CT: Yale University Press, 1974), 27, and chap. 5. For more observations of this kind, see David F. Wright, "Development and Coherence in Calvin's *Institutes*; The Case of Baptism *(Institutes* 4:15–4:16)," in *Adaptations of Calvinism in Reformation Europe,* ed. Mack P. Holt (Aldershot: Ashgate, 2007), 43–54; Mark E. Dever, *Richard Sibbes: Puritanism and Calvinism in Late Elizabethan and Early Stuart England* (Mercer, GA.: Mercer University Press, 2000), 186; Richard A. Muller, "The Covenant of Works and the Stability of Divine Law in Seventeenth-Century Reformed Orthodoxy: A Study in the Theology of Herman Witsius and Wilhelmus a Brakel," *Calvin Theological Journal* 29 (1994): 75–100; Alexandra Walsham, *Providence in Early Modern England* (Oxford: Oxford University Press, 1996), chap. 1 and pp. 152–56, emphasizing the "elastic and ambidextrous strands" (p. 17) of the doctrine of providence. Careful readings of sermons and treatises on predestination reveal the muted complexities of reflection and preaching on this topic. See, e.g., Greaves, *Theology & Revolution,* chap. 2; Arnold Hunt, *The Art of Hearing* (Cambridge: Cambridge University Press, 2011), chap. 7.

10. For exemplary responses to this task, see Joel Hurstfield, *Freedom, Corruption and Government in Elizabethan England* (Cambridge, MA: Harvard University Press, 1973); and A. S. P. Woodhouse, "Introduction," *Puritanism and Liberty* (Chicago: University of Chicago Press, 1951). Jonathan Scott emphasizes a similar "eclecticism" among advocates of republicanism in *Commonwealth Principles: Republican Writing of the English Revolution* (Cambridge: Cambridge University Press, 2004), 5.

11. Recent arguments in behalf of a more fluid understanding of orthodoxy appear in David Como, "Puritans, Predestination and the Construction of Orthodoxy in Early Seventeenth-Century England," in *Conformity and Orthodoxy in the English Church, c. 1560–1660,* ed. Peter Lake and Michael Questier (Woodbridge: Boydell, 2000), 64–87; and Peter Lake, "Puritanism, Familism, and Heresy in early Stuart England: The Case of John Etherington Revisited," in *Heresy, Literature, and Politics in Early Modern English Culture,* ed. David Loewenstein and John Marshall (Cambridge: Cambridge University Press, 2006), 82–107.

12. See also Collinson, "A Comment: Concerning the Name 'Puritan,'" *JEH* 10 (1980): 83–88 (suggesting that historians refrain from capitalizing the term); Michael P. Winship, "Were There Any Puritans in New England?" *NEQ* 74 (2001): 118–38.

13. Aspects of this argument have been contested by Peter Lake in *Anglicans and Puritans? Presbyterianism and English Conformist Thought from Whitgift to Hooker* (London: Unwin Human, 1988). Revisiting the back-and-forth between John Whitgift (defending the policies of Elizabeth I and some of her bishops) and Thomas Cartwright, who questioned those policies, Lake teased out serious differences. These had previously been identified in David Little, *Religion, Order and Law A Study in Pre-Revolutionary England* (New York: Harper Torchbooks, 1969. For another reading of the debate that illuminates differences, see John S. Coolidge, *The Pauline Renaissance: Puritanism and the Bible* (Oxford: Clarendon, 1970). My own analysis (chap. 2) builds on Little, Coolidge, and Lake. The Puritans as outsiders who acquire a "revolutionary" perspective from the Bible that eventually (inevitably?) prompted the coming of civil war in the 1640s is a perspective questioned by most historians of early modern Britain, for good reason. Hence my reluctance to use the phrase "Puritan Revolution" for the period 1640–60. That contradictions within the movement contributed to the breakdown of ecclesiastical and royal authority in the 1640s is, on the other hand, a legitimate assumption.

14. Conal Condren questions the meaning of "radical" in seventeenth-century historiography in *The Language of Politics in Seventeenth-Century England* (New York: St. Martin's, 1994), and Ethan Shagan underscores the multiple meanings of "moderation" in *The*

Rule of Moderation: Violence, Religion and the Politics of Restraint in Early Modern England (Cambridge: Cambridge University Press, 2011). Working in the shadow of Collinson, David Mullan describes the "Reformed piety" that was taught and experienced in Scotland as "on the one hand, focusing narrowly on individual salvation and tending toward a sectarian view of the church, while on the other hand attempting to harness the entire sinful nation, consisting of a majority of reprobates, in the service of God." Mullan, *Scottish Puritanism*, 8. As Alec Ryrie and Tom Schwanda remark in their "Introduction" to *Puritanism and Emotion in the Early Modern World* (Basingstock: Palgrave Macmillan, 2016), " 'Puritan' is a word both too useful to be abandoned and almost too weighed down with dubious intellectual baggage to be useful" (p. 2).

15. Jacqueline Eales, *Puritans and Roundheads: The Harleys of Brampton Bryan and the Outbreak of the English Civil War* (Cambridge: Cambridge University Press, 1990). In *Puritanism and the English Revolution 1 Marginal Prynne 1600–1669* (Aldershot: Greg, 1963/1991), William M. Lamont wrestles with the significance of labels such as "Arminian," with Prynne himself classified as a "moderate" who can be placed in an Anglican tradition dating from John Jewell.

16. Steve Hindle, *The State and Social Change in Early Modern England* (New York: St. Martin's Press, 2000); and Paul Slack, *From Reformation to Improvement: Public Welfare in Early Modern England* (Oxford: Clarendon Press, 1998).

17. Nigel Voak's careful study *Richard Hooker and Reformed Theology: A Study of Reason, Will and Grace* (Oxford: Oxford University Press, 2003), suggests some of the complexities of situating the would-be "Anglican" Hooker within the Reformed tradition.

18. The astonishing mutations of an "origins" perspective are described in Daniel T. Rogers, *As a City on a Hill: The Story of America's Most Famous Lay Sermon* (Princeton, NJ: Princeton University Press, 2018); and Abram van Engen, *The Meaning of America: How the United States Became the City on a Hill* (New Haven, CT: Yale University Press, forthcoming).

19. My graduate school classmate Norman Pettit deserves a nod for attempting something of this kind in *The Heart Prepared: Grace and Conversion in Puritan Spiritual Life* (New Haven, CT: Yale University Press, 1966), but (as Holifield and others would subsequently point out) misread several of his key sources.

20. In a less imaginative manner, I based *The Faithful Shepherd: A History of the Ministry in Seventeenth-Century New England* (1972) on a similar, if simpler, model. Later, after coming under the influence of British and French scholarship on popular religion, I turned to describing the colonists as "Elizabethans" in *Worlds of Wonder, Days of Judgment: Popular Religious Belief in Early New England* (New York: Knopf, 1989).

21. One way into this rhetoric is via *Images of English Puritanism: A Collection of Contemporary Sources 1589–1646*, ed. Lawrence A. Sasek (Baton Rouge: Louisiana State University Press, 1989). Another, more tantalizing approach is to explore nuances within "the figure of the puritan" in seventeenth-century English literature, as Kristen Poole does in *Radical Religion from Shakespeare to Milton Figures of Nonconformity in Early Modern England* (Cambridge: Cambridge University Press, 2000).

22. I was on the receiving end of popular anti-puritanism after publishing an op-ed piece in the *New York Times* (November 23, 2010) ostensibly about Thanksgiving but really an affirmation of Puritan social ethics. Dozens of email responses poured in, some expressing gratitude that I was taking the Puritans seriously but most insisting that Nathaniel Hawthorne (himself a Unitarian) was right and I was wrong. The leitmotif of my short essay was the nature of the meal served at the "first" Thanksgiving in 1621, and my assertion that the menu cannot be retrieved (true) was also challenged.

23. As I indicate in the substance of notes to chapter 5.

24. For another version of continuities, see Susan Juster, *Sacred Violence in Early America* (Philadelphia: University of Pennsylvania Press, 2016).

25. Williamson, *Scottish National Consciousness*.

26. For an introduction to their and others' points of view, see *The English Reformation Revised*, ed. Christopher Haigh (Cambridge: Cambridge University Press, 1987). See also Hunt, *Art of Hearing*.

27. I touch on some aspects of practice in chapters 4 and 9, and more extensively in *Worlds of Wonder*.

Chapter 1. From Protestant to Reformed

1. Andrew Pettegree, *Reformation and the Culture of Persuasion* (Cambridge: Cambridge University Press, 2005), 27; Claire Cross, *Church and People: England 1450–1660*, 2d ed. (Oxford: Blackwell, 1999), 58–63; Foxe, *Book of Martyrs*, 8:639–40. See also Margaret Spufford, *Contrasting Communities: English Villagers in the Sixteenth and Seventeenth Centuries* (Cambridge: Cambridge University Press, 1974), chap. 10.

2. Alfred W. Pollard, ed., *Records of the English Bible* (Oxford: Oxford University Press, 1911), 263, 279; Foxe, *Book of Martyrs*, 8:340.

3. John R. Knott Jr., *The Sword of the Spirit: Puritan Responses to the Bible* (Chicago: University of Chicago Press, 1980), 13; Pollard, *Records of the English Bible*, 90.

4. Foxe, *Book of Martyrs*, 7: 107, 218.

5. Jewell, quoted in Knott, *Sword of the Spirit*, 14, 29.

6. William Fulke, *A Brief and Plain Declaration concerning the Desires of All Those Faithful Ministers that Have and Do Seek for the Discipline and Reformation of the Church of England* (written c. 1573; [London?], 1584), reprinted in Leonard J. Trinterud, ed., *Elizabethan Puritanism* (New York: Oxford University Press, 1971), 248, 268.

7. Margo Todd, *Christian Humanism and the Puritan Social Order* (Cambridge: Cambridge University Press, 1987), 18, 28, 33–34.

8. In their introduction (pp. 3–32) to *Calvin and His Influence, 1509–2009* (New York: Oxford University Press, 2011), Irena Backus and Philip Benedict review some of the problems that arise around the terms "Calvinism" and "Reformed," a task addressed in other essays in this collection, especially Friedrich Wilhelm Graf, "Calvin in the Plural: The Diversity of Modern Interpretations of Calvinism, Especially Germany and the English Speaking World," pp. 255–66. For straightforward assertions of its hegemony, see James Kirk, *Patterns of Reform: Continuity and Change in the Reformation Kirk* (Edinburgh: T&T Clark, 1989), chap. 3; W. Stanford Reid, "Reformation in France and Scotland: A Case Study in Sixteenth-Century Communication," in *Later Calvinism: International Perspectives*, ed. W. Fred Graham, Sixteenth Century Essays and Studies 22 (Kirksville, MO: Sixteenth Century Journal Publishers, 1994), chap. 10; Anthony Milton, *Catholic and Reformed: The Roman and Protestant Churches in English Protestant Thought, 1600–1640* (Cambridge: Cambridge University Press, 1995), pt. 2, extremely useful for understanding the early decades (to the mid-1620s) and noting a reluctance to use the term "Calvinist." Richard L. Greaves emphasizes Knox's "ecumenical" stance as a means of freeing him from the label "Calvinist" at a moment in historical scholarship when this term was being used quite narrowly; *Theology & Revolution in the Scottish Reformation: Studies in the Thought of John Knox* (Grand Rapids, MI: Christian University Press, 1980), chap. 11. See below, chap. 4, for a more detailed discussion of Reformed theology and its place in the British reformations. For humanism and the project of reform, see J. K. Cameron, "The Renaissance Tradition in the Reformed Church: The Example of Scotland," in *Renaissance and Renewal in Christian History*, ed. Derek Baker, Studies in Church History 14 (Oxford: Blackwell, 1977):

251–69. General surveys of the Reformed tradition include Philip Benedict, *Christ's Churches Purely Reformed: A Social History of Calvinism* (New Haven, CT: Yale University Press, 2002); and, in much briefer compass, Graeme Murdock, *Beyond Calvin: The Intellectual, Political and Cultural World of Europe's Reformed Churches* (New York: Palgrave Macmillan, 2004).

9. Second thoughts about the longer-term significance of Lutheranism are many, based in part on the indebtedness of some of the Thirty-Nine Articles of the Church of England to the Augsburg Confession. For an overview, see David Scott Gehring, "From the Strange Death to the Odd Afterlife of Lutheran England," *HJ* 57 (2014): 825–844. See also Carl R. Trueman and Carrie Euler, "The Reception of Martin Luther in Sixteenth- and Seventeenth-Century England," in *The Reception of Continental Reformation in Britain*, ed. Polly Ha and Patrick Collinson, Proceedings of the British Academy 164 (Oxford: Oxford University Press, 2010), 63–81. The influence of the Reformed may be followed in Basil Hall, "Martin Bucer in England," in *Martin Bucer: Reforming Church and Community*, ed. D. F. Wright (Cambridge: Cambridge University Press, 1994), 144–60; David F. Wright, "Martin Bucer in England—and Scotland," in *Martin Bucer and Sixteenth Century Europe*, ed. Christian Krieger and Marc Lienhard, 2 vols. (Leiden: Brill, 1993), 2:522–32; Andrew Pettegree, *Foreign Protestant Communities in Sixteenth-Century London* (Oxford: Clarendon, 1986); Patrick Collinson, "The Elizabethan Puritans and the Foreign Reformed Churches in London," and "Calvinism with an Anglican Face: The Stranger Churches of Early Elizabethan London and Their Superintendent," both reprinted in Collinson, *Godly People: Essays on English Protestantism and Puritanism* (London: Hambledon, 1983). Students also arrived from overseas, most notably Rudolph Gualter. Claire Cross, "Continental Students and the Protestant Reformation in England in the Sixteenth Century," in *Reform and Reformation: England and the Continent c. 1500–1700*, ed. Derek Baker, Studies in Church History 2 (Oxford: Blackwell, 1979), 35–58. By the late 1560s and beyond, thousands of Dutch and French Protestant refugees were arriving in England and founding (mostly outside of London) more "stranger" churches. After Elizabeth I came to the throne, Peter Martyr Vermigli was invited to return, but he declined and died a short while later. In 1549 Cranmer, acting on a proposal by the moderate Lutheran Philip Melanchthon, invited him and other Continental Protestant leaders, including Calvin and Heinrich Bullinger, to England, in the hope that these "wise and godly men" could "take counsel together" to reconcile divergent theologies of the Eucharist and other matters, at a moment of severe pressure on Continental Lutherans and Reformed. Hastings Robinson, ed., *Original Letters Relative to the English Reformation* (Cambridge: 1846), 1:21–23; 2:713–14.

10. Christina Hallowell Garrett, *The Marian Exiles: A Study in the Origins of Elizabethan Puritanism* (Cambridge: Cambridge University Press, 1938); Dan G. Danner, *Pilgrimage to Puritanism: History and Theology of the Marian Exiles at Geneva, 1555–1560* (New York: Peter Lang, 1999); Andrew Pettegree, *Marian Protestantism: Six Studies* (Aldershot: Ashgate, 1996); Alec Ryrie, *The Origins of the Scottish Reformation* (Manchester: Manchester University Press, 2006), 126–28. For Melville, see Jack C. Whytock, *"An Educated Clergy": Scottish Theological Education and Training in the Kirk and Secession, 1560–1850* (Milton Keynes: Paternoster, 2007), chap. 3, and the references it contains. The ways in which John Foxe read, came to know personally, and was affected by other Reformed intellectuals during the years he lived on the Continent are a vivid reminder of exchanges and connections. For these, see Katharine R. Firth, *The Apocalyptic Tradition in Reformation Britain, 1530–1645* (Oxford: Oxford University Press, 1979), chap. 3; and for French connections among Scottish Protestants, chapter 4, below. Travel to and study in Protestant cities or seminaries in France continued; for example, Archibald Johnston (see

chap. 7) studied in France in early 1630s, connections that are touched on in Ole Peter Grell, *Calvinist Exiles in Tudor and Stuart England* (Brookfield VT: Scholar Press, 1996), chap. 11. Keith M. Brown provides an overview of the nobility and its overseas connections in *Noble Society in Scotland Wealth, Family and Culture, from Reformation to Revolution* (Edinburgh: Edinburgh University Press, 2000), chap. 8. The community of British exiles also included educated women such as Anne Lock, who translated several of Calvin's sermons while she lived abroad; after she returned, they were published. Murdock provides a broader overview of Reformed-linked exiles and refugees in *Beyond Calvin*), chap. 2.

11. Andrew Pettegree, "The Reception of Calvinism in Britain," *Calvinus Sincerioris Religionis Vindex Calvin as Protector of the Purer Religion*, ed. Wilhelm H. Neusner and Bruce G. Armstrong, Sixteenth Century Essays & Studies 36 (Kirksville, MO: Sixteenth Century Journal Publishers, 1997), 267–289; Francis Higman, "Calvin's Works in Translation," in *Calvinism in Europe, 1540–1620*, ed. Andrew Pettegree, Alastair Duke, and Gillian Lewis (Cambridge: Cambridge University Press, 1994), 82–99; his notes on the English translators indicate that most of them (e.g., John Field, Anthony Gilby, Laurence Tomson, Miles Coverdale) participated in the emergence of the Puritan movement. On Bullinger and his successor Rudolph Gualter and their international correspondence, see the references in Bruce Gordon, "Zurich and the Scottish Reformation: Rudolph Gualter's *Homilies on Galatians* of 1576," in *Humanism and Reform: The Church in Europe, England, and Scotland, 1400–1643*, ed. James Kirk, Studies in Church History: Subsidia 8 (Oxford: Blackwell, 1991), 207–20. For a more measured assessment of the availability of Bullinger's *Homilies* and John Foxe's *Book of Martyrs* in parish libraries, see John Craig, "Erasmus or Calvin? The Politics of Book Purchase in the Early Modern English Parish," in Ha and Collinson, *Reception of Continental Reformation*, 39–62. See also Howard Hotson, "'A Generall Reformation of Common Learning' and Its Reception in the English-Speaking World, 1560–1642," in ibid., 193–228.

12. Jane Dawson, "Calvinism and the Gaidhealtachd in Scotland," in Pettegree, Duke, and Lewis, *Calvinism in Europe*, 231–53; Arthur H. Williamson, *Scottish National Consciousness in the Age of James VI: The Apocalypse, the Union and the Shaping of Scotland's Public Culture* (Edinburgh: John Donald, 1979), 76–77.

13. A. F. Scott Pearson, *Thomas Cartwright and Elizabethan Puritanism, 1535–1603* (Cambridge: Cambridge University Press, 1925), chap. 4; Eleanor Rosenberg, *Leicester, Patron of Letters* (New York: Columbia University Press, 1955).

14. Preceded in 1537 by the "Matthew" Bible and substantially replaced in the seventeenth century by the "revised" or "King James" version. For that later period, it is sometimes argued that the politics of religion *within* the Puritan movement turned on which translation to use, an argument deftly contradicted by Charles Lloyd Cohen, *God's Caress: The Psychology of Puritan Religious Experience* (New York: Oxford University Press, 1986), 176 n. 58.

15. Basil Hall, "The Genevan Version of the English Bible: Its Aims and Achievements," in *The Bible, the Reformation and the Church: Essays in Honour of James Atkinson*, ed. W. P. Stephens (Sheffield: Sheffield Academic, 1995), 124–25, 139; David Daniell, *The Bible in English: Its History and Influence* (New Haven, CT: Yale University Press, 2003), chap. 22 (quotation, p. 374); Charles Eason, *The Geneva Bible: Notes on Its Production and Distribution* (Dublin: Eason & Son, 1937); Ian Green, *Print and Protestantism in Early Modern England* (Oxford: Oxford University Press, 2000), chap. 2 (providing revised figures on the number of printings). Importantly, Green minimizes the theological significance of the marginalia, most if not all of which could not be included in formats smaller than folio (pp. 74–75). He also notes that there were almost as many separate printings of the New Testa-

ment as of the entire Bible. See also Green, " 'Puritan Prayer Books' and 'Geneva Bibles': An Episode in Elizabethan Publishing," in *Transactions of the Cambridge Bibliographical Society* 11 (1998): 314–50, on abridged versions of the prayer book. The role of Theodore Beza's translation of the New Testament on the Geneva Bible and subsequently on the King James Version is traced in Irena Doruta Backus, *The Reformed Roots of the English New Testament: The Influence of Theodore Beza on the English New Testament* (Pittsburgh: Pickwick, 1980); it is worth noting that Laurence Tomson's translation of Beza's New Testament of 1576 replaced the 1560 Geneva version in some later editions.

16. Beth Quitslund, *The Reformation in Rhyme: Sternhold, Hopkins, and the English Metrical Psalter, 1547–1603* (Aldershot: Ashgate, 2008); data on the number of printings from Green, *Print and Protestantism*, 509.

17. Pettegree, *Reformation and the Culture of Persuasion*, chap. 3; Green, *Print and Protestantism*, 530–32; Jane Dawson, *John Knox* (New Haven, CT: Yale University Press, 2015), 126–27 (attributing this burst of publications to the exiles' desire to have "everything in hand for establishing a fully reformed Church in their own country"). The Geneva/Scottish liturgy is included in *The Works of John Knox*, ed. David Laing, 6 vols. (Edinburgh, 1846–54), 4:149–214.

18. Paul Christianson, *Reformers and Babylon English Apocalyptic Visions from the Reformation to the Eve of the Civil War* (Toronto: University of Toronto Press, 1978), 39–43 (indicating the influence of John Bale's *Image of the Two Churches;* see below); Katharine Firth, *The Apocalyptic Tradition in Reformation Britain, 1530–1645* (Oxford: Oxford University Press, 1979), chap. 3 (correcting, as do other scholars cited in this note, William Haller, *Foxe's Book of Martyrs and the Elect Nation* [New York: Harper and Row, 1963], which misunderstood Foxe to be speaking of the English nation). See also V. Norskov Olsen, *John Foxe and the Elizabethan Church* (Berkeley: University of California Press, 1973); Crawford Gribben, *The Puritan Millennium Literature and Theology, 1550–1682* (Milton Keynes: Paternoster, 2008), chap. 3; Jane E. Dawson, "The Apocalyptic Thinking of the Marian Exiles," in *Prophecy and Eschatology*, ed. Michael Wilks, Studies in Church History: Subsidia 10 (Oxford: Blackwell, 1994), 75–91.

19. Mine is not a definitive list; for other attempts, see Merwyn Johnson, "Calvin and Patterns of Identity in Reformed Theology," in *John Calvin and the Interpretation of Scripture*, ed. Charles Raynal, Calvin Studies 11 (Grand Rapids, MI: CRC Product Services, 2006), 355–67.

20. Calvin's reasoning about the order of the commandments, and the impact of this interpretation on British reformers, are described in Margaret Aston, *England's Iconoclasts*, vol. 1, *Laws against Images* (Oxford: Clarendon, 1988), 381–82, 397, 424, 435–37, and, more largely, chap. 7. Calvin's rejection of images, relics, and the like followed from his insistence that the finite cannot contain the infinite.

21. Murdock, *Beyond Calvin*, 10–14; James Kirk, "Iconoclasm and Reformation," *RSCHS* 24 (1992): 366–83; Margaret Aston, "Iconoclasm in England: Official and Clandestine," in *The Impact of the English Reformation 1500–1640*, ed. Peter Marshall (London: Arnold, 1997), 167–91; Keith Thomas, "Art and Iconoclasm in Early Modern England," in Kenneth Fincham and Peter Lake, eds., *Religious Politics in Post-Reformation England Essays in Honour of Nicholas Tyacke* (Woodbridge: Boydell, 2006), 16–40; Alexandra Walsham, *The Reformation of the Landscape Religion, Identity, and Memory in Early Modern Britain and Ireland* (Oxford: Oxford University Press, 2011), chap. 2.

22. John Calvin, *Institutes of the Christian Religion*, ed. John T. McNeill, trans. Ford Lewis Battles (Philadelphia: Westminster, 1960), bk. 1, chap. 4, pp. 99–110; Foxe, *Book of Martyrs*, 8:308. Debate remains intense among British theologians about the meaning of

the Eucharist to the first generation of reformers, especially Thomas Cranmer, and continues about Calvin. See, e.g., Brian A. Gerrish, *Grace and Gratitude: The Eucharist Theology of John Calvin* (Minneapolis: Fortress, 1993); Anthony N. S. Lane, "Was Calvin a Crypto-Zwinglian," in *Adaptations of Calvinism*, ed. Holt, 21–41.

23. Christopher Hill, *The English Bible and the Seventeenth-Century Revolution* (London: Allen Lane; New York: Penguin, 1993), 253–58; John N. King, *English Reformation Literature: The Tudor Origins of the Protestant Tradition* (Princeton, NJ: Princeton University Press, 1982), 144–51; G. J. Van De Poll, *Martin Bucer's Liturgical Ideas: The Strasbourg Reformer and His Connection with the Liturgies of the Sixteenth Century* (Asen: Van Gorcum, 1954); and see below, chaps. 2 and 3.

24. Christopher Ellwood, "Calvin, Beza, and the Defense of Marriage in the Sixteenth Century," in *Calvin, Beza and Later Calvinism*, ed. David Foxgrover (Grand Rapids, MI: CRC Product Services, 2006), 29–31; Martin Bucer, *De Regno Christi*, in *Melanchthon and Bucer*, ed. Wilhelm Pauck, Library of Christian Classics 19 (Philadelphia: Westminster, 1969), 194; Greaves, *Theology & Revolution*, 204. In modern Reformed circles, this argument is known as the regulative principle. Calvin and his Reformed contemporaries also drew on the history of the early church and what was said by the Church Fathers; see Irena Backus, "These Holy Men: Calvin's Patristic Models for Establishing the Company of Pastors," in *Calvin and the Company of Pastors*, ed. David Foxgrover (Grand Rapids, MI: CRC Product Services, 2004), 25–51. For more assertions by Knox of the primacy of Scripture, see G. D. Henderson, *The Scottish Ruling Elder* (London: James Clarke, 1935), 34–36. Richard Kyle provides a useful overview in *God's Watchman: John Knox's Faith and Vocation* (Eugene, OR: Pickwick, 2014), chap. 2.

25. Knott, *Sword of the Spirit*, chap. 1.

26. Calvin, *Institutes*, bk. 4, chap. 1.1 (pp. 1011–12).

27. Ibid., bk. 4, chap. 11.9 (pp. 1221–1223). In bk. 4, chap. 6.6, Calvin assigned to "doctors" the task of rebutting Catholic doctrine. In Scotland, the term became attached to faculty of the various Scottish colleges; in New England, the colonists preferred "teacher" (Catholicism not being an immediate threat) and attempted a dual ministry of pastor and teacher in each congregation, a practice that could not be sustained.

28. François Wendel, *Calvin: The Origins and Development of His Religious Thought*, trans. Philip Mairet (London: William Collins, 1963), chap. 5; James L. Ainslie, *The Doctrines of Ministerial Order in the Reformed Churches of the Sixteenth and Seventeenth Centuries* (Edinburgh: T&T Clark, 1940); Bucer, *De Regno Christi*, 194; Paul Avis, "The Church and Ministry," in *T&T Clark Companion to Reformation Theology*, ed. David M. Whitford (London: T&T Clark, 2012), 143–52.

29. Foxe, *Book of Martyrs*, 5:118 (tyranny). Calvin did not explicitly condemn the office of bishop. Backus, *Reformed Roots of the English New Testament*, 193. But see Calvin, *Institutes*, bk. 4, chap. 4.2–3 (1069–71) and bk. 4, chap. 11.9 (1221–22), for strictures about "worldly power."

30. Calvin, *Institutes*, bk. 4, chap. 1.15; Amy Nelson Burnett, *The Yoke of Christ: Martin Bucer and Christian Discipline*, Sixteenth Century Essays and Studies (Kirksville, MO: Sixteenth Century Journal Publishers, 1994), 6, citing Gottfried Hammann, *Entre la Secte et la Cite. Le Projet d'Eglise du reformateur Martin Bucer (1491–1551)* (Geneva: Labor et Fides, 1984); Michael F. Graham, *The Uses of Reform: "Godly Discipline" and Popular Behavior in Scotland and Beyond, 1560–1610* (Leiden: Brill, 1996), chap. 1. See also Benedict, *Christ's Churches Purely Reformed*.

31. Calvin, *Institutes*, bk. 4, chap. 1.7–8 (pp. 1022–23); chap. 12.5 (pp. 1232–33); chap. 1.15 (1029); chap. 12.12 (p. 1239); chap. 11.1–3 (pp. 1211–16). Harro Hopfl, *The Christian*

Polity of John Calvin (Cambridge: Cambridge University Press, 1982), 87–88, 100–102, noting also Calvin's assumption that the very being (authority) of the right kind of ministry would advance the work of discipline. As Burnett (*Yoke of Christ*, 4) and others have emphasized, the power of keys was being assigned to congregations rather than being a prerogative of the priesthood, as in Catholicism. Burnett also reminds us that church discipline was more about admonition than excommunication.

32. Martin Greschat, "The relation between church and civil community in Bucer's reforming work," in *Martin Bucer Reforming church and community*, ed. D. F. Wright (Cambridge: Cambridge University Press 1994), 17–31; *The Scots Confession 1560*, ed. G. D. Henderson (Edinburgh: St. Andrew Press, 1960), 70; Euan Cameron, "The 'Godly Community' in the Theory and Practice of the European Reformation," in *Voluntary Religion*, ed. W. J. Sheils and Diana Wood, Studies in Church History 23 (Oxford: Blackwell, 1986), 131–553 (noting, as well, the difficulties of specifying Calvin's and Luther's understanding of the church); Michael F. Graham, *The Uses of Reform: "Godly Discipline" and Popular Behavior in Scotland and Beyond, 1560–1610* (Leiden: Brill, 1996), chap. 1; Dewey D. Wallace Jr., *Puritans and Predestination: Grace in English Protestant Theology, 1525–1695* (Chapel Hill: University of North Carolina Press, 1982), 7; Calvin, *Institutes*, bk. 4, chap. 12.5 (p. 1232 and n. 8); Greaves, *Theology & Revolution*, chap. 3. According to article 23 of the Scots Confession of 1560 (p. 78), only those who "can try and examine themselves" can participate in Holy Communion.

33. W. P. Stephens, *The Holy Spirit in the Theology of Martin Bucer* (Cambridge: Cambridge University Press, 1970), chaps. 4, 7, esp. pp. 83–85, 161; Calvin, quoted in Timothy George, *John Robinson and the English Separatist Tradition* (Macon, GA: Mercer University Press, 2002), 99 (see also p. 98); John Craig, *A Shorte Summe of the Whole Catechisme* (1581), ed. Thomas Graves Law (Edinburgh: 1883), sig. C [1 verso]; Calvin, *Institutes*, bk. 4, chap. 1.17 (p. 1031); David Little, *Religion, Order, and Law: A Study in Pre-Revolutionary England* (New York: Harper and Row, 1969), 67–69. Theologically, Calvin and his heirs were insisting that the stages of justification and sanctification are really one and the same. See also Ronald S. Wallace, *Calvin's Doctrine of the Christian Life* (Edinburgh: Oliver and Boyd, 1959), pt. 3, chap. 2.

34. Little, *Religion, Order, and Law*, pt. 2, chap. 3 (quotation, p. 63). Little also emphasizes the inevitable persistence of the old order (coercion was inevitable) and Calvin's care to avoid the extreme of an Old Testament–style theocracy (pp. 54–56). The substance of Bucer's program is described in chapter 5, below.

35. Calvin, *Institutes*, bk. 4, chap. 1.17 (pp. 1031–40); Wallace, *Calvin's Doctrine*, 103–10 (quotation, p. 107) from Calvin's commentary on Ephesians 2:24; Hall, "Martin Bucer in England," 154–55. See also Little, *Religion, Order, and Law*, chap. 1, where "new order" is associated with voluntarism. Although the focus of Scott H. Hendrix, *Recultivating the Vineyard: The Reformation Agendas of Christianization* (Louisville, KY: Westminster John Knox, 2004) is on the Lutheran ambition to rechristianize Europe, the story he tells is pertinent to the politics of the Reformed.

36. Burnett, *Yoke of Christ*, chap. 7; Peter Iver Kaufman, *Redeeming Politics* (Princeton, NJ: Princeton University Press, 1990), chap. 6. As Alastair Duke succinctly puts it, "No thorough-going reformation in the Calvinist sense could take place without substantial support from the civil authorities." Duke, "Perspectives on International Calvinism," in Pettegree, Duke, and Lewis, *Calvinism in Europe*, 14.

37. Kirk, *Patterns of Reform*, 234 (quoting a 1548 statement by a Scottish Lutheran); Robinson, *Original Letters*, 2:715 (Calvin to Edward VI). Earlier, Martin Luther had appealed to the "Christian Nobility of the German Nation" to enact reform.

38. Kaufman, *Redeeming Politics*, passim.

39. Little, *Religion, Order, and Law*, 53 (noting a "constant tension" between church and civil society), and 72–73 (on coercion as sometimes warranted as well as unwelcome). Mark A. Hutchinson provides a similar framework for the aspirations of a small group of Protestant leaders in mid-to-late sixteenth-century Ireland in *Calvinism, Reform and the Absolutist State in Elizabethan Ireland* (London: Pickering and Chatto, 2015). Bruce Gordon, "Zurich and the Scottish Reformation: Rudolph Gwalther's *Homilies on Galatians* of 1576," in *Humanism and Reform: The Church in Europe, England, and Scotland, 1400–1643*, Studies in Church History: Subsidia 8 (Oxford: Blackwell, 1991), p. 213; Philip Broadhead, "In Defence of Magisterial Reformation: Martin Bucer's Writings against the Spiritualists, 1535," in *Discipline and Diversity*, ed. Kate Cooper and Jeremy Gregory, Studies in Church History 43 (Woodbridge: Boydell, 2007), 252–62.

40. The reformers took for granted that the thousand-year reign of Christ foretold in Revelation had already occurred; not until the beginning of the seventeenth century (see chap. 7) did this assumption give way to the millennium as happening in the present and future.

41. See, e.g., Arthur H. Williamson, *Apocalypse Then: Prophecy and the Making of the Modern World* (Westport, CT: Praeger, 2008), chap. 3.

42. Greaves, *Theology & Revolution*, 45; Jane E. A. Dawson, "The Apocalyptic Thinking of the Marian Exiles," in *Prophecy and Eschatology*, ed. Michael Wilks, Studies in Church History: Subsidia 10 (Oxford: Blackwell, 1994), 75–91; Firth, *Apocalyptic Tradition*, 124; Little, *Religion Order, and Law*, 72; Gribben, *Puritan Millennium*, 25–26, 73–74; Robinson, *Original Letters*, 1:21, 39; Adrian Chastain Weimer, *Martyrs' Mirror: Persecution and Holiness in Early New England* (New York: Oxford University Press, 2011), 5; Bernard McGinn, *Antichrist: Two Thousand Years of the Human Fascination with Evil* (New York: Columbia University Pres, 2000), chap. 8. The engraving on the title page of the Geneva Bible depicted the parting of the Red Sea, a "type" of what was to come for the true church.

43. This paragraph and those that follow draw on the following studies of apocalypticism in English culture: Richard Bauckham, *Tudor Apocalypse: Sixteenth-century Apocalypticism, Millenarianism and the English Reformation: From John Bale to John Foxe and Thomas Brightman* (Appleford: Sutton Courtney, 1978); Christianson, *Reformers and Babylon*; Firth, *Apocalyptic Tradition*; and Gribben, *Puritan Millennium*. Anti-popery also figures in this mix; see, e.g., Peter Lake, "Anti-popery: The Structure of a Prejudice," in *Conflict in Stuart England: Studies in Religion and Politics, 1603–1642*, ed. Richard Cust and Ann Hughes (London: Longman, 1989), 72–106. As Andrew Crome notes in *The Restoration of the Jews: Early Modern Hermeneutics, Eschatology, and National Identity in the works of Thomas Brightman* (Heidelberg: Springer, 2014), Luther overcame his initial reluctance to cite Revelation when he realized how useful it could be to a Protestant version of the history of the Christian church (p. 40). Catholics continued to emphasize the novelty of Protestantism, an argument the Irish Protestant James Ussher devoted himself to disproving, in part via the identification of the papacy with the Antichrist. Alan Ford, *James Ussher: Theology, History, and Politics in Early-Modern Ireland and England* (Oxford: Oxford University Press, 2007), chaps. 3, 6.

44. Firth, *Apocalyptic Tradition*, chap. 3.

45. Andrew Pettegree, "European Calvinism: History, Providence, and Martyrdom," in *The Church Retrospective*, ed. R. N. Swanson, Studies in Church History 33 (Woodbridge: Boydell, 1997), 227–52; Knott, *Sword of the Spirit*, 29.

46. Aston, "Iconoclasm in England" (attentive to vacillations of official policy punctu-

ated with spasms of iconoclasm); G. R. Elton, *Renewal and Reform: Thomas Cromwell and the Common Weal* (Cambridge: Cambridge University Press, 1973), 55 (anxieties about unchecked preaching); Bob Scribner, "Preconditions of Tolerance and Intolerance in Sixteenth-century Germany," in *Tolerance and Intolerance in the European Reformation*, ed. Ole Peter Grell and Bob Scribner (Cambridge: Cambridge University Press, 1996), 32–47.

47. *John Knox's History of the Reformation in Scotland*, ed. William Croft Dickinson, 2 vols. (London: Thomas Nelson, 1949), 1: li. The immensely complicated situation in Scotland is described more fully in Gordon Donaldson, *Scottish Church History* (Edinburgh: Scottish Academic Press, 1985), chap. 9.

48. Felicity Heal, "Economic Problems of the Clergy," in *Church and Society in England: Henry VIII to James I*, ed. Felicity Heal and Rosemary O'Day (London: Macmillan, 1977), 99–118; Rosemary O'Day, "Ecclesiastical Patronage: Who Controlled the Church?" in ibid., 137–55; Mark A. Hutchinson, *Calvinism, Reform and the Absolutist State in Elizabethan Ireland* (London: Pickering & Chatto, 2015), chap. 1; Jane Dawson, "Clan, Kin and Kirk: The Campbells and the Scottish Reformation," in *The Education of a Christian Society: Humanism and the Reformation in Britain and the Netherlands*, ed. N. Scott Amos, Andrew Pettegree, and Henk van Nierop (Aldershot: Ashgate, 1999), 211–42; Margaret James, "The Political Importance of the Tithes Controversy in the English Revolutions, 1640–1660," *History* 26 (1941): 1–18. Patrick Carter provides a useful overview in "Economic Problems of Provincial Urban Clergy during the Reformation," in *The Reformation in English Towns, 1500–1640*, ed. Patrick Collinson and John Craig (New York: St. Martin's Press, 1998), 147–85 . See also R. H. Pogson, "Revival and Reform in Mary Tudor's Church: A Question of Money," in *The English Reformation Revised*, ed. Christopher Haigh (Cambridge: Cambridge University Press, 1987), 139–56; and for an excellent case study, W. J. Sheils, " 'The Right of the Church': The Clergy, Tithe, and the Courts at York, 1540–1640," in *The Church and Wealth*, ed. W. J. Sheils and Diana Wood, Studies in Church History 24 (Oxford: Blackwell, 1987), 231–56.

49. Anthony Milton, *Catholic and Reformed: The Roman and Protestant Churches in English Protestant Thought, 1600–1640* (Cambridge: Cambridge University Press, 1995), 505. Simon Adams provides a succinct point of entry to the contradictions that accrued around foreign policy in "Spain or the Netherlands? The Dilemmas of Early Stuart Foreign Policy," in *Before the English Civil War: Essays on Early Stuart Politics and Government*, ed. Howard Tomlinson (London: Macmillan, 1983), 79–101.

50. Conrad Russell, "Arguments for Religious Unity in England, 1530–1650," in *Unrevolutionary England, 1603–1642* (London: Hambledon, 1990), 179–204. As Francis Lyall points out in *Of Presbyters and Kings: Church and State in the Law of Scotland* (Aberdeen: Aberdeen University Press, 1980), 4–5, Erastus took religious uniformity for granted and was not authorizing the civil state to pick and choose among doctrines or religious systems. In *The Religion of Protestants: The Church in English Society, 1559–1625* (Oxford: Clarendon, 1982), Patrick Collinson emphasizes (pp. 3–5) that, in the English context, Erastianism was tempered by rules about what all parties agreed was the jurisdiction of the church. For more on this topic, see chapters 2 and 8.

51. *Seconde Parte of a Register*, ed. Albert Peel (Cambridge: Cambridge University Press, 1915), 70, 74, 76; Jane Dawson, "Trumpeting Resistance: Christopher Goodman and John Knox," in *John Knox and the British Reformations*, ed. Roger A. Mason (Aldershot: Ashgate, 1998), 131–53; Collinson, *Religion of Protestants*, chap 6. Kevin Sharpe provides an acute reading of the politics of "conscience" from a monarch's point of view in "Private Conscience and Public Duty in the Writings of James VI and I," in *Public Duty and Private*

Conscience in Seventeenth-Century England: Essays Presented to G. E. Aylmer, ed. John Morrill, Paul Slack, and Daniel Woolf (Oxford: Clarendon, 1993), 77–100. The most careful study of the ideological and practical contours of state control of religion is Alexandra Walsham, *Charitable Hatred Tolerance and Intolerance in England, 1500–1700* (Manchester: Manchester University Press, 2006).

52. A question carefully surveyed in Peter Iver Kaufman, *Thinking of the Laity in Late Tudor England* (Notre Dame, IN: University of Notre Dame Press, 2004).

53. Helen C. White, *Social Criticism in Popular Religious Literature of the Sixteenth Century* (New York, 1944), 163; [John Penry], *A Treatise containing the Aequity of an Humble Supplication . . . , unto hir Gracious Maiestie* ([London], 1587], 46, 44. John Whitgift's venting about "the people" is a classic expression of contempt for their "inconstance." John Ayre, ed., *The Life and Acts of John Whitgift*, 3 vols. (Oxford, 1822), 120–22. See also George Gifford, *A briefe discourse of certaine points of the religion which is among the common sort of Christians, which may bee termed the countrie divinitie* (London, 1620).

54. The broader debate is reviewed in Geoffrey Parker, "Success and Failure during the First Century of the Reformation," *Past & Present* 136 (1992), 43–48. Second thoughts about any extreme view of "the people" as indifferent or hostile to Protestantism are summarized in Caroline Litzenberger, *The English Reformation and the Laity: Gloucestershire, 1540–1580* (Cambridge: Cambridge University Press, 1997), intro.; her analysis of the language in wills turns up a great many that were "ambiguous" in being neither explicitly Catholic nor Protestant. See also Peter Iver Kaufman, "English Calvinism and the Crowd: Coriolanus and the History of Religious Reform," *Church History* 75 (2006): 314–42. That Protestantism was adopted by the urban elite in western Europe is argued by Heinz Schilling (drawing on his own and others' scholarship) in *Religion, Political Culture, and the Emergence of Modern Society: Essays in German and Dutch History* (Leiden: Brill, 1992).

55. Arthur Dent, *The Plain Mans Path-way to Heaven* (London, 1612), 21. For an overview and perhaps overstatement of the culture wars of this period, see Keith Wrightson, "Alehouse, Order and Reformation in Rural England," in *Popular Culture and Class Conflict, 1590–1914: Explorations in the History of Labour and Leisure*, ed. Eileen Yeo and Stephen Yeo (Sussex: Harvester, 1981),1–27.

56. Alison Wall, "Patterns of Politics in England, 1558–1625," *HJ* 31 (1988): 947–63; *A Catechism Written in Latin by Alexander Nowell*, ed. G. E. Corrie (Cambridge, 1853), 175.

57. Kaufman, *Thinking of the Laity*, 94 and in general chaps. 3–4.

58. Barbara A. Johnson, *Reading "Piers Plowman" and "The Pilgrim's Progress": Reception and the Protestant Reader* (Carbondale: Southern Illinois University Press, 1992), chap. 3 (quotation, p. 79); Timothy Scott McGinnes, *George Gifford and the Reformation of the Common Sort: Puritan Priorities in Elizabethan Religious Life*, Sixteenth Century Essays and Studies 70 (Kirksville, MO: Truman State University Press, 2004), 73–76; Claire Cross, *Church and People: England, 1450–1660*, 2nd ed. (Oxford: Blackwell, 1999), 99–102; Jane Facey, "John Foxe and the Defence of the English Church," in *Protestantism and the National Church in Sixteenth Century England*, eds. Peter Lake and Maria Dowling (London: Croom Helm, 1987), 173–76 (quotation, p. 175); Kimberly Anne Coles, *Religion, Reform, and Women's Writing in Early Modern England* (Cambridge: Cambridge University Press, 2008), intro., chap. 1. The German version of this trope of the wise common man is touched on in Kat Hill, *Baptism, Brotherhood, and Belief in Reformation Germany: Anabaptism and Lutheranism, 1525–1585* (Oxford: Oxford University Press, 2015), 85. See also Litzenberger, *English Reformation and the Laity*, for a careful account of lay activism. For Separatists, see below, chapter 2.

59. Duke, "Perspectives on International Calvinism," 20; Cameron, "Godly Community."

60. William Bradford, *Of Plymouth Plantation, 1620–1647*, ed. Samuel Eliot Morison (New York: Knopf, 1952), 3 (echoing language in the *Book of Martyrs*, which Bradford quoted a page or two later).

61. As John Morrill has noted, the Scottish Reformation "developed first and foremost in accordance with local conditions, in response to the low level of Scottish state formation and in the absence of a godly prince either to shape or obstruct it. It was characterized by a strong parochial discipline, a powerful iconophobia and a clearly defined four-fold ministry of preacher, doctor, elder, deacon. It was the mirror image of the English church: radically decentralized, strong on discipline and preaching, slack in liturgical precision and confused in its relationship to the state." Morrill, "A British Patriarchy? Ecclesiastical Imperialism under the Early Stuarts," in *Religion, Culture and Society in Early Modern Britain Essays in Honour of Patrick Collinson*, ed. Anthony Fletcher and Peter Roberts (Cambridge: Cambridge University Press, 1994), 210.

62. Useful reflections: Euan Cameron, "Frankfort and Geneva: The European Context of John Knox's Reformation," in *John Knox and the British Reformations*, ed. Roger A. Mason (Aldershot: Ashgate, 1998), 51–73.

63. Pettegree, "European Calvinism: History, Providence, and Martyrdom"; Schilling, *Emergence of Early Modern Society*, pt. 2. Another aspect of confessionalization as *process* was a greater emphasis on the disciplining of social life and especially the behavior of church members.. Yet in contrast to the process in some of the German states or territories, its counterpart in England and Scotland did not include support for a more absolutist civil state. For an overview, see Thomas A. Brady Jr., "Confessionalization—The Career of a Concept," in *Confessionalization in Europe, 1555–1700: Essays in Honor and Memory of Bodo Nischan*, ed. John M. Headley, Hans J. Hillerbrand, and Anthony J. Papalas (Aldershot: Ashgate 2004), 1–20; and in the same volume, Heinz Schilling, "Confessionalization: Historical and Scholarly Perspectives of a Comparative and Interdisciplinary Paradigm," 21–35. As will be noted at various moments in the chapters that follow, parts of this program fared better than others. Likewise, in a persistently mixed or pluralist state such as England and Scotland, it was pursued only in part.

64. It is telling that John Foxe omitted this statement from his narrative of Rogers's martyrdom.

65. Laing, *Works of Knox*, 3:224; Roger A. Mason, "Knox, Resistance and the Royal Supremacy," in *John Knox and the British Reformations*, ed. Roger A. Mason (Aldershot: Ashgate, 1998), 154–75 (an essay that really demonstrates how Knox favored the independence of the church); Dawson, "Trumpeting Resistance"; W. Stanford Reid, "John Knox: The First of the Monarchomachs," in *The Covenant Connection from Federal Theology to Modern Federalism*, ed. Daniel J. Elazar and John Kincaid (Lanham, MD: Lexington, 2000), 119–41 (esp. p. 128); Glenn Burgess, *British Political Thought, 1500–1660* (London: Palgrave Macmillan, 2009). For the Lutheran, Dutch, and Huguenot side of the story, see Quentin Skinner, *The Foundations of Modern Political Thought*, 2 vols. (Cambridge: Cambridge University Press, 1978), 1, chaps. 7–9, noting as well the "constitutionalist" leanings of Calvinism.

66. Henry IV, who became monarch in 1589, was a Protestant but converted to Catholicism in a public ceremony in 1593. Had he not done so, entire regions and most of the nobility would have refused to acknowledge his authority.

67. The broader Reformed context out of which this dilemma emerged is sketched in Andrew Pettegree, "Humanism and the Reformation in Britain and the Netherlands," in *The Education of a Christian Society: Humanism and the Reformation in Britain and the Netherlands*, ed. N. Scott Amos, Andrew Pettegree, and Henk Van Nierop (Aldershot:

Ashgate, 1999), 1–18. The Catholic side of the story is described in Michael C. Questier, *Conversion, Politics and Religion in England, 1580–1625* (Cambridge: Cambridge University Press, 1996).

68. A partial answer to this question is provided by Darren Oldridge, "Protestant Conceptions of the Devil in Early Stuart England," *History* 85 (2000): 232–46.

69. I owe questions of this kind to James Simpson, *Under the Hammer: Iconoclasm in the Anglo-American Tradition* (Oxford: Clarendon, 2010). As Helen L. Parish points out, the "image of Antichrist as a permanent and spiritual presence in the world," which became "a central feature of English Protestant polemic," was a "departure from the traditional medieval legend" of the Antichrist. Parish, " 'By This Mark You Shall Know Him': Clerical Celibacy and Antichrist in English Reformation Polemic," in Swanson, *Church Retrospective*, 253.

70. Duke, "Perspectives on International Calvinism," 10. As Jane Facey has aptly pointed out, "How could a religion whose progress hitherto had been based on cells of true believers, who had often seen themselves as operating within and in opposition to a corrupt, indifferent, and sometimes hostile mass, transmute itself into the official ideology of an inclusive national church?" Facey, "John Knox and the Defence of the English Church," in Lake and Dowling, *Protestantism and the National Church*, 163. See also Kyle, *God's Watchman*, chap. 5 (on Knox's preference for the "little flock"). The deeper question—as much an aspect of Luther's theology as of Calvin's—is how a theological anthropology that excluded the majority of Christians from the scope of redemption could be reconciled with the sociology of an inclusive church.

Chapter 2. A Movement Emerges

1. *Zurich Letters*, 1–2; see also Sampson's letter of 1560 to Peter Martyr, ibid., 62–65; and *The Zurich Letters*, 2nd ser., ed. Hastings Robinson (Cambridge, 1845), 25–27, for Peter Martyr's advice that he not wear the surplice. Sampson's longer career in the church is described in John Strype, *Annals of the Reformation and Establishment of Religion*, 3 vols. (Oxford, 1834), vol. 1, pt. 2, chap. 43 (which includes Lawrence Humphrey; both died in 1589).

2. John Strype, *The Life and Acts of Matthew Parker, The First Archbishop of Canterbury in the Reign of Queen Elizabeth* (London, 1711), bk. 2, chap. 22–23; bk. 3, chap. 1. Humphrey eventually conformed, as noted in Strype, *Annals of the Reformation*, bk. 1, pt. 2:144.

3. Dickinson, *Knox's History of the Reformation*, 2:3; Alex Ryrie, "John Knox's International Network," in *International Religious Networks*, ed. Jeremy Gregory and Hugh McLeod, Studies in Church History: Subsidia 14 (Woodbridge: Boydell, 2012), 96–115. In the late 1580s, an English reformer was just as smitten with the city, describing Geneva as "the best reformed and most blessed Church and Citie of God that then was, or as yet is in all the world." Albert Peel, ed., *The Seconde Parte of a Register: Being a calendar of manuscripts under that title intended for publication by the Puritans about 1593*, 2 vols. (Cambridge: Cambridge University Press, 1915), 2:60.

4. Assessments of the progress of Protestantism from 1520s to the reign of Edward VI vary; for a judicious summary, see Nicholas Tyacke, "Introduction: Re-thinking the English Reformation," in *England's Long Reformation 1500–1800*, ed. Nicholas Tyacke (London: UCL Press, 1998), 1–32.

5. *Original Letters Relative to The English Reformation*, ed. Hastings Robinson, 2 vols. (Cambridge, 1846–47), 1:269; Ronald Hutton, "The Local Impact of the Tudor Reforma-

tion," in *The English Reformation Revised*, ed. Christopher Haigh (Cambridge: Cambridge University Press, 1987), 120–21; see also Ronald Hutton, *The Rise and Fall of Merry England: the Ritual Year, 1450–1700* (Oxford: Oxford University Press, 1994), 114–138. The hard-fought politics of reform (with Catholic-adhering bishops sitting in the House of Lords) of these years is more fully described in Felicity Heal, *Reformation in Britain and Ireland* (Oxford: Oxford University Press, 2003), pt. 2, chap. 8.

6. The unwinding of purgatory and attendant rites for the dead is carefully described in Peter Marshall, *Beliefs and the Dead in Reformation England* (Oxford: Oxford University Press, 2002).

7. Kenneth Fincham and Nicholas Tyacke, *Altars Restored: The Changing Face of English Religious Worship, 1547–c. 1700* (Oxford: Oxford University Press, 2007), 22–26; Robinson, *Original Letters*, 1:281–82; Jane Dawson, *John Knox* (New Haven, CT: Yale University Press, 2015), 72–75 (Knox was among those who objected to kneeling). In John Jewell's influential defense of the English Reformation, he spoke carefully about the Eucharist: "The bread and wine are holy and heavenly mysteries of Christ's body and blood and in them Christ, the true bread of eternal life, is so manifested as present to us that by faith we truly receive his body and blood. Not that the bread and wine change their 'nature' and are annihilated. On the contrary, they remain bread and wine. Yet . . . Christ is really present and by faith we really take his body and blood." John Jewell, *An Apologie of the Church of England* (1562 in Latin), reprinted in *English Reformers*, ed. T. H. L. Parker, Library of Christian Classics 26 (Philadelphia: Westminster, 1956), 5.

8. Foxe, *Book of Martyrs*, 5:696, 699; Claire Cross, *Church and People: England 1450–1660*, 2nd ed. (Oxford: Blackwell, 1999), 74. That an "evangelical establishment" was responsible for the changes under Edward VI is argued in Diarmid McCulloch, *Thomas Cranmer: A Life* (New Haven, CT: Yale University Press, 1996), 365–66, 463–64, 504–12.

9. It is worth emphasizing the scope of Elizabeth's authority. In T. E. Hartley's apt summary of her role, "the monarch and her advisors in the Privy Council . . . remained the centre of government. Parliament was called to 'give advice' for the safety of the Queen, the Church and the realm, as well as to grant money. It could not claim to be part of the policy-making government of the country. . . . The 'government,' in the person of the Queen herself, was elected only by God, and, as she was fond of pointing out, answerable to God alone." As he reminds us, it was possible to criticize the queen's policies, albeit indirectly. Hartley, *Elizabeth's Parliaments: Queen, Lords and Commons, 1559–1601* (Manchester: Manchester University Press, 1992), 3, 11.

10. Quoted in Basil Hall, "The Genevan Version of the English Bible: Its Aims and Achievements," in *The Bible, the Reformation and the Church: Essays in Honour of James Atkinson*, ed. W. P. Stephens (Sheffield: Sheffield Academic, 1995), 125; *Elizabethan Puritanism*, ed. Leonard J. Trinterud (New York: Oxford University Press, 1971), 208–14 (quotations, pp. 211, 212).

11. Norman L. Jones, *Faith by Statute: Parliament and the Settlement of Religion 1559* (London: Royal Historical Society, 1982), passim; the obstructionist tactics of bishops in the House of Lords has a central place in Jones's analysis, as does the government's attempts to placate moderate lay Catholics. See also Patrick Collinson, *The Elizabethan Puritan Movement* (London: Jonathan Cape, 1967), pt. 2, chap. 1; M. M. Knappen, *Tudor Puritanism: A Chapter in the History of Idealism* (Chicago: Chicago University Press, 1939), chap. 9; *Zurich Letters*, 1, 18; Daniel Eppley, *Defending Royal Supremacy and Discerning God's Will in Tudor England* (Aldershot: Ashgate, 2007), chap. 4 (noting the "reluctance" to include "doctrine" within the scope of the royal supremacy in the wake of the reinstating of Catholicism). The Act of Supremacy allowed the Crown in Parliament to

decide what counted as heresy, but only on the "authority" of Scripture or as settled by several councils or a convocation. The possibilities in play in 1559–60 are superbly described in Heal, *Reformation in Britain and Ireland*, 357–360. See also Dan G. Danner, *Pilgrimage to Puritanism: History and Theology of the Marian Exiles at Geneva, 1555–1560* (New York: Peter Lang, 1999), tracing what happened with the Marian exiles once they returned to England and, in the opening chapter, reviewing how historians have dealt with their role; and Andrew Pettegree, "The Marian Exiles and the Elizabethan Settlement," in Pettegree, *Marian Protestantism: Six Studies* (Aldershot: Ashgate, 1996). A persistent uneasiness of the former exiles is captured in a letter of 1566 from Edmund Grindal to Bullinger: "We who are now bishops, on our first return, . . . contended long and earnestly for the removal of those things that have occasioned the present dispute; but as we were unable to prevail, either with the queen or the parliament, we judged it best . . . not to desert our churches for the sake of a few ceremonies." Patrick Collinson, *Archbishop Grindal: 1519–1583: The Struggle for a Reformed Church* (Berkeley: University of California Press, 1979), 85.

12. Diarmid MacCulloch, *The Later Reformation in England: 1547–1603* (New York: St. Martin's, 1990), 6.

13. As in the so-called great controversy of the 1560s, a back-and-forth between clergy in the Church and English Catholics; it is described in Mary Morrissey, *Politics and the Paul's Cross Sermons, 1558–1642* (Oxford: Oxford University Press, 2011), 162–73. For Alexander Nowell's catechism, see John Strype, *Annals of the Reformation*, vol. 1, pt. 1, 525–29.

14. Strype, *Life of Parker*, app. 86–87; *Injunctions Giuen by the most reuerende father in Christ, Edmonde*, excerpted in *Religion & Society in Early Modern England: A Sourcebook*, 2d ed., ed. David Cressy and Lori Anne Ferrell (New York: Routledge, 2005), 104–7; *The Remains of Edmund Grindal, D.D.*, ed. William Nicholson (Cambridge, 1843), 134–36, 125; Patrick Collinson, *Archbishop Grindal*, chap. 11. See, in general, Walter Howard Frere, ed., *Visitation Articles and Injunctions of the Period of the Reformation*, vol. 3, *1559–1575* (London: Longmans, Green, 1910), 81–86 and passim.

15. Strype, *Annals of the Reformation*, vol. 3, pt. 2, 70; *Zurich Letters*, 2:147–48; Edward Cardwell, *Documentary Annals of the Reformed Church of England*, 2 vols. (Oxford, 1839), 1:235–40 (an "address made by some bishops and divines to queen Elizabeth against the use of images," asking her to "clearly purge the polluted church" (p. 237); Rosemary O'Day, *The English Clergy: The Emergence and Consolidation of a Profession 1558–1642* (Leicester: Leicester University Press, 1979), chaps. 3, 5; Roger B. Manning, *Religion and Society in Elizabethan Sussex: A Study of the Enforcement of the Religious Settlement, 1558–1603* (Leicester: Leicester University Press, 1969), chap. 4; Claire Cross, "Priests into Ministers: The Establishment of Protestant Practice in the City of York, 1530–1630," in *Reformation Principle and Practice: Essays in Honour of A. G. Dickens*, ed. Peter Newman Brooks (London: Scholar Press, 1980), 203–25.

16. *Zurich Letters*, 1:91.

17. "General notes of matters to be moved by the clergy in the next parliament and synod," in Strype, *Annals of the Reformation*, vol. l, pt. l, 473–84, a list that included drafting of a statement of "the principal grounds of Christian religion," prohibiting private baptisms except by ordained clergy, abolishing any rules about vestments, requiring more of godparents, asking more of ministers associated with "cathedral churches," stricter procedures for the appointing of ministers and repair of their "livings," and a tightening of rules for admission to the Eucharist. The complicated textual history of this moment includes another paper (Strype, *Annals of the Reformation*, vol. l, pt. 1, chap. 31) listing suggestions for re-

form. Cf. David J. Crankshaw, "Preparations for the Canterbury Provincial Convocation of 1562–63: A Question of Attribution," in *Belief and Practice in Reformation England: A Tribute to Patrick Collinson from His Students*, ed. Susan Wabuda and Caroline Litzenberger (Aldershot: Ashgate, 1998), 60–93.

18. Robinson, *Original Letters*, 1:160, 170–71; Knappen, *Tudor Puritanism*, chap. 6. Jane Dawson provides an acute description of disputes among the exiles in Frankfurt in *John Knox* (New Haven, CT: Yale University Press, 2015), chap. 7. All roads lead back to [anon.], *Brieff discours off the troubles begonne at Franckford* (1575), reprinted in Laing, *Works of Knox*, 4:9–40, followed by Knox's own "Narrative" of the dispute (pp. 41–49) and contemporary letters to Calvin from Sampson, Cox, and others; in light of the disputes of the 1560s and 1570s, it is telling that the more conservative group was willing to give up private baptisms, saints' days, the confirmation of children, and the surplice, although characterizing them as "in their own nature indifferent," a rebuke to those who regarded them as idolatrous leftovers from Catholicism (p. 56). Responding to the assertion that "religion" in England "was already brought to perfection," Knox identified errors and sins that remained in need of correction, one of them the imperative that anyone who had attended mass or otherwise "behaved . . . slanderously" should "first of conscience either purge them[selves], or shew some sign of repentance before the Congregation," a project taken up by the Separatists and again by some in early New England (pp. 44–45). The radicals in Frankfurt seem to have elevated the importance of "discipline" along Reformed lines and to have practiced (or expected to practice) a de facto congregationalism.

19. Peter Iver Kaufman, *Thinking with the Laity in Late Tudor England* (Notre Dame, IN: University of Notre Dame Press, 2004), chap. 3 (offering a tempered view of the process). As Beth Quitslund points out, the dispute in Frankfurt turned on "the relative value . . . of hierarchy, uniformity, and national community" versus "the imperative to scriptural purity." Quitslund, *The Reformation in Rhyme: Sternhold, Hopkins and the English Metrical Psalter, 1547–1603* (Aldershot: Ashgate, 2009), 118.

20. The word "only" was introduced into the description of the Eucharist in article 28 of the Thirty-Nine Articles—"only after an heavenly and spiritual manner"—to underscore the rupture with the Catholic doctrine of Real Presence.

21. O'Day, *English Clergy*, chap. 3 (on the diocese of Coventry and Litchfield, where Thomas Lever served as Archdeacon of Coventry with virtually a free hand to encourage advanced Protestantism); Peter Lake, "Matthew Hutton—A Puritan Bishop?" *History* 64 (1979): 182–204, esp. 185; Cardwell, *Documentary Annals*, 1:299; Collinson, *Archbishop Grindal*, chap. 9 and, for background, chap. 3. See also Hartley, *Elizabeth's Parliaments*, 84–85.

22. Caroline Litzenberger, "Defining the Church of England: Religious Change in the 1570s," in Wabuda and Litzenberger, *Belief and Practice*, 137–53; Susan Doran, "Elizabeth I's Religion: The Evidence of Her Letters," *JEH* 51 (2000): 699–720. For examples of the queen's indifference, if not hostility, to her bishops' advice about reform, see Strype, *Annals of the Reformation*, e.g., vol. 1, Pt. 1, chap. xviii; Strype, *Life of Parker*, bk. 3:402 (voicing Parker's dismay at "her Displeasure against" Alexander Nowell), chaps. 8, 13, app. 49–52. See also Alan Cromartie, *The Constitutionalist Revolution: An Essay on the History of England, 1450–1642* (Cambridge: Cambridge University Press, 2006), 116 (on her sacramental preferences) and 120–22 (emphasizing the importance of conciliating Habsburgs and local Catholics, and her "Henrican" instincts); Jane E. A. Dawson, "John Knox, Christopher Goodman and the 'Example of Geneva,'" in *The Reception of Continental Reformation in Britain*, ed. Polly Ha and Patrick Collinson (Oxford: Oxford University Press, 2010), 107–35; Felicity Heal, *Of Prelates and Princes: A Study of the Economic and Social Position of*

the Tudor Episcopate (Cambridge: Cambridge University Press, 1980), chap. 9; Melissa Franklin Harkrider, *Women, Reform and Community in Early Modern England: Katherine Willoughby, Duchess of Suffolk, and Lincolnshire's Godly Aristocracy, 1519–1580* (Woodbridge: Boydell, 2008), 116. As Joel Hurstfield points out in *Freedom, Corruption and Government in Elizabethan England* (Cambridge, MA; Harvard University Press, 1973), the leaders of church and government were unable to "solve the problems which for half a century . . . pressed for solution: namely to broaden the Church sufficiently to meet the reasonable demands of the moderate Puritans and to broaden the state sufficiently to meet the reasonable demands of the moderate Catholics" (101).

23. As is tellingly demonstrated in James C. Spaulding, "The Reformatio Legum Ecclesiasticarum of 1552 and the Furthering of Discipline in England," *Church History* 39 (1970): 162–71.

24. Agitation about religious policy in the House of Commons is a case in point. Repeatedly (1563, 1571–72, 1576, 1581, 1584–85, 1593, 1601) there was surprisingly broad support for easing any crackdown on nonconforming ministers, limiting the scope of subscription, and taking stronger action against pluralism and nonresidency, support described in Patrick Collinson, "Puritans, Men of Business, and Elizabethan Parliaments," *Parliamentary History* 7 (1988): 187–211, and in Hartley, *Elizabeth's Parliaments*, chap. 5.

25. *A parte of a register, contayninge sundrie memorable matters, written by divers godly and learned in our time, which stande for, and desire the reformation of our Church, in Discipline and Ceremonies, accordeinge to the pure worde of God, and the Lawe of our Lande* (n.p., [1593]), 55–72; Patrick Collinson, *The Religion of Protestants: The Church in English Society, 1559–1625* (Oxford: Oxford University Press, 1982), chap. 4; Collinson, "A Mirror of Elizabethan Puritanism: The Life and Letters of 'Godly Master Dering,'" in *Godly People: Essays on English Protestantism and Puritanism* (London: Hambledon, 1983), 289–323. Nowell's "official" catechism includes a passage indicating how conventional it was in these years to argue that "We are furthermore taught purely and sincerely to worship Christ . . . not with any earthly worship, wicked traditions, and cold inventions of men, but with . . . spiritual worship." *A Catechism Written in Latin by Alexander Nowell*, ed. G. E. Corrie (Cambridge, 1853), 168. Alan Cromartie points out that, in the same text, Nowell endorsed a version of discipline, as did Matthew Parker in the early going of Elizabeth's reign. Cromartie, *Constitutionalist Revolution*, 123–24. Accusations of "sedition" were already a commonplace by the 1570s; for one example, see Gregory D. Dodds, *Exploiting Erasmus: The Erasmian Legacy and Religious Change in Early Modern England* (Toronto: University of Toronto Press, 2009), 103–4.

26. "The humble petition of the Communalitie to their most renowned and gracious Soueraigne," in *A parte of a register*, 304–22; Peel, *Seconde Parte*, 1:50, 75–77, 2:163–65; Frere and Douglas, *Puritan Manifestos*, 149–51, 13; Strype, *Life of Parker*, 3:70; T. W. Davids, *Annals of Evangelical Nonconformity in the County of Essex* (London:, 1863), 79–80; Trinterud, *Elizabethan Puritanism*, 160. For an example of ministers weighing in, see John Stockwood, *A very fruiteful Sermon preched at Paules Crosse* (1579), sig. A3v (calling for the church to support "godly, paynefull and able teachers, whom it pleaseth God to use as the onely ordinary meanes by preaching of the worde to worke faith in the heartes of the hearers").

27. Claire Cross, *The Puritan Earl: The Life of Henry Hastings, Third Earl of Huntington, 1536–1595* (London: Macmillan, 1966), 10–11 and chaps. 1, 2, 5–7. Other dedications (ibid., 26–28) were offered by the likes of Francis Bunny and John Field. Sampson continued the tradition by dedicating a translation of the Huguenot colloquy at Poissy to Francis Hastings (ibid., 35–36), whose role as a patron of true religion is described in M. C. Cross,

"An Example of Lay Intervention in the Elizabethan Church," *Studies in Church History* 2, ed. G. J. Cuming (London: Nelson, 1965), 273–82.

28. John S. Coolidge, *The Pauline Renaissance in England Puritanism and the Bible* (Oxford: Clarendon, 1970), chap. 2 (quotation, p. 36); *Zurich Letters*, 1, 153–54, 158, 161–62, 164; Peel, *Seconde Parte*, 1: 55 ; Strype, *Life of Parker*, app. 76–84; William Fulke, *A Brief and Plain Declaration concerning the Desires of All Those Faithful Ministers* (1584)), reprinted in Trinterud, *Elizabethan Puritanism*, 271 (using edification to mean the right kind of "order"). With his customary astuteness, Diarmid MacCulloch singles out "these [biblical] texts because they exactly rehearse the Puritan attitude" to the state church. MacCulloch, *The Later Reformation in England 1547–1603* (New York: St. Martin's, 1990), 85–87 (quotation, p. 85). In chapter 3 of *The Pauline Renaissance*, Coolidge shows how a moderate Puritan such as William Perkins reconciled "edification" with conformity.

29. Patrick Collinson, "The Reformer and the Archbishop: Martin Bucer and an English Bucerian," *Journal of Religious History* 6 (1970–71): 305–30; J. E. Neale, *Elizabeth I and Her Parliaments, 1559–1581* (London: Jonathan Cape, 1953), 164–68; Norman L. Jones, "An Elizabethan Bill for the Reformation of the Ecclesiastical Law," *Parliamentary History* 4 (1985): 171–88; Collinson, *Archbishop Grindal*, pt. 3; *Zurich Letters*, 2nd ser., 1:169. For Richard Cox's practice as bishop, see Kenneth L. Parker and Eric J. Carlson, *"Practical Divinity": The Works and Life of Rev. Richard Greenham* (Aldershot: Ashgate, 1997), 16–17.

30. Benjamin Brook, *Lives of the Puritans*, 3 vols. (London, 1813), 1:146; Strype, *Life of Parker*, 3:65–6, 75–78; Peel, *Seconde Parte*, 1:142.

31. Elliot Rose, *Cases of Conscience: Alternatives Open to Recusants and Puritans under Elizabeth I and James I* (Cambridge: Cambridge University Press, 1975), 124–26, noting that a professional gown was consistent with rejecting the "idea of a separate spiritual estate" (p. 125).

32. Strype, *Life of Parker*, bk. 3, chaps. 8–9, app. 47–51; Frere, *Visitation Articles*, 3:171–80; *Documents Illustrative of English Church History*, ed. Henry Gee and William John Hardy (London: Macmillan, 1910), 467–75. The Advertisements encompassed a wide range of advice and rules about administering the sacraments of Holy Communion and baptism, the recognizing of Holy Days (essentially an anti-Catholic statement, as were other sections), the forming of clergy, and the like.

33. Peel, *Seconde Parte*, 1:68–9, 66, 54; Strype, *Life of Parker*, 3:76–84, Appendix, 43–47; *Zurich Letters*, 1:84–85, 141–43 (a bishop's take on a politics in which Catholics were meddling), 157–63. The dissidents were also being pressured by an aroused laity; see, e.g., Peel, *Seconde Parte*, 1: 53.

34. Peel, *Seconde Parte*, 1:57–58, 63, 158, 160–62; Strype, *Life of Parker*, 3:138–41. See also M. M. Knappen, *Tudor Puritanism: A Chapter in the History of Idealism* (Chicago: University of Chicago Press, 1939), chap. 10.

35. Peel, *Seconde Parte*, 1:51, 68–73; *A parte of a register*, 48–53; William Whittingham to Parker, in Strype, *Life of Parker*, 3:76–84 (questioning, among other matters, the argument of "indifferency"). For Laurence Humphrey, a crucial question was "whether those persons who have till now enjoyed their liberty, can with a safe conscience, by the authority of a royal edict, involve in this bondage both themselves and the church?" *Zurich Letters*, 1:152; see also Sampson to the same, ibid., 153–54. He undoubtedly knew of the martyred John Rogers's insistence that the true Christian must "speake and write against . . . unlawful laws . . . and he is bound in very conscience to do it." *Book of Martyrs*, quoted in Tom Betteridge, "From Prophetic to Apocalyptic: John Foxe and the Writing of

History," in *John Foxe and the English Reformation*, ed. David Loades (Aldershot: Ashgate, 1997), 222.

36. Collinson, *Elizabethan Puritan Movement*, 71–83; Strype, *Life of Parker*, bk. 3, pt. 2:144–48. That some matters were "indifferent" had already been asserted at the beginning of Elizabeth I's reign and was reasserted by Grindal and others in the context of the vestarian dispute; *Zurich Letters*, 1:175–76. Its connections with the royal supremacy are noted in Jacqueline Rose, *Godly Kingship in Restoration England: The Politics of the Royal Supremacy, 1660–1688* (Cambridge: Cambridge University Press, 2011), 30; the alternative, which emerged in the 1590s, was to steal a leaf from the presbyterians' book by tying episcopacy to divine law. Martin Luther had evoked the same principle against the fiercely iconoclastic Protestants in 1520s Germany, as had Philip Melanchthon in response to pressure on German Protestants to resume some Catholic practices. As Ethan H. Shagan has pointed out, John Whitgift (see below) was associating *adiaphora* with "moderation" in order to counter the connections Cartwright was making between edification and liberty. For Whitgift, a people-centered liberty would lead to anarchy, which a church headed by the monarch and organized hierarchically would always prevent. Shagan, *The Rule of Moderation: Violence, Religion and the Politics of Restraint in Early Modern England* (Cambridge: Cambridge University Press, 2011), 113–20.

37. Knappen, *Tudor Puritanism*, 200–202, paraphrasing Anthony Gilby, *A Pleasaunt Dialogue, betweene a Souldior of Barwicke, and an English Chaplaine* (Middleburgh, 1581); *An answere for the tyme, to the Examination put in print* ([Rouen], 1566), quoted in ibid., 203; Dan G. Danner, *Pilgrimage to Puritanism: History and Theology of the Marian Exiles at Geneva, 1555–1560* (New York: Peter Lang, 1999), 39–40, 65–67.

38. Neale, *Elizabeth I and Her Parliaments*, 191–217; *Proceedings in the Parliaments of Elizabeth I, 1558–81*, ed. T. E. Hartley (London: Leicester University Press, 1981), 220, 330–31, 362–63, 368. Agitation continued in the House of Common of 1576, for which see ibid., 422 (characterizing a petition on church discipline as an example of a "broadly-based, moderate anti-clericalism"); and for these years as a whole, Knappen, *Tudor Puritanism*, 226–34. The House of Commons repeatedly argued that measures involving religion should come before the Convocation and the queen just as firmly said no.

39. Of uncertain authorship, the *Second Admonition* has been attributed to various figures, including Cartwright, Christopher Goodman, and Throckmorton, with Thomas Sampson and Anthony Gilby as other possibilities. John Field's admiration for Gilby but, on the other hand, Gilby's lukewarm response to the tone of the *Admonition*, are noted in Cross, *Puritan Earl*, 133–34.

40. Patrick Collinson, "John Field and Elizabethan Puritanism," in *Godly People: Essays on English Protestantism and Puritanism* (London: Hambledon, 1983), 339; Frere and Douglas, *Puritan Manifestoes*, 8. Whoever wrote the preface to *An Admonition* (John Field?) complained about being "Slanderously" called "Puritanes, worse then the Donatistes." Ibid., 6.

41. Peel, *Seconde Parte*, 1:89, 83; Frere and Douglas, *Puritan Manifestos*, 21, 19; A. F. Scott Pearson, *Thomas Cartwright and Elizabethan Puritanism, 1535–1603* (Cambridge: Cambridge University Press, 1925), 76–77.

42. Strype, *Annals of the Reformation*, vol. 1, pt. 2:372–80; Pearson, *Thomas Cartwright*, 28–29, 42, 130–42, and in general chap. 2; H. C. Porter, *Reformation and Reaction in Tudor Cambridge* (Cambridge: Cambridge University Press, 1958), 140. The wider presence of Cambridge "puritanism" is described in David Hoyle, *Reformation and Religious Identity in Cambridge, 1590–1644* (Woodbridge: Boydell, 2007), 60–65; and Porter, *Reformation and Reaction*, chap. 10.

43. Frere and Douglas, *Puritan Manifestoes*, 11, 13–15, 20–30; Ayre, *Works of John Whitgift*, 2:455–59, 465–68, 495, 565–69; 3:330–39; Fulke, *Plain Declaration*, 267–72; Arnold Hunt, *The Art of Hearing: English Preachers and Their Audiences, 1590–1640* (Cambridge: Cambridge University Press, 2010), chap. 1 (filling out the "theory of preaching" on which the movement depended, noting some backtracking on free prayer when Separatists turned this concept against the state church, and noting (pp. 33–34) comparisons. See also Torrance Kirby, "Public Religion and Public Worship: The Hermeneutics of Common Prayer" (on Richard Hooker's incarnational understanding of symbols), chap. 3 of *Persuasion and Conversion: Essays on Religion, Politics and the Public Sphere in Early Modern England* (Leiden: Brill, 2013); Sharon L. Arnoult, " 'Spiritual and Sacred Publique actions': *The Book of Common Prayer* and the Understanding of Worship in the Elizabethan and Jacobean Church of England," in *Religion and the English People, 1500–1640*, ed. Eric Josef Carlson (Kirksville, MO: Thomas Jefferson University Press, 1988), 25–47; Glenda Goodman, " 'The Tears I Shed at the Songs of Thy Church': Seventeenth-Century Musical Piety in the English Atlantic World," *Journal of the American Musicological Society* 65 (2012): 691–725. The Genevan order of worship is described more fully in chapter 3, below. See also Horton Davies, *The Worship of the English Puritans* (Westminster: Dacre, 1948), chaps. 4 (noting differences with Reformed practices on the Continent), 5, 6, 9, and app. A; in the last of these, *A Booke of the Forme of Common Prayers* (1585) is compared with the Geneva-Scottish *Book of Common Order*.

44. Ayre, *Works of Whitgift*, 1:180, 192, 200–201, 203; Pearson, *Thomas Cartwright*, 89–90; Dodd, *Exploiting Erasmus*, 106–8. In *The Pauline Renaissance*, Coolidge offers a subtle reading of the differences between Cartwright and Whitgift on this point, differences made more explicit in John R. Knott Jr., *The Sword of the Spirit: Puritan Responses to the Bible* (Chicago: University of Chicago Press, 1980), 32–37; and detailed in Donald Joseph McGinn, *The Admonition Controversy* (New Brunswick, NJ: Rutgers University Press, 1949), pt. 1, chaps. 4–5. See also Peter Lake, *Anglicans and Puritans? Presbyterianism and English Conformist Thought from Whitgift to Hooker* (London: Unwin Hyman, 1988), 16–17. Whitgift was constrained by article 20 of the Thirty-Nine Articles, which specified that "it is not lawful for the church to ordain anything that is contrary to God's Word written," and article 6, which declared that Scripture contained everything necessary for salvation. That the principle of things indifferent went hand in hand with the royal supremacy was indicated by Grindal in 1567; see Nicholson, *Remains of Edmund Grindal*, 203, 206–7.

45. Frere and Douglas, *Puritan Manifestoes*, 9, 6, 15–18; Ayres, *Works of Whitgift*, 1:181, 185, 380–84, 387–88; 3:178; Lake, *Anglicans and Puritans?* 31, 34–37.

46. Ayres, *Works of Whitgift*, 1:171. As W. J. Torrance Kirby points out in *Richard Hooker, Reformer and Platonist* (Aldershot: Ashgate, 2005), 23–27, Hooker and Whitgift were more fully aligned with Reformed principles than Cartwright and the authors of the *Admonition* on this issue; the latter favored the position of Bucer and the "radical" Heidelberg theologians, namely, that outward structures were the doing of the Holy Spirit and "scripturally prescribed," i.e., matters of faith and righteousness. See also Kirby, *Richard Hooker's Doctrine of the Royal Supremacy* (Leiden: Brill, 1990), 80–86.

47. Peel, *Seconde Parte*, 1:86; Frere and Douglas, *Puritan Manifestoes*, 10. This definition of the church was relatively traditional, for it reiterated some of what was said in the nineteenth of the Thirty-Nine Articles and chapter 17 of the *Second Helvetic Confession*.

48. David Little, *Religion, Order, and Law: A Study in Pre-Revolutionary England* (New York: Harper Torchbooks, 1969), 91–92; Frere and Douglas, *Puritan Manifestoes*, 9–10, 17; Ayre, *Works of Whitgift*, 1:370–72, 139–41, 382–86; Fenner, *Counter-Poyson*, in *A*

parte of a register, 467, insisting that excommunication requires the consent of the people. "For Cartwright there was a practical assumption that the elect and the godly were roughly coterminous; that sooner or later God's people would start to act like God's people . . . ." Lake, *Anglicans and Puritans?* 41 (and more generally, pp. 28–42); for Bucer's thinking along these lines (which may have influenced Cartwright's), see chapter 5, below.

49. Ayre, *Works of Whitgift*, 3:404–5, 189, 297; Fulke, *Plain Declaration*, 298; Jacqueline Rose, "Kingship and Counsel in Early Modern England," *HJ* 54 (2001): 47–71; Rose, *Godly Kingship*, 52–53; Pearson, *Thomas Cartwright*, 95. For Fulke's daring as a fellow of a Cambridge college, see Porter, *Reformation and Reaction*, 115, 120–21. Field and Wilcox had already evoked the two-kingdoms framework (Frere and Douglas, *Puritan Manifestoes*, 30), as in arguing that divine law prohibited officers in the church from holding civil office or dispensing civil punishments, a point that would take on greater significance in the mid-seventeenth century.

50. A. F. Scott Pearson, *Church and State: Political Aspects of 16th Century Puritanism* (Cambridge: Cambridge University Press, 1928), 17; Frere and Douglas, *Puritan Manifestoes*, 93; Fulke, *Plain Declaration*, 246–47; Travers, quoted in Michael Fixler, *Milton and the Kingdom of God* (Evanston, IL: Northwestern University Press, 1964), 35. See also Little, *Religion, Order, and Law*, 96–99.

51. Rosamund Oates, "Puritans and the 'Monarchical Republic': Conformity and Conflict in the Elizabethan Church," *English Historical Review* 127 (2012): 819–43, an immensely important essay showing how these themes (up to and including a mild version of resistance theory) were shared by others in the church (e.g., Tobie Matthew).

52. Ayre, *Works of Whitgift*, 1:171; Frere and Douglas, *Puritan Manifestoes*, 9 (spelling modified).

53. Little, *Religion, Order, and Law*, 144–45; Ayre, *Works of Whitgift*, 3:313, 304–5; Eppley, *Defending Royal Supremacy*, 153; Rosendale, *Liturgy and Literature*, 52–54, 115. In *The Zurich Connection and Tudor Political Theology: Studies in the History of Christian Traditions* 131 (Leiden: Brill, 2007), W. J. Torrance Kirby associates Whitgift's political theology with what he terms a "Zwinglian-Erastian" framework that emphasizes authority in matters of religion as "co-extensive" or unified, that is, uniting church and state. See also W. J. Torrance Kirby, *Richard Hooker's Doctrine of the Royal Supremacy* (Leiden: Brill, 1990), chap. 3.

54. Ayre, *Works of Whitgift*, 2:239; Lake, *Anglicans and Puritans?* chap 2 and 55; John Young, *Sermon before the Queen* (1576), painting Puritans as overly "high-minded" and "ambitious" and placing them in the company of Jack Cade and Jack Straw, a reference I owe to Gregory D. Dodds, *Exploiting Erasmus: The Erasmian Legacy and Religious Change in Early Modern England* (Toronto: University of Toronto Press, 2009), 102–4. In a letter dating probably from 1575, Matthew Parker described a queen worried lest the "Puritans . . . undoe her" authority and himself struggling to "governe," having recently discovered that one of his visitations "wrought . . . a contention for obedience." The letter may also convey some of Parker's own doubts about the queen's high claims for the royal supremacy. See also Cromartie, *Constitutionalist Revolution*, 136 and chap. 5 passim. Stephen A. Chavura, *Tudor Protestant Political Thought, 1547-1603* (Leiden: Brill, 2011), 184–98, noting, too, that Anthony Gilby defended the principle that loyalty could be trumped by conscience. Ryan Reeves points out that Tudor "evangelicals" tried to divert this rhetoric by painting Catholics as seditious and, simultaneously, urging their own kind to obey the queen. Reeves, *English Evangelicals and Tudor Obedience, c. 1527-1570* (Leiden: Brill, 2014), 170–71, 180–81.

55. Ayre, *Works of Whitgift*, 1:370, 372 (the "disorder of . . . popular elections"); Dudley

Fenner, *A Counter-Poyson*, in *A parte of a register*, 431–33, 465–67; Fulke, *Plain Declaration*, 275; *A Directory of Church-government* (London, 1644), sig. A2r. The compelling analysis is Pearson, *Church and State*, chap. 3. See also Little, *Religion, Order, and Law*, 92–93 (on defending laypeople's role). Peter Lake suggests that the pairing of Protestant clericalism and the animus against Catholic-style authority helps explain "the peculiar balance . . . in the political structure of the Presbyterian system . . . while the authority conceded to the minister . . . was considerable it was scarcely unlimited." Lake, "Presbyterianism, the Idea of a National Church and the Argument from Divine Right," in Lake and Dowling, *Protestantism and the National Church*, 198; see also Lake, *Anglicans and Puritans?* 51–54. Tudor and radical Protestant/Reformed approaches to "obedience" are carefully surveyed in Reeves, *English Evangelicals and Tudor Obedience,* a study that, among others, recalibrates the Zurich-Geneva-Lutheran mix of ideas about resistance. See also Roger A. Mason, *Kingship and the Commonweal: Political Thought in Renaissance and Reformation Scotland* (East Linton: Tuckwell, 1998), chaps. 7–8 (esp. pp. 203–4); and John Guy, "The Elizabethan Establishment and the Ecclesiastical Polity," in *The Reign of Elizabeth I: Court and Culture in the Last Decade* (Cambridge: Cambridge University Press, 1995), 127–30 (emphasizing Whitgift's and the queen's uneasiness with the "mixed polity" endorsed by Cartwright).

56. The making of the "Book of Discipline" is described in S. J. Knox, *Walter Travers: Paragon of Elizabethan Puritanism* (London: Methuen, 1962), chap. 6; in chapter 7, he covers the broader story of presbyterian ecclesiology. See also Collinson, *Elizabethan Puritan Movement*, pt. 6, chap. 1; and the firsthand record of debate among one group of godly ministers, *Conferences and Combination Lectures in the Elizabethan Church: Dedham and Bury St Edmunds, 1582–1590*, ed. Patrick Collinson, John Craig, and Brett Usher, Church of England Record Society 10 (Woodbridge: Boydell, 2003).

57. Strype, *Annals of the Reformation*, vol. 1, pt. 1:314; Fulke, *Plain Declaration*, 244–47. Frere and Douglas, *Puritan Manifestoes*, 96.

58. Patrick Collinson, *Richard Bancroft and Elizabethan Anti-Puritanism* (Cambridge: Cambridge University Press, 2013), chap. 6; *Directory*, sig. A4 verso; Ayre, *Works of Whitgift*, 3:501; Peel, *Seconde Parte*, 2:41 (staying put). See also [Walter Travers], *A full and plaine declaration of the ecclesiasticall discipline* (Latin, 1574; English, 1584), 160–61, 179–80. Relying on the Dedham classis deliberations as well as other evidence of revisions or variations in the *Directory*, Patrick Collinson suggested that "Dedham leant, as it were instinctively, in the direction of a devolved independency." Collinson, Craig, and Usher, *Conferences and Combination Lectures*, ic. That the English "presbyterians" were not very presbyterian by comparison with the Scottish system is strongly argued in Carol Geary Schneider, "Godly Order in a Church Half-Reformed: The Disciplinarian Legacy, 1570–1641" (PhD thesis, Harvard University, 1986), pt. 1. Her point is well taken, but she overlooks the Reformed context of self-definition I regard as significant for the reformers in Scotland (see chap. 3) and the English "presbyterians." Another way of understanding the wavering within the Dedham classis is suggested by Heinz Schilling. With an eye on Continental practice, he suggests that the "late Calvinist Reformation," facing unexpected "pressures from hostile states," saw the emergence of a "conception of ecclesiology according to which each parish was a fully fledged church, capable of acting in any circumstances without seeking permission from a higher ecclesiastical authority." Heinz Schilling, "Calvinism as an Actor in the Early Modern State System around 1600,"in *Calvin and His Influence, 1509–2009*, ed. Irene Backus and Philip Benedict (New York: Oxford University Press, 2011), 161.

59. Puritan-linked themes persisted in catechisms, the Sternhold-Hopkins version of the psalms, collections of remarkable providences, and related genres. See, e.g., Quitslund, *Reformation in Rhyme*, chap. 5.

60. Strype, *Life of Parker*, bk. 4, 177–78; at the same time, he wrote a scathing letter to Grindal, ibid., 178–80. See also Edward Dering's letter to Lord Burghley, rebuking him for actions he had endorsed as chancellor of Cambridge University and urging him to "stand favorable" to Thomas Cartwright. Speaking as a prophet, Dering reminded Burghley that he was "set in Authoritie to serve the Lorde, not to serve your self," and that "Gods judgements" would "overtake" him if he faltered. Strype, *Life of Parker*, bk. 4, app. 122. Strype, *Life of Whitgift*, 1, chap. 8 (on tense relations in 1584, etc.); Strype, *Annals of the Reformation*, vol. 1:2, 151; Joshua Rodda, *Public Religious Disputation in England, 1558–1626* (Farnham: Ashgate, 2014), 113.

61. *A sermon preached before the queens Maiestie the 25 day of Februarie* (London, 1570), much reprinted thereafter; quotations from Trinterud, *Elizabethan Puritanism*, 150, 156–57, 148. See also Collinson, "Mirror of Elizabethan Puritanism"; Strype, *Life of Parker*, 3:219–25; John N. King, *Foxe's Book of Martyrs and Early Modern Print Culture* (Cambridge: Cambridge University Press, 2006), 116. Gradually, as well, the annotations in the Geneva Bible became more emphatic about the Antichrist and the apocalypse. Basil Hall, "The Genevan Version of the English Bible: Its Aims and Achievements," in Stephens, ed., *The Bible, the Reformation and the Church*, 144. In chapter 4 of *Tudor Protestant Political Thought, 1647–1603* (Leiden: Brill, 2011), Stephen A. Chavura traces the intersection between Protestant concepts of the Christian prince and royal "absolutism" in ways that make Puritan wrestlings with the royal supremacy more understandable.

62. Pearson, *Thomas Cartwright*, 115–17, 123–24; Collinson, *Elizabethan Puritan Movement*, pt. 3, chap. 5.

63. Collinson, *Elizabethan Puritan Movement*, 274; Gordon Donaldson, "Lord Chancellor Glamis and Theodore Beza," *Scottish Church History* (Edinburgh: Scottish Academic, 1985), chap. 11. *A Seconde Parte* remained in manuscript until edited by Peel, although eighteenth-century Dissenters such as Benjamin Brook drew upon it.

64. Collinson, Craig, and Usher, eds., *Conferences and Combination Lectures*, 89. The persistence of classis-like meetings in York is described in Roland. A. Marchant, *The Puritans and the Church Courts in the Diocese of York 1560–1642* (London: Longmans, Green, 1960), chaps. 3, 8; Manning, *Religion and Society*, chap. 10; Collinson, *Elizabethan Puritan Movement*, pt. 4, chap. 6.

65. Collinson, "John Field and Elizabethan Puritanism," 342 and passim; Collinson, *Elizabethan Puritan Movement*, pt. 4, chap. 5; Peel, *Seconde Parte*, 1:14–18; Pearson, *Thomas Cartwright*, 258–59.

66. Neale, *Elizabeth I and Her Parliaments*, 2:82, 160, 151, 154; Hartley, *Parliaments of Elizabeth I, Vol. 2: 1584–1589* (London: Leicester University Press, 1995), 45–47; Collinson, *Religion of Protestants* 41; William Hunt, *The Puritan Moment: The Coming of Revolution in an English County* (Cambridge, Mass.: Harvard University Press, 1983), chap. 4 (on petitions from Essex County).

67. As a reminder, the three were: (1) accepting the royal supremacy; (2) agreeing that the *Book of Common Prayer* was scriptural; and (3) accepting the Thirty-Nine Articles. The first and third were acceptable; the second was not. Whitgift's campaign and the scope of nonsubscription is described in Collinson, *Elizabethan Puritan Movement*, 243–72. Whitgift induced some of these to subscribe once he softened the meaning of the act, and local magnates did what they could to protect the clergy. The pushback against his agenda is described in Knappen, *Tudor Puritanism*, 271–80; and Diarmaid MacCulloch, *Suffolk and the Tudors: Politics and Religion in an English County, 1500–1600* (Oxford: Clarendon, 1986), 208–9, 216–17. For example, the nonconformist Richard Rogers was suspended by Whitgift, but "after Thirty Weeks I was Restored by Dr. Aylmer . . . to whome Sir Robert

Wroth Writ in favour of me." M. M. Knappen, ed., *Two Tudor Puritan Diaries* (Chicago: American Society of Church History, 1933), 29. Kenneth Fincham points out the structural and practical impediments to conformity in "Clerical Conformity from Whitgift to Laud," in *Conformity and Orthodoxy in the English Church, c. 1560–1660*, ed. Peter Lake and Michael Questier (Woodbridge: Boydell, 2000), 125–58.

68. Leland H. Carlson, *Martin Marprelate, Gentleman: Master Job Throkmorton Laid Open in His Colors* (San Marino: Huntington Library, 1981), 106; Strype, *Annals of the Reformation*, vol. 3.1:319–29 (on petitions in 1584; quotation, p. 322); Peel, *Seconde Parte*, 2:5–26.

69. Hartley, *Parliaments of Elizabeth I*, 2:334–38, 390–91, 439–69; a Puritan-linked "Supplication" to the Parliament of 1586–87 is included in Peel, *Seconde Parte*, 2:70–87, and the bills themselves are printed in ibid., 2:1–4, 196–98, 212–18. See also Hartley, ed., *Proceedings in the Parliaments of Elizabeth I, Vol. 3: 1593–1601* (Leicester: Leicester University Press, 1995), 163, 168, 486–87. Parliamentary politics of this period are described in Collinson, *Elizabethan Puritan Movement*, 307–8 and pt. 6, chap. 2 passim; Patrick Collinson, *Richard Bancroft and Elizabethan Anti-Puritanism* (Cambridge: Cambridge University Press, 2013), 55–57. "Now the time of toleration seemed to be past, and the course of so manie yeers seemed to call for the performance of the promise of reformation." Peel, *Seconde Parte*, 1:84, 304–11; Hartley, *Parliaments of Elizabeth I*, 2:439–69 (1589).

70. Pearson, *Thomas Cartwright*, 272–77; Knappen, *Tudor Puritanism*, 289–90; Joseph Black, ed., *The Martin Marprelate Tracts: A Modernized and Annotated Edition* (Cambridge: Cambridge University Press, 2010), xxii–xxiv.

71. Black, *Marprelate Tracts*, 115; accepting Throckmorton as their principal author, with John Penry (see below) possibly writing the final three in the series. Ibid., xxxv–xli. For an insightful discussion of the language of the tracts in the context of vernacular protest, see Collinson, "Ecclesiastical Vitriol: Religious Satire in the 1590s and the Invention of Puritanism," in *The Reign of Elizabeth I: Court and Culture in the Last Decade*, ed. John Guy (Cambridge: Cambridge University Press, 1995), 150–70. Their place in an expanding sphere of print-based controversy is described in Joad Raymond, *Pamphlets and Pamphleteering in Early Modern Britain* (Cambridge: Cambridge University Press, 2003), chap. 2.

72. Hoyle, *Reformation and Religious Identity*, 62. That bishops were the equivalent of robbers who misused the church's wealth for their personal benefit had already been emphasized in statements of the mid-1580s; Peel, *Seconde Parte*, 2:15–18.

73. Stuart Barton Babbage, *Puritanism and Richard Bancroft* (London; SPCK, 1962), chap. 1; Albert Peel, ed., *Tracts ascribed to Richard Bancroft* (Cambridge: Cambridge University Press, 1953); Collinson, "Ecclesiastical Vitriol"; Collinson, *Richard Bancroft*, chaps. 2–3; Morrissey, *Paul's Cross Sermons*, 208–13 (the emergence of this rhetoric, which associated the English presbyterians with "Brownists"); Collinson, *Elizabethan Puritan Movement*, pt. 8. See also Strype, *Life of Whitgift*, 1:559–60.

74. Collinson, *Elizabethan Puritan Movement*, 420–23; Peel, *Seconde Parte*, 1:84, 2:80; Porter, *Reformation and Reaction*, 143; *The Miscellany of the Wodrow Society*, ed. David Laing (Edinburgh, 1844), 1:483–85; Peel, *Tracts*, 70. Morrissey, *Paul's Cross Sermons*, chap. 7, traces this rhetoric from the 1560s onward. The intricate court politics behind these developments is described in Collinson, *Richard Bancroft*, chap 7. The contribution of English Catholics to a characterization of the reformers as political rebels is described in Peter Marshall, "John Calvin and the English Catholics," *HJ* 53 (2010): 849–70, an argument Catholics had been making about English Protestants since the 1550s, if not much earlier. See also Strype, *Annals of the Reformation*, vol. 1, pt. 1:166–68. The radicals emphasized their willingness to subscribe to two of the three Advertisements, but not the one involving

the *Book of Common Prayer*. Previously, Archbishop Parker had felt that the Admonition Controversy showed signs of becoming another uprising akin to the Anabaptist takeover of the city of Münster. Pearson, *Thomas Cartwright*, 104.

75. The transition from Whitgift's understanding of episcopacy in the 1570s to Bancroft and Bilson's much more firmly "divine right" in the 1590s is briefly sketched in Jacqueline Rose, *Godly Kingship in Restoration England: The Politics of the Royal Supremacy, 1660–1688* (Cambridge: Cambridge University Press, 2011), 56–60.

76. M. R. Sommerville, "Richard Hooker and His Contemporaries on Episcopacy: An Elizabethan Consensus," *Journal of Ecclesiastical History* 35 (1984): 177–87; John Guy, "Elizabethan Establishment and the Ecclesiastical Polity," in Guy, *Reign of Elizabeth I*, 126–27. Strype, *Annals of the Reformation*, vol. 1, pt. 1 166–68.

77. Easily misunderstood, in the 1570s this term referred to the practice of explicating Scripture by those capable of doing so, e.g., ordained and educated ministers. Its meaning broadened in the seventeenth century.

78. Collinson, *Archbishop Grindal*, chaps. 12–13; Guy, "The 1590s: The Second Reign of Elizabeth I," in Guy, *Reign of Elizabeth I*, 11–13.

79. Porter, *Reformation and Reaction*, 145. For a backward glance from the mid-1580s, emphasizing the lessons learned by the Marian exiles and the free discussion of reform of the early 1560s, see Peel, *Seconde Parte*, 2:83–84. As Collinson points out, "radical puritanism" persisted in "several pockets." *Elizabethan Puritan Movement*, 439 and more generally pt. 8/4. See also chapter 6, below.

80. *A parte of a register*, 382; John Udall, *A Demonstration of the Trueth of That Discipline* ([London, 1588]), sigs. a2–3; Peel, *Seconde Parte*, 2:10–12.

81. Hartley, *Parliaments of Elizabeth I*, 2:315 (modernized); Fulke, *Plain Declaration*, 257–59, a situation exacerbated by pluralism and nonresidency (ibid., 259). According to a census carried out by 1586, of 2,537 parishes, only 472 had "preachers," some of whom may not have preached very often. Peel, *Seconde Parte*, 2:70–87, 88–184.

82. R. C. Richardson, *Puritanism in North-west England: A Regional Study of the Diocese of Chester to 1642* (Manchester: Manchester University Press, 1972), chaps. 1–4 (quotation, p. 146); Pearson, *Thomas Cartwright*, 189; Cross, *Church and People*, 115–17, 134–39; Ron Fritze, "'A Rare Example of Godlyness Amongst Gentlemen': The Role of the Kingsmill and Gifford Families in Promoting the Reformation in Hampshire," in Lake and Dowling, eds., *Protestantism and the National Church*, 144–61; R. C. Richardson, "Puritanism and the Ecclesiastical Authorities: The Case of the Diocese of Chester," in *Politics, Religion and the English Civil War*, ed. Brian Manning (London: Edwin Arnold, 1973), 3–33; Hartley, *Parliaments of Elizabeth I*, 3:35; Strype, *Annals of the Reformation*, vol. 3, pt. 2:207–10; Cromartie, *Constitutionalist Revolution*, 116; Collinson, *Elizabethan Puritan Movement*, 14. Burghley's role in the religious politics of the 1590s is noted in John Guy, "The 1590s: The Second Reign of Elizabeth I?" in Guy, *Reign of Elizabeth I*, 6. This paragraph also draws on Mary Fulbrook, "Legitimation Crises and the Early Modern State: The Politics of Religious Toleration," in *Religion and Society in Early Modern Europe, 1500–1800*, ed. Kaspar von Greyerz (London: George Allen and Unwin, 1984), 146–56. The muddled situation on the ground is ably described in Roger Howell, Jr., *Newcastle upon Tyne and the Puritan Revolution* (Oxford: Clarendon Press, 1967), chap. 3.

83. Peel, ed., *Seconde Parte*, 1: 13–14; Morrissey, *Politics and the Paul's Cross Sermons*, chap. 6.

84. Quoted in Constantine Hopf, *Martin Bucer and the English Reformation* (Oxford: Basil Blackwell, 1956), 131; another version (1589) of the expansion of the reformers' program is quoted in Babbage, *Puritanism and Richard Bancroft*, 9.

85. Laing, *Works of Knox*, 6:402. In 1586, the Colloquy of Montbeliard made one more attempt prompted by political circumstances.

86. Glenn S. Sunshine, "Reformed Theology and the Origins of Synodical Polity: Calvin, Beza and the Gallican Confession," in *Later Calvinism: International Perspectives*, ed. W. Fred Graham, Sixteenth Century Essays and Studies 16 (Kirksville, MO: Sixteenth Century Journal Publishers, 1994); 141–58; Brian G. Armstrong, "*Semper Reformanda*: The Case of the French Reformed Church, 1559–1620," in ibid., 119–40; Derk Visser, "Establishing the Reformed Church: Clergy and Magistrates in the Low Countries 1572–1620," in ibid., 389–407 (noting that the plan of order drawn up in Emden in 1572 did not include any extra-congregational structures); Philip Benedict and Nicolas Forerod, *L'Organisation et L'Action des Eglises Reformees de France* (Geneva: Droz, 2012), intro. In 1561, Scottish accomplishments had been publicized in *The Confession of the Faythe and Doctrine . . . professed, by the Protestantes of the Realme of Scotlande*, and the ecclesiology of the Reformed international in *A Confession of Faythe, made by common consent of divers reformed Churches beyond the Seas*, which called for a ministry of pastors, deacons, and superintendents, all having "equal power" and coming to office "by election." I owe this bibliographical information to Champlain Burrage, *The Early English Dissenters in the Light of Recent Research*, 2 vols. (Cambridge: Cambridge University Press, 1912), 1:78. The French "discipline" of 1571 was among the documents included in Peel, *Seconde Parte* (numbers 44–45). See also Glenn Sunshine, "Discipline as the Third Mark of the Church: Three Views," *Calvin Theological Journal* 33 (1998): 469–80.

87. Andrew Pettegree, "European Calvinism: History, Providence, and Martyrdom," in *The Church Retrospective*, ed. R. N. Swanson (Woodbridge: Boydell, 1997), 227–52; Pettegree, "The Clergy and the Reformation: From 'Devilish Priesthood' to New Professional Elite," in *The Reformation of the Parishes: The Ministry and the Reformation in Town and Country*, ed. Andrew Pettegree (Manchester: Manchester University Press, 1993), 1–21; Pettegree, *Reformation and the Culture of Persuasion* (Cambridge: Cambridge University Press, 2005), chap. 8; Collinson, *Elizabethan Puritan Movement*, 293–94; Helga Robinson-Hammerstein, "Trinity College, Dublin, in the Early Seventeenth Century: Institutional Isolation and Foreign Contacts," in *Lines of Contact: Proceedings of the Second Conference of . . . Historians of Universities*, ed. John M. Fletcher and Hilde De Ridder-Symoens (Ghent: Universiteit Gent, 1994), 43–56. See also Heinz Schilling, *Religion, Political Culture and the Emergence of Early Modern Society: Essays in German and Dutch History* (Leiden: Brill, 1992), chap. 5; Collinson, *Elizabethan Puritan Movement*, chap. 2.

88. Cromartie, *Constitutionalist Revolution*, 123; Fulke, *Plain Declaration*, 271 (edification), 274–75 (authority curtailed).

89. *A parte of a register*, 62; Kaufman, *Thinking of the Laity*, chap. 4. For popular responses to clerical outspokenness, see below, chap. 4. After I had written these two paragraphs, I came on Alan Cromartie's argument that "the emergence . . . of an explicitly Presbyterian movement" can be understood as "an all-purpose cure for everything that hindered the spread of godliness, but especially for the shortage of adequate preachers." Cromartie, *Constitutionalist Revolution*, 125.

90. Robinson, *Zurich Letters*, 1:154; Peel, *Seconde Parte*, 1:71; 2:9; Hartley, *Parliaments of Elizabeth I*, 1:221–24. For Anthony Gilby's assertion of the priority of conscience in the mid-1550s, see Danner, *Pilgrimage to Puritanism*, 39; and for Gilby's wrestlings with this tension, see Chavura, *Tudor Protestant Political Thought*, 184–85. Another way of questioning the close relationship between episcopacy and the royal supremacy was to insinuate that theories of episcopacy as a divine office threatened the authority of the monarch, an argument revived in the 1640s. Lest we tip the balance too far in the direction of defiance, it is

important to keep in mind that, almost to a person, the dissenting clergy were willing to subscribe to the royal supremacy.

91. *Cartwrightiana*, ed. Albert Peel and Leland H. Carlson (London: George Allen and Unwin, 1951), 24, 27; see also Pearson, *Thomas Cartwright*, 148–50 (on Cartwright's advice c. 1576 to wear the surplice if doing so allowed someone to remain active in ministry) and 197–98; Strype, *Annals of the Reformation*, 4:67–73; Peter Lake, *Moderate Puritans and the Elizabethan Church* (Cambridge: Cambridge University Press, 1982), 77–92.

92. Patrick Collinson, *The Religion of Protestants: The Church in English Society 1559–1625* (Oxford: Clarendon, 1982), 3–6 (quotation, p. 4); Thomas Fuller, *The Church History of Britain*, 3 vols. (London, 1868), 2:503; Rose, *Godly Kingship*, 45–60; Cromartie, *Constitutionalist Revolution*, 124–25; Conrad Russell, "Parliament, the Royal Supremacy, and the Church," in *Parliamentary History* 19 (2000): 26–37. Tensions between secular and ecclesiastical authority were nothing new in the history of the Christian church in the West and flared up with special intensity in early sixteenth-century England, a story told in Kaufman, *Redeeming Politics*, and Richard Marius, *Thomas More: A Biography* (New York: Knopf, 1984), chap. 9.

93. Hartley, *Parliaments of Elizabeth I*, 2:339. See also Charles W. A. Prior, "Ecclesiology and Political Thought in England, 1580–c. 1630," *HJ* 48 (2005): 855–84.

94. As William M. Lamont has pointed out, the many references to "erastian" preferences and policies ignore what Thomas Erastus himself was arguing. Nonetheless, I employ the word as others in the seventeenth century were doing, to signify the impinging of the civil state on the church. Lamont, *Puritanism and the English Revolution: Vol. 1, Marginal Prynne, 1660–1669* (Aldershot: Gregg Revivals, 1991), chap. 7.

95. These questions reflect the influence on me of Jane Facey, "John Foxe and the Defence of the English Church," in Lake and Dowling, *Protestantism and the National Church*, 174–75; and Lake, "Presbyterianism, the Idea of a National Church and the Argument from Divine Right," in ibid., 196–97. The context includes the ambiguous relationship between the visible and invisible churches as described in certain sixteenth-century Reformed creeds, noted in Stephen Brachlow, *The Communion of Saints: Radical Puritan and Separatist Ecclesiology, 1570–1625* (Oxford: Oxford University Press, 1988), chap. 1.

96. Collinson, *Elizabethan Puritan Movement*, 132, see also p. 145.

97. In 1593 the laws repressing Catholicism were expanded to encompass "Brownists," not, however, without opposition. Hartley, *Parliaments of Elizabeth I*, 3:62–63, 168.

98. Timothy George, *John Robinson and the English Separatist Tradition* (Macon, GA: Mercer University Press, 1982), chap. 4; Frere and Douglas, *Puritan Manifestoes*, 19. B. R. White provides an overview in *The English Separatist Tradition: From the Marian Martyrs to the Pilgrim Fathers* (Oxford: Oxford University Press, 1971). In the early going, the Reformation in Europe also spawned groups that are sometimes described as "separatists" because they abandoned not yet fully reformed churches and set up communities of their own. Structurally, these groups resemble the Separatists described in this chapter, although there is no reason to assume any actual connections.

99. R. J. Acheson, *Radical Puritans in England 1550–1660* (London: Longman, 1990), 85. As we will see, another assumption of these groups was that the state church could never attain the requisite standard of holiness; "discipline" and/or "edification" was simply not possible.

100. The broadest definition may be Murray Tolmie's, which includes any "autonomous" congregation outside the framework of a parochial (state church) system. Tolmie, *The Triumph of the Saints: The Separate Churches of London, 1616–1649* (Cambridge: Cambridge University Press, 1977), chap. 1, a definition that suits the groups he is describing but not

the edgier "Separatism" of Henry Barrow. Just how fine the line can be is suggested by what we know about a group that formed around John Udall in the 1580s; as was noted in an investigation of his thinking and practice, "He has allowed some, whom he calls 'the children of God,' to be his disciples. This brotherhood refuse to mix with others, and many of them accompanied him to London, and communicated privately there." Peel, *Seconde Parte*, 2:45. As George Yule points out in *The Independents in the English Civil War* (Melbourne: Melbourne University Press, 1958), the category mashes together those who fully quit the state church and others who sought to reform it from outside, as it were, and retained a role for the state (pp. 7, 11–12).

101. Caroline Litzenberger, *The English Reformation and the Laity: Gloucestershire, 1540–1580* (Cambridge: Cambridge University Press, 1997), 143–53; Collinson, *Religion of Protestants*, chap. 6; Collinson, "The English Conventicle," in *Voluntary Religion*, ed. W. J. Sheils and Diana Wood, Studies in Church History 23 (Oxford: Blackwell, 1986), 223–59; Collinson, *From Cranmer to Sancroft* (London: Hambledon Continuum, 2006), chap. 6; and, for examples in 1570s Essex, Davids, *Annals of Evangelical Nonconformity*, 67–70. See also Michael E. Moody, "Trials and Travels of a Nonconformist Layman: The Spiritual Odyssey of Stephen Offwood, 1564–ca. 1635," *Church History* 51 (1982): 157–71; after dabbling in extra-church conventicles in England, Offwood tried out almost every variety of radical Puritanism in the Netherlands.

102. Preceded by the people described in Thomas Freeman, "Dissenters from a Dissenting Church: The Challenge of the Freewillers, 1550–1558," in *The Beginnings of English Protestantism*, ed. Peter Marshall and Alec Ryrie (Cambridge: Cambridge University Press, 2002), 129–56, describing them (p. 129) as "the first English Protestants to establish organized congregations which not only repudiated, but also challenged the authority of the Protestant clerical leadership."

103. *Zurich Letters*, 2:29–30, a group that would not admit anyone who had "backslid" unless that person repented; Brett Usher, " 'In a Time of Persecution': New Light on the Secret Protestant Congregation in Marian London," in *John Foxe and the English Reformation*, ed. David Loades (Aldershot: Scholar, 1997), 233–51; Collinson, Craig, and Usher, *Conferences and Combination Lectures*, liii; Foxe, *Book of Martyrs*, 8:443–49, 558–59; Cross, *Church and People*, 98–104. On historical memory, see Adrian Chastain Weimer, *Martyrs Mirror: Persecution and Holiness in Early New England* (New York: Oxford University Press, 2011), chap. 2.

104. *A parte of a register*, 23–37; John Strype, *The History of the Life and Acts of the Most Reverend Father in God, Edmund Grindal*, 2 vols. (London, 1821), 1:171–75; Brook, *Lives of the Puritans*, 1: 135; Burrage, *EED*, 2:13. Burrage argues (1:79–93) that the 1567 group should be classified as "independently Puritan," not Separatist. For John Knox's contacts with this group, see below, chap. 3. For an overview of this early period, see David Loades, "Anabaptism and English Sectarianism in the Mid-Sixteenth Century," in *Reform and Reformation: England and the Continent, c. 1500–1750*, ed. Derek Baker, Studies in Church History: Subsidia 2 (Oxford: Blackwell, 1979), 59–70.

105. John Craig, *Reformation, Politics and Polemics: The Growth of Protestantism in East Anglian Market Towns, 1500–1610* (Aldershot: Ashgate, 2001), 105, 105n. In 1590, the group associated with Barrow and Greenwood was also against having children baptized "according to the forme of baptisme ministred . . . in the Church of England, but are rather to be kept unbaptised." Burrage, *EED*, 2:21.

106. Browne, "A True and Short Declaration" in *The Writings of Robert Harrison and Robert Browne*, ed. Albert Peel and Leland Carlson (London: George Allen and Unwin,

1953), 405l,407, 412, 419, 39–40, 404. The *True Declaration* is, in part, Browne's narrative of his own spiritual history.

107. Burrage, *EED*, 1:105; Browne, *A Treatise of reformation without tarrying for anie* ([Middelburg], 1582); Peel and Carlson, *Writings of Browne*, 399, 419, 422; Coolidge, *Pauline Renaissance*, chap. 3. Browne is commonly credited with introducing congregational covenants, a point made by White, *English Separatist Tradition*, 54–56, but disputed by Brachlow, *Communion of Saints*, 50–52. A church imagined as a cluster of small-scale congregations and "free election" of ministers had figured in quasi-Separatist polemics as early as 1570, if not before; Peel, *Seconde Parte*, 1:71–72; and for strong assertions of this kind contemporary with Browne or from the mid-1580s, ibid., 2:33. John Udall's practice and thinking in the mid-1580s (Peel, *Seconde Parte*, 41–45) paralleled Browne's vision of a laity empowered to refuse anyone ordained by a bishop, "unlearned" men interpreting Scripture, and local congregations handling all matters of discipline.

108. Craig, *Reformation, Politics and Polemics*, chap. 4; Strype, *Annals of the Reformation*, vol. 3, pt. 1, 22; White, *English Separatist Tradition*, 61–64. See also Collinson, *Richard Bancroft*, 33–35.

109. Burrage, *EED*, 2:165. As White points out in *English Separatist Tradition*, 59, Browne regarded the magistrate in his capacity as a church member as subject to the same discipline as everyone else, another point on which he followed the lead of the presbyterians.

110. Peel and Carlson, *Writings of Robert Harrison*, 154–56.

111. Craig, *Reformation, Politics and Polemics*, 104–7; Henry Martyn Dexter, *The Congregationalism of the Last Three Hundred Years* (New York, 1880), 208–10. The local and national political tensions that coalesced in Bury are brilliantly explored in MacCulloch, *Suffolk and the Tudors*, chap. 6.

112. Strype, *Annals of the Reformation*, 4:244–45; Burrage, *Early English Dissenters*, 2:35.

113. White, *English Separatist Tradition*, 72–73; *The Writings of John Greenwood, 1587–1590, Together with the Joint Writings of Henry Barrow and John Greenwood, 1587–1590*, ed. Leland H. Carlson (London: George Allen and Unwin, 1962), 4.

114. Carlson, *Writings of John Greenwood*, 98 (from *The True Church and the False Church*, 1588); *The Writings of Henry Barrow, 1590–1591*, ed. Leland H. Carlson (London: George Allen and Unwin, 1966); 38, 46–47, 102–110 (quotation, p. 110); *A True Description out of the Word of God, of the Visible Church* ([Dordt], 1589), reprinted in Walker, *Creeds and Platforms*,, 33–40 (quotations, pp. 34, 40), Barrow, *A plaine refutation of M. Giffards reproachful booke* (London, 1591), 1–2; White, *English Separatist Tradition*, 71–79. In *Godly Republicanism: Puritans, Pilgrims, and a City on a Hill* (Cambridge, MA.: Harvard University Press, 2012), chap. 2, Michael P. Winship emphasizes this group's objections to presbyterianism. Debate continues about the exact meaning of the profession and other practices among this group. As of 1589, Greenwood had not had his eighteen-month-old son baptized. See also a document drawn up by the Amsterdam group c. 1603, "The Points of Difference," in which the "true visible Church" is described as "a company of people called and separated from the world . . . and joined together by voluntarie profession of the faith of Christ. . . . And that therefore no knowe Atheist, unbeliever, Heretique, or wicked liver, be received or retained." Walker, *Creeds and Platforms*, 78.

115. Carlson, *Writings of John Greenwood*, 297; Strype, *Annals of the Reformation*, 4:198–99; Burrage, *Early English Dissenters*, 2:43; Dexter, *Congregationalism*, 215, 224. Nonetheless, the Confession of 1596 that was Johnson's doing endorsed the authority of the civil state to "suppress and root out . . . all false ministries [and] abolish and destroy the

Idoll Temples . . . and all other monuments of Idolatrie and superstition." Walker, *Creeds and Platforms*, 71–72.

116. The basis in law for these executions is described in White, *English Separatist Tradition*, 89; the act itself, titled "The Act against Puritans," is included in Gee and Hardy, *Documents*, 492–98. Brought before the Court of High Commission in 1588, Penry subsequently published his own narrative of the back-and-forth: *Th'Appellation of John Penri unto the Highe Court of Parliament* (n.p., 1589). Albert Peel provides an overview of his life in *The Notebook of John Penry, 1593*, Camden Society 3rd Series 68 (Lodon: Royal Historical Society, 1944), with critical comments on previous versions of Penry's manuscripts.

117. Burrage, *EED*, 2:36–37, 136; Porter, *Reformation and Reaction*, 157–63; Strype, *Annals of the Reformation*, 4:187–92; Willem Nijenhuis, ed., *Matthew Slade 1569–1628 Letters to the English Ambassador* (Leiden: Leiden University Press, 1986), 75–76. In Amsterdam, the church had to deal with internal conflicts; for these, see White, *English Separatist Tradition*, chap. 7, and Michael E. Moody, "A Critical Edition of George Johnson's *A Discourse of Some Troubles and Excommunications in the Banished English Church at Amsterdam 1603*" (PhD thesis, Claremont Graduate School, 1979). The group also pondered emigrating to the New World.

118. Keith L. Sprunger, *Dutch Puritanism: A History of English and Scottish Churches of the Netherlands in the Sixteenth and Seventeenth Centuries* (Leiden: Brill, 1982), 53–54, a politics that continued into the 1630s.

119. Peel, *Seconde Parte*, 1:138–39 (referencing Anthony Gilby's response to a less intransigent Cartwright). The obverse of this principle was the assertion that no layperson should participate in the Lord's Supper if it was administered by the wrong kind of minister. Ibid., 2:43.

120. Peel and Carlson, *Cartwrightiana*, 60–75 (quotations, pp. 60, 61, 62); White, *English Separatist Tradition*, 56.

121. Peel, *Seconde Parte*, 2:87; and see, in general, Collinson, *Richard Bancroft*. The role of anti-puritanism in religious politics of the Caroline period is described in chapter 7, below.

122. Timothy Scott McGinnis, *George Gifford and the Reformation of the Common Sort: Puritan Priorities in Elizabethan Religious Life*, Sixteenth Century Essays and Studies 70 (Kirksville, MO: Truman State University Press, 2002), chap. 4; [Robert Browne], *An answere to Master Cartwright his letter for ioyning with the English Churches* (London, n.d.), in Peel and Carlson, *Cartwrightiana*, 49–58; Black, *Marprelate Tracts*, 204. In *English Presbyterianism, 1590–1640* (Stanford: Stanford University Press, 2011), Polly Ha emphasizes, quite wisely, the importance of "a single visible church" to the presbyterians (pp. 9–10). See also Edward H. Bloomfield, *The Opposition to the English Separatists, 1570–1625* (Washington, DC: University Press of America, 1981), chap. 5. Earlier, in 1568, Thomas Lever had debated the lawfulness of the church with a group of imprisoned Separatists and, although conceding that the surplice belonged "to the popish priesthood," had defended the lawfulness of the state church on the basis of the two "notes" of doctrine and the right administration of the sacraments. Peel, *Seconde Parte*, 1:55.

123. Peel, *Seconde Parte*, 2:203–4; Collinson, *Elizabethan Puritan Movement*, 390.

Chapter 3. Reformation in Scotland

1. Jane Dawson, *John Knox* (New Haven, CT: Yale University Press, 2015), chaps. 3, 8; (quotation, p. 151); Laing, *Works of Knox*, 6:239–41, 4:468; Jane E. A. Dawson, "John Knox, Christopher Goodman and the 'Example of Geneva,'" in *The Reception of Continental Ref-*

ormation in Britain, ed. Polly Ha and Patrick Collinson, Proceedings of the British Academy 164 (Oxford: Oxford University Press, 2010), 107–35. See also Richard L. Greaves, *Theology & Revolution in the Scottish Reformation: Studies in the Thought of John Knox* (Grand Rapids, MI: Christian University Press, 1980), 1–24 (suggesting that Knox owed his concept of authority more to the theologians of Zurich than to Calvin), 204; Richard G. Kyle, *God's Watchman: John Knox's Faith and Vocation* (Eugene, OR: Pickwick, 2014), chap. 6.

2. Knox, "A Vindication of the Doctrine that the Sacrifice of the Mass Is Idolatry" (c. 1550), in Laing, *Works of Knox*, 6:12; 3:206; 4:12. See also Katharine R. Firth, *The Apocalyptic Tradition in Reformation Britain, 1530–1645* (Oxford: Oxford University Press, 1979), chap. 4. In Jane Dawson's estimation, the political struggles that accompanied the waning of reform in the final months of the reign of Edward VI made Knox "deeply suspicious of any form of gradualism, and his fear of political accommodation and the dangers of compromise hardened into a rigid dogma." Dawson, *John Knox*, 79; see also her comments (p. 101) on his dissatisfaction with the Church of England. For the theme of "edification" or "commonwealth" in Knox's thinking, see Duncan Shaw, *The General Assemblies of the Church of Scotland, 1560–1600: Their Origins and Development* (Edinburgh: Saint Andrew, 1964), 21 n. 4.

3. Aberdeen's was a different kind of reformation, as Allan White demonstrates in "The Impact of the Reformation on a Burgh Community: The Case of Aberdeen," in *The Early Modern Town in Scotland*, ed. Michael Lynch (London: Croom Helm, 1987), 81–101. In *Aberdeen Before 1800: A New History*, ed. E. Patricia Dennison, David Ditchburn, and Michael Lynch (East Lothian: Tuckwell, 2002), the emphasis falls on the lingering Catholicism of the city's political elite and the city's muted Protestantism. Edinburgh's halting reformation is described in Michael Lynch, *Edinburgh and the Reformation* (Edinburgh: Donald, 1981). The violence in Perth and the reaction to it is described in *John Knox's History of the Reformation in Scotland*, ed. William Croft Dickinson, 2 vols. (New York: Philosophical Library, 1950), 1:161–63. See also Dawson, *John Knox*, 179–82.

4. Jane E. A. Dawson, "'The Face of Ane Perfyt reformed Kyrk': St Andrews and the Early Scottish Reformation," in *Humanism and Reform: The Church in Europe, England, and Scotland, 1400–1643*, ed. James Kirk, Studies in Church History: Subsidia 8 (Oxford: Blackwell, 1991), 413–36; Dickinson, *Knox's History of the Reformation*, 1:182–91; 161–63; Laing, *Works of Knox*, 6:23. Subsequently, Knox and Erskine of Dun criticized such "irregularitys" in response to the charge of inciting "rebellion." Robert Wodrow, *Collections upon the Lives of the Reformers and Most Eminent Ministers of the Church of Scotland*, 2 vols. (Glasgow, 1834), 1:17. Episodes of iconoclasm had arisen in Edinburgh in the context of Knox's visit of 1556 and John Willock's preaching; see Dickinson, *Knox's History of the Reformation*, 1:125, 128. Gripped by the same feelings, a mob entered St. Michael's, Linlithgow, on June 29, 1559, and "emptied all the niches, broke the holy-water 'stoup,' destroyed the altars, and in short kicked out of it everything which they deemed popish." John Ferguson, *Ecclesia Antiqua; or, The History of an Ancient Church* (Edinburgh: Oliver and Boyd, 1905), 52–53.

5. Michael Lynch, "From privy kirk to burgh church: An alternative view of the process of Protestantisation," in *Church, Politics and Society: Scotland, 1408–1929*, ed. Norman MacDougall (Edinburgh: John Donald,1983), 85–96; Roger Mason, "Covenant and Commonweal: The language of politics in Reformation Scotland," in ibid., 97–126; Clare Kellar, *Scotland, England, and the Reformation, 1534–61* (Oxford: Clarendon, 2003), 151 (suggesting that the "more extreme Protestant activists" were "clearly in a minority"). See also her

assessment of militance and its origins in the experience of the Scottish Marian exiles (chaps. 5 and 6).

6. John Coffey, "The Problem of Scottish Puritanism," in *Enforcing Reformation in Ireland and Scotland, 1550–1700*, ed. Elizabethanne Boran and Crawford Gribben (Aldershot: Ashgate, 2006), 66–90 (noting the belated appearance of the term in Scottish polemics, but emphasizing similarities); Margo Todd, "The Problem of Scotland's Puritans," in *The Cambridge Companion to Puritanism*, ed. John Coffey and Paul C. H. Lim (Cambridge: Cambridge University Press, 2008), 174–88. Shifts in historians' practice are visible in Coffey, *Politics, Religion and the British Revolutions: The Mind of Samuel Rutherford* (Cambridge: Cambridge University Press, 1997), esp. pp. 17–18; David George Mullan, *Scottish Puritanism, 1590–1638* (Oxford: Oxford University Press, 2000); and James Kirk, *Patterns of Reform: Continuity and Change in the Reformation Kirk* (Edinburg: T&T Clark, 1989). Coming into use: Jenny Wormald, "Ecclesiastical vitriol: The kirk, the puritans and the future king of England," in *The Reign of Elizabeth I: Court and Culture in the Last Decade*, ed. John Guy (Cambridge: Cambridge University Press, 1995), 171–91; Jamie Reid-Baxter, "Mr Andrew Boyd (1567–1636): A Neo-Stoic Bishop of Argyll and His Writings," in *Sixteenth-Century Scotland: Essays in Honour of Michael Lynch*, ed. Julian Goodare and Alasdair A. Macdonald (Leiden: Brill, 2008), 395–425 (Boyd objected to the practice of using this term to stigmatize critics of the state church). Just as perplexing is the custom of describing the more emphatic of the Scottish reformers either as "Presbyterians" or "Melvillians," so named because of the prominence of the minister and educator Andrew Melville in religious politics after 1575. Each of these terms is problematic, the first because the General Assembly waited until the drafting of the *Second Book of Discipline* (1578) to commit itself to an explicitly "Presbyterian" system; the second because it exaggerates the influence of a single minister, a point Alan R. MacDonald emphasizes in *The Jacobean Kirk, 1567–1625: Sovereignty, Polity and Liturgy* (Aldershot: Ashgate, 1998). See also Kirk, *Patterns of Reform*, chap. 6. The binary of presbyterian versus episcopalian seems irrelevant to an oddly hybrid state church.

7. Anthony Gilby, *An Admonition to England and Scotland, to Call Them to Repentance* (Geneva, 1558), in Laing, *Works of Knox*, 4:553–71; Kellar, *Scotland, England, and the Reformation*, chaps. 5–6 (noting the connections fashioned in Geneva and Frankfurt); Dawson, *John Knox*, 261–64; Gordon Donaldson, "The Scottish Presbyterian Exiles in England, 1584–8," *RSCHS* 14 (1960): 67–80.

8. Peterkin, *Records of the Kirk*, 178.

9. Gordon Donaldson, *The Scottish Reformation* (Cambridge: Cambridge University Press, 1960), chap. 3; Alec Ryrie, *The Origins of the Scottish Reformation* (Manchester: Manchester University Press, 2006), chap. 1. The economic disarray of the state church caused by lay patronage and, it must be said, the avarice of monasteries and abbeys, is briefly noted in J. H. Baxter, *Dundee and the Reformation*, Abertay Historical Society Publication 7 (Dundee: AHS, 1960), 11–12.

10. Mary Vershuur, *Politics or Religion? The Reformation in Perth, 1540–1570* (Edinburgh: Dunedin Academic Press, 2006); Ryrie, *Origins of the Scottish Reformation*, chap. 3 (quotation, p. 57); W. Stanford Reid, "Reformation in France and Scotland: A Case Study in Sixteenth-Century Communication" (emphasizing the importance of Scottish connections, and especially Knox's, with the French Huguenot), in *Later Calvinism: International Perspectives*, ed. W. Fred Graham, Sixteenth Century Essays and Studies 22 (Kirksville, MO: Sixteenth Century Journal Publishers, 1994), 195–214; Carol Edington, *Court and Culture in Renaissance Scotland: Sir David Lindsay of the Mount* (Amherst: University of Massachusetts Press, 1994).

11. Kirk, *Patterns of Reform*, chap. 1. Jane Dawson regards the layman Adam Wallace, executed for heresy in 1550, as "the first native Protestant within Scotland." Dawson, *Scotland Re-formed, 1488-1587* (Edinburgh; Edinburgh University Press, 2007), 184; Foxe, *Book of Martyrs*, 5:628–36. See also the sketch of John Willock in Wodrow, *Collections upon the Lives*, 1:99–116; active in Scotland in the 1550s, he was among the Scottish Protestants who found a haven in England.

12. Wodrow, *Collections upon the Lives*, 1:12–13; Ryrie, *Origins of the Scottish Reformation*, 109–13, chap. 6; Dickinson, *Knox's History of the Reformation*, 1:136–37; Laing, *Works of Knox*, 6:674–5. In places such as Dundee, Protestantism was more openly practiced by the late 1550s, as noted in Baxter, *Dundee and the Reformation*. For the 1550s period, Alec Ryrie offers a cautionary tale about the number of "privy kirks" of Protestants on the margins of a then-Catholic church. Ryrie, "Congregations, Conventicles and the Nature of Early Scottish Protestantism," *Past & Present* 191 (2006): 45–76.

13. Laing, *Works of Knox*, 4:524–28; Dickinson, *Knox's History of the Reformation*, 1:168; Carol Edington, "John Knox and the Castilians: A Crucible of Reforming Opinion?" in *John Knox and the British Reformations*, ed. Roger A. Mason (Aldershot: Ashgate, 1998), 29–50; David George Mullan, *Episcopacy in Scotland: The History of an Idea, 1560–1638* (Edinburgh: J. Donald, 1986), 12; Greaves, *Theology & Revolution*, 78–83, 207.

14. Kellar, *Scotland, England, and the Reformation*, 205 and chap. 6; Ryrie, *Origins of the Scottish Reformation*, chap. 7; Jane Dawson, "The Protestant Earl and Godly Gael: The Fifth Earl of Argyll (c. 1538–1573) and the Scottish Reformation," in *Life and Thought in the Northern Church c. 1100—c. 1700: Essays in Honour of Claire Cross*, ed. Diana Wood, Studies in Church History: Subsidia 8 (Woodbridge: Boydell, 1999), 337–63; Dawson, "Clan, Kin and Kirk: The Campbells and the Scottish Reformation," in *The Education of a Christian Society Humanism and the Reformation in Britain and the Netherlands*, ed. N. Scott Amos, Andrew Pettegree, and Henk van Nierop (Aldershot: Ashgate, 1997), 221–42; Dawson, *Scotland Re-formed*, 203–4. Campbell had entertained Knox during his preaching tour of 1555–56. Some six weeks later, a substantial group of craftsmen in St. Andrews added their names to a covenant that was being widely circulated, a text and moment described in Jane E. A. Dawson, "Bonding, Religious Allegiance and Covenanting," in *Kings, Lords and Men in Scotland and Britain, 1300-1625*, ed. Steve Boardman and Julian Goodare (Edinburgh: Edinburgh University Press, 2014), 161–62. That the substance of the 1559 covenant borrowed substantially from the "commonweal" tradition is demonstrated in Mason, "Covenant and Commonweal."

15. It remained so by comparison with England, for the documents of c. 1560–61 and the actions of two parliaments (1560, 1567) were never ratified by the country's monarch. Strictly speaking, therefore, these had an uncertain legal status.

16. Dickinson, *Knox's History of the Reformation*, 2:12.

17. See, e.g., John McCallum, *Reforming the Scottish Parish: The Reformation in Fife, 1560-1640* (Aldershot: Ashgate, 2010).

18. On the reformation parliament, see Alec Ryrie, *The Age of Reformation: The Tudor and Stewart Realms, 1485-1603* (London: Pearson Longman, 2009), 219; Keith M. Brown, "The Reformation Parliament," in *Parliament and Politics in Scotland, 1235-1560*, ed. Keith M. Brown and Roland J. Tanner (Edinburgh: University of Edinburgh Press, 2004), 203–31. James K. Cameron's "Introduction" to *The First Book of Discipline* (Edinburgh: Saint Andrew, 1972) traces the evolution of that text, which does not seem to have been printed until 1621. Debate persists about the "diversity" of the Reformation; see, e.g., A. C. Cheyne, *Studies in Scottish Church History* (Edinburgh: T&T Clark, 1999), chap. 1. Since

the story I am telling ends in the 1650s and his not for another two centuries, I emphasize consistency.

19. Dickinson, *Knox's History of the Reformation*, 2:27 For her own citing of conscience: Shaw, , *Acts and Proceedings*; 26, 89–91.

20. Shaw, *Acts and Proceedings* 26: 153; Kirk, *Patterns of Reform*, chap. 6. Up to this point, ministers had some legal responsibilities and bishops had sat in Parliament.

21. For an overview, see Maurice Lee Jr., *Government by Pen: Scotland under James VI and I* (Urbana: University of Illinois Press, 1980), chap. 1.

22. Keith M. Brown, *Noble Society in Scotland: Wealth, Family and Culture, from Reformation to Revolution* (Edinburgh: Edinburgh University Press, 2000), 235–39; Julian Goodare, *The Government of Scotland, 1560–1625* (Oxford: Oxford University Press, 2004), chap. 10; *The Political Works of James I*, ed. Charles Howard McIlwain (Cambridge, MA.: Harvard University Press, 1918), 24–25. Several of the more grisly examples of vengeance are described in Dawson, *John Knox*. Jenny Wormald's much more favorable view of the nobility is described and discounted in Keith M. Brown, "The Stewart Realm: Changing the Landscape," in *Kings, Lords and Men in Scotland and Britain, 1300–1625: Essays in Honour of Jenny Wormald*, ed. Steve Boardman and Julian Goodare (Edinburgh: Edinburgh University Press, 2014), 19–32.

23. Cameron, *First Book of Discipline*, 173; Laing, *Works of Knox*, 4:465–520 (quotation, p. 495); David Calderwood, *History of the Kirk of Scotland*, ed. Thomas Thomson, 7 vols. (Edinburgh, 1842–49), 1:360, 363; Jane E. A. Dawson, *Campbell Letters 1559–1583* (Edinburgh: Lothian Print, 1997), intro.; Dawson, "Clan, Kin and Kirk, 211–42 (quotation, p. 211); Jenny Wormald, "'Princes' and the Regions in the Scottish Reformation," in Macdougall, *Church, Politics and Society*, 65–84; Brown, *Noble Society*, especially part 2, "Family," and part 3, "Culture." See also Keith M. Brown, *Bloodfeud in Scotland, 1573–1625: Violence, Justice and Politics in an Early Modern Society* (Edinburgh: John Donald, 1986); Goodare, *Government of Scotland*, intro., chap. 1. In the 1560s, the Privy Council, all of them Protestants, became members of the General Assembly; in the longer run, assemblies and synods continued to include various kinds of officeholders. Shaw, *General Assemblies*, 41, chaps. 9–11.

24. Julian Goodare, "Scotland," in *The Reformation in National Context*, ed. Bob Scribner, Roy Porter, and Mikulas Teich (Cambridge: Cambridge University Press, 1994), 102–3, noting that "two thirds" of the elite ministers were from the Southeast, the more urban region of Scotland (p. 105). Circumstances blur the tidiness of this description, as noted by Laura A. M. Stewart, *Urban Politics and British Civil Wars Edinburgh, 1617–53* (Leiden: Brill, 2006), chap. 1.

25. Greaves, *Theology & Revolution*, 173. Michael Lynch's study of Edinburgh, which maps the differing agendas of the kirk, the city's merchants, and its guilds, details how "reformation" was muted in practice. See also Michael Lynch, "Introduction," in *The Early Modern Town in Scotland*, ed. Michael Lynch (London: Croom Helm, 1987); and Lynch, "Early Modern Scotland: Response: Old Games and New," *Scottish Historical Review* 73 (1994): 47–63. See also Allan White, "The Regent Morton's Visitation: The Reformation of Aberdeen, 1574," in *The Renaissance in Scotland: Studies in Literature, Religion, History and Culture Offered to John Durkan*, ed. A. A. MacDonald, Michael Lynch, and Ian B. Cowan (Leiden: Brill, 1994), 246–63 (in White's words, a town accustomed to combining "masterly activity . . . with judicious temporizing" when it came to religious politics [p. 252]).

26. Wodrow, *Collections upon the Lives*, 1:168–71; David Laing, ed., *Original Letters relating to the Ecclesiastical Affairs of Scotland*, 2 vols. (Edinburgh, 1851), lix. Too few min-

isters were available during the initial decade (some 250 or so, most of them priests who crossed over into Protestantism, for a church that encompassed some 1,080 parishes); and, for the more remote or Gaelic speaking or contested parts of Scotland, the situation remained dire for the rest of the century and beyond. Providing an adequate income for ministers remained an issue well into the seventeenth century despite recurrent protests by the Assembly; see, e.g., Shaw, *Acts and Proceedings*, 26:93, 97. The overall situation is described in Michael Lynch, "Preaching to the Converted? Perspectives on the Scottish Reformation," in *The Renaissance in Scotland*, ed. A. A. MacDonald et al. (Brill: Leiden, 1994), 401–43; Julian Goodare and Michael Lynch, "The Scottish State and Its Borderlands, 1567–1625," in *The Reign of James VI*, ed. Julian Goodare and Michael Lynch (East Linton: Tuckwell, 2000), 192–193; Michael Lynch, "James the VI and the 'Highland Problem,'" ibid., 208–27; and Goodare, *Government of Scotland*, chap. 10. James Kirk offers a slightly more optimistic tally for some areas of the Highlands; see *Patterns of Reform*, chap. 8.

27. Dawson, *John Knox*, 223, 245; 252–53; Greaves, *Theology & Revolution*, chap. 6; Laing, *Works of Knox*, 6:381–422; .

28. *The Autobiography and Diary of Mr James Melvill . . . , With a Continuation of the Diary*, ed. Robert Pitcairn, 2 vols. (Edinburgh: Wodrow Society, 1842), 1:11. Knox's part in an organized round of sermons (1553) rebuking the covetous Duke of Northumberland is described in Dawson, *John Knox*, 78–79; as Dawson points out, situations of this kind made it all the more imperative to preserve the church's authority in matters of discipline.

29. Alan R. MacDonald, "The Parliament of 1592: A Crisis Averted?" in *Parliament and Politics in Scotland, 1567–1707*, ed. Keith M. Brown and Alastair J. Mann (Edinburgh: Edinburgh University Press, 2005): 57–81.

30. Mullan, *Scottish Puritanism*, 16–19; Wodrow, *Collections upon the Lives*, 1:3; 76–77; Dawson, *John Knox*, 112–13.

31. Charles H. Haws, *Scottish Parish Clergy at the Reformation, 1540–1574*, Scottish Record Society n.s. 3 (Edinburgh: Scottish Record Society, 1972), v–xv; McCallum, *Reforming the Scottish Parish*, chap. 1.

32. An abridged version of Craig's *Shorter Catechism* (1591/2) was much more frequently reprinted. For an overview, see Ian Green, *Print and Protestantism in Early Modern England* (Oxford: Oxford University Press, 2000), 80–82.

33. Dawson, "The Protestant Earl," 351–54 (quotation, p. 352); Wodrow, *Collections upon the Lives*, 1:133–37; Felicity Heal, "Mediating the Word: Language and Dialectics in the British and Irish Reformations," *JEH* 56 (2005): 261–86 (describing other linguistic challenges).

34. A story told with considerable skill in Shaw, *General Assemblies*, a narrative that underscores the presence of the Privy Council and other lay officials (chap. 13) and is refreshingly realistic about the infrequent participation of delegates from synods at some distance from Edinburgh.

35. Dawson, *John Knox*, 126.

36. James Kirk, "'The Politics of the Best Reformed Kirk': Scottish achievements and English aspirations in church government after the Reformation," *Scottish Historical Review* 59 (1980): 22–53, esp. p. 30–31; Shaw, *General Assemblies*, chap. 4 (quotation, p. 22). See also Scott H. Hendrix, *Recultivating the Vineyard: The Reformation Agendas of Christianization* (Louisville, KY: Westminster John Knox, 2004); and Kyle, *God's Watchman*, chap. l. In Shaw's chapter, the emphasis falls on tensions between regents or monarchy and the General Assembly; but in chapter 5, the picture broadens to include a good deal of cooperation, especially with the Scottish Parliament.

37. No laying on of hands occurred during the service of ordination, for the true succession was not *within* the ministry as an order but doctrinal.

38. Cameron, *First Book of Discipline*, 96, 98–99, n. 16; Dickinson, *Knox's History of the Reformation*, 1:151, 157, 171–72; Dawson, *John Knox*, 45–46 (bishops as tyrants); Calderwood, *History of the Kirk*, 1:351; Laing, *Works of Knox*, 6:625 (1572).

39. *Creeds and Confessions of Faith in the Christian Tradition*, ed. Jaroslav Pelikan and Valerie Hotchkiss, 3 vols. (New Haven, CT: Yale University Press, 2003), 2:398; McCallum, *Reforming the Scottish Parish*, 37; Greaves, *Theology & Revolution*, 54–56; "The Order of Excommunication, and of Repentance" (1569) in Laing, *Works of Knox* 6:449–70. The French Reformed confession of 1559 and Belgic of 1561 also made discipline a mark of the church.

40. Its origins in a service book devised by Calvin and how it was used in England are described in *John Knox's Genevan Service Book, 1556: The Liturgical Portions of the Genevan Service Book*, ed. William D. Maxwell (Edinburgh: Oliver and Boyd, 1931). See also William McMillan, *The Worship of the Scottish Reformed Church, 1550–1638* (London: James Clarke, 1931), 63 (in general, a careful study demonstrating strong connections with the Reformed international). Millar Patrick, *Four Centuries of Scottish Psalmody* (Oxford: Oxford University Press, 1949), notes that an Edinburgh psalter of 1596 included psalms translated by a French colleague of Calvin and Beza's and included in the French psalter of 1561 (p. 53). Text in Laing, *Works of Knox*, 6:293–335.

41. Maxwell, *John Knox's Genevan Service Book*, 137 n. 8; Laing, *Works of Knox*, 6:544–48, adding, however, that the several "festivals" (Christmas, Easter, and the like) "obtain no place among us; for we dare not religiously celebrate any other feast-day than what the divine oracles have preached."

42. Gordon Donaldson provides a succinct overview, including details on actual practice, in "Reformation to Covenant," in *Studies in the History of Worship in Scotland*, ed. Duncan Forrester and Douglas Murray (Edinburgh: T&T Clark, 1984), chap. 3; McCallum, *Reforming the Scottish Parish*, 82–83; Patrick, *Four Centuries of Scottish Psalmody*; Dawson, *Scotland Re-formed*, 226–31, summing up changes in worship and noting that a modified version of godparents was retained; Linda Dunbar, *Reforming the Scottish Church: John Winram (c. 1492–1582) and the Example of Fife* (Aldershot: Ashgate, 2002), 71–74.

43. Shaw, *Acts and Proceedings*, 26:110–11; of more importance, the document was included in *A parte of a register* (1593).

44. Cameron, *First Book of Discipline*, 122. Where Knox and the first-generation reformers stood on this issue had become controversial by the 1620s (see chap. 6, below) and remains so among historians. In *The History of the Kirk of Scotland from the Year 1558 to August 1637* (Edinburgh, 1842), John Row insisted that Knox "inveighed aganis the autoritie and ambition of Bishops, both before, and especiallie after that Mr. Beza had written that letter to him concerning Bishops," citing others who felt the same way (pp. 414–19). The overall situation is reviewed in Mullan, *Episcopacy in Scotland*, 17–27. See also Greaves, *Theology & Revolution*, 78–80, 207 (arguing that Knox never explicitly repudiated the office). I agree with Sharon Adams, who insists (p. 131) in "The Conference at Leith: Ecclesiastical Finance and Politics in the 1570s," in Goodare and MacDonald, *Sixteenth-Century Scotland*, that "The system of oversight in operation after 1560 was thus a working compromise, which for practical reasons resembled the pre-Reformation structures in some respects. It did not, however, constitute a reformed episcopate. There is no evidence for the reformed church desiring reformed bishops through succession to vacant bishoprics prior to 1571." Gordon Donaldson argues otherwise in *Scottish Church History* (Edinburgh: Scot-

tish Academic Press, 1985), 90–93. This discussion is entangled with debate over the influence of Andrew Melville (see below, n. 60).

45. Kirk, " 'Politics of the Best Reformed Kirk,' " 29–30. In Strasbourg, Martin Bucer had
used the term "superintendent" for administrators charged with supervising clusters of
churches.

46. Dunbar, *Reforming the Scottish Church*, chap. 3; James Kirk, " 'Melvillian' Reform
in the Scottish Universities," in *The Renaissance in Scotland*, ed. A. A. MacDonald, Michael
Lynch, and Ian B. Cowan, 276–300; Gordon Donaldson, *Scotland: James VI to James VII*,
Edinburgh History of Scotland 3 (New York: Frederick A. Praeger, 1966), 149; Greaves,
Theology & Revolution, 191–202; "Of the Erection of Universities," in Cameron, *First Book
of Discipline*, 137–55, spelling out the curriculum and other aspects of the new system;
Thomas M'Crie, *Life of Andrew Melville*, 2nd ed., 2 vols. (Edinburgh, 1824), vol. 2, chap. 12;
Ernest R. Hollaway III, *Andrew Melville and Humanism in Renaissance Scotland, 1545–
1622* (Leiden: Brill, 2011). That he was "dominant" is questioned by Steven J. Reid in *Humanism and Calvinism: Andrew Melville and the Universities of Scotland, 1560–1625* (Aldershot: Ashgate, 2011).

47. Cameron, *First Book of Discipline*, 184. The difficult process of staffing churches and
establishing kirk sessions is described in McCallum, *Reforming the Scottish Parish*, chaps
1–2. See also Shaw, *Acts and Proceedings*, 26:437.

48. Margo Todd, *The Culture of Protestantism in Early Modern Scotland* (New Haven,
CT: Yale University Press, 2002), intro. and chap. 1 (quotation, p. 9); and Michael Graham,
*The Uses of Reform: "Godly Discipline" and Popular Behavior in Scotland and Beyond,
1560–1610* (Leiden: Brill, 1996). For more on this project, see chap. 5, below.

49. Dickinson, *Knox's History of the Reformation*, 1:194–95; Shaw, *Acts and Proceed-
ings*, 26:14; see also Mullan, *Episcopacy in Scotland*, 24–27; Dunbar, *Reforming the Scottish
Church*, chaps. 5, 6, and 8; W. J. Torrance Kirby, *The Zurich Connection and Tudor Political
Theology* (Leiden: Brill, 2007); Kirk, *Patterns of Reform*, chap. 6; Kirk, *Stirling Presbytery
Records, 1581–1587*, Scottish Historical Society Fourth Series 17 (Edinburgh, 1981), intro.

50. Shaw, *Acts and Proceedings*, 26:24, 137–38; 27:744.

51. Wodrow, *Collections upon the Lives*, vol. 1, pt. 2:340–58 (quotation, p. 340); Shaw,
Acts and Proceedings, 26:254. At this moment and continuing to the end of the century and
beyond, assemblies spent much of their time sorting out financial matters left over from the
Catholic period and encouraging the formation of a Protestant ministry. This assembly also
allowed Robert Pont to accept a judgeship in a state court, an interesting exception to two-
kingdoms theory.

52. As Alec Ryrie points out, the Concordat "failed because the General Assembly could
not hold the crown to its side of the bargain." Ryrie, *Age of Reformation*, 262.

53. Shaw, *Acts and Proceedings*, 26:293, 295–96, 301–4; William Scot, *An Apologetical
Narration of the State and Government of the Kirk of Scotland since the Reformation* (Edinburgh, 1856), 26–32 (detailing various complaints and procedures). For patronage (or
owning the income from a parish) as an issue, see below, chapter 8, and James Kirk, "Royal
and lay patronage in the Jacobean kirk, 1572–1600," in MacDougall, *Church, Politics and
Society*, 127–50.

54. Wodrow, *Collections upon the Lives*, 1:172; Gordon Donaldson, "Lord Chancellor
Glamis and Theodore Beza," in Donaldson, *Scottish Church History*, 120–36 (quotation, p.
128); S. J. Knox, *Walter Travers: Paragon of Elizabethan Puritanism* (London: Methuen,
1962), 39 n. 2; Pitcairn, *Diary of Mr. James Melvill*, 41, 55; Melville, quoted in Robert Cummings, "Andrew Melville, the 'Anti-Tami-Cami-Categoria,' and the English Church," in *Neo-
Latin Literature and Literary Culture in Early Modern* Scotland, ed. Steven J. Reid and

David McOrnish (Leiden: Brill, 2016), 174 (Melville himself was not present when this process got underway). Helpful light is thrown on its international contexts by Glenn S. Sunshine, "Reformed Theology and the Origins of Synodical Polity: Calvin, Beza and the Gallican Confession," in *Later Calvinism*, ed. Graham, 141–58. See also the essay by W. Stanford Reid, cited above (n. 10). A translation of Beza's dissection of episcopacy was published by Robert Waldegrave (London, c. 1585). In his introduction to the *Stirling Presbytery Records*, James Kirk argues (contradicting Gordon Donaldson and others) that the assembly had a clear understanding of what it wanted as an alternative to episcopacy.

55. Shaw, *Acts and Proceedings*, 26:90–91, 408, 530, 534, 536; Shaw, *General Assemblies*, 51–58; Mullan, *Episcopacy in Scotland*, 43–50. The process of preparing the text is described in Wodrow, *Collections upon the Lives*, 1:173–79.

56. *The First and Second Book of Discipline* ([Amsterdam], 1621); this, the first printing of the *Second Book of Discipline*, was the doing of David Calderwood (see chap. 6). In or around 1578, an assembly informed bishops that they were no longer to vote in Parliament without "a commission" from the assembly or "usurp any civil jurisdiction" of any kind. John Spottiswood, *A History of the Church of Scotland*, 3 vols. (Edinburgh, 1847–51), 2:258. Readers may have lingered on in some parishes.

57. Shaw, *Acts and Proceedings*, 26:577–78 (Shaw's spellings vary slightly from other versions of this statement). In 1582, the assembly rebuked James VI for "tak[ing] upon your Grace that spirituall power and authoritie which properlie belongeth to Christ, as onlie King and Head of his kirk." Quoted in Shaw, *General Assemblies*, 164 n. 2.

58. David Laing, ed., *The Miscellany of the Wodrow Society*, 1 (Edinburgh, 1844), 401–3. My awareness of this point was sharpened by Conrad Russell's brief comparison of the two state churches in *The Causes of the English Civil War* (Oxford: Clarendon, 1990), 35. See also Alan R. MacDonald, "Ecclesiastical Representation in Parliament in Post-Reformation Scotland: The Two Kingdoms Theory in Practice," *JEH* 50 (1999): 38–61 (indicating nuances of negotiations and shifts of opinion impossible to reproduce in my narrative); Shaw, *General Assemblies*, 84–88; Kirk, "Introduction," *Stirling Presbytery Records*, xxviii (and suggesting a "conciliar" model as a way around the strict binary of presbyterian and episcopal). This assembly quoted to James the assertion in the Scots Confession (article 11) that Christ was "the only Head of his Kirk, our just Lawgiver." Shaw, *General Assemblies*, 104 n. 2.

59. Pitcairn, *Diary of Mr. James Melvill*, 52; M'Crie, *Life of Andrew Melville*, 1:126–34 (including M'Crie's response), 137–39.

60. Mullan, *Episcopacy in Scotland*, 43–50. In part 1 of *Andrew Melville and Humanism*, Hollaway traces the development of the "legend" of Melville's influence, noting, along the way, the thinness of the evidence for some aspects of his life (e.g., his "Presbyterianism") and summarizing his administrative or advisory services; see especially pp. 315–29. Alan MacDonald takes on the legend in *The Jacobean Kirk: Sovereignty, Polity and Liturgy, 1567–1625* (Aldershot: Ashgate, 1998), esp. chap. 1; as does James Kirk in *Patterns of Reform*, chap. 6. Its development is described by Caroline Erskine, "The Making of Andrew Melville," in *Andrew Melville (1545–1633): Writings, Reception, and Reputation*, ed. Roger A. Mason and Steven J. Reid (Aldershot: Ashgate, 2014), 215–35. The Melville-blaming narrative enlivens the essays in Donaldson, *Scottish Church History* (see esp. pp. 93, 95, and 120); and Shaw, *General Assemblies*, 127ff. Never a parish minister, Melville was entitled by his rank in a university to participate in general assemblies. Duncan Shaw suggests that Melville was responsible for the abrupt appearance of the office of "doctor" in the Church of Scotland; ibid., chap. 14.

61. Maurice C. Lee, Jr., *Great Britain's Solomon: James VI and I in His Three Kingdoms* (Urbana: University of Illinois Press, 1990), 96; Ruth Grant, "The Brig o' Dee Affair, the

sixth earl of Huntly and the politics of the Counter-Reformation," in Goodare and Lynch, *Reign of James VI*, 93–109; Pitcairn, *Diary of James Melvill*, 129–32; Calderwood, *History of the Kirk*, 4:62–64; Arthur H. Williamson, *Scottish National Consciousness in the Age of James VI: The Apocalypse, the Union and the Shaping of Scotland's Public Culture* (Edinburgh: John Donald, 1979), 66–67. Subscription was tempered by allowing ministers to attach the phrase "agreeable to God's Word."

62. T. A. Kerr, "John Craig, Minister of Aberdeen, and King's Chaplain," in *Reformation and Revolution: Essays presented to the Very Reverend Principal Emeritus Hugh Watt*, ed. Duncan Shaw (Edinburg: St. Andrews, 1967) 117–20; Alan R. MacDonald, "The subscription crisis and church-state relations, 1584–1586," *RSCHS* 25 (1994): 222–55; MacDonald, *Jacobean Kirk*, chap. 2 (pointing out that James was not an English-style Erastian and that there was no serious attempt to enforce the acts); Gordon Donaldson, "Scottish Presbyterian exiles in England 1584–88," *RSCHS* 14 (1960), noting John Field's befriending of these exiles. Williamson underscores the divisions among the clergy as of 1585 in light of the fact that they "overwhelmingly signed" the acts. My narrative omits the reaction of James Melville to such men. Williamson, *Scottish National Consciousness*, 67.

63. Shaw, *Acts and Proceedings*, 27:765, 769, 771 (bishops yet again). In *Great Britain's Solomon*, chap. 2, Maurice Lee Jr. emphasizes Maitland's role in bringing the church and the king back together even though he continued to appoint bishops (Shaw, *Acts and Proceedings*, 27:822) and insisted on his right to decide when and where the General Assembly would meet.

64. Calderwood, *History of the Kirk*, 4: 254–67; Mullan, *Episcopacy in Scotland*, 59–60. Details of his career, some of them surprising, are described in Mullan, *Episcopacy in Scotland*, chap. 4; and Alan. R. MacDonald, "'Best of Enemies: Andrew Melville and Patrick Adamson, ca. 1574–1592," in Julian Goodare and Alasdair A. Macdonald, eds., *Sixteenth-Century Scotland: Essays in Honour of Michael Lynch* (Leiden: Brill, 2008), 257–76.

65. Calderwood, *History of the Kirk*, 5:119–20; a longer version appears in Pitcairn, *Diary of James Melvill*, 289–93. Attempts to have him excommunicated may be followed in Shaw, *Acts and Proceedings*, 27:775, 777–78, 782–84, 880; and Calderwood, *History of the Kirk*, 4 and 5.

66. Calderwood, *History of the Kirk*, 4:626, 647, 654–55; Shaw, *Acts and Proceedings*, 27:879 (a fast in 1588 prompted mainly by fears of a Catholic invasion). Grant, "Brig o' Dee Affair," is excellent on how James VI was attempting to balance the Catholic and Protestant nobility amid pressures arising out of the Counter-Reformation.

67. Wormald, "Ecclesiastical vitriol," 171–91; Gordon Donaldson, "The Attitude of Whitgift and Bancroft to the Scottish Church," *Transactions of the Royal Historical Society*, 4th ser., 24 (1942): 95–115; *The Miscellany of the Wodrow Society: Containing Tracts and Original Letters*, ed. David Laing (Edinburgh, 1844), 485–99, 505–20; Calderwood, *History of the Kirk*, 5:5–6, 73–77.

68. Text in *Scottish Historical Documents*, ed. Gordon Donaldson (Edinburgh: Scottish Academic Press, 1970), 160–61; Alan R. MacDonald, "The Parliament of 1592: A Crisis Averted," in *Parliament and Politics in Scotland, 1567–1707*, ed. Keith M. Brown and Alastair J. Mann (Edinburgh: Edinburgh University Press, 2005), 57–81; MacDonald, "Ecclesiastical representation in parliament," 33–61; and see Julian Goodare, "The admission of lairds to the Scottish parliament," *English Historical Review* 116 (2001): 1103–33. As has often been pointed out by historians, the "Golden Acts" did not abolish lay patronage, an issue that had moved to the forefront within the General Assembly.

69. Shaw, *Acts and Proceedings*, 27:1029–30; Calderwood, *History of the Kirk*, 5:408–11, 439–40; Pitcairn, *Diary of James Melvill*, 245 (another version reads "Christ Jesus, and his kingdome the kirk, whose subject King James the Sixt is, and of whose kingdome not a

kingdome not a king, nor a head, nor a lord, but a member." John Davidson's sermons and the renewal of covenant they prompted are described in chapter 5, below.

70. Described by John Row, a critic of the king, in *History of the Kirk*, 184–86.

71. Julian Goodare, "The Attempted Scottish *Coup* of 1596," in Goodare and MacDonald, *Sixteenth-Century Scotland*, 311–36; Roger A. Mason, *Kingship and the Commonweal: Political Thought in Renaissance and Reformation Scotland* (East Lothian: Tuckwell, 1998), 210–11. The most interesting analysis is that of Maurice Lee, who suggests that James's goal in the second half of the 'nineties was to gain significant control over the assembly. Lee, "James VI and the Revival of Episcopacy in Scotland, 1596–1600," *Church History* 43 (1974): 50–64. For other attempts at answering this question, see Mullan, *Episcopacy in Scotland*, 87–91; and Alan R. MacDonald, "James VI and the General Assembly, 1586–1618," in Goodare and Lynch, *Sixteenth-Century Scotland*, 170–85.

72. Donaldson, *Scotland*, 182; Mullan, *Episcopacy in Scotland*, 61; *Letters of Queen Elizabeth and King James VI*, ed. John Bruce, Camden Society 46 (London: J. B. Nichols, 1849), 63.

73. McIlwain, *Political Works of James I*, 23, 61. See also McIlwain, "Introduction," in ibid., xliii, xlv–xlvii, and "Appendix C: James and the Puritans," xc–xci. Roger A. Mason provides crucial context for these statements in "George Buchanan, James VI and the Presbyterians," in Mason, *Kingship and Commonweal*, 187–214. As Ronald G. Asch, points out, "Strict Calvinism had little to offer to a king in search of sacred kingship." See "Sacred Kingship in France and England in the Age of the Wars of Religion: From Disenchantment to Re-enchantment," in *England's Wars of Religion, Revisited*, ed. Charles W. A Prior and Glenn Burgess (Aldershot: Ashgate, 2011), 27–47 (quotation, p. 41). Nicholas Tyacke describes aspects of politicking on the English side as a change of regimes loomed in "Puritan politicians and King James VI and I, 1587–1604," in *Politics, Religion and Popularity in Early Stuart Britain: Essays in Honour of Conrad Russell*, ed. Thomas Cogswell, Richard Cust, and Peter Lake (Cambridge: Cambridge University Press, 2002), 21–44.

74. Wodrow, *Collections upon the Lives*, 1:235–37, 239.

75. *Narrative of the Life and Death of Robert Rollock*, in *Select Works of Rollock*, 2 vols., ed. William M. Gunn (Edinburgh, 1849), 1:lxxviii; Jamie Reid-Baxter, "Mr. Andrew Boyd (1567–1636): A Neo-Stoic Bishop of Argyll and His Writings," in Goodare and MacDonald, *Sixteenth-Century Scotland*, 399 (probably criticizing Robert Bruce); Lynch, "Preaching to the Converted," 301–43. Buchanan's thinking and his influence are summarized in Glenn Burgess, *British Political Thought, 1500–1660* (London: Palgrave Macmillan, 2009), 83–91. Goodare, "Attempted Scottish *Coup*," 327–28, underscores the very limited evidence of a Buchanan-Melville connection. See also Jenny Wormald, "The Headaches of Monarchy: Kingship and the Kirk in the Early Seventeenth Century," in Goodare and MacDonald, *Sixteenth-Century Scotland*, 365–93.

76. Shaw, *Acts and Proceedings*, 27:837; Calderwood, *History of the Kirk*, 2:413–16. A group biography is seriously needed, for most of these men had been exiled from to time, an experience that shaped their subsequent politics.

77. Williamson, *Scottish National Consciousness*, 68–69; Macdonald, *Jacobean Kirk*, 64. The text is included in Donaldson, *Scottish Historical Documents*, 150–53, and became important anew in the 1630s, for which see chap. 7, below.

78. Pitcairn, *Diary of James Melvill*, 506–804. In *The Reformation in Rhyme: Sternhold, Hopkins and the English Metrical Psalter, 1547–1603* (Aldershot: Ashgate, 2008), 33–36, Beth Quitslund sums up the Old Testament narrative on which the presbyterian party was depending; see also her commentary on Psalm 78 (pp. 36–40).

79. Row, *History of the Kirk*, 424–26.

80. Quoted in Russell, *English Civil War*, 42; Dickinson, *Knox's History of the Reformation*, 2:3; Calderwood, *Quaeres concerning the State of the Church of Scotland* 1621; repr., [London?], (1638), 3.

81. Williamson, *Scottish National Consciousness*, chap. 3.

82. Shaw, *General Assemblies*, 26–31; Dickinson, *Knox's History of the Reformation*, 2:116–30; John Craig, *A Shorte Summe of the Whole Catechisme*, ed. Thomas Graves Law (Edinburgh, 1883), xxvii–xxxii; Goodare, "Attempted Scottish *Coup*," 328–330. As the editor of Craig's catechism drily notes, Craig subsequently justified resistance to religious but not civil polity (p. xxxix).

83. Williamson, *Scottish National Consciousness*, 44. See also Crawford Gribben, *The Puritan Millennium: Literature & Theology, 1550–1682* (Dublin: Four Courts, 2000), comparing the "English tradition," which foregrounded the Christian prince, and the Scottish tradition, which was "always more radical" in its handling of the monarch (pp. 103–4). After Knox had his fingers burned by his objections to Mary Tudor, he represented himself (as he did in 1559 in a letter to a member of the nobility) as intending "neyther sedition, neyther yit rebellion against any just and lauchfull authoritie, but onlie the advauncement of Christes religion, and the libertie of this poore Realme." Laing, *Works of Knox*, 6:36. Jenny Wormald dates the "myth of the godly and embattled Kirk" loosely to the late 1630s and early 1640s, noting, however, that Calderwood and others turned it into a story of "the enemy within—the crown—which appeared to triumph." As my narrative suggests, James Melville and, before him, Davidson and Knox had employed the same narrative. Wormald, ed., *Scotland: A History* (Oxford: Oxford University Press, 2005), 145.

84. Donaldson, *Scottish Historical Documents*, 160–61; Goodare, "Attempted Scottish *Coup*," 329; Arthur Williamson, "George Buchanan and the Patriot Cause," and John Coffey, "George Buchanan and the Scottish Covenanters," both in Caroline Erskine and Roger A. Mason, eds., *George Buchanan: Political Thought in Early Modern Britain and Europe* (Farnham: Ashgate, 2012). Roger Mason captures some of the complexities of covenantal language in relationship to kingship in "Covenant and Commonweal: The Language of Politics in Reformation Scotland."

85. Shaw, *Acts and Proceedings*, 27:744; Arthur H. Williamson, "Empire and Anti-Empire: Andrew Melville and British Political Ideology, 1589–1605," in Mason and Reid, *Andrew Melville*, 75–100; David Calderwood, *The true history of the Church of Scotland from the beginning of the Reformation* (n.p., 1704), 146. Richard Greaves uncovers a "paradox" in Knox's understanding of Scottish national identity; in my version, paradox is less apparent than the themes I have emphasized in these paragraphs. Greaves, *Theology & Revolution*, chap. 11.

86. Dawson, "Bonding, Religious Allegiance and Covenanting," 167–70. Goodare, "Attempted Scottish *Coup*," 327–30 (on constitutionalism and quoting John Welsh's sermon).

Chapter 4. The Practical Divinity

1. J. T. Cliffe, *The Puritan Gentry: The Great Puritan Families of Early Stuart England* (London: Routledge and Kegan Paul, 1984), 14; Claire Cross, "The Genesis of a Godly Community: Two York Parishes, 1590–1640," in *Voluntary Religion*, ed. W. J. Sheils and Diana Wood, Studies in Church History 23 (Oxford: Blackwell, 1986), 213. The social correlates of godly Protestantism have been variously assessed, usually in the service of a larger argument. Some of these arguments and the evidence mobilized on their behalf are described in Margaret Spufford, "The importance of religion in the sixteenth and seventeenth centuries," in *The World of Rural Dissenters, 1520–1725*, ed. Margaret Spufford (Cambridge: Cambridge University Press, 1995), 1–102. This chapter omits the attempts

to uproot key "folk" and Catholic belief and practices, a process admirably described in Peter Marshall, *Beliefs and the Dead in Reformation England* (Oxford: Oxford University Press, 2002).

2. So Bunyan's pilgrim: "when he was walking in the Fields reading in his Book, and greatly distressed in his mind . . . he burst out, as he had done before , crying, *What shall I do to be saved?*" John Bunyan, *The Pilgrim's Progress* (1678), ed. W. R. Owens (Oxford: Oxford University Press, 2003), 11.

3. The emergence of the practical divinity occurred in the context of a broader anxiety about the spiritual health of second- and third-generation Protestants within the Lutheran and Dutch Reformed traditions. See, e.g., Eric Lund, "Second Age of the Reformation: Lutheran and Reformed Spirituality, 1550–1700," in *Christian Spirituality Post-Reformation and Modern*, ed. Louis Dupre and Don E. Saliers (New York: Crossroad, 1989), 218–27, emphasizing the Lutheran theologian Johann Arndt (1555–1621) and noting Dutch versions of the practical divinity; Harro Hopfl, *The Christian Polity of John Calvin* (Cambridge: Cambridge University Press, 1982), 23. The humanist sources of this emphasis on conduct or experience are emphasized in Patrick Collinson, " 'A Magazine of Religious Patterns': An Erasmian Topic Transposed in English Protestantism," in *Renaissance and Renewal in Christian History*, ed. Derek Baker, Studies in Church History 14 (Oxford: Basil Blackwell, 1977), 223–49.

4. William Ames, *The Marrow of Theology*, trans. and ed. John Eusden (Boston: Pilgrim, 1968), 77; Erasmus, quoted in Collinson, " 'A Magazine of Religious Patterns,' " 223; Arthur Dent, *The Plain Mans Path-way to Heaven* (London, 1612), 163; Hall, *AC*, 245; Arthur Hildersham, *Lectures upon the Fourth of John* (London, 1629), 7. "All the propositions of the Gospell be practical, as they say; . . . to bee drawne out into the manners and life everie day." Robert Rollock, *A Treatise of Gods Effectuall Calling* (London, 1603), 182. The context of theology as "practical" is described in Richard A. Muller, *Post-Reformation Reformed Dogmatics, Vol. 1: Prolegomena to Theology* (Grand Rapids: Baker Book House, 1987), chap. 6, and more broadly in Scott H. Hendrix, *Recultivating the Vineyard: The Reformation Agendas of Christianization* (Louisville, KY; Westminster John Knox, 2004), his deeper point being that the period of the two Reformations, Catholic and Protestant, saw a fresh insistence on vocation, or a more disciplined and substantial religious life, as the goal of laypeople as well as of those set apart as clergy or monastics. Disaffection with the spiritual health and expertise of ordinary people ran rife; see, e.g., Baird Tipson, *Hartford Puritanism: Thomas Hooker, Samuel Stone, and Their Terrifying God* (New York: Oxford, 2015), chap. 8, and what is said in chapter 1 of this book about "the people." At the beginning of *The Foundation of Christian Religion Gathered into Six Principles* (London, 1590), sig. A2r–v, William Perkins quoted several popular aphorisms that contradicted the workings of redemption. Ian Green offers a deft comparison of prayer-book piety and the practical divinity in *Print and Protestantism in Early Modern England* (Oxford: Oxford University Press, 2000), 312–14.

5. A 1580 survey of ministers throughout the English diocese of Chester reported that, "for the most part" they "are utterly unlearned." According to a more political survey of 1604, "only two-fifths of the ministers were described as being preachers." R. C. Richardson, *Puritanism in North-west England* (Manchester: Manchester University Press, 1972), 3. See also Alan Ford, *The Protestant Reformation in Ireland 1590–1641* (Dublin: Four Courts, 1997), chap. 2, for what may be the nadir.

6. *The Writings of John Bradford*, ed. Aubrey Townsend, 2 vols. (Cambridge, 1853), 1:127.

7. The "disciplinary" nature of the practical divinity is foregrounded in Theodore Dwight Bozeman, *The Precisionist Strain: Disciplinary Religion and Antinomian Back-*

lash in Puritanism to 1638 (Chapel Hill: University of North Carolina Press, 2004), and the genealogy he offers is an important supplement to what is sketched elsewhere in this chapter. According to the mid-seventeenth-century English minister Thomas Goodwin, "the chief work of the godly ministers . . . in this last age" has been to "spend most of their ministry in distinguishing men, by giving signs and marks of men's natural and regenerate estates," doing this because the churches could not rely on "the ordinance of excommunication" and other institutional means to keep the "unclean" from "church fellowship." Goodwin, *An Exposition of the Revelation* (c. 1639), reprinted in Robert Halley, ed., *The Works of Thomas Goodwin, D.D.*, 12 vols. (Edinburgh, 1861), 3:130–31. The task of defending orthodoxy against Catholic polemics, in particular, is noted in John Coffey, *Politics, Religion and the British Revolutions: The Mind of Samuel Rutherford* (Cambridge: Cambridge University Press, 1997), 74–75; and Tipson, *Hartford Puritanism*, chap. 4.

8. See, e.g., *Certain Most Godly, Fruitful and Comfortable Letters* (London, 1564), a collection assembled by Miles Coverdale of texts by Hooper, Bradford, and Cranmer, some of them previously published in Foxe's *Book of Martyrs*. Bradford's framing of the Christian life is briefly summarized in F. Ernest Stoeffler, *The Rise of Evangelical Pietism* (Leiden: Brill, 1971), 43–49; and Thomas Sampson's memories of him are included in Strype, *Annals of the Reformation*, vol. 3, pt. 2:192–96. Any "origins" thesis must acknowledge the long-standing rule that everyone participating in Holy Communion "examine ourselves whether we be true members of Christ," the "marks" thereof being (in the words of a catechism of c. 1563) "if we heartily repent us of our sins" and "rest upon a sure hope of God's mercy," "lead our life godlily hereafter," and "bear brotherly love to our neighbours." Alexander Nowell, *A Catechism Written in Latin*, ed. G. E. Corrie (1570; repr., Cambridge, 1853), 216. Citing the "well over eighty editions" of the Protestant evangelical Thomas Becon's spiritual writings, Alec Ryrie has proposed that these mark the debut of a generalized English Protestant piety well before the customary birthdate assigned the practical divinity; Ryrie, *Being Protestant in Reformation Britain* (Oxford: Oxford University Press, 2013), 5. Becon's importance is underscored in Jonathan Reimer, "Thomas Becon: Popular Devotional Writer," in *Sources of the Christian Self: A Cultural History of Christian Identity*, ed. James M. Houston and Jens Zimmermann (Grand Rapids: Eerdmans, 2018), noting "early modern editions of his writings" (p. 128), The overlap of early Tudor Protestantism and literary practice is described in John N. King, *English Reformation Literature: The Tudor Origins of the Protestant Tradition* (Princeton, NJ: Princeton University Press, 1979),

9. It has sometimes been suggested that the practical divinity emerged *after* the collapse of the presbyterian program in the late 1580s, to provide "a means, in the absence of a Presbyterian scheme of formal church discipline . . . to order the English people," for which see T. D. Bozeman, "The Glory of the 'Third Time': John Eaton as Contra-Puritan," *JEH* 47 (1996): 638–39, an argument reprised in Bozeman, *The Precisionist Strain*. This time line exaggerates the authority of English presbyterianism, ignores the groundwork being laid in the 1540s and early 1550s (see note 8, above), and implies a feat of conjuring, as though Perkins and his generation suddenly created densely complex modes of preaching and devotion. It is telling that John Cotton admired the spiritual history of the proto-Protestant martyr Thomas Bilney (d. 1531), as recorded in Foxe's *Book of Martyrs*, a book filled with other texts that anticipate or nurtured the practical divinity, as did the Second Helvetic Confession of 1569. Hall, *AC*, 94, 189. Early Elizabethan origins are sketched in Patrick Collinson, "A Mirror of Elizabethan Puritanism: The Life and Letters of 'Godly Master Dering,'" in Collinson, *Godly People: Essays on English Protestantism and Puritanism* (London: Hambledon, 1983), 289–323. In *Scottish Puritanism, 1590–1638* (Oxford: Oxford University Press, 2000), David George Mullan cites studies that uncover "a very

deeply rooted Scottish experiential strand of Calvinism stretching right back to the time of the Reformation" (p. 9), an argument he amplifies in the chapters that follow. See also Mullan, *Narratives of the Religious Self in Early-Modern Scotland* (Aldershot: Ashgate, 2010), for a detailed account of the inner lives of Scottish Protestants. My own reading led me back to John Bradford. In "The Development of a Puritan Understanding of Conversion" (PhD thesis, Yale University, 1972), Lynn Baird Tipson Jr. emphasizes, as I do, the role of Bradford, noting that William Perkins quoted him extensively. By the middle of the seventeenth century, an informal canon of books by "Affectionate, Practical" minister-theologians had come into being. The phrase is Richard Baxter's; see Gordon S. Wakefield, *Puritan Devotion: Its Place in the Development of Christian Piety* (London: Epworth, 1957), 3. For contemporary currents of the same kind within Lutheranism and the Reformed tradition, see Lund, "Second Age." For the practical divinity in Ireland, see Alan Ford, *The Protestant Reformation in Ireland 1590-1641* (New York: Peter Lang, 1987), chap. 8. In "Weak Christians, Backsliders, and Carnal Gospelers: Assurance of Salvation and the Pastoral Origins of Puritan Practical Divinity in the 1580s," *Church History* 70 (2001): 462–81, Michael P. Winship unfolds tensions within an emerging system he dates to the 1580s, a chronology anticipated in M. Charles Bell, *Calvin and Scottish Theology: The Doctrine of Assurance* (Edinburgh: Handsel, 1985), although slightly revised to 1590 in Mullan, *Scottish Puritanism*, and other studies. Rollock's contribution to Scottish theology is briefly described in Arthur H. Williamson, *Scottish National Consciousness in the Age of James VI: The Apocalypse, the Union and the Shaping of Scotland's Public Culture* (Edinburgh: John Donald, 1979), 76–77.

10. Claire Cross, *Church and People England 1450-1660*, 2nd ed. (Oxford: Blackwell, 1999), 138; Arnold Hunt, *The Art of Hearing English Preachers and Their Audiences, 1590–1640* (Cambridge: Cambridge University Press, 2010), 188. Anthony Fletcher details a similar thickening of ministers; Fletcher, "Puritanism in Seventeenth Century Sussex," in M. J. Kitch, ed., *Studies in Sussex Church History* (London: Leopard's Head, 1981), 144; Ryrie, *Being Protestant*, chap. 11. In *Practical Predestinarians in England, c. 1590-1640* (Burlington: Ashgate, 2013), Dixon suggests that the practical divinity came into being once evangelical Protestants in England had converted most of the people to Protestantism and the focus shifted to the Christian life and assurance, although he also attributes the growing importance of predestination to a "crisis of certainty in late medieval thought" (p. 15). That a disciplining-cum-evangelical program benefitted from a sense of crisis is noted by Ryrie, *Being Protestant*, chap. 15.

11. Luther and Lutheranism were more influential in the earliest phases of the English Reformation, an assertion that can be modestly qualified. Basil Hall, "The early rise and gradual decline of Lutheranism in England (1520–1600)," in *Reform and Reformation: England and the Continent c. 1500-c. 1750*, ed. Derek Baker, Studies in Church History: Subsidia 3 (Oxford: Blackwell, 1979), 103–31; Diarmaid McCullough, *Tudor Church Militant: Edward VI and the Protestant Reformation* (London: Allen Lane/Penguin, 1999), 99; McCullough, *Archbishop Cranmer*, 167–78; Duncan Shaw, *Renaissance and Zwinglian Influences in Sixteenth-Century Scotland* (Edinburgh: Edina, 2012); David Scott Gehring, "From the strange death to the odd afterlife of Lutheran England," *HJ* 57 (2014): 825–44. When Knox was asked by Continental Reformed leaders if theology in Scotland was consistent with their version, the answer was yes. Dickinson, *Knox's History of the Reformation*, 2:190.

12. In 1566, an exchange of letters between the kirk and Theodore Beza in Geneva exemplified the strong sense in Scotland of agreement on doctrine within the Reformed international. Laing, *Works of Knox*, 6:544–50, 562. The politics surrounding the Lambeth Articles is described in Peter Lake, *Moderate Puritans and the Elizabethan Church* (Cambridge: Cambridge University Press, 1982), chap. 9; see also H. C. Porter, *Reformation and*

Reaction in Tudor Cambridge (Cambridge: Cambridge University Press, 1958), chap. 16; David Hoyle, *Reformation and Religious Identity in Cambridge, 1590–1644* (Woodbridge: Boydell, 2007), 75–77 and chap. 3 passim. As Debora Shuger demonstrates in "The Mysteries of the Lambeth Articles," *JEH* 68 (2017): 306–25, the initial draft was modified by moderates. The Articles were in play at the Hampton Court conference (1604; see below, chap. 6) and the York House conference of 1626, for which see Jonathan D. Moore, *English Hypothetical Universalism: John Preston and the Softening of Reformed Theology* (Grand Rapids, MI: Eerdmans, 2007), chap. 6 and the references it includes.

13. *Creeds and Confessions of Faith in the Christian Tradition*, ed. Jaroslav Pelikan and Valerie Hotchkiss, 3 vols. (New Haven, CT: Yale University Press, 2003), 2:571–76. In chapters 1–4 of *Anti-Calvinists: The Rise of English Arminianism c. 1590–1640* (Oxford: Clarendon Press, 1987), Nicholas Tyacke reviews the support expressed before 1620 for certain Calvinist principles. That the delegation supported the decisions of the synod despite certain reservations is demonstrated in Anthony Milton's introduction to *The British Delegation and the Synod of Dort (1618–1619)*, Church of England Record Society 13 (Woodbridge: Boydell, 2005), noting, also, the compromises that figured in the making of the Dordtian points (p. xliii) and the "moderation" favored by the English delegation (p. xxxi); see also Milton, *Catholic and Reformed: The Roman and Protestant Churches in English Protestant Thought, 1600–1640* (Cambridge: Cambridge University Press, 1995), pt. 2, chap. 8. Stereotypical (and generally anti-Calvinist) interpretations of Dordt are reviewed in the essays brought together in *Revisiting the Synod of Dordt (1618–1619)*, ed. Aza Goudriaan and Freed van Lieburg (Leiden: Brill, 2011); these also detail some of the behind-the-scenes give-and-take that affected the wording of the Articles. For the Dutch context and its bearing on English policies, see Christopher Grayson, "James I and the Religious Crisis in the United Provinces 1613–19," in Baker, *Reform and Reformation*, 195–220.

14. Published initially in 1629 under the title *God no imposter nor deluder*.

15. Tyacke, *Anti-Calvinists*, 1; Nicholas Tyack, "Theology," in *The History of the University of Oxford: Vol. 4, Seventeenth-Century Oxford*, ed. Tyack (Oxford: Clarendon, 1997), chap. 10. The lay theologian Francis Rous anticipated Prynne in *Testis Veritatis* (1626), as did Simonds D'Ewes, for which see J. Sears McGee, *"An Industrious Mind": The Worlds of Sir Simonds D'Ewes (1602–1650)* (Stanford: Stanford University Press, 2015), chap. 6. Felicity Heal underscores differences of "doctrinal emphasis" between the Thirty-Nine Articles and the Scots Confession of 1560 in *Reformation in Britain and Ireland* (Oxford: Oxford University Press, 2003), 306–8. In part 2 of *Catholic and Reformed*, Milton notes the reluctance of English minister-theologians to call themselves "Calvinists," given the overtones this term had acquired in interconfessional polemics. His is also an excellent account of overseas connections that expands on C. M. Dent, *Protestant Reformers in Elizabethan Oxford* (Oxford: Oxford University Press, 1983). As Milton points out (p. 382), the English version of *Harmonia confessionum fide* was essentially a "Presbyterian" project that Whitgift tried to keep from being printed. The real importance of *Catholic and Reformed* is what it tells us about the presence of a "catholic" wing of the Church of England, perhaps not as widely preached or taught as the "practical divinity," but a presence that qualifies the argument cited at the outset of this endnote. Objections to some aspects of Calvinism were also ongoing; for James I's feelings of this kind, see Alan Cromartie, *The Constitutionalist Revolution: An Essay on the History of England, 1450–1642* (Cambridge: Cambridge University Press, 2006), chap. 6. David Hoyle makes a similar argument in *Reformation and Religious Identity*. David Como voices a more general dismay with binaries in "Puritans, Predestination and the Construction of Orthodoxy in Early Seventeenth-Century England," in *Conformity and Orthodoxy in the English Church, c. 1560–1660*, ed. Peter Lake and Michael Questier (Woodbridge: Boydell, 2000), 64–87. In *The Boxmaker's Revenge: "Orthodoxy,"*

"Heterodoxy," and the Politics of the Parish in Early Stuart London (Manchester: Manchester University Press, 2001), Peter Lake expands the scope of interministerial and popular levels of theological argument not touched on in this chapter. The more telling debates arise out of attempts to define the essence of Calvin's theology and to contrast his system with those of his successors, the so-called Calvin versus the Calvinists thesis. In the middle of the nineteenth century, German historians of doctrine claimed that Calvin's theology centered on the doctrine of election, with all else arranged accordingly. Of the many attempts to correct this thesis of a "central idea" and the Calvin versus Calvinists framework, the most vigorous may be Richard A. Muller's "Diversity in the Reformed Tradition," *Drawn into Controversie: Reformed Theological Diversity and Debates within Seventeenth-Century British Puritanism*, ed. Michael A G. Haykin and Mark Jones (Göttingen: Vandenhoeck & Ruprecht, 2011), 11–30; and *Calvin and the Reformed Tradition: On the work of Christ and the Order of Salvation* (Grand Rapids, MI: Baker Academic, 2012), chaps. 2–3; see also Muller, *Christ and the Decree* (1986; repr., Baker Academic, 2008), with a new preface that is essential reading; and Muller, *Post-Reformation Reformed Dogmatics*, 1: chap. 2. More recently, the literature is reviewed in Irena Backus and Philip Benedict, "Introduction," in *Calvin and His Influence, 1509–2009*, ed. Backus and Benedict (Oxford: Oxford University Press, 2011), 12–16; and in Hoyle, *Reformation and Religious Identity*, chap. 1. Beza as villain of the Calvin versus Calvinists framework is challenged in Raymond A. Blacketer, "The Man in the Black Hat: Theodore Beza and the Reorientation of Early Reformed Historiography," in *Church and School in Early Modern Protestantism: Studies in Honor of Richard A. Muller on the Maturation of a Theological Tradition*, ed. Jordan J. Ballor, David S. Sytsma, and Jason Zuidema (Leiden: Brill, 2013), 227–41. In the context of assessing Calvin's legacy, Scott M. Manetsch surveys pastoral, exegetical, and theological publications originating in Geneva or with the Company of Pastors, some of them (e.g., work by Simon Goulart and editions of Calvin's sermons) known to the larger Puritan community in Britain in *Calvin's Company of Pastors: Pastoral Care and the Emerging Reformed Church, 1536–1609* (Oxford: Oxford University Press, 2013), chap. 8.

16. As David Hoyle and other historians of Tudor-Stuart universities point out, the "disputation" required of all master's and doctoral students often overstated differences for the sake of academic argument. Hoyle, *Reformation and Religious Identity*, 17. The methods of disputation are more fully described in Joshua Rodda, *Public Religious Disputation in England, 1558–1626* (Aldershot: Ashgate, 2014). In *The Holy Spirit in the Theology of Martin Bucer* (Cambridge: Cambridge University Press, 1970), W. P. Stephens underscores the importance of context for understanding why Bucer could say different things at different moments.

17. On Song of Songs, see Tom Schwanda, *Soul Recreation: The Contemplative-Mystical Piety of Puritanism* (Eugene, OR: Pickwick, 2012), chap. 2; John Coffey, *Politics, Religion and the British Revolutions: The Mind of Samuel Rutherford* (Cambridge: Cambridge University Press, 1997), 80; and more generally, Barbara L. Lewalski, *Protestant Poetics and the Seventeenth-Century Religious Lyric* (Princeton, NJ: Princeton University Press, 1979). For a demonstration of biblical exegesis in the context of an arbitrary hermeneutic, see M.D.J. McKay, *An Ecclesiastical Republic: Church Government in the Writings of George Gillespie*, Rutherford Studies in Historical Theology (Carlisle: Paternoster, 1997).

18. Prescribed by many commentators on preaching; for one such statement, see Richard Bernard, *The Faithfull Shepheard* (London, 1607), 44; and more generally, Mary Morrissey, *Politics and the Paul's Cross Sermons, 1558–1642* (Oxford: Oxford University Press, 2011), 48–61. Tying sermons to Scripture was universally endorsed, not a peculiarity of one faction; for this point and others, see W. J. Sheils, "An Archbishop in the Pulpit: Tobie Matthew's Preaching Diary, 1606–1622," in *Life and Thought in the Northern Church c. 1100–*

c.1700, ed. Diana Wood, Studies in Church History: Subsidia 12 (Rochester, NY: Boydell, 1999), 395–96.

19. Porter, *Reformation and Reaction*, 311; Collinson, "Mirror of Elizabethan Puritanism," 293; Coffey, *Politics, Religion and the British Revolutions*, 70–77.

20. Lewalski, *Protestant Poetics*, chaps. 3–4; Mary Morrissey, "Elect Nations and Prophetic Preaching: Types and Examples in the Paul's Cross Jeremiad," in *The English Sermon Revised: Religion, Literature and History, 1600–1750*, ed. Lori Anne Ferrell and Peter McCullough (Manchester: Manchester University Press, 2000), 43–58; Theodore Dwight Bozeman, *To Live Ancient Lives: The Primitivist Dimension in Puritanism* (Chapel Hill: University of North Carolina Press, 1988), chap. 1; John R. Knott Jr., *The Sword of the Spirit: Puritan Responses to the Bible* (Chicago: University of Chicago Press, 1980), 7.

21. Mullan, *Scottish Puritanism*, 236–37; Greaves, *Theology & Revolution*, 10–13. In *Trinitarian Spirituality: John Owen and the Doctrine of God in Western Devotion* (Milton Keynes: Paternoster, 2007). Brian K. Kay identifies Aristotelian elements in the theology of John Owen, who may have been the most widely informed student of the Church Fathers in mid-seventeenth-century England. My unsystematic survey of the Scottish theologians turned up several who incorporated the Church Fathers into their work—e.g., Robert Boyd of Trochrigg, whose Latin commentary on Ephesians was published long after his death, and Samuel Rutherford, who also published in Latin; for Rutherford's citations, see Coffey, *Politics, Religion and the British Revolutions*, 73–74. Esther Chung-Kim provides a wider view of these appropriations (used, she notes, to validate objections to Catholic doctrine) in *Inventing Authority: The Use of the Church Fathers in Reformation Debates over the Eucharist* (Waco, TX: Baylor University Press, 2011).

22. Breward, *Work of Perkins*, 52–53 (noting that Augustine was cited more frequently than any other Church Father or theologian); Tyacke, *Anti-Calvinists*, 6, 34, 48, 50, 61; J. Stephen Yuille, *Puritan Spirituality: The Fear of God in the Affective Theology of George Swinnock* (Milton Keynes: Paternoster, 2007), 28; Richard Lovelace, "The Anatomy of Puritan Piety: Puritan Devotional Literature, 1600–1640," in *Christian Spirituality: Post-Reformation and Modern*, ed. Louis Dupre and Don. E. Saliers (New York: Crossroads, 1989), 294–323; Frank A. James III, "The Legacy of Peter Martyr and the Martyr Translation Project," in *John Calvin and the Interpretation of Scripture*, ed. Charles Raynal, Calvin Studies 10 and 11 (Grand Rapids, MI: CRC Product Services, 2006), 206–22, characterizing Vermigli as "first and foremost an Augustinian" (p. 219). Using the term "extreme Augustinianism," Baird Tipson attaches it to the English and eventually New England minister Thomas Hooker, who was debating Catholic and Protestant theologians about divine sovereignty and the economy of grace. Tipson, *Hartford Puritanism*, 4–5. *The Oxford Guide to the Historical Reception of Augustine*, ed. Karla Pollman, 3 vols. (Oxford: Oxford University Press, 2013) endorses the concept of Augustinianisms.

23. William K. B. Stoever, *"A Faire and Easie Way to Heaven": Covenant Theology and Antinomianism in Early Massachusetts* (Middletown, CT: Wesleyan University Press, 1978), 125; Hall, *AC*, 142, 194; John Cotton, *The Churches Resurrection, or the Opening of the First and 14 verses of the 20th Chap. of the Revelation* (London, 1642), 29; John Norton, *The Orthodox Evangelist* (Cambridge, MA: 1657), 144, 256, 261; Mark W. Elliott, "Melville, Rollock and Boyd on Paul's Epistle to the Romans," in *Andrew Melville (1545-1622) Writings, Reception, and Reputation*, ed. Roger A. Mason and Steven J. Reid (Aldershot: Ashgate, 2014), 108. For continuities with Aristotle and Acquinas, see David S. Sytsma, "The Logic of the Heart: Analyzing the Affections in Early Reformed Orthodoxy," in Ballor, Sytsma, and Zuidema, *Church and School*, 471–88. In the anti-Arminian *A Treatise tending to cleare the doctrine of justification* (Middleburgh, 1616), chap. 21, the Scottish minister John Forbes used Aristotle's four causes. Another premise was the congruence of what

could be learned from creation as God's doing and the remnants of mental and moral capacity in humankind, a congruence that validated the faculty of reason. Often overlooked, this aspect of the practical divinity is emphasized in Perry G. E. Miller, *The New England Mind: The Seventeenth Century* (Cambridge, MA: Harvard University Press, 1939); and more recently in Coffey, *Politics, Religion and the British Revolutions.*

24. Muller, *Post-Reformation Reformed Dogmatics,* 1, 42–46, identifies these figures. See also Muller, "Referencing and Understanding Calvin in Seventeenth-Century Calvinism," in Backus and Benedict, *Calvin and His Influence, 1509-2009,* 182–201. Brian G. Armstrong points out that Calvin was rarely cited in French Protestant debates of the early seventeenth century. *Calvinism and the Amyraut Heresy: Protestant Scholasticism and Humanism in Seventeenth-Century France* (Madison: University of Wisconsin Press, 1969), 188. A broader net would capture late medieval and early modern transmitters of "Augustinianism," many of them Catholics; for these and British Protestant citations of Aquinas and the like, see Frits G. M. Broeyer, "Traces of the Rise of Reformed Scholasticism in the Polemical Theologian William Whitaker (1548-1596)," in *Reformation and Scholasticism: An Ecumenical Enterprise,* ed. Willem J. van Asselt and Eef Dekker (Grand Rapids, MI: Baker Academic, 2001), 155–80. See also Robert Dodaro and Michael Questier, "Strategies in Jacobean Polemic: The Use and Abuse of St Augustine in English Theological Controversy," *JEH* 44 (1993): 432–49 (comparing Catholic and Protestant readings). Citations do not necessarily mean close knowledge of a given writer; for Calvin's practice, see Anthony N. S. Lane, *John Calvin: Student of the Church Fathers* (Edinburgh: T&T Clark, 1999). It is sometimes argued that what was said by the Zurich theologians, chief among them Bullinger, should be differentiated from what was said by theologians associated with Geneva.

25. More printings between 1587 and 1645, and twice as often as Calvin's *Institutes;* for its ideas and influence, see Anthony Milton, "The Church of England and the Palatinate, 1566–1642," in Ha and Collinson, eds., *Reception of Continental Reformation,* 140–42. The Heidelberg Catechism influenced Perkins (Muller, *Christ and the Decree,* 142) and was endorsed in the Scots Confession of 1560, which also reflects the influence of the First Helvetic Confession (1536). See also Jack C. Whytock, *"An Educated Clergy": Scottish Theological Education and Training in the Kirk and Secession, 1560–1850* (Milton Keynes: Paternoster, 2007), 71. Alexander Nowell's semiofficial catechism (1563, 1570) incorporated a great deal of Calvin's catechism. The holdings of college libraries at Oxford indicate "the increasing currency of the writings of Beza" and the like in the 1570s, a development seen as replacing a "hybrid theology" that included the Zurich reformers. Dent, *Protestant Reformers,* 92–102 (quotation, p. 92). For seventeenth-century citations of Calvin, see Richard A. Muller, "Reception and Response: Referencing and Understanding Calvin in Seventeenth-Century Calvinism," in Backus and Benedict, *Calvin and His Influence,* 182–201; Minna Prestwich, "Introduction," *International Calvinism 1541-1715,* ed. Prestwich (Oxford: Clarendon, 1985), p. 3 (noting the continuing republication of texts by Calvin up to 1640).

26. On Scots abroad (in Germany, the Netherlands, Geneva, and France): Thomas M'Crie, *Life of Andrew Melville,* 2nd ed., 2 vols. (Edinburgh, 1834), chap. 1; Robert Wodrow, *Collections upon the Lives of the Reformers and Most Eminent Ministers of the Church of Scotland* (Glasgow, 1848), vol. 2, pt. 2, noting that "most of the Protestant academies and schools in this part of France [the vicinity of Sedan] were filled with Scotsmen" (p. 86). For Ramism: Donald K. McKim, *Ramism in William Perkins' Theology* (New York: Peter Lang, 1987), pt. 2; Alan Ford, *James Ussher: Theology, History, and Politics in Early-Modern Ireland and England* (Oxford: Oxford University Press, 2007), 39–41; Tipson, *Hartford Puritanism,* chap. 7; Coffey, *Politics, Religion and the British Revolutions,* 67–69. It is doubtful that Ramean "logic" affected theological reasoning, a point on which I agree with

Muller, *Post-Reformation Reformed Dogmatics*, 1:254–56. On the other hand, any philo-sophical arguments on behalf of free will were potentially at odds with certain versions of divine sovereignty, a point underscored in Henri A. Krop, "Philosophy and the Synod of Dort: Aristotelianism, Humanism, and the Case against Arminianism," in *Revisiting the Synod of Dordt (1618–1619)*, ed. Aza Goudriaan and Fred van Lieburg (Leiden: Brill, 2011), 49–79. The role of humanism is emphasized in Margo Todd, *Christian Humanism and the Puritan Social Order* (Cambridge: Cambridge University Press, 1987); and less specifically although at great length in Ernest R. Holloway III, *Andrew Melville and Humanism in Renaissance Scotland, 1545–1622* (Leiden: Brill, 2011), which also touches on Melville's commitment to Ramism. R. Ward Holder sketches Calvin's dependence on humanist prac-tices and principles in "Calvin as commentator on the Pauline epistles," in *Calvin and the Bible*, ed. Donald K. McKim (Cambridge: Cambridge University Press, 2006), 237–45. For other categories and assumptions that informed theological work, see Miller, *New England Mind*, chapters 5–7, 9; William T. Costello, *The Scholastic Curriculum at Early Seventeenth-Century Cambridge* (Cambridge, MA.: Harvard University Press, 1958); Keith L. Sprunger, *The Learned Doctor William Ames: Dutch Backgrounds of English and Ameri-can Puritanism* (Urbana: University of Illinois Press, 1972); Norman Fiering, "Will and Intellect in the New England Mind," *WMQ*, 3d ser. 29 (1972): 515–58, and Fiering, *Moral Philosophy at Seventeenth-Century Harvard* (Chapel Hill: University of North Carolina Press, 1981). For topics in Reformed theology not discussed in this chapter, see Yuille, *Pu-ritan Spirituality*.

27. Green, *Print and Protestantism*, 305–11. Kimberly Anne Coles emphasizes the "late medieval" sources of Catherine Parr's piety after she became a Protestant, the influence on her of *The Imitation of Christ*, and the Catholic aspects of her *Prayers or meditacions*, which "remained popular beyond the end of the century," a publishing history she turns into the argument that "Catholic and Protestant modes of religious devotion were . . . neither as starkly contrasted nor as completely incompatible as is usually assumed." Coles, *Religion, Reform, and Women's Writing in Early Modern England* (Cambridge: Cambridge Univer-sity Press, 2008), chap. 2 (quotations, pp. 56–57).

28. Charles Hambrick-Stowe, *The Practice of Piety: Puritan Devotional Disciplines in Seventeenth-Century New England* (Chapel Hill: University of North Carolina Press, 1982), chap. 2; Lewalski, *Protestant Poetics*, chap. 5 (emphasizing differences over continuities); Knott, *Sword of the Spirit*, 64–65; Brad S. Gregory, "The 'True and Zealous Seruice of God': Robert Parsons, Edmund Bunny, and *The First Booke of the Christian Exercise*," *JEH* 45 (1994) 238–68; Alexandra Walsham, *Providence in Early Modern England* (Oxford: Oxford University Press, 1996), 104–5; Tessa Watt, "Piety in the pedlar's pack: Continuity and change, 1578–1630," in Spufford, *World of Rural Dissenters*, 248–49; Green, *Print and Prot-estantism*, 262–63; André Vauchez, *La spiritualité du Moyen Age occidental, VIII–XIII siècle* (Paris: Editions du Seuil, 1994); Susan C. Karant-Nunn, " 'Christians' Mourning and Lament Should Not Be Like the Heathens': The Suppression of Religious Emotion in the Reformation," in *Confessionalization in Europe, 1550–1700: Essays in Honor and Memory of Bodo Nischan*, ed. John M. Headley, Hans J. Hillerbrand, and Anthony J. Papalas (Al-dershot: Ashgate, 2004), 107–29; Jane E. A. Dawson, " 'Hamely with God': A Scottish View on Domestic Devotion," in *Private and Domestic Devotion in Early Modern Britain*, ed. Jessica Martin and Alec Ryrie (Burlington, VT: Ashgate, 2012), 33. Richard Lovelace points out that the makers of the practical divinity showed little interest in the "mystical" strains of the Catholic tradition emphasized by Helen C. White in *English Devotional Literature (Prose) 1600–1640* (Madison: University of Wisconsin Press, 1931) in Lovelace, "Puritan Piety," 294–98, an observation reiterated in Christine Peters, *Patterns of Piety: Women, Gender and Religion in Late Medieval and Reformation England* (Cambridge: Cambridge

University Press, 2003), chap. 8. (In mid-seventeenth-century England, the word "mystical" was being attached to godly writers such as Francis Rous and Henry Vane.) In *The Catholic Roots of the Protestant Gospel: Encounter between the Middle Ages and the Reformation* (Leiden: Brill, 1995), Stephen Strehle sketches Catholic and humanist contexts for Luther's turn toward interiority.

29. Ernest F. Kevan, *The Grace of Law: A Study in Puritan Theology* (Grand Rapids, MI: Reformation Heritage, 1993), 113–16; Brian Kay, *Trinitarian Spirituality: John Owen and the Doctrine of God in Western Devotion* (Milton Keynes: Paternoster, 2007), 52–53, noting also the presence of "sub-covenants" that varied from one theorist to another, a process described in Michael McGiffert, "Covenant, Crown, and Commons in Elizabethan Puritanism," in *The Covenant Connection: From Federal Theology to Modern Federalism*, ed. Daniel J. Elazar and John Kincaid (Lanham, MD.: Lexington, 2000), 163–86; and again in McGiffert, "Grace and Works: The Rise and Division of Covenant Divinity in Elizabethan Puritanism," *Harvard Theological Review* 75 (1982): 463–502. The covenantal thinking of William Ames is summarized in Joel R. Beeke and Jan van Vliet, "*The Marrow of Theology* by William Ames (1576–1633)," in *The Devoted Life: An Invitation to the Puritan Classics*, ed. Kelly M. Kapic and Randall C. Gleason (Downers Grove, IL: InterVarsity Press, 2004), 52–65.

30. Stoever, "*Faire and Easie Way*," 82 and chaps. 5–6; von Rohr, *Covenant of Grace*, chaps. 3 and 6; Muller, *Christ and the Decree*, 143; Breward, *Work of Perkins*, 210–12; Jeremy Schildt, "'In my private reading of the scriptures': Protestant Bible-reading in England, circa 1580–1720," in Martin and Ryrie, *Private and Domestic Devotion*, 206. As Ames pointed out in *The Marrow of Theology*, the new covenant (of grace) "requires no properly called or prior condition, but only a following or intermediate condition (and that to be given by grace as a means to grace)." *Marrow of Theology*, bk. 1.19, 151. See also Tipson, *Hartford Puritanism*, 160 n. 39 on faith as a condition, a topic he discusses again in chap. 9.

31. Bierma, *Covenant Theology of Caspar Olievanus*, 160–61 (quotation, p. 160), and for his influence on Perkins, 176–78; Peter Bulkeley, *The Gospel-Covenant; or, The Covenant of Grace Opened* (London, 1651), pt. 5, chap. 2; Norton, *Orthodox Evangelist*, 74; Richard A. Muller, "Perkins' *A Golden Chaine*: Predestinarian System or Schematized *Ordo Salutis?*" *Sixteenth Century Journal* 9 (1978): 78–79. In chapter 6 of "*Faire and Easie Way*," Stoever provides a superb analysis of secondary causes. The larger theological context is described in Francis Oakley, *Omnipotence, Covenant, and Order* (Ithaca, NY: Cornell University Press, 1984). Ames was among the Reformed theologians who reiterated the distinction between God's "absolute" and "ordaining or actual power." Ames, *Marrow of Theology*, 93.

32. Muller, "Perkins' *A Golden Chaine*." See also Dever, *Richard Sibbes*, 109–21, for a nuanced appraisal of the covenant of grace as conditional.

33. Breward, *Work of Perkins*, 393. For other uses of the analogy, see Wallace, *Puritans and Predestination*, 44–45 and, in general, chap. 3. Citing Romans 8:29, the Scottish minister William Cowper argued that "the linkes of the golden chaine of our Salvation are knit together inseparably by the hand of God . . . he that is sure of one is sure of all." Quoted in Mullan, *Episcopacy in Scotland*, 165; see also Gordon Marshall, *Presbyteries and Profits: Calvinism and the Development of Capitalism in Scotland, 1560–1707* (Oxford: Clarendon, 1980), 73–77 and Rollock, *Gods Effectuall Calling*, sig. *4v. The phrase "certaine steps and degrees" is from Richard Rogers, *The Practice of Christianity; or, An Epitomie of Seven Treatises*, 3rd ed. (London, 1627), 23. On conversion as lifelong, see Charles L. Cohen, *God's Caress: The Psychology of Puritan Religious Experience* (New York: Oxford, 1986), 14–15.

34. Prynne, *God no imposter nor deluder* (1629), quoted in Debora Shuger, *Religion in Early Stuart England, 1603–1638: An Anthology of Primary Sources* (Waco: Baylor University Press, 2012), 523; Krop, "Philosophy and the Synod of Dort," 73–77; David F. Wright,

"Calvin's Accommodating God," in *Calvinus Sincerioris Religionis Vindex Calvin as Protector of the Purer Religion*, ed. Wilhelm H. Neuser and Brian G. Armstrong, Sixteenth Century Essays and Studies 36 (Kirksville, MO: Sixteenth Century Journal Publishers, 1997), 3–19; Stoever, *"Faire and Easie Way*," chap. 1; Norton, *Orthodox Evangelist*, 43; Donald Sinnema, "God's Temporal Decree and Its Temporal Execution: The Role of This Distinction in Theodore Beza's Theology," in Mack P. Holt, ed., *Adaptations of Calvinism* in *Reformation Europe Essays in Honour of Brian G. Armstrong* (Aldershot: Ashgate, 2007), 55–78; Hildersham, *Fourth of John* (1629), 5–6; Strype, *Annals of the Reformation*, vol. 3, pt. 2:241. Stoever cautions that this language of stages must be handled carefully, since spiritual experience did not necessarily follow the sequences of Romans 8. Stoever, *"Faire and Easie Way*," 223 n12.

35. Kevan, *Grace of Law*, chaps. 1–3; Wendel, *Calvin*, 196–208.

36. Richard Rogers, *The Practice of Christianity. or An Epitomie of Seven Treatises* (3rd ed., London, 1627), sig. B3v; Townsend, *Writings of John Bradford*, 1. 216; Wendel, *Calvin*, 198; Kevan, *Grace of Law*, 124–25 (quoting William Twisse); Nowell, *A Catechism*, 141; Ames, *Marrow of Theology*, 175–76 ; Kevan, *Grace of Law*, 63–64, 49. The figure of Scripture (in this instance, penitential psalms) as a mirror is noted in Clare Costley King'oo, *Miserere Mei: The Penitential Psalms in Late Medieval and Early Modern England* (Notre Dame, IN: University of Notre Dame Press, 2012), 130. As Kevan rightly insists, the law as described in these paragraphs must not be translated into "legal" or "legalism," the first of these an epithet employed by mid-seventeenth-century "Antinomianism" (*Grace of Law*, 257–59; see chap. 9, below).

37. Rollock, *Gods Effectuall Calling*, 178; Gutherie, *A Short Treatise of The Christian's Great Interest* (1658; repr., Edinburgh, 1720), 35–36; Breward, *Work of Perkins*, 212; Kenneth L. Parker and Eric J. Carlson, *"Practical Divinity": The Works and Life of Revd Richard Greenham* (Aldershot: Ashgate, 1998), 146, 267; see also Kevan, *Grace of Law*, chap. 3; and Ronald S. Wallace, *Calvin's Doctrine of the Christian Life* (Edinburgh: Oliver and Boyd, 1959), pt. 2, chap. 5 (repentance as dying and rising with Christ, 50–77).

38. *Winthrop Papers* 1:165; Walsham, *Providence in Early Modern England*, chap. 2.

39. Townsend, *Writings of John Bradford*, 2:167; Graeme Murdock, *Beyond Calvin: The Intellectual, Political and Cultural World of Europe's Reformed Churches, c. 1540–1620* (London: Palgrave Macmillan, 2004), 23–25. As Richard Greaves points out in *Theology & Revolution* (chap. 3), reconciling divine sovereignty with free will and the sinfulness of humankind (the Fall) was not something John Knox and his successors could accomplish without, in the end, deferring to the concept of "mystery." For John Robinson's way of doing so, see Timothy George, *John Robinson and the English Separatist Tradition* (Macon, GA: Mercer University Press, [1982], 2005), chap. 5. Arthur Hildersham got around any determinism by combining election with the intermediary role of "means of grace." See Hildersham, *Fourth of John*, 6. For more on this problem, see chap. 9.

40. Eusden, Introduction," in Ames, *Marrow of Theology*, 27. Describing the gradual development of Knox's thinking, Greaves reminds us of the circumstances and sources that affected this process and the elements of uncertainty that clung to the doctrine. *Theology & Revolution*, 30–43. The fullest description of the doctrine in the context of the practical divinity is Leif Dixon, *Practical Predestinarians in England, c. 1590–1640* (Aldershot: Ashgate, 2014).

41. Statements emphasizing difference include Charles Bell, *Calvin and Scottish Theology: The Doctrine of Assurance* (Edinburgh: Handel, 1985), chap. 1; Alister E. McGrath, *Iustitia Dei: A History of the Christian Doctrine of Justification*, 3rd ed. (Cambridge: Cambridge University Press, 2005), 252–56 (comparing Calvin and Bucer); and the much criticized R. T. Kendall, *Calvin and English Calvinism to 1649* (Oxford: Oxford University

Press, 1979). See also David Foxgrover, "Self-Examination in John Calvin and William Ames," in *Later Calvinism: International Perspectives*, ed. W. Fred Graham, Sixteenth Century Essays and Studies 22 (Kirksville, MO: Sixteenth Century Journal Publishers, 1994), 451–69. In the 1630s, the Protestant ecumenist John Drury took for granted that "the principles and Doctrines of Practical Divinities . . . were more distinctly and plainly delivered in these Churches of Great Brittaine, than in all the rest of the Christian world besides," and contrasted its capacity to avoid the "endlesse maze of controversies and debates" with what he termed "Polemicall Divinities." Quoted in Tom Webster, *Godly Clergy in Early Stuart England: The Caroline Puritan Movement, c. 1620–1643* (Cambridge: Cambridge University Press, 1997), 258–59.

42. Breward, *Work of Perkins*, 308. E. Brooks Holifield sums up this "Calvinism," with an emphasis on its theme of accommodation, in *Theology in America Christian Thought from the Age of the Puritans to the Civil War* (New Haven, CT: Yale University Press, 2003), chap. 2.

43. An overview: Fred A. van Lieburg, "From Pure Church to Pious Culture: The Further Reformation in the Seventeenth-Century Dutch Republic," in Graham, *Later Calvinism*, 409–29, noting, for example, translations of Lewis Bayley's *The Practice of Piety* (p. 425 n. 20); Peter Damrau, *The Reception of English Puritan Literature in Germany* (London: Institute of Germanic and Romance Languages, University of London, 2006). Willem op 't Hof, *Engelse pietistiscdhe geschriften in het Nederlands, 1598–1622* (Rotterdam: Lindenberg, 1987), offers "a rough estimate for the period 1623–1699 of 260 new translation and, 580 editions" (quoted in Joel R. Beeke and Randall J. Pederson, *Meet the Puritans: With a Guide to Modern Reprints* (Grand Rapids, MI: Reformation Heritage, 2006), 743; they also cite 185 seventeenth-century Dutch printings of texts by Perkins, relying on J. van der Haar, *From Abbadie to Young: A Bibliography of English, mostly Puritan, Works, translated i/o Dutch Language* (Veenendall: Kool, 1980). See also Willem J. op 't Hof, "Puritan Emotions in Seventeenth-Century Dutch Piety," in *Puritanism and Emotion in the Early Modern World*, ed. Alec Ryrie and Tom Schwanda (Houndsmille: Palgrave Macmillan, 2016), 213–40. For the wider context, see Harm Klueting, "Problems of the Term and Concept 'Second reformation': Memories of a 1980s Debate," in *Confessionalization in Europe, 1555–1700: Essays in Honor and Memory of Bodo Nishan*, ed. John M. Headley, Hans J. Hillerbrand, and Anthony J. Papalas (Aldershot: Ashgate 2004), 37–49 (summarizing the wildly variant uses of the phrase, which include, among others, regimes switching to Protestantism in Germany in the early seventeenth century). See also Cornelis W. Schoneveld, *Intertraffic of the Mind: Studies in Seventeenth-Century Anglo-Dutch Translation with a Checklist of Books Translated from English into Dutch, 1600–1700* (Leiden: Brill, 1983); Anthony Milton, "Puritanism and the continental Reformed churches," in *The Cambridge Companion to Puritanism*, ed. John Coffey and Paul C. H. Lim (Cambridge: Cambridge University Press, 2008), 109–26; Helmer J. Helmers, *The Royalist Republic: Literature, Politics, and Religion in the Anglo-Dutch Public Sphere, 1639–1660* (Cambridge: Cambridge University Press, 2015), 66–68 (suggesting that the English term "further reformation" was appropriated in the Netherlands). The French context is sketched in Philip Benedict, "Print and the Experience of Ritual: Huguenot Books of Preparation for the Lord's Supper," in *Le Livre religieux et Ses Pratiques Etudes sur l'histoire du livre religieux en Allemagne et en France à l'epoque modern* (Göttingen: Vandenhoeck und Ruprecht, 1991), 110–130 (a reference I owe to Barbara Diefendorf).

44. Or simply write commitments to Reformed doctrines such as predestination out of the record as unauthentically Anglican; for such efforts, see Ford, *James Ussher*, 88–89; Peter Lake, "Serving God and the Times: The Calvinist Conformity of Robert Sanderson,"

Journal of British Studies 27 (1988): 81–116; Dixon, *Practical Predestinarians*, chap. 5; Daniel J. Steere, "A Calvinist Bishop at the Court of King Charles I," in *Adaptations of Calvinism in Reformation Europe: Essays in Honour of Brian G. Armstrong*, ed., Mack P. Holt (Aldershot: Ashgate, 2007); and, especially, Milton, *British Delegation*.

45. Preston, quoted in Shuger, *Religion in Early Stuart England*, 421. A fuller description than I am able to provide of any single practice exists for prayer; see Peter Iver Kaufman, *Prayer, Despair, and Drama: Elizabethan Introspection* (Urbana: University of Illinois Press, 1996); Green, *Print and Protestantism*, chap. 5; and Ryrie, *Being Protestant*, pt. 2; for an overall inventory, see Ian Green, "Varieties of Domestic Devotion in Early Modern English Protestantism," in Martin and Ryrie, *Private and Domestic Devotion*, 9–31. The most useful survey remains Wakefield, *Puritan Devotion*, seconded by Hambrick-Stowe, *Practice of Piety*; and Alex Ryrie, *Being Protestant*. See also Yuille, *Puritan Spirituality*, chap. 6 (using "godliness" as an inclusive category). For Scottish examples, which I mainly ignore in this chapter, see Dawson, "'Hamely with God': A Scottish View on Domestic Devotion," in Martin and Ryrie, *Private and Domestic Devotion*, 33–52, an essay that does double duty as an overview of "affective" divinity in Scotland; and Mullan, *Scottish Puritanism*. For music, Glenda Goodman, "'The Tears I Shed at the Songs of Thy Church': Seventeenth-Century Musical Piety in the English Atlantic World," *Journal of the American Musicological Society* 65 (2012): 691–725.

46. Foxe, *Book of Martyrs*, 7:200; Breward, *Work of Perkins*, 308, 312, 310, 314; Ames, *Conscience with the Power and Cases thereof* (London, 1639), 93. On psalm singing, see Beth Quitslund, *The Reformation in Rhyme: Sternhold, Hopkins, and the English Metrical Psalter, 1547–1603* (Aldershot: Ashgate, 2008), 124–25 and the corresponding endnotes.

47. *Letters of Samuel Rutherford*, ed. Andrew A. Bonar (1891; repr., Edinburgh: Banner of Truth Trust, 1984), 158. Isaac Ambrose, the English spiritual writer, was given to similar expressions. See Tom Schwanda, *Soul Recreation: The Contemplative-Mystical Piety of Puritanism* (Eugene: Pickwick, 2012), 86.

48. Michael McGiffert, ed., *God's Plot: The Paradoxes of Puritan Piety, Being the Autobiography and Journal of Thomas Shepard* (Amherst: University of Massachusetts Press, 1972), 26–27, 168; Dever, *Richard Sibbes*, chap. 6 (quotations, p. 143). See also Yuille, *Puritan Spirituality*, 89–85.

49. *Winthrop Papers* 1:166, 189, 203–4 (Winthrop himself craving Christ's kisses); *Select Works of Robert Rollock*, ed. William M Gunn, 2 vols. (Edinburgh, 1849–54), 2:6–7 (from a sermon series on the Passion of Christ, extolling his example of suffering). See also Schwanda, *Soul Recreation*, chap. 2; Thomas M'Crie, ed., *The Life of Mr. Robert Blair, Minister of St. Andrews* (Edinburgh: Wodrow Society, 1848), 122–25 (a dialogue between Christ and his "soul," fervent to the point of deserving M'Crie's phrase "divine raptures." For Sibbes's preaching on Song of Solomon and the Psalms, see Knott, *Sword of the Spirit*, chap. 2.

50. M. M. Knappen, ed., *Two Elizabethan Puritan Diaries by Richard Rogers and Samuel Ward* (Chicago: American Society of Church History, 1933), 64.

51. Breward, *Work of Perkins*, 237–46; Bonar, *Letters of Samuel Rutherford*, 110, 127. For broader studies of the motifs of pilgrim and the Christian life as marked by struggle, see Wendel, *Calvin*, 243–44; Mullan, *Scottish Puritanism*, chap. 4; Hambrick-Stowe, *Practice of Piety*, chap. 3. See also Wallace, *Calvin's Doctrine*, 127; Henry Scudder, *The Christians Daily Walke in holy Securitie and Peace*, 5th ed. (London, 1633), 5; John Downame, *The Christian Warfare* (1604), quoted in William Haller, *The Rise of Puritanism* (New York: 1938), 155–58; William Harrison, *Deaths Advantage Little Regarded* (1602), 56–58.

52. Gunn, *Works of Robert Rollock*, 2:38–39; Henry Smith, quoted in John L. Lievsay, "'Silver-Tongued Smith,' Paragon of Elizabethan Preachers," *Huntington Library Quarterly*

11 (1947): 23; Perkins, *A Salve for a Sicke Man,* (1595), 8, 9, 11; *Winthrop Papers,* 1:301; Adrian Chastain Weimer, *Martyrs' Mirror: Persecution and Holiness in Early New England* (New York: Oxford University Press, 2011).

53. McGiffert, *God's Plot,* 153; Arthur Searle, ed., *Barrington Family Letters, 1628–1632,* Camden Fourth Series 28 (London, 1983), 129. See also Gunn, ed., *Works of Robert Rollock,* 2:6–7.

54. Rogers, *Seven Treatises* (London, 1610), 422, quoted in Stoeffler, *Rise of Evangelical Pietism,* 61; *The Diary of Robert Woodford, 1637–1641,* ed. John Fielding, Camden Fifth Series 42 (Cambridge: Cambridge University Press, 2012), 14–15; see also Samuel Ward, *The Life of Faith,* 3rd ed., corrected (London, 1622), 56–57; Scudder, *Christians Daily Walke,* 20–21, and passim (the entire book is about the wise use of time). Cf. John Winthrop's statement in his spiritual reflections, "It is wonderful how the omission of the leaste dutie, or commission of evill, will quench grace and estrange us from the love of God." *Winthrop Papers* 1:162.

55. Breward, *Work of Perkins,* 207. Some of the qualities and paradoxes of self-examination are sketched in Kaufman, *Prayer, Despair, and Drama,* chap. 2. As Parker and Carlson point out, the emphasis on self-examination was in part a response to the disappearance of the Catholic rite of auricular confession. *"Practical Divinity,"* 63.

56. *John Knox's Genevan Service Book, 1556,* ed. William D. Maxwell (Edinburgh: OIiver and Boyd, 1931), 122; William Bradshaw, *A Preparation to the receiving of Christs Body and Blood* (1609), sig. B1v. Henry Smith's second sermon on the Lord's Supper ends with the words: "Now if you cannot remember all that I have said, yet remember the text, that is examine yourself" (quoted in Wakefield, *Puritan Devotion,* 43 n. 63. See also A[rthur] H[ildersam], *The Doctrine of Communicating Worthily in the Lords Supper* (London, 1630; often bound up with Bradshaw), 56–57. Green, *Print and Protestantism,* chap. 5, xviii, describes handbooks and their complexities. See also John E. Booty, "Preparation for the Lord's Supper in Elizabethan England," *Anglican Theological Review* 49 (1967): 131–48 (emphasizing the penitential context). How often laypeople communed is uncertain—in Scotland, perhaps once or twice a year, with exceptions; in England, where monthly communion was urged, the response varied. See J. P. Boulton, "The Limits of Formal Religion: The Administration of Holy Communion in Late Elizabethan and Early Stuart London," *London Journal* 10 (1984): 135–54. For practice as it varied elsewhere, see Raymond A. Metzger, "Reformed Liturgical Practice," in *A Companion to the Eucharist in the Reformation,* ed. Lee Palmer Wandel (Leiden: Brill, 2014).

57. [Richard Sibbes, ed.], *The Saints Cordialls As They were Delivered in Sundry Sermons . . . in the Citie of London, and else-where* (London, 1629), 288. One laymen's reflections on preparing for Communion is described in McGee, *"Industrious Mind,"* 90. Hesitations: Wakefield, *Puritan Devotion,* 117.

58. *The Diary of Samuel Rogers, 1634–1638,* ed. Tom Webster and Kenneth Shipps, Church of England Record Society 11 (Woodbridge: Boydell, 2004]), 162, 165; *The Notebooks of Nehemiah Wallington, 1618–1654: A Selection,* ed. David Booy (Aldershot: Ashgate, 2007), 243.

59. See, e.g., William Hinde, *A Faithful Remonstrance of the Holy Life and Happy Death of John Bruen* (1602).

60. Townsend, *Writings of Bradford,* 1:33, 35; Strype, *Annals of the Reformation,* 3:194–95. For another example of someone taking "brief notes of the condition of their souls" and reviewing them on a weekly basis, see M'Crie, *Life of Mr. Robert Blair,* 31.

61. Jacqueline Eales, *Puritans and Roundheads: The Harleys of Brampton Bryan and the Outbreak of the English Civil War* (Cambridge: Cambridge University Press, 1990), 49–52 (quotation, p. 51).; Rogers, *Seven Treatises,* 523, 519.

62. Dorothy M. Meads, ed., *Diary of Lady Margaret Hoby, 1599–1605* (Boston: Houghton Mifflin, 1930), 65, 64, 68–69, 71, 75, 153–54, 70, 216, 66, 168; a recurrent theme is the intrusion of the devil (e.g., 66). Thomas Cartwright was another writer she admired, as did her wider family and its connections; ibid., 247, n. 202. The remarkable pace of her reading is noted in Claire Cross, "The Religious Life of Women in Sixteenth-Century Yorkshire," in *Women in the Church*, ed. W. J. Sheils and Diana Wood, Studies in Church History 27 (Oxford: Blackwell, 1990), 323.

63. George Morison Paul, ed., *Diary of Sir Archibald Johnston of Wariston, 1632–1639* (Edinburgh: Scottish Historical Society, 1911), 117–23, 154, 169. Personal covenanting was common in Scotland after 1650 and especially after 1660; see David George Mullan, ed., *Protestant Piety in Early-Modern Scotland Letters, Lives and Covenants, 1650–1712* (Edinburgh: Scottish History Society, 2008), 5–7.

64. Paul S. Seaver, *Wallington's World: A Puritan Artisan in Seventeenth-Century London* (Stanford: Stanford University Press, 1985), 7, 11, 32–32, 35–36; Booy, *Notebooks of Nehemiah Wallington*, 10, 11, 17, 32, 48–49, 50, 81, 94, 243.

65. King'oo, *Miserere Mei*, 130; Wakefield, *Puritan Devotion*, 53, noting that "the Puritans believed in the Communion of Saints, which included the earthly fellowship of God's people, as well as the whole company of heaven."

66. The quantities of sermons heard by one man in 1630s England is noted in Fielding, *Diary of Robert Woodford*, 28–29. Gadding, which Fielding practiced, is noted in Ann Hughes, *Politics, Society, and Civil War in Warwickshire, 1620–1650* (Cambridge: Cambridge University Press, 1987), 72. Anthony Milton suggests, in "Religion and Community in Pre-Civil War England," that "gadding" appealed to others besides the godly, in *The English Revolution c. 1590–1720: Politics, Religion and Communities*, ed. Nicholas Tyacke (Manchester: Manchester University Press, 2007), 68.

67. William McMillan, *The Worship of the Scottish Reformed Church, 1550–1638* (London: James Clarke, 1932), chap. 25; Patrick Collinson, "Elizabethan and Jacobean Puritanism as Forms of Popular Religious Culture," in *The Culture of English Puritanism, 1560–1700*, ed. Christopher Durston and Jacqueline Eales (New York: St. Martins, 1996), 50–54; Collinson, *Richard Bancroft and Elizabethan anti-Puritanism* (Cambridge: Cambridge University Press, 2013), chap. 8; Webster, *Godly Clergy*, chap. 3; W. Ian P. Hazlett, "Playing God's Card: Knox and Fasting, 1565–66," in *John Knox and the British Reformations*, ed. Roger A. Mason (Aldershot: Ashgate, 1998), 176–98; Webster and Shipps, *Diary of Samuel Rogers*, xxxiv–xv; Peel and Carlson, *Cartwrightiana*, 134–36 (as its editors remark, Cartwright may not actually be its author).

68. Hastings Robinson, ed. *Original Letters Relative to the English Reformation* (Cambridge: 1846), 1:47; Frere and Douglas, *Puritan Manifestoes*, 13, 14 ; David Wright, "Infant baptism and the Christian community in Bucer," in *Martin Bucer: Reforming Church and Community*, ed. D. F. Wright (Cambridge: Cambridge University Press 1994), 95–106, esp. 97–98; Greaves, *Theology & Revolution*, 86–95; Pelikan and Hotchkiss, *Creeds and Confessions*, 2:399–400. The Aberdeen Confession of 1616 reiterated this argument, to which it added the assertion that baptism was "necessary to salvation, if it can be orderly had."

69. See, e.g., Kenneth Fincham, ed., *Visitation Articles and Injunctions of the Early Stuart Church*, 2 vols. (Woodbridge: Boydell, 1994), 1: 55.

70. I. M. Green, *The Christian's ABC: Catechisms and Catechizing in England c. 1530–1740* (Oxford: Clarendon, 1996), intro.

71. Alastair J. Mann, *The Scottish Book Trade, 1500–1720: Print Commerce and Print Control in Early Modern Scotland* (East Linton: Tuckwell, 2000), 48–49. Popular responses to the exercise are described (pessimistically) in Arnold Hunt, *The Art of Hearing: English*

Preachers and Their Audiences, 1590–1640 (Cambridge: Cambridge University Press, 2010), 237–39.

72. As Max Weber said. "a new type of man . . . entirely dependent upon himself, in terrible solitude, . . . No church, no preacher, no sacrament can help him in the decisive matter of his life." Quoted in Max Weber, *The Protestant Ethic and the "Spirit" of Capitalism and Other Writings*, ed. Peter Baehr and Gordon C. Wells (New York: Penguin, 2002), xii. For other studies that employ the binary of "collective" and "personal," the first being displaced by the second, see Marshall, *Beliefs and the Dead*, 276 n. 68. In his introduction to *Work of Perkins*, Ian Breward contradicts this argument (pp. 70–73), as do Cohen in *God's Caress* and Andrew Cambers in *Godly Reading: Print, Manuscript, and Puritanism in England, 1580–1720* (Cambridge: Cambridge University Press, 2011).

73. *Winthrop Papers*, 1:169; Fielding, "Opposition to the Personal Rule of Charles I: The Diary of Robert Woodford, 1637–1641," *HJ* 31 (1988): 774–75; Eales, *Puritans and Roundheads*, 57–59. See chapter 6 for more examples.

74. Ramona Wray, *Women Writers of the Seventeenth Century* (Horndon, Tavistock, Devon: Northcote House, 2004), chap. 3; Kate Narveson, *Bible Readers and Lay Writers in Early Modern England: Gender and Self-Definition in an Emergent Writing Culture* (Burlington, VT: Ashgate, 2012). I agree with Wray when she argues that "the formative role of mothers' advice books suggests that . . . it was perfectly possible for women to construct a legitimate and authoritative speaking voice" (p. 43), a possibility she confines to women who were dying, an argument that cannot account for Anne Locke. Cf. Patrick Collinson, "The Role of Women in the English Reformation illustrated by the Life and Friendships of Anne Locke," *Studies in Church History* 2, ed. G. J. Cuming (London: Thomas Nelson, 1965), 258–72; and Diane Willen, "Godly Women in Early Modern England: Puritanism and Gender," *JEH* 43 (1992): 561–80 (a broader response to assertions of Puritan misogyny). For a local expression of maternal responsibilities, see Philip Stubbes, *A christal glasse for Christian women* (1591; more than thirty editions by the 1690s), a tribute to his wife, who died in the aftermath of giving birth, detailing her visions, spiritual practices, and beliefs. Prose tributes to virtuous women abound; see, e.g., Booy, ed., *Notebooks of Nehemiah Wallington*, 87–88. See also Richardson, *Puritanism in North-west England*, 134–38, 105–14. Useful overviews include Jacqueline Eales, "Samuel Clarke and the 'Lives' of Godly Women in Seventeenth-Century England," in *Women in the Church*, ed. W. J. Sheils and Diana Wood, Studies in Church History 27 (1990), 365–76; Debra L. Parish "The power of female pietism: Women as spiritual authorities and religious role models in Seventeenth-Century England," *Journal of Religious History* 17 (1992): 33–46; and Susan Wabuda, "The woman with the rock: The controversy on women and Bible reading," in *Belief and Practice in Reformation England: A Tribute to Patrick Collinson from His Students*, ed. Susan Wabuda and Caroline Litzenberger (Aldershot: Ashgate, 1998), 40–59 (documenting the presence of "Jerome's model of the devote woman of letters" (p. 58). See also *Silent But for the Word: Tudor Women as Patrons, Translators, and Writers of Religious Works,* ed. Margaret Hannay (Kent, OH: Kent State University Press, 1985); Suzanne W. Hull, *Chaste, Silent and Obedient: English Books for Women, 1475–1640* (San Marino, CA.: Huntington Library, 1982). Anthony Fletcher casts a wider net in his description of "Women and Religion," *Gender, Sex and Subordination in England, 1500–1800* (New Haven, CT: Yale University Press, 1995), chap. 17, although drawing substantially on seventeenth-century godly sources.

75. Richardson, *Puritanism in North-west England*, 105; Fielding, *Diary of Robert Woodford*, 23–27; Keith M. Brown, *Noble Society in Scotland Wealth, Family and Culture, from Reformation to Revolution* (Edinburgh: Edinburgh University Press, 2000), 234–35. In "Prescription and Practice: Protestantism and the Upbringing of Children, 1560–1700,"

in *The Church and Childhood*, ed. Diana Wood, Studies in Church History 31 (Oxford: Blackwell, 1994), 325–46, Anthony Fletcher corrects the argument (common in American scholarship of the 1970s and 1980s) that Puritan households were grimly repressive or unloving.

76. Not yet adequately acknowledged, the category of "first conversion" is touched on in Cohen, *God's Caress*, 104, citing Richard Mather. The many others who used the term include John Goodwin, *Christ set forth in his Death, Resurrection, Ascension* (1651), sig. A2v; and Thomas Shepard, for which see McGiffert, *God's Plot*, 107. See also Morris Fuller, *The Life and Writings of Thomas Fuller*, 2 vols. (London, 1886), 1, 168.

77. Samuel Ward, *The Life of Faith*, 3d ed. (London, 1622), 33; William Perkins, *A graine of Musterd-Seede* (1597), addressed to "all troubled and touched consciences" to advise them on "the least measure of grace that can befall the true child of God" (sig. A4r–v); Breward, *Work of Perkins*, 230; Rogers, *Seven Treatises*, chap. 1; John Preston, *A Treatise of Effectuall Faith* (London, 1637); pagination continuous with Preston, *The Breast-Plate of Faith and Love*, 5th ed. (London, 1634), 121–53 (quotation, p. 134).

78. Shuger, ed., *Religion in Early Stuart England, 1603–1638*, 419–20; Booy, ed., *Notebooks of Nehemiah Wallington*, 192; [Sibbes], *Saints Cordialls*, 28; Dent, *Plain Mans Pathway*, 20; Pelikan and Hotchkiss, eds., *Creeds and Confessions*, 2:573.

79. Perkins, "To the Godly Reader," in *Briefe Discourse, Taken Out of Hier. Zanchius* (1592), quoted in W. B. Patterson, *William Perkins and the Making of a Protestant England* (New York: Oxford University Press, 2014), 96 n. 30; Calvin, *Institutes*, trans. Battles, bk. 3, chap. 2, sec. 15 (pp. 560–61); Joel Beeke, *The Quest for Full Assurance: The Legacy of Calvin and His Successors* (Edinburgh: Banner of Truth Trust, 1999), chap. 4; Dent, *Plain Mans Path-way*, 30; Wallace, *Puritans and Predestination*, 50. As Mark Dever points out, Calvin and his heirs took for granted the "objective" reality of the gospel promise that Christ will save those with faith. Within the practical divinity as in Calvin's own thinking, however, assurance was also "subjective," or a matter of personal assurance. Dever, *Richard Sibbes*, 163, an observation followed (pp. 165–170) by a close reading of Calvin and an extended critique of misreadings of Calvin on this point by R. T. Kendall and Perry Miller, among others, misreadings aligned with a "Calvin versus Calvinists" framework. Well-informed studies of assurance, although differing in how it is described, include Beeke, *Quest for Full Assurance*; Dever, *Richard Sibbes* (as noted in the index); Bozeman, *Precisionist Strain*, chaps. 7–8; Cohen, *God's Caress*, chaps. 4–5, Tipson, *Hartford Puritanism*, chap. 11, Stoever, *"Faire and Easie Way,"* chap. 7; and Michael P. Winship, *Making Heretics Militant Protestantism and Free Grace in Massachusetts, 1636–1641* (Princeton: Princeton University Press, 2002), chap. 1.

80. Breward, *Work of Perkins*, 228, 257; Rogers, *Practice of Christianity*, 7, 28; Dent, *Plain Mans Path-way*, 151–52; Gilby, *Briefe Treatise*, sig. A4v. See also Hildersham, *Fourth of John*, 9, insisting on the existence of "certain" signs. Timothy Rogers, *The righteous mans evidences from heaven; or, A treatise shewing how every man while he lives here may certainly know what shall become of him after his departure out of this life* (London, 1619; and much reprinted thereafter).

81. As analyzed by someone with no connections to the practical divinity, the non- (or anti-) Puritan English writer Robert Burton in his *Anatomy of Melancholy* (1638), it was godly preaching and its practice of "thunder[ing] out Gods Iudgments" and "wound[ing] mens consciences" that made people feel "they are almost at their wits end." See also Dixon, *Practical Predestinarians*, 26–32.

82. Eales, *Puritans and Roundheads*, 50; [John Hart], *Trodden down Strength, by the God of strength, or Mrs Drake Revived* (London, 1646); Winthrop, *Journal*, 229–30. This list could easily be lengthened; see, e.g., Peel and Carlson, *Cartwrightiana*, 107; Parker and

Carlson, *"Practical Divinity,"* 62; Mullan, *Scottish Puritanism*, 93–98; Greaves, *Theology & Revolution*, 67–68 (Elizabeth Bowes, Knox's mother-in-law); Fielding, *Diary of Robert Woodford*, 391 (a woman who, "in mighty horror," roared "sometimes most hideously . . . cryeinge out she was damn'd she was damn'd, she should be in hell"; and Lady Joan Barrington's nephew, as noted in Dever, *Richard Sibbes*, 162–63. More such episodes are assembled in John Stachniewski, *The Persecutory Imagination: English Puritanism and the Literature of Religious Despair* (Oxford: Clarendon, 1991), chap. 1, without, however, any suspicions on his part about their theatricality or the assumption that these were a consequence of the doctrine of election. Commenting on the "spiritual frailty" of the mid-sixteenth-century Englishwoman Elizabeth Bowes, Christine M. Newman, having noted that "a tendency toward spiritual chastisement formed a recurring theme in the history of reformation spirituality," suggests that "personal expressions of guilt and unworthiness may have drawn upon and been influenced by the wider spiritual attitudes and aspirations of the age." Newman, "The Reformation and Elizabeth Bowes: A Study of a Sixteenth-Century Northern Gentlewoman," in Sheils and Wood, *Women in the Church*, 333. See also Andrew Cambers, "Demonic Possession, Literacy and 'Superstition' in Early Modern England," *Past & Present* 202 (2009): 3–25; and Ryrie, *Being Protestant*, chap. 2.

83. Breward, *Work of Perkins*, 228, 285; Giles Firmin, *The Real Christian, or a Treatise of Effectual Calling* (Boston, 1742), 68; Ernest Axon, ed., *Oliver Heywood's Life of John Angier*, Chetham Society 97 (Manchester, 1937), 50; Tipson, *Hartford Puritanism*, 277–80; Dent, *Plain Mans Path-way*, 261; Albro, *Works of Shepard*, 1:57; Hall, *FS*, 65. See also Stachniewski, *Persecutory Imagination*, 152, and Kaufman, *Prayer, Despair, and Drama*, chap. 2. For terror as a theme of "godly" cheap print, see Hall, *Worlds of Wonder*, chap. 3.

84. *The Complete Works of Richard Sibbes, D.D.*, ed. Alexander Grosart, 7 vols. (Edinburgh, 1862–64), 1: 68–69, 40, 73; Ronald N. Frost, *"The Bruised Reed* By Richard Sibbes (1577–1635)," in Kapic and Gleason, *Devoted Life*, 79–91 (quotation, p. 82). The most careful reading of Sibbes on assurance is Mark Dever's in *Richard Sibbes*, 174–87, noting, for example, that he endorsed sanctification as one of its sources. See also Knott, *Sword of the Spirit*, chap. 2. A similar emphasis on divine love appears in Calvin, for which see Zachman, "Calvin's Sermons on Ephesians." Michael P. Winship links Sibbes, Culverwell, and Preston as critics of certain aspects of the practical divinity; see Winship, *Making Heretics*, 16–23. Simultaneously, Winship corrects (p. 269) overstatements of the kind that occur in Janice Knight, *Orthodoxies in Massachusetts: Rereading American Puritanism* (Cambridge, MA.: Harvard University Press, 1994). David Parnham depicts a Sibbes who uses terror: *Heretics Within: Anthony Wotton, John Goodwin, and the Orthodox Divines* (Eastbourne: Sussex University Press, 2014), 173. That English readers found Sibbes "comforting" is argued (using a single example) in L. E. Semler, "Creative Adoption in *Eliza's Babes* (1653): Puritan Refigurations of Sibbes, Herrick, and Herbert," in *Centered on the Word: Literature, Scripture, and the Tudor-Stuart Middle Way*, ed. Daniel W. Doerksen and Christopher Hodkins (Newark: University of Delaware Press, 2004), 319–45

85. [Ezekiel Culverwell], *A briefe answer to certaine objections against a treatise of faith* (London, 1620), sig. A4r; [Culverwell], *A Treatise of Faith* (1623), 145. Sibbes wrote a preface commenting the book.

86. Preston, *Breast-plate of Faith and Love*, 6–7, sig. A3v; Shuger, *Religion in Early Stuart England*, 426; McGee, *"Industrious Mind,"* 177. Divine love reappears as the theme of other sermon series, especially *Five Sermons on the Divine Love* (1640) and *Christ Set forth in his Death . . . Together with A Treatise discerning the Affectionate Tendernesse of Christ Heart once in Heaven, unto Sinners on Earth* (London, 1651). See also Wakefield's comments on Preston's love-centered preaching in *Puritan Devotion*, 2–94. Preston's preaching is appraised more fully in Moore, *English Hypothetical Universalism*.

87. Michael S. Horton, *"Of the Object and Acts of Justifying Faith* by Thomas Goodwin (1600–1680," in Kapic and Gleason, *Devoted Life*, 108–222.

88. Beeke, *Quest for Full Assurance*, 65–72 (reviewing the evidence and noting the Reformer's emphasis on the priority of Christ and free grace, and noting also the presence of the Holy Spirit as central to his understanding of assurance).

89. Stoever, *"Faire and Easie Way*," 126–29 and chap. 7; Parker and Carlson, *"Practical Divinity*," 290; Peel and Carlson, *Cartwrightiana*, 169; Cowper, quoted in Gordon Marshall, *Presbyteries and Profits: Calvinism and the Development of Capitalism in Scotland, 1560–1707* (Oxford: Clarendon, 1980), 74. See also "A catechism; containing certain questions and answers touching the doctrine of predestination . . . ," in Strype, *Annals of the Reformation*, vol. 3, pt. 2:239, (where it is argued that "to have either good will or good work is a testimony of the Spirit of God, which is given to the elect only," adding that the elect cannot "do as they list" but must "walk in such good works as God in Christ Jesus hath ordained them unto." See also Karen Bruhn, "'Sinne Unfolded': Time, Election, and Disbelief among the Godly in Late Sixteenth- and Early Seventeenth-Century England," *Church History* 77 (2008): 574–95. Thomas Shepard turned to sanctification as "mediate evidence of my faith and so of my peace." McGiffert, *God's Plot*, 110.

90. Herman J. Selderhuis, "Faith between God and the Devil: Calvin's doctrine of faith as reflected in his Commentary on the Psalms," in *John Calvin and the Interpretation of Scripture*, Calvin Studies 10 and 11, ed. Charles Raynal (Grand Rapids, MI: Calvin Studies Society, 2006), 188–205, especially 193–95; Bozeman, *Precisionist Strain* (emphasizing an "overall drift in it" to establish an "ever closer linkage of assurance and behavior, and its trademark demand for strictness and exactitude" (pp. 140–41). But see Alan C. Clifford, *Atonement and Justification: English Evangelical Theology, 1640–1790* (Oxford: Clarendon, 1990), 175–77, on Calvin's insistence on linking faith and works and on justification as "continuous" with sanctification.

91. *An Harmonie of the Confessions of the Faith of the Christian and Reformed Churches* (Cambridge, 1586), 255–56; Perkins, *Salve for a Sicke Man*, 17–18; Ames, *Marrow of Theology*, 200.

92. From Cartwright and Travers to Browne and Barrow, and on into the early seventeenth century with the radical Puritans and Separatists we take up in the next chapter, it was assumed that "true faith was more than simply intellectual assent: it must find expression in demonstrable obedience," which in turn was "evidence of saving faith." Stephen Brachlow, *The Communion of Saints: Radical Puritan and Separatist Ecclesiology, 1570–1625* (Oxford: Oxford University Press 1988), 20–21. For other useful reviews, see Mullan, *Scottish Puritanism*, chap. 3; Beeke, *Quest for Full Assurance*; and Stoever, *"Fair and Easie Way*," chap. 8. That assurance was entangled with social discipline is noted in chapter 5. See also chapter 9, below.

93. Sibbes, quoted in Stoever, *"Faire and Easie Way*," 154; Rutherford, *Letters*, 38. Three of the contributors to *Puritanism and Emotion* detail the place of "joy" or ""happiness" in the practical divinity: Karl Jones, "Thomas Goodwin and the 'Supreme Happiness of Man'"; Tom Schwanda, "The Saints' Desire and Delight to Be with Chreist"; and S. Bryn Roberts, "'Milke and Honey': Puritan Happiness in the Writings of Robert Bolton, John Norden and Francis Rous"; see also Kate Harveson, "Resting Assured in Puritan Piety: The Lay Experience," all in *Puritanism and Emotion in the Early Modern World*, ed. Alec Ryrie and Tom Schwanda (Houdsmills: Palgrave Macmillan, 2016).

94. Collinson, *Religion of Protestants*, 155, Breward, *Work of Perkins*, 41; Dent, *Plain Mans Path-way*, 127. That "contempt" affected every engaged minister in the Church of England at this time is suggested by the chapter headed "Contempt" (28) in George Her-

bert, *A Priest to the Temple, or the Country Parson* (1652; repr., London: Everyman's Library, [1908]). See also Kaufman, *Prayer, Despair, and Drama*, 54–57 (on the registers of Richard Greenham's ministry through his own eyes).

95. T. W. Davids, *Annals of Evangelical Nonconformity in the County of Essex* (London, 1863), 211; Dent, *Plain Mans Path-way*, 12; Parker and Carlson, "Practical Divinity," 23; for Cotton and Bernard, see chap. 6. See also Cornelius Burgess, *The First Sermon Preached to the Honourable House of Commons* (London, 1641), 78; Richard Bernard, *The Faithfull Shepherd* (London, 1621), 12–13. All such dichotomies of hate/love were reiterating the core dichotomy that Christ was hated/loved and that all true Christians are also hated/loved. For anticlericalism in this period, see Christopher Haigh, "Anticlericalism and Clericalism, 1580–1640," in *Anticlericalism in Britain c. 1500–1914*, ed. Nigel Aston and Matthew Cragoe (Stroud: Sutton, 2000), 18–41; and Haigh, *The Plain Man's Pathways to Heaven: Kinds of Christianity in Post-Reformation England, 1570–1640* (Oxford: Oxford University Press, 2007), chap. 1 and passim.

96. For ongoing Catholic critiques of Protestant spirituality, see, e.g., William Harrison and William Leigh, *Deaths Advantage Little Regarded and the Soules solace against sorrow* (London, 1602). See also *William Weston: The Autobiography of an Elizabethan*, trans. Philip Caraman (London: Longmans, Green 1955); an English Jesuit who returned to England in 1585, Weston singled out exorcisms he and other priests performed as a sign of "the majestic power of the Church over evil spirits and monsters" and therefore demonstrating "the difference between the two religions" (p. 27; see also p. 30 n. 10). He also reported episodes of someone being "overcome" by the "beauty" of the mass" (p. 35) and of people who, on their deathbeds, experienced "great comfort and joy" from Extreme Unction (p. 53). For context, see Alexandra Walsham, "In Sickness and in Health: Medicine and Inter-Confessional Relations in Post-Reformation England," in *Living with Religious Diversity in Early-Modern Europe*, ed. C. Scott Dixon, Dagmar Freist, and Mark Greengrass (Aldershot: Ashgate, 2009), 161–81.

97. Hopfl, *Christian Polity*, 90–94 (quotations, pp. 90–91, drawing on the *Ordonnances* of 1541 especially); Ronald S. Wallace, *Calvin's Doctrine of the Word and Sacraments* (Edinburgh: Oliver & Boyd, 1953), 84–85, 91; Calvin, *Institutes*, IV.i.5, IV.i.6; Hall, *FS*, chap. 1. See also Andrew Pettegree, "The clergy and the Reformation: From 'devilish priesthood' to new professional elite," in *The Reformation of the Parishes: The Ministry and the Reformation in Town and Country*, ed. Pettegree (Manchester: Manchester University Press, 1993), 1–21; Mullan, *Scottish Puritanism*, chaps. 1–2; and Margo Todd, *The Culture of Protestantism in Early Modern Scotland* (New Haven, CT: Yale University Press, 2002), chap. 8, for details of the situation—economic, theological, and otherwise—of the Scottish clergy.

98. Preston, *Breast-plate of Faith and Love*, 22–23; "The people would be exhorted to reverence and honour their Ministers chosen, as the servants and ambassadors of the Lord Jesus . . . whosoever rejecteth them, and despiseth their ministry . . . rejecteth and despiseth Christ Jesus." *Book of Discipline*, in Dickinson, *Knox's History of the Reformation*, 2:286. Catherine Davies describes this "clericalism" as voiced during the reign of Edward VI in Davies, *A Religion of the Word: The Defence of the Reformation in the Reign of Edward VI* (Manchester: Manchester University Press, 2002), 94–106.

99. Dent, *Plain Mans Path-way*, 336; Downame quoted in Patrick Collinson, "Shepherds, Sheepdogs, and Hirelings: The Pastoral Ministry in Post-Reformation England," in *The Ministry: Clerical and Lay*, eds. W. J. Sheils and Diana Wood, Studies in Church History 26 (Oxford: Blackwell, 1989), 195. Disputed by Whitgift in his debates with Cartwright and disputed anew by the Laudians of the 1620s and 1630s, the Puritan interpretation of

Romans had "drastic implications for the religious life of the Church of England." Hunt, *Art of Hearing*, 31 and, in general, chap. 2.

100. David Little, *Religion, Order, and Law: A Study in Pre-Revolutionary England* (New York: HarperTorchbooks, 1969), 89–91 (hence the rule that a sermon precede the sacrament); James K. Cameron, ed., *The First Book of Discipline* (Edinburgh: St. Andrew Press, 1972), 116.

101. Bernard, *Faithfull Shepherd*, chap. 7; Keith Thomas, "Cases of Conscience in Seventeenth-Century England," in *Public Duty and Private Conscience in Seventeenth-Century England: Essays Presented to G. E. Aylmer*, ed. John Morrill, Paul Slack, and Daniel Woolf (Oxford: Clarendon, 1993), 29–56. This chapter omits the ongoing task of disputing with apologists for Catholicism and deviant figures within the Reformed tradition that occupied such luminaries as James Ussher, William Ames, and William Perkins. A wider anxiety about allowing the unlearned to interpret Scripture is described in Kate Narveson, "'Their practice bringeth little profit': Clerical Anxieties about Lay Scripture Reading in Early Modern England," in Martin and Ryrie, eds., *Private and Domestic Devotion in Early Modern Britain*, 165–87.

102. Breward, *Work of Perkins*, 337; Lisa M. Gordis, *Opening Scripture: Bible Reading and Interpretative Authority in Puritan New England* (Chicago: University of Chicago Press, 2003), chap. 1; Green, *Print and Protestantism*, chap. 3. Catholic "insinuations" that Scripture was "inscrutable" are noted in Matthew Parker's preface to the Bishops Bible; John Strype, *The Life and Acts of Matthew Parker* (Oxford: 1831), 3: 237; to which Parker replied that Scripture was not "insuperable to them which with diligent searching labour to discern the evil from the good" (p. 239). Underlying assumptions about Spirit, Word, and biblical hermeneutics are described in Stephens, *Holy Spirit*, chap. 6; the introductory essays in William Perkins, *A Commentary on Galatians*, ed. Gerald Sheppard (New York: Pilgrim, 1989); Patrick Collinson, "The Coherence of the Text: How It Hangeth Together: The Bible in Reformation England," in *The Bible, the Reformation, and the Church: Essays in Honour of James Atkinson*, ed. W. Stephen (Sheffield: Sheffield Academic, 1999), chap. 7; and Jan Stievermann, *Prophecy, Piety, and the Problem of Historicity* (Tubingen: Mohr Siebeck, 2016), pt. 4; see also Wakefield, *Puritan Devotion*, chap. 2. As Calvin remarked in the *Institutes* (1.4–5), "simple folk" needed help in understanding the Bible lest they overlook its coherence. See also Green, *Print and Protestantism*, 106–7.

103. Tudor-period reformers called for Scripture to be interpreted according to its "literall sense," an assertion linked to their uneasiness with Catholic modes of exegesis and with classical or humanist poetics. A fuller history than I can provide would trace the anxieties about the uses of biblical tropes or figures in poetics. Some of this story is sketched in Coles, *Religion, Reform, and Women's Writing*, chap. 3.

104. Andrew Crome, *The Restoration of the Jews: Early Modern Hermeneutics, Eschatology, and National Identity in the Works of Thomas Brightman* (Heidelberg: Springer, 2014), chap. 2; see also Little, *Religion, Order, and Law*, p. 89 n. 129 and, in general, Knott, *Sword of the Spirit*, chap. 2 (noting Richard Sibbes's free use of tropes and figures); Darlene K. Fleming, "Calvin as commentator on the Synoptic Gospels," in *Calvin and the Bible*, ed. Donald K. McKim (Cambridge: Cambridge University Press, 2006), 131–63; Barbara Pitkin, "John Calvin and the Interpretation of the Bible," in *A History of Biblical Interpretation*, ed. A. J. Hauser and D. F. Watson, 2 vols. (Grand Rapids, MI: Eerdmans, 2003), 2:241–71; Mary Morrissey, "Ornament and Repetition: Biblical Interpretation in Early Modern English Preaching," in *The Oxford Handbook of the Bible in Early Modern England, c. 1530–1700*, ed. Kevin Killeen, Helen Smith, and Rachael Willie (Oxford: Oxford University Press, 2015), 303–16; Mason I. Lowance Jr., *The Language of Canaan: Metaphor and Symbol in*

New England from the Puritans to the Transcendentalists (Cambridge, MA: Harvard University Press, 1980), chaps. 2, 6; Stievermann, *Prophecy, Piety, and the Problem of Historicity*, pt. 4; Hunt, *Art of Hearing*, chap. 1 (not limited to godly, however). In *Hartford Puritanism*, chap. 7, Baird Tipson analyzes the hermeneutical consequences of Ramism. The argument that Puritans created a distinctive mode of writing known as the "plain style" does not stand up; for a prescient critique, see Lawrence Sasek, *The Literary Temper of the English Puritans* (Baton Rouge: Louisiana State University Press, 1961).

105. Mullan, *Scottish Puritanism*, 68–70. On the flowering of "spiritual" biographies in the mid-seventeenth century, see William Haller, *The Rise of Puritanism* (New York: Columbia University Press, 1938), chap. 2; and Patrick Collinson, "'A Magazine of Religious Patterns': An Erasmian Topic Transposed in English Protestantism," in *Godly People*, 498–525.

106. Parker and Carlson, *"Practical Divinity,"* chap. 5.

107. John N. King, *English Reformation Literature: The Tudor Origins of the Protestant Tradition* (Princeton, NJ: Princeton University Press, 1979), provides the necessary context. For Calvin's "anti-eloquence," see R. Ward Holder, "Calvin as commentator on the Pauline epistles," in *Calvin and the Bible*, ed. Donald K. McKim (Cambridge: Cambridge University Press, 2006), 243–44; see also Manetsch, *Calvin's Company of Pastors*, 156–73.

108. Ames, *Marrow of Theology*, 193; Breward, *Work of Perkins*, 315. For the broader context, see, in general, Darlene K. Fleming, "Calvin as commentator on the Synoptic Gospels," in McKim *Calvin and the Bible*, 131–63. Evoking an audience of "the meaner sort" or simpler folk" was a convention of political discourse as well as of religious, a trope that should never be translated into the categories of social history.

109. Breward, *Work of Perkins*, 341, 345; Hall, *FS*, 301–2; Whytock, *"An Educated Clergy,"* 75; Ames, *Marrow of* Theology, 191; Sargent Bush, *The Writings of Thomas Hooker: Spiritual Adventure in Two Worlds* (Madison: University of Wisconsin Press, 1980), 12–13, 16 (on their capacity). In *Sympathetic Puritans: Calvinist Fellow Feeling in Early New England* (New York: Oxford University Press, 2015), 124–25, Abram van Engen summarizes the advice in manuals and elsewhere on methods of making sermons "affective." This same emphasis on the Holy Spirit helps explain the insistence on free form prayer and, among Quakers, on spontaneous speech.

110. As Thomas Hooker did in his Chelmsford sermons. Tipson, *Hartford Puritanism*, 246–51. Arnold Hunt describes this tension more fully in *Art of Hearing* chap. 5.

111. Townsend, *Writings of Bradford*, 1:31; Dent, *Plain Mans Path-way*, 19, see also 40–42.

112. Hints of conflict and confusion occur in Haigh, *Plain Man's Pathways*, 71–78, 106–8.

113. Nowell, *A Catechism*, 217–18; *Barrington Family Letters, 1628–1632*, ed. Searle, 66–68, 85–86. As noted elsewhere in these letters, Lady Barrington suffered from "melancholy." See also Charles Thomas-Stanford, *Sussex in the Great Civil War and the Interregnum, 1642–1660* (London: (n.p., 1910), 28–29. The problem is not unique to Britain; for this same tension in sixteenth-century Germany, see Mattias A. Deuschle, "Ecclesiastical Jurisdiction, Ecclesiastical Discipline and Lived Morality before and after the Reformation in South-Western Germany," in *Sister Reformations II: Reformation and Ethics in Germany and in England*, ed. Dorothea Wendebourg and Alec Ryrie (Tubingen: Mohr Siebeck, 2014), 176.

114. Hunt, *Art of Hearing*, 267; Samuel Rawson Gardiner, ed., *Cases in Courts of Star Chamber*, Camden Society, n.s. 39 (1896), 198–238; Clarke, *Thirty-Two Eminent Divines*,

116. In *The Art of Hearing*, Arnold Hunt provides a fuller range of evidence, as does Haigh, *Plain Man's Pathways* (much of it taken from local records). See also Todd, *Culture of Protestantism*, chap. 8; Bernard Capp, *England's Culture Wars: Puritan Reformation and Its Enemies in the Interregnum, 1649–1660* (Oxford: Oxford University Press, 2012), intro. (describing the ministry of Richard Culmer in civil-war-period Kent); and Darren Oldridge, *Religion and Society in Early Stuart England* (Aldershot: Ashgate, 1998), chaps. 4, 6.

115. *Winthrop Papers* 3:143–43; *The Works of William Pemble* (London, 1635), 135. Hunt, *Art of Hearing*, chaps. 5–6, explores whether or how, in the context of political tensions, contemporary audiences or readers recognized the criticism implicit (or explicit) in certain biblical allusions; and the figure of minister as divisive rather than healing. See also Tipson, *Hartford Puritanism*, chap. 8, for Hooker's wrestling with this problem.

116. Calderwood, *History of the Kirk*, 4:95.

117. Christopher Haigh, "The Taming of Reformation: Preachers, Pastors, and Parishioners in Elizabethan and Early Stuart England," *History* 85 (2000): 572–88; Haigh, *Plain Man's Pathways*, 40ff.; Kaufman, *Prayer, Despair, and Drama*, 52–55. Richard Greenham went back and forth on this question, sometimes criticizing ministers who "use reaching, and excessive speaches to discredit" some aspect of behavior (p. 103), but preaching himself with "great zeal and fervency," a practice he justified "when the weightiness of the thing provoked [him] thereunto." Parker and Carlson, *"Practical Divinity,"* 143. See also Tipson, *Hartford Puritanism*, 261–62. Thomas Fuller's sketch of "the faithfull Minister" in *The Holy State* (London, 1642), 80–88, touches on this issue from the standpoint of a self-professed "moderate."

118. Possibly the least desirable of these possibilities; see, e.g, *The Diary of Samuel Rogers 1634–1638*, ed. Tom Webster and Kenneth Shipps, Church of England Record Society 11 (Woodbridge: Boydell, 2004), xxx–xxxii. For Thomas Shepard's discomfort, see McGiffert, *God's Plot*, 52.

119. A. J. Fletcher, "Puritanism in Seventeenth Century Sussex," *Studies in Suffolk Church History*, ed. M. J. Kitch (London: Leopard's Head,1981), 142; Patrick Collinson, *The Birthpangs of Protestant England: Religious and Cultural Change in the Sixteenth and Seventeenth Centuries* (London: Macmillan, 1985), 40; William Hunt, *The Puritan Moment: The Coming of Revolution in an English County* (Cambridge, MA.: Harvard University Press, 1983), 102–5; Cross, *Church and People*, 134–42; Paul Seaver, "Puritan Preachers and Their Patrons," in *Religious Politics in Post-Reformation England: Essays in Honour of Nicholas Tyacke*, ed. Kenneth Fincham and Peter Lake (Woodbridge: Boydell, 2006), 128–42; D. J. Lamburn, "The Influence of the Laity in Appointments of Clergy in the Late Sixteenth and Early Seventeenth Century," in Claire Cross, ed., *Patronage and Recruitment in the Tudor and Early Stuart Church* (York: University of York, 1996), 95–119; D. J. Lamburn, " 'Digging and Dunging': Some Aspects of Lay Influence in the Churches in Northern Towns," in *Life and Thought in the Northern Church c. 1100–c. 1700 Essays in Honour of Claire Cross*, ed. Diana Wood, Studies in Church History: Subsidia 12 (Woodbridge: Boydell, 1999), 365–80; Rosemary O'Day, "The law of patronage in early modern history," *JEH* 26 (1975): 247–60.

120. Complained of, however, at the Hampton Court conference of 1604 by some of the bishops and irritating to William Laud in the 1630s as an obstacle in the way of securing conformity. William Barlow, *The Summe and Substance of the Conference* (London, 1605), 53.

121. Paul Seaver, *The Puritan Lectureships: The Politics of Religious Dissent* (Stanford: Stanford Uiversity Press, 1970), chaps. 3–6, 125 (figure for London), 131 (context); as Seaver is careful to point out, conformists also held these positions. Even so, by the beginning of

the seventeenth century, the leaders of the church were regarding them as a bastion of nonconformity. See also Roger B. Manning, *Religion and Society in Elizabethan Sussex: A Study of the Enforcement of the Religious Settlement, 1558-1603* (Leicester: Leicester University Press, 1969), 76 (using a lectureship to get rid of someone already holding office); Beat Kumin, "Parish finance and the early Tudor clergy," in Pettegree, ed., *Reform of the parish*, 43-62.

122. Seaver, *Puritan Lectureships*, 88-92, 235-38, 251-55.

123. The complexities of the preacher–lay audience continuum are explored in detail in Hunt, *Art of Hearing*, noted in Dever, *Richard Sibbes*, 186, and, using a different methodology, analyzed in Cohen, *God's Caress*.

124. Production summarized in Tessa Watt, "Piety in the Pedlar's Pack: Continuity and Change, 1578-1630," in Spufford, *World of Rural Dissenters*, 235-72; see also Tessa Watt, *Cheap Print and Popular Piety, 1550-1640* (Cambridge: Cambridge University Press, 1991); *The Cambridge History of the Book in Britain, Vol. 4: 1557-1695*, ed. John Barnard and D. F. McKenzie (Cambridge: Cambridge University Press, 2002), 29, and for evidence about cost as a deterrent to ownership, pp. 56-57.

125. *Oliver Crowell's Letters and Speeches*, ed. Thomas Carlyle, 4 vols. (London, 1897), 1:101; Tipson, *Hartford Puritanism*, 36; William Row, *The Life of Mr. Robert Blair . . . containing His Autobiography*, ed. Thomas McCrie (Edinburgh, 1848), 19; Iain H. Murray, *The Puritan Hope: A Study in Revival and the Interpretation of Prophecy* (Edinburgh: Banner of Truth Trust, 1971), chap. 2. In a will he wrote in 1620, John Winthrop described himself as "washed from my sinnes, and . . . elected . . . to be a vessel of glory." *Winthrop Papers*, 2:249. So did Simonds D'Ewes, as noted in McGee, *"Industrious Mind,"* 177. Within the network of friends and family surrounding Brilliana and Robert Harley, people repeatedly referred to each other as being among the "elect." In his will, Francis Hastings affirmed that "Almighty God . . . hath chosen me to be his childe and predestinated me to eternall salvation." Claire Cross, "An Example of Lay Intervention in the Elizabethan Church," *Studies in Church History* 2, ed. M. C. Cummings, 275.

126. David Dickson, *True Christian Love* (Edinburgh, 1655), stanza 27.

127. William den Boer, "Defense or Deviation? A Re-Examination of Arminius's Motives to Deviate from the 'Mainstream' Reformed Theology," in Goudriaan and van Lieburg, eds., *Revisiting the Synod of Dordt*, 23-48; Aza Goudriaan, "The Synod of Dort on Arminian Anthropology," ibid., 81-106 (quotation, p. 104-5); Richard A. Muller, "God, Predestination, and the Integrity of the Created Order: A Note on Patterns in Arminius' Theology," in Graham, *Later Calvinism*, 431-46; Alan P. F. Sell, *The Great Debate: Calvinism, Arminianism and Salvation* (Grand Rapids, MI: Baker Book House, 1983), chaps. 1-2. What William Prynne understood as Arminianism is summarized in *Anti-Arminianisme*, 72-75.

128. Mark R. Shaw, "William Perkins and the New Pelagians: Another Look at the Cambridge Predestination Controversy of the 1590s," *Westminster Theological Journal* 58 (1996): 267-301; Porter, *Reformation and Reaction*, chap. 13; Lake, *Moderate Puritans*, chap. 9 (revising Porter's account of the behind-the-scenes politics); Hoyle, *Reformation and Religious Identity*, chap. 2 (correcting a few details in Lake); Mullan, *Scottish Puritanism*, chap. 7.

129. John Cotton, *The Way of Congregational Churches Cleared* (London, 1648), reprinted in *John Cotton on the Churches of New England*, ed. Larzer Ziff (Cambridge, MA.: Harvard University Press, 1968), 214-17 (quotation, p. 215); Jesper Rosenmeier, *"Spirituall Concupiscence": John Cotton's English Years, 1584-1633* (n.p.: Richard Kay, 2012), 103; *A treatise of Mr. Cottons . . . together with an examination thereof* (1646; written much earlier). Hearing from another minister that James Ussher wanted a copy of Cotton's "Dis-

course" on predestination, Cotton told Ussher that he was tempted by hypothetical universalism. But he also insisted that it was necessary to preach "Repentance, before Faith in the
Promises." Sargent Bush, ed., *The Correspondence of John Cotton* (Chapel Hill: University
of North Carolina Press, 2001), 111.

Chapter 5. A Reformation of Manners

1. Shaw, *Acts and Proceedings*, 27:1012–28 (quotations, p. 1026–27).

2. Ibid.; Laing, *Works of Knox*, 6:397; and see W. Ian P. Hazlett, "Playing God's Card:
Knox and Fasting," in *John Knox and the British Reformations*, ed. Roger A. Mason (Aldershot: Ashgate, 1998), 176–98 (filling out the political context).

3. *The Whole Works of James Ussher*, ed. Charles R. Elrington, 17 vols. (Dublin, 1847),
15:413–14, 418.

4. Taken for granted by fast-day preachers in England; see, e.g., Stephen Marshall, *A
Thanksgiving Sermon . . . July 28. 1648* (1648).

5. Chaderton, quoted in Sarah Bendall, Christopher Brooke, and Patrick Collinson, *A
History of Emmanuel College, Cambridge* (Woodbridge: Boydell, 1999), 33; Thomas Ball,
The Life of the Renowned Doctor Preston, ed. E. W. Harcourt (Oxford, 1885), 156–58; Alexandra Walsham, *Providence in Early Modern England* (Oxford: Oxford University Press,
1996), chap. 6.

6. Knox's version of covenantal rewards and punishments is summed up in Roger A.
Mason, "Knox, Resistance and the Royal Supremacy," in *John Knox and the British Refor-
mations*, ed. Mason, 154–75. On fasts from the vantage of the practical divinity, see Scudder,
Christians Daily Walke, chap. 5.

7. Robin Briggs, "The Catholic Puritans: Jansenists and Rigorists in France," in Donald
Pennington and Keith Thomas, eds., *Puritans and Revolutionaries: Essays in Seventeenth-
century History Presented to Christopher Hill* (Oxford: Clarendon, 1978), 333–54; Heinz
Schilling, *Civic Calvinism in Northwestern Germany and the Netherlands: Sixteenth to the
Nineteenth Centuries* (Kirksville, MO: Sixteenth-Century Journal Publishers, 1991), chap. 2.
Strong arguments against a distinctively "puritan" program figure in Steve Hindle, *The
State and Social Change in Early Modern England, c. 1550–1640* (London: Macmillan,
2000), chap. 7; and Paul Slack, *From Reformation to Improvement: Public Welfare in Early
Modern England* (Oxford: Clarendon, 1998). Both cite Puritan-connected programs of
"civic godliness" but emphasize broader contexts. Debate persists on the singularity of
Puritan-style rules about the Sunday Sabbath. In *The English Sabbath: A Study of Doctrine
and Discipline from the Reformation to the Civil War* (Cambridge: Cambridge University
Press, 1988), Kenneth Parker emphasizes the breadth of support for protecting it, an argu-
ment challenged by Alisdair Dougall in *The Devil's Book: Charles I, the Book of Sports, and
Puritanism in Tudor and Early Stuart England* (Exeter: University of Exeter Press, 2011).
See also (for common ground) Jonathan Barry, "Popular Culture in Seventeenth-Century
Bristol," in *Popular Culture in Seventeenth-Century England*, ed. Barry Reay (London:
Croom Helm, 1985), chap. 2. See also Patrick Collinson, *The Birthpangs of Protestant En-
gland: Religious and Cultural Change in the Sixteenth and Seventeenth Centuries* (New
York: St. Martin's, 1988), chap. 2. Any description of a common culture must slight the
many local peculiarities as well as those arising out of religious and intellectual debate or
the several different versions of culture ("elite," "learned," "plebian" and the like), all of them
evoked in Michael MacDonald and Terence R. Murphy, *Sleepless Souls: Suicide in Early
Modern England* (Oxford: Clarendon, 1990), intro. and chap. 6. As Debora Kuller Shuger
notes in *Habits of Thought in the English Renaissance: Religion, Politics, and the Dominant*

Culture (Berkeley: University of California Press, 1990), "despite their general agreement on doctrinal matters, the figures studied present an unexpected and at times drastic ideological pluralism" (p. 9).

8. Depending, as it does for the most part, on official narratives and prescriptive advice, this chapter describes everyday behavior through the eyes of the moralists. That social historians and, especially, historians of the family are given to reiterating truisms—for example, that Puritans were uncaring parents—that are not substantiated in the sources is also true. To cite a single example, in *Sexuality and Social Control: Scotland, 1660-1780* (Oxford: Blackwell, 1989), Rosalind Mitchison and Leah Leneman dismiss the reasoning of several major social historians about the contexts for premarital sex. The same problems dog every description of "popular religion" in this period. For exemplary second thoughts, see Martin Ingram, "The Reform of Popular Culture? Sex and Marriage in Early Modern England," in *Popular Culture in Seventeenth-Century England*, ed. Barry Reay (London: Croom Helm, 1985), chap. 4.

9. Roland A. Marchant, *The Church under the Law: Justice, Administration and Discipline in the Diocese of York, 1560-1640* (Cambridge: Cambridge University Press, 1969), 206; Stubbes, *Anatomie of Abuses*, quoted in Victor Harris, *All Coherence Gone* (Chicago: University of Chicago Press, 1949), 107; Alexander Walsham, " 'A Glose of Godlines': Philip Stubbes, Elizabethan Grub Street and the Invention of Puritanism," in *Belief and Practice in Reformation England: A Tribute to Patrick Collinson from his Students*, ed. Susan Wabuda and Caroline Litzenberger (Aldershot: Ashgate, 1998), 177–206; *The Books of Homilies: A Critical Edition*, ed. Gerald Bray (Cambridge: James Clarke, 2015), 96. As Walsham points out, Stubbes was not a Puritan, although often described as one by modern scholars who have not looked closely at his life story.

10. The following draws on David Underdown, *Revel, Riot, and Rebellion: Popular Politics and Culture in England, 1603-1660* (Oxford: Clarendon, 1985), chap. 5 and passim, a narrative emphasizing (pp. 123–24) "deep-rooted habits of participation and self-government" and a "culture shared by people in all areas" (119). See also Underdown, *A Freeborn People: Politics and the Nation in Seventeenth-Century England* (Oxford: Clarendon, 1996), an exemplary analysis of how commonplaces were appropriated at different times for different purposes; Susan Amussen, "Gender, Family and the Social Order, 1560–1725," in *Order and Disorder in Early Modern England*, ed. Anthony Fletcher and John Stevenson (Cambridge: Cambridge University Press, 1985), 196–217; E.M.W. Tillyard, *The Elizabethan World Picture* (London: Chatto and Windus, 1943); Walsham, *Providence in Early Modern England*; Helen C. White, *Social Criticism in Popular Religious Literature of the Sixteenth Century* (New York: Macmillan, 1944), chap. 2; Richard L Greaves, *Society and Religion in Elizabethan England* (Minneapolis: University of Minnesota Press,1981); Victor Harris, *All Coherence Gone: A Study of the Seventeenth-Century Controversy over Disorder and Decay in the Universe* (Chicago: University of Chicago Press, 1949); J. Sears McGee, *The Godly Man in Stuart England Anglicans, Puritans, and the Two Tables, 1620-1670* (New Haven, CT: Yale University Press, 1976), which balances difference with what was shared; and Marjorie Keniston McIntosh, *Controlling Misbehavior in England, 1370-1600* (Cambridge: Cambridge University Press, 1998); McIntosh broadened the chronological range of her study in response to assertions that dismay about disorder was something unusual in the Elizabethan period.

11. [John Trundle], *A Miracle, of Miracles* (London, 1614), 5.

12. *Elizabethan Puritanism*, ed. Leonard J. Trinterud (New York: Oxford University Press, 1971) 159; Robert Bolton, quoted in William M. Lamont, *Godly Rule: Politics and Religion, 1603-1660* (London: Macmillan, 1969), 49; Lorraine Daston and Katherine Park,

Wonders and the Order of Nature, 1150-1750 (New York: Zone, 1998); Thomas Edwards, *Gangraena* (1646); Baird Tipson, *Hartford Puritanism: Thomas Hooker, Samuel Stone, and Their Terrifying God* (New York: Oxford University Press, 2015), 252–55; Paul Slack, *The Impact of Plague in Tudor and Stuart England* (London: Routledge and Kegan Paul, 1985), 28–29. In *Foreign Bodies and the Body Politic: Discourses of Social Pathology in Early Modern England* (Cambridge: Cambridge University Press, 1998), Jonathan Gil Harris amplifies the discourse of disorder beyond what is said in this chapter.

13. Thomas Beard, *A Theatre of Divine Judgments* (London, 1631), 3. In late sixteenth-century Aberdeen, 16.3 percent of baptisms were of illegitimate children and an estimated twenty-five percent of births in the two decades after 1660 were illegitimate. *Aberdeen Before 1800 A New History*, ed. Patricia E. Dennison et al (East Lothian: Tuckwell Press, 2002), 118–19.

14. Bray, *Books of Homilies*, 347; Keith Wrightson and David Levine, *Poverty and Piety in an English Village: Terling, 1525-1700* (Oxford: Clarendon, 1995), 134–37. On intemperance: *Winthrop Papers* 2:114–15; Collinson, *Birthpangs*, 32, citing the Homily "Against Contention and Brawling"; Cardwell, *Documentary Annals*, 1:292; Strype, *Annals of the Reformation*, vol. 1, pt. 1:319; Beard, *Theatre of Divine Judgments*, chap. 25.

15. John Gauden, *The Love of Truth and Peace: A Sermon Preached before the Honourable House of Commons* (London, 1641), 10–17, noting that peace was contingent upon such adjacent qualities as "subjection . . . to the Will and Spirit of God" and unanimity and rule of law in civil affairs.

16. Strype, *Annals of the Reformation*, 4:292–93; Underdown, *Revel, Riot, and Rebellion*, chap. 2; Parker and Carlson, *"Practical Divinity,"* 76–77; Paul Griffiths, "Masterless Young People in Norwich, 1560-1645," in *The Experience of Authority in Early Modern England*, ed. Paul Griffiths, Adam Fox, and Steve Hindle (New York: St. Martin's, 1996), 146–86; George Herbert, *The Temple and A Priest to the Temple* (1652; repr., London: Everyman's Library, [1908]), 275. The most specific study of the masterless is A. L. Beier, *Masterless Men: The vagrancy problem in England, 1560-1640* (London: Methuen, 1985), which emphasizes the sharp increase in their numbers in the second half of the sixteenth century and the relationship between outcries of alarm and the "mutability" of the masterless at a moment "when those in power longed for stability" (p. 9). On idleness: James Kearney, "Idleness," in *Cultural Reformations: Medieval and Renaissance in Literary History*, ed. Brian Cummings and James Simpson, Oxford Twenty-First Century Approaches to Literature (Oxford: Oxford University Press, 2010), 570–88.

17. Harris, *Foreign Bodies*, chap. 5; see also Susan Dwyer Amussen, "The Gendering of Popular Culture in Early Modern England," in *Popular Culture in England, c. 15600-1850*, ed. Tim Harris (London: Macmillan, 1995), 48–68.

18. Quoted in Lawrence A. Sasek, *The Literary Temper of the English Puritans* (Baton Rouge: Louisiana State University Press, 1961), 59; William Tyndale, *The Obedience of a Christian Man*, ed. David Daniell (London: Penguin, 2000), p. 24. Cf. Alastair J. Mann, *The Scottish Book Trade, 1500-1720: Print Commerce and Print Control in Early Modern Scotland* (East Linton: Tuckwell, 2000), 20, 22, 41, 48–49 (on orders requiring Bibles and psalm books and destroying other books).

19. David S. Katz, *Philo-Semitism and the Readmission of the Jews to England, 1603-1655* (Oxford: Clarendon, 1982), 162; Conrad Russell, "Arguments for Religious Unity in England, 1530-1660," in *Unrevolutionary England, 1603-1642* (London: Hambledon, 1990), 179–204. Church leaders also endorsed an ethics of "civic harmony" grounded in the socio-theological "oneness" of the Christian community.

20. Bray, *Books of Homilies*, 510–12; Michael F. Graham, *The Uses of Reform: "Godly*

Discipline" and Popular Behavior in Scotland and Beyond, 1560–1610 (Leiden: Brill, 1996), 149; Strype, *Life of Parker*, 3:269.

21. John Walter, *Understanding Popular Violence in the English Revolution: The Colchester Plunderers* (Cambridge: Cambridge University Press, 1999), 5; Quitslund, *Reformation in Rhyme*, 47–49; Buchanan Sharp, "Rural Discontents and the English Revolution," in *Town and Countryside in the English Revolution*, ed. R. C. Richardson (Manchester: Manchester University Press, 1992), 257–58.

22. Trinterud, *Elizabethan Puritanism*, 150, an argument buttressed with an abundance of Old Testament references.

23. G. R. Elton, *Reform and Renewal Thomas Cromwell and the Common Weal* (Cambridge: Cambridge University Press, 1973); Hunt, *Art of Hearing*, 306–20 (covering, as well, crucial commonplaces about the body politic). In their respective histories of the state and "public welfare," Paul Slack and Steve Hindle extend the strengthening of the civil state and its greater activism on behalf of social betterment into the seventeenth century. Slack, *From Reformation to Improvement: Public Welfare in Early Modern England*; Hindle, *State and Social Change in Early Modern England*.

24. Patrick Collinson, *Archbishop Grindal, 1519–1583: The Struggle for a Reformed Church* (Berkeley: University of California Press, 1979), 240; Peel, *Seconde Parte*, 2:179, 20; *Certaine sermons appointed by the Queenes Majestie, to be declared and read . . . for the better understanding of the simple people* (1576), sig. A2v, r.

25. Walter Howard Frere, ed., *Visitation Articles and Injunctions of the Period of the Reformation*, 3 vols. (London, 1910), 3:82; William Gouge, quoted in Anthony Fletcher, *Gender, Sex, and Subordination in England, 1500–1800* (New Haven, CT: Yale University Press, 1995), 205; Ayres, *Works of Whitgift*, 1:159–160; Mullan, *Scottish Puritanism*, 245 and chap. 8; Collinson, *Religion of Protestants*, 154; Laura A. M. Stewart, *Urban Politics and British Civil Wars: Edinburgh, 1617–53* (Leiden: Brill, 2006), chap. 1.

26. Patrick Collinson, "Elizabethan and Jacobean Puritanism as Forms of Popular Culture," in *The Culture of English Puritanism, 1560–1700*, ed. Christopher Durston and Jacqueline Eales (New York: St. Martin's, 1996), 32–57. The political valences of fast days in mid-1620s England are noted in John F. Wilson, *Pulpit in Parliament Puritanism during the English Civil Wars, 1640–1648* (Princeton, NJ: Princeton University Press, 1969), chap. 2. John Bossy sketches an English "moral tradition" centered on peace in *Peace in the Post-Reformation* (Cambridge: Cambridge University Press, 1998), chap. 4.

27. Timothy Rosendale, *Liturgy and Literature in the Making of Protestant England* (Cambridge: Cambridge University Press, 2007), chap. 1. In Rosedale's words, the prayer book "was without parallel in contemporary England as a formalized and regularly and universally experienced expression of the relation between the individual and the sociopolitical order—and it was firmly under the control of the post-Reformation state" (p. 46).

28. *John Knox's Genevan Service Book, 1556*, ed. William D. Maxwell (Edinburgh: Oliver and Boyd, 1931), 122; John E. Booty, "Preparation for the Lord's Supper in Elizabethan England," *Anglican Theological Review* 49 (1967): 131–48; Alexander Nowell, *A Catechism Written in Latin* (1570; repr., Cambridge, 1853), 216.

29. [William Harrison], *Deaths Advantage Little Regarded* (London, 1602), 17–20; Stubbes, quoted in A. J. Beier, *Social Thought in England, 1480–1730: From Body Social to Worldly Wealth* (New York: Routledge, 2016), 267, and see pts. 1 and 3 for the ideology of society as a "body"; *Winthrop Papers*, 2:282–95.

30. Albert Peel and Leland H. Carlson, eds., *Cartwrightiana* (London: Allen and Unwin, 1951), 164–65; Ian Green, *The Christian's ABC: Catechisms and Catechizing in England c. 1530–1740* (Oxford: Clarendon 1996), chap. 10 (indicating the method of in-

terpretation that drove these expansive interpretations); Parker and Carlson, *"Practical Divinity,"* 270–75.

31. *The First and Second Prayer Books of Edward VI* (London: J. M. Dent, 1910), 385; ; Strype, *Life of Parker,* 3:59–62 (linking sins with God correcting us); Strype, *Annals of the Reformation,* vol. 1, pt. 1:481–83; Marchant, *Church under the Law,* chap. 1; Martin Ingram, *Church Courts, Sex and Marriage in England, 1570–1640* (Cambridge: Cambridge University Press, 1987), 4 (summing up the Puritan critique); Peel, *Seconde Parte,* 2:201 (requesting, c. 1586, "that Excommunicateion be not used for money matters"); Beier, *Masterless Men,* chap. 1. Neither Ingram nor Marchant endorses the thesis that church courts were tools of nascent "industrious classes," as Christopher Hill has argued.

32. Margo Todd, *Christian Humanism and the Puritan Social Order* (Cambridge: Cambridge University Press, 1987), 132, 134, 137, and passim; Ronald S. Wallace, *Calvin's Doctrine of the Christian Life* (Edinburgh: Oliver and Boyd, 1959), emphasizing Calvin's concept of "moderation."

33. Ingram, "Reformation of Manners in Early Modern England," in Griffiths, Fox, and Hindle, *Experience of Authority,* 47–88; Ingram, "Ridings, Rough Music, and the 'Reform of Popular Culture' in Early Modern England," *Past & Present* 105 (1984): 79–113. In *The Puritan Moment: The Coming of Revolution in an English County* (Cambridge, MA: Harvard University Press, 1983), William Hunt ties moral reform to Puritanism. See also Robert Tittler, *The Reformation and the Towns in England: Politics and Political Culture, c. 1540–1640* (Oxford: Clarendon, 1998), 336–38.

34. Nowell, *A Catechism,* 201–2.

35. Hindle, *State and Social Change,* 63–64; A. L. Beier, "Poverty and Progress in Early Modern England," *The First Modern Society: Essays in English History in Honour of Lawrence Stone,* ed. A. L. Beier, David Cannadine, and James M. Rosenheim (Cambridge: Cambridge University Press, 1989), 201–39; trends also noted in R. B. Outhwaite, *The Rise and Fall of the English Ecclesiastical Courts, 1500–1860* (Cambridge: Cambridge University Press, 2006), chaps. 5–6; Ingram, *Church Courts,* chap. 2; Wrightson and Levine, *Poverty and Piety,* 114. They also point out that the actual extent of vagrancy was nowhere near what moralists said it was like. See also Alastair MacLachlan, *The Rise and Fall of Revolutionary England: An Essay on the Fabrication of Seventeenth-Century History* (New York: St. Martin's, 1966), 135 (summarizing Christopher Hill's metaphors of "bestiality and disorder" and "undercurrent[s] of incipient rebellion bubbling away" beneath the surface of Stuart political life).

36. Richard L. Greaves, "Concepts of political obedience in late Tudor England: Conflicting perspectives," *Journal of British Studies* 22 (1982) 23–34.

37. Heinz Schilling, *Religion, Political Culture and the Emergence of Early Modern Society: Essays in German and Dutch History* (Leiden: Brill, 1992); Beat Kumin, "The Fear of Intrusion: Communal Resilience in Early Modern England," in *Fear in Early Modern Society,* ed. William G. Naphy and Penny Roberts (Manchester: Manchester University Press, 1997), 118–36; Clive Holmes, *Seventeenth-Century Lincolnshire,* History of Lincolnshire 7 (Lincoln: History of Lincolnshire Committee, 1980), chap. 2; Underdown, *Revel, Riot, and Rebellion,* esp. chap. 5; Eric Josef Carlson, *Marriage and the English Reformation* (Oxford: Blackwell, 1994), 156, 165, 168. Any reference to "community" runs the risk of confusing ideology or projection with what happened on the ground. Warnings and second thoughts include Craig Muldrew, "From a 'light cloak' to an 'iron cage': Historical changes in the relation between community and individualism," in *Communities in Early Modern England: Networks, Place, Rhetoric,* ed. Alexandra Shepard and Phil Withington (Manchester: Manchester University Press, 2000), 156–77; and Steve Hindle, "Exclusion crises: Pov-

erty, migration and parochial responsibility in English rural communities, c. 1560–1550," *Rural History* 7 (1996): 125–49. Prescription, meaning, and practice figure as well in Michael Lynch, *Edinburgh and the Reformation* (Edinburgh: Donald, 1981); Joseph P. Ward, "Religious Diversity and Guild Unity in Early Modern London," in *Religion and the English People, 1500–1640: New Voices, New Perspectives*, ed. Eric Josef Carlson (Kirksville, MO: Thomas Jefferson University Press, 1998), 77–98; Phil Withington, "Views from the Bridge: Revolution and Restoration in Seventeenth-Century York," *Past & Present* 170 (2001): 121–51, and the literature cited at p. 124 n. 17; Keith Wrightson, "The Politics of the Parish in Early Modern England," in Griffiths, Fox, and Hindle, *Experience of Authority*, 10–46; Wrightson and Levine, *Poverty and Piety*, 139; Raymond Gillespie, "Godly Order: Enforcing Peace in the Irish Reformation," in *Enforcing Reformation in Ireland and Scotland, 1550–1700*, ed. Elizabethanne Boran and Crawford Gribben (Aldershot: Ashgate, 2006), 184–227; Derek Hirst, "Local Affairs in Seventeenth-Century England," *HJ* 32 (1989): 437–48, and the books cited therein. Willem Frijhoff underscores the presence of practical tolerance in a confessionally divided Netherlands in "The threshold of toleration: Interconfessional conviviality in Holland during the early modern period," in Frijhoff, *Embodied Belief: Ten Essays on Religious Culture in Dutch History* (Hilversum: Uitgeverij Verloren, 2002), chap. 2, esp. pp. 41–44; see also his emphasis on the "ecumenicity of everyday life" (p. 35). Patriarchy was also variable in its implications and consequences, as Margaret Ezell points out in *The Patriarch's Wife: Literary Evidence and the History of the Family* (Chapel Hill: University of North Carolina Press, 1987), challenging a then hegemonic "feminist" reading of the term.

38. Margaret Spufford, "The importance of religion in the sixteenth and seventeenth centuries," in Spufford, ed. *The World of Rural Dissenters, 1520–1725* (Cambridge: Cambridge University Press, 1995), 13–15, an assertion based in part on Christopher Marsh's study, "Family of Love," in the same volume; Muriel C. McClendon, *The Quiet Reformation: Magistrates and the Emergence of Protestantism in Tudor Norwich* (Stanford: Stanford University Press, 1999), chaps. 6–7; Anthony Fletcher, "Prescription and Practice: Protestantism and the Upbringing of Children, 1560–1700," in *The Church and Childhood*, ed. Diana Wood, Studies in Church History 31 (Oxford: Blackwell, 1994), 325–46; Anthony Fletcher, *A County Community in Peace and War: Sussex, 1600–1660* (London, Longman, 1975), 140; Outhwaite, *Rise and Fall*, chap. 6 (citing demographic studies); Wrightson and Levine, *Poverty and Piety*, 128–32 (noting how many instances of premarital pregnancy or births occurred in the context of courtship), a point substantiated in Ingram's survey of popular attitudes and practices (*Church Courts*, chap. 4). Ian W. Archer, *The Pursuit of Stability: Social Relations in Elizabethan London* (Cambridge: Cambridge University Press, 1991) comes at this from the point of view of "stability" and consensus. See also Cynthia B. Herrup, *The Common Peace Participation and the Criminal Law in Seventeenth-century England* (Cambridge: Cambridge University Press, 1987), chaps. 2–4 (on local participation).

39. As Julian Goodare points out, sheriffs in Scotland "all held their offices heritably," and for this and other reasons were "well placed to ignore royal demands." Goodare, *The Government of Scotland, 1560–1625* (Oxford: Oxford University Press, 2004), 176; other aspects of local autonomy are described in chapter 8, below.

40. Peter Lake, "The politics of 'popularity' and the public sphere: The 'monarchical republic' of Elizabeth I defends itself," in *The Politics of the Public Sphere in Early Modern England*, ed. Peter Lake and Steven Pincus (Manchester: Manchester University Press, 2007), 59–94; Alexandra Gajda, *The Earl of Essex and Late Elizabethan Political Culture*

(Oxford: Oxford University Press, 2012), passim; Steve Hindle, "The Keeping of the Public Peace," in Griffiths, Fox, and Hindle, eds., *Experience of Authority*, 213–48.

41. Beard, *Theatre of Divine Judgments*, chap. 3; [Harrison], *Deaths Advantage Little Regarded*, 40. Henry Burton, *The Seven Vials* (1628), sig. a3r; John Cotton, quoted in Hall, *ARP*, 107. See also Mullan, *Episcopacy in Scotland*, 89. In *Rhetoric, Politics and Popularity in Pre-Revolutionary England* (Cambridge: Cambridge University Press, 2013), Markku Peltonen describes a nervousness about excessive power in the hands of kings.

42. McCallum, *Reforming the Scottish Parish*, 48–51; he sees the surge in other parishes at the same time as tied to the arrival of ministers as impassioned as James Melville (pp. 53–54). For panics, see, e.g., Walsham, *Providence in Early Modern England*, 142; David Underdown, *Fire from Heaven: Life in an English Town in the Seventeenth Century* (New Haven, CT: Yale University Press, 1992), 90. The "General Observations for the Plantation of New England" John Winthrop and others put together in 1629 to support the founding of Massachusetts cited the success of Catholic forces during the Thirty Years War and signs of moral decay in England itself—in effect, signs that a reformation of manners was being overtaken by corruption. *Winthrop Papers*, 2:111–12. Witch hunts as a feature of moral panics are described in Brian P. Levack, *Witch-hunting in Scotland: Law, Politics and Religion* (New York: Routledge, 2008), 55 and passim.

43. Hartley, *Parliaments of Elizabeth I*, 2:314; *Commons Debates, 1621*, ed. Wallace Notestein, Frances Helen Reif, and Hartley Simpson, 7 vols. (New Haven, CT: Yale University Press, 1935), 4:53. Other expressions of this kind are noted in Underdown, *Fire from Heaven*, 62, 64, 169.

44. Slack, *From Reformation to Improvement*, 30. For overviews: Hunt, *Puritan Moment*; Collinson, *Birthpangs of Protestant England*, chaps. 2–3; Christopher Hill, *Society and Puritanism in Pre-Revolutionary England* (London: Secker and Warburg, 1964); Ingram, "Reformation of Manners in Early Modern England." The best survey of local efforts and the complexities that encumbered godly reform is Bernard Capp, "Republican reformation: Family, community and the state in Interregnum Middlesex, 1649–60," in *The Family in Early Modern England*, ed. Helen Berry and Elizabeth Foyster (Cambridge: Cambridge University Press, 2007), 40–66.

45. Hill, *Society and Puritanism*, is a classic statement of the social discipline thesis tied to the aspirations of "the middling." For the context of this argument, see MacLachlan, *Rise and Fall of Revolutionary England*. In an overlapping version of this argument, Puritanism becomes the instrument of an aggressive "culture" of a "godly minority" (to quote David Underdown) displeased with "traditional popular culture." The merits of this argument are real, but it is also easily questioned. See, e.g., Sharp, "Rural Discontents and the English Revolution," in Richardson, *Town and Countryside*, chap. 10; Margaret Spufford, "Puritanism and Social Control?" in *Order and Disorder in Early Modern England*, ed. Anthony Fletcher and John Stevenson (Cambridge: Cambridge University Press, 1985),41–57, an essay with significant implications for this chapter as a whole. In *Weber's Protestant Ethic: Origins, Evidence, Contexts*, ed. Hartmut Lehmann and Guenther Roth (Washington, DC: Catholic University Press, 1993), the contributors provide multiple contexts and corrections, especially David Zaret, "The Use and Abuse of Textual Data," 245–69 (addressing a contemporary sociologist's recuperation of the thesis); and Kaspar von Greyerx, "Predestination, Covenant, and Special Providence," 273–84. See also the editors' introduction to *Max Weber: The Protestant Ethic and the "Spirit" of Capitalism and Other Writings*, ed. and trans. Peter Baehr and Gordon C. Wells (New York: Penguin, 2002); Beier, *Masterless Men*, 5; T. H. Breen, "The Non-Existent Controversy: Puritan and Anglican Attitudes upon Work and Wealth," *Church History* 35 (1966): 273–871; and C. John Sommerville, "The

Anti-Puritan Work Ethic," *Journal of British Studies* 20 (1981): 70–81. Paul Seaver finds no evidence for a singular Puritan/Protestant anxiety-driven ethic in the spiritual and economic practices of Nehemiah Wallington; Seaver, *Wallington's World: A Puritan Artisan in Seventeenth-Century London* (Stanford: Stanford University Press, 1985), 126.

46. Cornelius Burgess, *The First Sermon, Preached To The Honourable House of Commons* (1641), repr. in *The English Revolution: Fast Day Sermons to Parliament, 1640–41* (London: Cornmarket, 1970), 11, 13; John Row, *History of the Kirk of Scotland: From the Year 1558 to August 1637* (Edinburgh, 1842), 35. The key scholarly study of this expansive interpretation is McGee, *Godly Man*, chap. 2.

47. Hall *ARP*, 99 (a statement by Henry Vane Jr.).

48. Ayres, *Works of Whitgift*, 1: 264, 270; A. F. Scott Pearson, *Thomas Cartwright and Elizabethan Puritanism* (Cambridge: Cambridge University Press, 1928), 90–92; Scudder, *Christians Daily Walke*, chap. 6; Richard J. Ross, "Distinguishing Eternal Law from Transient Law: Natural Law and the Judicial Laws of Moses," *Past & Present* 217 (2012): 79–11. See also note 8, above. Patrick Collinson cautions against overemphasizing the connections between sabbatarianism and Puritanism in "The Beginnings of English Sabbatarianism," in *Studies in Church History* 1, ed. C. W. Dugmore and C. Duggan (1964): 207–21, an argument reversed in Dougall, *Devil's Book*. See also John H. Primus, *Holy Time: Moderate Puritanism and the Sabbath* (Macon, GA: Mercer University Press, 1989), especially his summary of Nicholas Bownde's emphatic version (pp. 72–81), which made its way into the Westminster Directory of Worship.

49. Samuel Clarke, *The Lives of Two and Twenty Eminent Divines* (London, 1660), 30; idem, *The Lives of Sundry Eminent Persons* (1683), 7 (a reference I owe to Ann Hughes). For other examples, see Michael McGiffert, ed., *God's Plot: The Paradoxes of Puritan Piety, Being the Autobiography and Journal of Thomas Shepard* (Amherst: University of Massachusetts Press, 1972), 52–53; M'Crie, *Life of Mr. Robert Blair*, 68; Richard Baxter, *The Reformed Pastor*, ed. Hugh Martin (London: SCM, 1956), 10; Peel, *Seconde Parte*, 2:179; Samuel Ward, *Wo to Drunkards* (1622), 43. Nehemiah Wellington was capable of evoking the voice of a "faithfull Minister . . . cry[ing] down . . . sinnes and abomindations." Booy, *Notebooks of Nehemiah Wallington*, 248.

50. Dickinson, *Knox's History of the Reformation*, 2: 263; Hooker, quoted in Tipson, *Hartford Puritanism*, 179.

51. William Fulke, *A Brief and Plain Declaration* (1584), in Trinterud, *Elizabethan Puritanism*, 248–49.

52. As John McCallum pointes out in *Reforming the Scottish Parish: The Reformation in Fife, 1560–1640* (Aldershot: Ashgate, 2010), chap. 2.

53. [Henry Burton], *The Protestation Protested* (1641), 406; Timothy Rogers, *Two Puritan Diaries*, ed. M. M. Knappen (Chicago: ASCH, 1933), 72; Bossy, *Peace in the Post-Reformation*, 94–96 (quoting John Rogers of Dedham and others). The fullest, most acute descriptions of this ethics are those of Abram van Engen, "Origins and Last Farewells: Bible Wars, Textual Form, and the Making of American History," *NEQ* 86 (2013): 543–92; van Engen, *Sympathetic Puritans: Calvinist Fellow Feeling in Puritan New England* (New York: Oxford University Press, 2015), to which could be added the 1547 Homily on "Christian Love and Charity."

54. Walsham, *Providence in Early Modern England*, 2, 15–20.

55. Greaves, *Theology & Revolution*, chap. 10; Underdown, *Fire from Heaven*, chap. 6.

56. John Norden, *A progresse of piety* (1599; repr., 1847), 87. Law reform does not figure in the list of issues in Scotland.

57. Fletcher, *Gender, Sex, and Subordination*, chap. 4.

58. *Melanchthon and Bucer*, ed. Wilhelm Pauck, Library of Christian Classics 19 (Philadelphia: Westminster, 1969), 175. Bucer had already initiated disciplinary-style reform in Strasbourg, possibly borrowing some of his ideas from local Anabaptists. Michael F. Graham summarizes this phase of his life in *Uses of Reform*, 13–19. Willem van't Spijker, "Bucer's influence on Calvin: Church and community," in *Martin Bucer: Reforming Church and Community*, ed. D. F. Wright (Cambridge: Cambridge University Press, 1994), 32–44 (quotations, p. 42); Martin Greschat, "The relation between church and civil community in Bucer's reforming work," in ibid., 17–31.

59. Pauck, ed. *Melanchthon and Bucer*, 197, 219, 205, 237, 263, and passim.

60. A "commonwealth" or commonweal ethics to be practiced by the Christian prince runs throughout the book; see, e.g., 182–83.

61. David F. Wright, "Martin Bucer and England—and Scotland," in *Martin Bucer and Sixteenth Century Europe*, ed. Christian Krieger and Marc Lienhard, 2 vols. (Leiden: Brill, 1993), 530–31 (citing the scholarship of James Kirk); Patrick Collinson, "The Reformer and the Archbishop: Martin Bucer and an English Bucerian," *Journal of Religious History* 6 (1971): 305–30; Collinson, *Archbishop Grindal, 1519–1583: The Struggle for a Reformed Church* (Berkeley: University of California Press, 1979), 96; Strype, *Life of Matthew Parker*, 3:316–19. See also Alan Cromartie, *The Constitutionalist Revolution: An Essay on the History of England, 1450–1642* (Cambridge: Cambridge University Press, 2006), 123–24; and M. E. Vanderschaaf, "Archbishop Parker's efforts toward a Bucerian Discipline in the Church of England," *Sixteenth-Century Journal* 8 (1977): 85–103.

62. George Gillespie, *Aarons Rod Blossoming* (London, 1646), sig. A1v; Paul Chang-Ha Lim, *In Pursuit of Purity, Unity, and Liberty: Richard Baxter's Puritan Ecclesiology in Its Seventeenth-Century Context* (Leiden: Brill, 2004), 13. See also Nicholas Thompson, "Martin Bucer and Early Seventeenth-Century Scottish Irenicism," in *The Reception of Continental Reformation in Britain*, ed. Polly Ha and Patrick Collinson (Oxford: Oxford University Press, 2010), 167–91. Alan Cromartie suggests that the importance Bucer assigned to "discipline" prompted Matthew Parker and Alexander Nowell to emphasize it as well. Cromartie, *The Constitutionalist Revolution: An Essay on the History of England, 1450–1642* (Cambridge: Cambridge University Press, 2006), 121–22.

63. Shaw, *Acts and Proceedings*, 26:302; Margo Todd, ed., *The Perth Kirk Session Books, 1577–1590* (Woodbridge: Boydell, 2012), 39–44, 62; Graham, *Uses of Reform*, 48; Dewey Wallace, "George Gifford, Puritan Propaganda and Popular Religion in Elizabethan England," in *Sixteenth Century Journal* 9 (1978): 27–49; Tipson, *Hartford Puritanism*, chap. 3 (quotations, pp. 64–65), 252–58.

64. Ryan M. Reeves, *English Evangelicals and Tudor Obedience, c. 1527–1570* (Leiden: Brill, 2014).

65. Claire Cross, *The Puritan Earl: The Life of Henry Hastings, Third Earl of Huntington, 1536–1595* (London: Macmillan, 1966), 280, 156, 124–27. For reform elsewhere in late Elizabethan England, see Muriel C. McClendon, *The Quiet Reformation: Magistrates and the Emergence of Protestantism in Tudor Norwich* (Stanford: Stanford University Press, 1999), 209–37.

66. Other examples than those that follow are described in Slack, *Poverty & Policy*, 146–52; and the case studies brought together in Patrick Collinson and John Craig, eds., *The Reformation in English Towns, 1500–1640* (New York: St. Martin's, 1998), with excellent bibliographical notes.

67. John S. Craig, "'The Cambridge Boies': Thomas Rogers and the 'Brethren' in Bury St. Edmunds," in *Belief and Practice in Reformation England*, ed. Wabuda and Litzenberger, 154–76; John Craig, *Reformation, Politics and Polemics: The Growth of Protestantism in East Anglian Market Towns, 1500–1610* (Aldershot: Ashgate, 2001), chap. 4 (quota-

tions, pp. 129–30); Collinson, *Religion of Protestants*, 158–59; Samuel Clarke, *The Lives of Sundry Eminent Persons in This Age* (London: Thomas Simmons, 1683), 165–82.

68. Dedham orders, printed in Patrick Collinson, John Craig, and Brett Usher, eds., *Conferences and Combination Lectures in the English Church: Dedham and Bury St. Edmunds, 1582–1590* (Woodbridge: Boydell, 2003), 128–30 (quotation, p. lvii; see also pp. l–lxxiv for a history of the town in the late sixteenth century.

69. Underdown, *Fire from Heaven*, chap. 4.

70. Frances Rose-Troup, *John White, the Patriarch of Dorchester* (New York, 1930), 418–20.

71. Dent, *Plain Mans Path-way*, 151, 156, 146.

72. Scudder, *Christians Daily Walke*, 56, 12, 171, 147–77. The connections are also carefully spelled out in J. Stephen Yuille, *Puritan Spirituality: The Fear of God in the Affective Theology of George Swinnock* (Milton Keynes: Pasternoster, 2007), chaps. 5–7.

73. James K. Cameron, *The Book of Discipline* (Edinburgh: Saint Andrew, 1972), 165; Laing, *Works of Knox*, 6:449–70 (quotation, p. 449), 405; Greaves, *Theology & Revolution*, chap. 10; Shaw, *Acts and Proceedings*, 26:137–38; 27:853–54, 858 (1583), 871–72; Row, *History of the Kirk of Scotland*, 137–38.

74. McCallum, *Reforming the Scottish Parish*, chap. 2 (summarizing, as well, the work of Michael F. Graham); Todd, *Perth Kirk Session Books*.

75. Based on the "Table of Statues" in Francis Lyall, *Of Presbyters and Kings: Church and State in the Law of Scotland* (Aberdeen: Aberdeen University Press, 1980), 197–98; Calderwood, *History of the Kirk*, 5:409–11. See also Geoffrey Parker, "The 'Kirk By Law Established' and the Origins of 'The Taming of Scotland': St Andrews 1559–1600," in *Perspectives in Scottish Social History: Essays in Honour of Rosalind Mitchison*, ed. Leah Leneman (Aberdeen: Aberdeen University Press, 1998), 1–32, noting shifts in rigor in the 1590s. In Edinburgh and probably in other towns, steps were taken by the local government to remedy the "indigent poor," as noted in Stewart, *Urban Politics and the British Civil Wars*, 34–35.

76. Maxwell, *Knox's Genevan Service Book*, 122–23; Robert Bruce, *The Mystery of the Lord's Supper: Sermons on the Sacrament preached in the Kirk of Edinburgh by Robert Bruce in A.D. 1589*, translated and edited by Thomas F. Torrance (London: James Clarke, 1958), 154–55; Craig, *Shorte Summe*. A glance at kirk sessions records show parishes purchasing thousands of tokens at a time.

77. Robert Wodrow, *Collections upon the Lives of the Reformers and Most Emininent Ministers of the Church of Scotland*, 2 vols. (Edinburgh, 1834–1838), 2:18–22; Graham, *Uses of Reform*, 144–45, 161.

78. G. D. Henderson, *The Scottish Ruling Elder* (London: James Clarke, 1935), 111–15; Stewart, *Urban Politics and British Civil Wars*, chap. 2. As Margo Todd has emphasized, the Perth kirk sessions were staffed by "a remarkable number of men, from an impressively broad swathe of urban society" including craftsmen and merchants as the largest categories; as well, she points out that "most members of the community would have cause to appear before the session," some in need of correction but many others there to complain about neighbors or secure the right to be married. Todd, *Perth Kirk Session Books*, 27.

79. "Ourder of Excommunication and Public Repentance" in Laing, *Works of Knox*, 455–59; Ivo Macnaughton Clark, *A History of Church Discipline in Scotland* (Aberdeen: W. & W. Lindsay, 1929), chaps. 3, 5; Todd, *Perth Kirk Session Books*, 39–43. Other historians agree. According to McCallum, *Reforming the Scottish Parish*, the records reveal a "very striking absence of significant numbers of cases of communion-absence, heterodoxy,

superstition, open dissent, or recusancy" (p. 202). Attempts to quantity and rank order misbehavior that caught the eye of these church courts generally indicate that sex (fornication outside of marriage) attracted more attention than any other social or moral offense, with breaches of the Sabbath, disorders, and the persistence of Catholic or folk practices in second or third place. Overall, the records demonstrate the immense importance of clarifying the legal and social significance of marriage.

80. M'Crie, *Life of Mr. Robert Blair*, 65–66.

81. Todd, *Perth Kirk Sessions Books*, 310, n. 62 (a response to an outbreak of the plague).

82. Keith Thomas, "Puritans and Adultery: The Act of 1650 Reconsidered," in Pennington and Thomas, eds., *Puritans and Revolutionaries*, 257–82. That adultery *was* pursued at a local level in the 1650s is indicated in Bernard Capp, "Republican reformation: Family, community and the state in Interregnum Middlesex, 1649–1660," in *The Family in Early Modern England*, ed. Helen Berry and Elizabeth Foyster (Cambridge: Cambridge University Press, 2007), 40–66.

83. Hall, *ARP*, chap. 4; Bruce Lenman, "The Limits of Godly Discipline in the Early Modern Period with Particular Reference to England and Scotland," in *Religion and Society in Early Modern Europe, 1500–1800*, ed. Kaspar von Greyerz (London: George Allen and Unwin, 1984), 123–45 (an essay important also for its references to secondary and primary sources); Philip Benedict, *Christ's Churches Purely Reformed: A Social History of Calvinism* (New Haven, CT: Yale University Press, 2002), chaps. 14–15; and for other evidence, Haigh, *Plain Man's Pathways*, 71–72; McCallum, *Reforming the Scottish Parish*, chap 3..

Chapter 6. Royal Policies, Local Alternatives

1. James Doelman, *King James I and the Religious Culture of England* (Cambridge: D. S. Brewer, 2000), 63; Strype, *Annals of the Reformation*, 4:498–99. According to the former Separatist George Johnson (Francis Johnson's brother), "It is prophecied he [James] shall pull the pope out of his throne, and many godly hope and expect the work that he, as a Christian prince, shall ... hate the whore always." Quoted in Michael Moody, "A Critical Edition of George Johnson's *A Discourse of Some Troubles and Excommunications in the Banished English Church at Amsterdam* 1603" (PhD thesis, Claremont Graduate School, 1979), 227–29. See also Timothy George, *John Robinson and the English Separatist Tradition* (Macon, GA: Mercer University Press, 2005), 70 (quoting a sermon by Robinson extolling James "by whose raigne there is great hope of the contynuance of peace and the gospell to be preached"). James was also known to be someone who enjoyed theological disputation, as noted by Joshua Rodda, *Public Religious Disputation in England, 1558–1628* (Aldershot: Ashgate, 2014), chap. 5.

2. Gee and Hardy, *Documents*, 508–11.

3. Patrick Collinson, "The Jacobean Religious Settlement: The Hampton Court Conference," in *Before the English Civil War: Essays on Early Stuart Politics and Government*, ed. Howard Tomlinson (London: Macmillan, 1983), 27–51 (quotation, p. 31); Champlin Burrage, *The Early English Dissenters in the Light of Recent Research* (1550–1641), 2 vols. (Cambridge, 1912), 2:146–48; *An Abridgement of that Booke which the ministers of Lincoln diocess delivered to his Maiestie* ([London], 1605), 17, 43–44. Something of a compendium of fifty years of debate within the Church of England and the Reformed international, this petition opened with a long list of writers and texts, citing, among others, William Fulke, Richard Hooker, the troubles at Frankfurt, the *Book of Martyrs*, the texts of the Admonition controversy, and the heavyweights of the Reformed tradition. In *English Presbyterianism, 1590–1640* (Stanford: Stanford University Press, 2011), Polly Ha makes a case for a continuing "Presbyterian" presence in England after 1590; see especially chap. 6. Surveys that

demonstrate such a presence include W. J. Sheils, *The Puritans in the Diocese of Peterborough, 1558–1610* (Northampton: Northamptonshire Record Society, 1979), and the English town studies previously cited in chapter 5. See also Josias Nichols, *The Plea of the Innocent: Wherein is auerred, that the ministers & people falslie termed puritanes, are injuriouslie slaundered* (Middleburgh, 1602), a vigorous recapitulation of Elizabethan-period complaints.

4. Looking ahead to the Scottish insurgency of 1638, Conrad Russell makes a telling observation: "One of Charles's major errors was believing that James had carried the Royal Supremacy far enough in Scotland for him to treat it as an established and recognized fact." Russell, *The Causes of the Civil War* (Oxford: Clarendon, 1990), 48; see also chap. 9 for Russell's astute summary of the personal strengths and weaknesses of Charles I. Jenny Wormald compares the Scottish policies of father and son (the latter, in her words, unable to grasp the "practicalities" of on-the-ground politics in the country) in "The Headaches of Monarchy: Kingship and the Kirk in the Early Seventeenth Century," in *Sixteenth-Century Scotland: Essays in Honour of Michael Lynch*, ed. Julian Goodare and Alasdair A. MacDonald (Leiden: Brill, 2008), 365–93.

5. John S. Morrill, "The Religious Context of the English Civil War," *Transactions of the Royal Historical Society*, 5th ser. 34 (1984): 155–78. For a remarkably well-informed survey of the problems of this project, see Russell, *Causes of the Civil War*, chap. 2; and, more recently, Glenn Burgess, "Introduction," *England's Wars of Religion, Revisited*, ed. Charles W. A. Prior and Glenn Burgess (Aldershot: Ashgate, 2011). That English practices and authority were not fully implanted in Scotland after 1603 is shown by Julian Goodare, *The Government of Scotland, 1560–1625* (Oxford: Oxford University Press, 2004), chap. 2 and passim.

6. T. W. Davids, *Annals of Evangelical Nonconformity in the County of Essex, From the Time of Wycliffe to the Restoration, with Memorials of the Essex Ministers who were ejected or silenced in 1660–1662* (London: 1863), 130; Diana Newton, *The Making of the Jacobean Regime: James VI and I and the Government of England, 1603–1605* (Woodbridge: Boydell, 2005), 60–70; *King James VI and I: Political Writings*, ed. Johann P. Sommerville (Cambridge: Cambridge University Press, 1994), 138–39; W. B. Patterson, *King James VI and I and the Reunion of Christendom* (Cambridge: Cambridge University Press, 1997). Other attempts at Protestant-led ecumenism are sketched in the essays in *Conciliation and Confession: The Struggle for Unity in the Age of Reform, 1415–1648*, ed. Howard P. Louthan and Randall C. Zachman (Notre Dame: University of Notre Dame Press, 2004).

7. Stuart Babbage, *Puritanism and Richard Bancroft* (London: SPCK, 1962), 48, 60; Doelman, *King James I*, 7; Calderwood, *History of the Kirk*, 7:217. Realizing that William Barlow's semi-official description of the conference (see below, note 9) was a political document, historians have assessed the outcome of the conference quite differently, some treating it as an example of James's "moderation" and others as manifesting his emphasis on the royal supremacy. For the first, see Newton, *Making of the Jacobean Regime*; for the second, see Alan Cromartie, "King James and the Hampton Court Conference," in *James VI and I: Ideas, Authority, and Government*, ed. Ralph Houlbrooke (Aldershot: Ashgate, 2006), 61–80, arguing that the king made "no concessions," a critique, in part, of Kenneth Fincham and Peter Lake, "The Ecclesiastical Policy of King James I," *Journal of British Studies* 24 (1985): 169–207, an argument reiterated in Cromartie, *The Constitutionalist Revolution: An Essay on the History of England, 1450–1642* (Cambridge: Cambridge University Press, 2006), chap. 6. See also Nicholas Tyack, *Anti-Calvinists: The Rise of English Arminianism c. 1590–1640* (Oxford: Clarendon, 1987), chap. 1; Babbage, *Puritanism and Richard Bancroft*, chap. 2. Arnold Hunt regards the outcome as "a fairly comprehensive defeat for the puritan cause," although tempered by James's willingness to do something about private

baptism, the Sabbath, and bits of the prayer book. Hunt, "Laurence Chaderton and the Hampton Court Conference," in *Belief and Practice in Reformation England: A Tribute to Patrick Collinson from His Students*, ed. Susan Wabuda and Caroline Litzenberger (Aldershot: Ashgate, 1998), 223. See also B. W. Quintrell, "The Royal Hunt and the Puritans, 1604–1605," *Journal of Ecclesiastical History* 31 (1980): 41–58; Collinson, *Elizabethan Puritan Movement*, pt. 8, chaps. 4–5; Collinson, "The Jacobean religious settlement: The Hampton Court Conference," in *Before the English Civil War: Essays on Early Stuart Politics and Government*, ed. Howard Tomlinson (London: Macmillan, 1983), 27–51; Collinson, *Richard Bancroft and Elizabethan Anti-Puritanism* (Cambridge: Cambridge University Press, 2013), chap. 11; and Charles Howard McIlwain, ed., *The Political Works of James I* (Cambridge, MA: Harvard University Press, 1918), 330–31.

8. In addition to Chaderton and Rainolds, the group included John Knewstub and Michael Sparks. A more emphatically Puritan group headed by Arthur Hildersham, Stephen Egerton, and Edward Fleetwood, acting in the name of some thirty ministers, "delivered . . . some ten demands and requests" of a more "radical" kind. According to Hunt, "Chaderton and the Hampton Court Conference," 212–13 n. 10, this group may have been "in close touch with Chaderton and the other puritan speakers." The story itself derives from Samuel Clarke, *The Lives of Thirty-Two Divines* (London, 1677), 116. Collinson, "The Jacobean Religious Settlement," 190 n. 30, suggests that Walter Travers, Francis Marbury, and John Knewstub were probably included in the delegation. James rebutted the group's request for further discussion.

9. John Strype, *The Life and Acts of John Whitgift, D.D.*, 3 vols. (Oxford:, 1822), 3:402–9; William Barlow, *The Sum and Substance of the Conference . . . at Hampton Court, January 14, 1603* (London, 1604), 6–9, 13–14, 17–18, 23–26, 36, 46–47, 72; Gee and Hardy, *Documents*, 512–15; Babbage, *Puritanism and Richard Bancroft*, 55, 66 and chap. 2. For moderation itself as polemical, see Lori Anne Ferrell, *Government by Polemic: James I, the King's Preachers, and the Rhetoric of Conformity, 1603–1625* (Stanford: Stanford University Press, 1998). Unhappy with the outcome of Hampton Court, Henry Jacob pleaded for another go around in the surreptitiously printed *A Christian and Modest Offer of a Most Indifferent Conference, or Disputation* ([London], 1606).

10. Kenyon, *Stuart Constitution*, 120–21 (proclamation of 16 July 1604); James I to the Parliament of 1610, quoted in Jenny Wormald, "James VI and I, *Basilikon Doron* and *The Trew Law of Free Monarchies*: The Scottish Context and the English Translation (1610)," 37, in *The Mental World of the Jacobean Court*, ed. Linda Levy Peck (Cambridge: Cambridge University Press, 1991), 37. Bringing James I's self-understanding into focus (given that two of the most cited of his texts have a Scottish context) is handled with admirable exactitude in Wormald, "James VI and I," and two other essays in the same collection: Paul Christianson, "Royal and parliamentary voices on the ancient constitution," ibid., 71–98, and J. P. Sommerville, "James I and the divine right of kings: English Politics and continental theory," 55–70. Andrew Thrust emphasizes the king's dislike of parliaments in "The Personal Rule of James I, 1611–1620," in *Politics, Religion and Popularity in Early Stuart Britain: Essays in Honour of Conrad Russell*, ed. Thomas Cogswell, Richard Cust, and Peter Lake (Cambridge: Cambridge University Press, 2002), 84–102. See also Cromartie, *Constitutionalist Revolution*, chap 6 (on the nature of James's "absolutism"). Differences of opinion on this matter are assessed in Roger A. Mason, *Kingship and the Commonweal: Political Thought in Renaissance and Reformation Scotland* (East Lothian: Tuckwell, 1998), chap. 8.

11. Kenyon, *Stuart Constitution*, 11–12; Barlow, *Summe and Substance*, 82; Babbage, *Puritanism and Richard Bancroft*, 253; Newton, *Making of the Jacobean Reign*, 88–89; McIlwaine, ed., *Political Works of James I*, 20. See also Glenn Burgess, *British Political*

Thought, 1500–1660: The Politics of the Post-Reformation (London: Palgrave Macmillan, 2009), chap. 4 (qualifying James's "absolutism" and astutely noting certain limits to the royal supremacy in matters of religion); John Cramsie, "The Philosophy of Imperial Kingship and the Interpretation of James VI and VI," in Houlbrooke, *James VI and I*, 43–60.

12. Kenneth Fincham, *Prelate as Pastor: The Episcopate of James I* (Oxford: Clarendon, 1990), 62–63; Cromartie, *Constitutionalist Revolution*, 165–67; Babbage, *Puritanism and Richard Bancroft*, chap. 8 and pp. 285–86; Kenyon, *Stuart Constitution*, 126–28; Maija Jansson, *Proceedings in Parliament, 1614 (House of Commons)* (Philadelphia: American Philosophical Society, 1988), xxi. Francis Hastings was a near counterpart to Throckmorton in James's first two parliaments; see M. C. Cross, "An Example of Lay Intervention in the Elizabethan Church," *Studies in Church History* 2, ed. G. J. Cuming (London: Nelson, 1965), 273–82. The legislative record is crisply described in Stephen Foster, *The Long Argument: English Puritanism and the Shaping of New England Culture, 1570–1700* (Chapel Hill: University of North Carolina Press, 1991), 114–19. As Conrad Russell points out in *Parliaments and English Politics, 1621–1629* (Oxford: Oxford University Press, 1979), "It is remarkable how hard it is to discover 'a puritan opposition' in the 1620s, especially in the last years of King James" (p. 26).

13. Newton, *Making of the Jacobean Regime*, 60–66. His indifference to the plight of his daughter Elizabeth is summarized in Anthony Milton, *Catholic and Reformed: The Roman and Protestant Churches in English Protestant Thought, 1600–1640* (Cambridge: Cambridge University Press, 1995), 506–7, in the context of a broader description of the politics of "Protestant internationalism."

14. Edward Cardwell, ed., *Synodalia: A Collection of Articles of Religion, Canons, and Proceedings of Convocations, in the Province of Canterbury, From the Year 1547 to the Year 1717*, 2 vols. (Oxford: Oxford University Press, 1842), 1:245–329; Gerald Bray, ed., *The Anglican Canons, 1529–1947* (Woodbridge: Boydell/Church of England Record Society, 1998), 820–22; Ayres, *Works of Whitgift*, 1:207–8; Fincham, *Prelate as Pastor*, 64–66, and arguing (p. 220) that "the episcopate strictly observed the letter of this canon"; Babbage, *Puritanism and Richard Bancroft*, chaps. 3–4; Jane Rickard, "The Word of God and the Word of the King: The Scriptural Exegeses of James VI and I and the King James Bible," in Houlbrooke, *James VI and I*, 135–49.

15. See, e.g., Newton, *Making of the Jacobean Regime*, chap. 4, focused on the Lincolnshire petition of 1604. Unusually, a few of these petitions were printed and reached a wider audience, as noted in Babbage, *Puritanism and Richard Bancroft*, chap. 2.

16. Quintrell, "Royal Hunt," passim; Roger B. Manning, *Religion and Society in Elizabethan Sussex: A Study of the Enforcement of the Religious Settlement, 1558–1603* (Leicester: Leicester University Press, 1969), 207–12; Babbage, *Puritanism and Richard Bancroft*, chap. 12. Region-by-region studies of the numbers of ministers suspended, deprived, or complained of include Clive Holmes, *Seventeenth-Century Lincolnshire*, History of Lincolnshire 7 (Lincoln: History of Lincolnshire Committee, 1980), 92–94 (sixty-one ministers reported for not wearing a surplice or doing ceremonies, foot-dragging bishops, a mere eight deprived); Fincham, *Prelate as Pastor*, chap. 7 (proposing between seventy-three and eighty-three); William Hunt, *The Puritan Moment: The Coming of Revolution in an English County* (Cambridge, MA: Harvard University Press, 1983), 109, noting that, in Essex County, the campaign led to forty-four ministers being charged with nonconformity, twenty-five suspended, and ten deprived, adding that, for "the entire period from 1603 to 1610, sixteen . . . including six lecturers" were deprived; and Sheils, *Puritans in the Diocese of Peterborough*, 82–84, 99–106. Stephen Foster proposes a much higher figure—closer to 300—for the country as a whole (*Long Argument*, pp. 99–106). See also Babbage, *Puritanism and Richard Bancroft*, chap. 6. Kenneth Fincham paints a marvelously acute picture

of the confusion about structure, purpose, and authority within the state church and the bearing of this confusion on enforcement in "Clerical Conformity from Whitgift to Laud," in *Conformity and Orthodoxy in the English Church, c. 1560–1660*, ed. Peter Lake and Michael Questier (Woodbridge: Boydell, 2000), 125–58, a confusion also described in Perez Zagorin, *The Court and the Country: The Beginning of the English Revolution* (London: Routledge and Kegan Paul, 1969), 163–70, with useful comments by contemporaries. For Hutton, see Peter Lake, "Matthew Hutton—A Puritan Bishop?" *History* 64 (1979): 182–204. The practices of "evangelical bishops" are described in Fincham, *Prelate as Pastor*, 215, 229–30 257–58.

17. The "deeply ambiguous" nature of their Protestantism is emphasized in scholarship cited by Alan Ford, "James Ussher and the Creation of an Irish Protestant Identity," in *British Consciousness and Identity: The Making of Britain, 1533–1707*, ed. Brendan Bradshaw and Peter Roberts (Cambridge: Cambridge University Press, 1998), chap. 6.

18. Alan Ford, *The Protestant Reformation in Ireland, 1590–1641* (Dublin: Four Courts, 1997), chaps. 2–4; Crawford Gribben, *The Irish Puritans: James Ussher and the Reformation of the Church* (Auburn, MA: Evangelical, 2009), chap. 1; Alan Ford, " 'Force and Fear of Punishment': Protestants and Religious Coercion in Ireland, 1603–33," in *Enforcing Reformation in Ireland and Scotland, 1550–1700*, ed. Elizabethanne Boran and Crawford Gribben (Aldershot: Ashgate, 2006), 91–130; and more generally, Alan Ford, *James Ussher: Theology, History, and Politics in Early Modern Ireland and England* (Oxford: Oxford University Press, 2007), 41–48 (on Trinity College).

19. J. M. Barkley, "Some Scottish bishops and ministers in the Irish Church, 1605–35," in *Reformation and Revolution: Essays Presented to The Very Reverend Principal Emeritus Hugh Watt*, ed. Duncan Shaw (Edinburgh: St. Andrews, 1967), 141–59; Gribben, *Irish Puritans*, 61; M'Crie, *Life of Mr Robert Blair*, 116, a story that may exaggerate the bishop's leniency. Alan Ford reviews the evidence in *James Ussher*, 164–73. John McCafferty casts a skeptical eye on assumptions about stirrings of "independence," nonconformity, Scottish sources for the 1615 articles, and Irish "puritanism"; instead, he finds bishops committed to uniformity but willing to compromise with those who preferred a different mode of worship. McCafferty, "When Reformations Collide," in *The Stuart Kingdoms in the Seventeenth Century: Awkward Neighbours*, ed. Allan I. Macinnes and Jane Ohlmeyer (Dublin: Four Courts Press, 2002), 186–203.

20. Ford, *Protestant Reformation*, chap. 7; Ford, *James Ussher*, 111–12, 116–17; Philip S. Robinson, *The Plantation of Ulster: British Settlement in an Irish Landscape, 1600–1670* (Dublin: Gill and Macmillan, 1984).

21. Elizabethanne Born, ed., *The Correspondence of James Ussher, 1600–1656*, 3 vols. (Dublin: Irish Manuscripts Commission, 2015), 1:90; 230–31; 2:433, 544. Ward was a frequent correspondent.

22. Charles Hardwick, *A History of the Articles of Religion* (Cambridge, 1859), chap. 8 and app. p. 6; Ford, *James Ussher*, 109, chaps. 4 (noting other important changes from English practice), 7 (assigning Ussher the most important role in drafting the articles and noting the appearance of covenant theology); Capern, "The Caroline Church, James Ussher, and the Irish Dimension," *HJ* 39 (1996): 57–85. In *The Reconstruction of the Church of Ireland Bishop Bramhall and the Laudian Reforms, 1633–1641* (Cambridge: Cambridge University Press, 2007), John McCafferty questions the importance of Ussher (pp. 62, 89). As Gribben points out (*Irish Puritans*, 37–47), this was the first Reformed confession to associate the papacy with the Antichrist. See also Ford, "Ussher and Irish Identity," 200–201; and R. G. Asch, "Antipopery and ecclesiastical policy in early seventeenth-century Ireland," in *Archiv für Reformationsgeschichte*, 83 (1992): 258–301. No minister in Ireland had to subscribe to the Articles.

23. W. B. Patterson, "William Perkins as Apologist for the Church of England," *JEH* 57 (2006), 252–53; David Hoyle, *Reformation and Religious Identity in Cambridge, 1590–1644* (Woodbridge: Boydell, 2007), 65, 111; Tessa Watt, *Cheap Print and Popular Piety, 1560–1640* (Cambridge: Cambridge University Press, 1991). Bibliographical data on editions appears in Ian Green, *Print and Protestantism in Early Modern England* (Oxford: Oxford University Press, 2000). Claire Cross's summary of the end of the sixteenth and beginning of the seventeenth centuries emphasizes the growing number of lectureships, the swelling of enrollments at Oxford and Cambridge, the presence of bishops who supported evangelical preaching, the limited impact of the canons of 1604, and James I's credentials as a Protestant. Cross, *Church and People: England 1450–1660*, 2nd ed. (Oxford: Blackwell, 1999), 141–42. Nonetheless, evangelical ministers remained in short supply. Cf. Jacqueline Eales, *Puritans and Roundheads: The Harleys of Brampton Bryan and the Outbreak of the English Civil War* (Cambridge: Cambridge University Press, 1990), 56 (figures from a survey of 1603).

24. One of the themes of the essays in *The World of Rural Dissenters, 1520–1725*, ed. Margaret Spufford (Cambridge: Cambridge University Press, 1995), is the capacity of dissenters, some of them quite radical, to live at ease in their communities. For a careful assessment of the "two culture" paradigm, see Patrick Collinson, *The Birthpangs of Protestant England Religious and Cultural Change in the Sixteenth and Seventeenth Centuries* (New York: St. Martin's, 1988), chap. 5. See also W. J. Sheils, "Catholics and their Neighbours in a Rural Community: Egton Chapelry 1590–1780," *Northern History* 25 (1998): 109–33; Tom Webster, *Godly Clergy in Early Stuart England: The Caroline Puritan Movement, c. 1620–1643* (Cambridge: Cambridge University Press, 1997). Part 3, and for the broader context, C. Scott Dixon, "Introduction: Living with Religious Diversity in Early Modern Europe," in *Living with Religious Diversity in Early-Modern Europe*, ed. C. Scott Dixon, Dagmar Freist, and Mark Greengrass (Aldershot: Ashgate, 2009), 1–20. For self-representations: Brian Manning, "Religion and Politics: The Godly People," in *Politics, Religion and the English Civil War*, ed. Manning (London: Edward Arnold, 1973), chap. 3.

25. *The Autobiography of Richard Baxter*, ed. N. H. Keeble (London: Dent, 1974), 6; Jacqueline Eales, "Sir Robert Harley, K.B. (1579–1656) and the 'Character' of a Puritan," *British Library Journal* 15 (1989): 134–57 (quotation, p. 150); Eales, *Puritans and Roundheads*, passim. Eales provides an overview of an ongoing Puritan presence tied to patronage, the book trades, and local ventures in "A Road to Revolution: The Continuity of Puritanism, 1559–1642," in *The Culture of English Puritanism, 1560–1700*, ed. Christopher Durston and Jacqueline Eales (New York: St. Martin's, 1996), chap. 6. See also Margo Todd, "'An act of discretion': Evangelical Conformity and the Puritan Dons," *Albion* 18 (1986) 581–99. The essays brought together in *The Culture of English Puritanism*, although not uniformly convincing, amplify the argument of this paragraph.

26. As Mary Morrissey points out in *Politics and the Paul's Cross Sermons, 1558–1642* (Oxford: Oxford University Press, 2011), esp. chaps. 5–6, anti-Catholicism, including the assertion that the papacy was the Antichrist, was a "constant" from the reign of Elizabeth I, although voiced more sharply at certain moments and not always turned against Catholics themselves. According to James Ussher, "Rome is not to cease from being Babylon, till her last destruction shall come upon her; and that unto her last gasp she is to continue in her spiritual fornications, alluring all nations unto her superstition and idolatry." Quoted in Gribben, *Irish Puritans*, 47. The longer history of identifying the papacy with Antichrist is described in C. A. Patrides, *Milton and the Christian Tradition* (Oxford: Clarendon, 1966), 270 n.1.

27. Sheila Lambert, "Richard Montagu, Arminianism and Censorship," *Past & Present* 124 (1989): 36–68; see also Julian Davies, *The Caroline Captivity of the Church: Charles I*

and the Remoulding of Anglicanism, 1625–1641 (Oxford: Clarendon, 1992), 113–15; John Rushworth, *Historical Collections of private matters of state* (London, 1659), 209–11; Milton, *Catholic and Reformed*, intro.

28. Peter Lake, "The Significance of the Elizabethan Identification of the Pope as Antichrist," *JEH* 31 (1980): 161–78; and, especially, Peter Lake, "Anti-popery: The Structure of a Prejudice," in *Conflict in Stuart England: Studies in Religion and Politics, 1603–1642*, ed. Richard Cust and Ann Hughes (London: Longman, 1989), 72–106.

29. Thomas Cogswell, *The Blessed Revolution: English Politics and the Coming of War, 1621–1624* (Cambridge: Cambridge University Press, 1989), prologue, 51, 298–99; *Original Letters relating to the Ecclesiastical Affairs of Scotland*, ed. David Laing, 2 vols. (Edinburgh, 1851), 2:729–30; Jason White, *Militant Protestantism and British Identity, 1603–1642* (London: Pickering and Chatto, 2012), chap. 2 (noting how the corruption associated with the Duke of Buckingham fed a larger scenario of corruption and crypto-Catholicism); Alan Ford, "'Force and Fear of Punishment': Protestants and Religious Coercion in Ireland, 1603–33," in Boran and Gribben, *Enforcing Reformation*,100–113. Milton, *Catholic and Reformed*, 45, noting as well resistance to its "extreme" versions. See also Irony Morgan, *Prince Charles's Puritan Chaplain* (London: Allen and Unwin, 1957), 43 (citing Samuel Clarke's description of the "most intimate affections between Sibbes, Preston, and Ussher"). Scott published two sequels before fleeing to the Netherlands, where he ministered to one of the garrison churches until he was assassinated in 1628. Rushworth, *Historical Collections*, 85–89; Markku Peltonen, *Rhetoric, Politics and Popularity in Pre-Revolutionary England* (Cambridge: Cambridge University Press, 2013), chap. 9. The broader context is sketched in Richard Cust, "News and Politics in Early Seventeenth-Century England," *Past & Present* 112 (1986): 60–90.

30. Tyacke, *Anti-Calvinists*, chap. 3; Susan Holland, "Archbishop Abbot and the Problem of 'Puritanism,'" *HJ* 37 (1994): 23–43.

31. Sarah Bendall, Christopher Brooke, and Patrick Collinson, *A History of Emmanuel College, Cambridge* (Woodbridge: Boydell, 1999), 224–25.

32. His career is described in Morgan, *Prince Charles's Puritan Chaplain*.

33. Patrick Collinson, "Lectures by Combination: Structures and Characteristics of Church Life in Seventeenth-Century England," *Godly People: Essays on English Protestantism and Puritanism* (London: Hambledon, 1983), 467–98; *Conferences and Combination Lectures in the Elizabethan Church, 1582–1590*, ed. Patrick Collinson, John Craig, and Brett Usher, Church of England Record Society 10 (Woodbridge: Boydell, 2003), intro.; Manning, *Religion and Society*, chap. 1; Patrick Collinson, "The English Conventicle," in *Voluntary Religion*, ed. W. J. Sheils and Diana Wood, Studies in Church History 23 (Oxford: Blackwell, 1986), 223–59. See also Webster, *Godly Clergy*, pt. 1; R. C. Richardson, "Puritanism and the Ecclesiastical Authorities: The Case of the Diocese of Chester," in *Politics, Religion and the English Civil War*, ed. Brian Manning (London: Edward Arnold, 1973), 3–33.

34. Shepard, *Confessions*, 74, 83, 94. For examples of "churches within churches," see Foster, *Long Argument*, 164.

35. David Booy, ed., *The Notebooks of Nehemiah Wallington, 1618–1654: A Selection* (Aldershot: Ashgate, 2007), 21–23; Ann Hughes, "Thomas Dugard and His Circle in the 1630s: A 'Parliamentary-Puritan' Connexion?" *HJ* 29 (1986): 771–93; *The Diary of Robert Woodford, 1637–1641*, ed. John Fielding, Camden Fifth Series 42 (Cambridge: Cambridge University Press, 2012), 32–39, and passim. Webster describes a more specialized "sociability" in *Godly Clergy*, pt. 1, and in his introduction to *The Diary of Samuel Rogers 1634–1638*, ed. Tom Webster and Kenneth Shipps, Church of England Record Society 11 (Woodbridge: Boydell 2004). David Scott provides a wealth of details about intersecting networks in "Yorkshire's Godly Incendiary: The Career of Henry Darley during the Reign of Charles I,"

in *Life and Thought in the Northern Church, c.100–c.1700: Essays in Honour of Claire Cross*, ed. Diana Wood, Studies in Church History: Subsidia 12 (Rochester, NY: Boydell, 1999), 435–64.

36. Edward Bloomfield, *The Opposition to the English Separatists, 1570–1625* (Washington, D.C: University Press of America, 1981), 72–76; W. B. Patterson, "William Perkins as an apologist for the Church of England," *JEH* 57 (2006): 242–69. See, among other case studies, J. F. Merritt, "The pastoral tightrope: A puritan pedagogue in Jacobean London," in Cogswell, Cust, and Lake, *Politics, Religion and Popularity*, 143–61; and Dever, *Richard Sibbes*, 85–95. The other side of the story includes presbyterian-linked advocacy and debate traced in Polly Ha, *English Presbyterianism*; and touched on in Hunter Powell, *The Crisis of British Protestantism: Church Power in the Puritan Revolution, 1638–44* (Manchester: Manchester University Press, 2015). Peter Lake has emphasized the attempts among some Puritan-linked ministers to restrain intracommunity conflict. Lake, *The Boxmaker's Revenge: "Orthodoxy," "Heterodoxy" and the Politics of the Parish in Early Stuart London* (Manchester: Manchester University Press, 2001), 221–42. Mark E. Dever, *Richard Sibbes: Puritanism and Calvinism in Late Sixteenth and Early Seventeenth-Century England* (Macon: Mercer University Press 2000), 85–95.

37. Thomas Goodwin et al., *An Apologeticall Narration, Humbly Submitted to the Honourable Houses of Parliament* (London, 1643 [1644]), 4; Thomas Edwards, *Antapologia; or, A full answer to the Apologeticall narration* (London, 1644), 30 (for Edwards, the phrase denoted nonconformity not yet under pressure from Laudianism); Thomas Edwards, *Gangraena; or, A Catalogue and Discovery of many of the Errours, Heresies, Blasphemies and pernicious practices of the Sectaries of this time* (London, 1646), pt. 1, 76; John Geree, *The Character of an Old English Puritan, or Nonconformist* (London, 1646); Robert Baillie, *A Dissuasive from the Errours of the Time* (London, 1645), 55; David Dickson, *Truths Victory over Errour* (Glasgow, 1649; repr., Edinburgh: Banner of Truth Trust, 2007), 58; see also Henry Burton's self-description (c. 1626) as "conformable [and] none of the refractories," quoted in Tyacke, *Anti-Calvinists*, 187. Kenneth Fincham contrasts an "old conformity" to the "new" envisioned by William Laud and others in the 1630s; Fincham, *Conformity and Orthodoxy*, 146.

38. Ethan H. Shagan, *The Rule of Moderation: Violence, Religion and the Politics of Restraint in Early Modern England* (Cambridge: Cambridge University Press, 2011), pt. 2, chap. 4; Peter Lake, *Moderate Puritans and the Elizabethan Church* (Cambridge: Cambridge University Press, 1982), chaps. 1, 3; Bendall, Brooke, and Collinson, *History of Emmanuel College*, 185.

39. Hoyle, *Reformation and Religious Identity*, 110–11 and, in general, chap. 4; Peter Lake, "Moving the Goal Posts? Modified Subscription and the Construction of Conformity in the Early Stuart Church," in Lake and Questier, *Conformity and Orthodoxy*, 179–205; Polly Ha, "Spiritual Treason and the Politics of Intercession: Presbyterians, Laudians and the Church of England," in *Puritans and Catholics in the Trans-Atlantic World, 1600–1800*, ed. Crawford Gribben and Scott Spurlock (London: Palgrave Macmillan, 2016), 66–88. It is worth remembering Thomas Cartwright's advice in *The Rest of the Second Replie* (1577) that it was better to wear the surplice than to suffer deprivation; for other statements of the same kind, see A. F. Scott Pearson, *Thomas Cartwright and Elizabethan Puritanism, 1535–1603* (Cambridge: Cambridge University Press, 1925), 148–50. The reappraisals of nonconformity as radical or moderate (or compromised) include Mark E. Dever, "Moderation and Deprivation: A Reappraisal of Richard Sibbes," *JEH* 43 (1992): 396–413.

40. Isabel MacBeath Calder, ed., *Letters of John Davenport, Puritan Divine* (New Haven: Yale University Press, 1937), 19, 13–14, 23–28; Ole Peter Grell, *Brethren in Christ: A Calvinist Network in Reformation Europe* (Cambridge: Cambridge University Press,

2011), chap. 4. Francis J. Bremer provides more details on Davenport's religious politics in the 1620s in *Building a New Jerusalem: John Davenport, a Puritan in Three Worlds* (New Haven: Yale University Press, 2012), chaps. 4–5.

41. Nicholas Byfield, *A Commentary; or, Sermons upon the Second Chapter of the First Epistle of Saint Peter* (Londeon, 1623), 563, 586 (a reference I owe to Carole Schneider). Cf. Webster, *Godly Clergy*, 159.

42. Hunt, "Chaderton and the Hampton Court Conference," 213, 215–17, 219–21, 227; Bendall, Brooke, and Collinson, *History of Emmanuel College*, 185; Lake, *Moderate Puritanism and the Elizabethan Church*, chap. 1. See also Kevin Sharpe, "Private Conscience and Public Duty in the Writings of James VI and I," in John Morrill, Paul Slack, and Daniel Woolfe, eds., *Public Duty and Private Conscience in Seventeenth-Century England* (Oxford: Oxford University Press, 1993), 77–100.

43. Dickinson, *Knox's History of the Reformation*, 2:28; William Perkins, *The Whole Treatise of the Cases of Conscience*, quoted in Helen C. White, *Social Teachings in Popular Religious Literature of the Sixteenth Century* (New York: Macmillan, 1944), 177 (endorsing passive resistance); *A parte of a register*, 87–93. At another moment (1588), Hildersham acknowledged having preached without allowance in ways that nurtured "discontent with the state," practices he recanted in the presence of church officials. Peel, *Seconde Parte*, 2:259–60.

44. Bradshaw, *English Puritanisme* (1605), 1–3; Lake, *Moderate Puritans*, 265–68 and chap. 11; Bremer, *Building a New Jerusalem*, 104.

45. *Thomas Hooker Writings in England and Holland, 1626–1633*, eds. George H. Williams et al. (Cambridge, MA: Harvard University Press, 1975), 324–25.

46. Burrage, *EED*, 2:148–51; Row, *History of the Kirk*, 410. For other references to conscience, see Willliam Ames, *The Marrow of Theology*, trans. and ed. John Eusden (Boston: Pilgrim, 1968), 42–44; John Robinson, quoted in George, *John Robinson*, 113–14; and J. I. Packer, "The Puritan Conscience," in *Puritan Papers, Vol. 2: 1960–1963*, ed. J. I. Packer (Phillipsburg, NJ: P&R, 2001), 237–58; Charles Lloyd Cohen, *God's Caress: The Psychology of Puritan Religious Experience* (New York: Oxford University Press, 1986), 120–22.

47. Sargent Bush, Jr., *The Correspondence of John Cotton* (Chapel Hill: University of North Carolina Press, 2001), 120, 122, 133–34. See also Sargent Bush, Jr., "Epistolary Counseling in the Puritan Movement: The Example of John Cotton," in *Puritanism: Transatlantic Perspectives on a Seventeenth-Century Anglo-American Faith*, ed. Francis J. Bremer (Boston: Massachusetts Historical Society, 1993), 127–46. Chauncy apologized to the Court of High Commission for refusing to practice the ceremonies; subsequently, he penned a "retraction" written "before his going to New England in 1641." Chauncy, *The Retraction of Mr. Charles Chancy* [*sic*] (1641).

48. Jesper Rosenmeier, *"Spiritual Concupiscence": John Cotton's English Years, 1584–1633* (Lincoln, Eng.: Richard Kay, 2012), 143; Cotton, "To the Godly Reader," in Hildersham, *Fourth of John*.

49. Robert Sanderson, *Ten Sermons: 1. Ad Clerum* (London, 1627), quoted in Rosenmeier, *"Spiritual Concupiscence,"* 92–94 (he was critical of Cotton, specifically). Sanderson was drawing on popular anti-puritanism of the kind described in Haigh, *Plain Man's Pathways*. For Sanderson's broader moderation (he defended Reformed theology throughout the 1620s and 1630s), see Peter Lake, "Serving God and the Times: The Calvinist Conformity of Robert Sanderson," *Journal of British Studies* 27 (1988): 81–116.

50. A story told in Rosenmeier, *"Spiritual Concupiscence,"* chap. 6.

51. Bush, *Correspondence*, 95–96, 98–101. In English period sermons published as *A Briefe Exposition of the whole Book of Canticles* (1648), Cotton had described separatism as sinful (pp. 31–32). Responding to his Scottish critic Robert Baillie, who had questioned

Cotton's reputation as an emphatic nonconformist, he insisted that he "forbore all the Ceremonies alike at once, many years before I left England." John Cotton, *The Way of the Churches of Christ Cleared* (London, 1648), reprinted in Larzer Ziff, *John Cotton on the Churches in New England* (Cambridge, MA: Harvard University Press, 1968), 117.

52. Raymond Phineas Stearns, *Strenuous Puritan: Hugh Peter, 1598–1660* (Urbana: University of Illinois Press, 1954), 41–43; Eales, *Puritans and Roundheads*, 57–58.

53. Stephen Brachlow, *The Communion of Saints: Radical Puritan and Separatist Ecclesiology, 1579–1625* (Oxford: Oxford University Press, 1988), 61.

54. Gregory D. Dodds, *Exploiting Erasmus: The Erasmian Legacy and Religious Change in Early Modern England* (Toronto: University of Toronto Press, 2009), 163–65.

55. Calderwood, *History of the Kirk*, 6:264–67, 270–71; *A Declaration of the iust causes of his Maiesties proceeding against those Ministers, Who are now lying in prison, attainted of high Treason. Set foorth by his Maiesties Counsell of his kingdome of Scotland* (1606); Alan R. MacDonald, "James VI and the General Assembly, 1586–1618," in *The Reign of James VI*, ed. Julian Goodare and Michael Lynch (East Lothian: Tuckwell, 2000), 179–80. Some of these men eventually returned to their parishes in Scotland.

56. Thomas M'Crie, *Life of Andrew Melville*, 2 vols. (Edinburgh 1824), 2:126–27 (noting, also, a protest Melville and others made to the Parliament against this step); David Calderwood, *The true history of the Church of Scotland* ([Edinburgh?], 1678), 527–31. The behind-the-scenes politicking (for and against the king's ministers) connected with the treatment of the Aberdeen dissenters is described in Maurice Lee Jr., *Government by Pen: Scotland under James VI and I* (Urbana: University of Illinois Press, 1980), 51–56.

57. MacDonald, *Jacobean Kirk*, chap. 5; Pitcairn, *Autobiography and Diary of Mr James Melvill*, ed., Robert Pitcairn, 2 vols. (Edinburgh, 1842), 648–88 (clarifying that the authority of the king in church affairs was the heart of the issue); David George Mullan, *Episcopacy in Scotland: The History of an Idea, 1560–1638* (Edinburgh: John Donald, 1986), 98–102.

58. Glenn Burgess, *British Political Thought, 1500–1660: The Politics of the Post-Reformation* (New York: Palgrave Macmillan 2000), 143; Gordon Donaldson, *Scottish Historical Documents* (Edinburgh: Scottish Academic Press, 1970), 176–77; John Spottiswood, *The History of the Church of Scotland*, 3 vols. (Edinburgh: 1831), vol. 1, lviv; Pitcairn, *Autobiography and Diary of Mr James Melvill*, 627; Shaw, *Acts and Proceedings*, 27:1218–19.

59. Lee, *Government by Pen*, chap. 3; MacDonald, *Jacobean Kirk*, 180–81 (on manipulation); Mullan, *Episcopacy in Scotland*, 119 (on bishops cooperating with synods) Spottiswood, *History of the Church*, vol. 1, xxxviii–ix; Vaughan T. Wells, "Constitutional Conflict after the Union of the Crowns: Contention and Continuity in the Parliaments of 1612 and 1621," in Brown and Mann, *Parliament and Politics*, 82–100. Wormald, "Headaches of Monarchy."

60. Donaldson, *Scottish Historical Documents*, 151; Jane E. A. Dawson, "John Knox, Christopher Goodman and the 'Example of Geneva,'" in *The Reception of Continental Reformation in Britain*, ed. Polly Ha and Patrick Collinson (Oxford: Oxford University Press, 2010), 107–35; Gordon Donaldson reviews the king's push for liturgical reform and its consequences in "Reformation to Revolution," in Duncan Forrester and Douglas Murray, eds., *Studies in the History of Worship in Scotland* (Edinburgh: T&T Clark, 1984), chap. 4.

61. *Original Letters relating to the Ecclesiastical Affairs of Scotland*, 2 vols. (Edinburgh, 1851); 2:569, 658–60, 662–63; Calderwood, *History of the Kirk*, 7:249. The substance of the Articles and reactions to them are described in Ian B. Cowan, "The Five Articles of Perth," in *Reformation and Revolution: Essays presented to . . . Hugh Watt*, ed. Duncan Shaw (Edinburgh: Saint Andrew, 1967),

62. Shaw, *Acts and Proceedings*, 27:1539, 1544–47.

63. Ibid., 1547–50; Gordon Donaldson, *Scotland: James V–James VII* (1965; repr., Edinburgh: Mercat, 1987), 210; Spottiswood, *History of the Church*, 1: xc

64. See, e.g., Laura Stewart, "'Brothers in Treuth': Propaganda, Public Opinion and the Perth Articles Debate in Scotland," in Houlbrooke, *James VI and I*, 151–68; Stewart, "The political repercussions of the Five Articles of Perth: a reassessment of James VI and I's religious policies in Scotland," *Sixteenth Century Journal* 38 (2007): 1013–36. See also the very useful analysis by John D. Ford, "Conformity in Conscience: The Structure of the Perth Articles Debate in Scotland, 1618–38," *JEH* 46 (1995): 256–77; Ford, "The Lawful Bonds of Scottish Society: The Five Articles of Perth, the Negative Confession and the National Covenant," *HJ* 37 (1994): 45–64. According to the *Dictionary of Scottish Theology and History* (Downers Grove, IL: InterVarsity, 1993), the term "non-conformity" in Scottish religious history should be reserved for the period after 1660.

65. M'Crie, *Life of Mr. Robert Blair*, 11–15. See also William Scot, *An Apologetical Narration of the State of the Kirk of Scotland* (Edinburgh: Wodrow Society, 1846).

66. *The First and Second Books of Discipline* ([n.p.], 1621); Calderwood, *The Altar of Damascus* (n.p., 1621), 14, 10, 163; Row, *History of the Kirk*, 320–32.

67. M'Crie, *Life of Mr. Robert Blair*, 15; Row, *History of the Kirk*. See also Julian Goodare, "The Scottish Parliament of 1621," *HJ* 38 (1995): 29–52; Calderwood, *History of the Kirk*, 7:460–507.

68. The Aberdeen Confession of 1616 included the statement that "the Kirk of Scotland . . . is one of the most pure Kirks under heaven this day, both in respect of truth in doctrine, and purity in worship," a statement possibly qualified by the words that followed, "and therefore, with all our hearts we adjoin ourselves thereto, and to the religion publicly professed therein by the king's majesty." Shaw, *Acts and Proceedings*, 27:1531.

69. Calderwood, *History of the Kirk*, 7:313–15; Shaw, *Acts and Proceedings*, 27:1390 (for an encomium of 1606). See also Charles MacInnes, *Charles I and the Making of the Covenanting Movement, 1625–1641* (Edinburgh: J. Donald, 1991), on flexibilities and a quieting of unrest and foreign problems; Margo Todd, "Bishops in the kirk: William Cowper of Galloway and the puritan episcopacy of Scotland," *Scottish Journal of Theology* 57 (2004): 300–312; Mullan, *Episcopacy in Scotland*, chap. 7.

70. Calderwood, *History of the Kirk*, 7:285; Mullan, *Religious Controversy in Scotland: 1625–1639* (Edinburgh: Lothian, 1998), 139 n. 11; Williamson, *Scottish National Consciousness*, 92; Mullan, *Episcopacy in Scotland*, 155–66 (on pro-Perth history writing by Cowper, Lindsay, and others).

71. John Forbes, *Certaine Records Touching the Estate of the Kirk in the Years MDCV and MDCVI* (Edinburgh, 1846), 299–334n; Mullan, *Scottish Puritanism*, 72–84; Mullan, *Episcopacy in Scotland*, 130–31.

72. Laing, *Original Letters*, 2:711–12; Balfour, *Works*, 2:91, 99; Coffey, *Politics, Religion and the British Revolutions*, 41–42, 192–98; Helga Robinson-Hammerstein, "Trinity College, Dublin, in the Early Seventeenth Century: Institutional Isolation and Foreign Contacts," in *Lines of Contact: Proceedings of the Second Conference of . . . Historians of Universities*, ed. John M. Fletcher and Hilde De Ridder-Symoens (Ghent: Universiteit Gent, 1994), 43–56; David Stevenson, "Conventicles in the Kirk, 1619–37: The Emergence of a Radical Party," *RSCHS* 18 (1974): 99–114. Laura A. M. Stewart provides more details about local networks hostile to Perth in *Urban Politics and British Civil Wars: Edinburgh, 1617–53* (Leiden: Brill, 2006), chaps. 2 and 5; and in Stewart, *Rethinking the Scottish Revolution: Covenanted Scotland, 1637–1651* (Oxford: Oxford University Press, 2016), chap. 1.

73. Keith L. Sprunger, *Dutch Puritanism: A History of English and Scottish Churches*

of the Netherlands in the Sixteenth and Seventeenth Centuries (Leiden: Brill, 1982), 26 and passim; Ha, *English Presbyterianism*, chap. 6. As a member of the local classis, the English Church had to accept its supervision of who became the congregation's ministers. See also Alice Clare Carter, *The English Reformed Church in Amsterdam in the Seventeenth Century* (Amsterdam: Scheltema and Holkema, 1964).

74. Geoffrey Nuttall, *Visible Saints: The Congregational Way, 1640–1660* (Oxford: Basil Blackwell, 1957), 9–10, correcting Raymond P. Stearns, *Congregationalism in the Dutch Netherlands: The Rise and Fall of the English Congregational Classis, 1621–1635* (Chicago: University of Illinois Press, 1940), and challenging the category of non-Separatist Congregationalism described in Perry Miller, *Orthodoxy in Massachusetts, 1630–1650* (Cambridge, MA: Harvard University Press, 1933). See below, chapter 7, for more discussion of this question as it bears on the "origins" of congregationalism in New England.

75. I follow Carole Schneider, who regards these "Congregationalist" renderings of church order as akin to the casual "presbyterianism" of Cartwright and Travers, a point I make myself in chapter 8. She points out, as well, that Bradshaw and others of his thinking aimed their fire at episcopacy, not presbyterianism. Schneider, "Godly Order in a Church Half-Reformed: The Disciplinarian Legacy, 1570–1641" (PhD thesis, Harvard University, 1986), chap. 5. See also Burrage, *EED*, 1, chap. 12. The traditional story, still revered by denominational historians, may be found in Walker, *Creeds and Platforms*.

76. *The Pilgrim Press*, ed. R. Breugelmans (Neiuwkoop: De Graaf, 1987); Keith L. Sprunger, *Trumpets from the Tower: English puritan printing in the Netherlands, 1600–1640* (Leiden: Brill, 1994); Baynes, *The Diocesans Tryall*, quoted in Benjamin Hanbury, *Historical Memorials relating to the Independents or Congregationalists*, 3 vols. (London, 1839–1844), 2:244; Keith Sprunger, *The Learned Doctor William Ames: Dutch Backgrounds of English and American Puritanism* (Urbana: University of Illinois Press, 1972), 232–35, chap. 10; Alastair J. Mann, *The Scottish Book Trade, 1500–1720: Print Commerce and Print Control in Early Modern Scotland* (East Linton: Tuckwell, 2000), chap. 3. Other signs of historical memory—in this case, references to Travers, Chaderton, and Edward Dering's sermon of 1570, among others—occur in George Johnson, *A Discourse of Some Troubles and Excommunications in the Banished English Church at Amsterdam* (Amsterdam, 1603).

77. Marchant, *Puritans and the Church Courts*, 141–42; George, *John Robinson*, chap. 3 (quotation, p. 85); Stephen Wright, *The Early English Baptists, 1603–1649* (Woodbridge: Boydell, 2006), chap. 1.

78. Burrage, *EED*, 2:173.

79. James Robert Coggins, *John Smythe's Congregation English Separatism, Mennonite Influence, and the Elect Nation Studies in Anabaptist and Mennonite History No. 32* (Waterloo, ON: Herald, 1991), detailing Smythe's theology as it developed over time and re-dating the pamphlets Smythe and others were issuing; he also suggests that Smythe's group briefly merged with the Ainsworth-Johnson congregation. In *The English Separatist Tradition: From the Marian Martyrs to the Pilgrim Fathers* (Oxford: Oxford University Press, 1971), chap. 6, B. R. White covers the same events. In his introduction to *The Life and Writings of Thomas Helwys* (Macon, GA: Mercer University Press, 2009), Joe Early Jr., describes Helwys's theological relationship to Smythe as it evolved over time and touches briefly on his activities once he returned to England (quotations, 166–70, 179). In *Francis Johnson and the English Separatist Influence* (Macon, GA: Mercer University Press, 2011), Scott Culpepper surveys several of the attempts to impose order on Smythe's "curious theological formation" (pp. 186–214), a task undertaken, in the main, by historians of English Baptists.

80. The authoritative study of Robinson is George, *John Robinson*. To William Prynne,

an "Erastian" at heart who favored Presbyterianism, Ames was a theological ally because of his objections to Dutch-style Arminianism. Prynne, *Anti-Arminianism; or, The Church of Englands Old Antithesis to New Arminianisme* (1630), 22. Parker's theorizing is nicely summarized in Ha, *English Presbyterianism*, 70–73, in the context of Ha's assertion that English-style presbyterianism incorporated congregationalist elements; for John Paget's evocations of Parker on synods, see ibid., 91–92; and for the two men's personal relationship, see Benjamin Brook, *Lives of the Puritans*, 3 vols. (London, 1813), 2:239. That Presbyterians were a presence in the Netherlands is emphasized by Ha, "Genevan-Jesuits: Crypto Presbyterianism in England," in *Insular Christianity Alternative Models of the Church in Britain and Ireland, c. 1570–c.1700*, ed. Robert Armstrong and Tadhg Ó hAnnracháin (Manchester: Manchester University Press, 2013), chap. 3. According to Sprunger, *Dutch Puritanism*, 227, Bradshaw may have been thinking of parishes as the units out of which the visible church was constructed.

81. Forbes's politics are briefly described in Ha, *English Presbyterianism*, 126–28.

82. Burrage, *EED*, vol. 1, chap. 12 (covering, e.g., the covenanting in Rotterdam); Stearns, *Strenuous Puritan*, 75–78; Sprunger, *Dutch Puritanism*, 162–68, 226–31; Thomas Edwards, *Antapologia; or, A Full Answer to the Apologeticall Narration* (London, 1644), 40–41, 141–51; Bremer, *Building a New Jerusalem*, 141 (on requirements for membership). At the reorganizing moment in Rotterdam, John Forbes preached, solicited the group's assent to the new covenant, and laid hands on Peter, as did all the other ministers present. Burrage, *EED*, 1:300–303. The infighting and inconsistencies among these exiles were highlighted in Edwards, *Antapologia*.

83. Burrage, *EED*, 2:165; *Anno Domini 1616, A confession and protestation of the faith of certaine Christians in England* (Amsterdam, 1616), passim; Henry Jacob, *An humble supplication for toleration and libertie to enjoy and observe the ordinances of Christ Iesus* ([Amsterdam], 1609). The workings of his church and its longer history are described in Murray Tolmie, *The Triumph of the Saints: The Separate Churches of London, 1616–1649* (Cambridge: Cambridge University Press, 1977), chaps. 1–2; and Jacob's ecclesiology in Stephen Brachlow, *The Communion of Saints: Radical Puritan and Separatist Ecclesiology 1570–1625* (Oxford: Oxford University Press, 1988).

84. Brachlow, *Communion of Saints*, pp. 132–35 and chap. 6, noting that the description of criteria for membership in Edmund S. Morgan, *Visible Saints: The History of a Puritan Idea* (New York: New York University Press, 1963) left out "sanctification" as a requirement for becoming a church member. In *English Presbyterianism*, Ha characterizes Jacobs's project as a "silent ecclesiastical revolution . . . as revolutionary as Luther's Reformation" (p. 7).

85. In manuscript exchanges of c. 1610 between Jacob and "Presbyterians" insisting on the existence of a visible catholic church, his critics characterized Jacob and others of his thinking as advocates of "independency," a term that would burst into prominence in the 1640s. Ha, *English Presbyterianism* 52.

86. Burrage, *EED*, vol. 1, chaps. 12–13; 2:163.

87. See above, chapter 2, on William Axton's congregationalist-style ideas as revealed in Peel, *Seconde Parte of a Register*, 1:68–73.

88. [Bradshaw], *English Puritanisme*, sig. A4r; Burrage, *EED*, 1:291, 2:165 (on Robinson/Jacob); Tolmie, *Triumph of the Saints*, 9; A. C. Carter, "John Robinson and the Dutch Reformed Church," in *Studies in Church History 3*, ed. G. J. Cuming (Leiden: Brill, 1966), 232–41; John Cotton, *The Way of the Churches of Christ, Cleared* (1648), reprinted in Ziff, *John Cotton on the Churches of New England*, 183–84. Timothy George downplays any change of mind, as does B. R. White. George, *John Robinson*, 159–66; White, *English Sepa-*

ratist Tradition, 155–59. Cf. Robinson, *A Treatise od the Lawfulnes of hearing Ministers in the Church of England* ([Leiden], 1634).

89. Ames, *Marrow of Theology*, 179–80. This paragraph owes a great deal to Brachlow, *Communion of Saints*, chap. 3; and George, *John Robinson*, 107–13, 136–52. As the allusions to 1 Peter 2:5 and parts of Ephesians indicate, Robinson was thinking of the visible church as "always *ecclesia in via*: in the process of being 'built up' or torn down, of growing toward holiness or of relapsing into decay." George, *John Robinson*, 109.

90. Edward Arber, *The Story of the Pilgrim Fathers, 1606-1623* (London, 1897), 280–81.

91. Walker, *Creeds and Platforms*, 88, 92. How newcomers were admitted to the Plymouth church in the 1620s is unknown; in a statement dating from 1634, Edward Winslow said that the church was requiring "reason of that faith & hope they have in Christ . . . together with a good testimony of an honest life." Jeremy Bangs, *Edward Winslow . . . a Documentary Biography* (Boston: New England Historical and Genealogical Society, 2004), 150.

92. Williams et al., *Thomas Hooker Writings in England and Holland*, 280, 284–85.

93. Calder, *Letters of John Davenport*, 44–46; Bremer, *Building a New Jerusalem*, 116–29 (clarifying that Davenport did not share Hooker's stringency about baptism), 137. Davenport's other activities in the Netherlands are described in ibid., chap. 9.

94. Seaver, *Puritan Lectureships*, 115; Tyacke, *Anti-Calvinists*, 102–5; Gee and Hardy, *Documents*, 516–18; Milton, *Catholic and Reformed*, 58–59. On Montagu in the context of waverings on Dordt-style Calvinism: ibid., 428–31; Cromartie, *Constitutionalist Revolution*, 171–74.

Chapter 7. A New Sion? Reform, Rebellion, and Colonization c. 1625–1640

1. Thomas M'Crie, *The Life of Mr. Robert Blair, Minister of St. Andrews* (Edinburgh: Wodrow Society, 1848), 3, 35–38, 105–8, 140–46. Robert Baillie, who studied under Blair, credited him with nurturing Baillie's "early love towards the ancient oppressed Discipline of our Church" and with strengthening his memories of those "who had lived and dyed in opposition to Episcopall usurpations." Robert Baillie, *An Historical Viindication of the Government of the Church of Scotland* (London, 1646), sig. A2v. Samuel Rutherford and John Livingston, another of the Scottish ministers in Ireland, also met with John Winthrop, Jr., for which see John Coffey, *Politics, Religion and the British Revolutions: The Mind of Samuel Rutherford* (Cambridge: Cambridge University Press, 1997), 198. John McCafferty reminds us not to trust every word of Blair's memoirs, which he wrote in the early 1660s. McCafferty, "When reformations collide," in *The Stuart Kingdoms in the Seventeenth Century: Awkward Neighbours*, ed. Allan I. Macinnes and Jane Ohlmeyer (Dublin: Four Courts, 2002), 198.

2. A statement that deserves modest qualification if civil war in Scotland between 1565 and 1573 is included, for the party that supported James VI included both Protestants and Catholics, as did the party supporting Mary Stuart.

3. The details, with how they figured in the rhetoric of anti-popery, are beautifully spelled out in Caroline M. Hibbard, *Charles I and the Popish Plot* (Chapel Hill: University of North Carolina Press, 1983).

4. The emergence of this group may be dated to the 1590s; see Peter Lake, "Lancelot Andrewes, John Buckeridge, and avant-garde conformity at the court of James I," in *The Mental World of the Jacobean Court*, ed. Linda Levy Peck (Cambridge: Cambridge University Press, 1991), 113–33; see also Lake, "Defining Puritanism—again?" in *Puritanism:*

Transatlantic Perspectives on a Seventeenth-Century Anglo-American Faith, ed. Francis J. Bremer (Boston: Massachusetts Historical Society, 1993), 3–29. See also T. M. Parker, "Arminianism and Laudianism in Seventeenth-Century England," in *Studies in Church History* 1, ed. C. W. Dugmore and Charles Duggan (London: Nelson, 1964), 20–34; Kenneth Fincham and Nicholas Tyacke, *Altars Restored: The Changing Face of English Religious Worship, 1547–c1700* (Oxford: Oxford University Press, 2007), chap. 3; Nicholas Tyacke, *Anti-Calvinists: The Rise of English Arminianism c. 1590–1640* (Oxford: Clarendon, 1987), chap. 5 and passim; Tyacke, "Lancelot Andrewes and the Myth of Anglicanism," in *Conformity and Orthodoxy in the English Church, c. 1560–1660*, ed. Peter Lake and Michael Questier (Woodbridge: Boydell, 2000), 5–33; and Anthony Milton, "The creation of Laudianism: a new approach," in *Politics, Religion and Popularity in Early Stuart England Essays in Honour of Conrad Russell*, ed. Thomas Cogswell, Richard Cust, and Peter Lake (Cambridge: Cambridge University Press, 2002), chap. 8. That perfectly conformable "Anglicans" distrusted the new group is noted in Calvin Lane, *The Laudians and the Elizabethan Church: History, Conformity, and Religious Identity in Post-Reformation England* (London: Pickering and Chatto, 2013), chap. 1 and passim. In *Catholic and Reformed: The Roman and Protestant Churches in English Protestant Thought, 1600–1640* (Cambridge: Cambridge University Press, 2002), Anthony Milton proposes a more complex array of factions: two associated with the Puritan wing of the church, and three relating to conformists, one of them a party he terms the Laudians. Historically, the question—of much importance to High Church Anglicans—is whether the Laudians were innovators or were in continuity with certain predecessors. Historians have also wondered whether some features of this program were more important than the whole. David Hoyle questions any simple description of factionalism in *Reformation and Religious Identity in Cambridge, 1590–1644* (Woodbridge: Boydell, 2007), chap. 5.

5. Milton, *Catholic and Reformed*, pt. 2, chap. 8; Tyacke, *Anti-Calvinists*, provides a wealth of details. See also Tyacke, "Archbishop Laud," in Tyacke, *Aspects of English Protestantism, c. 1530–1700* (Manchester: Manchester University Press, 2001), chap. 8. The charges brought against Laud during the trial that resulted in his execution in 1645 made no reference to Arminianism. That a critique of predestination was *not* central to the Laudian program is argued in Darren Oldridge, *Religion and Society in Early Stuart England* (Aldershot: Ashgate, 1998), chap. 2. Alan Cromartie qualifies the anti-Calvinism of Laud in "The Mind of William Laud," in *England's Wars of Religion, Revisited*, ed. Charles W. A. Prior and Glenn Burgess (Aldershot: Ashgate, 1988), 75–100.

6. In *The Caroline Captivity of the Church: Charles I and the Remoulding of Anglicanism, 1625–1641* (Oxford: Clarendon, 1992), Julian Davies attributes the Laudian agenda to the king's wish "to realize his highly personal notion of sacramental kingship by exploiting his prerogative as Supreme Governor of the Church" (p. 3); simultaneously, Davies notes (p. 12) the king's indifference to theology. On the other hand, Fincham and Tyacke attribute the policy of repositioning the communion table to "Laudians," pointing out that the king "was not co-opted aboard until, at the earliest, the mid-1630s." *Altars Restored*, 176. For the historiographical context, with Davies's *Caroline Captivity* as foil, see Kenneth Fincham, "The Restoration of Altars in the 1630s," *HJ* 44 (2001): 919–40; Anthony Milton, *The British Delegation and the Synod of Dort (1618–1619)* (Woodbridge: Boydell, 2005), xix; and for the special example of the reissuing of the Book of Sports, Alistair Dougall, *The Devil's Book: Charles I, the Book of Sports and Puritanism in Tudor and Early Stuart England* (Exeter: University of Exeter Press, 2011), chap. 5 (arguing that the king was responsible for its being reissued). Gregory D. Dodds argues that Laud and his allies were situated within an Erasmian tradition and owed little to the Dutch Arminians. Dodds, *Exploiting Erasmus: The*

Erasmian Legacy and Religious Change in Early Modern England (Toronto: University of Toronto Press, 2009), 194–95.

7. Milton, *Catholic and Reformed*, 85–87; Tyacke, *Anti-Calvinists*, 182; on baptism, Fincham and Tyacke, *Altars Restored*, 130–31; Anthony Milton, "'Anglicanism' by Stealth: The Career and Influence of John Overall," in *Religious Politics in Post-Reformation England: Essays in Honour of Nicholas Tyacke*, ed. Kenneth Fincham and Peter Lake (Woodbridge: Boydell, 2006), 159–76; Tyacke, *Anti-Calvinists*, chaps. 5–7 and the references in these chapters; John Fielding, "Arminianism in the Localities: Peterborough Diocese, 1603–1642," in *The Early Stuart Church, 1603–1642*, ed. Kenneth Fincham (Stanford: Stanford University Press, 1993), 93–113; Fincham and Tyacke, *Altars Restored*, 13–21, chaps. 4–6. As Arnold Hunt has observed, the Laudian program "amounted to a radical downgrading of the role of preaching which went far beyond anything previously seen in the Elizabethan or Jacobean Church." Hunt, *The Art of Hearing: English Preachers and Their Audiences, 1590–1640* (Cambridge: Cambridge University Press, 2010), 43.

8. Lori Anne Ferrell, "Kneeling and the body politic," in *Religion, Literature, and Politics in Post-Reformation England, 1540–1688*, ed. Donna B. Hamilton and Richard Strier (Cambridge: Cambridge University Press, 1996), 70–92, esp. 85–92; Milton, *Catholic and Reformed*, chap. 9 (a careful reading of theories of episcopacy and the argument for things indifferent); Kenyon, *Stuart Constitution*, 147–49 (Laud's speech of 1637); Charles W. A. Prior, "Ecclesiology and Political Thought in England, 1580–c.1630," *HJ* 48 (2005): 855–84 (noting how customary this assumption was). See also Peter Lake, "The Laudian Style: Order, Uniformity, and the Pursuit of the Beauty of Holiness in the 1630s," in Fincham, *Early Stuart Church*, 161–85; and Ronald G. Asch, "Sacred Kingship in France and England in the Age of the Wars of Religion: From Disenchantment to Re-enchantment," in Prior and Burgess, *England's Wars of Religion*, 27–47. The Laudian program is placed in a broader context in Alexandra Walsham, *The Reformation of the Landscape: Religion, Identity, and Memory in Early Modern Britain and Ireland* (Oxford: Oxford University Press, 2011), chap. 4.

9. Milton, *Catholic and Reformed*, pt. 1, chaps. 1–2; Breward, *Work of Perkins*, 210. See also Peter Lake, "The Laudians and the Argument from Authority," in *Court, Country and Culture: Essays on Early Modern British History in Honor of Perez Zagorin*, ed. Bonnjelyn Young Kunze and Dwight D. Brautigam (Rochester: University of Rochester Press, 1992), 149–75. Iain M. MacKenzie provides a useful analysis of the meaning of "order" as the theological category on which unity or uniformity depended in *God's Order and Natural Law: The Works of the Laudian Divines* (Aldershot: Ashgate, 2002).

10. John McCafferty, *The Reconstruction of the Church of Ireland: Bishop Bramhall and the Laudian Reforms, 1633–1641* (Cambridge: Cambridge University Press, 2007), chap. 5 (quotation, p. 177); Jack Cunningham, *James Ussher and John Bramhall: The Theology and Politics of Two Irish Ecclesiastics of the Seventeenth Century* (Aldershot: Ashgate, 2007), chap. 8; *The Anglican Canons, 1529–1947*, ed. Gerald Bray (Woodbridge: Boydell / Church of England Record Society, 1998), 485–531.

11. Tyacke, *Anti-Calvinists*, 184; Hoyle, *Reformation and Religious Identity*, 182–83, 192–95; *The History of Oxford University, Vol. 4: Seventeenth-Century Oxford*, ed. Nicholas Tyacke (Oxford: Clarendon, 1997), 584–95, and continuing into the early 1640s; Dougall, *Devil's Book*, 146–47; Paul Seaver, *The Puritan Lectureships: The Politics of Religious Dissent 1560–1662* (Stanford: Stanford University Press, 1970), chap. 8. The scope of censorship (licensing) and other effects on the book trades are described in S. Mutchow Towers, *Control of religious printing in early Stuart England* (Woodbridge: Boydell, 2003); Peter McCullough, "Making Dead Men Speak: Laudianism, Print, and the Works of Lancelot An-

drewes, 1626–1642," *HJ* 41 (1998): 401–24; and Anthony Milton, "Licensing, Censorship, and Religious Orthodoxy in Early Stuart England," *HJ* 41 (1998): 625–51.

12. Gee and Hardy, *Documents*, 528–32. Books by Laudians critical of a "Puritan" view of the Sabbath are listed in Debora Shuger, ed., *Religion in Early Stuart England, 1603–1638: An Anthology of Primary Sources* (Waco, TX: Baylor University Press, 2012), 816 n. 2. Kenneth L Parker paints Laud as a strong defender of the Sunday Sabbath in *The English Sabbath: A Study of Doctrine and Discipline from the Reformation to the Civil War* (Cambridge: Cambridge University Press, 1988), chap. 7.

13. T. W. Davids, *Annals of Evangelical Nonconformity in the County of Essex* (London, 1863), chap. 6; Seaver, *Puritan Lectureships*, chaps. 7–8; *Winthrop Papers*, 3:261, 371–75; Richard Cust, "Anti-Puritanism and Urban Politics: Charles I and Great Yarmouth," *HJ* 35 (1992): 1–26. Alternatively, the "metropolitan visitation of 1634 and 1635" was the "defining event of the Laudian period," a point made in Oldridge, *Religion and Society*, chap. 4 (quotation, p. 39) See also Fincham and Tyacke, *Altars Restored*, 214–15, and Matthew Reynolds, *Godly Reformers and Their Opponents in Early Modern England Religion in Norwich, c. 1560–1643* (Woodbridge: Boydell, 2005), chap. 9; Roland A. Marchant, *The Puritans and the Church Courts in the Diocese of York, 1560–1642* (London: Longmans, 1960) chaps. 4–5. That Laud was less punitive than Wren and others in the diocese of London and that the rules about what could be preached were not that constraining is demonstrated in Ann Hughes, "A Moderate Puritan Negotiates Religious Change," *JEH* 65 (2014): 761–79, an assessment she shares with Davies, *Carolinian Captivity*.

14. Edward Cardwell, *Synodalia: A Collection of Articles of Religion, Canons, and Proceedings of Convocations*, 2 vols. (Oxford, 1842), 1:380–415; quotations, pp. 382–83, 384, 389–90, 402–3, 406; Tyack, *Anti-Calvinism*, 236–39. Charles W. A. Prior points out that some contemporaries understood the canons of 1640 to violate an ambiguous but working consensus about the relationship between civil or common law and church law. Prior, "Canons and Constitutions," in Prior and Burgess, *England's Wars of Religion*, 101–23.

15. *The Works of the Most Reverend Father in God, William Laud*, ed. William Scott and James Bliss, 6 vols. (Oxford, 1857), 6, pt. 1, 42; Tyacke, *Anti-Calvinists*, 57. For other expressions of this theme, see Tyack, *Anti-Calvinists*, 140–41, 156, 167, 186. See also the references to "puritans" in the index to Fincham and Tyacke, *Altars Restored*. This argument dates from the 1560s and 1570s, when English Catholics were doing their best to characterize Calvin and Calvinism as rebellious. Cf. Peter Marshall, "John Calvin and the English Catholics, c. 1565–1640," *HJ* 53 (2010): 849–70.

16. Montagu, quoted in Polly Ha, "Spiritual Treason and the Politics of Intercession: Presbyterians, Laudians and the Church of England," in *Puritans and Catholics in the Trans-Atlantic World, 1600–1800*, ed. Crawford Gribben and Scott Spurlock (London: Palgrave Macmillan, 2016) , 66–88 (quotation, p. 72); Margo Todd, "Anti-Calvinists and the republican threat in Early Stuart Cambridge," in the same book, 85–105; Dwight Brautigan, "Prelates and Politics: Uses of 'Puritan,' 1625–1640," *in Puritanism and Its Discontents*, ed. Laura Lunger Knoppers (Newark: University of Delaware Press, 2003), 49–66 (quotation from Brooke, pp. 53–54); Anthony Milton, *Laudian and Royalist Polemic in Seventeenth-Century England: The Career and Writings of Peter Heylyn* (Manchester: University of Manchester Press, 2007), chaps. 1–3; John Rushworth, *Historical Collections . . . Beginning the Sixteenth Year of King James, First Part*, vol. 2 (London, 1659), 585–86, 593–95; Gee and Hardy, *Documents*, 533–54; Milton, *Catholic and Reformed*, 516–21; Davies, *Caroline Captivity*, 13 (emphasizing "popularity").

17. Michael C. Questier, ed., *Newsletters from the Caroline Court, 1631–1638: Catholi-

cism and the Politics of the Personal Rule, Camden Fifth Series 26 (Cambridge: Cambridge University Press, 2005), 181.

18. Ann Hughes, *Politics, Society and Civil War in Warwickshire, 1620–1660* (Cambridge: Cambridge University Press, 1987), 79; Christopher Haigh, *The Plain Man's Pathways to Heaven: Kinds of Christianity in Post-Reformation England, 1570–1640* (Oxford: Oxford University Press, 2007), 115–17, 137–38; Dougall, *Devil's Book*, chap. 5 (noting Laud's own indifference to enforcing the rule that ministers read the Book of Sports to their parishes); John Fielding, "Arminianism in the Localities: Peterborough Diocese, 1603–1642," in Fincham, ed., *Early Stuart Church*, 93–113; Oldridge, *Religion and Society*, 57; Seaver, *Puritan Lectureships*, 95–96, characterizing Laud's instructions about lecturers as ineffectual.

19. The most telling demonstration of this point is Milton, *Catholic and Reformed*, a book critical to understanding why the House of Commons in 1640–41 moved so readily to unwind the Laudian program. As one British historian of the period of personal rule (1629–early 1640) has noted, "Without a meeting of parliament, it was difficult for people . . . to express an ideological opposition to the government." Fielding, "Opposition to the Personal Rule of Charles I: The Diary of Robert Woodford, 1637–1641," *HJ* 31 (1988): 783.

20. Ward, quoted in Hoyle, *Reformation and Religious Identity*, 150; *Proceedings of the Short Parliament of 1640*, ed. Esther S. Cope and Wilson H. Coates, Camden Fourth Series 19 (London: Camden Society, 1977), 147. Associating Laud with the papacy figured in anti-royalist propaganda of the 1640s and his trial on charges of treason; for a taste of this propaganda, see David Brady, *The Contribution of British Writers between 1560 and 1830 to the Interpretation of Revelation 13.16–18* (Tubingen: Mohr Siebeck, 1983), 99–102. Walsham cautions against interpreting the 1631 edition of Beard as anti-monarchical. *Providence in Early Modern England*, 110.

21. Fincham and Tyacke, *Altars Restored*, chaps. 4–5; Dougall, *Devil's Book*, chap. 6; Anthony Fletcher, *A County Community in Peace and War: Sussex, 1600–1660* (London: Longman, 1975), chap. 4; *The Diary of Robert Woodford, 1637–1641* , ed. John Fielding, Camden Fifth Series 42 (Cambridge: Cambridge University Press, 2012), 59–61; Cust, "Anti-Puritanism and Urban Politics"; Claire Cross, "Achieving the Millennium: The Church in York during the Commonwealth," in *The Province of York*, ed. G. J. Cumming, Studies in Church History 4 (Leiden: Brill, 1967), 122–42 (despite its title, this essay also details the resistance of the town's leaders in the 1630s to Archbishop Neile and others); Daniel J. Steere, "A Calvinist Bishop at the Court of King Charles I," in *Adaptations of Calvinism in Reformation Europe Essays in Honour of Brian G. Armstrong*, ed. Mack P. Holt (Aldershot: Ashgate, 2007), 193–218; Alfred Kingson, *East Anglia and the Great Civil War* (London, 1897), 28.

22. Seaver, *Puritan Lectureships*, 144–45; Hughes, *Politics, Society and Civil War*, 79.

23. Hibbard, *Charles I and the Popish Plot*, is an indispensable survey of the emergence of this rhetoric and the complexities surrounding the Catholic presence in the court of Charles I. See also Stephen Brachlow, *The Communion of Saints: Radical Puritan and Separatist Ecclesiology, 1570–1625* (Oxford: Oxford University Press, 1988), chap. 2; and Marc Schwartz, "Lay Anglicanism and the Crisis of the English Church in the Early Seventeenth Century," *Albion* 14 (1982): 1–18.

24. As Michael P. Winship has pointed out, aspects of this argument were already circulating under Elizabeth I; Winship, *Godly Republicanism: Puritans, Pilgrims and a City on a Hill* (Cambridge, MA: Harvard University Press, 2012), chap. 1. Beyond the time frame of this chapter, John Walter describes the power of the same theme in *Understanding Popular Violence in the English Revolution: The Colchester Plunderers* (Cambridge: Cambridge

University Press, 1999), pt. 3, chap. 5 (noting, as well, popular resentment of gentry and aristocratic control of clerical appointments. See also Robert von Freideburg, "The Continental Counter-reformation and the Plausibility of the Popish Plots, 1638–1642," in Prior and Burgess, *England's Wars of Religion*, 49–73.

25. Conrad Russell, "The Parliamentary Career of John Pym, 1621–9," in *The English Commonwealth, 1547–1640: Essays in Politics and Society*, ed. Peter Clark, Alan G. R. Smith, and Nicholas Tyacke (Leicester: Leicester University Press, 1979), 147–66.

26. Conrad Russell, *Parliaments and English Politics, 1621–1629* (Oxford: Clarendon, 1979), 206–8, 229–33, 248, 462–65. Historical memory figured in this outburst, with Pym citing Bucer, Foxe, the Lambeth Articles, and the Synod of Dordt. See also Anthony Fletcher, *The Outbreak of the English Civil War* (London: Edward Arnold, 1981), xix–xxiv (summing up assertions of a popish plot and its connections with Arminianism and Catholicism).

27. *Commons Debates for 1629 Critically Edited*, ed. Wallace Notestein and Frances Helen Relf (Minneapolis: University of Minnesota, 1921), 12–14; the men who spoke after Rous echoed these themes. See also J. Sears McGee, "Sir Simonds D'Ewes: A 'respectable conservative' or a 'fiery spirit'? in Prior and Burgess, *England's Wars of Religion*, 147–67.

28. Arthur Williamson, *Scottish National Consciousness in the Age of James VI: The Apocalypse, the Union, and the Shaping of Scotland's Public Culture* (Edinburgh: J. Donald, 1979), 21–28 (on Napier), 93; Paul Christianson, *Reformers and Babylon: English apocalyptic visions from the reformation to the eve of the civil war* (Toronto: University of Toronto Press, 1978), 97–100 (quotation, p. 99); Katherine Firth, *The Apocalyptic Tradition in Reformation Britain, 1530–1645* (Oxford: Oxford University Press, 1979), chap. 4.

29. Dent, *The ruine of Rome; or, An Exposition upon the Revelation* (1603), sig. A4v; Jeffrey K. Jue, *Heaven upon Earth: Joseph Mede (1586–1638) and the Legacy of Millenarianism* (Dordrecht: Springer, 2006); Howard Hotson, *Johann Heinrich Alsted, 1588–1638: Between Renaissance, Reformation, and Universal Reform* (Oxford: Clarendon, 2000). See also R. G. Clouse, "The Rebirth of Millenarianism," in *Puritans, the Millennium and the Future of Israel: Puritan Eschatology 1600–1660*, ed. Peter Toon (Cambridge; James Clarke, 1970), 42–65, noting, among other features, Alsted's dispensationalism and, in an astrological work of 1628, his reliance on planetary conjunctions to emphasize the importance of 1642–43.

30. Andrew Crome, *The Restoration of the Jews: Early Modern Hermeneutics, Eschatology, and National Identity in the Works of Thomas Brightman* (Heidelberg: Springer, 2014), 16–22 (quotation, p. 18) For a longer view of this project, see Richard Cogley, "The Most Vile and Barbarous Nation of all the World': Giles Fletcher the Elder's the Tartars, or Ten Lost tribes," *Renaissance Quarterly* 58 (2000): 781–814; Cogley, "The Fall of the Ottoman Empire and the Restoration of Israel in the 'Judeo-centric' Strand of Puritan Millenarianism," *Church History* 72 (2003): 304–32 (noting that this "Judeo-centric" focus was one among several strands of millenarianism); A. H. Williamson, "The Jewish Dimension of the Scottish Apocalypse," in *Menasseh Ben Israel and his World*, ed. Y. Kaplan et al. (Leiden: Brill, 1989), 7–30.

31. Brightman, *A Revelation of the Revelation That Is* (Amsterdam, 1615), A3r; 160–61, and passim; Williamson, *Scottish National Consciousness*, 174.

32. Brightman, *Revelation*, sig. A2r; H[enry] B[urton], *The Seven Vials* (London, 1628), 88.

33. Firth, *Apocalyptic Tradition*, chaps. 4–5; Hotson, *Paradise Postponed*, 87, 93 n. 23; Crawford Gribben, *The Puritan Millennium: Literature and Theology, 1550–1682* (Dublin: Four Courts, 2000), 33; Johannes van den Berg, "Joseph Mede and the Dutch Millenarian

Daniel Van Laren," in *Prophecy and Eschatology*, ed. Michael Wilks, Studies in Church History: Subsidia 10 (Oxford: Oxford University Press, 1994), 111–22 (suggesting that William Ames was familiar with Brightman). For Scotland a little later, see James K. Cameron, "The Commentary on the Book of Revelation by James Durham (1622–58)," in Wilks, ed., *Prophecy and Eschatology*, 123–30; Sanderson, quoted in Debora Shuger, *Religion in Early Stuart England, 1603-1638: An Anthology of Primary Sources* (Waco, TX: Baylor University Press, 2012) 247. Richard Cogley has accumulated a great many more references, to appear in his study of the motif of the conversion of the Jews.

34. John White, *The Planters Plea; or, The Ground of plantations examined . . . for the satisfaction of those that question the lawfulnesse of the action* (London, 1630), 15–16; *Letters of the Lady Brilliana Harley*, ed. Thomas Taylor Lewis (New York: AMS, 1968), 41; Fielding, *Diary of Woodford*, 289. William Twisse told Mede after realizing the older man was endorsing ceremonies, "the time of the slaughtering of the witnesses had arrived," a passage "widely interpreted as a prophecy of the final bloody confrontation with Rome." Hoyle, *Reformation and Religious Identity*, 192. See also Crawford Gribben, "The Church of Scotland and the English Apocalyptic Imagination, 1630 to 1650," *Scottish Historical Review* 88 (2009): 34-56.

35. Prynne, *Anti-Arminianism*, 22; [John Bastwick], *The Litany of John Bastwick* (1637); William M. Lamont, *Puritanism and the English Revolution, Vol. 1: Marginal Prynne, 1600-1669* (Aldershot: Gregg Revivals, 1991), chaps. 1–2; Christianson, *Reformers and Babylon*, chap. 4; Tyacke, *Anti-Calvinists*, 158; Adrian Chastain Weimer, *Martyrs Mirror: Persecution and Holiness in Early New England* (New York: Oxford University Press, 2011), 13–14.

36. *Notebooks of Nehemiah Wallington, 1618-1654: A Selection*, ed. David Booy (Cambridge: Cambridge University Press, 2007), 121–23 (subsequently, he was reading a printed account of sufferings); *Winthrop Papers* 3:485–87; *Calendar of State Papers, Domestic Series, of the reign of Charles I, 1625-1649* (London, 1868), 11:287, 332. Prynne's reception en route to his imprisonment is described in ibid., 433–34.

37. Booy, *Notebooks of Wallington*, 122, 116.

38. David Quinn, "The First Pilgrims," *WMQ* 3rd. ser. 23 (1966): 360–90, tracing late sixteenth-century suggestions and petitions by Separatists; Babette Levy, "Early Puritanism in the Southern and Island Colonies," *Proceedings of the American Antiquarian Society*, n.s. 70 (1960): 69–348; Winthrop, *Journal*, 405–6, 426–27, 719–21. The broader arc of settlements attempted or sustained is sketched in Arthur H. Williamson, "An Empire to End Empire: The Dynamic of Early Modern British Expansion," in *The Uses of History in Early Modern England*, ed. Paulina Kewes (San Marino, CA: Huntington Library, 2006), 241–42. See also Karen Kupperman, "Errand to the Indies: Puritan Colonization from Providence Island through the Western Design," *WMQ* 3rd ser. 45 (1988): 70–99. Some people characterized by a minister as "very superstitious" settled on the eastern margins of New England. [Thomas Hutchinson], A *Collection of Original Papers relating to the History of the Colony of Massachusetts Bay* (1767), 112–13.

39. Valerie Pearl, *London and the Outbreak of the Puritan Revolution: City Government and National Politics, 1625-43* (Oxford: Oxford University Press, 1961), 162–169 (on Feoffees), 7; Rosemary O'Day, "Yorkshire's Godly Incendiary: The Career of Henry Darley during the Reign of Charles I," in *Life and Thought in the Northern Church c. 1100–c. 1700: Essays in Honour of Claire Cross*, ed. Diana Wood, Studies in Church History: Subsidia 12 (Woodbridge: Boydell, 1999), 435–64, an essay that also traces Darley's political connections to Lord Brooke and some of the Scottish insurgents.

40. In *Congregational Communion Clerical Friendship in the Anglo-American Puritan*

Community, 1610–1692 (Boston: Northeastern University Press, 1994), chap. 4, Francis J. Bremer fills out the details of these contexts and connections. Others in England had claims on the region, as noted in Jeremy Dupertuis Bangs, *Edward Winslow: New England's First International Diplomat* (Boston: NEHGR, 2004), 140–59.

41. Roger Thompson, *Mobility and Migration: East Anglican Founders of New England, 1629–1640* (Amherst: University of Massachusetts Press, 1994), estimating that, at a minimum, a third of the emigrants from East Anglia traveled in groups (p. 201); Susan Hardman Moore, *Pilgrims: New World Settlers and the Call of Home* (New Haven: Yale University Press, 2007), 22. Stephen Foster suggests that the earliest to arrive were not as "militant" as those who arrived mid-decade or later, an argument linked to his discerning a "religious radicalism" emerging in the 1620s and 1630s among an alienated laity. The major problem with this thesis is that the core elements of the "Congregational Way" had been clarified by 1634 or, at the latest, by the close of 1635. Moreover, the second phase also included laity and ministers who, then and later, were not especially radical. Foster, *The Long Argument: English Puritanism and the Shaping of New England Culture, 1570–1700* (Chapel Hill: University of North Carolina Press, 1991), chap. 4 (quotation, p. 139).

42. Shepard, *Confessions*, 47, 64, 84; Clifford K. Shipton, "The Autobiographical Memoranda of John Brock, 1636–1659," *Proceedings of the American Antiquarian Society* 53 (1944): 96; *Letters from New England: The Massachusetts Bay Colony, 1629–1638*, ed. Everett Emerson (Amherst: University of Massachusetts Press, 1976), 175–77; *Winthrop Papers* 2:293.

43. *A Letter of Many Ministers in Old England, Requesting the judgment of their Reverend Brethren in New England . . . Together with their answers thereunto returned, anno 1639* (1643), 2; "An Epistle Written by the Elders" (unpaginated); Calder, *Letters of John Davenport*, 39; Thomas Shepard and John Allin, *A Defense of the Answer* (1648), 20. The "primitivism" of the colonists is carefully described in Theodore Dwight Bozeman, *To Live Ancient Lives: The Primitivist Dimension in Puritanism* (Chapel Hill: University of North Carolina Press, 1988), coupled with a critique of the "millenarianism" some have imputed to them. See also Abram van Engen, "Origins and Last Farewells: Bible Wars, Textual Form, and the Making of American History," *NEQ* 86 (2013): 547–92, and the references cited therein.

44. *Winthrop Papers* 2:127–28, 199; 3:36; Bush, *Correspondence*, 183, 217, 210; Emerson, *Letters from New England*, 141, 94–98; John Davenport, *A Sermon Preach'd at The Election . . . 1669* (Cambridge, MA, 1670), 15.

45. *Recs. MBC*, 1, 79–80, 86; Hall, *ARP*, 116–17.

46. Bush, *Correspondence*, 243–49; Hall, *ARP*, 117–18; Gribben, *Puritan Millennium*, 50.

47. Bush, *Correspondence*, 369.

48. Emerson, *Letters from New England*, 97. The political and social circumstances noted in this paragraph are elaborated on in Hall, *ARP*, intro., chap. 1.

49. White, *Planters Plea*; John Cotton, *Gods Providence to His Plantation* (London, 1630); [anon.], *The Humble Request of His Majesties loyall subjects . . . to the rest of their Brethren in and of the Church of England* (London, 1630), reprinted in *Winthrop Papers*, 2:231–33 (quotation, p. 232). White was curiously candid. Responding to assertions that some of the ministers being recruited by the company were "Separatists," he acknowledged their nonconformity but characterized them as "semi-Separatists" (pp. 61–62). See also "Reasons to prove a necessitye of reformation . . . without an absolute separation," *Winthrop Papers* 3:10–14, a fragment dated c. March 1631.

50. Bush, *Correspondence*, 143–47 (quotation, p. 144). Responding to the Scottish Presbyterian Robert Baillie (see chap. 8), who wanted to associate the "Congregational Way" of

the colonists with Separatists, Cotton reemphasized the irrelevance of Plymouth to the ministers at Salem. Ibid., 147 n. 2. In sermons he preached in Boston, England, he had been characterizing separation from the state church as a sin. Cotton, *A Briefe Exposition of the whole Book of Canticles* (London, 1648), 31–32. The influence of the Plymouth church on the newcomers at Salem is emphasized in Winship, *Godly Republicanism*, chap. 6; whereas Perry Miller dismissed it in *Orthodoxy in Massachusetts, 1630–1650: A Genetic Study* (Cambridge, MA: Harvard University Press, 1933). In *The Way of the Churches of Christ in New England Cleared* (1648), Cotton rejected Baillie's genealogy. My sense of the evidence leads me to conclude that any conversations of c. 1629 had little or no bearing on the decisions being made in mid-1630s Massachusetts, an assumption I share with Stephen Foster, who insists (p. 151) in *The Long Argument* that the "New England Way was . . . a further and continuing development in America of an ongoing and long-running English process of adjustments," although also citing (pp. 153–54) the influence of William Bradshaw, William Ames, and the like, as Cotton himself was doing in the 1640s.

51. Winthrop, *Journal*, 50, 146–49; *Winthrop Papers* 3:10–14, 146–49; Bush, *Correspondence*, 211–23 (John Cotton's summary of Williams's disdain for how churches were being organized). In *Master John Cottons Answer to Master Roger Williams* (1644), Cotton disputed Williams's version of the events leading up to his banishment, highlighting Williams's "vehemence" and quasi-Separatism in particular; as the nineteenth-century editor of the *Answer* acknowledged, the issue in 1633–35 was not liberty of conscience. *The Complete Writings of Roger Williams*, 7 vols. (New York: Russell and Russell, 1963), 2:40–65. See also *The Correspondence of Roger Williams*, ed. Glenn W. LaFantasie, 2 vols. (Hanover: University Press of New England, 1988), 1:12–23.

52. Hall, *FS*, 104; *Winthrop Papers*, 3:54, 101, 175–77; Winthrop, *Journal*, 142, 144–45.

53. *Winthrop Papers*, 2:267, 200; LaFantasie, *Correspondence of Roger Williams*, 1:42, 45–52; Bush, *Correspondence*, 220. In another letter written soon after this one, Cotton revisited the differences between Separatism and the colonists' self-understanding. Ibid., 238–41.

54. In 1640 John Winthrop was still swatting down assertions that the colonists' rules about church membership were intrinsically Separatist. *Winthrop Papers*, 4:169–71, and in the mid-1640s English and Scottish Presbyterians revived this issue as part of their campaign against Independency (see chap. 8).

55. *Winthrop Papers*, 3:139; Roger Williams, *The Bloudy Tenent of Persecution, Washed and Made Clean*, ed. Richard Groves (Macon, GA: Mercer University Press, 2001), 136–53, 112, 20. (The "Model" survives only because Williams incorporated it into a book of his own.) See also Cotton, *Briefe Exposition*, 165, 178, 180. That the ministers were acutely aware of unpleasant alternatives is apparent not only from the "Model" and Cotton's exegesis of Revelation but also from comments of the kind made by Thomas Allen in a letter (1642) to Cotton: "But how dangerous that [power of magistrates] may prove we have seene by exper. In Engl. where authority from Rom. 13.1 . . . have laid such burdens as the churches were not able to beare." Bush, *Correspondence*, 369.

56. William H. Whitmore, *The Colonial Laws of Massachusetts* (Boston, 1887), 57–59.

57. [John Davenport], *A Discourse about Civil Government in a New Plantation Whose Design Is Religion* (Cambridge, MA, 1663), 7–8; [Richard Mather], *Church-Government and Church-Covenant Discussed, In an Answer of the Elders of the severall Churches in New-England to two and thirty Questions, sent over to them by divers Ministers* (London, 1643), 35. The rules laid out in the "Model" were incorporated into the "Body of Liberties."

58. Williams et al., *Thomas Hooker Writings*, 284, 285; see also chap. 6. Pressed by Robert Baillie about his letter of 1630, Cotton insisted in *The Way of Congregational Churches Cleared* (1648),pt. 1, 18–20, that before he arrived in Massachusetts he had

"learned of Mr Parker, and Mr. Baynes (and soon after of Dr. Ames), that the Ministers of Christ and the Keys . . . are given to each particular Congregational Church respectively." For other assertions of this genealogy, see Hall, *FS*, 82; and for Baillie's skepticism, ibid., 83 n. 27.

59. *Winthrop Papers*, 2:178–80; Keith L. Sprunger, "William Ames and the Settlement of Massachusetts Bay," *NEQ* 39 (1966): 66–79; *Winthrop Papers*, 3:167. In *Puritan Crisis: New England and the English Civil Wars, 1630–1670* (New York: Garland, 1989), Francis J. Bremer notes (p. 221) that the term "Congregational" was used for the first time in Cotton's *The Way of the Congregational Churches Cleared* (1648), but Geoffrey Nuttall pushes this date back to 1641, when "Congregational Way" was used in *A Glimpse of Sions Glory*. Nuttall, *Visible Saints: The Congregational Way, 1640–1660* (Oxford: Blackwells, 1957), 8, n. 4.

60. John Cotton, *An Exposition upon the Thirteenth Chapter* (1655), 221.

61. [Mather], *Church-Government and Church-Covenant*, 41–42; Thomas Hooker, *A Survey of the Summe of Church-Discipline* (1648), 7–8.

62. Cotton, *The True Constitution of a Particular Visible Church* (1642), 7 (written c. 1635); [Mather], *Church-Government and Church-Covenant*, 77.

63. Cotton, *True Constitution*, 6; [Mather], *Church-Government and Church-Covenant*, 56–57; *Letter of Many Ministers*, 3–4.

64. Albro, *Works of Shepard*, 2:65; *The Record of Baptisms, Marriages and Deaths, and Admissions to the Church . . . in the Town of Dedham, Massachusetts*, ed. Don Gleason Hill (Dedham, MA, 1888), 2.

65. Cotton, *True Constitution*, 8.

66. Edward Lambert, *History of the Colony of . . . New Haven* (New Haven, 1834), 10; Samuel Sewall, *The History of Woburn, Middlex County, Mass.* (Boston, 1868), 21; Lemuel Shattuck, *A History of the Town of Concord, Middlesex County, Massachusetts* (Boston, 1835), 151.

67. Walker, *Creeds and Platforms*, 131.

68. Hill, *Record of Baptisms*, 2:1–15. Gifts to congregations are described in Hall, *ARP*, 135–37; and the workings of this ethics in the Cambridge congregation in ibid., chap. 5.

69. Winthrop, *Journal*, 168–70.

70. Ibid., 169–70; Albro, *Works of Shepard*, 2:65, 24–26.

71. [Mather], *Church-Government and Church-Covenant*, 19–21, 23–24, to which he added the criterion of good "conversation"; Albro, *Works of Shepard*, 1: cxxix (see also Winthrop, *Journal*, 173). That congregations may have understood "profession" in different ways is argued in Michael G. Ditmore, "Preparation and Confession: Reconsidering Edmund S. Morgan's *Visible Saints*," *NEQ* 67 (1994): 298–319. Francis J. Bremer at once reaffirms the significance of the exercise and questions referencing such statements as being about "conversion"; he questions, too, the extent to which this requirement was employed. Bremer, " 'To Tell What God Hath Done for Thy Soul': Puritan Spiritual Testimonies as Admissions Tests and Means of Edification," *NEQ* 87 (2014): 625–65. For doubts at a later moment, see Baird Tipson, "Samuel Stone's 'Discourse' against Requiring Church Relations," *WMQ*, 3rd ser. 46 (1989): 786–99. Argument about this matter is hampered by the paucity of church records for the 1630s, indiscriminate references in modern scholarship to "conversion," a reluctance to take at face value assertions that some of "weak faith" were being admitted, and differing perspectives on the import of words such as "profession." News from New England that being baptized or a member in good standing of the Church of England did not count is part of the equation—significant but confusing because the sense of shock in England and the reports themselves had a political flavor. What seems certain is that the gathered congregations were not aspiring to merge the visible and invis-

ible churches; as Thomas Shepard pointed out in the 1630s, hypocrites were inescapably included, a fact that irritated Anne Hutchinson. Missing from most accounts of this process is any recognition of edification as itself close cousin of conversion and something only a sanctified community could pursue, a point made effectively by Stephen Brachlow in his analysis of practice among the exile congregations in the Netherlands (see chap. 6). See also Willliam Rathband, *A briefe narration of some church courses . . . in the churches lately erected in New*-England (1644), 8 (on what is required): "knowledge of principles of religion," then adding, "Yet they confide not therein, nor can be satisfied therewith, without a verbal declaration . . . touching the manner of his Conversion from point to point, and what evidences he can shew truth of his grace, of his sound faith, and sincere repentance." "Profession" is how the organizers of the Dedham church spoke most often of what they were expecting. To English observers, the real stumbling block was the refusal to acknowledge baptism as sufficient.

72. *The Legacy of a Dying Mother to her Mourning Children, Being the Experiences of Mrs. Susanna Bell* (London, 1673), 47–55, excerpted in Moore, *Pilgrims*, 5.

73. According to the group letter of 1637, "Fare more" heads of households had been admitted than not, an assertion linked to another blaming the gap between population and membership on the learning curve lay colonists were experiencing. In *A Dissausive from the Errours of the Times* (1645), Robert Baillie reported that 'three quarters" were outside (p. 73). My attempt to answer this question for Cambridge in the 1640s led me to a minimum of sixty percent and possibly as high as eighty. Hall, *ARP*, 171.

74. Winthrop, *Journal*, 275; Shepard, *Confessions*, 131.

75. A point I owe to Abram van Engen. See also Karen Ordahl Kupperman, "Definitions of Liberty on the Eve of the Civil War; Lord Say and Sele, Lord Brooke, and the American Puritan Colonies," *HJ* 32 (1989): 17–33.

76. Hall, *ARP*, chap. 1. None of the colonies founded in the Chesapeake took this step.

77. For commentary and analysis of actual procedures, see G. B. Warden, "Law Reform in England and New England, 1620 to 1660," *WMQ*, 3d ser. 35 (1978): 668–90; William K. Holdsworth, "Law and Society in Colonial Connecticut, 1636–1672" (PhD diss., Claremont University, 1974); Gail Sussman Marcus, " 'Due Execution of the Generall Rules of Righteousnesse': Criminal Procedures in New Haven Town and Colony, 1638–1658"; and John M. Murrin, "Magistrates, Sinners, and a Precarious Liberty: Trial by Jury in Seventeenth-Century New England," both in *Saints and Revolutionaries: Essays on Early American History*, ed. David D. Hall, John M. Murrin, and Thad W. Tate (New York: W. W. Norton, 1984), pt. 2. See also Hall, *ARP*, chap. 4 and the citations it includes.

78. John Cotton, *A Sermon . . . Deliver'd at Salem, 1636* (Boston, 1713); Hall, *AC*, 412, 121.

79. Ibid., 55, 336, 209.

80. Ibid., 162, 163, 172. In an entry (early March, 1637), Winthrop noted that Wheelwright "inveighed against all that walked in a covenant of works , as he described it to be . . . and called them anti-christs." Winthrop, *Journal*, 210; earlier, he noted that "it began to be as common here to distinguish between men, by being under a covenant of grace or a covenant of works." Ibid., 209.

81. *Recs. MBC*, 1:115, 117, 349–57; Winthrop, *Journal*, 102–3.

82. *Recs. MBC*, 1:142–43, 168, 129 (maintenance); Walker, *Creeds and Platforms*, 118; Hall, *FS*, 124–27.

83. Hill, *Record of Baptisms*, 9–10; Winthrop, *Journal*, 288. An order in 1632, prohibiting a minister from "further gathering a church within this patent," was repealed the following year. *Recs MBC*, 1, 100.

84. Walker, *Creeds and Platforms*, 118; *Winthrop Papers*, 3:223–25; "Thomas Shepard Election Sermon, in 1638," *NEHGR* 24 (1870): 361–66.

85. *Winthrop Papers*, 3:160; *New Englands First Fruits . . . 2 Of the progresse of learning, in the colledge at Cambridge* (1643).

86. *A Letter of Many Ministers in Old England, Requesting the judgment of their Reverend Brethren in New England* (1640); Bush, *Correspondence*, 264–66. See also B. Richard Burg, "A Letter of Richard Mather to a Cleric in Old England," *WMQ*, 3rd ser. 29 (1972): 81–98.

87. David George Mullan, ed., *Religious Controversy in Scotland, 1625–1639* (Edinburgh: Scottish Historical Society, 1998), 5–8; Mullan, *Scottish Puritanism, 1590–1638* (Oxford: Oxford University Press, 2000), chap. 7; Maurice Lee Jr., *The Road to Revolution: Scotland under Charles I, 1625–37* (Urbana: University of Illinois Press, 1985), 199.

88. Charles MacInnes, *Charles I and the Making of the Covenanting Movement* (Edinburgh: John Donald, 1991), chaps. 3–4; Gordon Donaldson, *Scotland James VI to James VII* (New York: Frederick A. Praeger, 1966), chap. 16; Lee, *Road to Revolution*, chap. 4 (emphasizing the consequences of disputes among the Scottish nobility and the narrowing of Charles's connections); Balfour, *Works*, 2:181–84.

89. Donaldson, *Scotland: James VI to James VII*, 309–10; Julian Goodare, *The Government of Scotland, 1560–1625* (Oxford: Oxford University Press 2004), 131–33.

90. The two petitions are printed in John Row, *The Historie of the Kirk of Scotland* (Edinburgh, 1842), 153–55, 352–62. See also Peter Donald, *An Uncounselled King Charles I and the Scottish Troubles, 1637–1641* (Cambridge: Cambridge University Press, 1990), chap. 1; Lee, *Road to Revolution*, 128, 157–58, 162; *Scottish Historical Documents*, ed. Gordon Donaldson (Edinburgh: Scottish Academic Press, 1970), 191–94; MacInnes, *Charles I*, 138, 140 (on the damage done by the sentencing of Balmerino), in his eyes "the single most important event transforming . . . a political faction into a national movement," an argument reinforcing his insistence that the issues posed in 1633 were as much political as strictly religious.

91. William McMillan, *The Worship of the Scottish Reformed Church, 1550–1638* (London: James Clarke, 1931), 106–7; Fincham and Tyacke, *Altars Restored*, 156–57. Joong-Lak Kim cautions that Charles and his father were not actually insisting on complete uniformity, an argument I regard as overstated. Kim, "The Scottish-English-Romanish Book: The character of the Scottish Prayer Book of 1637," in *The Experience of Revolution in Stuart Britain and Ireland Essays for John Morrill*, ed. Michael J. Braddick and David L. Smith (Cambridge: Cambridge University Press, 2011), chap. 1. For a strongly negative interpretation, see Baillie, *Letters and Journals*, 1:4.

92. Bray ed., *Anglican Canons*, 532–52 (quotation, p. 533).

93. Row, *Historie of the Kirk*, 409; Baillie, *Letters and Journals*, 1:17–21; John Earl of Rothes, *A relation of Proceedings concerning the Affairs of the Kirk of Scotland* (Edinburgh, 1830), 198–200; *Diary of Sir Archibald Johnston of Wariston, 1632–1639*, ed. George M. Paul (Edinburgh: Edinburgh University Press, 1911), 265; Rushworth, *Historical Collections . . . Second Part* (1680), 1:39; Baillie, *Letters and Journals*, 1: 23. Laura Stewart places these events within a broader popular politics new to seventeenth-century Scotland. Stewart, *Urban Politics and the British Civil Wars: Edinburgh, 1617–1653* (Leiden: Brill, 2006), chap. 1. For other signs of activism, including the return of ministers from Ireland, see Macinnes, *Charles I*, 155–61.

94. *Letters of Samuel Rutherford*, ed. Andrew A. Bonar (1891; repr., Edinburgh: Banner of Truth Trust, 1984), 129; David Stevenson, "Conventicles in the Kirk, 1619–37: The Emergence of a Radical Party," *Records of the Scottish Church History Society* 18 (1974): 99–114;

Mullan, *Religious Controversy*, 82–120; Laura A. M. Stewart, *Rethinking the Scottish Revolution Covenanted Scotland, 1637–1651* (Oxford: Oxford University Press, 2016), chap. 1; Jason White, *Militant Protestantism and British Identity, 1603–1642* (London: Pickering and Chatto, 2012), chap. 4.The parallels included a retort to the royalist rhetoric of anti-puritanism; rightly understood, "puritans" were "truly Protestant" and "tenacious of just liberty," not "men of anti-monarchicall principles." Mullan, *Religious Controversy*, 31.

95. Peterkin, *Records of the Kirk*, 1:176. Wariston, *Diary*, 265, 275. The narrative that follows draws on David Stevenson, *The Scottish Revolution, 1637–44: The Triumph of the Covenanters* (Newton Abbot: David and Charles, 1973).

96. David Stevenson, *Scottish Covenanters and Irish Confederates: Scottish-Irish Relations in the Mid-seventeenth Century* (Belfast: Ulster Historical Foundation, 1981), 26–27; Stewart, *Urban Politics and the British Civil Wars*, chap. 6 (quotation, p. 266); M'Crie, *Life of Blair*, 150–51. As Stevenson indicates in *Scottish Covenanters and Irish Confederates*, Argyll's politics were affected by long-standing grievances between the Campbells and the mostly Irish-based MacDonalds.

97. The politics of those who hesitated to endorse either the religious agenda of the king or the insurgency of 1638, including attempts to enlighten Charles I on the depth of feeling in Scotland, are sketched in John Scally's profile of James Hamilton, the king's principal advisor on Scottish affairs. Scally, "Counsel in Crisis: James, third Marquis of Hamilton and the Bishops' Wars, 1638–1640," in *Celtic Dimensions of the British Civil Wars*, ed. John R. Young (Edinburgh: John Donald, 1997), 18–34.

98. Donald, *Uncounseled King*, chap. 2; Rothes, *Relation of Proceedings*, 318–323; *The Government of Scotland under the Covenanters 1637–1651*, ed. David Stevenson (Edinburgh: Pub. Scottish Historical Society ser. 4 v. 18 1982), Introduction; Gardiner, *Constitutional Documents*, 124–34.

99. Donaldson, *Scotland*, 313–14; Rothes, *Relation of Proceedings*, 39.

100. Gardiner, *Constitutional Documents*, 124, 129, 133; see also Calderwood, quoted in Peter Donald, "The Scottish National Covenant and British Politics, 1638–1640," in *The Scottish National Covenant in Its British Context*, ed. John Morrill (Edinburgh: Edinburgh University Press, 1990), 90; Glenn Burgess, *British Political Thought, 1500–1660* (London: Palgrave Macmillan, 2009), 188 (noting how covenantal language enabled the insurgents to justify self-defense (p. 189).

101. Paul, *Diary of Sir Archibald Johnston*, 330–31, 327–28; Mullan, *Religious Controversy*, 132–36; Baillie, *Letters and Journals*, 1:62 (a glowingly optimistic report); Rothes, *Relation of Proceedings*, 103–10 (noting, as well, ministers who refused to read the text aloud); Balfour, *Works*, 2:270. Taking the covenant in the royal burgh of Peebles is described in Ronald Ireland, *The Bloody Covenant Crown and Kirk in Conflict* (Stroud: History Press, 2010), 96–101.

102. Rutherford, *Letters*, 128–29, 199, 570. See also Margaret Steele, "The 'Politick Christian': The Theological Background to the National Covenant," in Morrill, ed., *Scottish National Covenant in its British Context*, 51–54; Gribben, *Puritan Millennium*, 101–5.

103. Baillie, *Letters and Journals*, 1:95; Alexander Henderson, *Sermons, Prayers, and Pulpit Addresses, by Alexander Henderson, 1638*, ed. R. Thomson Martin (Edinburgh, 1867), .

104. This range of opinions may be discerned in Walter Makey, *The Church of the Covenant, 1637–1651: Revolution and Social Change in Scotland* (Edinburgh: John Donald, 1979), 9, 14–15; Lee, *Road to Revolution*, chap. 7; Williamson, *Scottish National Consciousness*, chap. 7; Macinnes, *Charles I*, chap. 7; Williamson, "The Scottish Constitution, 1638–51: The Rise and Fall of Oligarchic Centralism," in Morrill, *Scottish National Covenant*, 106–33; J. R. Young, "The Scottish parliament and the Covenanting revolution: The emer-

gence of a Scottish commons," in Young, *Celtic Dimensions*, 164–84, cautioning that the Covenant was neither fully "national or cohesive." The process of tamping down some of the language in the initial draft is noted in Rothes, *Relation of Proceedings*, 72–73.

105. Edward J. Cowan, "The Making of the National Covenant," in Morrill, *Scottish National Covenant*, 76–82; Donaldson, *Scotland*, 314 (noting the contradiction I also emphasize).

106. Rothes, *Relation of Proceedings*, 96–98. "The National Covenant was not a private league of rebellious subjects, nor even an aristocratic reaction against the personal rule of Charles I, but a nationalist manifesto asserting the independence of a sovereign people under God." Macinnes, *Charles I*, 173. The dynamics of the insurgency and, of more importance, the actual language of the National Covenant and the more proximate sources of political theology on which Archibald Johnston was relying, include George Buchanan and an early seventeenth-century Dutch theorist's justification of the revolt in the Netherlands. Cf. John Coffey, "Samuel Rutherford and the Political Thought of the Scottish Covenanters," in Young, *Celtic Dimensions, 75–95.*

107. Steele, "The 'Politick Christian': The Theological Background to the National Covenant," in Morrill, *Scottish National Covenant*, 41–43 (quotations, pp. 41, 57); Dickinson, *Knox's History of the Reformation*, 2:271; Henderson, *Sermons, Prayers, and Pulpit Addresses*, 28, 50–51, 67, 205–6, 211.

108. Peterkin, *Records of the Kirk*, 85–86.

109. Ibid., 99–106, 142–43, 147. Donald, *Uncounselled King*, chaps. 5–6, covers in detail the king's negotiations—usually at second hand—with revolutionaries and royalists in Scotland.

110. Peterkin, *Records of the Kirk*, 128–93.

111. *Diary of Sir Archibald Johnston Lord Wariston 1639*, Scottish Historical Society Publications 26 (1896), 38–39. My narrative scants the efforts of the Covenanter government to influence public opinion in England, for which see S. Waurechen, "Covenanter Propaganda and Conceptualization of the Public During the Bishops' Wars, 1638–1640," *HJ* 52 (2009): 63–86; and White, *Militant Protestantism*, chap. 4.

112. *Aberdeen before 1800: A New History*, ed. E. Patricia Dennison, David Ditchburn, and Michael Lynch (East Linton: Tuckwell, 2002), 240, 44–45. The faculty in Glasgow also rejected the Covenant. Baillie, *Letters and Journals*, 1:63, 96–97 (describing the delegation to Aberdeen).

113. Peterkin, *Records of the Kirk*, 264. See also Mullan, *Scottish Puritanism*, chap. 9 on the implications of this transition.

114. *The Remonstrance of the Nobility, Barrones, Burgesses, Ministers and Commons within the Kingdome of Scotland, Vindicating them and their proceedings from the crymes, wherewith they are charged by the late Proclamation in England, Feb. 27.* 1639 (Edinburgh, 1639). The process leading to the "Treaty of Berwick" and its various interpretations are described in Donald, *Uncounselled King*, chap. 4; and Stevenson, *Scottish Revolution*, chap. 4. The text of the treaty is included in Balfour, *Works*, 2:327–28 (one of them the king's insistence that the terms of the treaty be kept secret). Charles's uneasiness is apparent in ibid., 2:329–36.

115. Stevenson, *Government of Scotland*, intro.; Stevenson, *Scottish Revolution*, chaps. 5–6; John R. Young, "The Scottish Parliament and the Covenanting Revolution: The Emergence of a Scottish Commons," in Young, *Celtic Dimensions*, 164–81; Young, "The Scottish parliament and the Covenanting heritage of constitutional reform," in *The Stuart Kingdoms in the Seventeenth Century: Awkward Neighbors*, ed. Allan I. Macinnes and Jane Ohlmeyer (Dublin: Four Courts, 2002), 226–50.

Chapter 8. The End of the Beginning, 1640–1656

1. *The Notebooks of Nehemiah Wallington, 1618–1654: A Selection*, ed. David Booy (Aldershot: Ashgate, 2007), 125–26, 238; Caroline M. Hibbard, *Charles I and the Popish Plot* (Chapel Hill: University of North Carolina Press, 1983), 126. That a Catholic faction at court was soliciting money and possibly soldiers from Spain to help Charles I is described in ibid., chap. 5.

2. Booy, *Notebooks of Wallington*, 128–31.

3. See, e.g, Cornelius Burgess, *The First Sermon, Preached to the Honourable House of Commons . . . Novemb. 17. 1640* (London, 1641); Henry Burton, *Englands Bondage and Hope of Deliverance: A Sermon Preached before the Honourable House of Parliament* (1641); John Coffey, "England's Exodus: The Civil War as a War of Deliverance," in *England's Wars of Religion, Revisited*, ed. Charles W. A. Prior and Glenn Burgess (Aldershot: Ashgate, 2011), 253–80; John F. Wilson, *Pulpit in Parliament: Puritanism during the English Civil Wars, 1640–1648* (Princeton: Princeton University Press, 1969), chap. 6. Of the many iterations of this theme at earlier moments, Edward Dering's *A Sermon Preached before the Quenes Maiestie* (1570) stands out.

4. Goodwin, *A Glimpse of Sions Glory*, reprinted in *Puritanism and Liberty Being the Army Debates (1647–9)*, ed. A.S.P. Woodhouse (Chicago: University of Chicago Press, 1951), 233–37. Attributed to various of the Independents who decamped to the Netherlands, but usually ascribed to Goodwin, the alternatives are noted in Mark E. Bell, *Apocalypse How? Baptist Movements during the English Revolution* (Macon: Mercer University Press, 2000), 69, n. 22. See also John Coffey, *John Goodwin and the Puritan Revolution Religion and Intellectual Change in 17th-Century England* (Woodbridge: Boydell, 2006), 89; Crawford Gribben, *The Puritan Millennium: Literature and Theology 1550–1682* (Dublin: Four Courts, 2000), 48–49, 69, n. 22. This sense of the times was endorsed by Alexander Henderson in *The Unlawfulnesse and Danger of Limited Prelacie* (1641), noting that "divine Providence is about some great worke" (pp. 18–19).

5. George Gillespie, *A Sermon Preached . . . March 27, 1644*, reprinted in *Sermons Preached before the English Houses of Parliament by the Scottish Commissioners to the Westminster Assembly*, ed. Chris Coldwell (Dallas: Naphtali, 2011), 301, 304. For fuller analysis of this sermon, see Gribben, *Puritan Millennium*, chap. 5. In 1642, Samuel Rutherford poured his own sense of excitement that God was "mak[ing] us eye-witnesses of his last Marriage-glory on earth," a reference to the common cause of the two state churches, into *A peaceful and temperate plea for Pauls presbyterie in Scotland* (1642), sig. A2r.

6. Booy, *Notebooks of Wallington*, 25–26, 238, 125, 128, 129, 131, 294.

7. A story told with remarkable clarity in John Walter, *Covenanting Citizens: The Protestation Oath and Popular Political Culture in the English Revolution* (Oxford: Oxford University Press, 2017).

8. See, in general, John Morrill, "The War(s) of the Three Kingdoms," in *The New British History: Founding a Modern State, 1603–1715*, ed. Glenn Burgess (London: Tauris, 1999), 65–91, laying out the "inter-penetration of events" and how reforming the one meant disrupting the other; J. S. Morrill, "The Religious Context of the English Civil War," *Transactions of the Royal Historical Society*, 5th ser. 34 (1984): 155–78; Glenn Burgess, "Introduction: Religion and the Historiography of the English Civil War," in Prior and Burgess, *England's Wars of Religion*, 1–25 and the scholarship he cites; Conrad Russell, *Unrevolutionary England, 1603–1642* (London: Hambledon, 1990), pt. 4; and George Yule, *Puritans in Politics: The Religious Legislation of the Long Parliament 1640–1647* (Appleford: Sutton Courtenay Pres, 1976), intro. As J. P. Kenyon points out, "the pace of the crisis visibly accelerated in 1640" in response to the Bishops' Wars, the "insanely provocative . . . canons" of that year,

and the arrival of Wentworth in London, among other circumstances. Kenyon, *Stuart Constitution*, 176.

9. Hibbard, *Charles I and the Popish Plot*, chap. 8, especially 173–74, 188–89.

10. Events and attitudes traced in Michael Mendle, *Henry Parker and the English Civil War: The Political Thought of the Public's "Privado"* (Cambridge: Cambridge University Press, 1995), chaps 4–5; George Yerby, *People and Parliament Representative Rights and the English Revolution* (London: Palgrave Macmillan, 2008). That the leaders of the House of Commons had a well-thought-out program of constitutional reform was taken for granted some forty or fifty years ago. The inadequacies of this assumption are detailed in the notes and introductions to Kenyon, *Stuart Constitution*. The structural aspects of anti-Catholicism and anti-Laudianism are deftly described in John Walter, *Understanding Popular Violence in the English Revolution: The Colchester Plunderers* (Cambridge: Cambridge University Press, 1999), pts. 3 and 4.

11. Conveniently included in Gardiner, *Constitutional Documents*, 202–32; the same collection includes other measures Parliament endorsed at this time. The political and religious allegiances of the gentry are sketched in Barry Coward, "The Experience of the Gentry, 1640–1660," in R. C. Richardson, ed., *Town and Countryside in the English Revolution* (Manchester: Manchester University Press, 1992), chap. 8, emphasizing (pp. 200–201) the unity of Parliament when it came to eliminating Laudian innovations, but the gentry's moderation or conservativism when it came to abolishing an inclusive state church. Anthony Fletcher underscores the impact of "parliamentary factionalism" on an institution that depended on consensus, with late 1641 as a tipping point; Fletcher, *The Outbreak of the English Civil War* (London: Edward Arnold, 1981), chap. 4.

12. The horror stories reaching London of how Protestants were being treated, all of them exaggerating the extent and substance of inter-religious atrocities, are sampled in *The Journal of Sir Simonds D'Ewes From the First Recess of the Long Parliament to the Withdrawal of King Charles from London*, ed. Willson Havelock Coates (Hamden, CT: Archon, 1970), 283–84.

13. Kenyon, *Stuart Constitution*, 222–26.

14. Michael J. Braddick, "History, liberty, reformation and the cause: Parliamentarian military and ideological escalation in 1643," in *The Experience of Revolution in Stuart Britain and Ireland Essays for John Morrilll*, ed. Michael J. Braddick and David L. Smith (Cambridge: Cambridge University Press, 2011), 117–34.

15. David Wootton, "From rebellion to revolution: The crisis of the winter of 1642–43 and the origins of civil war radicalism" (1990); reprinted in *The English Civil War*, ed. Richard Cust and Ann Hughes (London: Arnold, 1997), chap. 13; David Scott, *Politics and War in the Three Stuart Kingdoms, 1637–49* (New York: Palgrave Macmillan, 2004), chap, 3 (quotation, p. 86). The following paragraphs radically abridge the substance of Scott's description of Parliamentary factions, war aims, the king's intentions, the political situation in Ireland, and much else. In passing, however, it should be noted that Parliamentary "Independents" and "Presbyterians" were never identical with the quasi-denominational groups I refer to under those names. Debates about who stood for what in the House of Commons may be sampled in George Yule, *The Independents in the English Civil War* (Cambridge: Cambridge University Press, 1958).

16. John Morrill, "Introduction," in Morrill, *Revolution and Restoration*, 8.

17. Morrill, "Religious Context," 11–16, making a useful distinction between "constitutionalist" and "religious" agendas of reform and how the two intersected and diverged in the 1640s. I have slightly altered the sense of Morrill's distinction.

18. Wallace Notestein, ed., *The Journal of Sir Simonds D'Ewes, From the Beginning of the Long Parliament to the Opening of the Trial of the Earl of Stafford* (New Haven: Yale

University Press, 1923), 7–8. The best guide to the politics of the popish plot in the run-up to the Long Parliament and during its early years is Hibbard, *Charles I and the Popish Plot*.

19. An overview: John Morrill, "The attack on the Church of England in the Long Parliament, 1640–42," in *History, Society and the Churches: Essays in honour of Owen Chadwick*, ed. Derek Beales and Geoffrey Best (Cambridge: Cambridge University Press, 1985), 105–24.

20. Maija Jansson et al., *Proceedings in the Opening Session of the Long Parliament*, 7 vols. (Rochester, NY: University of Rochester Press, 2000), 1:619; *Mr Grimstons Speech in Parliament upon the Accusation and Impeachment of William Laud* (1641), 2.

21. Shaw, *History of the Church*, 1:21, 47–54; Notestein, *Journal of D'Ewes*, 70–71. See also Fletcher, *Outbreak of the English Civil War*, chaps 3, 6.

22. John Rushworth, *Historical Collections . . . Third Part (1721)*, 1:93–97, 135–42; Fletcher, *Outbreak*, 92–104; Notestein, *Journal of D'Ewes*, 282; Shaw, *History of the Church*, 1, 16–27.

23. *A Copie of the Proceedings of some worthy and learned Divines, appointed by the Lords to meet at the Bishop of Lincolnes in Westminster: Touching Innovations in the Doctrine and Discipline of the Church of England, Together with considerations upon the Common Prayer Book* (London, 1641); Shaw, *History of the Church*, 1: 65–75; Notestein, *Journal of D'Ewes*, 339–42; Alan Ford, *James Ussher Theology, History, and Politics in Early-Modern Ireland and England* (Oxford: Oxford University Press, 2007), chap. 10. Petitions on behalf of episcopacy and the *Book of Common Prayer* continued to arrive; see Judith Maltby, *Prayer Book and People in Elizabethan and Early Stuart England* (Cambridge: Cambridge University Press, 1998). My narrative omits ongoing attempts by certain bishops to adapt episcopacy to practices such as toleration, a story told in part in Anthony Milton, "Coping with alternatives: religious liberty in royalist thought, 1643–47," in *Insular Christianity: Alternative models of the Church in Britain and Ireland, c. 1570–1700*, ed. Robert Armstrong and Tadhg Ó hAnnracháin (Manchester: University of Manchester Press, 2013), chap. 8.

24. Greville, *A Discourse opening the Nature of that Episcopacie, which is exercised in England* (1641); [John Milton], *Of Reformation touching Church-Discipline* (1641), the first of three tracts in which Milton assailed episcopacy; [Henry Vane], *Reasons Why the Hierarchy or Governement of the Church by Arch-Bishops . . . ought to be Removed* (1641), recalling (p. 2) the project of a "thorough reformation" in "Queen Elizabeths days" and citing the troubles at Frankfurt (p. 3).

25. William Prynne, *The Antipathie of the English Lordly Prelacie, Both to Regall Monarchy, and Civill Unity . . . the first Part* (London, 1641); [SMECTYMNUUS], *An Answer to a Booke Entituled, An Humble Remonstrance* (1641), 103, 10–12.

26. Henderson, *The Unlawfullness and Danger of Limited Prelacie, or Perpetuall Presidencie in the Church, Briefly Discovered* (n.p., 1641), sig. A2v, 1, 7, 8, 19; for other Scottish diatribes, see F. N. McCoy, *Robert Baillie and the Second Scots Reformation* (Berkeley: University of California Press, 1974), chap. 4; [Robert Baillie], *Prelacie is Miserie; or, The Suppressing of Prelaticall Goverment and establishing of Provintiall, and nationall Sinods* (1641).

27. Kenyon, *Stuart Constitution*, 17; *The Letters, Speeches and Proclamations of King Charles I*, ed. Sir Charles Petrie (London, Cassell, 1935), 117; Morris Fuller, *The Life, Times and Writings of Thomas Fuller*, 2 vols. (London, 1886), 1:281; *Letters of King Charles the First to Queen Henrietta Maria*, ed. John Bruce, Camden Society 63 (1856), 7, 19, 22–23. See also Anthony Milton, "Sacrilege and compromise: Court divines and the king's conscience, 1642–1649," in Braddick and Smith, *Experience of Revolution*, chap. 7. My narrative scants the support within Parliament for episcopacy and, especially, the *Book of Common*

Prayer and the petitions it received on behalf of both. See, e.g., Coates, *Journal of D'Ewes*, 290.

28. Parliament voted in January 1643 to abolish all aspects of episcopal office, a bill the king refused to endorse. Thereafter, its fate rested in the hands of the Westminster Assembly.

29. Anthony Fletcher, *A County Community in Peace and War: Sussex 1600–1660* (London: Longmans, 1975), 253 , 253; Burgess, *First sermon*, 38; Eales, *Puritans and Roundheads*, 104; Shaw, *History of the Church*, 1.

30. Shaw, *History of the Church*, 1:110–11; 2: chap. 4. More emerge from the sketches of ministers in A. G. Matthews, *Walker Revised: Being a Revision of John Walker's Sufferings of the Clergy during the Grand Rebellion, 1642–1660* (Oxford: Clarendon, 1948).

31. Ian Green, "The persecution of 'scandalous' and 'malignant' parish clergy during the English Civil War," *English Historical Review* 94 (1979): 507–51; Fiona McCall, "Scandalous and Malignant? Settling Scores against the Leicestershire Clergy after the First Civil War," *Midlands History* 40 (2015): 220–41 (sketching a wider variety of complaints, some justified, others not); Fiona McCall, *Baal's Priests: The Loyalist Clergy and the English Revolution* (Aldershot: Ashgate, 2013), 6–7; Christopher Durston, "Policing the Cromwellian Church: The Activities of the County Ejection Committees, 1654–1659," in *The Cromwellian Protectorate*, ed. Patrick Little (Woodbridge: Boydell, 2007), 188–205; Jim Sharpe, " 'Scandalous and Malignant Priests' in Essex: The Impact of Grassroots Puritanism," in *Politics and People in Revolutionary England: Essays on Honour of Ivan Roots* (Oxford: Blackwell, 1986), 253–73, provides local details. See also Jacqueline Eales, " 'So many sects and schisms': Religious diversity in Revolutionary Kent, 1640–60," in *Religion in Revolutionary England*, ed. Christopher Durston and Judith Maltby (Manchester: Manchester University Press, 2006), 230. The wider program is described in G. B. Tatham, *The Puritans in Power: A Study in the History of the English Church from 1640 to 1660* (Cambridge: Cambridge University Press, 1913), chaps. 4–5; Nicholas Tyacke, ed., *The History of the University of Oxford, Vol. 4: Seventeenth-Century Oxford* (Oxford: Oxford University Press, 1997), chaps. 10, 14, 15; Sarah Bedell, Patrick Collinson, and Christopher Brooke, *A History of Emmanuel College, Cambridge* (Woodbridge: Boydell, 1999), chap. 8.

32. Rushworth, *Historical Collections . . . Third Part (1721)*, 1:284; Fletcher, *Outbreak*, 109–11; Margaret Aston, "Puritans and Iconoclasm, 1560–1660," in *The Culture of English Puritanism, 1560–1700*, ed. Christopher Durston and Jacqueline Eales (New York: St. Martin's, 1996), chap. 3; Julie Spraggon, *Puritan Iconoclasm during the English Civil War* (Woodbridge: Boydell, 2003), 63, 65; Firth and Rait, *Acts and Ordinances*, 1: 265–66, 425–26; John Walters, "Abolishing Superstition with Sedition? The Politics of Popular Iconoclasm in England, 1640–1642," *Past & Present* 183 (2004): 79–123; Keith Lindley, *Popular Politics and Religion in Civil War London* (Aldershot: Scholar, 1997), chap. 2.

33. Spraggon, *Puritan Iconoclasm*, chaps. 3–7; Eales, *Puritans and Roundheads*, 115; *The Journal of William Dowsing*, ed. C. H. Evelyn White (Ipswich, 1885), 7–9; John Morrill, "William Dowsing and the Administration of Iconoclasm in the Puritan Revolution," in *The Journal of William Dowsing: Iconoclasm in East Anglia during the Civil War*, ed. Trevor Cooper (Woodbridge: Boydell and Brewer, 2001), 1–28; Morrill, "A Liberation Theology? Aspects of Puritanism in the English Revolution," in Laura Lunger Knoppers, ed., *Puritanism and Its Discontents* (Newark, DE: University of Delaware Press, 2003), 35–39; Lindley, *Popular Politics*, chap. 6. Iconoclastic practice in this period (including Scotland) is also described in Alexandra Walsham, *Reformation of the Landscape: Religion, Identity, and Memory in Early Modern Britain and Ireland* (Oxford: Oxford University Press, 2011), 125–47.

34. Morrill, "Attack on the Church of England," emphasizing the depth of hostility to

Laudianism in the early going, an argument directed at Shaw, *History of the Church*, who insisted (chap. 1) that no one really wanted presbyterianism to replace episcopacy; Rushworth, *Historical Collections . . . Third Part*, 1:385–86. The mood of the more moderate is suggested by Edward Dering's suggestion (September 1641) that "narrow is the way between papism on the one hand, and Brownism on the other." Ibid., 394.

35. Charles A. Prior, "Canons and Constitutions," in Prior and Burgess, eds., *England's Wars of Religion, Revisited*, 101–23, esp. 111; Kenyon, *Stuart Constitution*, 215.

36. Gordon Donaldson, "The emergence of schism in seventeenth-century Scotland," in *Schism, Heresy and Religious Protest*, ed. Derek Baker, Studies in Church History 9 (Cambridge: Cambridge University Press, 1972), 277–93; Henderson, *The Government and Order of the Church of Scotland* (Edinburgh, 1641), 61–62 and passim; Baillie, *Letters and Journals*, 1:305–7; "Our desires concerning unity of religion, and uniformity of church government," reprinted in W. M. Hetherington, *History of the Westminster Assembly of Divines* (New York, 1853), 301–7; Peterkin, *Records of the Kirk*, 325.

37. [Henry Burton], *Christ on his Throne; or, Christs Church-government briefly laid downe* (1640), 51, 53–55 (summary).

38. Virginia Bernhard, "Religion, Politics, and Witchcraft in Bermuda, 1651–55," *WMQ* 67 (2010): 677–708; Baillie, *Letters and Journals*, 2:204–5.

39. Ann Hughes, *Gangraena and the Struggle for the English Revolution* (Oxford: Oxford University Press, 2004). The transatlantic exchanges are summarized in Benjamin Hanbury, *Historical Memorials Relating to the Independents, or Congregationalists: From their rise to the restoration of the monarchy, A.D. MDCLX*, 3 vols. (London, 1841), vols. 2–3, and evoked in American-written biographies of John Cotton, John Davenport, and Richard Mather. Hunter Powell returns to them and, especially, the disputes that arose around Cotton, in *The crisis of British Protestantism: church power in the Puritan Revolution, 1638–44* (Manchester: Manchester University Press, 2015), chaps. 4–6. Powell also discerns a rough consensus among putative Independents and English Presbyterians as of c. 1641, a consensus George Yule extends into mid-1647 in *Puritans in Politics*, 208–11. See also Kenyon, *Stuart Constitution*, 230. In *Discord in Zion: The Puritan Divines and the Puritan Revolution* (The Hague: Martinus Nijhoff, 1973), especially chaps 2–3 and p. 33, Tai Liu argues exactly the opposite with regard to Independency.

40. G.S.S. Yule, "Puritan piety in the Long Parliament," in *Popular Belief and Practice*, ed. G. J. Cuming and Derek Baker, Studies in Church History 8 (Cambridge: Cambridge University Press, 1972), 187–94 (quotation, p. 189); Thomas Case, *Gods Rising, His Enemies Scattering* (1644), 46; Edmund Calamy, *Englands Looking-Glasse* (1642), 46–47; Thomas Wilson, *Jerichoes Down-Fall, As it was Presented in a Sermon . . . before the Honourable H of C . . . Sept. 20. 1642* (1643), 4.

41. Carol Schneider, "Godly Order in a Church Half-Reformed: The Disciplinary Legacy, 1570–1641 (PhD thesis, Harvard University, 1986), chap. 6; Fletcher, *Outbreak*, 115 and, in general, chap. 3.

42. Francis J. Bremer, *Congregational Communion: Clerical Friendship in the Anglo-American Puritan Community, 1610–1692* (Boston: Northeastern University Press, 1994), 132; Powell, *Crisis of British Protestantism*, chap. 2. The points of agreement Powell identifies could have come straight from Walter Travers's *Directory of Church-government*, a genealogy Powell overlooks. To Robert Baillie's surprise, the possibility of a middle ground on which the Scots and the more Congregational-tilting English could agree was possible as late as mid-1644. Baillie, *Letters and Journal*, 2: 230. Outside of London, however, new-style Independents were founding churches that broke with the parish model, as noted in Joel Halcomb, "A Social History of Congregational Religious Practice during the Puritan Revolution" (PhD thesis, Cambridge University, 2010), 29–30. See also Carole Schneider,

"Roots and Branches: From Principled Nonconformity to the Emergence of Religious Parties," in Bremer, ed., *Transatlantic Puritanism*, 167–200.

43. Kenyon, *Stuart Constitution*, 223 (the same proposition asked the king to "consent to laws for the taking away of innovations and superstitions, and of pluralities, and against scandalous ministers"); Fuller, *Life, Times and Writings*, 1:215; Chad Dixhoorn, ed., *The Minutes and Papers of the Westminster Assembly, 1643–1652*, 5 vols. (Oxford: Oxford University Press, 2012), 1:3–7. Dixhoorn provides an acute summary of the questions taken up by the Assembly: I: 81-88.

44. Bills to abolish episcopacy were discussed, debated, and endorsed in December 1642 and January 1643, but held in abeyance in the context of negotiations with the king.

45. The Parliamentary ordinance of July 18 cited the popish plot and announced the Westminster Assembly, but was mainly about how the Scottish army in Ireland would be paid and other arrears made good. No specific reference was made to uniformity of religion in both countries. Firth and Raitt, *Acts and Ordinances*, 1:192–202.

46. In October 1642, at a moment when the Long Parliament was hoping the king would assent to an assembly of divines, the Long Parliament insisted that it was not intending to "reject" the *Book of Common Prayer* but only to "take . . . out of it, . . . what shall be evil . . . or at least . . . unnecessary and burthensome," a policy replaced by a law abolishing its use in church services. Rushworth, *Historical Collections . . . Third Part*, 2: 47.

47. Gardiner, *Constitutional Documents*, 267–71; Baillie, *Letters and Journals*, 2:90, noting also that Alexander Henderson drafted the first version and attributing the hesitations of the English to "keeping of a doore open in England to Independencie"; Dixhoorn, *Minutes*, 1, 82. Henry Vane Jr., one of the English delegates who negotiated the new alliance, is credited with inserting the phrases "Word of God" and "according to the same Holy Word and" into Article 1 on purpose, in the hope that these would forestall any straightforward project of uniformity. In her biography of Vane, Violet A. Roper credits this story to the royalist historian Edward Hyde (Clarendon), noting that it "cannot be proved." *Sir Henry Vane the Younger* (London: Athlone, 1970), 23–24. In *Jus Divinum: The Westminster Assembly and the Divine Right of Church Government* (Kampen: Kok, 1969), J. R. De Witt cites the same phrase from other texts of the period, also to the end of discounting this story (pp. 44–50). That the ritual of taking the Covenant meant different things to different people is noted by Tai Liu. Liu, *Discord in Zion*, 26. Differences are also apparent in the documents printed as *A Letter From the Assembly of Divines in England, to the Generall Assembly in Scotland, Together with the Answer of the Generall Assembly of Scotland, Thereunto* (1643). See also Chad Dixhoorn, "Scottish influence on the Westminster assembly: A study of the synod's summoning ordinance and the Solemn League and Covenant," *RSCHS* 37 (2007): 55–88.

48. Baillie, *Letters and Journals*, 2:186; Dixhoorn, *Minutes*, 1, app. l, noting revisions by Lords and Commons in the wording of the ordinance as it was being drafted. The assertions of state authority echoed Article 21 of the Thirty-Nine Articles, which specified that "general councils" could meet only at "the commandment and will of princes."

49. Invitations were extended to a few bishops and ministers associated with episcopacy, but with a single (brief) exception, no one of this persuasion turned up. Dixhoorn, *Minutes*, 1, Biographical dictionary (pp. 106–47).

50. Dixhoorn, *Minutes*, 1, apps. 45, 15. The text of December 1644 was published in London and Edinburgh in 1647 as *Propositions concerning church-government*. Initially, Parliament rejected the assembly's advice about ordination, but protests by the Scots and a petition from most of the ministers in London saved the day. Baillie, *Letters and Journals*, 2: 198, 221.

51. Shaw, *History of the Church*, vol. 1, chap. 2, details the workings of the assembly, a

story also told in Benjamin Breckinridge Warfield, *The Westminster Assembly and Its Work* (1932; repr., Grand Rapids: Baker, 2003), chap. 2. Parliament edited the Propositions (finally published in 1647) in the version endorsed by the assembly, stripping sections on church censures, synods, councils, divorce and the like. For details, see Walker, *Creeds and Platforms*, 350 n. 5.

52. Peterkin, *Records of the Kirk*, 419; James Hasting Nichols, *Corporate Worship in the Reformed Tradition* (Philadelphia: Westminster, 1968), 99–103, 421–22. As Nichols points out, the leaders of the kirk tweaked what was specified about administering Holy Communion, specifying that "congregations be still tried and examined before the Communion" and a "Sermon of Preparation" be preached the day before.

53. *A Directory for the Publique Worshp of God* (1646), 20–21; Alan Clifford, "The Westminster Directory of Public Worship," in *The Reformation of Worship: Papers read at the 1989 Westminster Conference* (London: Westminster Conference, 1989), 53–75; Gordon Donaldson, "Covenant to Revolution," *Studies in the History of Worship in Scotland*, ed. Duncan B. Forrester and Douglas M. Murray (Edinburgh: T&T Clark, 1984), 52–64; Firth and Raitt, *Acts and Ordinances*, 1:582.

54. De Witt, *Jus Divinum*, 67–69; Powell, *Crisis of British Protestantism*, chap. 3 (arguing that there were "various Presbyterian positions" and pointing out that the Independents had their own version of a visible catholic church).The debate on the keys may be sampled in Dixhoorn, *Minutes*, 2, sessions 84–86.

55. Dixhoorn, *Minutes*, 2: sessions 161–75; De Witt, *Jus Divinum*, pt. 2.

56. Hetherington, *Westminster Assembly*, 175; Shaw, *History of the Church*, chap. 2; William M. Abbott, "Ruling Eldership in Civil War England, the Scottish Kirk, and Early New England: A Comparative Study of Secular and Spiritual Aspects," *Church History* 75 (2006): 38–68; Baillie, *Letters and Journals*, 2:205.

57. Dixhoorn, *Minutes*, 5:128; Baillie, *Letters and Journals*, 2:205, 236.

58. Dixhoorn, *Minutes*, 5:133; 1:31. An enduring anxiety about protecting the sacrament seems to have flared up anew in the early 1640s; see, e.g., John Owen, *The Principles of the Doctrine of Christ . . . the knowledge whereof is required . . . before any person be admitted to the sacrament of the Lords Suppe*r (1645).

59. Dixhoorn, *Minutes*, 3:99–123; l:31–34; Hetherington, *Westminster Assembly*, chap. 4; Baillie, *Letters and Journals*, 2:267, 307, 315; Yule, *Puritans in Politics*, chap. 7. Ofir Haivry objects to casual references to "erastianism" as if Selden were disassociating church and state. Haivry, *John Selden and the Western Political Tradition* (Cambridge: Cambridge University Press, 2017), chap. 10. See also William Lamont, *Marginal Prynne, 1600–1669* (London: Routledge and Kegan Paul, 1963), chap. 7. After some indecision, the Independent members of the Assembly had supported the premise that Scripture provided a *jure divino* model of church government. De Witt, *Jus Divinum*, 148.

60. De Witt, *Jus Divinum*, passim. The core of his argument is summarized in De Witt, "The Form of Church Government," in *To Glorify and Enjoy God: A Commemoration of the 350th Anniversary of the Westminster Assembly*, ed. John L. Carson and David W. Hall (Edinburgh: Banner of Truth Trust, 1994), 145–68.

61. William Prynne, *A Vindication of foure Serious Questions of Grand Importance* (London, 1645); De Witt, *Jus Divinum*, 112; Milton, "On the enforcers of conscience under the Long Parliament"; Gribben, *Puritan Millennium*, chap. 6; Robert Baillie, *An Historical Vindication of the Government of the Church of Scotland* (1646), 15–17 (responding as well to complaints about the strictness of moral discipline and accusations that people were excommunicated in large numbers); *Sion College: What it is, and doeth* (London, 1648), 1.

62. Gillespie, *Aarons Rod Blossoming: or, The Divine Ordinance of Church-Government*,

Vindicated (1646), sig. a2v. See also Ann Hughes, "'The remembrance of sweet fellowship': Relationships between English and Scottish Presbyterians in the 1640s and 1650s," in Armstrong and Ó hAnnracháin, *Insular Christianity*, chap. 9.

63. Lucidly described in Chad Van Dixhoorn, "Politics and religion in the Westminster Assembly and the 'grand debate,'" in Armstrong and Ó hAnnracháin, eds., *Insular Christianity*, 129–48. As Warfield emphasizes (*Westminster Assembly*, 40 n. 78), Parliament "was of the strongest conviction, in even its most Puritan element, that the Church derived all its authority and jurisdiction from the State."

64. Firth and Raitt, *Acts and Ordinances*, 1, 879–83; Baillie, *Letters and Journals*, 2:377; Robert Dale, *History of English Congregationalism* (London, 1907) 295–96; de Witt, "The Form of Church Government."

65. Anonymous; attributed on title page to "sundry ministers," and sometimes assigned to Edmund Calamy. See also James Durham, *The Dying Man's Testament to the Church of Scotland* (Edinburgh, 1659), chap. 13; "The humble remonstrance and Petition of the Lord Mayor" urging Parliament not to "let loose the Golden Reins of Discipline and Government in the Church" and to suppress "all private and separate Congregations," quoted in Raymond Phineas Stearns, *The Strenuous Puritan: Hugh Peters, 1598–1660* (Urbana: University of Illinois Press, 1954), 285. This campaign is described more fully in Sarah Mortimer, *Reason and Religion in the English Revolution The Challenge of Socinianism* (Cambridge: Cambridge University Press, 2010), chap. 7, and Hughes, *Gangraena*, chap 5.

66. "Thomas Shepard to Hugh Peter," *American Historical Review* 4 (1898): 105–7; Yule, *Puritans in Politics*, 226–28. John Goodwin became a central figure on the anti-presbyterian, pro-toleration side in this back-and-forth, for which see John Coffey, *John Goodwin and the Puritan Revolution: Religion and Intellectual Change in 17th-Century England* (Woodbridge: Boydell, 2006), chaps. 4–5. For a fuller inventory of printed and spoken examples of heresiography, see Hughes, *Gangraena*, chap. 4. Like so many others touched on in this book, the categories used by modern historians to describe these people are often off the mark. Leo Damrosch offers telling examples in *The Sorrows of the Quaker Jesus: James Naylor and the Puritan Crackdown on the Free Spirit* (Cambridge, MA: Harvard University Press, 1996), 6–14. Portent-mongering aimed at women is described in Julie Crawford, *Marvelous Protestantism: Monstrous Births in Post-Reformation England* (Baltimore: Johns Hopkins University Press, 2005), chap. 4.

67. Immediately after it assembled in July 1643, the Westminster Assembly was warning Parliament that "Swearing and Drunkenness" were increasing, as were "Fornication, Adultery, and Incest" and the "Prophanation of . . . the Lords-Day." Alarmist rhetoric of this kind should be taken with a large grain of salt, but it seems likely that, with formal means of discipline in abeyance, popular behavior was deteriorating. Rushworth, *Historical Collections . . . Fourth Part*, 1:344; *Historical Collections . . . Third Part*, 2:344. For an overview: Christopher Durston, "Puritan Rule and the Failure of Cultural Revolution, 1645–1660," in Durston and Jacqueline Eales, eds., *Culture of English Puritanism*, chap. 7; Durston, "'Preaching and sitting still on Sundays': The Lord's Day during the English Revolution," in *Religion in Revolutionary England*, ed. Christopher Durston and Judith Maltby (Manchester: University of Manchester Press, 2006), 205–25. Bernard Capp opens *England's Cultural Wars: Puritan Reform and Its Enemies in the Interregnum, 1649–1660* (Oxford: Oxford University Press, 2012) with the story of a rector in Kent at war with his parisioners over godly discipline. Other stories of failure follow, alongside some of relative success.

68. Ann Hughes, "'The public profession of these nations': the national Church in Interregnum England," in Durston and Maltby, *Religion in Revolutionary England*, 93–114;

Judith Maltby, "Suffering and surviving: The civil wars, the Commonwealth and the formation of 'Anglicanism,' ," in ibid., 158–80; Judith Maltby, " 'The Good Old Way': Prayer Book Protestantism in [the] 1640s and 1650s," in *The Church and the Book*, ed. R. N. Swanson, Studies in Church History 38 (Woodbridge: Boydell, 2004), 233–56. See also Ann Hughes, "The Frustrations of the Godly," in *Revolution and Restoration: England in the 1650s*, ed. John Morrill (London: Collins and Brown, 1992), chap. 4; Christopher Durston, " 'Preaching and Sitting Still on Sundays': The Lord's Day during the English Revolution," in Durston and Maltby, *Religion in Revolutionary England*, 205–25.

69. *The Autobiography of Richard Baxter*, ed. N. H. Keeble (London: Dent, 1974), chap. 7. See, in general, Shaw, *History of the Church*, 2, chaps. 3 and 4; Wilfred W. Biggs, "The Controversy Concerning Free Admission to the Lord's Supper," *Transactions of the Congregational Historical Society* 16 (1949–951): 176–89; Yule, *Puritans in Politics*, app. 2 ("The Extent of the Presbyterian System"); Charles E. Surman, "Presbyterianism under the Commonwealth: The Wicksworth Classis Minutes, 1651–1658," *Transactions of the Congregational Historical Society* 15 (1945–48): 163–76; M. C. Cross, "Achieving the Millennium: The Church in York during the Commonwealth," in *The Province of York*, ed. G. J. Cuming, Studies in Church History 4 (Leiden: Brill, 1967), 122–42.

70. *The Diary of Thomas Larkham, 1647–1669*, ed. Susan Hardman Moore, Church of England Record Society 17 (Woodbridge: Boydell, 2011), intro.; Paul Chang-Ha Lim, *In Pursuit of Purity, Unity, and Liberty Richard Baxter's Puritan Ecclesiology in Its Seventeenth-Century Context* (Leiden: Brill, 2004), 92–93; *The Autobiography of Henry Newcome, M.A.*, ed. Richard Parkinson, 2 vols., Chetham Society 27 (1857), 1:16, 20, 25 (preaching a preparation sermon); Coffey, *John Goodwin*, 102–7; W. J. Sheils, "Oliver Heywood and His Congregation," in *Voluntary Religion*, ed. W. J. Sheils and Diana Wood, Studies in Church History 23 (Oxford: Blackwell, 1986), 261–78. The Presbyterians' premise that the church was inclusive made it next to impossible for them to ally with Independents who regarded it as gathered—in Presbyterian eyes, a version of Separatism.

71. Derek Hirst, "The Failure of Godly Rule in the English Republic," *Past & Present* 132 (1991): 33–66; Alex Craven, " 'Contrarie to the Directorie': Presbyterians and People in Lancashire, 1646–53," in *Discipline and Diversity*, ed. Kate Cooper and Jeremy Gregory, Studies in Church History 43 (Woodbridge: Boydell, 2007), 331–41.

72. *Autobiography of Richard Baxter*, 79–81, 83, pt. 2, chap. 1. Baxter's religious politics are carefully described in Lim, *In Pursuit of Purity, Unity, and Liberty*.

73. Sectary as a pejorative antedates the 1640s, appearing, for example, in Visitation Articles of the Elizabethan period.

74. *The Sermons of the Right Reverend Robert Sanderson* (1840), 235. The most insightful description of the heresiographers is Hughes, *Gangraena*, which also covers (chap. 3) the turmoil produced by itinerant ministers elsewhere in England. For an overview of Baptist women who preached, see Curtis W. Freeman, *A Company of Women Preachers: Baptist Prophetesses in Seventeenth-Century England: A Reader* (Waco: Baylor University Press, 2011), Introduction.

75. Lindley, *Popular Politics*, chap. 4; Valerie Pearl, *London and the Outbreak of the Puritan Revolution: City Government and National Politics, 1625–1642* (Oxford: Oxford University Press, 1961).

76. Rushworth, *Historical Collections . . . Third Part* (1691), 1:144; Michael J. Braddick, "Prayer Book and Protestation: Anti-Popery, Anti-Puritanism and the Outbreak of the English Civil War" (describing the outburst of petitions, the founding of the first newsbook, and other aspects of a near-revolution in the world of print) in Prior and Burgess, eds., *England's Wars of Religion,*, 125–146; Walter, *Understanding Popular Violence*,

and, especially, John Walter, *Covenanting Citizens: The Protestation Oath and Popular Political Culture in the English Revolution* (Oxford: Oxford University Press, 2017). See also Jason Peacey, *Print and Public Politics in the English Revolution* (Cambridge: Cambridge University Press, 2013). These studies built in various ways on Lindley, *Popular Politics.*

77. Figures I owe to Joad Raymond, *Pamphlets and Pamphleteering in Early Modern Britain* (Cambridge: Cambridge University Press, 2003), 163. See also the essays included in *News, Newspapers, and Society in Early Modern Britain*, ed. Joad Raymond (London: Frank Cass, 1999). David Zaret has somewhat lower figures, though he is just as emphatic about the jump in scale: Zaret, *Origins of Democratic Culture: Printing, Petitions, and the Public Sphere in Early-Modern England* (Princeton: Princeton University Press, 2000), especially chaps. 7–8. There is room for disagreement about the birth of a "public sphere" or "public opinion"; for an argument that this antedates the 1640s, see Pauline Croft, "The Reputation of Robert Cecil: Libels, Political Opinions and Political Awareness in the early Seventeenth Century," *Transactions of the Royal Historical Society*, 6th ser. 1 (1991): 43–69. The distinctiveness of the 1640s is emphasized in Braddick, "History, liberty, reformation, and the cause," 122–24. Parliamentary attempts to reestablish licensing are noted in Firth and Rait, *Acts and Ordinances*, 1:184–86.

78. Raymond, *Pamphlets and Pamphleteering*, 157 (quoting *The Humble Remonstrance of the Company of Stationers* [1643]). The actual quantity is less dramatic than these numbers suggest. Production measured by sheet count remained unchanged, but the shift to pamphlets enabled printers to publish more titles.

79. Yule, *Puritans in Politics*, 216; Crawford Gribben, *John Owen and English Puritanism Experiences of Defeat* (Oxford: Oxford University Press, 2016), 67; J. C. Davis, "The Levellers and Christianity," in *Politics, Religion and the English Civil War*, ed. Brian Manning (London: Edward Arnold, 1973), 225–40; John Coffey, "Puritanism and Liberty Revisited: The Case for Toleration in the English Revolution," in *Heresy, Literature and Politics in Early Modern British Culture*, ed. David Loewenstein and John Marshall (Cambridge: Cambridge University Press, 2006), chap. 5. Hence the first printings in London or first openly printed version of the Mar-prelate tracts, the end-time speculations of Thomas Brightman, the story of the "troubles" at Frankfurt in the 1550s, the "Antinomian" theologizing of John Eaton and others (see chap. 9) transferred from manuscript to print, and Walter Travers's description of church government.

80. The ever-shifting tides of opinion about these groups is touched on in Jason Peacey, "The parliamentary context of political radicalism in the English revolution," in *Radical Voices, Radical Ways: Articulating and Disseminating Radicalism in Seventeenth- and Eighteenth-Century Britain*, ed. Laurent Curelly and Nigel Smith (Manchester: Manchester University Press, 2016), 151–69; Peacey's endnotes cite a range of recent opinion. As Ann Hughes points out, "historians" are generally "more excited by sectaries who took Calvinist ideas to radical conclusions" than they are by "the orthodox godly" who seem too "elitist" and preach a "complex theology of despair." Hughes, "Frustrations of the Godly," 76.

81. Edwards's career is sketched in Hughes, *Gangraena*, 31–54; Edwards, *Reasons against the Independant Government of Particular Congregations: As also, against the Toleration of such Churches to be erected in this Kingdom* (1641), sig. *2v.

82. Baillie, *Letters and Journals*, 2:216; Paul C. H. Lim, *Mystery Unveiled: The Crisis of the Trinity in Early Modern England* (Oxford: Oxford University Press, 2012), 89.

83. The authoritative study of how he came by his stories is Hughes, *Gangraena*, esp. chap. 2.

84. Edwards *Gangraena*, sig. a1v, 23, 27, 84, 86–87; Hughes, *Gangreana*, 96. It has been estimated that as many as three hundred women assumed the mantle of prophetess; see,

e.g, Patricia Crawford, "Women's Published Writings 1600–1700," in *Women in English Society, 1500–1800*, ed. Mary Prior (London: Methuen, 1985), 211–82.

85. Edwards, *Gangraena*, 25, 28–31.

86. As noted by Christopher Hill, *The World Turned Upside Down: Radical Ideas during the Puritan Revolution* (New York: Viking, 1972), 149; see also *The testimony of William Erbery, left upon Record for the Saints of succeeding Ages* (1658).

87. John Clarke, *Ill-Newes from New-England* (1652), reprinted in *Collections of the Massachusetts Historical Society*, 4th ser. 2 (1854): 19.

88. Torrance Kirby, "Apocalyptics and Apologetics: Richard Helgerson on Elizabethan England's Religious Identity and the Formation of the Public Sphere," in *Forms of Association Making Publics in Early Modern Europe*, ed. Paul Yachin and Marlene Eberhart (Amherst: University of Massachusetts Press, 2015), 58–73; Peter Lake, "Puritanism, Familism, and Heresy in early Stuart England: The case of John Etherington revisited," in Loewenstein and Marshall, *Heresy, Literature and Politics*, chap. 4; Phyllis Mack, *Visionary Women: Ecstatic Prophecy in Seventeenth-Century England* (Berkeley: University of California Press, 1992), chap. 3; Mark E. Bell, *Apocalypse How? Baptist Movements during the English Revolution* (Macon: Mercer University Press, 2000), chap. 2. Foxe had embedded a dispensationalist reading of history in the *Book of Martyrs*, for which see John N. King, *Foxe's Book of Martyrs and Early Modern Print Culture* (Cambridge: Cambridge University Press, 2006), 38–39. Essential background is provided by Geffrey F. Nuttall, *The Holy Spirit in Puritan Faith and Experience* (Oxford: Blackwell, 1946); see especially pp. 18–19, and chaps. 3, 6, and 7.

89. R. J. Acheson, *Radical Puritans in England, 1550–1660* (London: Longman, 1990), 61–63; J. Stanley Lemons, "Roger Williams: Not a Seeker But a 'Witness in Sackcloth'," *NEQ* 88 (2015): 693–714.

90. That Quakerism was different in kind from Puritanism is argued in Melvin B. Endy Jr., "Puritanism, Spiritualism, and Quakerism: An Historiographical Essay," in *The World of William Penn*, ed. Richard S. Dunn and Mary Maples Dunn (Philadelphia: University of Pennsylvania Press, 1986), chap. 16.

91. *The Journal of George Fox: A revised edition*, ed. John L. Nickalls (London: Religious Society of Friends, 1952), 24; Hugh Barbour and Arthur O. Roberts, eds., *Early Quaker Writings, 1650–1700* (Grand Rapids: Eerdmans, 1973), 93; John R. Knott Jr., *The Sword of the Spirit: Puritan Responses to the Bible* (Chicago: University of Chicago Press, 1980), 34. See, in general, Christopher Hill, *The English Bible and the Seventeenth-Century Revolution* (London: Allen Lane Penguin, 1993) and, more concretely, Andrew Bradstock, "Digging, Levelling, and Brawling": The Bible and the Civil War Sects," in *The Oxford Handbook of the Bible in Early Modern England, c. 1530–1700*, ed. Kevin Lilleen, Helen Smith, and Rachel Willie (Oxford: Oxford University Press, 2015), 397–411. In *The Light in Their Consciences: Early Quakers in Britain, 1646–1666* (University Park: Pennsylvania State University Press, 2000), chaps. 1–2, Rosemary Moore notes the presence of Quaker-like attitudes as early as the mid-1640s.

92. The full story is told in William C. Braithwaithe, *The Beginnings of Quakerism* (London, 1912).

93. Stephen Wright, *The Early English Baptists, 1603–1649* (Woodbridge: Boydell, 2006), chaps. 1–2; Murray Tolmie, *The Triumph of the Saints: The Separate Churches of London, 1616–1649* (Cambridge: Cambridge University Press, 1977), chaps. 3–4; Bell, *Apocalypse How?* chaps. 3, 6, and pt. 3, chaps. 9–11 (covering Seventh-Day Baptists and other splinter groups); Winthrop, *Journal*, 286. For the rest of his long life, Williams never affiliated with a congregation or church.

94. Wright, *Early English Baptists*, 89–95, 120–21, noting also (p. 127) the pressures on

the group to reaffirm something akin to orthodoxy in response to the Westminster Assembly; Matthew C. Bingham, "English Baptists and the Struggle for Theological Authority, 1642–1646," *JEH* 68 (2017): 546–69.

95. *Confessions of Faith, and Other Public Documents . . . of the Baptist Churches of England in the 17th Century*, ed. Edward Bean Underhill (London, 1854), 27–48 (the 1646 version); Bell, *Apocalypse How?*, chaps. 4–5. Stephen Wright and Bell agree that the Confession did not speak for everyone.

96. The Levellers were suppressed by the government in 1649, and the Fifth Monarchists were largely ignored by Cromwell.

97. A figure I owe to Halcomb, "Social History of Congregationalist Religious Practice." Cromwell became directly involved in securing the right kind of ministers for Ireland, where every minister who took over a parish or congregation was paid by the state. In 1650 he appealed to the ministry in New England to move there, and in 1651 the Irish government wrote John Cotton to the same end. Eventually, two of Richard Mather's sons, Samuel and Increase, took up posts in the country, as did Thomas Patient, who stayed only briefly in New England before returning to England and becoming a prominent Baptist. St. John D. Seymour, *The Puritans in Ireland, 1647–1661* (Oxford: Clarendon, 1969), 62–63.

98. [Henry Burton], *Christ on his Throne* (1640), 52–58, sig. C[1]4; Edwards, *Reasons against the Independant Government of Particular Congregations*; *The Correspondence of John Owen (1616–1683) With an account of his life and work*, ed. Peter Toon (Cambridge: James Clarke, 1970), 19–20; Geoffrey F. Nuttall, *Visible Saints: The Congregational Way, 1640–1660* (Oxford: Basil Blackwell, 1957), "Historical Introduction." Connections forged in England among the ministers who left for New England and those who brought Independency into being in England are sketched in Francis J. Bremer, *Congregational Communion: Clerical Friendship in the Anglo-American Puritan Community, 1610–1692* (Boston: Northeastern University Press, 1994), chap. 6. See also Powell, *Crisis of British Protestantism*, chaps. 4–6; Polly Ha, "Religious Toleration and Ecclesiastical Independence in Revolutionary Britain, Bermuda and the Bahamas," *Church History* 84 (2015): 807–27. Owen's understanding of the church and his unwavering insistence on the regulative principle are described in Graham Harrison, "John Owen's Doctrine of the Church," in *John Owen—The Man and His Theology*, ed. Robert W. Oliver (Phillipsburg, NJ.: Evangelical Press, 2002), 157–89.

99. Robert S. Paul, *An Apologeticall Narration* (Philadelphia: United Church, 1963), 10, 3–4, 24, 11–12; Coffey, *John Goodwin*, 123. See also Nuttall, *Visible Saints*, chaps. 3–4; Wright, *Early English Baptists, 1603–1649*, 111–13. Yule, *Independents*, 61, pointing out how much of a "composite" (if political views are included) they were.

100. William L. Sachse, "The Migration of New Englanders to England, 1640–1660," *American Historical Review* 51 (1948): 251–78; Bremer, *Congregational Communion*, passim; Susan Hardman Moore, " 'Pure folkes' and the Parish: Thomas Larkham in Cockermouth and Tavistock," in Wood, *Life and Thought*, 489–509. My narrative omits shifts in practice and principle that moved some Independents (or, in New England, Congregationalists) closer to moderate Presbyterians, a story touched on in Hall, *FS*, 118–19; Bremer, *Congregational Communion*, chap. 8; and in chapter 9, sec. 3, below.

101. Coffey, *John Goodwin*, 59–61.

102. Ibid., 61; Katherine Chidley, *The Justification of the Independent Churches of Christ* (1641), "To the Christian Reader," 5, 24–25. The longer history of the Chidleys and their son Daniel as activists is described in Ian Gentles, "London Levellers in the English Revolution: The Chidleys and Their Circle," *JEH* 29 (1978): 282–309; and Peter Elliott,

"Dueling Ecclesiologies: 1640s Religious Independency in Katherine Childley's Separatism vs. Thomas Edwards's Presbyterianism," *Journal of Religious History* 41 (2017): 326–45. See also Murray Tolmie, *The Triumph of the Saints: The Separate Churches of London, 1616–1649* (Cambridge: Cambridge University Press, 1977), chap. 5.

103. Edward Bean Underhill, ed., *The Records of a Church of Christ Meeting in Broadmead, Bristol, 1640–1687* (London, 1847), 1–19.

104. Ibid., 18; Claire Cross, "'He-Goats before the Blocks': A Note on the Part Played by Women in the Founding of Some Civil War Churches," in *Popular Belief and Practice*, ed. G. J. Cuming and Derek Baker, Studies in Church History 8 (Cambridge: Cambridge University Press, 1972), 195–203.

105. John Rogers, *Ohel or Beth-shemesh* (London, 1653), 15, 19–20, 50–58, 1. See also Gribben, *Puritan Millennium*, chap. 7; Gribben, *God's Irishmen: Theological Debates in Cromwellian Ireland* (Oxford: Oxford University Press, 2007), 57–59.

106. Yule, *Puritans in Politics*, 209–10; Williams, quoted in Yule, *Independents*, 10. As Blair Worden has pointed out, "The Independents . . . were not committed to the principle, [as] became evident at those moments when . . . they sought to make common cause with the Presbyterians against the sectaries." Worden, "Toleration and the Cromwellian Protectorate," in *Persecution and Tolerance*, ed. W. J. Sheils, Studies in Church History 21 (Oxford: Blackwells, 1984), 206, n. 29. (For more on toleration as it was endorsed or qualified by Independents, see chap. 9.) On the other hand, John Goodwin was a "radical" when it came to toleration, as noted in Coffey, *John Goodwin*, 112. In chapter 1 of *Puritans in Politics*, Yule finds it necessary to divide the Independents into various groupings; his are politically driven, to the end of sorting out the role of the Independents in the Long Parliament and afterwards. His nuanced understanding of their policy of toleration has influenced this paragraph. He instances, for example, the assumption among moderate Independents that the Old and New Testaments were really a whole, an argument rejected by Roger Williams, the Baptists, and the Levellers (p. 72). That there was no *necessary* relationship between Independency and toleration is demonstrated by the practice of the New England colonists.

107. Bremer, *Congregational Communion*, chap. 8, noting also certain moments of cooperation between Presbyterians and Congregationalists; W. R. Owens, "'Antichrist must be Pulled Down': Bunyan and the Millennium," in *John Bunyan and His England, 1628–88*, ed. Anne Laurence, W. R. Owens, and Stuart Sim (London: Hambledon, 1990), 77–94; Liu, *Discord in Zion*, chap. 3.

108. Coward, "Experience of the Gentry," 211. Fifth Monarchist and Quaker outbursts of apocalypticism and Cromwell's reaction to the first of these, especially, are described in Katharine Gillespie, "Prophecy and Political Expression in Cromwellian England," in *The Oxford Handbook of Literature and the English Revolution*, ed. Laura Lunger Knoppers (Oxford: Oxford University Press, 2012), chap. 24.

109. Mortimer, *Reason and Religion in the English Revolution*, chap. 7 (tracing the tensions between toleration as Owen and others understood it and hopes for some sort of boundaries). Owen spelled out his understanding of the role of the state in a statement (1649) summarized in Peter Toon, ed., *Correspondence of John Owen*, 28–29.

110. Ann Hughes, "The Frustrations of the Godly," in Morrill, *Revolution and Restoration*, chap. 4; Mortimer, *Reason and Religion*, chap. 8; Liu, *Discord in Zion*, chap. 4. See also Margaret James, "The Political Significance of the Tithes Controversy in the English Revolution, 1640–1660," *History* 26 (1941–42): 1–18; Moore, *Diary of Thomas Larkham*, 19.

111. Walker, *Creeds and Platforms*, chap. 12.

112. Laura A. M. Stewart sketches "the collapse of consensus" in Edinburgh, a process

driven in part by the extraordinary financial needs of the Covenanter government and the success of the Engagers who came to power at the end of 1647, in *Urban Politics and the British Civil Wars Edinburgh, 1617-53* (Leiden: Brill, 2006), chap. 7. See also Allan I. Macinnes, "Scottish Gaeldom, 1638-1651: The Vernacular Response to the Covenanting Dynamic," in *New Perspectives on the Politics and Culture of Early Modern Scotland*, ed. John Dwyer, Roger A. Mason, and Alexander Murdoch (Edinburgh: John Donald, 1982), 59-94.

113. John R. Young, *The Scottish Parliament, 1539-1661: A Political and Constitutional Analysis* (Edinburgh: John Donald, 1996), 94.

114. Peterkin, *Records of the Kirk*, 434-35; Baillie, *Letters and Journal*, 2:255-57; Baillie expressed his unhappiness with the pace of reform and the unwillingness of Parliament to suppress errors in fast-day sermons he preached in 1644 and 1645, summarized in McCoy, *Robert Baillie*, 101-4.

115. For Samuel Rutherford's pessimistic comments on the Long Parliament and popular willingness to ignore idolatry, see *The Trial and Triumph of Faith* (1645; repr., Edinburgh: Banner of Truth Trust, 2001), 8-9.

116. Crawford Gribben, "The Church of England and the English Apocalyptic Imagination, 1630-1650," *Scottish Historical Review* 88 (2009): 34-56; Edwards, *Gangraena*, pt. 1, 43, 49 (citing speeches by Independents).

117. David Stevenson, *Revolution and Counter-Revolution in Scotland, 1644-1651* (London: Royal Historical Society, 1977), 19-54, 82-85; Mark Napier, *Memoirs of the Marquis of Montrose*, 2 vols. (Edinburgh, 1856), 1: app. (p. 52).

118. Stevenson, *Revolution and Counter-Revolution*, 27-28, 41-42, 46-47; John R. Young, "The Covenanters and the Scottish Parliament, 1639-51: The Rule of the Godly and the 'Second Scottish Reformation,'" in *Enforcing Reformation in Ireland and Scotland, 1550-1700*, ed. Elizabethanne Boran and Crawford Gribben (Aldershot: Ashgate, 2006), chap. 5; Young, *Scottish Parliament, 1639-1661*, 137; *The Records of the Commissions of the General Assemblies*, ed. Alexander F. Mitchell and James Christie, 3 vols., Publications of the Scottish Historical Society, 11, 25, and 58 (1892-1909), 1:33; 37-38.

119. Rushworth, *Historical Collections, . . . Fourth Series, One*, 253-54. My narrative omits most of the details of a very complex politics which descended into accusations (not without reason) that one faction of Scots was conspiring with the king against the Long Parliament. The details may be followed in Stevenson, *Revolution and Counter-Revolution*.

120. Thomas M'Crie, *The Life of Mr. Robert Blair* (Edinburgh, 1848), 185-95; *The Papers Which passed First between his Majesty and Mr. Alexander Henderson at Newcastle, An. Dom. 1646*, included in *Reliquae Sacrae Carolinae* (The Hague, 1650). The Newcastle Propositions are excerpted in Gee and Hardy, *Documents*, 567-69.

121. Peterkin, *Records of the Kirk*, 450-52, 468-72.

122. John Coffey, *Politics, Religion and the British Revolutions: The Mind of Samuel Rutherford* (Cambridge: Cambridge University Press, 1997), 247; chap. 6.

123. Mitchell and Christie, *Records of the Commissions*, 1:79-97.

124. Baillie, *Letters and Journals*, 3:18; Rushworth, *Historical Collections . . Fourth Series, Part Two*, 769-70; Gordon Donaldson, *Scottish Historical Documents* (Edinburgh: Scottish Academic Press, 1970), 214-18.

125. Stevenson, *Revolution and Counterrevolution*, 96-97, 113, and chap. 3; McCoy, *Robert Baillie*, chap. 8; Gardiner, *Constitutional Documents*, 347-52; Young, *Scottish Parliament*, chap. 8; Peterkin, *Records of the Kirk*, 496-505; Mitchell and Christie, *Records of the Commissions*, 2:10, arguing also (pp. 18-19) that Hamilton and his allies were interfering with the kirk's privilege of deciding cases of conscience.

126. Stevenson, *Revolution and Counter-Revolution*, 123–25, 130–31; Stevenson, "Deposition of Ministers in the Church of Scotland under the Covenanters, 1638–51," *Church History* 40 (1975): 321–35 (documenting the breadth of the purge in 1649–50); Young, *Scottish Parliament*, chaps. 9–11; Peterkin, *Records of the Kirk*, 587–90; Balfour, *Works*, 4:20; Baillie, *Letters and Journals*, 2:451.

127. Balfour, *Works*, 4:67, 93–94, 98–102. In the circle of royalists gathered around the young king, it was said that signing the covenant would make him guilty of his father's execution. Ibid., 523.

128. The sorry tale of Charles II's dealings with the Scottish government and its with him may be followed in *Letters and Papers Illustrating the Relations between Charles the Second and Scotland in 1650*, ed. Samuel Rawson Gardiner (Edinburgh, 1894); the documents assembled in Balfour, *Works*, 4; and *Diary of Archibald Johnston of Wariston, 1650–54*, vol. 2, ed. D. H. Fleming (Edinburgh: Scottish Historical Society, 1919).

129. Balfour, *Works*, 4:92–94, to which he added (pp. 92–93) the pledge that he had "sincerely" signed the Covenant and would "have no friends or enemies, but these of the covenant."

130. Balfour, *Works*, 4:99–103.

131. For the larger story of non-presbyterian initiatives, see, in part, W. Ivan Joyh, "The Entry of Sects into Scotland," in *Reformation and Revolution*, ed. Duncan Shaw (Edinburgh: St. Andrews, 1967), 178–211. As early as 1640, some ministers and parishes in the southwest were adopting free-form prayer and other practices, to the dismay of the General Assembly. See, e.g., Sharon Adams, "The Making of the Radical South-West: Charles I and his Scottish Kingdom, 1625–1649," in *Celtic Dimensions of the British Civil Wars*, ed. John R. Young (Edinburgh: John Donald, 1997), chap. 4. My narrative does not include the "western" or "Whiggamore" protest against the alliance with the king, which is partly documented in Balfour, *Works* 4:141–60.

132. Young, *Scottish Parliament*, chap. 12; Balfour, *Works*, 4:88, 278, 298. The penalizing of malignants may be followed in ibid., vols. 3–4, a process often marked by dissent among the nobility about how severe the penalties should be.

133. R. Scott Spurlock, *Cromwell and Scotland: Conquest and Religion, 1650–1660* (Edinburgh: John Donald, 2007), is an excellent account of this entire period. For several years, "no Communions" took place in Glasgow because of infighting about the "grounds of seclusion." Robert Wodrow, *Collections upon the lives of the reformers and most eminent ministers of the Church of Scotland*, 2 vols. (Edinburgh, 1834–1838), 2:26. Local conflict over ministers is described in John Ferguson, *Ecclesia Antiqua or, the History of an Ancient Church* (Edinburgh, 1803), chap. 6.

134. *Oliver Cromwell's Letters and Speeches with Elucidations*, ed. Thomas Carlyle, 4 vols. (London, 1897), 1:329; 4:64; Blair Worden, "Providence and Politics," *Past & Present* 109 (1985): 55–99. John Morrill casts a skeptical eye on Cromwell's religious history in "The Making of Oliver Cromwell," in Morrill, ed., *Oliver Cromwell and the English Revolution* (London: Longmans, 1990), 19–48. But see Colin Davis, "Cromwell's religion," in ibid., chap. 7; and Davis, "Against Formality: One Aspect of the English Revolution," *Transactions of the Royal Historical Society* 3 (1993): 265–88.

135. Blair Worden, "Oliver Cromwell and the Sin of Achan," in *Cromwell and the Interregnum: The Essential Readings*, ed. David L. Smith (Oxford: Blackwell, 2003), 58. (In Psalm 7, an "old man" pleads with God to be a "refuge" and celebrates his own "faithfulness.") Insightful studies include Robert S. Paul, *The Lord Protector: Religion and Politics in the Life of Oliver Cromwell* (Grand Rapids: Eerdmans, 1664), 300–301; and John Morrill, "The Making of Oliver Cromwell," in *The Nature of the English Revolution: Essays by John*

Morrill (London: Longman, 1993), chap. 6. Policy toward the Jews is ably described in Andrew Crome, *Christian Zionism and English National Identity, 1600–1850* (Cham: Springer / Palgrave Macmillan, 2018), chap. 3. See also Achsah Guibbory, *Christian Identity, Jews, and Israel in Seventeenth-Century England* (New York: Oxford University Press, 2010), chap. 7. Aspirations for a reformation of manners during this period are described in Capp, *England's Culture Wars*.

136. Roger Howell Jr., reviews the sharply different judgments of Cromwell in his own day and underscores the contradictions inherent in his social and political agenda. Howell, "Cromwell and English liberty," in *Freedom and the Puritan Revolution: Essays in History and Literature*, ed. R. C. Richardson and G. M. Ridden (Manchester: Manchester University Press, 1986), 25–44. See also Howell, " 'Who needs another Cromwell?' The Nineteenth-Century Image of Oliver Cromwell," in R. C. Richardson, ed., *Images of Oliver Cromwell: Essays by and for Roger Howell* (Manchester: Manchester University Press, 1993), chap. 6. Cromwell's reputation for duplicity is validated from personal experience in Lucy Hutchinson, *Memoirs of the Life of Colonel Hutchinson*, ed. N. H. Keeble (London: Dent, 1995), 238–39. For dilemmas, Paul, *Lord Protector*, chaps. 17 and 20.

137. Carlyle, *Cromwell's Letters and Speeches*, 1: 228; Barry Coward, *The Cromwellian Protectorate* (Manchester: Manchester University Press, 2002), 59 and, more generally, chap. 3. David L. Smith illuminates Cromwell's political impasse in "Oliver Cromwell and the Protectorate Parliaments," in *The Cromwellian Protectorate*, ed. Patrick Little (Woodbridge: Boydell, 2007), 14–31; and in "Cromwell and Religious Reform," *Parliamentary History* 19 (2000): 39–48 (quotations, pp. 42–43).

138. Blair Worden, "Toleration and the Protectorate," in *God's Instruments: Political Conduct in the England of Oliver Cromwell* (Oxford: Oxford University Press, 2013), 5.

139. Gribben, *God's Irishmen*, 43 (and, in general, chaps. 1 and 4). Cf. Austin Woolrych, "The Cromwellian Protectorate: A Military Dictatorship?" in Smith, *Cromwell and the Interregnum*, chap. 3. Thanks to Ann Hughes's gentle questioning, I excised comments of my own along these lines.

140. *Winthrop Papers*, 5:206–7.

141. Stevenson, *Revolution and Counter-Revolution*, 140–43; Brian P. Levack, *Witch-hunting in Scotland: Law, Politics and Religion* (New York: Routledge, 2008), chap. 4; and for the specifically religious definition of witchcraft in Scotland, see chap. 1; James Sharp, *Witchcraft in Early Modern England* (Edinburgh; Pearson Education, 2001), 70–73. See also Liu, *Discord in Zion*, passim; Gretchen E. Minton, " 'The same cause and like quarrell': Eusebius, John Foxe, and the Evolution of Ecclesiastical History," *Church History* 71 (2002): 715–42.

Chapter 9. Change and Continuity

1. Shepard, *Confessions*, 102–5.

2. Obadiah Holmes, "Last Will & Testimony," printed in Edwin S. Gaustad, ed., *Baptist Piety: The Last Will & Testimony of Obadiah Holmes* (New York: Arno, 1980), 72–82.

3. David Parnham, *Heretics Within: Anthony Wotton, John Goodwin, and the Orthodox Divines* (Brighton: Sussex Academic, 2014); Theodore Dwight Bozeman, *The Precisionist Strain Disciplinary Religion and Antinomian Backlash in Puritanism to 1638* (Chapel Hill: University of North Carolina Press, 2004), chap. 10; David R. Como, *Blown by the Spirit: Puritanism and the Emergence of an Antinomian Underground in Pre-Civil War England* (Stanford: Stanford University Press, 2004); Dewey D. Wallace Jr., *Puritans and*

Predestination: Grace in English Protestant Theology, 1525–1695 (Chapel Hill: University of North Carolina Press, 1982), 114–16.

4. See, e.g., Arnold Hunt, *The Art of Hearing English Preachers and Their Audiences, 1590–1640* (Cambridge: Cambridge University, 2010), chap. 7, and Leif Dixon, *Practical Predestinarians in England, c. 1590–1640* (Burlington: Ashgate, 2013). John Coffey summarizes the difficulties of defining orthodoxy at midcentury in "A ticklish business: Defining heresy and orthodoxy in the Puritan revolution," in *Heresy, Literature, and Politics in Early Modern English Culture*, ed. David Loewenstein and John Marshall (Cambridge: Cambridge University Press, 2006), 108–36.

5. Ball's *Short Catechisme containing the Principles of Religion* (c. 1615) was frequently reprinted in the seventeenth century. My assessment stems in part from reading Alexander F. Mitchell, ed., *Catechisms of the Second Reformation* (London, 1886). See also Douglas F. Kelly, "The Westminster Shorter Catechism," in *To Glorify and Enjoy God: A Commemoration of the 350th Anniversary of the Westminster Assembly*, ed. John L. Carson and David W. Hall (Edinburgh: Banner of Truth Trust, 1994), chap. 5.

6. The history of the Savoy Declaration may be followed in Walker, *Creeds and Platforms*, chap. 12; and Crawford Gribben, *John Owen and English Puritanism: Experiences of Defeat* (Oxford: Oxford University Press, 2016), 197–99. See also Sarah Mortimer, *Reason and Religion in the English Revolution: The Challenge of Socinianism* (Cambridge: Cambridge University Press, 2010) 196–200 and 221–26, for the bearing of Socinianism on John Owen's agenda.

7. This tweaking of high Calvinism was favored by some of the English delegates to the Synod of Dordt, as Anthony Milton points out in *Catholic and Reformed: The Roman and Protestant Churches in English Protestant Thought, 1600–1640* (Cambridge: Cambridge University Press, 1995), 420. See also Jonathan D. Moore, *English Hypothetical Universalism: John Preston and the Softening of Reformed Theology* (Grand Rapids, MI: Eerdmans, 2007).

8. Wallace, *Puritans and Predestination*, 133; Brian G. Armstrong, *Calvinism and the Amyraut Heresy: Protestant Scholasticism and Humanism in Seventeenth-Century France* (Madison: University of Wisconsin Press, 1969), chap. 1 and passim.

9. Peter Lake, "Puritanism, Familism, and Heresy in Early Stuart England: The Case of John Etherington Revisited," in Loewenstein and Marshall, *Heresy, Literature, and Politics*, 82–107 (quotation, p. 93); Prynne, *Anti-Arminianisme*, 28.

10. *Thomas Hooker: Writings in England and Holland, 1626–1633*, ed. George H. Williams et al. (Cambridge: Harvard University Press, 1975), 144–45. The letters passing back and forth between James Ussher and his many correspondents record several disputes and discussions both private and public. *The Correspondence of James Ussher, 1600–1656*, ed. Elizabethanne Boran, 3 vols. (Dublin: Irish Manuscripts Commission, 2015). The best brief survey of opinion in the 1630s and 1640s is Wallace, *Puritans and Predestination*, chaps. 3–4.

11. Ann Hughes, "The Pulpit Guarded: Confrontations between Orthodox and Radicals in Revolutionary England," in *John Bunyan and His England, 1628–88*, ed. Anne Laurence, W. R. Owens, and Stuart Sim (London: Hambledon, 1990), 31–50; John Coffey, *John Goodwin and the Puritan Revolution: Religion and Intellectual Change in Seventeenth-Century England* (Woodbridge: Boydell, 2006), chaps. 7–9; Phil Kilroy, "Radical Religion in Ireland, 1641–1660," in *Ireland from Independence to Occupation, 1641–1660*, ed. Jane H. Ohlmeyer (Cambridge: Cambridge University Press, 1995), chap. 10; E. Brooks Holifield, *The Covenant Sealed: The Development of Puritan Sacramental Theology in Old and New England, 1570–1720* (New Haven: Yale University Press, 1974), chap 4. See also Parnham, *Heretics*

Within, chaps. 3–4; Gribben, *John Owen*; Crawford Gribben, "Robert Leighton, Edinburgh Theology and the Collapse of the Presbyterian Consensus," in *Enforcing the Reformation in Ireland and Scotland, 1550–1700*, ed. Elizabethanne Boran and Crawford Gribben (Aldershot: Ashgate, 2006), chap. 6.

12. T. D. Bozeman, "The Glory of the 'Third Time': John Eaton as Contra-Puritan," *JEH* 47 (1996): 638–54; Como, *Blown by the Spirit*, chap. 6; Michael P. Winship, *Making Heretics: Militant Protestantism and Free Grace in Massachusetts, 1636–1641* (Princeton, NJ: Princeton University Press, 2002), 264 n. 30. As Tim Cooper has pointed out, Eaton and Robert Towne, another member of the Antinomian "underground," continued to endorse a certain role for the law. Cooper, *Fear and Polemic in Seventeenth-Century England Richard Baxter and Antinomianism* (Aldershot: Ashgate, 2001), 22–24.

13. Christopher Hill surveys the emergence of these writers in "Antinomianism in 17th-century England" and "Dr. Tobias Crisp, 1600–43," reprinted in *The Collected Essays of Christopher Hill, Vol. 2: Religion and Politics in 17ᵗʰ Century England* (Amherst: University of Massachusetts Press, 1986). J. C. Davis has identified Antinomian motifs in the speculations of some of the Levellers. Davis, "The Levellers and Christianity," in *Politics, Religion, and the English Civil War*, ed. Brian Manning (London: Edward Arnold, 1973), chap. 6.

14. Robert Baillie depended heavily on *A Short Story* for the stories he incorporated into *A Dissuasive against the Errours of the Time* (1645), and Thomas Edwards cited it in *Gangraena*, as did Ephraim Pagitt in *Heresiography* (1645); cf. Hughes, *Gangraena*, 83 n. 91; Edwards, *Gangraena*, 1: 3. Other texts emerging from the controversy are printed in Hall, *AC*; unprinted texts are described in Hall, *Ways of Writing: The Practice and Politics of Text-Making in Seventeenth-Century New England* (Philadelphia: University of Pennsylvania Press, 2008), chap. 2, where I also contextualize the *Short Story*.

15. Edwards, *Gangraena*, 16–17; Cooper, *Fear and Polemic*, intro., chap. 1; see esp. pp. 113–14. As Cooper points out, pairing Antinomian and "Libertine" was incorrect but effective polemically. The term itself had come into use in sixteenth-century Lutheran circles when debate erupted about the relationship between law and gospel. Luther's affirmations of free grace became something of an icon to the Antinomian "underground" of c. 1620, even though he repudiated the more extreme views of fellow Lutherans. This chapter does not include the "mystics" or "spiritual" writers who emerged during this period, one of them Henry Vane Jr., whose theology is described in David Parnham, "Politics Spun Out of Theology and Prophecy: Sir Henry Vane on the Spiritual Environment of Public Power," *History of Political Thought* 22 (2001): 53–83, and more fully in *Sir Henry Vane, Theologian: A Study in Seventeenth-Century Religious and Political Discourse* (Madison, NJ: Fairleigh Dickinson University Press, 1997), where (p. 12) Vane is described as presenting "himself as a 'witness' of light, as a spiritualist, as one dispensing advanced wisdoms in the epistemological setting of an imminent and apocalyptic age of the Spirit," a role others were claiming in this period. See also Nigel Smith, *Perfection Proclaimed: Language and Literature in English Radical Religion, 1640–1660* (Oxford: Clarendon, 1989).

16. Herbert J. McLachlan, *Socinianism in Seventeenth-Century England* (London, 1951), chaps. 1–3, 8; Mortimer, *Reason and Religion*, chap. 2.

17. Dixhoorn, *Minutes*, 3: 614; Nigel Smith, "'And if God was one of us': Paul Best, John Biddle, and anti-Trinitarian heresy in seventeenth-century England," in Loewenstein and Marshall, *Heresy, Literature, and Politics*, 160–84; Hughes, *Gangraena*, 159–64; Paul C. H. Lim, *Mystery Unveiled: The Crisis of the Trinity in Early Modern England* (Oxford: Oxford University Press, 2012), chap. 1, pt. 2:174–81, and passim. The response of Parliament is summarized in W. K. Jordan, *The Development of Religious Toleration in England, Vol. 3: 1640–1660* (Cambridge, MA: Harvard University Press, 1938), 88–91.

18. Sarah Hutton, "Iconisms, Enthusiasm and Origen: Henry More Reads the Bible," in *Scripture and Scholarship in Early Modern England*, ed. Ariel Hessaye and Nicholas Keene (Aldershot: Ashgate, 2006), 192–207. In *Puritans and Predestination*, 120–28, Wallace describes "Anglican" Arminians of the 1640s and 1650s whose anti-Calvinism resembled that of the Great Pew Circle. See also Adrian Johns, "The Physiology of Reading and the Anatomy of Enthusiasm," in *Religio Medici: Medicine and Religion in Seventeenth-Century England*, ed. Ole Peter Grell and Andrew Cunningham (Aldershot: Scholars, 1996), 136–70; and Ronald A. Knox, *Enthusiasm: A Chapter in the History of Religion, With Special Reference to the Seventeenth and Eighteenth Centuries* (Oxford: Oxford University Press, 1950), chap. 8.

19. McLachlan, *Socinianism*, chap. 5; Mortimer, *Reason and Religion*, chap. 3, noting (p. 75) that Chillingworth described himself as a Trinitarian; J. Sears McGee, *The Godly Man in Stuart England: Anglicans, Puritans, and the Two Tables, 1620–1670* (New Haven, CT: Yale University Press, 1976), chap. 4. In *From Puritanism to the Age of Reason: A Study of Changes in Religious Thought within the Church of England, 1660–1700* (Cambridge: Cambridge University Press, 1950), G. R. Cragg pursues these tendencies beyond 1660.

20. David Parnham, "John Saltmarsh and the Mystery of Redemption," *Harvard Theological Review* 104 (2011): 265–98; David Parnham, "The Dismantling of 'High Presumption': Tobias Crisp Dismantles the Puritan *Ordo Salutis*," *JEH* 56 (2005): 50–74. See also Leo Solt, *Saints in Arms: Puritanism and Democracy in Cromwell's Army* (Stanford: Stanford University Press 1959), chap. 2.

21. Henry Jessey, *Exceeding Riches of grace, advanced by the spirit of grace* (London, 1647), reprinted in *A Company of Women Preachers: Baptist Prophetesses in Seventeenth-Century England, A Reader*, ed. Curtis W. Freeman (Waco, TX: Baylor University Press, 2011), 173, 174, 186, 189, 204, 207, 209–10, sig. a2r–v.

22. *Letters of Samuel Rutherford*, ed. Andrew Bonar (Edinburgh: Banner of Truth Trust, 1984), 194; Samuel Rutherford, *The Trial and Triumph of Faith* (1645; repr., Carlisle, PA: Banner of Truth Trust, 2001), 102, 23–25, 91–93, 102, 110, 174–75; Rutherford, *A Survey of the Spiritual Antichrist* (1648), 238.

23. Rutherford, ibid., 237–38. In *Ane Catechisme* (included in Mitchell, *Catechisms of the Second Reformation*), Rutherford responded to the question "What is the condition of the covenant?" by citing "saving and true faith." This answer prompted an imaginary respondent to ask, "But wee must pay the duetie of faith, and therefore it seemeth the covenant is not free?" to which Rutherford answered, "Yea, for all that it is most free, for our Lord payeth for us and maketh us believe." Insisting at another moment that sinners can do nothing before they are "made new creatures," he also endorsed "preparation" under the law (pp. 174, 178, 200–201).

24. [Isaac Ambrose], *The Complete Works of that Eminent Minister of Gods Word Mr. Isaac Ambrose* (1674), 41, 15, 88–90, 95–114.

25. Wallace, *Puritans and Predestination*, 135; Thomas Gataker, *Shadowes without Substance, or Pretended new Lights . . . In way of Rejoynder unto Mr John Saltmarsh* (1646), 13, 18, 20; Gataker, *Antinomianism Discovered and Confuted: And Free-Grace As it is held forth in Gods Word . . . maintained* (1652).

26. Peterkin, *Records of the Kirk*, 475. The debates and negotiations out of which it emerged are described in Benjamin B. Warfield, *The Westminster Assembly and Its Work* (New York: Oxford University Press, 1932), chap. 2; and Chad B. Van Dixhoorn, "Reforming the Reformation: Theological Debate at the Westminster Assembly, 1643–1652" (PhD thesis, Cambridge University, 2004).

27. Warfield, *Westminster Assembly*, 160. Warfield describes in detail the making of

chapter 3 of the Confession (ibid., chap. 2), indicating continuities and differences from the Lambeth and Irish Articles, a Westminster committee report, and the final wording of this chapter, a table he borrowed from E. Tyrell Green, *The Thirty-Nine Articles and the Age of the Reformation* (London: Wells Gardner, Darton, 1896). In chapter 3, Warfield covered the doctrine of "holy Scripture"; and in chapter 5, the doctrine of "inspiration."

28. Again, an idiom that some ministers endorsed and others questioned. See, e.g., Carl R. Trueman, *John Owen: Reformed Catholic Renaissance Man* (Aldershot: Ashgate, 2007), chap. 3.

29. The distinction between two orders of time is described more fully in Donald Sinnema, "God's Temporal Decree and Its Temporal Execution: The Role of This Distinction in Theodore Beza's Theology," in Mack P. Holt, ed., *Adaptations of Calvinism in Reformation Europe: Essays in Honour of Brian G. Armstrong* (Aldershot: Ashgate, 2007), 55–78.

30. Light is shed on the relationship between faith and justification by what was said by members of the Westminster Assembly when it was deciding to approve or modify the statement, "in general apprehension, faith goes before justification" (Dixhoorn, *Minutes* 2: [Oct 43], 172–78), a debate entangled in explanations of how "preparatory works" differed from those that occur after faith and the relationship between justification, which in the abstract was God's doing, and its "actual" unfolding in human time.

31. All quotations taken from *The Confession of Faith and Larger and Shorter Catechisms* (Glasgow: Free Presbyterian Church of Scotland, 1976).

32. Dickson, *Truths Victory over Error: A Commentary on the Westminster Confession of Faith*, trans. and ed. John R. De Witt (Edinburgh: Banner of Truth Trust, 2007), 71, 82–83, 113-14.

33. Ibid., 73, 71, 86, 89, 110 (citing 2 Pet. 1:10), 112; Adam Martindale, *Divinity-Knots unloosed* (1649), 6.

34. The Confession may also be read as a retort to hypothetical universalism, for it implies that the scope of the Atonement is limited to the elect (chap. 11) and does not use the words "sufficient" and "efficient." During the assembly itself, Edmund Calamy argued on behalf of that terminology. Calamy, quoted in Alan C. Clifford, *Atonement and Justification: English Evangelical Theology, 1640-1790, An Evaluation* (Oxford: Clarendon, 1990), 75.

35. Walker, *Creeds and Platforms*, chap. 12. For these changes, see also Gribben, *John Owen*, 197–99. Although committed to a strong doctrine of the Holy Spirit, Owen objected to how it was being employed by radical Spiritists, for which see Sinclair B. Ferguson, "John Owen and the doctrine of the Holy Spirit," in *John Owen—The Man and His Theology*, ed. Robert W. Oliver (Phillipsburg, NJ: Evangelical, 2002), 101–29.

36. Gribben, *John Owen*, 115–17. Their respective positions on justification are described in Trueman, *John Owen*, chap. 4.

37. Paul Chang-Ha Lim, *In Pursuit of Purity, Unity, and Liberty: Richard Baxter's Puritan Ecclesiology in Its Seventeenth-Century Context* (Leiden: Brill, 2004), chap. 5.

38. Ibid., noting, among other texts, Baxter's *Confession of Faith* (1655), where he questioned Owen's understanding of the Atonement. As Lim points out (chap. 6), the statement of doctrine Baxter included in *Christian Concord* struck several contemporaries as inadequately Trinitarian. See also N. H. Keeble, " 'Take heed of being too forward in imposing on others': Orthodoxy and heresy in the Baxterian tradition," in Loewenstein and Marshall, eds., *Heresy, Literature, and Politics*, 282–305, an essay of great value for carrying the story toward to the end of the seventeenth century.

39. Gribben, *John Owen*, 153.

40. He is often classified as a "moderate Calvinist." See, e.g., Wallace, *Puritans and Predestination*, 132–44.

41. *The Autobiography of Richard Baxter*, abr. J. M. Lloyd Thomas and ed. N. H. Keeble (London: Dent, 1974), 10; Lim, *Pursuit of Purity*, 31.

42. M'Crie, *Life of Mr. Robert Blair*, 21–24, 115; *Winthrop Papers*, 3:338–44.

43. Trapnel, *A Legacy for Saints*, reprinted in Freeman, *Company of Women Preachers*, 527–29, 491.

44. Turner, *Choice Experiences*, reprinted in Freeman, *Company of Women Preachers*, 319, 323, 333, and passim. Hansard Knollys, who spent a few years in New England before returning to his homeland, where he became a Baptist and Fifth Monarchist, narrated a similar transition from being a "formal Professor, a legal performer of Holy Duties" and living "a Life of Works, and not of Faith" to a life directed by the Holy Spirit, a story told in *The life and death of . . . Mr Hansard Knollys* (1692).

45. John H. Taylor, "Some Seventeenth-Century Testimonies," *Transactions of the Congregational Historical Society* 16 (1949–51), 64–77; John Rogers, *Ohel or Beth-Shemesh* (1653), 393–94, 402–7, 410.

46. A telling example because it narrates so fully the practices and experiences associated with the practical divinity is Norman Penney, ed., *Experiences in the Life of Mary Pennington (written by herself)* (Philadelphia: Biddle, 1910).

47. John Bunyan, *Grace Abounding and The Life and Death of Mr Badman*, ed. G. B. Harrison (London: Everyman's Library, 1979), 12, 14–15, 225, 28, 30, 48; Roger Pooley, "Grace Abounding and the New Sense of the Self," in *John Bunyan and His England, 1628–1688*, ed. Anne Laurence, W. R. Owen, and Stuart Sim (London: Hambledon, 1990), 105–14 (quotation, p. 109); Richard L. Greaves, *John Bunyan* (Grand Rapids, MI: Eerdmans, 1969), chap. 3, noting, among other matters, Bunyan's insistence on linking faith and justification. Roger Sharrock points out that when Bunyan revised *Grace Abounding*, he added more "mystical" moments. Sharrock, "Spiritual Autobiography: Bunyan's *Grace Abounding*," in Laurence, Owen, and Sim, *John Bunyan and His England*, 100–101.

48. Ambrose, *Complete Works*, 232.

49. Baxter, *The Reformed Pastor*, ed. Hugh Martin (London: SMC, 1956), 28, 51, 53–54, 56–57, 61, 64.

50. Lim, *Pursuit of Purity*, 32–34 (noting the relationship between Baxter's objections to Separatism and his idealizing of the church as means of grace).

51. David M. Powers, *Damnable Heresy: William Pynchon, the Indians, and the First Book Banned (and Burned) in Boston* (Eugene, OR: Wipf and Stock, 2015), chaps. 11, 12, 15. At the urging of the government, John Norton replied to Pynchon in the London-printed *A Discussion of that Great Point in Divinity, The Sufferings of Christ* (1653). For Stoughton, see *Winthrop Papers* 6:113–30, and for other disputes recorded in manuscripts, David D. Hall, "Scribal Publication in Seventeenth-Century New England: An Introduction and a Checklist," *Proceedings of the American Antiquarian Society* 116 (2006): 29–80; Hall, "Scribal Publication in New England: A Second Checklist," in ibid., 118 (2008): 267–96; Sargent Bush Jr., "After Coming Over: John Cotton, Peter Bulkeley, and Learned Discourse in the Wilderness," *Studies in the Literary Imagination* 27 (1994): 7–22.

52. Hall, *AC*, 46–59 (the initial questions, with Cotton's answers; the "Elders Reply" and Cottons' "Rejoynder" follow, 60–151); *God's Plot: The Paradoxes of Puritan Piety, Being the Autobiography and Journal of Thomas Shepard*, ed. Michael McGiffert (Amherst: University of Massachusetts Press, 1972), 65. See also Stoever, *"Fair and Easie Way,"* 52–53, and *Winthrop Papers* 3:324–26 (a statement by the Boston congregation, c. December 1636). That assurance of salvation and how it was validated lay at the heart of the controversy was established by Stoever, *"Faire and Easie Way,"* 169–74 and passim; and suggested in Hall, *AC*, 11–19. That Cotton was an authentic Calvinist, whereas the "legal" ministers were seeking a theological means of controlling lay behavior and stumbled on "preparation," is argued

in Perry G. E. Miller, "'Preparation for Salvation' in Seventeenth-Century New England," *Journal of the History of Ideas* 4 (1943): 259–86. The critiques include Stoever, *"Faire and Easie Way,"* app.: Preparation for Salvation; Tipson, *Hartford Puritanism,* chap. 10; and Abram van Engen, *Sympathetic Puritans: Calvinist Fellow Feeling in Early New England* (New York: Oxford University Press, 2015), chap. 2. That the "witness of the Spirit" was open to various interpretations is noted in Geoffrey F. Nuttall, *The Holy Spirit in Puritan Faith and Experience* (Oxford: Blackwell, 1946), chap. 3. See also Stoever, *"Faire and Easie Way,"* 120–22.

53. Bozeman, *Precisionist Strain,* chap. 11 (the most trustworthy reading of the early sermons). For overviews that vary in their emphasis, see ibid., chaps. 12–13; David Parnham, "John Cotton Reconsidered: Law and Grace in Two Worlds," *JEH* 64 (2013): 296–34; Winship, *Making Heretics;* Stoever, *"Faire and Easie Way,"* chap. 3; and Michael J. Colacurcio, *Godly Letters: The Literature of the American Puritans* (Notre Dame, IN: University of Notre Dame Press, 2006), chap. 7. Misleading or erroneous scholarship is noted in Tipson, *Hartford Puritanism,* chap. 1. The "antinomian element" in Anthony Wotton's doctrine of justification, the musings of John Preston, and John Goodwin's sermons of the 1630s— focused, like Cotton's, on differentiating the covenant of grace from the covenant of works and denying the necessity of preparation—may be pertinent. Parnham, *Heretics Within,* chap. 6 (esp. pp. 185–88).

54. John Cotton, *A Sermon Preached . . . At Salem* (Boston, 1713), 30–33; Hall, *AC,* 32.

55. Cotton, *A Treatise of the Covenant of Grace, As it is dispensed to the Elect Seed, effectually unto Salvation: Being the Substance of divers Sermons preached upon Act. 7.8* (London, 1671), 11, 36–37, 19–20, 31, 19; Hall, *AC,* 36, 176–77, 181–83, 402–5, 128–30, 49. In his response to Robert Baillie, he acknowledged that during the synod he withdrew his objections to certain arguments, and he admitted that some in his congregation had been voicing "Erroneous and Hereticall opinions," which he should have been quicker to correct. He also tried to put some distance between himself and Anne Hutchinson. Ibid., 407, 425, 408–9, 413–14. Whether he really changed his mind about assurance and the golden chain remains unclear.

56. Philip Gura, *A Glimpse of Sion's Glory Puritan Radicalism in New England, 1620–1660* (Middletown, CT: Wesleyan University Press, 1984), 61; Hall, *AC,* 160–62; Sargent Bush Jr., "Wheelwright's Forgotten 'Apology': The Last Word in the Antinomian Controversy," *NEQ* 64 (1991): 22–45; Winship, *Making Heretics,* 90–91; chap. 6 (detailing the struggle within the General Court to pursue Wheelwright for "sedition" or for "heresy"). Cotton revisited the 1637 sermon in a letter of 1640; see Sargent Bush Jr., "'Revising what we have done amisse': John Cotton and John Wheelwright, 1640," *WMQ,* 3rd ser. 45 (1988), 733–50 .

57. Ill-informed appropriations of Hutchinson abound. The exceptions include Amanda Porterfield, *Female Piety in Puritan New England The Emergence of Religious Humanism* (New York: Oxford University Press, 1982), chap. 3 .

58. Hall, *AC,* 271–72.

59. Ibid., 227, 236.

60. Ibid., 263, 316, 371, 412. The *Short Story* includes a summary of theological opinions attributed to her, one of them her assertion that the injunction to "worke out our salvation with feare" was "spoken onely to such, as are under a Covenant of works" (pp. 301–3). The ministers charged with questioning her in the run-up to her church trial prepared another list (pp. 351–52).

61. Hall, *AC,* 271, 337–38. Cotton was not as startled as others were to hear her say these things. See also George Selement, "John Cotton's Hidden Antinomianism: His Sermon on Revelation 4:1–2," *NEHGR* 129 (12975): 278–94.

62. Hall, *AC*, 229, 238. The ministers also questioned how the term "hypocrite" was being used (p. 223).

63. Ibid., 243, 236, 232.

64. Ibid., 228. The importance of order or "ordained" is illuminated in Stoever, *"Faire and Easie Way*," chap. 7.

65. Albro, *Works of Shepard*, 1: cxxix; Van Engen, *Sympathetic Puritans*, chap. 2. The central importance of "love" in Puritan discourse had previously been noted by J. Sears McGee, *The Godly Man in Stuart England: Anglicans, Puritans, and the Two Tables, 1620–1670* (New Haven, CT: Yale University Press, 1976), and Charles L. Cohen, *God's Caress: The Psychology of Puritan Religious Experience* (New York: Oxford University Press, 1986), without, however, tying this concept to the debates of 1636–37 or to l John 3:14. Cotton dismissed this argument (Hall, *AC*, 183), as did Tobias Crisp.

66. Shepard, for one, did not trust a supposedly repentant Cotton. Cf. McGiffert, *God's Plot*, 74.

67. Peter Bulkeley, *The Gospel-Covenant; or, The Covenant of Grace Opened* (1651), 98–99 and passim; Norton, *Orthodox Evangelist*, 318. Another local response worth noting was voiced by Henry Dunster in his relation to the Cambridge church. Familiar with the synod of 1637 and its contexts, he insisted that there are no "revelations without the word" and no doorway to Christ except through the "ordinances." Obedience, which he translated into "holy" walking, was central to being a true Christian; anyone who "saith he hath faith and hath no obedience" (that is, repudiated the law) should not be allowed into a congregation. On this point he was emphatic: a "life in Christian obedience," or "sanctification," was an intrinsic part of the pathway to eternal life. Shepard, *Confessions*, 160–61.

68. Ostensibly a defense of the "morality of the Sabbath," the *Treatise* also covers "the great controversy whether the law be a rule of life to a believer" and revisits the relationship between justification and sanctification, the place of "duties" in the work of redemption, and "how the gospel requires doing." Among other assertions, Shepard insists that "believers are rational creatures . . . and therefore have some inherent power . . . to act." Albro, *Works of Shepard*, 3: 96–97, 241, 247.

69. McGiffert, *God's Plot*. 101.

70. Albro, *Works of Shepard*, 1: cxxvii–cxxx; 2:19.

71. Ibid., 2:25, 92, 243–44.

72. Hall, *AC*, 74, 73; Albro, *Works of Shepard*, 2:77–78.

73. Ibid., 40–49, 84, 85; Colacurcio, *Godly Letters*, 375. In chap. 5, Colacurcio describes Shepard's "Activist Calvinism" as manifested in two earlier sermon series. Winship describes a more legalistic Shepard in *Making Heretics*.

74. McGiffert, *God's Plot*, 40–46, 198–99.

75. Shepard, *Confessions*, 104, 59, 65–69, 33–34. The most careful reading of these texts is Charles Cohen's in *God's Caress*, chaps. 6–8.

76. See, e.g., John Goodwin, *Certain Select Cases Resolved: Specially tending to the comfort of Believers* (1651).

77. Hall, *ARP*, chap. 5; McGiffert, *God's Plot*, 106, 114, 121.

78. Charles M. Andrews, *The Colonial Period of American History: The Settlements II* (New Haven: Yale University Press, 1936), chap. 8.

79. See in general, Francis J. Bremer, *Puritan Crisis: New England and the English Civil Wars, 1630–1670* (New York: Garland, 1989); James O'Toole, "New England Reactions to the English Civil Wars," *NEHGR* 129 (1975): 238–49; and Timothy J. Sehr, *Colony and Commonwealth: Massachusetts Bay, 1649–1660* (New York: Garland, 1989), chaps. 1, 4. In 1645, a Parliamentary committee told the government in Bermuda to allow a limited ver-

sion of toleration, but never addressed any of the orthodox colonies in New England in the same manner.

80. *Winthrop Papers* 5:356. Winslow's efforts are briefly described in Hall, *Worlds of Wonder*, chap. 2. See also his letter to Winthrop (June 1646) warning him to be "better prepared . . . to stave off prejudice," created by petitions to the Committee on Plantations in the Long Parliament. *Winthrop Papers*, 5: 87.

81. Disputes lie at the heart of Sumner Chilton Powell, *Puritan Village: The Formation of a New England Town* (Middletown, CT: Wesleyan University Press, 1967). On the other hand, the founders of Woburn, Massachusetts in the early 1640s were intentionally ethical, as were those of Lancaster, practices too commonly ignored by historians. Cf. Hall, *ARP*, chap. 2.

82. For details, see ibid., chaps. 1, 2, and 4.

83. Cf. Hall, *ARP*, chap. 2; [Thomas Hutchinson], *A Collection of Original Papers Relative to the History of the Colony of Massachusetts-Bay* (Boston, 1769), 211.

84. Doubts acknowledged with unusual frankness in *New Englands First Fruits* (1643), 24–26.

85. *Winthrop Papers* 5:42–45; Bernard Bailyn, *The New England Merchants in the Seventeenth Century* (Cambridge, MA.: Harvard University Press, 1955); Edward Johnson, *The Wonder-Working Providence of Sions Savior in New England*, ed. J. Franklin Jameson (New York: Scribners, 1910), 209–12; Sehr, *Colony and Commonwealth*, chap. 5. Bailyn's thesis of hostility between merchants and the "traditionalism" of the ministers and their allies among the magistrates is revisited in Louise A. Breen, *Transgressing the Bounds: Subversive Enterprises among the Puritan Elite in Massachusetts, 1630–1690* (New York: Oxford University Press, 2001). For an alternative, see Mark E. Peterson, *The Price of Redemption: The Spiritual Economy of Puritan New England* (Stanford, CA: Stanford University Press, 1997); and Mark A. Valerie's subtle reading of "Providence in the Life of John Hull: Puritanism and Commerce in Massachusetts Bay, 1650–1680," *Proceedings of the American Antiquarian Society*, n.s., 118 (2008): 55–116.

86. Walker, *Creeds and Platforms*, 169–70; Winthrop, *Journal*, 628. Critical comments on the document are noted in Hall, *FS*, 116–17.

87. Baillie, *Letters and Journals*, 2: 146; Walker, *Creeds and Platforms*, 233.

88. Winthrop, *Journal*, 421; Hall, *FS*, 106.

89. John Cotton, *The Keyes of the Kingdome* (1644), repr. in Ziff, *John Cotton*, 75; Hall, *FS*, 112–13; Walker, *Creeds and Platforms*, 220; Edwards, *Antapologia*, 294; Bremer, *Congregational Communion*, chap. 7. Whether these rules altered congregational governance is questioned by James F. Cooper, *Tenacious of Their Liberties: The Congregationalists in Colonial America* (New York: Oxford University Press, 1999), 83.

90. Walker, *Creeds and Platforms*, 236–37. B. R. Burg places the wording of this chapter in the context of ministerial anxieties about interference by the magistrate in church affairs, or "erastianism." *Richard Mather of Dorchester* (Lexington: University Press of Kentucky, 1976), chap. 5. Ongoing scuffles are described in Hall, *FS*, chap. 6.

91. Walker, *Creeds and Platforms*, 198, 205–6, 221–23; Baird Tipson, "Invisible Saints: The 'Judgment of Charity' in the Early New England Churches," *Church History* 44 (1975): 460–71; Thomas Shepard and John Allin, *A Defence of the Answer to the Nine Questions* (1648), sig. D1v–D2r. Like their fellow Independents in England, Shepard and Allin also rejected the concept of a universal visible church. One way of viewing the phrasing about charity is to revisit the figure of the hypocrite that been disparaged by Hutchinson and Cotton in the 1630s. Partly in response to English critics, Cotton alleged that he and his fellow ministers would "rather 99 Hypocrites should perish through presumption, then one hum-

ble soul belonging to Christ, should sinke under discouragement or despaire." Cotton, *The Way of the Churches of Christ in New-England* (1645; written earlier), 58. In the same section (pp. 56–58), Cotton defended the importance of requiring more than mere "externall profession" of prospective members since, in his words, they should be "saints by calling," but simultaneously endorsed admitting those of "weak faith."

92. Increase Mather, *The First Principles of New-England Concerning the Subject of Baptisme & Communion of Churches* (Cambridge, MA, 1675), 2–3; [Mather], *Church-Government*, 22; *Winthrop Papers*, 4:211 The same correspondent observed that "rather would I live with breade and water . . . then . . . not being admitted in to the Congregation." He also suggested allowing grandparents as "the seede unto whome the Covenant apprterteine."

93. Burg, *Richard Mather*, 110; Bulkeley, *Gospel-Covenant*, pt. 2, esp. 154–59; John Cotton, *Certain Queries Tending to accommodation and communion of Presbyterian & Congregationall Churches* (1654), 13. See also Bush, *Correspondence*, 405. In mid-1645, John Winthrop wrote out a summary of reasons for preserving infant baptism (emphasizing Gen. 17), probably in response to Baptist statements but an intriguing sign of theological currents to which Mather was also responding. *Winthrop Papers* 5: 32.

94. Albro, *Works of Shepard*, 1:2; McGiffert, *God's Plot*, 35; Mather, *A Farewel Exhortation* (Cambridge, MA, 1657), 9–10; Mather, *First Principles*, 24–26; Walker, *Creeds and Platforms*, 256. See also Albro, *Works of Shepard*, 3:522–24, 536. Increase Mather was responding to accusations that the new policy was an "invention." His critics could cite his father Richard and John Cotton's assertions of c. 1643 against the new policy, an embarrassing circumstance Mather circumvented by complaining that Cotton's *Way of the Churches* was a corrupt text.

95. *Public Records of the Colony of Connecticut*, ed. J. Hammond Trumbull, 2 vols. (Hartford, 1850), 2:54–55; Walker, *Creeds and Platforms*, 291–93. Extracts from the "result" of this synod, *A Disputation Concerning Church-Members and their Children in Answer to 21 Questions* (1659), are included in Walker, *Creeds and Platforms*, chap. 11. Paul R. Lucas covers this and related issues on a regional basis in *Valley of Discord Church and Society along the Connecticut River, 1636–1725* (Hanover, NH: University Press of New England, 1976), chaps. 2–4.

96. Walker, *Creeds and Platforms*, chap. 11, where the relevant publications and manuscripts are listed. Theological reasons for and against are described in Holifield, *Covenant Sealed*, chaps. 5–6. The fullest survey of how congregations responded is Robert G. Pope, *The Half-Way Covenant: Church Membership in Puritan New England* (Princeton, NJ: Princeton University Press, 1969).

97. Mary McManus Ramsbottom, "Religious Society and the Family in Charlestown, Massachusetts, 1630 to 1740" (PhD, Yale University, 1987), a close reading of church records in the service of the argument (p. 88) that "church affiliation was fundamentally a social act and a family concern"); Bulkeley, *Gospel-Covenant*, 162. For more details on this process and its theological contexts, see Ann S. Brown and David D. Hall, "Family Strategies and Church Membership: Baptism and the Lord's Supper in early New England," in *Lived Religion in America: Toward a History of Practice*, ed. David D. Hall (Princeton, NJ: Princeton University Press, 1997), 47–82, and the literature cited in the notes. See also Katherine Gerbner, "Beyond the 'Halfway Covenant': Church Membership, Extended Baptism, and Outreach in Cambridge, Massachusetts, 1656–1667," *NEQ* 85 (2012): 281–301.The mature version of this system is beautifully described in Douglas L. Winiarski, *Darkness Falls on the Land of Light: Experiencing Religious Awakenings in Eighteenth-Century New England* (Chapel Hill: University of North Carolina Press, 2017), pt. 1.

98. Bradford, *Plymouth Plantation*, 26 (alluding as well to cannibalism); Jenny Hale Pulsipher, *Subjects unto the Same King: Indians, English, and the Contest for Authority in Colonial New England* (Philadelphia: University of Pennsylvania Press, 2005), intro., chap. 1. In *American Passage: The Communications Frontier in Early New England* (Cambridge, MA.: Harvard University Press, 2013), chapter 1, Katherine Grandjean describes the circumstances that led to the "Pequot War"; and in chapter 3, interactions with New Netherland and inter-tribal disputes of the 1640s and 1650s. The epidemics are described in Neal Salisbury, *Manitou and Providence: Indians, Europeans, and the Making of New England, 1500–1643* (New York: Oxford University Press, 1984). William Bradford complained about Dutch incursions in Connecticut in the 1630s; see, e.g., Bradford, *Plymouth Plantation*, 257–60.

99. Situations noted in *Winthrop Papers* 5:19–20, 101, 111, 534, and other places in this and the subsequent volume of *Winthrop Papers*. The larger story is narrated from the colonists' perspective in Alden Vaughn, *New England Frontier: Puritans and Indians, 1620–1675* (Boston: Little, Brown, 1965). The history of the New England Confederation is reappraised in Neal F. Dugre, "Repairing the Breach: Puritan Expansion, Commonwealth Formation, and the Origins of the United Colonies of New England, 1630–1643," *NEQ* 91 (2018): 382–417. Factors bearing on its activities and colonial diplomacy are described (with special attention to the French in Canada) in Laurie Henneton, "'Fear of Popish Leagues': Religious Identities and the Conduct of Frontier Diplomacy in Mid-17th Century Northeastern America," *NEQ* 91 (2018), 356–83.

100. Michael P. Clark, ed., *The Eliot Tracts* (Westport, CT: Praeger, 2003), 259. The authoritative study of Eliot's agenda as a missionary (up to 1675) is Richard W. Cogley, *John Eliot's Mission to the Indians before King Philip's War* (Cambridge, MA: Harvard University Press, 1999). See also Charles L. Cohen, "Conversion among Puritans and Amerindians: A Theological and Cultural Perspective," in *Puritanism: Transatlantic Perspectives on a Seventeenth-Century Anglo-American Faith*, ed. Francis J. Bremer (Boston: Massachusetts Historical Society, 1993), 233–56; William Kellaway, *The New England Company, 1649–1776: A Missionary Society to the American Indians* (London: Longmans, 1961), and William S. Simmons, "Conversion from Indian to Puritan," *NEQ* 52 (1979): 197–218. In *Dry Bones and Indian Sermons: Praying Indians in Colonial America* (Ithaca: Cornell University Press, 2004), Kristina Bross ably explicates the politico-international aspects of the missionary project.

101. *Recs. MBC* 3:281; the ordinance to this effect also included the provision that Indians who "come amongst the English, to inhabite in any of theire plantations" and do so "civilly & orderly" would have the same access to town lands as anyone else. As well, the statute endorsed the Indians' ability to sue the colonists in civil courts (ibid., 281–82; see also 386). Simultaneously, the government was attempting to limit the sale of alcohol to Native Americans (ibid., 308).

102. John Eliot, *A Late and Further Manifestation of the Progress of the Gospel Amongst the Indians in New-England* (1655).

103. David J. Silverman, *Faith and Boundaries: Colonists, Christianity, and Community among the Wampanoag Indians of Martha's Vineyard, 1600–1871* (New York: Cambridge University Press, 2005). Hiacoomes's spiritual history was narrated in Experience Mayhew, *Indian Converts; or, Some Account of the Lives and Dying Speeches of a considerable Number of the Christianized Indians of Martha's Vineyard* (1727), 1–12.

104. Responses sampled in Sehr, *Colony and Commonwealth*, 30–32. Simultaneously some of the ministers in New England were lamenting the explosion of theological diversity in England and the apparent paralysis of the government and orthodox clergy. Thomas

Shepard wrote in this fashion to Hugh Peter in 1645. "Thomas Shepard to Hugh Peter," *American Historical Review* 4 (1898): 105–7.

105. Edwards, *Gangraena*, 97.

106. Winthrop, *Journal*, 383, 383n, 483, 476–78, 481; *Winthrop Papers*, 5:13, 224, 247. Gorton's heterodox theology is described in Gura, *Glimpse of Sion's Glory*, chap. 10.

107. Winthrop, *Journal*, 517; *Recs. MBC* 2:85; Hall, *ARP*, 123. The authoritative account of Baptists and how they were treated before 1660 is William G. McLoughlin, *New England Dissent, 1630–1833: The Baptists and the Separation of Church and State*, vol. 1 (Cambridge, MA: Harvard University Press, 1971), chaps. 1–2, noting, as well, the common ground both sides occupied (p. 28).

108. *Winthrop Papers*, 5:23–25.

109. Cotton, *The Bloody Tenent, Washed, And Made White* (1647), 8; Bush, *Correspondence*, 496–504. Earlier, in 1645, the Massachusetts government had insisted in response to English criticism that "such as differ from us only in judgment, in point of baptism or some other points of lesser consequence, and live peaceably amongst us . . . have no cause to complaine," noting that the law had not been employed against them. [Hutchinson], *Collection of Original Papers*, 216. Colonial responses to criticism coming from England are described in Gura, *Glimpse of Sion's Glory*, chap. 8; and Perry Miller, *Orthodoxy in Massachusetts, 1630–1650* (Cambridge, MA: Harvard University Press, 1933), chap. 8. The trope of "persecution" is reviewed and discounted by Alan S. Rowe, "The Problem of Toleration in Early Massachusetts," *Journal of Religious History* 42 (2018): 200–221. Theological contexts and the politics that emerged around toleration in early Massachusetts are carefully described in Andrew R. Murphy, *Conscience and Community: Revisiting Toleration and Religious Dissent in Early Modern England and America* (University Park: Pennsylvania State University Press, 2001), chaps. 1–2.

110. *Recs. MBC* 3:415–16; Carla Pestana, "The City upon a Hill under Siege: The Puritan Reception of the Quaker Threat to Massachusetts Bay," *NEQ* 56 (1985): 323–53; and Gura, *Glimpse of Sions Glory*, chap. 5. Why Quakers (or "Friends") were regarded in England and the colonies as so menacing is suggested in Rosemary Moore, *The Light in Their Consciences: Early Quakers in Britain, 1646–1666* (University Park: Pennsylvania State University Press, 2000), chap. 7.

111. *Winthrop Papers*, 6:353; see also Frederick Freeman, *The History of Cape Cod*, 2 vols. (Boston, 1858), 1:199 (a woman ordered to apologize publicly for calling another woman a witch). Every pre-1660 case is included in David D. Hall, *Witch-Hunting in Seventeenth-Century New England: A Documentary History, 1638–1692* (Boston: Northeastern University Press, 1991); for initiatives on the part of the accused, see the case involving Winifred Holman and her daughter (1659–60) in Cambridge, which included their suit for defamation and strong support from church members. Two or possibly three of the women executed before 1660 had been accused of infanticide. Assertions that women were unfairly treated within the legal system are discounted in Cornelia Hughes Dayton, "Was There a Calvinist Type of Patriarchy? New Haven Colony Records Reconsidered in the Early Modern Context," in *The Many Legalities of Early America*, ed. Christopher L. Tomlin and Bruce H. Mann (Chapel Hill: University of North Carolina Press, 2001), 337–56.

112. *Letters of John Davenport, Puritan Divine*, ed. Isabel MacBeath Calder (New Haven, CT: Yale University Press, 1937), 82; Bush, *Correspondence*, 459–61; Clark, *Eliot Tracts*, 263. Cotton's prophecy (written c. 1640 as a warning against decline!) appears in *An Exposition upon the Thirteenth Chapter of the Revelation* (1656), 93.

113. For details, see Susan Hardman Moore, *Pilgrims: New World Settlers and the Call of Home* (New Haven, CT: Yale University Press, 2007); and Moore, *Abandoning America: Life-stories from Early New England* (Woodbridge: Boydell Press, 2013).

114. *New Englands First Fruits*, 26; *Winthrop Papers*, 5:115, 126. Whether the colonists could sustain a viable identity as martyrs is a question Adrian Chastain Weimer addresses in *Martyrs Mirror: Persecution and Holiness in Early New England* (New York: Oxford University Press, 2011).

115. *Winthrop Papers*, 2:294–95; Winthrop, *Journal*, 115, 121, 125–28; Bradford, *Plymouth Plantation*, 367–71, 255–54.

116. W. DeLoss Love, *Fast and Thanksgiving Days of New England* (Boston, 1895), 127; Albro, *Works of Shepard*, 1, cxlii–cxliv. Church discipline faltered and civil courts took over much of the work of policing social behavior.

117. Both are included in *The Poems of Michael Wigglesworth*, ed. Ronald A. Bosco (Lanham, MD: University Press of America, 1989) (quotation, p. 29). See also David Powers, *Good and Comfortable Words: The Coded Sermon Notes of John Pynchon and the Frontier Preaching Ministry of George Moxon* (Eugene, OR; Wipf and Stock, 2017), 27–28 (complaints dating from 1649). The amplitude and contexts of "declension" are described in Hall, *FS*, chaps. 8 and 10; and the misbehavior of "youth" may be sampled in *Recs. MBC*, 3:316–17, 353. That the colonists were alarmed by the possibility of succumbing to "Indianness" is described in John Canup, *Out of the Wilderness: The Emergence of an American Identity in Colonial New England* (Middletown, CT: Wesleyan University Press, 1990).

118. Sylvester Judd, *History of Hadley* (Hadley, MA, 1905), 73–75. Adrian Chastain Weimer has uncovered many more manuscript petitions dating from 1664–65 and describes them in " 'Our precious liberties and privillidges': The Restoration of Charles II and the 1664–1665 Petition Campaign in Massachusetts-Bay," *NEQ* (forthcoming, 2019).

119. In *Toward Democracy: The Struggle for Self-Rule in European and American Thought* (New York: Oxford, 2016), James Kloppenberg assigns a special significance to the making of town and colony governments (Rhode-Island's in particular) in early New England in the larger story he tells.

Epilogue: Legacies

1. David J. Appleby, "From Ejectment to Toleration in England, 1662–89," in *The Great Ejectment of 1662: Its Antecedents, Aftermath, and Ecumenical Significance*, ed. Alan P. F. Sell (Eugene, OR: Pickwick, 2012), 67–124, an essay noting remarkable variations in practice and shifts in state policy.

2. Among other limitations, Merton and Weber both depended on a single Puritan writer, Richard Baxter. Responses to Walzer are cited in Hall, *ARP*, 203 n. 37. Some of those to Weber are cited in chapter 5.

3. With one exception (Richard Baxter), no mainstream Puritan texts are included in *Divine Right and Democracy: An Anthology of Political Writing in Stuart England*, ed. David Wootton (Harmondsworth: Penguin, 1986). The "Calvinist political tradition" is succinctly described in Harro M. Hopfl, "The Ideal of *Aristocratia Politiae Vicina* in the Calvinist Political Tradition," in *Calvin and His Influence, 1509–2009*, ed., Irena Backus and Philip Benedict (Oxford: Oxford University Press, 2011), 46–66.

4. Richard Floyd, *Church, Chapel and Party Religious Dissent and Political Modernization in Nineteenth-Century England* (New York: Palgrave Macmillan, 2008), is an excellent guide to this process before 1850, which Floyd summarizes in a concluding chapter that provides a wealth of bibliographical citations to scholarship on the religious aspects of nineteenth-century party politics. I am grateful to Brent Sirota for calling this book to my attention.

5. See., e.g., Patrick Collinson, "Towards a Broader Understanding of the Early Dissenting Tradition," in *The Dissenting Tradition: Essays for Leland H. Carlson*, ed. C. Robert Cole and Michael E. Moody (Athens: Ohio University Press, 1975), 3–38.

6. Anti-Catholicism may be among the more enduring of these legacies, which Paul Dudley, a wealthy Bostonian, attempted to perpetuate in the Dudleian lectureship he endowed in 1750. One of the four subjects he required speakers to address was "The detecting and convincing and exposing the idolatry of the Romish Church, their tyrannous usurpations, damnable heresies, fatal errors, abominable superstitions, and other crying wickednesses in their high places, and finally that the Church of Rome is that mystical Babylon, that man of sin, that apostate church spoken of in the New Testament."

7. The inventiveness of antebellum Amerian writers when it came to describing the Puritan past is ably described in Lawrence Buell, *New England Literary Culture from Revolution through Renaissance* (Cambridge: Cambridge University Press, 1986). This epilogue incorporates only a small fraction of the evidence he provides. Equally well done are two recent books that trace the appropriations of John Winthrop's "Charitie Discourse" of 1630: Daniel T. Rogers, *As a City on a Hill: The Story of America's Most Famous Lay Sermon* (Princeton, NJ: Princeton University Press, 2018); and Abram van Engen, *The Meaning of America: How the United States Became the City on a Hill* (New Haven, CT: Yale University Press, forthcoming). See also Jonathan Beecher Field, "Puritan Acts and Monuments," in *American Literature and the New American Studies*, ed. Bryce Traister (Cambridge: Cambridge University Press, 2017), chap. 10; Richard M. Gamble, *In Search of the City on a Hill: The making and unmaking of an American myth* (London: Continuum, 2012).

8. Lucy Hutchinson, *Memoirs of the Life of Colonel Hutchinson*, ed. N. H. Keeble (London: Everyman/Dent, 1995), 64–65; see also her paean to the ethical qualities of her husband (pp. 27–30).

9. Brent Sirota, *Christian Monitors: The Church of England and the Age of Benevolence, 1680–1730* (New Haven, CT: Yale University Press, 2014). See also Richard P. Gildrie, *The Profane, the Civil, and the Godly: The Reformation of Manners in Orthodox New England, 1679–1749* (University Park: Pennsylvania State University Press, 1994).

10. An agenda described more fully in Daniel Walker Howe, *What Hath God Wrought: The Transformation of America, 1815–1848* (New York: Oxford University Press, 2007), chap. 5. This was not, however, a truly Puritan-style reformation of manners, which would have required the unflinching cooperation of the state.

11. *The Autobiography of Lyman Beecher*, ed. Barbara M. Cross, 2 vols. (Cambridge, MA.: Harvard University Press, 1960), vol. 1, chaps. 37–39; Kathryn K. Sklar, *Catharine Beecher: A Study in American Domesticity* (New York: Norton, 1973).

12. The unwinding of this agenda is sketched in Robert Wuthnow, *After Heaven: Spirituality in America since the 1950s* (Berkeley: University of California Press, 1998). Unwinding of the Sunday Sabbath began before World War I, for which see Alexis McCrossen, *Holy Day, Holiday: the American Sunday* (Ithaca: Cornell University Press, 2000). Trends in British evangelicalism are described in David W. Bebbington, *Evangelicalism in Modern Britain: A History from the 1730s to the 1980s* (London: Allen and Unwin, 1989).

13. In these paragraphs I pass by the evidence assembled in Dewey D. Wallace Jr., *Shapers of English Calvinism, 1660–1714* (Oxford: Oxford University Press, 2011).

14. A story told in Daniel D. Williams, *The Andover Liberals: A Study in American Theology* (New York: King's Crown, 1941). The shifting contours of theology among English Presbyterians are described in *The English Presbyterians: From Elizabethan Puritanism to Modern Unitarianism*, ed. C. G. Bolam et al. (London: Allen and Unwin, 1968), chaps. 2, 3, and 6, especially.

15. Ibid., chap. 4.

16. Useful studies of theological and intellectual change include Peter Byrne, *Natural Religion and the Nature of Religion: The Legacy of Deism* (New York: Routledge, 1989); Conrad Wright, *The Beginnings of Unitarianism in America* (Boston: Starr King, 1955); Hans W. Frei, *The Eclipse of Biblical Narrative: A Study in Eighteenth and Nineteenth-*

Century Hermeneutics (New Haven, CT: Yale University Press, 1974); Matthew Kadane, "Original Sin and the Path to the Enlightenment," *Past & Present* 235 (2017): 105–40, and H. Shelton Smith, *Changing Conceptions of Original Sin: A Study in American Theology since 1955* (New York: Scribner's, 1955). As the mid-nineteenth-century Presbyterian theologian John W. Nevin pointed out, his fellow Presbyterians knew next-to-nothing of Calvin's commitment to the visible church and its sacraments and favored a revivalism that the founders of the Reformed tradition would have repudiated. James H. Nichols, *Romanticism in American Theology: Nevin and Schaff at Mercersburg* (Chicago: University of Chicago Press, 1961).

17. Charles H. Foster, *The Rungless Ladder: Harriet Beecher Stowe and New England Puritanism* (Durham: Duke University Press, 1954); for an alternative understanding of Stowe's relationship to doctrine, see Peter J. Thuessen, *Predestination: The American Career of a Contentious Doctrine* (New York: Oxford University Press, 2009).

18. Richard E. Brantley, "The Common Ground of Wesley and Edwards," *Harvard Theological Review* 83 (1990): 271–303. More light is thrown on Wesley's practice by Carol Acree Cavalier, "Reading literature with prayer: the uses of Milton and Bunyan in 18th-century Anglo-American devotional practice" (PhD thesis, Cornell University, 2000). The European aspects of this story are sketched in essays on the situation in the Netherlands, France, and Germany in Backus and Benedict, eds., *Calvin and His Influence.* Most pertinent to my story is David Bebbington, "Calvin and British Evangelicalism in the Nineteenth and Twentieth Centuries," 282–305.

19. Matthew Kadane, *The Watchful Clothier: The Life of an Eighteenth-Century Protestant Capitalist* (New Haven, CT: Yale University Press, 2013); Edward W. Emerson, *Life and Letters of Charles Russell Lowell* (Boston: Houghton Mifflin, 1907), 17, 20, 193.

20. Two exceptions to this rule are Irish Catholic "memories" of the battle of Drogheda (1649), when Cromwell's army captured and killed everyone in the town, and the post-1660 tragedies associated with the Covenanter remnant in Scotland.

21. For a broader perspective on this topic, see D. W. Bebbington, "Religion and national identity in nineteenth century Wales and Scotland," in *Religion and National Identity*, ed. Stuart Mews, Studies in Church History 18 (Oxford: Blackwell, 1982), 489–503.

22. A perspective on Scott I owe to John McWilliams, *Revolution and the Historical Novel* (Lanham, MD: Lexington, 2018). See also Colin Kidd, *Subverting Scotland's Past: Scottish whig historians and the creation of an Anglo-British identity, 1689-c. 1830* (Cambridge: Cambridge University Press, 1993), chap. 11.

23. Robert G. Ingram, "Representing and Misrepresenting the History of Puritanism in Eighteenth-Century England," in *The Church on Its Past*, ed. Peter D. Clarke and Charlotte Methuen, Studies in Church History 49 (Woodbridge: Boydell, 2013), 205–18.

24. Thomas Carlyle, *Oliver Cromwell's Letters and Speeches, With Elucidations*, 4 vols. (1845; repr., London, 1897), 1:1–11. For attempts at depicting Cromwell during his lifetime and shortly thereafter, see *Constructing Cromwell: Ceremony, Portraits, and Print, 1645–1661*, ed. Laura Lunger Knoppers (New York: Cambridge University Press, 2000). Matthew Arnold, another great cultural critic, was responsible for identifying the Puritans as "Philistines" whose culture was irreparably second-rate. John Netland, "Of Philistines and Puritans; Matthew Arnold's Construction of Puritanism," in *Puritanism and Its Discontents*, ed. Laura Lunger Knoppers (Newark, DE: University of Delaware Press, 2003), 67–82.

25. Timothy Lang, *The Victorians and the Stuart Heritage: Interpretations of a Discordant Past* (Cambridge: Cambridge University Press, 1995), chaps. 3–4 (quotations, pp. 167–70).

26. The historians who became known as "revisionists," chief among them Conrad Russell, argued that the political system took for granted that parliaments would cooperate

with the monarchy and that consensus far outweighed any partisan issues. In this telling of the tale, financial strain (the gap between expenses and income) on the monarchy was at the root of Charles I's problems. Russell offered a nuanced version of these arguments that takes account of religion in *The Causes of the English Civil War* (Oxford: Clarendon, 1990). See also Richard Cust and Ann Hughes, "Introduction: After Revisionism," in *Conflict in Early Stuart England: Studies in Religion and Politics, 1603–1642*, ed. Richard Cust and Ann Hughes (London: Longman, 1989). Post-revisionist possibilities include Nicholas Tyacke, "The Puritan Paradigm of English Politics, 1558–1642," *HJ* 53 (2010): 527–50; Michael P. Winship, "Freeborn (Puritan) Englishmen and Slavish Subjection: Popish Tyranny and Puritan Constitutionalism, c. 1570–1606," *English Historical Review* 124 (2009): 1050–74; and the scholarship noticed in Catherine Gimelli Martin, *Milton among the Puritans: The Case for Historical Revisionism* (Aldershot: Ashgate, 2010), intro. and chap. 1, where she reviews some of the more important contradictions in the equation "puritanism = democracy."

27. Webster, "First Settlement of New England," in *The Works of Daniel Webster*, 6 vols. (Boston, 1869), 1:1–50. See also Paul D. Erickson, "Daniel Webster's Myth of the Pilgrims," *NEQ* 57 (1984): 44–64.

28. Baird Tipson, *Hartford Puritanism: Thomas Hooker, Samuel Stone, and Their Terrifying God* (New York: Oxford University Press, 2015), chap. 1; Michael Besso, "Thomas Hooker and His May 1638 Sermon," *Early American Studies* 10 (2012): 194–225.

29. Walker, *Creeds and Platforms*, chap. 18 (quotations, pp. 562–63, 561); David D. Hall, "Calvin and Calvinism within Congregational and Unitarian Discourse in Nineteenth-Century America," in *John Calvin's American Legacy*, ed. Thomas J. Davis ((New York: Oxford University Press, 2010), chap. 6.

30. *The Works of William Ellery Channing, D.D.*, 6 vols. (New York, 1848), 1:218 and passim; Walker, *Creeds and Platforms*, chap. 6.

31. Charles Wentworth Upham, *Salem witchcraft; with an account of Salem Village, and a history of opinions on witchcraft and kindred subjects* (Boston, 1867).

32. Lawrence Buell deals in a far richer way with Hawthorne's "puritanism" in *New England Literary Culture*, chap. 11.

33. Ellis, *The Puritan Age and Rule* (Boston, 1888), chaps. 4, 5, 8, 9, Note on the "Salem Witchhunt," pref. (quotation, p. 27).

34. Charles Francis Adams, *Three Episodes of Massachusetts History*, 2 vols. (Boston, 1894), 1:367–68.

35. The most famous example in American cultural history is probably H. L. Mencken's essay "Puritanism as a Literary Force," in *A Book of Prefaces* (New York: Knopf, 1917).

36. Perry Miller, "Thomas Hooker and the Democracy of Connecticut" (1931), reprinted in *Errand into the Wilderness* (Cambridge, MA: Harvard University Press, 1956); "'Preparation for Salvation' in Seventeenth-Century New England" (1943), repr. in *Nature's Nation* (Cambridge, MA: Harvard University Press, 1967); *The New England Mind: The Seventeenth Century* (Cambridge, MA: Harvard University Press, 1939); *The New England Mind: From Colony to Province* (Cambridge, MA: Harvard University Press, 1953), 397, 412–13, and chap. 25. What Miller said about Cotton Mather has been challenged by David Levin and Richard Lovelace, and others (noted in chaps. 4 and 9), have dismantled his interpretation of John Cotton, preparation for salvation, and the covenant theology, although in less-well-informed hands his narrative continues to be reiterated.

37. See, e.g, David Bebbington, "The Evangelical Discovery of History," in Clarke and Methuen, *The Church on Its Past*, 330–64.

A NOTE ON THE TYPE

{≈≈≈≈≈}

THIS BOOK has been composed in Miller, a Scotch Roman typeface designed by Matthew Carter and first released by Font Bureau in 1997. It resembles Monticello, the typeface developed for The Papers of Thomas Jefferson in the 1940s by C. H. Griffith and P. J. Conkwright and reinterpreted in digital form by Carter in 2003.

Pleasant Jefferson ("P. J.") Conkwright (1905–1986) was Typographer at Princeton University Press from 1939 to 1970. He was an acclaimed book designer and AIGA Medalist.

The ornament used throughout this book was designed by Pierre Simon Fournier (1712–1768) and was a favorite of Conkwright's, used in his design of the *Princeton University Library Chronicle.*